Dan Urman, Ph.D. (1979) New York University, is Senior Lecturer at Ben-Gurion University. He has directed numerous surveys and excavations in Israel, and has published books on the Golan and the Shephelah in the Roman and Byzantine periods.

Paul V.M. Flesher, Ph.D. (1988) Brown University, directs Religious Studies at the University of Wyoming. He has published on synagogues, targums, and early Rabbinic Judaism, including his book *Oxen, Women, or Citizen? Slaves in the System of the Mishnah*.

ANCIENT SYNAGOGUES

STUDIA
POST-BIBLICA

GENERAL EDITOR

DAVID S. KATZ (Tel Aviv)

VOLUME 47, 2

ANCIENT SYNAGOGUES

Historical Analysis and Archaeological Discovery

EDITED BY

DAN URMAN

AND

PAUL V.M. FLESHER

VOLUME TWO

E.J. BRILL

LEIDEN · NEW YORK · KÖLN

1995

The paper in this book meets the guidelines for permanence and durability of the Committee on Production Guidelines for Book Longevity of the Council on Library Resources.

Library of Congress Cataloging-in-Publication Data

Ancient synagogues : historical analysis and archaeological discovery, vol. 1 /
edited by Dan Urman and Paul V.M. Flesher
p.   cm. — (Studia post-Biblica, ISSN 0169-9717 ; v. 47, 1)
[Vol. 2 includes bibliographical references and indexes.]
ISBN 9004102426 (vol. 1)
ISBN 9004102434 (vol. 2)
ISBN 9004099042 (set)
1. Synagogues—Palestine—History. 2. Synagogues—Middle East–
–History. 3. Synagogue architecture—Palestine. 4. Synagogue
architecture—Middle East. 5. Palestine—Antiquities. 6. Middle
East—Antiquities.   I. Urman, Dan. II. Flesher, Paul Virgil
McCracken. III. Series.
BM653.A495   1994
296.6'5'09015—dc20   94-36799
                                                                              CIP

Die Deutsche Bibliothek – CIP-Einheitsaufnahme

Ancient synagogues : historical analysis and archaeological discovery
/ ed. by Dan Urman and Paul V.M. Flesher. - Leiden ; New
York ; Köln : Brill, 1994
  (Studia post-Biblica ; Vol. 47, 1)
  ISBN 90-04-10242-6
NE: Urman, Dan [Hrsg.]; GT

ISSN   0169-9717
ISBN   90 04 10242 6 (*vol. 1*)
ISBN   90 04 10243 4 (*vol. 2*)
ISBN   90 04 09904 2 (*set*)

PRINTED IN THE NETHERLANDS

TABLE OF CONTENTS

VOLUME TWO

Plates

LIST OF FIGURES, SECTION V

LIST OF FIGURES, SECTION VI

SECTION V

THE SYNAGOGUE'S INTERNAL AESTHETICS

ART OF THE ANCIENT SYNAGOGUES IN ISRAEL

ASHER OVADIAH*

This article deals with the relief and mosaic art of the ancient synagogues of Israel (ranging in date between the third and eighth centuries C.E.) and specifically with two aspects of this art—the ornamental and icono-graphic—which invite certain questions:

1.   What was the attitude of the rabbinic teachers to the plastic arts in general and to the figurative motifs in particular? How did they reconcile the latter (i.e. the figurative motifs) with the Second Commandment: "You shall not make for yourself any sort of carved image or any sort of like-ness..." (Ex. 20:4)?

2.   To what degree were the figurative representations and ornamental motifs intended to be symbolic or didactic?

3.   Did a specifically Jewish art exist in antiquity?

In the prevailing absence of adequate evidence, these questions will not always admit of definitive and clear-cut answers. We shall thus use rabbinic writings to supplement archaeological data.

RELIEF ART IN SYNAGOGUES

Most of the synagogues in the Galilee and Golan regions were built in the third century C.E., while others were constructed—according to the archaeo-logical evidence—during the fourth and fifth centuries C.E.[1]

As a general rule the facades of these synagogues were lavishly decorated with relief carving to create an impression of grandeur. However, their inte-riors were kept simple and free of adornment so as not to distract the wor-shipper's attention from his prayers and devotion. The relief carvings were confined almost exclusively to the lintels and jambs of doors and windows and to the decoration of the architraves, friezes, and so on. These relief carv-ings constitute a major discovery, for they clearly prove that the synagogue art of the mishnaic and talmudic periods, in contravention of the biblical prohibition regarding human representation, was rich in figurative motifs

---

* In memory of my father-in-law Rabbi Abraham Sofer (Schreiber). His life work: Redaction of the writings of Rabbi Menahem ben Solomon Meiri.

[1] See Kohl and Watzinger; Avigad, "Synagogues"; Avi-Yonah, "Architecture"; Avi-Yonah, "Ancient Synagogues"; and Ma'oz, "Synagogues."

(i.e. human and animal representations) in addition to 'permitted' geometric and plant designs. These ornamental carvings are infused with the Hellenistic and Roman spirit dominating the intellectual life and education of the architects, artists and donors of the synagogue building; this is equally evident throughout the architecture and art of the pagan temples of the Eastern Mediterranean region (Syria, Lebanon, Transjordan and Israel).[2]

Scholarly opinion at first viewed these ornamental relief carvings as the work of 'apostate' Jewish artists (stemming from and sanctioned by 'apostate' Jewish communities) or, alternatively, as "bestowed" on the Jews by Roman emperors in a gesture of goodwill which would have been ungracious (and unwise) to reject. But the evidence of the wall-paintings of the Dura-Europos synagogue,[3] along with the colored floor mosaics of the Israel synagogues,[4] clearly prove that figurative carvings were not banned for synagogue ornamentation by the Jews in general, or, specifically, by the Jews of the Galilee and Golan regions, who evidently did not regard them as offending against the Second Commandment. At the same time the Jews took care not to produce any three-dimensional sculptures for their synagogues. The sole exceptions are the lion sculptures at Capernaum, Chorazin, and Kefar Bar'am, apparently symbolizing the 'lion of Judah.'[5]

The relief decorations of the Galilean and Golan synagogues embrace a very rich and varied range of subjects, forms and motifs, be they architectural, geometrical, plant, human or animal. The repertoire also includes such typical Jewish motifs as the menorah, Torah Ark, incense shovel, *lulab* and *ethrog*. Also found are the Magen David (Shield/Star of David), Seal of Solomon (a five-pointed star), amphora and various zodiacal signs. Of special note is the basalt-carved throne known as *kathedra di-Moshe* (Seat of Moses). Examples were found in the synagogues of Chorazin[6] and Hammath-Tiberias.[7] These thrones are sumptuously orna-

---

[2] H.C. Butler, *Publications of an American Archaeological Expedition to Syria in 1899-1900, Architecture and Other Arts* (New York, 1903); D. Krencker and W. Zschietzschmann, *Römische Tempel in Syrien* (Berlin-Leipzig, 1938); C.H. Kraeling, ed., *Gerasa—City of the Decapolis* (New Haven, 1938), pp. 125ff.; A. Ovadiah, M. Fischer, I. Roll and G. Solar, "The Roman Temple at Kedesh in Upper Galilee," *Qadmoniot* 15, no. 4 (60) (1982): 121-125.

[3] See Sukenik, *Dura-Europos*.

[4] See M. Avi-Yonah, "Mosaic Pavements in Palestine," *Quarterly of the Department of Antiquities in Palestine* 2 (1933): 136-181; 3 (1934):26-47, 49-73; 4 (1935): 187-193; E. Kitzinger, *Israeli Mosaics of the Byzantine Period* (New York, 1965).

[5] See Goodenough, vol. 1, pp. 189, 203; E. L. Sukenik, "The Present State of Ancient Synagogue Studies," *Bulletin, Louis M. Rabinowitz Fund for the Exploration of Ancient Synagogues*, vol. 1 (Jerusalem, 1949), pp. 18-21; see also G. Orfali, *Capharnaüm et ses ruines* (Paris, 1922), p. 63. The exact placement of these statues in the synagogue is still in dispute.

[6] Goodenough, vol. 3, fig. 544.

[7] Goodenough, vol. 3, fig. 568.

mented, especially the one found in the Chorazin synagogue. Yet, despite the ornamentation—rosette-decorated back and carvings on the armrests—the style tends to be rather stiff and rustic.

The architectural motifs of the relief repertoire include the aedicula, conch, Torah Ark and Syrian gable. The function and placing of the actual aedicula are still under discussion. In the southern part of the nave of the Capernaum synagogue, between the southernmost pillars and the central entrance, there are indications of some kind of structure. According to Kohl and Watzinger, the structure was an aedicula inside which stood a Torah Ark.[8] In Roman architecture, aediculae or niches, topped with a gable or arch, were a common ornamental device for decorating wall areas. Examples of this architectural ornamentation with its hint of the 'baroque' can be observed in various second and third century roman buildings.[9]

The conch was a common ornament at the top of aediculae and niches as well as within small gables. The conch usually radiates upwards in the eastern Roman empire and downwards in the west.[10] In the synagogues of Israel, the conch invariably radiates upwards. Ornamental conches have been found in the synagogues of Capernaum, Chorazin, Umm el-Qanâṭir, Arbel, Rafid, and elsewhere, with those at Capernaum and Chorazin especially large and not carved within gables.[11] In these two synagogues the conches apparently surmounted actual aediculae. In the synagogue of Dura-Europos, in the center of the west wall, is an aedicula surmounted by a conch bearing the Aramaic inscription "*bet aronah*" (Torah shrine).[12]

The conch as an ornament surmounting a niche appears at Caesarea Philippi (Panias/Banias),[13] and is commonly encountered in Roman architecture.[14] It may be safely stated that the conch motif was taken over by the synagogue from the pagan world for purely ornamental purpose with no symbolical content intended.

---

[8] Kohl and Watzinger, p. 38, abb. 73 (on p. 37), pls. II, IV (above).

[9] See for example: Kohl and Watzinger, abb. 285-287 (on pp. 150-151); E. Weigand, *Das sogenannte Praetorium von Phaena*. Würzburger Festgabe für H. Bulle (Stuttgart, 1938), pp. 71-92; L.C. Cummings, "The Tychaion at is-Sanamen," *American Journal of Archaeology* 13 (1909): 417 ff; H.C. Butler, *Ancient Architecture in Syria—Southern Syria (Publications of the Princeton University Archaeological Expeditions to Syria in 1904-5 and 1909)*, Division II, Section A, Part 5 (Leyden, 1915), pp. 308 ff.; Section A, Part 7 (Leyden, 1919), p. 410, ill. 352; Lyttelton, *Architecture*, pls. 4, 50, 115, 132, 133, 139, 140, 142, 162, 173, 174, 182, 190, 191, 199, 204.

[10] Kohl and Watzinger, p. 152.

[11] Goodenough, vol. 3, Figs. 462, 463, 479, 497, 498, 499, 502, 508, 521, 526, 527, 533, 538, 539, 540, 548, 573, 617.

[12] Sukenik, *Dura-Europos*, pl. IV; Kraeling, *Synagogue*, p. 269, fig. 78, pl. XLII(3).

[13] D. Amir, *Banias—From Ancient till Modern Times* (Kibbutz Dan, 1968), photos 24, 25, 28 (on pp. 33, 34, 35) (in Hebrew).

[14] Lyttelton, *Architecture*, pls., 50, 53, 143, 144, 162; M. Bratschkova, "Die Muschel in der antiken kunst," *Bulletin de l'Institut Archéologique Bulgare* 12 (1938): 1-131 (esp. p. 14).

The Torah Ark occurs as an architectural motif in the synagogues at
Capernaum, Chorazin, Peki'in, Khirbet Shema' and elsewhere, taking the
form of a shrine-like structure with a sloping roof and carved doors
surmounted by a gable.[15] The same form of Torah Ark is depicted in synagogue floor mosaics of a later date. The Torah Arks appearing in the synagogue reliefs and mosaics are similar to the cabinets, specifically scroll
cabinets, known in the Roman world. Carved on the synagogue frieze at
Capernaum is a shrine in the form of a small temple mounted on wheels resembling a Roman temple in its construction. This type of structure was no
doubt borrowed from Roman architecture for ritual and ornamental purposes
in the synagogue. The shrine depicted at Capernaum is most likely a Torah
Ark, since a passage in the Mishnah describes how on fast days and holy
days the Torah Ark was taken to an open space within the city:

> They used to bring out the ark (containing the Torah scrolls—according to
> R. Ovadiah from Bartenura) into the open space in the town and put wood-
> ashes on the ark and the heads of the President and the Father of the court
> (author's parentheses).[16]

This literary testimony indicates that during mishnaic times the Torah Ark
was mobile, a point further borne out by the shrine-on-wheels depicted in
the Capernaum synagogue frieze. Only one similar movable shrine (ark) is
known—that depicted in a wall-painting of the Dura-Europos synagogue—
though evidently there the Ark of the Covenant and not the Torah Ark is intended.[17]

The Syrian gable, adopted as an ornamental element by synagogue
builders under the influence of Syrian-Roman architecture,[18] appears in the
synagogue at Capernaum, Kefar Bar'am, ed-Dîkkeh, and Umm el-Qanâṭir.[19]

The non-figurative motifs in synagogue decoration are drawn from the
Hellenistic, Roman and Oriental repertoires. This range embraces a broad
and varied gamut of designs, including patterns known as: egg-and-dart, meander and interlace, dentils, bead-and-reel, and loop. All of these are
Hellenistic-Roman designs, most of which are geometrical. The use of these

---

[15] See Kohl and Watzinger, pp. 34 (abb. 68), 40 (abb. 76), 51 (abb. 100:1), 142-143
(abb. 280-282); Goodenough, vol. 3, figs. 471, 472, 497, 560, 573; E. M. Meyers, "The
Synagogue at Khirbet Shema'," in Levine, *ASR*, p. 72.

[16] Mishnah, Taanit 2:1.

[17] Sukenik, *Dura-Europos*, pl. IV; Goodenough, vol. 3, fig. 602.

[18] See Kohl and Watzinger, pp. 147-152; see also S. Butler Murray, *Hellenistic
Architecture in Syria* (Princeton, 1917), pp. 12-14; D.S. Robertson, *A Handbook of Greek and
Roman Architecture*, 2nd ed. (Cambridge, 1964), pp. 226-227; R. Vallois, *L'architecture
hellénique et hellénistique à Délos jusqu'à l'éviction des Déliens (166 av. J.-C.)* (Paris,
1944), pp. 364-373; L. Crema, *L'architettura romana* (Turin, 1959), pp. 139-145.

[19] Kohl and Watzinger, pp. 100 (abb. 191), 124 (abb. 251), 134 (abb. 272), pls. III, V,
VI.

elements and their incorporation into the architectural decoration of the synagogue bring to mind public buildings and temples of the Hellenistic-Roman world, where this type of architectural ornamentation originated. Such an extensive borrowing of pagan decorative motifs serves to underline the total dependence of the synagogue builders and artisans on foreign, non-Jewish artistic patterns and sources. Despite the derivative character of these synagogue decorations, they point to a refined aesthetic sense and an awareness of the effectiveness of modelled decoration.

The plant motifs in the architectural decoration include acanthus leaves, lattice-work, vine-trellis, wreaths, garlands and rosettes, as well as some of the 'Seven Species' of the Land of Israel, such as bunches of grapes, pomegranates, dates, olives and ears of wheat. The use of these elements in architectural decoration did not originate with the synagogue; in carving, workmanship and style, they embody and reflect the qualities typical of the ornamental art of the Hellenistic-Roman world. In their new architectural-ornamental context, these motifs lose whatever symbolical meaning they may have possessed and become purely elements of architectural surface decoration.

Figurative representations frequently appear in the synagogue decorations: signs of the zodiac, victories, angels and cherubim, Herucles, Medusa, soldiers, grape-gatherers, grape-treaders, and so on.[20] The animal representations include eagles and lions, and also legendary beasts such as griffins (a hybrid beast with an eagle's head and lion's body), centaurs, a beast that is half-horse and half fish, as well as fish, birds, and so on. The figurative and other motifs are, like the non-figurative, geometrical and floral, inspired by and borrowed from the decorative repertoire of Classical, Hellenistic and Roman art.

The motifs that are specifically Jewish in character form a distinct assemblage within the ornamental repertoire of the synagogue, strikingly different from other decorative elements. Despite the assessments of some scholars, we believe that the data are insufficient to permit of any evaluation of the symbolical significance and/or apotropaic function of the Magen David and Seal of Solomon in the Capernaum synagogue.[21] However, the incorporation and integration of these two 'Jewish' motifs into the general decorative repertoire emphasize their sole function as elements of architectural ornamentation.[22]

---

[20] See Kohl and Watzinger; Ma'oz, "Synagogues"; Goodenough, vol. 3, figs. 459-461, 475, 487-489, 492-494, 501, 509-511, 513-515, 517, 522, 523-525, 531, 534, 536, 538, 541, 548, 569.

[21] Kohl and Watzinger, pp. 184-185, 187 ff.; Goodenough, vol. 7, pp. 198-200.

[22] Only in the Middle Ages did the *Magen David* (Shield of David) become a Jewish symbol; see G. Scholem, "The Curious History of the Six-Pointed Star," *Commentary* 8 (1949): 243-251.

The effacing of many of the figurative depictions of the synagogue decorations makes it difficult to evaluate the quality of their carving. In the few cases where these depictions have been preserved intact one can detect considerable technical carving skill, as for instance, on the eagle motif of the cornice at Capernaum or on the lintel at Gush Halav.[23] However, the artistic quality of these depictions is consistently inferior, with the shallow relief, the lack of proportion and plasticity typical of Oriental Roman sculptural art, as in the grape-gathering scene on the frieze at Chorazin and in the human and animal depictions in various synagogues in the Golan.[24] The sculptural treatment of the plant motifs, especially the acanthus and vine scrolls, derives from Oriental Roman art. The acanthus and vine leaves, as well as the garlands, are carved in low relief in a highly stylized though rather lifeless manner. The sculptors and carvers endeavored to create three-dimensionality by means of light-and-shade effects resulting from sharply differentiated treatment of the various surfaces of the relief. Among the various synagogue buildings, and sometimes even within the same building, differing sculptural styles can be observed. This is particularly evident in the treatment of the Corinthian capitals, for instance. Some of the garlands in the Capernaum synagogue are vividly plastic and realistic, while others are purely stylized. Variations in stylistic treatment are due to different hands at work. The decorative elements of the cornices point to efforts on part of the provincial carvers to copy the intricate mouldings of the Roman imperial period, such as egg-and-dart, *cyma*, bead-and-reel, dentils, etc. Due to the artists' remoteness from the major artistic centers, however, they could hardly even be expected fully to comprehend the correct placing of certain decorative elements, or to prevent a certain degree of deterioration in workmanship.

As can be seen, the synagogue decorations incorporate both Jewish and pagan motifs. The pagan motifs, borrowed from Classical, Hellenistic and Roman art, were applied in a new context by local artists who in details of their work betray the influence of Oriental tradition. The presence of typical pagan motifs and subjects among the synagogue decorations has always occasioned puzzlement and invited questions, with scholars searching for an explanation of their presence in the synagogue context. Opinions are divided. The explanation favoured by most scholars views the decorative motifs in the synagogue (except for those connected with Jewish subjects) as purely ornamental, with no sort of symbolic meaning. The minority opinion, whose major advocate was E. R. Goodenough, is that these motifs did

---

[23] See Kohl and Watzinger 34 (abb. 65-66), 110 (abb. 210); Goodenough, vol. 3, figs. 475, 522.

[24] See Kohl and Watzinger, p. 50 (abb. 99b); Goodenough, vol. 3, fig. 488; Ma'oz, "Synagogues."

have a symbolic or apotropaic meaning.[25] Goodenough does not exclude the
Jewish motifs from this general view. He argues that any interpretation of
the symbolism of the synagogue decorations must take into account the fact
that the same or similar motifs appear on many Jewish gravestones and
sarcophagi of this period (third—fifth centuries C.E.). Nor can one, in his
opinion, ignore the prevailing *zeitgeist* which was permeated by religious
symbolism, equally affecting Jews and gentiles. Just as anyone else, the
Jews were desirous of apotropaic symbols, a longing achieving expression
in their synagogue ornamentation.

The pagan motifs among the synagogue decorations—regardless of their
possible symbolic and/or apotropaic meaning—provide conclusive evidence
as to the tolerant attitude of the spiritual leaders of the Galilee and Golan
congregations during this period (third—fifth centuries C.E.). As for the
figurative representations, what evidently favoured their inclusion in the ornamental repertoire was their not constituting three-dimensional free-standing sculpture (except for the lion figures), but merely shallow relief depictions, to which the biblical prohibition did not apply. Since these relief
decorations were on the outside walls of the synagogue (often on its facade),
but in any case not inside the building, they were regarded as purely architectural ornamentation which did not detract from the building's sacred purpose and function. One recalls the case of the statue of Aphrodite in the
public bath at Acre where Rabban Gamaliel came to bathe:

> Proklos the son of Philosophos asked Rabban Gamaliel in Acre while he
> was bathing in the Bath of Aphrodite, and said to him, "It is written in
> your Law. And there shall cleave nought of the devoted thing in thine
> hand. Why then dost thou bathe in the Bath of Aphrodite?" He answered:
> "One may not answer in the bath." And when he came out he said, "I came
> not within her limits: she came within mine!" They do not say, "Let us
> make a bath for Aphrodite," but "Let us make an Aphrodite as an adornment
> for the bath."[26]

Apparently for the Jews there was no connotation of idolatry in an
Aphrodite statue in a public bath-house. Since in this particular context no
one was likely to worship it or prostrate himself at its feet, it was permissible to bathe in its presence.[27] Something about the enlightened attitude of
the Jewish sages towards aesthetic matters can be learned from this incident.

---

[25] Goodenough, vol. 1, pp. 30-31, 178-179; vol. 4, pp. 3-48.

[26] Mishnah, Abodah Zarah 3:4.

[27] About the nature of idolatry see Babylonian Talmud, Keritot 3b; see also D. Kotlar, *Art
and Religion* (Jerusalem and Tel Aviv, 1971), p. 91 and n. 88.

> Behold in the synagogue of *Shaph-weyathib* in Nehardea a statue was set
> up; yet Samuel's father and Levi entered it and prayed there without worry-
> ing about the possibility of suspicion![28]

This passage in the Babylonian Talmud makes it clear that even a synagogue housing a statue was not thereby disqualified to serve as a place of
public worship. Another talmudic passage relates that two of the most eminent Babylonian rabbis, Rav and Samuel, came to pray in this Nehardean
synagogue with its imperial statue.[29]

In our investigations we have not found any literary-historical or archaeological evidence to support a tendency to view decorative motifs as fraught
with symbolical meaning. Within the synagogue context these motifs, especially the figurative, appear to have an architectural-decorative function
only. Conceived and executed according to the aesthetic concepts of the
time, these elements formed an integral part of the embellishments of the
region's architecture. The repertoire of motifs in the synagogue also included some purely Jewish designs which require special consideration.
Given the circumstances and socio-political conditions of the post Second-
Temple period in which these synagogues were erected, one perceives in
these Jewish motifs a didactic purpose and the expression of Jewish identity,
a desire both to adorn and remember. Thus the Temple utensils and the
'Seven Species' are commemorated and at the same time brought to the
forefront of the worshipper's attention. We see no symbolic intent here.

The moderate, tolerant and perhaps even sympathetic attitude of the rabbinic teachers to the plastic arts, including figurative motifs, came up at a
certain stage against the opposition of zealot circles, who resorted to force-
ful means to eradicate the sculpture of figures. Their hostile attitude resulted
in the defacing—sometimes to the point of destruction—of all figurative
representations within their reach, making identification of the surviving
carvings difficult. By way of example, this iconoclasm wrought destruction
on the figurative representations in the synagogue of Capernaum, Kefar
Bar'am, Rama and Chorazin. The archaeological data suggest that these
iconoclasts may have been a localized phenomenon arising in a few
settlements in Galilee, where they operated in an organized fashion. It may
be that in these settlements a new, more conservative generation of leaders
took over, who were intolerant of figurative art.

---

[28] Babylonian Talmud, Abodah Zarah 43b.
[29] Babylonian Talmud, Rosh Hashanah 24b.

MOSAIC ART IN SYNAGOGUES

The main artistic vehicle in synagogues dated to a period between the mid-fourth and the seventh centuries C.E. was the polychrome mosaic floor.[30] Unfortunately few Jewish literary sources of the mishnaic and talmudic periods make any mention of the plastic arts. But those which do help us understand rabbinic attitudes towards artistic expression.

R. Yohanan, who lived in the Holy Land in the third century C.E., did not protest when his contemporaries began to paint on walls.[31] On the other hand, he did not hesitate to dispatch a person whose name was Bar Drosay to smash all the statues in the baths in Tiberias because incense seems to have been burned to them.[32] R. Abun (or Abin), head of the foremost *bet midrash* (theological school) in Tiberias during the first half of the fourth century C.E., also forbore from restraining his contemporaries from decorating mosaic pavements.[33] It is also told of R. Abun that he showed to another rabbi, whose name was Mane, the magnificent gates he had installed in the Great Theological School in Tiberias. This provoked R. Mane's disapproval, for he considered the gates to be luxury items.[34] One may attribute to R. Abun the following saying from the *Abba Gurion Midrash*, portion A: "R. Abun said: a woman prefers regarding beautiful forms to feasting on fatted calves." E. E. Urbach, in making reference to R. Yohanan and R. Abun, adds:

> In both cases (of R. Yohanan and R. Abun) the designs in question were reproductions of forms that had previously been regarded as forbidden. If these paintings and adornments were introduced into private houses for aesthetic reasons, it is not surprising that they should also have found their way into synagogues and cemeteries. The Sages themselves referred to the works of painters and sculptors to give vividness to their ideas and their expositions of biblical texts.[35]

---

[30] For the various sites see the *Encyclopedia of Archaeological Excavations in the Holy Land,* M. Avi-Yonah and E. Stern (eds.), 4 vols. (Jerusalem, 1975-1978) [Eds.—Now in a new edition. See NEAEHL]; Levine, *ASR.*

[31] Palestinian Talmud, Abodah Zarah 3:4, according to the Leningrad manuscript (=f. 42d).

[32] Palestinian Talmud, Abodah Zarah 4:4.

[33] Palestinian Talmud, Abodah Zarah 3:4, according to the Leningrad manuscript (=f. 42d); see also J.N. Epstein, "Additional Fragments of the Jerushalmi," *Tarbiz* 3 (1931): 15-16, 20 (in Hebrew); S. Klein, "When was Mosaic Pictorial Art Introduced into Palestine?", *BJPES* 1, no. 2 (1933): 15-17 (in Hebrew); Urbach, "Idolatry," pp. 236 f.

[34] Palestinian Talmud, Sheqalim 5:4; see *ibid., Qorban ha-'Edah,* on a similar statement relating to R. Hoshaya "and they shall not be strict as to the drawing in the synagogue building."

[35] Urbach, "Idolatry," pp. 236-237.

Additional support for the depiction of animate figures is found in Tosefta, *Abodah Zarah* 5:2: "R. Eleazar ben R. Zadok says: All the faces were in Jerusalem, except only the human face."[36] This would indicate that objections to portraying animals had long been discontinued. R. Yohanan and R. Abun even seem to have permitted the portrayal of human forms.

Synagogue mosaics, occupying as they do a special place in the art of the period, are rich in geometric, plant and figurative designs which create a 'carpet of stone.' A series of themes may be distinguished based on the following iconographic depictions: the biblical scene, the zodiac, and the Torah Ark flanked by menorahs.

Some mosaics depict biblical scenes. These include the Binding of Isaac (Beth Alpha), King David as Orpheus (Gaza Maiumas), Daniel in the Lions' Den (Na'aran and Khirbet Susiya) and Noah's Ark (Gerasa in Jordan and Mopsuhestia in Cilicia, Asia Minor).[37] Of the biblical scenes mentioned, Daniel in the Lions' Den at Na'aran near Jericho is of special historical interest. Although the scene was defaced, it may be identified on the basis of a clear inscription "Daniel Shalom." The synagogue at Na'aran was apparently built in the middle of the sixth century, during the reign of Justinian I or possibly slightly later, during Justin II's reign. The vicious attitude of the rulers towards the Jews of *Eretz Israel*, with its repression and stringent royal edicts, permitted the erection of only a very limited number of synagogues. The use of the Daniel story in the Na'aran pavement reflects the troubles of the time, namely the instability and the precarious position of the Jewish community in the Byzantine Empire. The Jews' refusal to submit to royal decrees mirrors Daniel's resistance to the king's will, and thus a certain degree of symbolism may be distinguished in the choice of Daniel in the Lions' Den for the Na'aran mosaic.

A purely pagan motif appearing on mosaic floors is the zodiac wheel with Helios in the center[38] and personifications of the four seasons in the corners (Beth Alpha, Na'aran, Hammath-Tiberias, Ḥusifah [a.k.a. Hosefa or Isfiyah] and apparently Khirbet Susiya as well).[39] Karl Lehmann sees in some cases the reflection of domed ceilings on mosaic floors.[40] Perhaps this was still perceived as the mirror reflection of the domed ceiling in those synagogues where the zodiac wheel appears. The zodiacs occur despite the

---

[36] Cf. also Palestinian Talmud, Abodah Zarah 3:1.

[37] A. Ovadiah, "Ancient Synagogues in Asia Minor," *Proceedings of the 10th International Congress of Classical Archaeology* (Ankara, 1978), pp. 864-866, pls. 279 (fig. 18), 280.

[38] Cf. M. Dothan, "The Figure of Sol Invictus in the Mosaic of Hammath-Tiberias," in Hirschberg, pp. 130-134.

[39] The Seasons also appear by themselves in the Villa at Beth Guvrin; they are depicted within round medallions which are arranged in a vertical row.

[40] Cf. K. Lehmann, "The Dome of Heaven," *Art Bulletin* 27 (1945): 1-27.

saying of the sages that "there is no (planetary) luck (or fate) in Israel."[41] An alternative explanation comes from the midrashic literature, where there are indications of personification of the sun. For example, Numbers Rabbah 12:4 interprets the phrase "the chariot of it (was) purple" in Song of Songs 3:10 as: "The chariot of it purple—*argaman*. 'Chariot' signifies the sun, which is set on high and rides on a chariot, lighting up the world. This accords with the text, 'the sun, which is as a bridegroom coming out of his chamber,' etc." (Psalms 19:6-7).[42] A similar indication is found in Pirqei de Rabbi Eliezer 6: "The sun is riding on a chariot and rises with a crown as a bridegroom...and he is as a bridegroom coming out of his canopy."[43] Despite these attempts at explanation, the significance of the zodiac wheel depicted on mosaic pavements of ancient synagogues remains obscure in the absence of literary or archaeological evidence as to its function. Attempts to view the wheel of the zodiac as calendar[44] (an acceptable explanation) or as fraught with cosmic symbolism (somewhat less likely) are still tentative.[45] However, an additional possibility exists, that of an astrological interpretation. The discovery of magic texts inscribed on bits of metals in the apse of the Ma'on synagogue (some of which have lately been opened, read and deciphered), together with additional amulets from *Eretz Israel* and the bowls inscribed with spells from Babylonia indicates that the border between orthodox Judaism and magical and astrological practices was somewhat blurred.[46] It is of interest to note that the zodiac wheel has not been found in churches or Christian complexes in *Eretz Israel* of the early Byzantine period. At this moment, the zodiac must be regarded as exclusive to ancient synagogues.

The Torah Ark flanked by two seven-branched menorahs also forms a common motif in synagogue mosaic pavements (Beth Alpha, Na'aran, Beth-Shean, Hammath-Tiberias and Khirbet Susiya; the mosaic from Jericho synagogue shows the Torah Ark without its flanking menorahs).

---

[41] Babylonian Talmud, Shabbath 156a-156b.

[42] English Translation: J. J. Slotki, *Midrash Rabbah—Numbers I, V* (London: Soncino Press, 1939), p. 458.

[43] The dating of Pirqei de Rabbi Eliezer has recently been subjected to question; this may be a work of considerably later date than hitherto believed.

[44] Cf. M. Avi-Yonah, "The Caesarea Inscription of the Twenty-Four Priestly Courses," in *The Teacher's Yoke: Studies in Memory of Henry Trentham* (Waco, TX, 1964), pp. 45-57; *idem*, "La mosaïque juive dans ses relations avec la mosaïque classique," *La Mosaïque Gréco-Romaine (Paris, 29 août-3 septembre 1963)* (Paris, 1965), vol. 1, pp. 325-330; *idem, Art in Ancient Palestine* (Jerusalem, 1981), pp. 396-397.

[45] G. Guidoni Guidi, "Considerazioni sulla simbologia cosmica nell'arte giudaica—lo zodiaco," *Felix Ravenna* 117 (1979): 131-154; Goodenough, vol. 8, pp. 215-217.

[46] I am grateful to Professor Joseph Naveh of the Hebrew University in Jerusalem who most kindly communicated verbally this important information and the suggestion of linking the zodiac wheel in ancient synagogues with astrological concepts of the same period. See also M. Smith, "Helios in Palestine," *Eretz Israel* 16 (1982): 199-214 (Non-Hebrew Section).

The Ark of the Law appears on mosaic floors in a form similar to that carved in stone, i.e. generally as a decorated chest with a double-leaved door topped with a gable (as at Naʿaran), a conch (Beth-Shean) or a gable enclosing a conch (as at Beth Alpha, Hammath-Tiberias and Khirbet Susiya). A *parochet* (Torah Ark curtain), often rendered very realistically with various decorative motifs, is depicted at either side of the Ark or in front of it. At Beth Alpha two lions, possibly symbolizing guardian beasts, also flank the Torah Ark.

An important detail of synagogue mosaic is the menorah.[47] All synagogue menorahs, be they carved in stone or depicted on mosaic floors, take the same general form. The menorah rests on three legs which join to form a central shaft terminating in a central branch. Six branches emerge from the central shaft to support six lamps, as is the description in the book of Exodus.[48] While the stone-carved menorah is generally rendered schematically, in mosaics an attempt is made to depict "its flowers, its knobs and its cups" in more detail. Additionally, the flames of the seven lamps are portrayed with the central flame burning vertically, while in certain cases the flames of the six flanking lamps are drawn to the central flame. This convention follows the tradition of Exodus 25:37: "And thou shalt make the lamps thereof, seven; and they shall light the lamps thereof, to give light over against it."[49] Successfully-drawn menorahs which reveal the artist's attempt to convey details are to be found in Beth-Shean and Hammath-Tiberias. The Samaritan synagogue of the fifth century C.E. at Shaʿalbim has a mosaic pavement depicting a hummock (apparently Gerizim, the mountain sacred to the Samaritans) flanked by two seven-branched menorahs larger in size than the mountain proper. A number of mosaics portray one menorah only (Beth-Shean, Jericho, Maʿon, Maʿoz Ḥayyim, Gerasa, etc.). At times two menorahs are symmetrically depicted flanking the Torah Ark as at Beth Alpha, Naʿaran, Beth-Shean, Hammath-Tiberias, etc. It is worth noting that the Maʿon menorah is of exaggerated size and flanked by two lions. The location of the menorah within the mosaic floor is not fixed: in some cases it will occur near the wall facing Jerusalem (Beth Alpha, Naʿaran, Hammath-Tiberias, Khirbet Susiya and Maʿon), placed at either side of the Torah Ark or elsewhere on the floor (Beth-Shean, En-Gedi, Hammath-Tiberias—later stage, Ḥusifah, Jericho, Kefar Qarnaim[50] and

---

[47] Regarding the menorah see H. Strauss, "The Fate and Form of the *Menorah* of the Maccabees," *Eretz Israel* 6 (1960): 122-129; A. Negev, "The Chronology of the Seven-Branched Menorah," *Eretz Israel* 8 (1967): 193-210.

[48] Exodus 25:31-39; 37:17-24.

[49] See Rashi on Exodus 25:37.

[50] S. Goldschmidt, "Synagogue Remains at the Mound of Kefar Qarnaim," *Eretz Israel* 11 (1973): 39-40, pl. VIII; M. Avi-Yonah, "Places of Worship in the Roman and Byzantine Periods," *Antiquity and Survival* 2, nos. 2-3 (1957): 262-272, fig. 14.

Ma'oz Hayyim). The menorahs occur in conjunction with typical Jewish motifs such as the *lulav* (palm-branch), *ethrog* (citron), *machta* (incense shovel) and shofar (ram's horn).

Over and above the main decorative subjects described above, synagogue mosaic pavements, or the borders thereof, were embellished with various motifs. A few examples: the mosaic pavements at Gaza Maiumas and Ma'on show animals, vegetal forms and still life within medallions consisting of intertwining vine-trellises emerging from an amphora; geometric patterns also occur on these floors. The border of the Beth Alpha mosaic displays birds, animals, fish, bread-baskets, cornucopiae, bunches of grapes, bowls of food and blossoms. The northern mosaic floor panel of the nave of the Na'aran synagogue depicts animals and various birds, including one in a cage. There are additional motifs, such as the lion and the bull at the entrance to the Beth Alpha synagogue, the two lions flanking the main inscription in the Hammat Gader mosaic,[51] the same beasts flanking the Ma'on menorah, and the Greek inscriptions at the entrance to the Hammath-Tiberias synagogue. The standard of workmanship varies from one pavement to the next.

The artistic merit of composition and drawing of the mosaic pavements is not uniform. The arrangement of the mosaic surface is not complex, and planning is generally simple. Most of the mosaics exhibit a simple and popular craftmanship, creative, powerful and dynamic, usually based on Oriental elements. This art is fairly close to the contemporaneous official Byzantine-Christian mode in its aesthetic conception, composition, style and decorative repertoire.

In the nave of the Hammath-Tiberias synagogue, a division into three panels makes its first appearance. The panel closest to the location of the actual Torah Ark shows a symmetrical composition with a central Torah Ark flanked by two menorahs, each accompanied with a shofar, a *machta* and the Four Species. The central panel displays the wheel of the zodiac, and only the biblical scene is lacking. On the third panel appear Greek inscriptions with the names of donors, set between two confronted lions rendered with a good measure of naturalism. This pavement is unique not only by reason of the innovative tripartite composition and the primary importance of the depictions, but also for its Classical conception and technical and artistic excellence. The mosaic is executed in a broad spectrum of shades. The gradual color transitions create areas of light and shadow, and the general impression is one of delicacy with a certain depth in the depicted figures. The naturalistic rendering and proportions of the individualistic

---

[51] E. L. Sukenik, "The Ancient Synagogue of el-Hammeh," *Journal of the Palestine Oriental Society* 15 (1935): 125-128.

figures are well thought out. All these elements are evidence of a skill hitherto unknown in *Eretz Israel*. It is interesting to note that the figures stand separately with no base line or background, as was common in the fourth century. In seeking parallels for the human and animal forms here depicted, we must of necessity have recourse to Antioch.[52] A mosaic artist or artists may have been brought from Antioch to Hammath-Tiberias, to be assisted on the spot by local artists. The composition at Hammath-Tiberias forms an earlier and less mature stage than that of Beth Alpha, which constitutes the zenith in area division and adaptation of themes.

Of the synagogue mosaic floors discovered in Israel, the floor from En-Gedi is unique in its artistic design and religious conception. This artistic uniqueness lies in the *emblematic* composition of the mosaic. While it may seem uncomplicated (a large polychrome carpet form), the central design commands the entire hall, making of it one single unit and drawing the eye to its central motif of four birds within a round medallion. The stance of the birds seems to draw the eye to the *bemah* and to the rectangular niche for the Torah Ark set into the north wall of the building. Not only is a comprehensive plan of this sort not found in other synagogues; we have not encountered its like in mosaic pavements found in buildings of other types in *Eretz Israel*.

The various inscriptions from the west aisle of the synagogue lend to the 'Ein Gedi mosaic its specific religious flavor, mirroring as they do the religious notions of the local Jewish community it served. Unlike in other synagogues, these inscriptions not only mention donors to the synagogue but also list the fathers of mankind according to 1 Chron. 1:1-4, and provide a verbal description of the twelve signs of the zodiac. The description is undoubtedly tendentious and hints at the religious zealousness of the Jewish community at En-Gedi, its conservative outlook and its strict attitude towards certain figurative depictions. This stood in direct contrast to the moderate attitude of contemporary Jewish communities in *Eretz Israel*, which permitted the portrayal of the wheel of the zodiac—at times in daring nudity like that in the synagogue at Hammath-Tiberias. In the En-Gedi mosaic, the names of the months, which follow the names of the constellations, hint that the signs of the zodiac are to be perceived as directly connected with the months of the year, and the Hebrew calendar should be adapted to the solar year, so that Jewish holidays can be celebrated in their proper season, e.g. Passover in the spring and Tabernacles in the autumn.[53] It seems, then, that the verbal representation of the zodiac instead of the figurative one, was created in order not to violate the religious commandment.

---

[52] Cf. D. Levi, *Antioch Mosaic Pavements,* 2 vols. (Princeton, 1947).

[53] Cf. *supra,* n. 44.

The figurative synagogue mosaics are devoid of any element that could offend the religious sensibilities of the worshippers, even when purely pagan figures or motifs, like the signs of the zodiac and Helios, are considered. The figures are not depicted freely as in the case of three-dimensional sculpture, and thus are distorted and partial.[54] During that period pagan motifs lost their original significance and were no longer revered or worshipped.[55]

The halakah exhibits a rather tolerant traditional approach to art, albeit with certain reservations. Figurative representation in relief or mosaic is permissible; prohibition applies to free-standing sculpture especially when the statue incorporates a personal attribute of the figured portrayed, such as a staff, a bird, or a sphere.[56] The encouragement of the moderate aspect of the halakic approach—itself so firmly anchored in tradition—gave rise to a tolerant attitude towards painting and sculpture, reflected by R. Yohanan and R. Abun. This sharp turn in attitude towards art but serves as indirect evidence for the contemporary disapproval of sculpture and drawing, echoing the disputes between teachers of halakah on matters of aesthetic-pictorial value and mirroring their substantive differences in general outlook and pragmatic and philosophical modes of thought.

Urbach, rejecting Goodenough's thesis that synagogue art was totally foreign to the spirit of normative-traditional Judaism, sides with Sukenik's view that synagogue ornamentation in no way hints at the existence of a "liberal-reform" Judaism.[57] It appears that normative-traditional Judaism had no fear of decorative aesthetic representations either overtly expressed or indirectly indicated. By way of example, one of the Jewish dirges recited on the eve of the Ninth of Av, includes an allegorical description of the heavenly host weeping over the destruction of Jerusalem and of the First and Second Temples, with additional mention of the zodiac and its twelve signs, most truly of pagan character: "...and the heavenly host lamented...even the constellations shed tears."[58] Then as now the image of the zodiac occupied a place in Jewish tradition. One may conclude that Jewish tradition displays a moderate and tolerant approach to art—be it relief or mosaic. Judaism has always recognized the aesthetic yearnings of mankind and has sought to harness them in the service of God. Only when aesthetics diverge into idolatrous worship are they prohibited. It is quite conceivable that the disputes among the sages resulted additionally in creating differing attitudes with regard to art and artistic values. The attitude taken by the sages towards art

---

[54] Cf. Babylonian Talmud, Abodah Zarah 43b.

[55] Cf. Urbach, "Idolatry," p. 236.

[56] Cf. Mishnah, Abodah Zarah 3:1.

[57] Urbach, "Idolatry," p. 151 and n. 5; Goodenough, vol. 1, p. 180; Sukenik, *Dura-Europos*, p. 3.

[58] While the date and author of this *piyyut* (hymn) are not known, its meter dates it to medieval times or perhaps even earlier.

differs from generation to generation, fluctuating according to their *Weltanschauung* and mode of thought from moderate and tolerant to orthodox and stringent. The approach of teachers of religion in the mishnaic and talmudic period to art in general and to the three-dimensional figurative in particular was also subject to variation.[59]

An interesting phenomenon encountered in the Na'aran synagogue's mosaic pavement is the defacing of the figures. This was apparently carried out deliberately in the middle of the seventh century C.E., and seems to be the work of a strict local iconoclastic movement prompted by ideological religious motives as was a similar movement operating in Galilee. If indeed this defacing was carried out by some radical religious sect, objecting on halakic grounds to figurative representations, the non-figurative ornamentation of the synagogue in nearby Jericho attributed to the seventh century is a response to the defacing of the Na'aran figures. This response takes the form of a mosaic pavement of simple design consisting only of a colored carpet of geometric patterns and stylized organic motifs. In the center appears the Torah Ark, represented in a flat and stylized manner and a round medallion framing a menorah, shofar and *lulav* above a Hebrew inscription "Peace upon Israel."

Some scholars reject the existence of a Jewish iconoclastic movement inspired by halakic prohibitions.[60] Indeed, in spite of the tendency to ascribe the defacing of the Na'aran figures to a local Jewish iconoclastic movement, it is also possible that the figures were defaced by Moslem zealots.[61] The phenomenon of Moslems defacing figures may be noted in the case of the mosaic pavement of the Kursi church on the north-east bank of the Lake of Galilee.[62] Was this the result of its Christian surroundings? A number of the Church Fathers are known to have been as strict as some of the mishnaic and talmudic sages, at times even surpassing them in their severity and zealous tenacity in condemnation of pagan motifs or human and animal forms. Thus Tertullian of Carthage (160?-220?) and Eusebius of Caesarea (260-339) were sworn enemies of figurative representation; Clement of Alexandria (150-215) prohibited the wearing of signet rings with a human or animal form on the bezel; Epiphanius (born in Beth Zadok near Beth Guvrin-Eleutheropolis, 320-403) tore into shreds with his own hands a hanging in a church in the Holy Land which was decorated with forms, that is, human figures.[63] The 36th Canon of the Church Council of

---

[59] Cf. Sukenik, *ASPG*, p. 64.

[60] S. Klein, *Toldot ha-Yishuv ha-Yehudi be-Eretz-Israel* (= *The History of the Jewish Settlement in Eretz-Israel*) (Tel Aviv, 1950), pp. 36-37 (in Hebrew).

[61] *Ibid.*, n. 94 (on p. 37).

[62] V. Tzaferis and D. Urman, "Excavations at Kursi," *Qadmoniot* 6, no. 2 (22) (1973): 62-64 (in Hebrew).

[63] See E. J. Martin, *A History of the Iconoclastic Controversy* (London, 1930), p. 134.

Elvira in Spain in c. 306 C.E. prohibited the use of human figures in churches.[64]

A portion of the figurative representations in synagogues listed above are instructive in intent, a purpose achieved by the visual portrayal of some of the most famous biblical stories. In this graphic form worshippers could be taught selected episodes from the Bible.[65] We feel that to the extent that symbolism is to be found in the biblical scenes or in other motifs decorating synagogue mosaics, this symbolism must equally be distinctly expressed and clearly reflected in Jewish literary sources. Should there be no such correlation between the written material and the visual representation, it is rather the educational aspect of the mosaic picture, with the notion they are meant to convey, that should be studied. If, however, the symbol can be perceived as expressing an abstract idea, the biblical scenes appearing in synagogues may to a certain extent be regarded as symbolizing the ways of the Divine Providence—forgiveness and redemption. The shofar, for example, symbolizes forgiveness and redemption while recalling the Binding of Isaac.[66] Should this symbolism actually be implied, it must of necessity be viewed within the relevant historical context with all its political and social realities, as well as being interpreted in its historical aspects with their primary task of bringing to mind and permanently recording.[67] It is universally acknowledged that certain circumstances give rise to specific

---

[64] On this matter see C. J. Hefele, *Histoire des Conciles* 1:1 (Paris, 1907), pp. 212-264; E. Bevan, *Holy Images* (London, 1940), pp. 105 f., 113-116. For the attitude of the Church Fathers to art and its use in churches, see F. Cabrol et H. Leclercq, *Dictionnaire d'archéologie chretienne et de liturgie* (Paris, 1926), vol. 7, cols. 11-31, *s.v.* "Iconographie"; vol. 7, cols. 51-62, s.v. "Idolatrie"; H. Koch, *Die altchristliche Bilderfrage nach den literarischen Quellen* (Göttingen, 1917); W. Elliger, *Die Stellung der alten Christen zu den Bildern in den ersten 4 Jahrhunderten* (Leipzig, 1930).

[65] The instructive value attributed by the Church to the portrayal of episodes from the sacred writings is reflected in the response of Nilos of Mt. Sinai to a query broached by Olympiodoros the Eparch in the early fifth century. Olympiodoros asked whether the lives of the saints to whom he sought to dedicate a church might be portrayed in paintings to be further embellished with animals and plants; Nilos replied that themes from the sacred writings should be painted so that individuals untutored in these religious works could learn of the deeds of the Church Fathers from the paintings. See J. P. Migne, *Patrologiae Graecae*, vol. 79 (Paris, 1865), col. 577.

[66] See Genesis Rabbah 56:9.

[67] In my opinion the seven-branched menorah is not to be considered as symbolic, but rather as an instructive element both recalling and perpetuating the past of the Jewish world and emphasizing Jewish identity. Philo of Alexandria and Josephus Flavius attributed symbolic significance to the menorah, regarding it as having a cosmic connotation and representing the seven planets. Philo even expands upon this symbolism, stating that the menorah represents the heavens which, like itself, bear lights. It must be stressed that reference here is not to the traditional orthodox sources which alone represent the tenets held by the religious establishment. It is to be noted that no hint of cosmic or other symbolism is encountered in the Mishnah or the Talmud. See Philo, *Quis Rerum Divinarum Heres*, 216-227 (The Loeb Classical Library, IV, [London-New York, 1932], 390-397); Josephus, *War* V, 217 (The Loeb Classical Library, III, [London-New York, 1928], 266-267).

symbolism in an attempt to derive from those symbols strength and encouragement.[68]

Over and above the unique character of the Jewish motifs—the Torah Shrine, the menorah, the shofar, the *machta*, the *lulav* and the *ethrog* occasionally appear on reliefs and mosaic floors—the ornamentation of ancient synagogues draws its inspiration from decorative, iconographic and stylistic sources of the non-Jewish Greek-Roman world and the Orient. The logical conclusion is that in discussing the embellishment of synagogues of the Roman and early Byzantine periods in the Holy Land we are not concerned with Jewish Art. The artwork of the synagogues, as much as the actual synagogue building, is eclectic and indicates a merging of different artistic elements borrowed from other sources. It is difficult to speak of the originality of the depictions in the synagogues or about an original composition which affects and influences the surroundings. It would appear that the art of the synagogues is introverted; it is influenced without being influential, absorbing or borrowing but not contributing or inspiring.

The Jewish creative spirit in ancient times can be seen in religious law (halakah), in the midrashim, and in religious philosophy but not in the plastic arts or in aesthetic form.

---

[68] Cf. D. Landau, *From Metaphor to Symbol* (Ramat-Gan, 1979), p. 215 (in Hebrew).

VICARIOUS SACRALITY:
TEMPLE SPACE IN ANCIENT SYNAGOGUES

JOAN R. BRANHAM

The metaphysical concept of 'the sacred'—as it manifests itself in palpable, physical terms—has long absorbed historians of art, architecture, and religion. Especially alluring to thinkers in the Jewish and Christian traditions is the notion that the holy makes its mundane appearance under various architectonic guises, such as the Tabernacle in the Wilderness, the Temple structures in Jerusalem, or the monumental worship spaces in Christendom.[1] More recently, scholars have addressed the issue of sacred space as it bears on the institution of the synagogue in late antiquity.[2] While this previously neglected area is finally coming to the fore, few academic treatments have applied compelling, theoretical approaches to define the ambiguous and elusive rubric 'sacred space' in the Jewish context of Roman-Byzantine Palestine. Prior analyses of sacred space usually misinterpret this multi-dimensional phenomenon as a monolithic, unchanging, and self-evident notion and thus lead to simplistic and unequivocal pronouncements that the synagogue 'is' or 'is not' a sacred *topos*.

This article seeks out the ambiguities and shifting associations of synagogue art, architecture, and liturgy. Specifically, I aim to ferret out the nuances evoked by the locution 'sacred space' and to relate them to the late-antique synagogue and its influential forebear, the Jerusalem Temple. In his recent study on symbolic discourse, Jacob Neusner writes that "no Judaic structure beyond A.D. 70 ignored the Temple, and all Judaisms both before and after A.D. 70 found it necessary to deal in some way with, to situate

---

[1] For example, see G. van der Leeuw, *Phänomenologie der Religion* (Tübingen, 1933; 2nd ed., 1955); M. Haran, *Temples and Temple Service in Ancient Israel* (Oxford: Clarendon, 1978); R. L. Cohn, *The Shape of Sacred Space* (Chico, CA: Scholars Press, 1981) B. M. Bokser, "Approaching Sacred Space," *HTR* 78:3-4 (1985): 279-299; J. Gammie, *Holiness in Israel* (Minneapolis: Fortress, 1989); R. Otto, *Das Heilige* (Munich, 1947); and J. Scott and P. Simpson-Housley, *Sacred Places and Profane Spaces: Essays in the Geographics of Judaism, Christianity, and Islam* (New York: Greenwood Press, 1981).

[2] Most notable are S. J. D. Cohen's two articles: "The Temple and the Synagogue," *The Temple in Antiquity*, ed. T. G. Madsen (Provo, UT: Brigham Young University, 1984), pp. 151-174; and "Pagan and Christian Evidence on the Ancient Synagogue," Levine, *SLA*, pp. 159-181. See also S. Safrai, "The Temple and the Synagogue," *Synagogues in Antiquity*, eds. A. Kasher, A. Oppenheimer, and U. Rappaport (Jerusalem: Yad Yitzak ben Zvi, 1987), pp. 31-51 (in Hebrew), and my article "Sacred Space Under Erasure in Ancient Synagogues and Early Churches," *Art Bulletin* 74:3 (1992): 375-394.

themselves in relationship to, that paramount subject."[3] In the spirit of this observation, the present essay traces the way in which the ancient synagogue constantly negotiates between two opposing forces: the assertion of its own legitimacy and integrity as an independent and viable liturgical institution, and the acknowledgment of its perpetual bond and deference to the Jerusalem Temple tradition. The definition of sacred space in Judaism is, in fact, fundamentally associated with the histories of the consecutive Temple structures that existed in Jerusalem. The tentative transference, then, of sanctity from the Temple tradition to the developing synagogue organization introduced in this latter establishment a new, yet fluctuating expression of 'Temple space,' thereby endowing it with what I call 'vicarious sacrality.' By figuratively staging Temple sacrality in liturgically important parts of the synagogue—primarily around the Torah shrine—the Jews of late antiquity enabled the synagogue to participate in the sanctity associated with the Temple, thus rendering the synagogue a 'surrogate Temple' at times. This holiness, vicariously assumed by the synagogue, depended not only on the meaning of sacred space as it was conjured in the Temple, but also necessitated artistic and architectural elements—such as figural representations of the Temple and chancel screens that conceived and defined spatial entities—to indicate that symbolic sphere. The literary and material evidence reveals, however, that while the Jewish community attributed to the synagogue certain Temple attributes, it also affirmed the fundamental differences inherent in the two separate institutions. The ability to develop and maintain two distinct yet converging identities in the synagogue, then, lies at the heart of the phrase 'vicarious sacrality' and constitutes the subject of this article.

The works of Mircea Eliade, René Girard, and Jonathan Z. Smith provide crucial theoretical models for examining these two ancient Jewish worship spaces. For example, Eliade's classic formulation of sacred space, with its emphasis on sacred mountains, hierophany, and divine rupture within profane space, situates the Jerusalem Temple as a *locus* of holiness while essentially excluding the synagogue from such characterization. This discrimination represents not only a twentieth-century interpretation but reflects some ancient rabbinic attitudes toward the institution of the synagogue as well.[4] Talmudic passages often reveal rabbinic ambivalence about the status of the synagogue—a status that is redefined and forged anew after 70 C.E.—as the Jews grapple with the synagogue's liturgical role in the shadow of its untouchable forerunner, the Temple. Such tension between

---

[3] Neusner, *Symbol*, p. 187.

[4] See L. I. Levine's discussion of the relationship between the rabbinic class and the synagogue as a communal place in "The Sages and the Synagogue in Late Antiquity: The Evidence of the Galilee," in Levine, *GLA*, pp. 201-222. See also S. J. D. Cohen's article about rabbinic disdain toward and insularity from the institution of the early synagogue, "The Place of the Rabbi in Jewish Society of the Second Century," in Levine, *GLA*, pp. 157-173.

what began as two very different institutions, embodying antithetical associations to sacrality, creates what critic René Girard describes as a competitive relationship between a subject and its rival—the synagogue and the Temple—for a commonly desired object, namely, sanctity. This rivalry plays a considerable role in the problematic rapport between ancient synagogues and their Promethean antecedent, the Jerusalem Temple.

Jonathan Z. Smith revises Eliade's well-known definitions of sacred and profane in order to develop a more complex notion of sacred space in late antiquity. Smith claims that two types of sanctity existed at this time. One was tied to the singularly-placed Temple model that embodied God's presence while the other was associated with a Diasporic model that allowed for a diffusion of sacred spaces in multiple locations. I maintain that both of these genres of sacred space were at work in a dynamic and sometimes conflicting relationship within synagogues in late antiquity.

To ground the ensuing discussion of somewhat abstract and theoretical conjectures, this paper focuses on the iconography and spatial arrangements of Jewish synagogues of the first to seventh centuries, as well as on the Jewish literature of the period from Babylonia and Palestine. The literary, epigraphic, and material evidence does not present any unified or consistent cultural tradition. In fact, it has become commonplace in Judaic studies to perceive 'ancient Judaism' as 'ancient Judaisms.'[5] I insist, moreover, that Judaism in late antiquity reveals constant equivocations, indeterminacies, and pluralisms both in its appropriation of the past and in its formulation and treatment of the notion of the sacred.

SYNAGOGUE AND TEMPLE: MONSTROUS DOUBLES

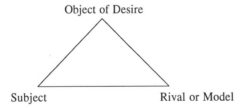

Object of Desire

Subject   Rival or Model

In his book, *Violence and the Sacred*, René Girard develops a theory about competitive relationships that proves helpful in interpreting the synagogue's struggle with the Temple's legacy. His hypothesis consists of a three-way paradigm in which there exist (1) a subject, (2) a superior rival, and (3) an

---

[5] Neusner has made this point in several places. Most recently, see Neusner, *Symbol*, p. 175.

object of desire. I have diagrammed this configuration in the preceding manner.

The subject desires a particular object, Girard maintains, because the subject's rival *initially* desires the same object, not because the object is in any way inherently desirable. The subject perceives the rival as a model and therefore values what the rival values—the way, for example, an apprentice follows a master, yearning for equal achievement as well as similar status and respect. Since desire is mimetic, Girard argues, and the subject imitates the rival, who plays the dominant role, the subject learns to covet the rival's object.[6] In human terms, Girard sees the desired object as a mode of 'being.' The rival is thus "endowed with superior being" and the subject perceives its own being enhanced by attaining the identical object.[7]

While the synagogue and Temple are not human characters playing out a mortal, psychological battle, the Jewish community's perception of them is subject to this same cognitive drama. These structural entities represent human institutions that conform to anthropomorphic creation and intervention. The synagogue is not, therefore, a sentient being conducting some sort of personal relationship with the Temple. The rabbis, community leaders, and artisans *are*, however, conscious subjects and they project their own ambivalences, perceptions, and desires on the formative synagogal institution, its changing art, and its developing liturgy. By investing the synagogue and its historical precursor, the Jerusalem Temple, with human-constructed notions—such as sacrality or competition—the Jewish community transforms the synagogue and Temple into anthropomorphic constructs. In considering the synagogue and Temple within Girard's paradigm on mimetic desire and rivalry, therefore, I alter his terminology from 'subject' to 'subject-construct' and from 'rival' to 'rival-construct' to reflect the extent to which societal dynamics mold the significations attached to the synagogue and Temple. In analyzing the so-called 'monstrous relationship' between the synagogue and Temple, then, I implicitly refer to the human motives and yearnings that influence and configure that relational meaning.

With these revisions in place, the synagogue and Temple lend themselves to the taxonomy that Girard traces in his own work for literary-mythical personages. Girard's triangular system, now projected onto the relationship between the late-antique synagogue and the Jerusalem Temple, suggests a modified triangle:

---

[6] Girard, *Violence*, p. 145. Compare with Girard's theories of sacrifice and scapegoating which are generally considered more controversial and problematic.

[7] Girard, *Violence*, p. 146.

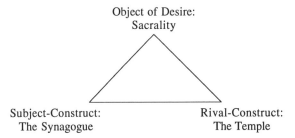

Object of Desire:
Sacrality

Subject-Construct: Rival-Construct:
The Synagogue   The Temple

In this configuration, we see that the synagogue's relationship to sacrality is formally and intimately linked to the Temple's rapport with sanctity. To fully understand the interdependent parts of this arrangement and the tie that binds them, I will examine the following separately: (1) Eliade's theoretical notions of sacred space, (2) the Temple's association with that popular definition of sacrality, and (3) the synagogue's rapport with sacred space as reformulated by Smith. Then I will insert these constructed relationships into the diagram proposed here for a comparative reading of the two institutions.

SACRED SPACE AS RUPTURE

Mircea Eliade's ground-breaking work, *The Sacred and the Profane*, states at the outset: "For religious man, space is not homogeneous; he experiences interruptions, breaks in it; some parts of space are qualitatively different from others."[8] This fundamental notion of space as heterogeneous, that is to say, the perception of physical realms as essentially differentiated from other sensible areas—in significance and self-definition—stands at the theoretical core of this essay. 'Spatial difference' for both primitive and modern societies, Eliade maintains, lies in its association with a divine presence. Exodus 3:5, for example, in which YHWH cautions Moses, "Do not come closer. Remove your sandals from your feet, for the place on which you stand is holy ground," illustrates Eliade's direct correlation between hierophany and spatial sacrality.[9] The manifestation of a transcendent reality, then, distinguishes a holy site from the otherwise profane, homogeneous, and undifferentiated zone around it. In Eliade's words, "Every sacred space implies a hierophany, an irruption of the sacred that results in detaching a territory from the surrounding cosmic milieu and making it qualitatively different."[10] Moreover, such a sacred revelation constitutes what Eliade designates as the "real unveiling itself" or "a revelation of being."[11] Space

---

[8] Eliade, *Sacred*, p. 20.

[9] All Biblical translations in this article are my own.

[10] Eliade, *Sacred*, p. 26.

[11] Eliade, "Architecture," p. 107.

that is 'real' provides a point of orientation, a fixed center, for the expanse of chaotic 'nonreality' encircling it. A qualitative break in the spatial consistency of the mundane does not, therefore, merely indicate topographical intrusion, but "ontological rupture and transcendence."[12]

While divine rupture can take place almost anywhere in the terrestrial realm, at least theoretically, Eliade's examination of ancient cultures leads him to associate qualitative breaks with sacred mountains. "The Sacred Mountain—where heaven and earth meet—is situated at the center of the world."[13] Therefore, Eliade translates *Dur-an-ki*—the term given to Babylonian sanctuaries atop mountain peaks—as the "Bond of Heaven and Earth." These sacred places represent the navel or omphalos of the earth and connect it to transcendent spheres.[14] Furthermore, a sanctuary built on the site of a rupture is assimilated into the qualitative break in space. This means that just as a hierophany transforms the physical ground from a mundane to sacred status—as in the burning-bush episode—so sacred space renders any architectural structure built within its limits qualitatively different. Eliade elaborates, "Every temple or palace—and by extension, every sacred city or royal residence—is a Sacred Mountain, thus becoming a Center."[15] The humanly constructed city or temple is itself, therefore, regarded as the juncture of heaven and earth and thereby acts as the point of passage from one level to another.[16]

While such metaphysical rupture may assume any number of physical forms, a specifically unique architectural feature often signifies the threshold between the dual worlds. Communication with the heavenly realm occurs through this symbolic opening by which passage from one cosmic region to another is made possible.[17] An example of such transition takes place in Genesis 28:12-22 when Jacob sees a ladder in his dream. Its base rests on the earth and its apogee reaches into the heavens. Angels ascend and descend the ladder and YHWH stands above it. When Jacob awakes he exclaims, "Surely the Lord is present in this place and I did not know it!... How sublime is this place! This is no other than the house of God, and that is the gateway to heaven." The Jacob/ladder paradigm incorporates all of the ingre-

---

[12] Eliade, "Architecture," p. 124.

[13] Eliade, *Myth*, p. 12.

[14] Eliade, *Myth*, p. 16. J. Z. Smith calls for a closer reading of the evidence and contends that the word *Dur-an-ki*, which Eliade translates as "Bond of Heaven and Earth," probably implies the scar or navel "left behind when heaven and earth were forcibly separated in creation." The relationship of the earthly and heavenly realm, in this case, is not one of intersection and union, rather one of severing and disjunction. See Smith, *Map*, p. 99.

[15] Eliade, *Myth*, p. 12.

[16] Eliade, "Architecture," p. 108.

[17] Certain images, such as the *universalis columna* and gateway, represent for Eliade the idea of "center within rupture" and symbolize the *axis mundi*. See Eliade, *Sacred*, p. 37.

dients of Eliadian rupture. First, there is a qualitative break in mundane space accompanied by a hierophany. Second, the ladder represents the instrument of passage at the threshold where the divine world makes contact with the human realm. Finally, the text states that Jacob sets up a stone, pours oil on it, and renames the location *bet-el*, 'house of God.' In Jacob's makeshift, quarried edifice, the stone marks the spot where the ladder's base rested and symbolically represents a foundation stone, thus standing in a synecdochal relationship to the entire, albeit improvised, architectural complex he dubs 'house of God.'

THE JERUSALEM TEMPLE: CUTTING SPACE

The aforementioned elements—space differentiated through hierophany, mountains as primary locations for rupture, and architectural structures as thresholds between human and divine worlds—play key roles in interpreting the Jerusalem Temple as sacred space *par excellence*. Drawing from rabbinic sources, Eliade attributes the symbolism of 'center,' for example, to Zion and the Jerusalem Temple. While Mishnah Kelim 1:8, 9 delineates the degrees of holiness that increase as one moves from the outer court areas toward the Holy of Holies, the early medieval text Midrash Tanhuma, Qedoshim 10 similarly states:

> Just as the navel is found at the center of a human being, so the land of Israel is found at the center of the world...and it is the foundation of the world. Jerusalem is at the center of the land of Israel, the Temple is at the center of Jerusalem, the Holy of Holies is at the center of the Temple, the Ark is at the center of the Holy of Holies, and the Foundation Stone is in front of the Ark, which spot is the foundation of the world.[18]

According to certain rabbinic attitudes then, the Temple Mount serves as a sacred mountain in its geographic centrality to the world.[19] It is the founding place of creation and the site of two topographically distinct divine ruptures. While the *devir* or Holy of Holies represents the dwelling place of the Divine Presence (or *shekinah*, to use later rabbinic terminology)—and hence marks the meeting place of heaven and earth—the altar area and the sacrifices performed there signify the threshold through which the two worlds communicate. Moreover, just as the Exodus passage demands a human gesture in response to divine presence at the burning bush, so the priests in the

---

[18] These rabbinic traditions echo Ezekiel 38:12, where the people of Israel are "gathered from the nations" and "dwell at the center of the earth."

[19] See R. L. Cohn's work on sacred landscapes in biblical texts in Cohn, pp. 38 ff. and 63ff.

Jerusalem Temple administered sacred ritual barefoot.[20] The Temple's association to that which is ontologically real, then, creates a point of orientation and reference to which all nonreal entities in the surrounding so-called
profane space are obligated.[21] Indeed, the site of the Jerusalem Temple, even
after its destruction in 70 C.E., generates the point of physical orientation to
which all other Jewish religious edifices will refer.

Eliade's formulation of the sacred as that which is both set apart or de-
tached from mundane space, as well as that which is associated with or
linked to divine presence, is reflected in the Hebrew linguistic tradition.
Detachment, for instance, is revealed in the root for 'holy' or 'sacred'—*qdsh*
(קדש)—which means 'to be cut off' or 'to be separated.'[22] The linguistic
implications of 'being cut off' materialize in both the liturgical actions and
communal building enterprises undertaken by ancient Israelite culture. At
Sinai, for example, the mandate is given in Deut. 14:2: "You are a *set-apart*
people to the Lord your God, and the Lord has chosen you to be a special
possession to himself, out of all peoples that are upon the earth" (כי עם קדוש
אתה ליהוה אלהיך ובך בחר יהוה להיות לו לעם סגלה מכל העמים אשר על פני האדמה).
"You are a set-apart people to the Lord" expresses the multivalent associations contained in the word *qdsh* (קדש). "You are set apart" qualitatively cuts
the Israelites off from other people while "to the Lord" sanctifies or conse-
crates this group of people by associating them with the divine. In this
sense, the people of Israel represent a 'sacred rupture' in the homogeneity of
men. As Jon Levenson has observed:

> Much of the biblical law, especially from the Priestly sources, evidences a
> desire to establish a clear and durable border between the Israelites and the
> Canaanites among whom they lived (Lev. 20:22-26). All the social pres-
> sure in biblical times encouraged Israel to stress what set her apart from her
> neighbors, for example, the experience of the Exodus, rather than what she
> shared with them.[23]

---

[20] See Haran, "Vestments," p. 1068. He states, "Shoes are not included among the
priestly vestments and the priests evidently ministered barefoot as was obligatory in a holy
place."

[21] In his book *Sinai and Zion*, J. D. Levenson tests the applicability of Eliade's categories
within the context of the biblical tradition. He asserts that Sinai, rather than Zion, initially
receives the attributions of a sacred mountain. In Exodus 19, YHWH physically appears at
Sinai with all the quaking drama of an anthropomorphic God. Sinai, however, marks more
than just the place of divine rupture. Through the institution of covenant, it denotes the site of
direct contact between human beings and the transcendent. Only later is the significance of
Sinai and Moses assimilated into and subsumed under the tradition of Zion and David (p. 17).
Levenson's definition of Sinai as sacred mountain, therefore, is not limited to the place of
hierophany, but encompasses a broader theory of sacred space that involves "a place where
effective decrees are issued." See Levenson, p. 111.

[22] Jastrow, p. 49; and BDB, pp. 871-874.

[23] For a discussion of 'separation' and 'difference' in the Hebrew Bible, see Levenson,
p. 120. He defines Israel as a tribe qualitatively different from other nations simply by its

This identity of distinction becomes paramount in the Talmudic era when the rabbis stressed social peculiarity. Levenson points out that at this time, "the Jews were already...radically and visibly distinct from their neighbors. They dressed differently, abstained from foods others consumed, and observed a radically different rhythm of life."[24] The Hebrew term for holy, *qdsh*, denotes, therefore, both detachment and linkage in its respective relationship to mundane and ontological realities.

In architectural terms, one of the primary linguistic signifiers used for the Jerusalem Temple is *bet hamiqdash* (בית המיקדש), 'the house that is set apart' or 'the house that is cut off.' Similarly, the word *temenos* (plural *temene*)—used to designate the precincts of a Greek temple—derives from the Greek verb *temno* (τέμνω), which means 'to cut,' hence 'to cut off' a space.[25] A Greek *temenos* originally signified any geographical domain marked off for any special purpose.[26] *Temenos* gradually came to mean almost exclusively, however, "a piece of land marked off from common uses and dedicated to a god, a precinct."[27] A *temenos* represents, therefore, a discrete space that is associated with divinity and is isolated and 'cut off' from all other regions. Moreover, most *temene* contain stone markers to indicate that the area is a site of divine rupture (as in the case of Jacob's post-dream stone pillar).[28] The third-century coin depicting the Temple of Men at Antioch (PL. 17a), for example, exhibits a lattice-work screen dividing the sacred building and its statue from the surrounding area. In fact, low fences of stone or wood appear frequently on Roman coins in order to indicate the sanctity of temples.[29] Various scholarly interpretations have suggested that these barriers were used to hinder people and animals from entering sacred grounds and that ritual participants provisionally tied sacrificial animals to the posts located on such fences.[30] These screens were low enough to be

---

connection to and covenant with the transcendent reality at Sinai. Furthermore, it is a category of difference that lies in the area of holiness, p. 53.

[24] Levenson, p. 121.

[25] See R. Parker's discussion of the meaning of *temenos*, from its secular origins associated with land 'cut off' for a king to the post-Homerian usage as land 'cut off' for the gods, in Parker, pp. 160-163. Also see J. P. Brown's discussion of *temenos* and חמנה in Brown, "*Templum*," p. 427. For an explanation of *temenos* planning in Greek temples, see Scully, pp. 54-55.

[26] See Burkert, p. 86.

[27] See Liddell & Scott, p. 1774. Also see Wright, p. 225.

[28] See Burkert, pp. 84-85. According to J. and L. Robert, the Greek word for such barriers—*kagkellos* (κάγκελλος)—is a transcription of the Latin *cancellus* and appears in a number of inscriptions in Asia Minor during the Imperial period. For κάγκελος, see Robert & Robert, pp. 47-48; and Liddell & Scott, p. 848.

[29] For other examples, see *Coins*, pp. 9, 18-19, 144-146, and 264-265.

[30] See Will, p. 259; and Corbett, p. 153, note 29. See Scully's description of a "high wall" marking the *temenos* of Asklepieion at Corinth in Scully, p. 207, fig. 405.

trespassed, however, and so they probably functioned at a symbolic level as well as at a level of security. Moreover, their permeable nature allowed the non-participant visual entry into the sacrificial rituals taking place on the other side of the balustrade.[31] In physically cutting off an area, therefore, these low walls delineated, marked out, and intensified the qualitative uniqueness of a space.[32]

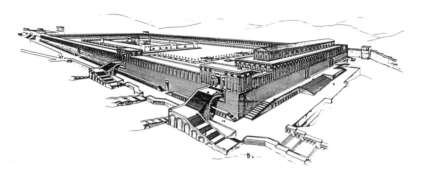

FIG. 19 Reconstruction of Herod's Temple in Jerusalem. The Temple *soreg* surrounds the inner courts (Meir Ben-Dov).

The Second Temple in Jerusalem comprised similar architectural features that 'cut off' sacred spaces from less holy ones. Both Josephus and Mishnah Middot 2:3 speak of a *soreg* (סורג) that divided the inner Temple courts from the outer ones.[33] The *soreg* carried both Greek and Latin inscriptions that described the law of purification and warned Gentiles not to enter the area.[34] Meir Ben-Dov's reconstruction of the Temple courts (FIG. 19) illustrates the probable location of the balustrade.[35] Whereas the Greek term *temenos* comes from the verb 'to cut,' the Hebrew noun *soreg* originates from the verb סרג, meaning 'to gird.' סרג also means 'to weave' and 'to knit,' indicating that the Jerusalem Temple partition was probably a lattice-work wall.

---

[31] For a discussion of vertical screenings that varied the degree of visual restrictions, see Martienssen, pp. 6-7.

[32] Smith, *Place*, p. 104.

[33] See Josephus, *JW* 5.5, 2 nos. 193-194. See other references to this barrier in Josephus, *JW* 4.3, 10 nos. 182-183 (τῶν βεβήλων); *JW* 6.2, 4 nos. 124-128; Josephus, *JA* 15.11, 5 no. 417; *JA* 12.3, 4 no. 145; Josephus, *AA* 2.8 no. 103. See also Philo, *Gaius*, 31 no. 212. Also consult Schürer, vol. 2, pp. 284-286.

[34] See E. P. Sanders' discussion of Gentiles and purity in Sanders, *Judaism*, pp. 72-76. For the warning sign, see Bickerman, "Warning," pp. 210-211; and Segal, "Warning," pp. 79-84.

[35] See Ben-Dov, p. 109.

Based on this etymological evidence pointing to 'lattice-work,' on a comparative analysis of contemporary pagan dividers (such as the one in PL. 17b), and on the material evidence that remains (in the Rockefeller and Istanbul museums), I have revised previous reconstructions of the *soreg* and propose an alternative version in FIG. 20.[36]

FIG. 20 Alternative reconstruction of the Jerusalem Temple *soreg* (author).

The Jerusalem Temple *soreg* separated and girded, therefore, the areas most associated with sacrality. We are now able to place the Jerusalem Temple and its physical indicators of sanctity within Girard's model. The Temple represents the primary, authoritative model for the synagogue; it is, in essence, the *arche*-tecture for subsequent structures conveying sanctity. The mode of superior being that the Temple enjoys is the status of sacred space, paralleling Eliade's theory that any sacred rupture in mundane space implies a 'revelation of being.' Sacrifices in the altar area enable human communication with the divine and the *shekinah* even finds spatial abode inside the Temple's precincts, within a designated room, the Holy of Holies. The simple presence of a functioning Temple in Jerusalem, in fact, connotes the political *well-being* of the nation of Israel, and hence, a mode of eminent being. The object of desire with which the Temple has become synonymous, therefore, is the translation of human contact with the divine into architectural and liturgical terms; that is to say, the manifestation of a hierophany into physical signage.

---

[36] For initial evidence on the *soreg* fragments, see Schwabe, pp. 359-368; and Iliffe, pp. 1-3.

THE SYNAGOGUE: SACRED OR PROFANE?

The late-antique synagogue does not share in the definition of sacred space
that Eliade associates with the Jerusalem Temple. Instead, the synagogue
embodies contradictory notions. On the one hand, it can only be a lesser
institution that never actually competes with the tradition of sacrality monopolized by the Temple. Sacred space in the Jewish tradition is decisively
linked to and defined in terms of experiences and realities in which the synagogue does not share. For example, no special, forbidden chamber privately
embraces the Divine Presence there. The synagogue takes on numerous
forms in unlimited *loci*, as opposed to a singular design in a 'centered'
place. And ritual purity, as well as shoeless attendance, are not required in
the synagogue. In fact, the early-medieval rabbinic assertion in Exodus
Rabbah 2:6, "Wherever the *shekinah* appears one must not go about with
shoes on," seems to suggest a 'divine absence' in the synagogue because
synagogue participants normally wore shoes. Moreover, the Hebrew signifiers used in conjunction with the Temple and the synagogue—*bet hamiqdash* (בית המיקדש) 'house of the sacred' or 'house that is set apart' and *bet
hakeneset* (בית הכנסת) 'house of the congregation'—reflect the essential *difference* in their relation to a divine presence.[37] Such nomenclature couples
qualitative distinctness with the former and common ground accessible to all
with the latter. Moreover, the synagogue is not marked off by boundary indicators comparable to the *temenos* of the Temple. As Shaye Cohen has
pointed out, synagogues differed from the Temple in certain fundamental
ways: cult, personnel, and place. While Jews regarded the Jerusalem Temple
to be the center of the earth, God's throne, and the very symbol of the entire
cosmos, Cohen argues that synagogues were, in contrast,

> built throughout the Greco-Roman world in both Palestine and the
> Diaspora, both before the destruction of the temple and after it.
> Synagogues were not built in holy places. They were built anywhere and
> everywhere: even a private home could be converted into a synagogue.
> Surely these humble structures were not cosmic centers in any sense of the
> term.[38]

Synagogues do not, therefore, require a *genius loci*; they may be reproduced
worldwide. Nor do synagogues carry a tradition of "rupture" equal to that of
Mount Moriah where sacrifices are carried out as a means of liaison with
God. In fact, according to the third-century Rabbi Eleazar ben Pedat, all contact and communication between God and Israel seems impossible in post-
70 C.E. synagogues. B. Berakot 32b states, "From the time the Temple was

---

[37] See M. Hengel's study of nomenclature associated with the synagogue in Hengel,
"Proseuche," pp. 27-54.

[38] See Cohen, "Temple," p. 154.

destroyed, an iron wall has cut Israel off from its Father in Heaven."[39] In addition, synagogues do not boast a pedigree comparable to that of Mount Sinai's—the historic place of covenant between human and divine. Post-Temple synagogues lack, in essence, any intimate connection to sacred mountains except one, and that is their consignment to pay homage to Jerusalem's Temple Mount by means of orientation. In the early years of the Common Era, synagogue facades and doors consistently open toward Jerusalem. By the fourth and fifth centuries, synagogues succumb to another set of orientation rules by angling their most important walls, designed for the placement of Torah scrolls, toward the Temple Mount.[40] Both cases of orientation situate the synagogue in a relationship of *perpetual deference* to the Temple's memory and place this later and 'secondary' institution in the area Eliade designates as 'profane nonreality' circumscribing the Temple Mount. In relation to Girard's competitive triangle, then, the synagogue plays the role of the apprentice, yearning for the object of desire associated with its rival the Temple: sacrality.

On the other hand, the post-Temple synagogue represents the only worship establishment available to the Jews and by default inevitably assumes some of the liturgical and spatial sacrality initially monopolized by the Jerusalem Temple. Drawing from Ezekiel, early medieval sources refer to the synagogue, for example, as a 'little Temple' *miqdash me'at* (מקדש מעט), reflecting both the nostalgia and reverence that Byzantine Jews still carry for the Temple—despite its absence from Jerusalem for hundreds of years—and the amount of sanctity that they are willing to allocate the synagogue through such nomenclature.[41] The rabbis even hold that prayer from the lips replaces sacrifices from the altar and B. Sotah 38b claims that neither the ark in the synagogue, nor a partition of iron, can separate the people of Israel from their Father in heaven.[42]

In addition to the liturgical significance that synagogues gained from the fourth to sixth centuries, the development and increasing presence of one decisive element—the chancel screen—differentiated spatial conceptions in synagogues. The synagogue *soreg*—similar in form and function to the *soreg* that existed in the Jerusalem Temple—changed homogeneous synagogue space into a heterogeneous realm by 'cutting off' and defining areas oriented toward the Temple Mount. The synagogue chancel thus distin-

---

[39] See Bokser, "Wall," pp. 349-374.

[40] See Landsberger, p. 183.

[41] See B. Megillah 29a and Leviticus Rabbah 6:2. Also consult Levine, "Sanctuary," p. 81.

[42] See Y. Ber. 5:1, 8d. See also Levine, "Sages," p. 206.

guished certain zones (often already chiseled out by apses and niches) from other spatial entities in the same building.[43]

The Babylonian Talmud narrates two stories that reveal the significance of such physical dividers in their ability to set apart the presence of a sacred object, much like the *soreg* in the Jerusalem Temple. The following examples describe material barriers located interestingly enough in domestic settings, not in actual synagogues. B. Berakot 25b-26a tells us that R. Ahai entered the bridal chamber of his newly married son and was horrified to see that the nuptials would be consummated in the presence of a Torah scroll. He exclaims to the bride's family:

> Had I not come now, you would have endangered the life of my son, for it has been taught: It is forbidden to have marital intercourse in a room in which there is a scroll of the Law or *tefillin*, until they are taken out or placed in one receptacle inside of another.

Sexuality in this instance is considered a profane activity because it might have taken place in the presence of a sacred object. Just as sexuality is forbidden in ancient Jewish, Greek, and Roman temple *temene*, it is also prohibited in any space made sacred by a holy object. The placement of the Torah scroll in a receptacle within the same room allowed for the creation of two spatially distinct areas, one profane and one sacred. The passage continues, further illustrating the necessity of segregating space for the Torah scroll:

> R. Joshua b. Levi said: For a scroll of the Law it is necessary to make a partition (*mehitza*, מחיצא) of ten [handbreadths]. Mar Zutra was visiting R. Ashi, and he saw that in the place where Mar the son of R. Ashi slept there was a scroll of the Law and a partition of ten [handbreadths] was made for it. He said to him: Which authority are you following? R. Joshua b. Levi, is it not? I presume that R. Joshua b. Levi meant this to apply only where one had not another room, but your honor has another room! He replied: I had not thought of it.

In these passages, two modes of physical barriers—a receptacle intended for the containment of the Torah scroll and a low wall of approximately 40 inches—symbolically represent entirely separate spatial entities. Likewise, the term 'divider,' *mehitza* (מחיצא), is based on the root *hutz* (חוץ), 'outside,' hence the meaning to place something 'outside' of a space by means of a partition. In addition to *mehitza*, the term *soreg*, denoting both the balustrade in the Temple and screens that separated the Torah shrine from the rest of synagogue interiors, derives from the verb *srg* (סרג), meaning both "to gird" and "to interlace or weave."[44] The linguistic bivalence revealed by

---

[43] See Hachlili, *Art*, pp. 187-191; and Foerster, "Menorah," p. 196.

[44] Jastrow, pp. 1022-1023.

the term *soreg*—that which is circumscribed or 'girded,' as well as that which is 'woven' together—evokes a unique tension inherent to such barriers. At one level, their visual and *formal structure* often take the form of a woven lattice-work screen, like the Jerusalem Temple *soreg* (FIG. 20) and the permeable chancel barriers from Tiberias and the synagogue at Gaza (PLS. 17b and 18a). The lattice-work conceptually symbolizes the point at which sacred and secular are knitted together in union. At another level, however, the *spatial context* of chancel screens, seen in the reconstruction of the synagogue *bemah* at Khirbet Susiya (PL. 18b), defines them as the force that severs sacred from secular space, inhibiting one from infiltrating the other.[45] This notion of architectural juncture, as both uniting and dividing, mirrors Mircea Eliade's theory of architectural threshold between two qualitatively different spaces. He states:

> The threshold that separates the two spaces also indicates the distance between two modes of being, the profane and the religious. The threshold is the limit, the boundary, the frontier that distinguishes and opposes two worlds—and at the same time the paradoxical place where those worlds communicate, where passage from the profane to the sacred world becomes possible. Hence their great religious importance, for they are symbols and at the same time vehicles of passage from the one space to the other.[46]

Like a threshold that signifies separation and continuity then, the *soreg* or the *mehitza* in front of the Torah scrolls creates the 'edge' necessary for the existence and definition of two distinct yet interrelated spatial realities.

Epigraphic evidence in Greek, Latin, Hebrew, and Aramaic further reveals the increasing sacrality attributed to synagogue space in conjunction with synagogue screens in late antiquity. An early seventh-century chancel screen from Ashkelon, for example, reads, "Kyros has presented to God and to the holy place (ἁγίω τόπω) for his salvation."[47] A sixth-century inscription located on the mosaic floor of the Gaza synagogue (PL. 19a), acknowledges the wood merchants who contributed to this "most holy place" (ἁγιωτ[άτω] τόπω).[48] The synagogue at Hamman Lif refers to itself as *sancta sinagoga*[49]

---

[45] This is Ze'ev Yeivin's reconstruction in Yeivin, "Susiya," pp. 93-98.

[46] Eliade, *Sacred*, p. 25.

[47] See Sukenik, "el-Hammeh," p. 155. Sukenik accepts a 604 C.E. dating on this screen, which is now the property of the Deutsches Evangelisches Institut für Altertumswissenschaft des Heiligenlands and on loan to the Israel Museum. See Lifshitz, p. 55, no. 70; and Frey, vol. 2, pp. 151-152, no. 964.

[48] See Ovadiah, "Gaza," p. 195 and Ovadiah "Synagogue," pp. 130-131. See also Lifshitz, pp. 58-59, no. 73.

[49] See Biebel, "Hamman Lif," pp. 541-551.

and other Diaspora synagogues—Stobi,[50] Side in Pamphylia,[51] and Philadelphia in Lydia[52]—define each of their spatial compositions as "holy place."[53] In Byzantine Palestine, synagogues at Beth-Shean,[54] Naʻaran,[55] Hammath-Tiberias,[56] Kefar Hananiah,[57] and Gerasa[58] all reveal epigraphic evidence confirming the sacred quality of these structures. Four inscriptions from synagogues in Egypt alone refer to "holy place"[59] and inscriptions listing the twenty-four Priestly courses that once functioned in the Temple appear at Caesarea, Beit el-Khader in Yemen, and Kissufim.[60] Another such inscription commemorating the hieratic caste of the Temple, reported by Sukenik but now lost, appears directly on a chancel screen from Ashkelon.[61] And in another Palestinian case, a chancel screen fragment found near the synagogue site at Gaza carries the Greek inscription:

> For the salvation of Jacob the son of Lazarus, X, his son, in gratitude to God has renovated the structure of the apse of this holy place (ἁγίου τόπου)

[50] At Stobi, the terms ἁγίῳ τόπῳ and ἁγίων refer to sacred place and sanctuary. See Frey, vol. 1, pp. 504-507, no. 694; and Lifshitz, pp. 18-19, no. 10.

[51] At Side, a marble plaque identifies the building as "the very holy, first synagogue," ἁγιωτάτ[ης] πρώτης συναγωγης, Lifshitz, p. 37, no. 36; and Frey, vol 2, pp. 38-39, no. 781.

[52] At Lydia: "To the very holy synagogue of the Hebrews," ἁγιοτ[άτη] [σ]υναγωγη των Ἑβραίων. See Lifshitz, p. 31, no. 28; and Frey, vol. 2, pp. 18-19, no. 754.

[53] See A. T. Kraabel's discussion of the development of sacred space in Diaspora synagogues in Kraabel, p. 495. J. T. Burtchaell also comments on the increasing sanctity of Roman synagogues, stating that they were considered *aedes sacra*, sacred edifices. The synagogue was defined as a *religionis locus*; theft or destruction of funds or of documents from its premises was classified as *sacrilegium*; the synagogue retained rights of asylum or sanctuary; it was immune from most intrusions from civil authorities; and no religious symbols from outside traditions could be imposed on it. See Burtchaell, p. 226; and Juster, vol. 1, pp. 456-472.

[54] Here the inscription reads: "Remembered be for good all the members of the holy congregation who endeavored to repair the holy place" (אתרה קדישה). See Bahat, "Beth-Shean," p. 85.

[55] The Aramaic inscription here also reads אתרה קדישה. See Naveh, pp. 136.

[56] Once again, אתרה קדישה, Dothan, *Hammath Tiberias*, pp. 53-54.

[57] Here the inscription mentions אתרה קדישה on a bronze hanging lamp. See Frey, vol. 2, pp. 164-165, no. 980.

[58] See Lifshitz, p. 70, no. 78; and Frey, vol. 2, pp. 103-104, no. 867.

[59] One inscription from the time of the Ptolemies mentions "sacred precincts" ἱερὸν περίβολον. See Lifshitz, p. 76, no. 87; Frey, vol. 2, pp. 360-361, no. 1433. Three others refer to ἁγίῳ τόπῳ: Lifshitz, p. 77, nos. 88, 89, 90; Frey, vol. 2, pp. 362-64, nos. 1435, 1436, 1437.

[60] See Avi-Yonah, "Courses," pp. 137-139; and Levine, *Caesarea*, p. 44.

[61] This screen has unfortunately been lost, but the inscription was recorded by Sukenik in Sukenik, "el-Hammah," pp. 156-157. See also Goodenough, vol. 1, pp. 220-221; and Frey, vol. 2, p. 150, no. 962.

together with its screen (καγκέλλω) from the ground up in the month of March...[62]

This inscription incontestably associates spatial sacrality—designated epigraphically as "holy place"—with the two architectural features that received renovation during the sixth century, the apse and the screen.

In addition to the plethora of inscriptional evidence pointing to sacrality in synagogues, Talmudic passages, such as B. Sotah 40a, allude to the qualitative difference between synagogal spatial settings by stating that the priestly class, the *kohanim*, "had their faces toward the people and their backs toward the *shekinah*." Moreover, texts like B. Megillah 29a and B. Berakot 6a-b, state that the Divine Presence can now be discovered in the synagogue. These comments further encroach upon the uniqueness of the Temple by *deferring* the sacrality of the Temple, embodied in the *shekinah*'s presence, spatially and temporally to the institution of the synagogue. And B. Sotah 40a claims that before reciting the priestly blessing, the *kohanim* removed their shoes in order to ascend the synagogue platform—a mimetic reference to Biblical traditions associated with holy ground and Temple rituals performed barefoot.[63]

In spite of such affirmations to validate the synagogue's liturgical role and to link the synagogue with the Divine Presence, the synagogue in late antiquity never shares the uniquely prestigious position once enjoyed by the Temple. B. Berakot 32b juxtaposes significant texts that are attributed to R. Eleazar and that comment on the importance of Temple sacrifice: "From the day on which the Temple was destroyed the gates of prayer have been closed" and "Prayer is more efficacious than offerings, as it says, 'To what purpose is the multitude of your sacrifices unto me?'" (Is. 1:11). Such ambivalence and seemingly contradictory attitudes toward the role of the Temple and the status of sacrifice during the post-Temple era places the Jewish tradition at a theological impasse. To fill the lacuna left by the Temple, the synagogue necessarily appropriates its ritual and ontological importance. In doing this, however, the synagogue must rival and threaten the tradition of the constructed Temple model—whether it remains standing or has been destroyed. Moreover, the tangible and formal marking of sacrality represents the object of desire to which the synagogue is indentured.

---

[62] This reading follows Sukenik's reconstructed translation in Sukenik, "el-Ḥammah," pp. 158-159. Sukenik inserts καγκέλλω where the screen is broken to indicate the self-referential nature of the inscription. See also Lifshitz, pp. 56-57, no. 72; and Frey, vol. 2, pp. 152-154, no. 966.

[63] S. Safrai comments that "the ruling that the priests must ascend barefoot added *an element of the Temple atmosphere* to its execution in the synagogue" (emphasis mine). See Safrai, "Gathering," p. 10. See my analysis of this Temple priestly gesture in Branham, "Sacred Space," p. 392.

The incomparable phenomenon of the late-antique synagogue appears, therefore, to elude preconceived notions of sacred space as formulated by Eliade and routinely attached to the Temple. Furthermore, the relationship between its spatial composition and that of the Jerusalem Temple demands the formulation of new typologies and definitions in order to interpret the religious and architectural meaning of its space.

WITH AND WITHOUT PLACE

In his book *Map is not Territory*, Jonathan Z. Smith develops a theory of space very different from that of Eliade's and asks, "Has not the illuminating category of the 'Center' been too narrowly discussed in literal terms of geographical symbolism?"[64] Instead, Smith argues for a theory built on the difference between a caste-run cult and an individual-based religion, between topographical centers and geographical peripheries. The discrepancy between these extremes gives rise to the opposing categories of "locative" and "utopian." He defines the locative as that which conforms to a location or emphasizes the centrality of a place.[65] It is associated with a world that knows its limits and boundaries and maintains the integrity and character of place. Ancient temple structures with bounded *temene*, such as the Temple in Jerusalem, illustrate this locative religious mode because they employ a highly defined ritual system with a set of rules that maintain a closed and static society. Smith describes systems of this kind as centripetal, compact, bound, and native. Furthermore, Smith asserts that part and parcel of this world view is the idea of hierarchy. Just as every element belongs to the character of a certain group or place, each member occupies a specific position within the system. Liturgical traditions that prohibit the presence of foreigners or ritually impure participants, such as menstruating women, are examples of this system.[66] Integral to the success of the totality, then, is "each individual's keeping his place."[67]

In contrast to the concept of 'central-locative,' Smith sets forth the idea of "peripheral-utopian" or "the value of being in no place."[68] The word 'utopian' is etymologically derived from the Greek, *ou topos*, 'no place.' Here Smith emphasizes boundless, free, undefinable, and vast territories. Instead of corresponding to an ordered, rational world, the u-topian is often

---

[64] Smith, *Map*, p. 98.

[65] Smith, *Map*, pp. 101-102.

[66] See S. J. D. Cohen's treatment of this problem in Cohen, "Menstruants," pp. 273-299; and in my forthcoming book, *Sacred Space in Ancient Jewish and Early Medieval Architecture* (Cambridge: Cambridge University Press, 1996).

[67] Smith, *Map*, p. 138.

[68] Smith, *Map*, p. 101.

characterized by the chaotic.[69] Smith relates the story of Alexander the Great, who continually tested the boundaries of his empire and trespassed their limits. When he encountered the sages of India, the world conqueror inquired why they stood before him stamping the earth with their feet. To protest Alexander's military exploits, they replied that "every man can possess only so much of this earth's surface as this we are standing on."[70] While the attitude of the sages illustrates Smith's category of the 'locative,' emphasizing a highly defined center with articulated limits and rules, Alexander the Great's position typifies the nature of 'rebellion.'[71] The edges of his empire were not closed and compact, but made up of diffuse, dynamic, and differentiated space; the fringes were open and u-topian, without locative cohesiveness.

In relation to the synagogue and the Temple, it is not difficult to identify the locative as the singularly 'placed' and hierarchically structured institution on the Temple Mount and the u-topian as the unlimited, ubiquitous, and varied worship structures scattered throughout the land of Israel and the Diaspora. Intrinsic to Smith's categories of the locative and u-topian, as he applies them to late antiquity, however, is the shift from the former to the latter. He states that a significant change in emphasis takes place from the ceremonial life of temple systems to that of individuals. This institutional shift—from a closed, compact society to an open arrangement based on the individual—implies a change in topography as well as in theology. Such an 'anthropologic' shift constitutes a unique transition where the centralized city or temple wall no longer protects individuals from evil. Rather, the association with a religious society or human group will save him or her from an evil perceived in human terms, embodied in other people.[72] Smith designates this anthropologic system as a diasporic model, a movement from static to mobile, from centralized to peripheral, from native to perpetual exiles.[73]

---

[69] It is difficult to dissociate Smith's term 'utopian' from its more familiar reference to an "ideal situation." While certain societies, adopting what Smith calls a u-topian system of de-centralization, may have in fact believed that they were headed toward an ideal solution, Smith employs the word primarily to suggest that their spiritual focus was not limited to a single place. To make more apparent his reference to its linguistic source, I have hyphenated the word: 'u-topos.'

[70] Smith, *Map*, p. 102.

[71] Smith, *Map*, p. 186.

[72] Joseph Gutmann asserts that this was the impetus for the formation of the synagogue. The Pharisaic emphasis on the individual's ability to influence his or her salvation through the observance of law, halakah, led to the origins of the synagogue in the second century B.C.E. See Gutman, *Synagogues*, pp. 3-4. See Steven Fine's discussion of post-Temple time as "non-sacred time" or *zman ha-zeh* in Fine, "Holy Place," p. 11.

[73] Smith, *Map*, p. 131. Problems arise from Smith's categories because he speaks in general of "the religious life of Late Antiquity" (p. 186) without completely clarifying the religious groups to which he refers. While most of his book addresses early Judaism and

At first glance, the mere existence of pre-70 C.E. synagogues attests to what Smith earmarks as a shift from the 'character of place' toward the 'u-topian,' that is, toward disparate and peripheral locations. Although the origins of the synagogue are still indeterminate and the archaeological evidence questionable, it is clear from the New Testament and other literary sources that this communal institution developed and began to gain strength while the Temple in Jerusalem was still functioning in a centralized, 'locative' religious system.[74] This diffused system was not new, however, to the Jewish people. Before attempts under Josiah in the seventh century B.C.E. to centralize worship in Jerusalem, ancient Israelite existence was symbolized by wilderness and vast territorial expanses. These areas were dotted with regional altar sites to YHWH, such as those at Shechem, Bethel, and Shiloh. Initially, therefore, the Israelites were steeped in a 'u-topian' system, without a permanent place. The first shift, then, was the reverse of what Smith describes: from u-topian existence, embodied in localized sanctuaries, to locative stasis in the one Jerusalem Temple.

It is pointless to speculate whether the Jewish people would have executed a complete shift from worship in the Jerusalem Temple to the more anthropologic and highly ubiquitous institution of the synagogue had the Herodian Temple continued to function on its Mount. Although the Qumran community and early Christian groups had already de-centered their religious orientation away from the Temple, Smith's generic reference to a "shift of late antiquity" proves somewhat ill-suited when applied to the Jewish tradition. By political-historical compulsion rather than by choice, the Jews unwillingly made this radical dispersive shift after the destruction of the Temple in 70 C.E. Furthermore, while Smith devises his two categories to set the stage for the great uni-directional detour in late antiquity, the successive shifts from one category to the other present a more complicated picture of the period. Multiple reversals, from the establishment of a decentralized, diasporic cult to the simultaneous and unrelenting references to and yearnings for a locative existence, more accurately characterize the relationship of the synagogue and the Temple. This tension, then, between a u-topian model and a locative prototype—that is to say, between a community orga-

---

Christianity, his chapter on the "anthropological shift" is devoted to a Graeco-Egyptian, Hellenistic figure. In cryptic footnotes (pp. 187-188, nos. 66-67), he mentions the "secret society" of the synagogue (his only reference to the institution) as well as the communities of early Christianity and Qumran. Yet the religious world of late antiquity was teeming with diverse religious groups irreducible to a single phenomenon. Within Judaism itself several movements were at work and they were not undergoing a monolithic metamorphosis. As R. MacMullen has described it, "It was a proper melting pot." For a discussion of religious diversity in the first three centuries C.E., see MacMullen, esp. pp. 1-12.

[74] See Flesher, "Synagogues," pp. 67-81. See also Chiat, "First-Century," pp. 49-60.

nization in multiple locations without a structured, caste system and a hierarchical institution defined spatially and ontologically as *real* and set apart—becomes an internalized tension within the late-antique synagogue, itself. Through its development, the synagogue maintains both a u-topian, communal nature while tentatively introducing within its parameters a locative model, a model bound to and defined in terms of the spatial sacrality of the Jerusalem Temple. The desire in late antiquity, therefore, to reconstruct a locative presence—that is, the Temple's presence—in the spatial and liturgical panorama of the synagogue may be understood in terms of merged or coalesced identities as well as displaced, vicarious sacrality. Jewish chancel screens, Temple liturgy, and iconographic representations of the Temple all play decisive roles in staging locative, spatial sacrality in late-antique synagogues.

RIVALRY AND THE DOUBLE BIND

We now arrive at a comparative analysis of the subject-construct, the syna-gogue, and the rival-construct, the Temple, within the Girardian model of mimetic desire and monstrous doubles. The triangular relationship, as thus proposed, reflects what Girard calls the "double-bind imperative." Girard claims that tension arises from the constructed rival's assumed authority, which by its very nature as a superior being implicitly conveys to any fol-lower, "Imitate me! Desire what I desire!" But when the constructed subject does start to imitate the rival and become similar to it, there is inevitable conflict as opposed to harmony. The more comparable the two become, the more intense the contention. The rival, who seemed to once encourage imi-tation simply by assuming the role of the model

> is surprised to find himself engaged in competition. He concludes that the disciple has betrayed his confidence by following in his footsteps. As for the disciple, he feels both rejected and humiliated, judged unworthy by his model of participating in the superior existence the model himself en-joys.[75]

Threatened by the subject-construct, the rival forbids the appropriation of what it considers "*my* object" and decrees, "Don't imitate me." This gives rise to the double-bind imperative, a directive to imitate and yet not to imi-tate.[76]

The synagogue as perceived by the Jewish community is, in this sense, subject to a twofold predicament. First, in order to gain legitimacy and pro-vide Judaism with a viable religious alternative to a Temple left in ruins,

---

[75] Girard, *Violence*, p. 146.
[76] Girard, *Violence*, p. 147.

the synagogue must imitate the Temple in order to achieve the same object
of desire: meaningful contact with God and the physical manifestation of
sanctity. One example of such imitation shows up in Tosefta Megillah
4:22, which states that synagogue entrance ways should be located on the
eastern wall *to mirror the Jerusalem Temple's orientation.*[77]

The other side of Girard's double-bind theory prevails, nevertheless, when
the art of the synagogue comes too close to representing its model's sacred
and venerated tradition. The rival's expression, "Don't imitate me" is revealed in rabbinic prohibitions (B. Menahot 28b, B. RH 24a, B. AZ 43a)
that explicitly warn against the exact replication of symbolically-charged
objects, such as the Temple menorah. Distorted menorahs, like the five-
branched menorahs at Capernaum and the nine-branched menorahs at Beth-
Shean and 'Ein Nashot (PL. 19b), deviate from the traditional seven-branched
form. In other cases, menorah representations exhibit a three-legged base
instead of the supposed solid one described by Josephus or depicted on the
Arch of Titus (PL. 20a).[78] Beth Alpha displays two menorahs (PL. 20b),
both with deviated genres of tri-legged bases, different even from each
other.[79] Hence, synagogue art reveals the desire, on the one hand, to
appropriate the heritage of the Temple, and therefore its legitimacy, and the
impetus, on the other hand, to deviate from the veritable form of the *ur-*
object, thereby actually *expropriating* certain charged Temple images.

In the end, Girard claims that each of the rivals merges its own identity
with the other and ultimately perceives the other as its mirror image, as its
"monstrous double." He comments:

> In the collective experience of the *monstrous double* the differences are not
> eliminated, but muddied and confused. All the doubles are interchangeable,
> although their basic similarity is never formally acknowledged.[80]

Such "confused differences" call to mind the juxtaposition of Temple motifs
and synagogue images in the art of late-antique synagogues. The Beth Alpha
mosaics (PL. 20b), for example, are visual landmarks to "Eliadian rupture"—that is to say, a tribute to the tradition of the Jerusalem Temple—but
within the parameters of synagogue space. The top portion of the three
mosaic panels depicts a portal-type shrine in the middle of a liturgical
arrangement, flanked by lions, veils, incense shovels, the *ner tamid* (eternal
flame), menorahs, and cherubim-like birds. In his book, *The Sacred Portal,*

---

[77] See M. Chiat's list of synagogues with eastern-oriented doors in Chiat, *Handbook*, p.
338.

[78] See Sperber, "Menorah," pp. 135-159; and Meyers, *Menorah*.

[79] See Hachlili, "Composition," where she states "the inclination to depict unidentical
objects or animals within heraldic design must have been intentional as it would have been
just as easy to portray completely identical designs," p. 66.

[80] Girard, *Violence*, p. 161.

Bernard Goldman likens this composition to ancient Near Eastern images of door/shrine motifs found on seals and scarabs and indicates that the portal itself represents rupture and discontinuity in space. Along the lines of Eliade's interpretation of threshold, Goldman says that

> throughout ancient art the portal is stressed above that of any other architectural feature...it is a pictograph for sacredness. Whatever appears framed in the door is thereby cloaked in sanctity. It is a small step, indeed, to translate the door frame into an aedicula, a shrine, or a sacred niche.[81]

This interpretation of the aedicula structure as a sign of sacred manifestation allows for the broader identification of the top panel of the Beth Alpha mosaics as (1) a model of the destroyed Temple of Jerusalem, (2) the innermost sanctuary of the Temple, or (3) a structure present within the synagogue itself. Arguing for the symbolization of Temple sanctity within the synagogue, Goldman remarks:

> The flowered curtains which stood before the Holy-of-Holies...lions, birds, menorah, ritual utensils, and trees are gathered together, assembled about the pedimented sacred portal; the basic meaning of the portal as the palace-shrine of the heavenly Dweller is never lost. As the architectural concretion of God's house, it holds His Tablets, His Torah. It is the Temple because it also holds God's seat and footstool. And, as the heavenly precinct, its doors close upon the realm of the pious dead who are gathered under His throne.[82]

Whereas the other mosaic panels on the same floor exhibit written titles to identify Abraham, Isaac, the ram, and the twelve figures of the zodiac, this panel displays no titulary labels to associate it with any specific structure. The depiction of the portal in essence speaks for itself. Goldman concludes that the artists who signed the work, Marianos and Hanina, purposefully designed this panel "to provide a sense of admission, entry into the most holy precincts whose only language is that of the symbol."[83] In this phrase, we finally meet the dual significance of Goldman's assessment of the sacred portal. The doorway is simultaneously the vehicle for hierophany, that is the passage way through which YHWH enters the human realm, and the mortal gateway to a more sacred domain. Similar then to the figuration of 'rupture' and 'passage' in Jacob's dream of the ladder, the symbolic language of the portal indicates a two-way traffic.

The middle mosaic panel at Beth Alpha—devoted to the seasons of the year, the months of the zodiac, and the clockwork of day and night—does not signify the ontologically *real* heavens, evoked in the first panel, but

---

[81] Goldman, pp. 73 and 82.
[82] Goldman, p. 124.
[83] Goldman, p. 65.

rather denotes the temporal workings of our own cosmos.[84] Fruits and grains from earthly fields appear as attributes beside personified Summer, Fall, Winter, and Spring. Even the presence of Helios clinches the association with the earth's sun—a heavenly body bound to our own global sky and planetary system. The middle panel symbolizes, therefore, a heavenly realm one level lower than the celestial arrangement depicted in the top panel.

The third and final panel completes the cosmic stratification by illustrating an event that occurs in mundane, earthly territory—the *aqedah* or the binding of Isaac. The hand of God not only intercedes at the appropriate moment in the pictorial narrative, but actually breaks through the formal borderline distinguishing the mosaic panels containing the heavenly and terrestrial worlds. Such 'Eliadian rupture'—the appearance of a divine presence in a mortal environment—acts as the link between the three mosaic sections, formally and iconographically uniting them under one program. This three-part mosaic stresses in narrative form God's intervention from the High Heavens to the earthly heavens and finally to the human realm.[85]

VICARIOUS SACRALITY

The evocation of the heavenly/Jerusalem Temple tradition within synagogue space allows Beth Alpha to participate in the sacrality associated with divine rupture.[86] Only the re-creation of 'symbolic Temple space' within the realm of the synagogue enables this subordinate institution to take part in the sacred—a notion that remains irretrievably bound to the Temple's proprietorship. The synagogue's link with Temple sacrality should not be seen as a literal transference of Temple space to the synagogue apse, but instead might be perceived in terms of a 'vicarious' rapport; that is to say that by definition, the synagogue takes the place of another in its "imagined participation in the experience of another." The Temple's sacrality is, therefore, displaced and *deferred* to the synagogue until the Temple is rebuilt. In this sense, the synagogue's artistic and liturgical representations of the Temple become mnemonic referents to Temple space, figuratively and vicariously reconstructing its presence in the synagogue's own domain.

Finally, according to René Girard's theory of rivalry, the tension created between the monstrous doubles—the Temple and the synagogue—precipi-

---

[84] Josephus attributes similar cosmic symbolism and time in the form of a zodiac to the Jerusalem Temple. See Josephus, *JA* 3.7 and Cohen, "Temple," p. 170.

[85] See Schapiro, p. 28.

[86] Similarly, the images of the sacrifice of Isaac, the Temple facade, and the Temple menorah on the Torah shrine at Dura Europos link this synagogue in the Diaspora to the whole architectural and religious history of its ancestor in Jerusalem.

tates a condition of ultimate interchangeability, substitution, and violent opposition. He explains:

> The model considers himself too far above the disciple, the disciple considers himself too far below the model, for either of them even fleetingly to entertain the notion that their desires are identical—in short, that they might indeed be rivals. To make the reciprocity complete, we need only add that the disciple can also serve as a model, even to his own model.[87]

The reciprocity that Girard implies suggests that the synagogue possibly acted as a rival organization while the Temple still stood in Jerusalem. This reversal gives weight to Smith's suggestion that late-antique Judaism saw a willed shift from locative to u-topian societal structures. Communities like Qumran and the early Christians were certainly turning away from the Jerusalem Temple, asserting that the Divine Presence had long since deserted the polluted Temple Mount. Instead, they gravitated toward organizations conceived of and structured much like the late-antique synagogue—a contending and reforming model. Girard concludes, "When all differences have been eliminated and the similarity between two figures has been achieved, we say that the antagonists are *doubles*. It is their interchangeability that makes possible the act of sacrificial substitution."[88] The culmination of this multifarious and tension-filled relationship is the sacrifice of one of the rivals. The Temple, once the place of sacrifice, paradoxically becomes the sacrifice itself for the development of the synagogue. Without this sacrifice, the synagogue would never rise to the incontestable place that it occupies as the principle place of religious worship in late-antique Jewish society. And it is the rabbis' task to make this substitution possible by endowing the synagogue with crucial import. One early-medieval tradition claims, therefore, that the actual building materials from the Temple of Solomon comprised the physical structure of a synagogue. Sherira ben Hanina, the tenth-century Gaon of Pumbedita, said that when Israel was exiled to Babylon, King Jehoiachin built a synagogue in Nehardea, using for its foundation earth and stones brought from the Temple in Jerusalem.[89] This endeavor physically to in*corpora*te the Temple's *being* into the synagogue legitimates the synagogue's status through the physical and symbolic appropriation of Temple attributes. Such appropriation witnessed its extreme denouement in 19th-century reform Judaism when the synagogue completely assumed the theological role that the Temple once held. The synagogue—and not the rebuilding of the third Temple—was seen as the ultimate instigator of a utopian age (here, I use 'utopian' in the ideal sense

---

[87] Girard, *Violence*, p. 147.

[88] Girard, *Violence*, p. 159.

[89] See The Letter of Rav Sherira Gaon (אגרת רב שרירא גאון), written in 992 C.E. and cited in Gutmann, *Sanctuary*, p. 1.

of the word) and in an attempt to eclipse its powerful precursor even appropriated the nomenclature 'Temple' as its signifier.

CONCLUSION

The iconographic, architectural, and ritual manifestations of sanctity in ancient Jewish religious spaces reveal a set of complex relationships that existed between the synagogue and its forebear, the Jerusalem Temple. Sacred and profane categories in architecture—like other conjured descriptions, such as 'anxious,' 'vicarious,' and 'competitive'—are essentially human constructs. As such, they illustrate the ways in which communities invest objects, institutions, and histories with their own anxieties and perceptions. Talmudic evidence, for example, reveals the shifting status of sacrality in the synagogue. Tosefta Megillah 3:18 illustrates a rabbinic desire, notably a tentative one, to attribute sacrality to early synagogues:

> One does not act lightly in synagogues; one does not enter them in the heat because of the heat, in the cold because of the cold, or in the rain because of the rain. One does not eat in them, nor drink in them, nor sleep in them, nor walk around in them nor relax in them, but one does read and study and preach in them.[90]

This rabbinic text does not assert that the synagogue is a *locus* of sacrality in concrete or definitive terms. Nor does it directly mention the character of Temple space—a spatial reality that these injunctions, if followed, come close to creating. Instead, this passage demonstrates a hesitant legal attempt to distinguish synagogues from common, secular structures. The goal of this code of conduct—the establishment of synagogue sacrality—remains, however, unarticulated.

In iconographic and architectural terms, the late-antique synagogue evoked sacred space within its walls through the mimetic representation of Temple imagery, liturgy, and heterogeneous space. Temple objects appear, for example, in the Beth Alpha synagogue mosaics next to what is most likely a Torah shrine, thereby combining the trappings of the two different organizations and conflating the heavenly/Temple world with synagogue iconography. Moreover, the mosaic panel that exhibits these 'muddied' complexions—bringing to mind René Girard's paradigm of rivalry and confused identities—is situated closest to the apsidal arrangement that geographically projects toward Jerusalem. The incorporation of Temple motifs into synagogue imagery and space implies, therefore, vicarious

---

[90] This passage appears in both Y. Megillah 3:74a and B. Megillah 28a-b. See Safrai, "Gathering," p. 7.

synagogal participation, by means of symbolic representation, in the sanctity once allocated to the Jerusalem Temple.

Such artistic evidence, together with certain Talmudic *topoi*, make explicit the Jewish community's efforts to assign to the post-70 C.E. synagogue at least some of the sacred status initially dominated by the Temple. As an institution that is perpetually *different* from and *deferent* to the destroyed Temple, the synagogue paradoxically becomes the place of *deferred* Temple sacrality.[91] The Temple's unique association with the Divine Presence and its sacrificial means of communicating with God are deferred after its destruction—spatially, temporally, and formally—to the liturgy and space of the synagogue. Special parts of this space, qualitatively distinguished by markers of the sacred such as synagogue *soregim* are, however, placed under erasure to denote the inadequate representation of true Temple space.[92] The synagogue must therefore yield itself up to an existence in the shadow of the Temple tradition and at the same time it must work as a viable, authentic place of worship, sequestering the Temple's ability both to communicate with God and to express that sacred connection in visible, structural signs.

[91] A subtext to my discourse on the "difference" between the Temple and the synagogue revolves around the words "difference" and "deferring," with obvious allusions to J. Derrida's essay, "La Différance." See Derrida, p. 8. I add to this polysemia the notion of 'deference.'

[92] See Branham, "Sacred Space," pp. 390-393.

REREADING THE REREDOS:
DAVID, ORPHEUS, AND MESSIANISM IN THE
DURA EUROPOS SYNAGOGUE[*]

PAUL V. M. FLESHER[1]

A scholarly consensus holds that the Jews at Dura Europos—a walled city on the Euphrates destroyed in 256 C.E.—held messianic beliefs; they believed that a messiah from the lineage of King David would come in the future to bring peace upon the world.[2] According to the consensus, the main evidence for these Jews' messianic beliefs derives from the middle scene of the synagogue's reredos, its large central painting located directly above the Torah Shrine. This scene depicts a figure, identified as David, playing a lyre before some animals. The artist, it has been argued, has cast David in the classic form of Orpheus, who is often depicted playing a lyre to pacify wild animals. By portraying David in this manner, the Dura Jews thus present David not as the biblical David, but as an ideal figure who can only be the future messiah.

Although scholars have subjected the details of the David scene to much debate, little discussion has occurred of whether this scene actually constitutes evidence for messianism. The identification of David with Orpheus has led inexorably to the conclusion that the synagogue's artist depicted David as a messiah.

This article considers whether the synagogue's paintings—the David scene in particular—reveal a belief in a future Jewish messiah; it thus provides an evaluation of the claims that Dura's Jews were messianic. The

[*] This paper is dedicated to Warren Moon, who was my main conversation partner about the art in the Dura synagogue for several years. He died unexpectedly in 1992.

[1] I want to acknowledge the support I have received for this research: Northwestern University provided funds in the form of a University Research Grant as well as access to its ATG Media Studio; Clifford Tarrance of *Memethink* helped me enter the photograph into computer form; Andy Bryson of the Center for Teaching Excellence and the computing support staff of the College of Engineering at the University of Wyoming assisted me in the final stages of the project. Susan B. Downey and Caroline McCracken-Flesher read drafts of this essay and made many helpful comments, and I thank them.

[2] The scholars who are most strongly identified with this position are A. Grabar, "Le thème religieux des fresques de la synagogue de Doura," *Revue de l'histoire des religions*, 122 (1941)159-72; Du Mesnil, *Les peintures*; Stern, "Orpheus"; Wischnitzer, *Theme*; Goodenough, esp. vols. 5 and 9-11; and Goldstein. Kraeling, in Kraeling, *Synagogue*, pp. 62-65, 214-27, also adheres to this view but he does not articulate it strongly. See also J. Leveen, *The Hebrew Bible in Art* (London, 1944).

study will center on several questions. It begins by reopening the debate
concerning the David scene's details and analyzing whether the artist portrayed David as Orpheus. With the help of computer-assisted image processing, we will subject the elements of the scene to close scrutiny, evaluating
the form of each, and sometimes even questioning their existence. Next, we
shall question the automatic equation of 'Orphic' David with the messiah by
analyzing the place of messianism in Orphism and whether Orpheus figures
as a messiah. From there, we shall briefly visit the question of whether
messianic themes appear in other paintings in the Dura synagogue, and conclude with a discussion of the role of messianic notions in different types of
Judaism prior to and during the time of the Dura Europos synagogue.

The results of these analyses uniformly reveal that the claims for messianic ideas in the David scene in particular and among Dura's Jews in general are vastly overstated. Far from building a solid case for messianism,
scholars have built a tower of cards. The case has been constructed of mis-
identified and imagined objects in the painting itself, faulty reasoning, and
historical and religious confusion. None of the evidence scholars have identified from the synagogue's artwork points to messianic beliefs among Dura's
Jews.

COMPUTER ANALYSIS OF THE DAVID FIGURE

The main problem with the messianic interpretation of the David scene is
that it rests upon a highly confused painting. The reredos, in which the
David scene appears, was repainted several times during the life of the synagogue. Each time the artists painted on top of previous images rather than
removing them. When archaeologists uncovered the reredos, the sunlight affected the paint, bringing out the layers underneath. Within a short time, all
layers appeared together in mass confusion, with images in one layer over-
laping those of another, and at times images in earlier layers showing
through better than those in later layers. Furthermore, a red wash used by
one ancient artist to cover an earlier painting now infuses the whole painting, even though it has faded in places to let earlier images show through. A
high degree of confusion thus reigns in the reredos, with many images obscured or faded.[3] Nowhere is this more apparent than in the so-called David

---

[3] Most of the problems with the reredos have come from the paint's reaction to exposure
to the elements. In addition, the painting has lost further surface material due to the paint
flaking off and to cracks and gouges in the surface (Kraeling, *Synagogue*, pp. 62, 216-17). It
seems to me, however, that the damage to the painting since discovery has been vastly
overstated. Goldstein practically suggests that the painting was redone by its restorers and is
now unreliable for analysis (Goldstein, pp. 100-101), while Stern states that when the reredos
was moved from its original location, it lost its analytic value (Stern, p. 2). Goodenough
despairs of any analysis of the reredos bearing fruit (Goodenough, vol. 9, p. 90). My

scene. Scholars have claimed to see up to six different animals, but they have agreed neither on the specific animals represented nor even on the total number. Only two animals now appear to the naked eye. The image of David has faded and become so obscured that only its barest outline can be seen. To add to this confusion, no photographs of the reredos were taken at the time of its discovery; we possess only tracings, field notes, and sketches.[4] Later, when the wall was removed for display in Damascus in 1933-34, Herbert Gute painted copies of each picture and photographs were made.[5] There is thus no unquestionable or objective record of the reredos' details before it reacted to the exposure to sunlight, or even from the period between its discovery and its removal. Current interpretations of the David scene thus rest upon subjective descriptions which cannot be checked for accuracy.

But all is not lost. Computer-assisted image enhancement has brought new powers of analysis to works of art. Even moderately powerful personal computers can now analyze artwork in ways unavailable just a decade ago. By applying computerized techniques of image processing to the reredos, we can enhance its obscured, faded, and damaged images. These techniques enable us to view the painting's minute details and to see—with a greater degree of certainty than heretofore possible—the remains of any images present when the photograph was taken.[6]

For this study, I used the best available photograph of the reredos, that taken by Fred Anderreg for the color plates of volume 11 of Goodenough's

---

computer-assisted analysis of the painting has found little damage which caused the total loss of valuable data. This is not to overlook the confusion caused by the painting's discovery or the scratches and holes in the painting—both ancient and modern—but by and large these problems affect only small parts of each image; they rarely result in the loss of an entire object.

[4] In the season the reredoes was discovered, 1932-33, H. Pearson made tracings (Kraeling, *Synagogue*, p. 62, n. 148). But these, for some reason, only depict the tree-vine and the objects underneath it. Pearson's tracing can be seen in Goodenough, vol. 11, figs. 73 and 76; and in Goldstein, pp. 102-3, figs. 2 and 4. Other scholars made sketches (Du Mesnil, "Le Deux synagogues," p. 88, fig. 11, reproduced in Goodenough, vol. 11, fig. 77 [see also fig. 75]; and in Goldstein, pp. 102-3, fig. 5) and notes (Kraeling cites C. Hopkin's field notes in Kraeling, *Synagogue*, p. 224, n. 886). See also Du Mesnil, *Les peintures*, p. 49.

[5] H. Gute painted copies of the synagogue paintings in 1934, before they were moved and cleaned. Kraeling, *Synagogue*, uses these as its color plates, while Goodenough, in vol. 11, reproduces these in black and white (figs. 323-49). Although Gute's paintings have played a key role in the debate, neither the early photographs nor the infrared photographs taken by Anderegg have been consulted. See Hopkins, *Discovery*, pp. 207-8, 212.

[6] Several different types of Apple Company's Macintosh II have been used during this research, which was completed on a Centris/Quadra 650. In all cases, the software used has been Adobe Photoshop, developed by Adobe Systems Inc.

Jewish Symbols in the Greco-Roman World.[7] It captures the state of the reredos in the early 1960's while on display at the National Museum in Damascus, Syria. In the photograph, the figure of David has faded, with only faint outlines visible to the naked eye. The figure is obscured by the red wash as well as by several dark-green leaves of a vine (a product of a different artistic moment). Only two of the animals mentioned by various scholars remain visible, the lion and the 'duck,' which is actually a dove.

The goal of my research was to analyze the details of the David figure in the Dura synagogue's reredos and to search for the animals that observers have claimed to see. Through trial and error I discovered that the outlines of the figures provided the most information about the images, rather than other artistic features such as color or technique. The following description can be most easily understood by consulting the two photographs in Plate 21 and the drawing based on them found at the end of this essay (FIG. 21). The two photographs were produced by different methods of image enhancement. The first provides clearer outlines of the image than the second, but the images are essentially the same.

To create these images, the initial steps were the same. I borrowed a photo transparency from Princeton University Press and used a high-quality color scanner with a light hood to scan the image into the computer (where it was stored in TIFF format). Using Adobe System's Photoshop, I then removed the areas of the reredos outside the middle range where the images of David and the animals were found.

Once the picture was in computer form, I used Photoshop's features of Color Separation and Brightness/Contrast to determine which color contained the artistic information about the David figure. It turned out that most of the information appeared in the red layer, with a tiny amount in the green layer and none in the blue layer.[8] Happily, the latter two layers also contained most of the 'noise,' dirt, scratches, discolorations, and other damage to the picture. So I deleted the green and blue layers and converted the red layer into black-and-white. I then enhanced the contrast between the dark and light areas to make the figure's outlines stand out.

At this stage, I applied different techniques to produce the two pictures in PL. 21. For the first picture (PL. 21a), I used Photoshop's Sharpening tool

---

[7] The image of the reredos comes from the transparency used to produce the photograph of the reredos in Goodenough, vol. 11, plate IV, courtesy of Princeton University Press. This photograph of the reredos after the synagogue wall was reconstructed in the Damascus museum was taken by Fred Anderegg specifically for the 1964 publication of volume 11. According to Clark Hopkins, this was because the existing photographs of the paintings "were not considered quite adequate for the illustrations" (Hopkins, "Excavations," p. 19). Kraeling dealt with this problem by publishing Gute's paintings. I want to thank Princeton University Press for permission to study the photograph.

[8] I also tried CMYK analysis, but this produced poorer results.

to trace the edges of the figure. This brought the outlines of the figure into sharp delineation, without affecting the rest of the picture. The effect was to cause the lines of the David figure to stand out from the rest of the picture. To create the second picture (PL. 21b), I applied Photoshop's different sharpening filters to the whole picture several times. This had the effect of heightening all dark/light contrasts in the picture—bringing out both the lines of the David image and any other line or contrasting area, whether part of the painting or a product of the centuries of deterioration. So although David has been emphasized, so has all the 'garbage' in the picture.[9] After the enhancement was complete, both pictures were 'printed' to a digitized slide printer (essentially a computerized 35mm camera) and developed.

Looking at both the pictures in PL. 21 and the drawing in FIG. 21, we can see that the image of David revealed by computer analysis is similar to descriptions by previous observers, but it differs in several details, both important and minor.[10] The figure is seated, with crossed legs, resting a lyre on his left leg. A tunic drapes down David's front to rest across his knees. This gives his torso a roughly triangular shape. The tunic seems to be a light red, but this may be affected by the red wash that suffuses the entire painting. A phrygian cap sits on the top of David's head, which is covered with dark hair. Unfortunately, I cannot make out any details of the face. A chlamys is fastened just below the neck, but it must go down David's back, for it appears on neither side of him. Some viewers have seen the chlamys coming down David's right side (the viewer's left), but this is just a dark stain on the painting. The chlamys under David's neck, like the lyre, appears in yellow tones. David's upper right arm comes straight down before the viewer and then bends at the elbow to cross to the lyre on the left. The sleeve of the tunic ends just below the elbow. David is apparently wearing dark trousers that end just below the knee in light-colored boots. This can be seen best on his right leg, the left leg (on the viewer's right) could not be brought out by the techniques I used. David sits on a stool that

---

[9] The reason for creating the two pictures is to show that different levels of human involvement in the enhancement process reveal essentially the same image. In the first picture, I had to identify the outlines of the David figure and enhance them 'by hand.' In the second picture, the computer adjusted all elements of the picture equally, without my selecting any specific area.

[10] Some differences lead me to believe that some of the artists who provided renderings of the image could not see it very well. In fact, I suspect that the drawing published by Du Mesnil is a rather free rendition, with the artist filling in absent details and altering the figure's pose. The drawing, for example, depicts a thin-waisted David, who holds a small lyre high in his arms. To help the right arm reach high enough, Du Mesnil changes the slope of the upper arm and shifts the body back to balance the lyre. Gute's painting is generally more accurate, but he draws the curves of the lyre incorrectly and lacks the bottom of the figure. These drawings appear in many publications; in addition to works already cited, see Goodenough, vol. 11, figs. 74, 77, and 323.

has crossed legs. It is apparently covered by a cushion or a cloth which ends in a roll on the (viewer's) left side.

David balances a large lyre on his left knee with his left hand (which cannot be seen behind the lyre). The lyre's upper ends curve towards each other, with the left one ending even with David's hair and the right extending a bit higher. There appears to be a hole in the sounding box at the level of David's shoulder.

The most significant discovery of the computer analysis concerns the area behind David's right shoulder in the upper left corner of the image. Previous scholars all agreed that something was painted here. In his paintings, Gute placed an eagle, while Kraeling later claimed to see both an eagle and a horizontal bar suggesting the back of a throne.[11] The computer-enhanced image, however, shows not a bird, but a shepherd's crook—a long, straight pole with three-quarters of a circle on the end. The crook has not been observed by previous viewers, but the computer-enhancement brings it out quite clearly. The mistaking of a crook for an eagle makes me wonder how well this image could be seen even shortly after discovery.[12]

The absence of the eagle brings us to the second area in which computer enhancement assists our analysis of the David scene, namely, the suggested presence of different animals before David. This has been an area of scholarly disagreement. Gute's painting depicts three—the aforementioned eagle, the lion and the dove. Du Mesnil saw a monkey between David and the lion as well as a bird and another (unidentified) animal in the area to the right of the lion.[13] Kraeling saw none of Du Mesnil's animals and discounted the dove by claiming it was simply an oddly shaped area which the red wash had not covered; he suggested it had not actually been painted into the scene.[14] Goodenough took an inclusive view, accepting the lion, the eagle, and the duck (my "dove") as well as the monkey and the other bird seen by Du Mesnil.[15]

One of the animals usually seen by these scholars in this scene we now know never existed, the eagle. But what about the other animals that scholars have identified? The computer analysis reveals only two, the lion and the dove. The lion stands out more than any image in the reredos and so requires no further discussion. The dove, by contrast, has been more controversial. Kraeling, as we mentioned above, held that it was merely an oddly shaped

---

[11] Kraeling, *Synagogue*, p. 223.

[12] I cannot explain why Kraeling thought the eagle was yellow (Kraeling, p. 223).

[13] See the discussion of whether the monkey is a dog in Du Mesnil, *Les peintures*, pp. 49-51; and Goodenough, vol. 9, pp. 90-91 and figs. 82, 85-87.

[14] Kraeling, pp. 223-224.

[15] Goodenough, vol. 9, p. 93. See also Du Mesnil, "Le Deux synagogues," pp. 87-89.

damaged area.[16] But the computer analysis reveals that the dove was actually painted onto the reredos. Both the bird's beak and eye have been painted and part of its body has been outlined in black—the top of the head, back of the neck, some of the back and part of the tail feathers. This partial outline is similar to that of the lion, whose torso, head and tail received outlining, even though its legs did not.

No evidence reveals any of the three animals identified solely by Du Mesnil. Computer analysis finds no traces of a monkey (or any other creature) between David and the lion. An odd-shaped leaf appears there as well as a lightening of the red wash—perhaps a result of flaking paint—also in an unusual shape.[17] Perhaps Du Mesnil mistook one of these for a monkey. To the right of the lion and the dove there is nothing. I used all the techniques of image enhancement I applied to the David image—techniques designed to heighten contrast, eliminate 'garbage,' and otherwise distinguish images—and no animals, portions of animals, or other objects appeared. Thus only two animals appear in this scene with David, the lion and the dove.[18]

The computer-enhanced analysis of the depiction of David in the reredos of the Dura synagogue reveals that this David was presented as the biblical David, and shows that the scene does not fit the usual form of 'Orpheus playing to the animals.' Let me briefly discuss the negative side first—that this scene does not depict David as Orpheus. The first feature in this scene that militates against the identification of David as Orpheus is the shepherds' crook behind David's back. According to Warren Moon, a historian of Roman art, Orpheus never appears with a shepherd's crook.[19] Indeed, the elements of Orpheus' mythic stories consistently depict him as a singer and musician, and never as a herdsman. Orpheus used music to persuade the gods of the underworld to allow him to bring his dead wife back from Hades, and for mourning his dead wife in a way that wooed to him animals, plants and even rocks. Because of his continuing, mournful singing, angry women cut off his head, which then continued to sing and mourn. His inclusion in the voyage of the Argo with Jason also stems from his musical talents. Orpheus is thus constantly portrayed as a musician by his myths, never as a

---

[16] See Kraeling, p. 224.

[17] The odd-shaped leaf can be seen at the far right in the photos in PL. 21.

[18] The computer analysis reveals a David scene surprisingly similar to that painted by Gute. He indicated three animals: the lion and the dove/duck (on which the computer concurs), and the eagle, which the computer revealed as a shepherds crook. None of the animals or objects suggested by other scholars were seen by Gute or by my computer analysis.

[19] Private conversation, May 1992. This has held true for all the Orpheus images I have examined.

herdsman.[20] Since the Orpheus myths and the artistic representations of him agree that he was not a shepherd, the presence of the shepherd's crook in the synagogue reredos militates against identifying David as Orpheus.

The second aspect of the David scene relates to the animals. All undamaged scenes of Orpheus that depict him playing to animals show him surrounded by a multitude of animals. The Orpheus mosaic in Tripoli's "House of Orpheus" contains twenty animals, the Orpheus Mosaic in Paphos reveals thirteen.[21] Even the Jerusalem mosaic has eight animals, as well as two satyrs.[22] This holds true for all the other late-antique images of Orpheus and the animals I have studied.[23] So the appearance of only two animals in this scene does not suggest Orpheus, but, on the contrary, indicates that David is not Orpheus.

So if the elements of this scene do not indicate David as Orpheus, what do they suggest? They present David as a composite of the different stages of his life, as presented in the biblical record. First, the shepherd's crook indicates his boyhood occupation of tending his father's sheep, while the lion represents one of the beasts that he protected the sheep against. David in fact mentions his shepherd's prowess against lions to King Saul in 1 Samuel 17:34-36. Second, the harp symbolizes his early relationship to Saul when he was brought to court to play his harp to calm Saul's troubled emotions (1 Sam. 16:14-23). Third, the kingly hat and dress clearly identify David as

---

[20] See W. S. Anderson "The Orpheus of Virgil and Ovid: *flebile nescio quid*," pp. 25-50 in Warden, *Orpheus*; Linforth, *Arts*; F. Graf "Orpheus: A Poet Among Men," pp. 80-106 in J. Bremmer, ed., *Interpretations of Greek Mythology* (Totowa, NJ: Barnes & Noble, 1986).

[21] See R. B. Bandinelli, *Rome: the Late Empire, Roman Art AD 200-400* (London: Thames and Hudson, 1971), p. 260; and *The Conservations of the Orpheus Mosaic at Paphos, Cyprus* (Burbank, CA: Getty Conservation Institute, 1991), plate 1.

[22] See M. Avi-Yonah, *Art in Ancient Palestine* (Jerusalem: Magnes, 1981) pp. 319-20 and plates 50-51. The same observation about animals applies to the Orpheus depictions cited by Goodenough, vol. 9, pp. 91-92, and vol. 11, figs. 82-88.

[23] Unfortunately, it is difficult to make a systematic comprehensive survey of all images of Orpheus from antiquity. Perhaps when *Lexicon Iconographicum Mythologiae Classicae* reaches 'O,' we will be able to be more comprehensive. In addition to images and objects in other sources cited elsewhere in this essay, I have studied images of Orpheus playing to the animals in the following places: D. S. Neal, *Roman Mosaics in Britain* (London: Society for the Promotion of Roman Studies, 1981), pp. 109-112, plate 83; L. Budde, *Antike Mosaiken in Kilikien*, Band 1 (Recklinghausen: Verlag Aurel Bongers, 1969), pp. 169, 174, 178 and 191; S. Charitonidis, L. Kahil, and R. Ginouvès, *Les Mosaïqes de la Maison du Ménandre a Mytilène* (Bern: Francke Verlag, 1970), pp. 17-25, 90-1, plates 1, 9-14; Stern, "Orphée"; P. E. Bourguet, *Early Christian Art* (New York: Reynal & Co., 1971), pp. 52-53, 64-65, 90-91, & 188-189; B. Walters, "The Restoration of an Orphic Temple in England," *Archaeology* 35, no. 6 (1982): 36-43; M. Grant & J. Hazel, *Gods and Mortals in Classical Mythology* (Springfield, MA: G. & C. Merriam Co., 1973), p. 309; K. Kilinski, II, *Classical Myth in Western Art* (Dallas, TX: Southern Methodist Univ., 1985), pp. 26 & 85. See also the citations in the "Selective Catalogue of Figurative Mosaics" in K. M. D. Dunbabin, *The Mosaics of Roman North Africa* (Oxford: Clarendon, 1978), pp. 254-277; and in M. Rochelle, *Mythological and Classical World Art Index* (Jerrerson, NC: McFarland & co., 1991), pp. 155-157.

the King of Israel. Other elements of this scene play 'double-duty' by point-ing to David's benevolent rule over his people. The crook indicates David as the shepherd of his people Israel. As Psalms 78:71 states, "He [i.e., God] chose David his servant, and took him from the sheepfolds…to be the shep-herd of Jacob his people, of Israel his inheritance." Thus David in the rere-dos scene carries the crook, the symbol of his royal shepherding. The lion represents the lion of Judah, symbolizing the People Israel in David's care. The dove by the lion thus becomes the symbol of the peace of David's reign.

The David scene in the Dura synagogue can therefore be explained as a portrayal of the important roles David played during his lifetime. No ele-ment in the scene requires the interpreter to reach to Orpheus for explana-tion. And, since the identification of David as an Orphic figure provided the basis for understanding this scene as messianic, the idea that this is a mes-sianic scene no longer stands. This scene depicts David as the biblical David, not David as Orpheus or David as Messiah.

Computer-enhanced analysis of the David scene in the Dura synagogue's reredos has enabled us to see that the scholarly identification of David as Orpheus has been incorrect. But could we have ascertained the error of seeing messianic notions in the David scene without the computer? The answer is yes, for the arguments identifying messianism with Orpheus or Orphism have seriously misunderstand their character.

ORPHEUS AND MESSIAH, ORPHISM AND MESSIANISM

Although the computer has been helpful in showing that the David of the reredos is not Orpheus, we do not need the computer to show that even if David was Orpheus we could not validly conclude that he was David the messiah. Obviously, if the myths about Orpheus depicted him as a messiah, or as a figure who would arrive in the future to change the world, or even as a prophetic forerunner of a messiah, there would be a link between Orpheus and messianism. But there are no such myths. Nothing in the stories about Orpheus or in the Orphic mysteries which claim him as founder stands out as messianic. As we mentioned above, Orpheus was known for his musical talents by which he performed his famous deeds and which ultimately led to his death. From this perspective, then, there is no link between Orpheus and any messianic expectations.[24]

Similarly, Orphism—the movement that sees Orpheus as its founder—contains no messianic beliefs. The Greek writers who used Orphic ideas—such as Plato, Eudemos, and Euripides—put forth no concepts of a messiah

---

[24] See note 20.

or of a divine national redemption.[25] The oracular poems produced by Orphism and attributed to Orpheus himself, similarly reveal neither messiah nor messianic age. Nothing in the Orphic writings suggests that identifying the Dura synagogue's David as Orpheus leads to the conclusion that this David is the messiah.

So where does the notion that Orphism is messianic come from? I trace the idea to a confusion in the concept of eschatology, for eschatology appears in both Orphism and messianism—although in different ways. Eschatology has acquired multiple meanings, but two in particular concern us here. The basic meaning of eschatology is the study of 'final things.' As applied to Orphism, the focus is on the end of each individual human, that is, their deaths. Orphism focuses on the life of the soul after the body's death, the judgment of the individual's actions during life, and the reward or punishment of the soul that will be given for them.[26] Of course, Orphism then prescribes the type of actions people should carry out while alive in order to get a favorable judgement after death. So Orphism is eschatological in that it is concerned with a person's life after death, or to put it in Christian terms, with an individual's resurrection.[27]

When we look at messianic religions—whether exemplified by Christianity or by Judaism—we find that they are also deemed eschatological, but in a different way. In these contexts, eschatology refers to 'final things' in terms of the 'end time,' that is, the end of the cosmos as it is known. This second understanding of eschatology is concerned with the radical transformation of the cosmos into a 'new age' in which God will wipe out all evil and institute a new cosmic order. This transformation is usually accomplished in an apocalyptic manner and is often initiated by a messiah. This messiah is an individual with other-worldly powers who plays a key role in the transformation. This second understanding of eschatology may include within it the concept of resurrection or life-after-death, but not necessarily. By confusing the two different types of eschatology, scholars have

---

[25] See, on Plato. Larry J. Alderink, *Creation and Salvation in Ancient Orphism* (Chico, CA: Scholars Press, 1981). See also the relevant sections of: L. Moulinier, *Orphée et l'Orphisme a l'Époque Classique* (Paris: Les Belles Lettres, 1955); Boulanger; V. D. Macchioro, *From Orpheus to Paul* (New York: Henry Holt and Co., 1930); Linforth, *Arts*; M. Detienne, "The myth of 'Honeyed Orpheus,'" in R. L. Gordon, ed., *Myth, religion and society* (Cambridge: Cambridge, 1981), pp. 95-110; and W. K. C. Guthrie, *Orpheus and Greek Religion* (London: Methuen & Co., 1935).

[26] Boulanger has a chapter in his book on Orphism's notion of life after death. He gives it the title "L'Orphisme et L'Eschatologie Chrétienne." See Boulanger.

[27] See Linforth, *Arts*; M. L. West, *The Orphic Poems* (Oxford: Clarendon, 1983); W. Burkert, "Craft Versus Sect: The Problem of Orphics and Pythagoreans," in B. F. Meyer and E. P. Sanders, eds., *Jewish and Christian Self-Definition* (Philadelphia: Fortress, 1982), vol. 3, pp. 1-22; L. J. Alderink, "Orphism," in *ABD*, vol. 5, pp. 48-50.

led themselves to believe that Orphism was eschatological in the messianic
sense rather than just in the notion of resurrection.

This confusion can be seen in E. R. Goodenough's interpretation of a judaized Orphic oracle. Orphic oracles apparently became quite popular in the
hellenistic period, even among those outside of Orphism. The hellenized
Jew Aristobolus, who lived in Alexandria sometime between the second century B.C.E. and the first century C.E., is attributed a judaized Orphic
poem.[28] Goodenough discusses this oracle at length, showing that its pagan
character was recaste as the 'Mystery of Moses.'[29] But a close look at this
Jewish-Orphic oracle still reveals no interest in the messiah or even in a future age; it looks rather to the past and to God's helping of Israel through
Moses. Thus not even the Jewish use of Orphic material contains any explicit messianic connotations. Even though Goodenough recognizes this
point, he ignores it in his desire to link Orphic David with messianism. At
the end of his discussion of Orpheus, he transforms his understanding of
David as Orpheus into David as messiah through sleight of hand.
Goodenough's argument is that David as Orpheus is a mystic—an initiate
into the mysteries. Goodenough then links mysticism and messianism in
the final paragraph of his discussion of the David scene. He posits that the
presence of mysticism necessarily entails the presence of messianism,
"mysticism is in its true sense 'realized eschatology'" (vol. 9, p. 104). Here
Goodenough substitutes the messianic understanding of eschatology for the
Orphic eschatology of life-after-death. Even though he has only shown that
the oracle is a reworking of Orphism with its eschatology of resurrection, he
concludes that it contains the eschatology of messianic expectations.
Although he makes no attempt to demonstrate the presence of a messianic
eschatology, he concludes that the synagogue's David is the messiah because he is Orpheus. Obviously, once understood, Goodenough's discussion
fails to make the case that David as Orpheus is David the messiah.

Goodenough, although unsuccessful, at least attempted to seek an aspect
of Orphism that might link Orpheus with messianism and then tie that element into details of Dura's David scene. Other scholars have simply ignored
the scene's details to interpret the painting more in line with the biblical
text. Both H. Stern and J. Goldstein are interested in David's supposed
Orphic character only to the extent it identifies the David figure as a messiah.[30] Once they make this identification, they ignore the figure's details.
Indeed, they reduce the scene to just two symbolic elements, namely, messiah and animals. This enables them to argue that the scene depicts Isaiah

---

[28] See M. Lafargue, "Orphica," in *OTP*, vol. 2, pp. 795-802; and A. Y. Collins,
"Aristobulus," in *OTP*, vol. 2, pp. 831-842.

[29] Goodenough, vol. 9, pp. 95-8.

[30] See Stern, "Orpheus," p. 4 and Goldstein, pp. 111-112.

11:1-9, claiming in particular that it depicts Is. 11:6: "The wolf shall dwell
with the lamb, and the leopard shall lie down with the kid, and the calf and
the lion and the fatling together." The David figure represents the "shoot
from the stump of Jesse" (Is. 11:1), that is, the messiah, while the lion and
the dove represent the peaceful animal behavior mentioned in verse six. But
the problem with this interpretation is that Dura's David scene contains
nothing which points specifically to this passage. Stern even admits this
point when he says, "In the synagogue it [i.e., the David scene] has been
used to illustrate not the actual prophecy of Isaiah, but, in a more general
sense, the Golden Age of the Messiah" (Stern, p. 4, brackets mine). But if
this Isaianic passage had been the referent for the Dura artist, the painting
should imitate the passage in more details. Only one of the animals mentioned in Is. 11:6-8 appears in the panel. No matching of a carnivorous animal with its prey takes place.[31] Furthermore, Isaiah depicts the future
Davidic king as neither a musician nor a shepherd.[32] These significant differences between Isaiah 11 and the synagogue painting, then, indicate that
painting does not represent the passage and thus precludes the passage's use
for identifying this scene as messianic. Furthermore, since Orpheus and
Orphism had no messianic elements, Stern's and Goldstein's initial assumption that David equals Orpheus equals the messiah does not hold.

So why have scholars persisted in their belief that an Orphic David must
be the messiah when nothing about Orpheus or Orphism reveals any messianic implications? In a nutshell, the explanation lies in Christian adoption
of Orphic imagery and the simplistic notion that Christianity must have followed Judaism's lead in this adoption. But there is a multitude of evidence
that Christianity took this material directly from Orphism, while there is
very little evidence that Judaism had more than occasional contact with it.

By the fourth or fifth century C.E., Christianity had taken over much
Orphic imagery, in both artistic and literary forms. In representational art,
Christ began to be depicted as an Orphic type in mosaics, paintings, frescos,
and sculpture. The most frequent image was that of Christ as Orpheus playing to the animals. In Christian theological literature, important thinkers
such as Clement and Eusebius, discussed Christ as a superior type of
Orpheus.[33] Clement explicitly described Orpheus as prefiguring Christ, in
some ways like the Old Testament prophets. E. Irwin argures that for
Clement, "the taming of beasts is an allegory, not of Orpheus, but of the

---

[31] As it does in several Christian mosiacs which depict the Isaiah passage. Several of
these are cited by Stern, "Orpheus," p. 5. Every one of these portrayals of Isaiah 11 have at
least one pair of carnivore and prey. None appear in the Dura synagogue's David scene.

[32] Goldstein's argument follows the same lines as Stern's with the addition of some
comments about the vine that he believes was part of the final composition.

[33] See Irwin, "Song"; Boulanger, pp. 117-134; and Murray, "Christian Orpheus."

activity of the Word [i.e., Christ] in dealing with mankind."[34] Christ uses the Word as an instrument to calm the bestial non-Christians. Eusebius picks up on this imagery and sees the "Word...who is 'all-wise' and 'all-harmonious' strikes up 'odes and epodes' which 'soften the fierce, angry passions of the souls of Greeks and barbarians.'"[35] So through its artists and its thinkers, Christianity reveals a long, continuous tradition of presenting Christ as an Orpheus-type. Moreover, this tradition stems from key church theologians, not from fringe or heretical elements.

It is also important to note that Christian thinkers brought David into the identification of Jesus and Orpheus. Since the gospels never portrayed Christ as a musician, these thinkers reached back to David—Jesus' supposed ancestor—and attributed "David's musical skill allegorically to Christ."[36] Thus Christianity had a tradition of linking David and Orpheus as part of its identification of Christ and Orpheus.

In contrast to the accepted Christian link between Christ and Orpheus—a link that continued into the Middle Ages—the evidence for Orphic influence on Judaism is quite small. Apart from the short Aristobulus poem mentioned above (and its related copies and revisions) there are no Jewish texts that incorporate any Orphic beliefs into Judaism. In the earlier part of the century, some scholars identified the Essenes and Therapeutae with Orphism, but with the discovery and analysis of the Dead Sea Scrolls, this identity no longer can be supported.[37] Indeed, the Jews did not even preserve Aristobulus' oracle; that was done by the Christians. Furthermore, the oracle only mentioned doctrines; it never mentioned Orpheus nor identified any Jewish hero with him.

The artistic evidence for linking Orphism and Judaism is no more substantial. There are only two images, to my knowledge, that have been identified as Jewish depictions of David as Orpheus: the one at Dura and a sixth-century floor mosaic in a Gaza synagogue.[38] We have just shown that Dura's David is not an Orphic figure. The Gaza synagogue simply provides an image of King David with a harp and the mosaic remains of (perhaps) two animals; the rest of the image has been destroyed. So the image is not

---

[34] Irwin, "Song," p. 54. Brackets mine.

[35] Irwin, "Song," p. 56.

[36] Irwin, "Song," p. 57; see also pp. 54-55..

[37] Boulanger, pp. 70-75; and V. D. Macchioro, *From Orpheus to Paul* (New York: Henry Holt & Co., 1930), pp. 188-189. D. M. Kosinsky (*Orpheus in Nineteenth-Century Symbolism* [Ann Arbor, MI: UMI Research Press, 1989], p. 7) states that the apocryphal Psalm 151 found at Qumran is "the earliest identification of David with Orpheus" in Judaism. What she takes as fact has been a matter of debate from its initial suggestion. F. M. Cross in fact definitively demonstrated the fallacy of this identification more than ten years earlier. For discussion and bibliography see Cross' "David, Orpheus, and Psalm 151:3-4," in *BASOR* 231 (Oct., 1978): 69-71.

[38] See Ovadiah, "Synagogue."

complete enough to provide any reliable interpretation. Moreover, since it was constructed several centuries after the Dura, it does not constitute an artistic antecedent. In Judaism prior to or during the third century C.E., therefore, no artistic tradition of depicting David as Orpheus can be demonstrated.[39]

So essentially what has happened is that the messianic character has been read back from Christianity onto Orpheus and then onto David. Christ as Orpheus became Orpheus the Christ, i.e., Orpheus the messiah. Once the Dura synagogue's David was identified as Orpheus, it was only a short step to identifying 'Orphic' David as David the messiah. This faulty link was strengthened by the Christian practice of also linking David—as a messianic forerunner—to Orpheus. These two linkages—albeit in Christianity and not in Judaism—explain the persistence of scholars thinking that identifying Dura's David as Orpheus meant that David was therefore the messiah. This persistence essentially constitutes the 'christianization' of Dura's Judaism.

MESSIANISM IN THE ART OF THE DURA SYNAGOGUE

Up to this point of the essay, I have focused solely on the David scene within the reredos and have shown that there is no reason to identify it as messianic from either the image itself or from its supposed association with Orpheus and Orphism. But we have not yet completed our investigation. To be absolutely sure that no rationale remains for interpreting the David figure as messianic, we need to examine the other paintings for messianic themes—both the other scenes of the reredos and the other paintings around the room. Perhaps they provide a reason for interpreting Dura's David as a messiah.

In its final configuration before the synagogue's destruction, the bottom picture of the reredos contained two scenes in which a person sits on a couch before a group of people. In one, twelve figures surround the couch, in the other a man and two boys stand before it. Scholars have interpreted these scenes as Jacob blessing his twelve sons, described in Gen. 49, and Jacob blessing the two sons of Joseph, found in Gen. 48. Up to this point, I think these identifications are correct. But several scholars, including Stern, Goodenough, and Goldstein, go a step further to argue that the portrayal of these scenes is inherently messianic.[40] Stern states that Gen. 49 "contains

---

[39] A similar point has been by Sister Charles Murray in a reexamination of Stern, "Orphée." See Murray, "Christian Orpheus." Stern's reply, "De l'Orphée juif et chrétien," on p. 28 of the same volume fails to rebut her point. Concerning his reference to the apocryphal Psalm 151 from Qumran, see note 37 above.

[40] Kraeling, p. 226, sees the upper panel as a messianic reading of Gen. 49:10-11, but not the lower.

the most famous Messianic prophecy in the Old Testament" (Gen. 49:9-11).
This is true, assuming a certain interpretive context. At the time of its
composition, Gen. 49:9-11 was not messianic.[41] Rather, looking forward
from Jacob's time, it refered to the uniting of the people Israel under the
first Judahite king. That is to say, it constitutes a prophecy of the first, biblical King David. It is not until many centuries later that it came to be seen
as a prophecy for a Davidic messiah. The early Christians for whom the
passage became "famous"—in Stern's words—are well known for seeing
these verses as messianic.

To be fair to Stern, Gen. 49:9-11 acquired messianic overtones in post-
Temple Jewish writings as well. These do not support the claim, however,
that the reredos' representation of Gen. 49 is messianic. Genesis Rabbah, for
example, has a few messianic comments, one of which interprets Gen.
49:10 as a messianic prophecy predicting Hillel as a Davidic "messiah" (GR
98:8).[42] But this does not bolster Stern's case. One problem is that this text
was composed in Palestine (not Babylonia) a century or more after Dura's
destruction. More tellingly, the interpretation itself is specific to local-
Palestinian concerns because the designation of Hillel as a Davidic messiah
stems from the politics of the Palestinian Patriarch; it constitutes an attempt to bolster the Patriarch's authority within the Jewish community.
This is not the type of messiah which Stern sees in the Dura reredos.

The targums to the book of Genesis reveal stronger support for a messianic interpretation of the Genesis passage than Genesis Rabbah. These
texts provide clear evidence of Jewish interpretation of Gen. 49:9-11 which
foresees a future Messiah who will arrive to alter the current situation.[43]
One of the Palestinian Targums to the Pentateuch, Targum Neofiti, probably stems from the second century C.E., early enough to have been known
by Dura's Jews. But Neofiti's interpretation of Gen. 49:9-11 did not provide
the conceptual basis for the reredos in Dura's synagogue. Stern's argument
makes it quite clear that the reredos' messiah is peaceful. Orpheus was a
symbol of heavenly peace and so, according to Stern, the David/
Orpheus/messiah represents the coming of peace to the world. The targum's
messianic interpretation of Gen. 49:9-11, by contrast, is one of violence and
war:

> How beautiful is King Messiah who is to arise from among those of the
> house of Judah. He girds his loins and goes forth to battle against those
> that hate him; and he kills kings with rulers, and makes the mountains red

---

[41] See Skinner, *Genesis*, pp. 518-24, and von Rad, *Genesis*, pp. 424-6.

[42] See Neusner, *Messiah*, pp. 138-9.

[43] Targum Onkelos has a similar interpretation, but it is less useful since it was not
composed until the fourth century.

from the blood of their slain and makes the valleys white from the fat of the warriors. His garments are rolled in blood.

Targum Neofiti to Gen. 49:11[44]

A messiah who "makes the mountains red" from the blood of slain enemies and whose clothes are covered with blood is not a peaceful messiah. This interpretation of Gen. 49 could not have formed the interpretive background to the Dura synagogue's reredos.

It is much more likely that the synagogue's blessing scenes were painted on the basis of the biblical understanding of the two chapters, rather than later messianic speculation. The key to this lies in the choice of the two scenes, Jacob's blessing of his twelve sons and Jacob's blessing of Joseph's sons. Stern and others have argued that the former blessing is messianic—based primarily on an interpretation of Gen. 49:10-11. These verses refer to the coming descendant of the tribe of Judah who will be a king and a messiah. As the above-quoted targum to Gen. 49:11 indicates, this interpretation was current among Jews during the existence of the Dura synagogue. But the artist's decision to include a second scene—that of Jacob blessing his grandsons, Ephraim and Manasseh—provides the first hint that depicting messianic expectations was not the artist's goal. Stern, Goldstein, Wischnitzer and others provide no support for interpreting this scene as messianic. Apparently they overlooked a suggestion by A. Grabar which sees this as following Targum Pseudo-Jonathan's interpretation of Exodus 40:9-11.[45] Pseudo-Jonathan recasts these verses to suggest that the King Messiah from Judah will redeem Israel and the Messiah of Ephraim will overcome Gog and his confederates at the end of days.

But once again the narrow focus on trying to find support for a messianic interpretation of the reredos has led scholars to ignore the obvious details of the painting. These two blessing scenes are not of Judah and Ephraim, as the messianic interpretation suggests. The scenes depict Jacob blessing all twelve sons and both of Joseph's sons. Any interpretation of the scenes must account for the fourteen recipients of blessings, not just two.

So how should the two blessing scenes of the lower register of the reredos be understood? These paired scenes represent the establishment of the people Israel. The fourteen individuals receiving blessings are the founding

---

[44] This quote is taken from M. McNamara, *Targum Neofiti 1: Genesis* (Collegeville, MN: Liturgical Press, 1992), p. 220. For further discussion of messiah and the targums, see Neusner, *Messiah*, pp. 239-48; S. H. Levey, *The Messiah: An Aramaic Interpretation* (Cincinnati, OH: Hebrew Union College, 1974). On Gen. 49 in the targums, see R. Syren, *The Blessings in the Targums: A Study on the Targumic Interpretations of Genesis 49 and Deuteronomy 33* (Abo: Abo Akademi, 1986).

[45] A. Grabar, "Les Fresques de la Synagogue de Doura-Europos," *CRAI* (1941): 77-90, esp. 82. The problem with Grabar's argument is that Targum Pseudo-Jonathan was composed several centuries after Dura's destruction.

fathers of the tribes of Israel. The scenes refer to the past and depict the
unity of all Jews through their common ancestry. This emphasis on the
peoplehood of Israel is an important theme in nearly every form of Judaism.
It would have been particularly significant to Dura's Jews, who would have
been constantly reminded of Israel's scattered condition by their isolation in
an out-of-the-way diaspora town like Dura.

Moving from the lower register of the reredos to the upper, we find it
contains a court scene—a figure seated on a throne surrounded by fifteen
men.[46] I follow Kraeling and others in understanding this scene as David
crowned as king over the thirteen tribes. These are accompanied by David's
two priests Zadok and Abiathar—who represent the tribe of Levi. This provides the completion for the theme of Israel's unity begun in the lower register. David was not part of the founding fathers, coming many generations
afterwards. But his kingship provided the unity that founders could not. Let
me explain. Abraham, Isaac, and Jacob were each a single, unchallenged
ruler of their children. With the division into tribes headed by Jacob's children, the leadership became divided, with each tribe having its own head.
David's rise to kingship over all the tribes restored the unity that had been
lost. David's unifying power comes from his position over all the tribes and
their leaders. In this position he becomes a forefather himself, indeed, the
chief of the forefathers.

From the bottom up, then, the reredos depicts the story of the formation
of Israel's nationhood. In the lower register, the blessings of Jacob represent
the foundation of the people. Above that comes the David presented as a
composite of his historical roles: shepherd, musician, and king. The upper
register depicts his place as the forefather—a ruler of equals—and the restoration of the unity of the people Israel. The reredos is clearly a nationalistic
painting, emphasizing the unity of the people Israel.

Before closing our discussion of the reredos, we must address one last aspect, namely, the tree-vine (hereinafter called a tree).[47] This is because many
scholars have placed the tree in the final version of the reredos and identified
it as the Tree of Life. But this is not accurate, in my view. The tree formed
the original painting of the reredos, before any of the figures we have dis-

---

[46] Du Mesnil suggested that there might be fourteen figures, while Gute painted fifteen.
Kraeling follows Gute, and argues that the scene was painted in two stages. The earlier
scene consisted only of the seated king and two court figures before him, as in the other
scenes of kings in the Dura synagogue. In the later scene, the artist added thirteen more
figures. Computer analysis of the upper register, however, reveals evidence for only thirteen,
although much of the upper part of the painting has been destroyed since its discovery. The
figures that cannot be confirmed are in the damaged areas. See Goodenough, vol. 11, plate
IV and figure 323; Kraeling, *Synagogue*, p. 226, n. 894 and plates XXXV & LXXV; Du
Mesnil, *Les peintures*, p. 44.

[47] For discussion and relevent bibliography, see Kraeling, *Synagogue*, pp. 62-65, 214-27;
Goldstein, pp. 101-109.

cussed were added. When the red wash was applied to the painting, it covered
the tree completely. Confusion has reigned in scholarly interpretation, however, because the dark-colored leaves have shown through the succeeding
coats of paint across the reredos, interfering with the later scenes. This led
Du Mesnil to posit that some leaves were later painted back over new
scenes. But Pearson's ability to trace a single, connected tree—rather than
disconnected branches—suggests this did not happen. Furthermore, computer analysis indicates that the leaves' color remains the same throughout
the reredos, which suggests that the leaves were painted at the same time.
The tree, then, was fully painted out before later scenes were added. It has no
place in the interpretation of the final design of the reredos. Neither the tree
nor the appearance of David as Orpheus (now disproven) provides an interpretive background for the reredos which would point to its messianic character.

If we turn to the other paintings in the synagogue, we continue to find a
distinct lack of messianic themes. Indeed, a careful reader of the decades of
scholarship concerning messianism in the paintings in the Dura synagogue
will have noticed an interesting phenomenon. No painting apart from the
reredos has a history of being cited as messianic. This is because none of
them contain any clear messianic themes. They depict miracles performed by
God—parting the Reed Sea and drowning the Egyptians through Moses;
raising the widow's dead son through Elijah; destroying the idols in the
temple of Dagon; raising the dry bones—as well as scenes with the Temple
and its forerunner the Tabernacle, but nothing that stands out as messianic.
Kraeling identified the Ezekiel scene of raising the dry bones into living
people as the eschatological "Restoration of National Life," but nothing in
the painting requires messianic or even eschatological interpretation.[48]
Kraeling's interpretation of this panel, like Wischnitzer's approach to all the
synagogue's paintings, presupposes the presence of messianic ideas in order
to see them there.[49] Similarly, Goodenough's interpretation of the "Closed
Temple" reads messianism into the scene, rather than drawing it out.[50]
Detailed refutations of these suggestions are not necessary. None of the
paintings have any direct, thematic appeal to messianic ideas.

The notion that the Dura Jews were messianic, then, draws support from
none of the synagogue's paintings. The lack of interest in the messiah
throughout the synagogue's art also suggests that the reredos lacks mes-

---

[48] Kraeling, *Synagogue*, pp. 178-94

[49] See Wischnitzer, *Theme*. Despite the title of this volume, *The Messianic Theme in the
Paintings of the Dura Synagogue*, Wischnitzer often makes a poorer case for the messianic
interpretation of the reredos and the Ezekiel sequence than previous scholars. See also R.
Wischnitzer-Bernstein, "The Conception of the Resurrection in the Ezekiel Panel of the Dura
Synagogue,' *JBL* 60 (1941): 43-55.

[50] Goodenough, vol. 10, pp. 42-73.

sianic interests. This is because the reredos is the central painting of the
synagogue and as such it would reflect the overall themes of the room and
set a central focus for them. It would be odd for an artist to set up messianic
themes in the room's central painting and then fail to carry them through in
any other painting. To be sure, many of the paintings are missing and we
have no knowledge of what their contents may have been. But if messianism was important enough to provide the main focus of the synagogue's
central painting, it should also appear in the other preserved paintings, since
we have remains of more than half. Since it does not, the non-reredos paintings in the synagogue do not lead us to expect messianic themes in the
reredos itself.

MESSIANISM AND JUDAISM

This brings us to our final question. If there is no messianism in the Dura
synagogue paintings, why have scholars been so persistent in seeing it
there? The persistence comes from the wide-spread, scholarly notion that
messianic ideas appeared throughout Judaism at this period and for several
centuries prior. J. Goldstein makes an explicit case when he argues that
there is a *prima facie* reason for seeing messianic themes in the Dura reredos
because strong messianic beliefs permeated the Judaism of this period.[51] In
recent years, however, there have been several studies of messianic ideas in
the different types of Judaism during the Second-Temple and rabbinic
periods. These studies have shown that not all types of Judaism were
messianic. Indeed, most Jewish groups did not incorporate messianic ideas
into their thinking.

One recently published work, *Judaisms and their Messiahs at the Turn of
the Christian Era*, edited by J. Neusner and W. S. Green, surveys the literary
evidence of different types of Judaism during or just prior to the first century. William Green sums up the results of the different studies:

> Any [scholarly] notion of a messianic belief or idea in ancient Judaism
> necessarily presupposes that "messiah" was a focal and evocative native
> category for ancient Jews. But a review of Israelite and early Judaic litera-
> ture, the textual record produced and initially preserved by Jews, makes
> such a conclusion dubious at best....Most of the Dead Sea Scrolls and the
> Pseudepigrapha, and the entire Apocrypha, contain no reference to "the
> messiah." Moreover, a messiah is neither essential to the apocalyptic
> genre nor a prominent feature of ancient apocalyptic writings....
> The Maccabean documents, which disdain the revival of the Davidic dy-
> nasty ignore the term. There is no messiah in Jubilees, nor in Enoch 1-36
> and 91-104, nor in the Assumption of Moses, nor in 2 Enoch nor in the

---

[51] Goldstein, pp. 109-111.

Sibylline Oracles....The messiah is absent from Josephus' description of
Judaism in both *Antiquities* and *Against Apion*, and also from the writings
of Philo.[52]

Messiahs appear, by contrast, only in Ben Sira, Psalms of Solomon 17, a
few scrolls from Qumran, Josephus' *War*, and once in the Similitudes of
Enoch. Two early second-century C.E. texts, Second Baruch and Fourth
Ezra, likewise contain several references to the messiah.[53] So 'messiah' fails
to comprise a central category in different types of Judaism of the Second-
Temple period; it instead occurs infrequently. It does not infuse Jewish belief, but instead appears occasionally, usually in writings by people on the
periphery of Jewish society.

The situation after the Temple's destruction is similar. Jacob Neusner
studied the approaches of rabbinic texts to messianic ideas in his *Messiah in
Context*.[54] He discovered that messianic references appear strongly only in
fourth- and fifth-century texts such as the Palestinian Talmud (and later in
the Babylonian Talmud) and Genesis Rabbah and Leviticus Rabbah.[55]
Among earlier rabbinic texts, those which had been, or might have been,
composed at the time of the painting of the Dura synagogue, messianic
ideas appear much less regularly. The Mishnah and the Tosefta make a couple of references to the messianic age, but they do not build their conception
of the world and cosmos around it.[56] Indeed, the authors of each text built a
systematic Judaism in which a messiah could play no role. Midrashim such
as Sifra and Sifre Numbers do not even mention the messiah, while the
Mekilta and Sifre Deuteronomy have only occasional references to the messianic age.[57] So while there are messianic ideas and even messianic-based
movements among Jews in the centuries prior to the painting of the Dura
synagogue, these appear occasionally, rather than systematically. There is
widespread ignoring of messianic ideas in all periods.[58] For the Dura Jews,
then, no *prima facie* expectation exists that they should hold messianic be-

---

[52] See Green, "Question," pp. 2-3. Brackets mine.

[53] For dating of these texts, see the discussions in *OTP*, vol. 1, pp. 520, 616-7.

[54] See Neusner, *Messiah*. Neusner's work on rabbinic Judaism has been criticized by E.
P. Sanders (*Jewish Law from Jesus to the Mishnah* [Philadelphia: Trinity Press International,
1990], pp. 309-31). More recently, C. Evans in "Mishna and Messiah 'in Context': Some
Comments on Jacob Neusner's Proposals" (*JBL* 112, no. 2 [1993] 267-89), has specifically
attacked *Messiah in Context* and Neusner's approach to understanding messianic concepts in
rabbinic Judaism. Neusner has reponded in "The Mishna in Philosophical Context and Out of
Canonical Bounds" (*JBL* 112, no. 2 [1993] 291-304).

[55] See Neusner, *Messiah*, pp. 79-97, 138-43, 167-190. As we mentioned above, messianic
ideas also appear in the Palestinian Targums, composed at the earliest in the second century
C.E.

[56] See Neusner, *Messiah*, pp. 17-41, 53-73.

[57] See Neusner, *Messiah*, pp. 131-137.

[58] The largest 'Jewish' group of this period that held messianic beliefs were the
Christians.

liefs. Any existence of messianic themes in the artwork needs to be demonstrated, not assumed *a priori*.

CONCLUSION

This study removes all the supports for interpreting the Judaism of Dura's Jews as messianic. First, the computer-assisted image analysis of the synagogue's David scene provides solid evidence against the identification of David as Orpheus. Second, the essay's next section reveals that neither Orpheus nor Orphism had messianic stories or doctrines associated with them. So even if the David figure is Orpheus, that does not lead to the conclusion that he was David the messiah. Third, the following analysis shows in addition that none of the other pictures in the Dura synagogue have explicit messianic associations. So if David is a messianic figure, his scene stands alone; no other painting in the synagogue depicts messianic themes. Consequently, far from being a key belief, a messiah remains relatively unimportant at Dura. Finally, to explain why scholars have persisted in reading the reredos as messianic, I argue that they assumed that all forms of Judaism are messianic. Our discussion shows that this is not the case. Instead, I suggest that the reredos' David scene is an indication of the national unity of the Jewish people, despite their scattered circumstances across the diaspora. The unity comes from their past—their nationhood and their peoplehood—and unites them under their first king, King David, rather than the multiplicity of the twelve tribes.

FIG. 21 Free-hand rendition of David in the reredos of the Dura synagogue.

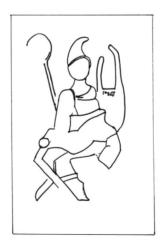

THE MOSAIC WORKSHOP OF GAZA
IN CHRISTIAN ANTIQUITY

ASHER OVADIAH[*]

The aim of this study is to examine the question of whether the town of Gaza formed a regional center for the production of artistic mosaics.[1] Using the methods of history and archaeology, we will examine the period from the start of the Byzantine era and extending into the sixth century A.D. This period includes the reigns of the Byzantine Emperors Anastasius (491-518), Justin I (518-527), and Justinian I (527-565). The era in which these three emperors reigned was a time of prosperity and relative political stability in the Byzantine Empire. Gaza benefited from this and became a flourishing city in the cultural, intellectual, and economic domains. It fulfilled the function of an eminent cultural center for the district along the southern coastal plain of the Holy Land, while the other settlements mentioned below had a rural character.[2]

We know through literary sources that from the fifth century A.D. Gaza was an important town in the Christian world. It was famous for its schools and its academy of rhetoric, and many important personages lived there and practiced their craft.[3]

---

[*] This essay was originally published as "Les Mosaïstes de Gaza dans l'Antiquité Chrétienne," *Revue Biblique* 82 (Octobre 1975): 552-557. The translation appears by permission of the author and the Editor, *Revue Biblique*. It was translated by Dr. Fiona Ritchie.

[1] My teacher, the late Prof. M. Avi-Yonah, has already stated "that both the earlier Maʿon and later Shellal pavements are the products of the same workshop, which was probably located at Gaza (the center of the region)," see *Rabinowitz Bulletin*, vol. 3, p. 34. See also the article in *La Mosaïque Gréco-Romaine, II* (Vienne 30 Août-4 Septembre 1971; Paris: A. & J. Picard, 1975), pp. 377-383.

[2] For general information about Gaza, see: Stephen of Byzantium, s.v. *Gaza*; M. A. Meyer, *History of the City of Gaza* (New York: Columbia University Press, 1907); G. Downey, *Gaza in the Early Sixth Century* (Norman, OK: University of Oklahoma Press, 1963); S. Assaf and L. A. Mayer, eds., *Sepher ha-Yishuv*, 2 vols. (Tel Aviv, 1939-44) (in Hebrew); J. Braslavski (Braslavi), *Le-Heker Arzenu—ʿAvar u-Seridim* (Tel Aviv: Hakibbutz Hameuhad, 1954) (in Hebrew); J. Braslavski (Braslavi), *Mi-Rezuʿat ʿAzzah ʿad Yam Suf* (1957) (in Hebrew).

[3] One of the most important was Procopius of Gaza, who was active during the reign of the Emperor Anastasius. Other outstanding personalities were Porphyrius, Bishop of Gaza, a powerful, active and influential figure (346-420); Choricius, a disciple of Procopius, was a scientist and rhetorician whose activity occurred primarily between 520 and 540; Marcianus, Archbishop of Gaza, who was a fellow disciple of Choricius. In connection with these figures, we can mention other less-famous lettered men who brought some personal touches

On the Madaba map (sixth century), Gaza appears as a large fortified town with colonnaded streets crossing at its center and with large squares, a great church, and a theater (or *nymphaeum*). These appear in the traditional style of classical architecture of the Graeco-Roman world.[4] The port of Gaza was called "New Town" (*Maioumas Neapolis*), that is to say, Maritime Gaza or Gaza Maiumas. It is under this name, Μαιουμας καὶ Νεαπόλις, that it appears on the Madaba map, with buildings and streets which meet at right angles.[5] This town, faithful to Christianity long before the capital, was also called Constantia from the fourth century.[6] It was here that the ancient Gaza synagogue was discovered. With Tiberias and Zoar, the town formed one of the three great centers of pilgrimage in the Holy Land at the beginning of the Byzantine period.

Some Christian sources reveal the existence in Gaza of churches whose remains have still not been discovered. One of these churches, the Eudoxiana, from the name of the Empress Eudoxia, is described in detail in *The Life of Porphyry*.[7]

The mosaics of a second church, founded in the sixth century and dedicated to St. Sergius, are described at length by Choricius in a panegyric addressed to Marcian, the bishop of Gaza who had the idea of founding the church and had contributed to its building.[8] The dome, pendentives, apses, arches, walls, floors and baptistry were decorated with rich mosaics of high artistic quality. They bear witness to the rank and skill of the artist (or group of artists). This church contained so many mosaic panels that Choricius deems it impossible to describe them all in his panegyric honoring the bishop. He decides, therefore, to omit the motifs on the lower part of the walls and directs the visitor to contemplate the artistry of the ceiling vaults. The dramatic descriptions of Choricius—which included the central

---

to the intellectual and cultural world of Gaza. These include John of Gaza, Zosimus, Aeneas, Timothy and the bishop Zachary of Mitylene, originally from Gaza. All these people were active during the course of the fifth and sixth century. One of the best known writers who studied in the Gaza schools was Procopius of Caesarea; he became the Secretary of State for Justinian the First and the most important historian of Justinian's reign. These brilliant intellectuals made Gaza into a cultural center of exceptional cultural importance.

[4] See Avi-Yonah, *Madaba*, p. 74, pl. 9.

[5] See Avi-Yonah, *Madaba*, pp. 74f., pl. 9; see also Sozomenus, *Hist. Eccl.*, II, 5, in *PG*, LXVII (Paris, 1864), col. 948; ibid., V, 3, col. 1221.

[6] "...ὃν Μαιουμᾶν προσαγορεύουσιν, εἰσάγαν δεισιδαιμονοῦν, καὶ τὰ ἀρχαῖα πρὸ τούτου θαυμάζον, εἰς Χριστιανισμὸν ἀθρόον πανδημεὶ μετέβαλε" (Sozomenus, *PG*, LXVII [Paris, 1864], cols. 948, 1221).

[7] Marcus Diaconus, *Vita S. Porphyrii Episcopi Gazenzis*, in *PG*, LXV (Paris, 1864), cols. 1211-1254. See also Mark the Deacon, *The Life of Porphyry, Bishop of Gaza*, translated with introduction and notes by G. F. Hill (Oxford, 1913); and *Vie de Porphyre, évéque de Gaza*, edited and translated by H. Grégoire and M. A. Kugener (Paris: Les Belles Lettres, 1930).

[8] See also Choricius, translated by R. W. Hamilton, in *PEFQS* (1930): 178-191.

events of the life of Christ: His Passion, His Glorification, and Ascension—brought the mosaics alive to his readers.

Choricius also describes the mosaics of a third church, that of St. Stephen. In particular, the mosaic in the apse depicted the founder holding a model of the church and a picture of St. John the Baptist. The cupola was entirely filled with the figure of Jesus Pantocrator. On the mosaic pavement of the eastern colonnade which led to the church appeared fruits, plants, birds, pots, and other items. The artist had reproduced these motifs with precision and great mastery. These representations once again evidence the skill of the artists of the Gaza workshop.

From this review of the literary evidence for mosaic artists in Gaza, we turn to the archaeological evidence. Central to our argument are the four polychrome mosaic pavements, composed of round medallions, discovered in sites on the southern coastal plain:[9]

1. The synagogue of Maritime Gaza, which can be dated by the mosaic inscription to 508/9 A.D.[10] (See PL. 22.)

2. The Hazor church (in Judea), which can be dated to 512 A.D. by one of the Greek inscriptions on the mosaic.[11] (See PL. 23.)

3. The Synagogue of Ma'on (Nirim). According to the archaeological finds, especially the coins, it was built no later than 538 A.D.[12] (See PL. 24.)

4. The Shellal church, which can be dated to 561/2 A.D. by one of the Greek inscriptions on the mosaic.[13] (See PL. 25.)

---

[9] The motif of round medallions made of a vine-trellis coming out of an amphora is not restricted to these four mosaics. They appear in many other mosaics discovered in Israel and elsewhere. This composition is found in a form at one and the same time asymmetric and symmetric. See R. P. Hinks, *Catalogue of Greek, and Roman Paintings and Mosaics in the British Museum* (London: British Museum, 1934), pp. LIII f.; D. Levi, *Antioch Mosaic Pavements*, vol. 1 (Princeton: Princeton University Press, 1947), pp. 511-515. A catalogue of these pavements has been prepared by F. M. Beibel, "Mosaics," in C. H. Kraeling, ed., *Gerasa, City of the Decapolis* (New Haven: ASOR, 1938), p. 303, n. 27. See also F. van der Meer, *Atlas of the Early Christian World* (London: Nelson, 1958), nos. 141, 263. Some other specimens have been discovered at Sede Nahum (*RB* 64 [1957]: 261; Yeivin, below, note 11, p. 46; the file of the site is in the archives of the Israel Department of Antiquities and Museums); Beth-Shean (*RB* 78 [1971]: 585-586 and pl. XXVIIb; D. Bahat, *Qadmoniot* 5, no. 2 [18] [1972]: 56 [in Hebrew]); Matta' (A. Ovadiah, Ruth Ovadiah, S. Gudovitz, *RB* 83 [1976]: 421-431, pls. xxxviii-xli); Tiberias (unpublished; *RB* 63 [1956]: 97); Kurnub (A. Negev, *CNI* 17, no. 4 [1966], Photos).

[10] A. Ovadiah, *Qadmoniot* 1, no. 4 (1968): 120-124, pls. 3-4 (in Hebrew); A. Ovadiah, *IEJ* 19 (1969): 193-198, pls.15-18.

[11] S. Yeivin, *A Decade of Archaeology in Israel, 1948-58* (Istanbul: Nederlands Historish-Archaeologish Institut, 1960), p. 45. The records of the site are in the Archives of the Israel Department of Antiquities and Museums (unpublished).

[12] M. Avi-Yonah, *Rabinowitz Bulletin*, vol. 3, pp. 25-35. Cf. *RB* 65 (1958): 421-422 and pl. XII.

[13] A. D. Trendall, *The Shellal Mosaic* (Canberra: Australian War Memorial, 1957).

The mosaics of Ma'on and Shellal have striking resemblances.[14] The pavements are composed of five vertical rows of round medallions, linked together by rings. At both sites, an amphora appears in the central medallion near the main entrance to the vestibule. It is flanked by two peacocks, each one filling two medallions. The motifs of the central axis are identical, while the lateral medallions are decorated with similar animals. The accent is placed more on symmetry at Ma'on than at Shellal, since at Ma'on the animals are identical on each side. Despite the geographical proximity of the two pavements, the similarity in the decoration of their details and their execution, they are separated in time by at least twenty-five years.

At Gaza and Hazor, the pavements have been executed according to the same artistic canon: the space is divided into three vertical rows of round medallions. Again, the central row provides the axis of symmetry. Unlike Ma'on and Shellal, these pavements' medallions are not linked by rings. At Gaza and Hazor, the medallions in the central row are decorated with still life and animals, while at Ma'on and Shellal there are no animals in that row.[15] At Gaza, as at Hazor, the decoration is not always rigorously enclosed in the frame of the medallion and the animals sometimes stray outside its boundaries. In this way, the accent is put on realism and freedom, and the animals which follow each other recall hellenistic prototypes influenced by the East. One should note that at Gaza the animals of the central row are turned towards the right and left; they do not all face in the same direction, contrary to the other lateral rows.

Despite the differences in detail, the disposition of the motifs is similar in the mosaic pavements of the four buildings. In all four, the decoration is oriented towards the main entrance, and the first medallion in the axis of symmetry is decorated with an amphora from which tangled vines—trellis' emerges (in Gaza, this part of the pavement near to the entrance has been destroyed, but one can imagine that there also was an amphora). In the four pavements, the axis of symmetry is underlined by closed medallions in the central row, while the medallions in the lateral rows are slightly open; in the Gaza pavement, for example, the depictions in the central row of still life and of animals, which turn left or right, emphasize the axis of symmetry. By contrast, the animals represented in the lateral medallions are shown in an antithetical manner. (It is interesting to note in all these medallions the absence of any human figures.) They include a wide range of birds, wild and savage animals, and domesticated animals—the images stem from the same repertoire, without a doubt. Moreover they are drawn with talent, pre-

---

[14] The resemblance between the two mosaic pavements has been partially treated by Avi-Yonah, in *Rabinowitz Bulletin*, vol. 3, pp. 32-33.

[15] At Gaza, the Greek inscription is inscribed in one of the round medallions of the central row.

cision, and skill. Some representations are to be found in three out of four pavements (although they might have originally appeared in the fourth and have since been destroyed): the bird in a cage (Gaza, Ma'on, Shellal); the basket of fruit (Hazor, Ma'on, Shellal); savage animals chasing other animals (Gaza, Hazor, Shellal).

Above, we noted a close relationship between the pavements of Gaza and Hazor on the one hand and between those of Ma'on and Shellal on the other. The mosaic pavements of Gaza and Hazor are earlier than those of Ma'on and Shellal. In addition, the animals on the Gaza pavement are represented in a more realistic fashion, in a much freer style and executed to a higher artistic standard. At Hazor, at least judging by the little that remains of the mosaic, it is possible to state that there is a strong tendency towards realism; for instance, the hare on the basket of grapes and the hounds pursuing the doe. At Ma'on, by contrast, the animals do not stray outside the medallion frame, which is without doubt the sign of a more conservative and severe conception. The animal figures become individual images within the circular frames, with the exception of the symbolic representations of peacocks flanking the amphora, the palm trees, the lions, and the menorah. We should not, however, leave unremarked the realistic treatment of several details, such as, a hen laying an egg, a double basket full of grapes—all irregularly shaped—and the peacock tails. A conception similar to that of Ma'on can be seen at Shellal. If there remains here a certain tendency towards realism—such as the birds pecking the grapes in the double basket—it must be pointed out that the grapes are very stylized. Similarly, none of the animals steps out of its frame and the peacocks' tails are also highly stylized.

From all that we have said so far, it turns out that we can see a certain evolution of style: from the realism of the mosaic pavement of Gaza, the earliest of the four, towards a progressive tendency towards stylization in the Shellal mosaic, the most recent. The number of rows of medallions is proportional to the dimensions of the pavement and must not be considered as a development of three rows of medallions (Gaza, Hazor) to five (Ma'on, Shellal).

The four pavements of mosaic studied here present all the characteristics usually associated with this type of ornamentation. However, a certain number of characteristics are common and make up a homogeneous group: the representation of the amphora in the central medallion near the entrance; the importance given to the axis of symmetry by the particular motifs; the insistence placed on symmetrical composition by the representation of the animals in an antithetic and rhythmical way; the variety of still lifes, birds, domestic animals, wild and ferocious animals; the absence of human figures; the realism of the depiction which denotes sharp and penetrating observation, seasoned with humor.[16]

Taking account of the grandeur, the position and locality of Gaza at this time, and the witness of written sources and archaeological finds, we can conclude that Gaza housed in the early Byzantine period, a central mosaic workshop whose clientele was both Jewish and Christian. This center produced mosaics full of color and variety for the synagogues and churches, but the artists or artisans remained anonymous; we can determine neither their identity nor their religion.[17] One thing is certain, however, their workmanship was of high artistic quality. We can therefore suppose that it produced both the mosaic pavements at the settlements mentioned above, and it is possible that it may have influenced the decoration in other sites.[18]

---

[16] Cf. C. R. Morey, *Early Christian Art* (Princeton: Princeton University Press, 1953), pp. 54 f., 58 f.

[17] See Downey (above, note 2), pp. 6-8.

[18] To the above citations, one can add, F. M. Abel, "Gaza au VIe siècle d'après le rhéteur Chorikios," *RB* 40 (1931): 5-31. See also Ovadiah, *MPI*.

SECTION VI

PUBLIC STRUCTURES AND JEWISH COMMUNITIES
IN THE GOLAN HEIGHTS

DAN URMAN

PREFACE

The study of Jewish archaeological remains in the region today called the Golan Heights began in the 1880's with the journeys and surveys of L. Oliphant and G. Schumacher. Oliphant was actually the first to report the existence of Jewish public buildings in the Golan, which he called 'synagogues,' comparing their artifacts with those of similar buildings previously discovered in the Galilee. Therefore, in their 1905 expedition investigating Galilean synagogues, H. Kohl and C. Watzinger included the remains of the Jewish public buildings Oliphant and Schumacher had discovered at Kh. Dîkkeh and Umm el-Qanâṭir. The short exploratory excavations these two scholars and their staff conducted under the auspices of the Deutsche Orient-Gesellschaft at Kh. Dîkkeh and Umm el-Qanâṭir are, for all practical purposes, the first excavations conducted at sites in the region.

After the First World War, the Sykes-Picot Agreement led to the separation of the Land of Israel from Syria, with Palestine coming under the British Mandate, while Syria and Lebanon passed into French control. This new geopolitical reality caused a decades-long hiatus in the investigation of Jewish sites in the Golan. With the exception of single archaeologist, investigators of sites in Palestine never took the trouble to go up to the Golan, whereas their colleagues in Syria had no interest in this marginal region and certainly none in this subject.[1] The events of the thirties and forties, during which the independent states Syria and Israel came into being, essentially closed the Golan Heights region to investigators for about twenty years. Indeed, the Golan Heights became a closed Syrian military area on the confrontation line between the two countries.

Only after the Six Day War in 1967, during which the area was captured by the Israel Defense Forces (I.D.F.), was research at the Golan sites renewed. A short time after the battles ceased, the Association for the Archaeological Survey of Israel initiated surveys in the area. At first, two teams were sent, led by C. Epstein and S. Gutman. These teams worked in the area for about four months and registered dozens of sites hitherto unknown. Among these were a number with Jewish artifacts, such as Dabûra and Qîsrîn. In addition to the Epstein and Gutman teams, the author was

---

[1] The exception was E. L. Sukenik, who, in 1928 visited Umm el-Qanâṭir and in 1932, during his excavations at the synagogue at Ḥammat Gader (which was included in the British Mandate), visited, recorded, and published important details about the remains of the Jewish public buildings at Mazra'at Kanaf and Kh. er-Rafîd.

sent at the head of a third team to conduct a fundamental survey of the dozens of abandoned Syrian villages and army camps, most of which had been erected on top of archaeological remains. This team discovered hundreds of decorated architectural items and dozens of inscriptions previously unreported. A significant number of these finds originated in Jewish sites or Jewish structures. In October 1968, the author was appointed as Staff Officer in Charge of Archaeological Affairs in the Golan Heights. This appointment enabled him to continue the surveys in the region—a region that had already begun to change with the settling in of the I.D.F. and the erection of the first Israeli settlements. In addition, he initiated systematic archaeological excavations at a number of the region's Jewish sites, such as Qîsrîn and Ghâdriyye. Immediately upon assuming his position, the author began collecting the hundreds of architectural items and the dozens of ancient inscriptions of the region and cataloging them in the Golan Antiquities Collection he established at Quneiṭra. (This collection is now in the Museum at Qaṣrîn.) In 1972, the author was appointed as Secretary of the Association for the Archaeological Survey of Israel and M. Ben-Ari succeeded him in the Golan. In this new appointment, the author continued his surveys of the region's Jewish sites until 1976.

The Yom Kippur War in 1973, in which a large part of the region was captured by the Syrian Army and then recaptured by the I.D.F., added another layer to the transfiguration the Golan experienced during the late sixties and the early seventies. Most of the abandoned Syrian villages disappeared from the area. Their agricultural peripheries, which generally were a direct continuation of their use on the peripheries of the ancient sites, were severely damaged during the rapid development the region experienced.

In 1975-1976, M. Ben-Ari and S. Bar-Lev completed the excavation and restoration work that the author had begun at Qîsrîn, and in 1976, S. Gutman began his important excavations at Gamala. There he uncovered the oldest structure in Palestine identified as a synagogue.

At the end of the 1970's, a team headed by C. M. Dauphin began to work at various sites in the Golan, and Z. Ma'oz replaced M. Ben-Ari in the civilian position of the Golan District Archaeologist. These investigators began a new stage in the investigation of the region's rabbinic-period, Jewish sites while differing among themselves about the questions of the scope and the dating of the Jewish settlement in the Golan.[2] We shall not involve ourselves in these disagreements but only note that although no files of the archive of the Staff Officer in Charge of Archaeological Affairs in the Golan Heights were opened to C. Dauphin (according to a personal conversation with her), these were at the disposal of Ma'oz by virtue of his

---

[2] See Dauphin, "Gaulanitis" and Ma'oz, "Communities."

position. He made selective use of them at best, however, even though he published several articles on Jewish settlement in the Golan. (These have peculiar conclusions which we shall discuss later.) Ma'oz initiated excavations at the Jewish public buildings at Mazra'at Kanaf, 'Ein Nashôt, and Dâbiyye and presently continues his work in the Golan for the Israel Antiquities Authority. At the end of the 1980's, R. Arav began archaeological excavations at the site known as et-Tell and which he identifies (following a number of many early investigators) as the site of Bethsaida. Nevertheless, to our regret, no clearly Jewish finds have been uncovered at the site to indicate that this is indeed the site of this important Jewish village from the second-temple and rabbinic periods.

It seems that the importance of the Golan Heights to the study of the Jewish communities in Palestine and Syria in general, and the investigation of remains of public buildings from the second-temple and rabbinic periods in particular, is no longer in any doubt. At the region's southern boundary, at Ḥammat Gader, archaeologists excavated the only structure in Palestine where an inscription which unambiguously attests that the building served as a 'gathering [place]'—that is, a 'synagogue'—was found *in situ*. In the heart of the Golan, at Gamala, the oldest Jewish public building in Palestine and Syria was unearthed, upon whose identification as a 'synagogue' scholars agree. The discoveries at Dabûra and at Qîsrîn have introduced a new dimension into the investigation of the construction of Jewish public buildings in the rabbinic period, namely, archaeological and epigraphic finds of a *bet midrash* and perhaps also of a hall for *se'udot mitzvah*—meals celebrating the fulfillment of certain religious rituals.[3] Furthermore, archaeologists have uncovered in the region the traces of several important Palestinian sages who lived between the late second century and the mid fourth century C.E. These contribute to our understanding of the density of Jewish settlement in this region in the period under discussion.

In the following chapters, we shall begin by surveying what is known from written sources about the existence and history of Jewish communities in the Golan during the second-temple and rabbinic periods. Next, the major part of this essay will be devoted to a review of the Jewish archaeological and epigraphic finds discovered at various Golan sites. Also included are the finds discovered by my survey teams between 1968-1972, most of which has yet to be published because it was 'buried' in the files of the 'Staff Officer in Charge of Archaeological Affairs in the Golan Heights.' We will also discuss several sites whose names are known from the written historical sources, but which have not yet been definitively located.

---

[3] On this, see my article "The House of Assembly and the House of Study: Are They One and the Same?" in vol. 1, pp. 232-255.

We have divided the description of sites—that is, the evidence of ancient communities—into three chapters: 'Upper Golan,' 'Lower Golan,' and the 'District of Sûsîta.' This division comes first and foremost from their treatment by Josephus and the rabbinic literature as geographic-physical and/or as geographic-administrative units.[4] The scheme we are implementing here can also lead us to more solid conclusions on different aspects of Jewish settlement in the Golan region during the stages of the second-temple and rabbinic periods.

In my opinion, the archaeological investigation of ancient Jewish communities in the Golan Heights region is still in its infancy; not even the remains uncovered to date have been fully utilized. Therefore, it would be an error to attempt a summary of our knowledge of Jewish settlement in the Golan. Hence we will conclude our discussion with a chapter devoted to the question of whether there is any typology to be seen in the Jewish public buildings so far discovered in the Golan, and whether we can, by means of such a typology, arrive at a chronological scheme.

---

[4] See my discussion of the Josephan material in Urman, "Toponym Golan."

JEWS IN THE GOLAN—HISTORICAL BACKGROUND

Evidence concerning the existence of Jewish communities in the Golan first appears during the reign of Judas Maccabaeus, in the second century B.C.E. In 1 Maccabees 5:3-13, 24-54 and 2 Maccabees 10:24-37 and 12:10-31, we read about the campaign of Judas Maccabaeus and his brother Jonathan who took their forces across the Jordan to rescue the Jewish communities in Northern Gilead and Southern Bashan from pagan oppressors. Among the places to which Judas and his forces laid siege was Χασφών or Κασπείν (1 Maccabees 5:26, 5:36; 2 Maccabees 12:13), which scholars identify with Khisfîn.[1] We are told that Jews in these towns and villages were liberated, but no indication is given of what happened to them or whether they ever returned to their former homes.

In the years 83-81 B.C.E., Alexander Jannaeus conquered Northern Gilead and the Golan, annexing these areas to his kingdom. According to Josephus, Jannaeus' conquest was violent, and he conquered the towns of Gaulana, Seleucia, and Gamala among others (*War* I §§ 104-105, and *Antiquities* XIII §§ 393-394). Complementary evidence from Syncellus (*Chronographia* I § 558, ed. Dindorf) informs us that Hippos should be added to this list of conquered towns. Apparently after this conquest, the population of Jews in the Golan increased under the patronage of Hasmonean rule. Evidence of new occupation by Jews following Jannaeus' campaigns comes to light as archaeological work continues in the Golan. In his excavations at Mazra'at Kanaf, for instance, Z. Ma'oz exposed the remains of a Seleucid observation tower, part of a complex that fell to Alexander Jannaeus in 81 B.C.E.[2] In place of the tower, a fort was constructed and settled by Jews. The fort was continually occupied (with some building changes) until the Great Revolt in 66 C.E.[3] The discovery of coins of Alexander Jannaeus at el-'Âl has raised the possibility that Jews settled there in the aftermath of Jannaeus' campaign in the Golan.[4] The most impressive data was brought to light in the excavations at Gamala, which expanded at the time of Jannaeus' expedition.[5]

---

[1] Cf. Avi-Yonah, *Gazetteer*, p. 48. For further details concerning this identification, see below in our discussion on the finds at Khisfîn.

[2] Ma'oz, "Golan Synagogues," p. 149; Ma'oz, "Horvat Kanaf—1," p. 807; Ma'oz, "Horvat Kanaf—2," p. 848.

[3] See previous note, especially Ma'oz, "Golan Synagogues," p. 149.

[4] See Gibson and Urman, p. 70.

[5] See Gutman, *Gamala-3*, pp. 61 ff.

In 63 B.C.E., Pompey conquered the Golan. Some of the pagan settlements, ruined by Jannaeus' campaigns, were reconstructed and their populations regained their rights. We know specifically about the rebuilding of Hippos (Josephus *War* I § 156; *Antiquities* XIV § 75). The extent to which the development of Jewish settlements declined in the Golan following Pompey's victory and the terms established by Gabinius remains unclear (*War* I § 170; *Antiquities* XIV § 86-88). Jews in the Golan enjoyed a new era of development ,with the rise of Herod the Great (37-34 B.C.E.). In the year 30, Octavian granted to Herod the areas of the towns of Gadara and Hippos (*War* I § 396; *Antiquities* XV § 217), and in 23 B.C.E., Augustus added all the area south of Damascus, including the Batanaea (Bashan), Trachonitis (Trachon), Auranitis (Haurân), and Gaulanitis (Golan) (*War* I § 398; *Antiquities* XV §§ 343-345). In 20 B.C.E., the territory of Paneas (Baniâs) was also annexed to Herod's kingdom (*Antiquities* XV § 360).

It seems that already in Herod's time—and certainly during the rule of his successors—Jewish communities were established at various sites in the Golan. From Josephus we know only of the settlement project initiated by Herod in Batanaea, where he placed a Babylonian Jew by the name of Zamaris, with his kinsfolk and horsemen (*Antiquities* XVII §§ 23-29). However, some inscriptions uncovered in our surveys may add to the picture. Certain of the epigraphs which indicate the presence of Jews—for example, in Bâb el-Hawâ, Quneiṭra and Ṣûrmân—conceivably date from the time of Herod and his dynasty.

Upon Herod's death in 4 B.C.E., the Golan passed into the rule of his son Philip. He established his capital in Paneas (Baniâs), which was henceforth called Caesarea Philippi (*Antiquities* XVII § 189; XVIII § 28). Another town was built by Philip north of the Sea of Galilee, in the location of Bethsaida, which he named Julias, after Julia, Augustus' daughter (*Antiquities* XVIII § 237). In 50-98 C.E., it was included within the territory ruled by Agrippa II (*War* II § 573; *Vita* § 187).

It is noteworthy that Josephus was the first to use the name Gaulanitis (=Golan) in describing a territory, or district, in contradistinction to the biblical use of this name for a city of refuge in the Bashan.[6] Josephus' designation of the Golan probably originated with a Roman administrative division enacted after the Great Revolt. At the same time, however, Josephus reflects the Jewish conception which regards Jewish sites in the Golan as inseparable from the Jewish Galilee. So, for instance, he calls Judas, founder of the "fourth philosophy" party and a native of Gamala, "Judas the Galilean" (*Antiquities* XVIII §§ 4-10, 23). Josephus also refers to Gamala as

---

[6] See Urman, "Toponym Golan," pp. 6-12.

a site in the Galilee, a feature which appears in later Jewish sources as well (e.g., M. Arakin 9:6; Sifra, Behar 4:1).

The failure of the Great Revolt against the Romans resulted in the destruction of some Jewish communities in the Golan, particularly Gamala (*War* IV §§ 62-83). But the fact that Seleucia and Sogane—two Golan strongholds fortified by Josephus—surrendered without a fight (*War* IV §§ 2, 4) might suggest that most of the communities went unharmed, having been persuaded to submit by Agrippa II. It is reasonable to suppose that even those communities which fought and suffered damage where later rehabilitated, with the king's assistance.

In the first generation after the revolt, when Agrippa II continued to hold sway over the Golan, we find evidence in rabbinic literature of a Jewish population in urban centers at the western margin of the Golan—the towns of Caesarea Philippi and Bethsaida. Thus, for instance, the Tosefta (Sukkah 1:9) and the Babylonian Talmud (Sukkah 27b) reveal that R. Eliezer ben Hyrcanus—one of his generation's most eminent sages—was a guest in the sukkah of Yohanan ben R. Ilai in Caesarea Philippi. Also in the Babylonian Talmud (Shabbat 21a), we read the tale of two elders who stayed in Seidan (=Saida=Bethsaida), one of the School of Hillel, the other of the School of Shammai.

Bethsaida had its share of celebrated rabbis, including Rabbi Hananiah ben Hakinai, a student in the Yavnean generation and a pupil of Rabbi Aqiba (Tos. Niddah 6:6; B. Niddah 52b; B. Ketubot 62b), Abba Yudan of Saidan (Tos. Yeb. 14:7; Tos. Oh. 18:7), Abba Gurion of Saidan (Y. Qidd. 4, 66c; B. Qidd. 82a), and in the fourth or fifth generation also Rabbi Yosi Saidaniah (Y. Ket. 11:7, 34c; Y. Ber. 4:4, 8a). It seems that the Jewish community of Saidan was the hiding place of Rabbi Simeon ben Gamaliel II during the suppression of the Bar-Kokhba Revolt, and he visited Saidan (Bethsaida) frequently after the rebellion. In our sources, Rabbi Simeon continually refers to events that occurred, or were reported to him, during his stay in Saidan (M. Gittin 7:5; Tos. Gittin 1:10; Tos. AZ 3:7; Y. Sheq. 6, 50a).

A passage datable to the era of Rabbi Simeon ben Gamaliel II's son, Rabbi Judah ha-Nasi, suggests that Jews constituted the majority of Bethsaida's populace in that period (Y. AZ 5:5, 44d):

> One who places wine on a wagon....Rabbi Hanina said: "An incident [which took place] in one wagon of the house of Rabbi (=Judah ha-Nasi) that went more than four miles. The incident was brought before the sages and they permitted (the use of that wine). [They] said, 'the incident took place on the highway of Saidan and it [i.e., Bethsaida's area] was completely [populated by people] of Israel....'"

And indeed, between the surveys by Oliphant and Schumacher and those by
Epstein, Gutman, and the author after the 1967 war, remains of more than a
dozen Jewish communities—some displaying ruins of splendid Jewish public structures—have been discovered within "four miles" of Bethsaida: Kh.
ed-Dîkkeh, Kh. er-Rafîd, Jarabâ, Dardâra, "Horvat Zawîtan", Kh.
Zumâimîra', Yahûdiyye, es-Salabe, el-Hûseiniyye, Batrâ, Wâkhsharâ, Kh.
Khawkha, Zeita, Mazra'at Kanaf, Deir 'Azîz.

With the exception of Kh. ed-Dîkkeh and Mazra'at Kanaf, no archaeological excavations have yet been conducted at these sites. It is likely that if the
date of establishment of these Jewish communities is not the period following Jannaeus' conquest (as the evidence of Mazra'at Kanaf indicates), or during the reign of the Herodian dynasty, then these settlements should be
ascribed to the migration of Jews from Judaea in the aftermath of the Bar
Kokhba Revolt and its suppression during the 130's and 140's C.E. Towards
the end of the second century, Rabbi Judah ha-Nasi received by tenancy 2000
units of land (of unspecified size) in the area (Y. Sheb. 6:1, 36d).

During the time of R. Judah ha-Nasi, Rabbi Eliezer ha-Qappar—or Bar-
Qappara—had a *bet midrash* located in Dabûra. In our discussion of the inscriptions from this site, we will note the importance of this sage and his
disciples, and the possibility that some of the surviving *halakot* and
midrashim were composed and/or edited in his school. In Y. Shabbat 6:2, 8a
and Y. San. 17:1, 28a, for example, we learn of a rule forbidding a Jew to
wear new shoes or sandals on the day of Shabbat, unless "he was wearing
them the previous day." This norm was probably established in the interest
of preserving the enjoyment of Sabbath ("the foot is not used to the shoe,
the shoe is not used to the foot"). As the discussion unfolds, the three most
important schools in the generation following Rabbi Judah ha-Nasi's death
convey their opinions of the distance a Jew should walk, wearing his new
shoes or sandals, prior to the Shabbat:

> How much should they be walked in? The students of Bar-Qappara's school
> say, "[As far as the distance from] Bar-Qappara's school [to] the school of
> Rabbi Hoshaya [the Great]." The people [students] of Sepphoris say, "[The
> distance from] the synagogue of the Babylonians (to) the apartment of
> Rabbi Hama Bar Hanina. [These are two well-known buildings in
> Sepphoris]." The Tiberians say, "[The distance from] the *Sidra Rabbah*
> [i.e., the great *bet midrash* in Tiberias] [to] the store of Rabbi Hoshaya [of
> Tiberias]."

This text, together with that of Y. Ter. 10:3, 47a, in which Rabbi Yohanan
states "when we went over to Rabbi Hoshaya the Great in Qîsrîn to study
the Torah...," led us to excavate the remains of the monumental Jewish public building in Qîsrîn, and to suggest the identification of that site in the
Golan with the Qîsrîn in which the school of Rabbi Hoshaya the Great was

located.[7] Hoshaya was a student of Bar-Qappara, whom tradition labeled the "father of the Mishnah" (Y. Qidd. 1:3, 60a; Y. Yeb. 3:3, 4d; Y. Ket. 9:1, 32d). This identification supported by the discovery of Rabbi Abun's tombstone in Qîsrîn in the Golan (the same Rabbi Abun, according to the Zohar Ḥadash, Midrash ha-N'elam to the Book of Ruth 29a, had spent all of his life in Qîsrîn), opens new research prospects concerning the rabbis of Qîsrîn and their contributions to the creation of rabbinic literature. The arrangement and editing of some of the first Yerushalmi tractates are thought by S. Lieberman to have taken place in Qîsrîn.[8] In his opinion, "the Qîsrîn Yeshiva never ceased, from the time of Hoshaya the Great (and perhaps also Bar-Qappara) to the days of Rabbi Yosi Bar (A)bun,"[9] who may well have been the son of Rabbi Abun, known to us from his tombstone.[10]

It is worth remarking that within three miles of Qîsrîn in the Golan, more than ten sites have been surveyed in which remains of Jewish public buildings were in evidence. Each site will be treated in the chapter devoted to the Lower Golan sites. As we will indicate at several points in the following chapters, we do not accept the later dates attributed to the remains of Golan Jewish public structures by Z. Ma'oz. In our view, several of those ancient ruins can be traced to the aftermath of the Bar Kokhba revolt. Certainly, Jewish communities continued to flourish in the Golan heights during the years spanned by the careers of Rabbi Judah ha-Nasi, Bar-Qappara, Rabbi Hoshaya the Great, Rabbi Yoḥanan, and Rabbi Abun. In the time of Rabbi Yosi Bar Abun, the Gallus Revolt erupted (351 C.E.), leaving signs of its destruction in some Golan sites (Tell el-Jûkhadâr,[11] Qîsrîn[12]). Echoes of the worsened conditions for Jews can be heard in Y. Sheb. 6:1, 36d:

> Rabbi Huna wanted to free Yavlona (=Gavlona=Golan)[13] [from the religious duties that depend on the land]. He approached Rabbi Mana, saying to him: "Here it is—sign it." And he did not agree to sign it. The following day Rabbi Ḥiyya Bar Madayya stood with him (i.e., Rabbi Mana), saying to him: "You did right in not signing, [because] Rabbi Yonah, your father, used to say, Antoninus leased to Rabbi [i.e., Rabbi Judah ha-Nasi] two thousand *doshnin* [i.e., units of land] [there]. Therefore we will eat but we will not work in Syria and it is exempt from tithes since it is like the gentile fields."

---

[7] Urman, "Bar Qappara—2," pp. 163-172.

[8] See Lieberman, *Caesarea*, pp. 9 ff.; Lieberman, *Siphré Zutta*, pp. 92-136.

[9] Lieberman, *Caesarea*, p. 10.

[10] See Hyman, *Toldoth*, vol. 2, p. 717.

[11] See Urman, "Hellenistic," p. 460.

[12] Urman, "Hellenistic," pp. 457-458.

[13] See Klein, "Estates," pp. 545-556.

Qîsrîn excavations—as well as those conducted by Ma'oz in sites such as
Mazra'at Kanaf, 'Ein Nashôt, and Dâbiyye—make it clear that at some point
after the Gallus Revolt the Jewish sites in the Golan were rebuilt and continued until the Arab conquest and perhaps even later. Information about
Jewish communities in the Golan that derives from literary sources comes
to an end in around 375 C.E., with the publication of the Palestinian
Talmud in Tiberias.

It is conceivable—but not verifiable on the basis of available data—that
following the destruction of some of the Jewish communities in the Gallus
Revolt, some Christian communities grew up in what had been densely
Jewish areas—for example, in Na'aran and 'Ein Semsem, both on the road
leading from Dabûra to Qîsrîn.[14] Systematic archaeological excavations
would be required to confirm (or disprove) this hypothesis.

We may summarize our discussion of Jews in the Golan by taking note
of the list of "forbidden towns in the District of Sûsîta," as preserved in the
Tos. Sheb. 4:10 (66, 4-6) and Y. Demai 2:1, 22d. A more reliable version
of this list was revealed in a mosaic inscription in the floor of the Jewish
public building at Rehob:[15]

> The forbidden towns in the territory of Sûsîta: 'Ayyanosh, and 'Ein Ḥarrah
> (or 'Ein Ḥaddah), and Dembar 'Iyyon, and Ya'arot (or Ya'arut), and Kefar
> Yaḥrib (or Kefar Iaḥriv), and Nob, and Ḥasfiya, and Kfar Ṣemaḥ, and Rabbi
> (Judah ha-Nasi) permitted [or released] Kfar Ṣemaḥ.

This list testifies that during the third and the fourth centuries C.E., seven
large Jewish communities were in existence within the District of Sûsîta.
The rabbis therefore obligate their Jewish populations to keep the laws of
the Sabbath Year, and prohibit the consumption of fruit grown by Jewish
farmers at these sites during the Sabbath Year.

In many of his publications on the Golan Jewish settlements, Ma'oz
systematically ignored the existence of the Rehob list, and dated some
Jewish finds from sites in the District of Sûsîta to the late Byzantine and/or
Early Arab periods.[16] In our view, there is no reason to doubt the antiquity
of the Jewish communities in the (dominantly pagan and later Christian) territory of the District of Sûsîta (Hippos). Indeed, we can point to Khisfîn,
which is already mentioned in the time of Judas Maccabaeus, as well as to
evidence of continuous Jewish presence in Sûsîta itself, despite adversities
suffered in the Great Revolt (*War* II §478). We cannot take up here the ques-

---

[14] For further information on Na'arân and 'Ein Semsem, see the sections on these sites in
Gregg and Urman.

[15] See Sussmann, "Beth-Shean" and Sussman, "Rehob."

[16] See for example his datings for the Jewish finds from Fîq in Ma'oz, *Golan* (rev. ed.),
pp. 36-37 and Ma'oz, "Golan—2," p. 545.

tion of the list's date. However, in the chapter devoted to the sites in the District of Sûsîta we will discuss each settlement mentioned in this important rabbinical list.

For our purposes, it is noteworthy that at the end of the list this statement occurs: "and Rabbi permitted Kfar Ṣemaḥ." It seems that this exemption from obligation also reflects a demographic change that took place in a settlement in the District of Sûsîta around 200 C.E.; for the Jewish population in Kfar Ṣemaḥ decreased, and consequently was excused from the Sabbath-year rule by Rabbi Judah ha-Nasi.

These last comments about the territory of Sûsîta and the fortunes of particular sites like Kfar Ṣemaḥ, may serve to caution us against too-general and uniform assumptions about Jewish communities in the Golan. Our repeated reference to the 'Golan' or the 'Golan Heights,' should not blind us to the reality that within this larger geographical area, individual Jewish communities lived under different and distinctive conditions, affected no doubt by changes in governance, ethnic and religious dynamics peculiar to their own villages and towns, interactions with neighbors, and the like. Our knowledge of these communities will be enhanced as archaeological research in the Golan proceeds, and as discoveries especially of Jewish inscriptions— in Hebrew, Aramaic, or Greek—continue.

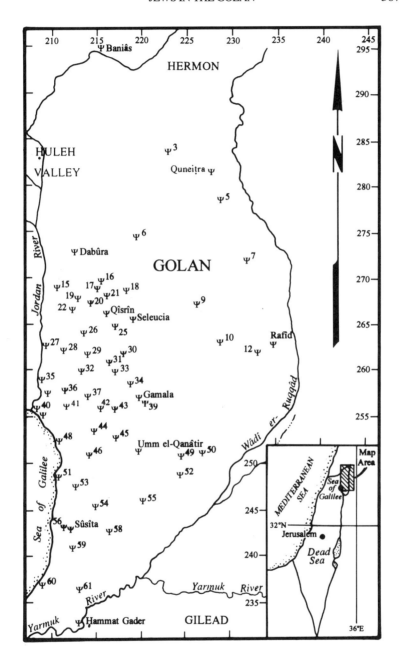

JEWISH COMMUNITIES IN THE GOLAN DURING THE ROMAN AND/OR
BYZANTINE PERIOD (LINDA MARSTON)

THE UPPER GOLAN

BANIÂS (PANEAS, CAESAREA PHILIPPI)

The ruins of Baniâs constitute the largest ancient settlement on the north-west edge of the Golan, at coordinates 2145/55-2945/49. In surveys conducted after the Six Day War in 1967 by Y. Olami[1] and the author,[2] the area of the early site was estimated at about 700 dunams.

It is not our intention here to enter into all that is known about this important site from the various historical sources,[3] nor even to describe the history of its investigation or the finds unearthed so far.[4] Paneas, Caesarea Philippi, or Caesarion—as the place was sometimes designated in rabbinic literature—was a gentile city throughout its existence. Yet, a number of attestations in the written historical sources reveal the existence of Jewish communities in this city at different times—and it is to these that we shall devote this discussion.

The first testimony appears in Josephus, in his *Vita* §§ 49-61, where he describes an attempt by Varus,[5] an aide of King Herod Agrippa II, to harm the Jewish population of Caesarea Philippi, which in those days served as Agrippa's capital city. According to Josephus' story, many Jews were killed in the city at the initiative of this Varus.[6] At his orders, Jews were prevented from leaving the city so they could not report to Agrippa the misdeeds of his aide.[7] The King finally heard what Varus had done, relates

---

[1] Y. Olami, "Baniâs," *Special Surveys Reports*, Archive of the Association for the Archaeological Survey of Israel, Israel Antiquities Authority, Jerusalem, 1968 (in Hebrew).

[2] D. Urman, "Baniâs," *Reports of the Staff Officer in Charge of Archaeological Affairs in the Golan* (from 1968-1972), Archive of the Israel Antiquities Authority, Jerusalem (in Hebrew). See also Urman, "Golan—1," pp. 3-4; Urman, *List*, p. 2; Urman, *Golan*, p. 187, Site #3 and the note for this site on page 210.

[3] For a comprehensive historical survey of this site, see Amir, *Banias*. This pioneering work now requires updating and corrections, but at present, this study is all that is available.

[4] Since the mid-1980's, surveys and excavations have been conducted intermittently at Baniâs by M. Hartal, Z. Ma'oz, and V. Tsaferis. Since, to the best of our knowledge, these efforts have uncovered no Jewish finds thus far, we can only refer the reader to their statements in the *Archaeological Newsletter of the Israel Antiquities Authority* beginning with vol. 4.

[5] Called Noarus in *War* II §§ 481ff.

[6] *Vita* § 53.

[7] *Vita* § 53.

Josephus, "The king meanwhile, hearing that Varus intended to massacre in one day the Jewish population in Caesarea (Philippi), numbering many thousands, including women and children, recalled him and sent Aequus Modius to take over the command (in Caesarea Philippi)...."[8] This description makes the great extent of the Jewish community there clear—a community that apparently began back in the days of Philip the Tetrarch, the son of Herod the Great (4 B.C.E.-34 C.E.).

Some of the city's Jewish residents were religiously observant—a point revealed by Josephus in relating his confrontations with John of Giscala. He describes how John overcharged the city's Jews for oil:

> This knavish trick John followed up with a second. He stated that the Jewish inhabitants of Caesarea Philippi, having, by the king's order, been shut up by Modius, his viceroy, and having no pure oil for their personal use, had sent a request to him to see that they were supplied with this commodity, lest they should be driven to violate their legal ordinances by resort to Grecian oil. John's motive in making this assertion was not piety, but profiteering of the most barefaced description; for he knew that at Caesarea two pints were sold for one drachm, whereas at Gischala eighty pints could be had for four drachms. So he sent off all the oil in the place....John by this sharp practice made an enormous profit.[9]

In spite of the injuries to the Jewish community at Caesarea Philippi during the Great Rebellion, the community survived for at least a generation afterwards. Evidence of this comes from Tosefta Sukkah 1:9 and B. Sukkah 27b, where it is related that Rabbi Eliezer ben Hyrcanus, one of that generation's most eminent sages, was a guest in the *sukkah* of Yohanan ben Rabbi Ilai in Caesarea Philippi.

After the death of King Herod Agrippa II (ca. 100 C.E.), we have no direct information about the continuity of the existence of the Jewish community there until the twelfth century.[10] Apparently it gradually declined over the generations until it finally disappeared during the Crusades.

As indicated in note 4, the archaeological excavations conducted sporadically at Baniâs in the last decade have yet to unearth any clearly Jewish artifacts. Still, in light of our knowledge of the site,[11] we believe that the moment the various excavators broaden their excavations beyond the area of the Temple of Pan and the Crusader fortress and cross the stream westward to dig in the residential areas of the city itself, Jewish remains will be found. We hope such finds will shed light on the history of the Jewish community of Baniâs which remains shrouded in darkness.

---

[8] Thus in *Vita* § 61. In the parallel version found in *War* II § 483, Varus' deposition is mentioned, but not the name of his successor.

[9] *Vita* §§ 74-76.

[10] Amir, *Banias*, pp. 39 ff.

[11] See above, note 2.

SOGANE (Σωγάνη)

Sogane was a Jewish settlement on the Golan during the second-temple period whose location has yet to be identified with certainty. Josephus mentions Sogane as one of the two villages in the Golan (along with the city of Gamala) which he fortified when he was commander of the rebellion in Galilee.[12] From Josephus' description, it seems that Sogane was well defended by nature, but despite the defenses of both nature and Josephus, the men of this village chose not to fight the Romans.[13] As a result, Josephus apparently decided not to give a more detailed description from which we might have learned more about this village's exact location. Nevertheless, Josephus points out that Sogane was in the 'Upper Golan.'[14]

Following Schumacher's report on the existence of the remnants of a wall at Yahûdiyye (see my discussion of this village below), various scholars suggested identifying Sogane with Yahûdiyye.[15] Still, the difficulty with this identification lies in the fact that Yahûdiyye lies in the heart of the 'Lower Golan,' while Sogane is to be sought in the 'Upper Golan.'[16] A more plausible suggestion was made about ten years ago by my late friend and colleague, Zvi Ilan.

In October-November 1983, Ilan conducted a survey at a ruin called Sûjen or Siyâr es-Sûjen which lies at coordinates 2153-2903. As a result of this survey, Ilan suggested identifying Sogane with the ruins at Sûjen.[17] According to his report:

> The ruin is on a low hill on a slope facing the Huleh Valley. Its area is 7-10 dunams and there are agricultural terraces built around it. There are a number of ancient buildings in the ruin that were in use until recently. On the west side, a outer wall was discerned extending for tens of meters. Most of the shards collected there are of the Roman-Byzantine period, a few are Iturean ('Golan ware') and of the Middle Ages.[18]

It is difficult for us to express a definitive opinion on the Ilan's suggestion. From the standpoint of the site's location, it certainly lies in the region defined by Josephus as the 'Upper Golan.' We must wait, however, until systematic archaeological excavations are held at the site, from which we may learn more concerning the actual location of Sogane.

---

[12] *War* II § 574; *Vita* § 187.

[13] *War* IV § 4.

[14] *War* IV § 2. On the division of the Golan into 'Upper' and 'Lower' in the works of Josephus, see Urman, "Toponym Golan," pp. 6-12.

[15] See, for example, Avi-Yonah, *Gazetteer*, p. 152.

[16] See above, note 14.

[17] Ilan, "Kh. Sûjen," p. 5; Ilan, *Israel*, p. 95.

[18] Ilan, "Kh. Sûjen," pp. 4-5.

BÂB EL-HAWÂ

Bâb el-Hawâ is a small abandoned Syrian village built in the 1950's on an ancient ruin at coordinates 2229-2834.

The first to report on the existence of the ancient ruin at Bâb el-Hawâ was P. Bar-Adon, who settled and worked in this region of the Golan in the 1920's. In 1933, he published a Greek inscription which he found in the nearby Circassian village of Manṣûra, and raised the possibility that it originated in the large ruin at Bâb el-Hawâ, having heard from the veteran residents of Manṣûra that this ruin had served them as a quarry when they had built their homes back in the 1880's.[19] The inscription, which mentions a deaconess named Severa, was found on fragments of a lintel that undoubtedly belonged to a Christian building that existed there in the sixth century.[20]

S. Gutman surveyed the ruin immediately after the Six Day War (1967) and found pottery from the Roman and Byzantine periods.[21] Various architectural items that Gutman and his team found incorporated into the homes of the village of Manṣûra were also attributed by them to the site at Bâb el-Hawâ.[22]

In 1968 and again in 1971, the author and his team surveyed Bâb el-Hawâ and Manṣûra. Like the previous investigators, we also concluded that the settlement in Manṣûra has no remains from the Roman and Byzantine periods, and that all the items found in the Circassian village originated, as P. Bar-Adon reported, in the ruin of Bâb el-Hawâ.[23]

Our survey revealed that the area of the Bâb el-Hawâ ruin is about 80 dunams, and that the remains form one of the largest settlements in the northern Golan of the Roman and Byzantine periods. In addition to the pottery reported by Gutman, we also found Iron Age II shards. In the homes of the new village, we found no decorated architectural items or inscriptions. These were found in secondary use in the homes of the village of Manṣûra. In addition to the lintel fragments with the inscription published by P. Bar-

---

[19] Bar-Adon, "Golan," pp. 187-188.

[20] Bar-Adon, "Golan," pp. 187-188. And also see Schwabe, "Golan," pp. 189-190; Gregg and Urman, Inscription #235.

[21] Epstein & Gutman, p. 261, Site #41.

[22] Epstein & Gutman, p. 261, Site #42.

[23] D. Urman, "Bâb el-Hawâ and Manṣûra," *Special Surveys Reports*, Archive of the Association for the Archaeological Survey of Israel, Israel Antiquities Authority, Jerusalem (in Hebrew); D. Urman, "Bâb el-Hawâ and Manṣûra," *Reports of the Staff Officer in Charge of Archaeological Affairs in the Golan* (from 1968-1972), Archive of the Israel Antiquities Authority, Jerusalem (in Hebrew); Urman, *List*, p. 6; Urman, *Golan*, pp. 190, 211, Sites #43-44.

Adon, we found two lintels with Greek inscriptions which also attest to the existence of a Christian community at Bâb el-Hawâ in the sixth century.[24]

Another Greek inscription, whose existence at Manṣûra was reported by N. Zakai of Kibbutz Hagoshrim, was preserved on a tombstone. It reads: "Aνϵανας ἔτ(ος) α" which translates as: "Aneanas, One year old." Wuthnow links this name, Aneanas, with several others: Aνϵιανη, Aννϵιανη, Aννιανος[25] and quite possibly the one-year-old was a Jew.[26]

Another Jewish find was uncovered at Bâb el-Hawâ when M. Hartal conducted archaeological excavations there from 1988 to 1990.[27] According to his report, an elongated structure of about 180 square meters was exposed in the center of the site. Hartal claims that this Byzantine period building was in use from the fourth to the seventh centuries, having been erected atop debris of an Iron Age II structure. Antiquities recovered within the building were numerous and varied; some shards with Greek inscriptions (no details are given), nearly 800 ceramic lamps (decorated with floral and geometric patterns, figures of animals, and crosses), and more than 900 coins (mostly dating from the fourth to the sixth centuries). Among numerous glass vessels and remnants of jewelry (such as beads, cross-shaped pendants, and bronze and bone earrings), a fragment of a glass bracelet was found which bore the impression of a five-branched candelabrum. In Hartal's view, this bracelet—which implies the Jewish identity of its owner—is an exception to the impression gained from the site's many cross-shaped pendants and lamps decorated with crosses: ancient Bâb el-Hawâ's population was Christian.[28]

The Christian inscriptions at Manṣûra, along with the finds of Hartal's excavations, reveal that in the late Byzantine period the settlement at Bâb el-Hawâ was mostly populated by Christians. Yet, from the gravestone of the infant Aneanas and the menorah found on the glass bracelet discovered by Hartal, we learn that Jews also dwelt in this large settlement. It is possible that originally the settlement at Bâb el-Hawâ was already Jewish during the second-temple period (for further discussion, see the following section on Quneiṭra), but that in the course of the Byzantine period the number of Jews there diminished and the settlement became Christian. I am sure that if Hartal or others would continue the excavations at Bâb el-Hawâ, we would gain additional Jewish finds from this important site.

---

[24] For further details about these lintels and their inscriptions see Gregg and Urman, Inscription #234 and Inscription #236.

[25] Wuthnow, pp. 22-23; Gregg and Urman, Inscription #233.

[26] For further discussion of this name and of the forms of the name approximating it see our discussion, below, of the inscriptions found at Quneiṭra.

[27] Hartal, "Bâb el-Hawâ," pp. 6-8.

[28] Hartal, "Bâb el-Hawâ," pp. 6-8.

QUNEIṬRA (SARISAI)

Quneiṭra (located at coordinates 227-281) was until 1967 the Golan's district capital and its largest town. The nucleus for the modern town's growth was a *khân* (dating from the Ottoman period) on the principal road from Damascus to the Benot Ya'aqov Bridge and beyond, into western Palestine. Circassians began to settle around this *khân* during the latter half of the nineteenth century, making extensive use of the building stones from the then-visible remains of the Roman and Byzantine settlement. G. Schumacher found Quneiṭra to be the military headquarters and administrative center of the region.[29] In the late 1940's, the Syrian government commenced the construction of military camps here, and the population tripled, reaching 15,000 by 1967. Today most of Quneiṭra is in ruins because of wartime destruction there in 1967 and 1973.

The first to publish archaeological finds from Quneiṭra was Schumacher.[30] The finds he published—some of which were relocated by the author in surveys conducted in the town after 1967—are mostly Christian and apparently date to the latter part of the Byzantine period.[31] In 1911, G. Dalman and P. Lohmann visited the place and copied a dozen ancient inscriptions in Greek, which Dalman published two years later.[32] Some of these inscriptions were likewise relocated after the Six Day War.[33] Half of the inscriptions published by Dalman were found on tombstones—four of them undoubtedly of Christians.[34] On a lintel and two lintel fragments, segments of inscriptions were found, also Christian, from the Byzantine period.[35] One complete inscription was copied from a pagan altar,[36] while another came from a boundary marker.[37] In this last inscription, Diocletian, Maximian, Constantius, and Galerius—the tetrarchy in power between 293-305—are mentioned, and giving the inscription's a firm dating. In addition to the four rulers, the inscription cites the name of a local official, Aelius, and the names of the villages between whose fields the boundary stone was set: Sarisai and Berniki (Σαρισῶν καὶ Βερνίκης). As Dalman pointed out, one of the two village names is the ancient name of Quneiṭra (see further on this below).[38]

---

[29] Schumacher, "Dscholan," p. 304; Schumacher, *Jaulân*, pp. 207-208.

[30] Schumacher, "Dscholan," pp. 305-307; Schumacher, *Jaulân*, pp. 209-214.

[31] Gregg and Urman, the section on Quneiṭra.

[32] See Dalman, "Inschriften," pp. 249-254, Inscriptions #1-12.

[33] Gregg and Urman, the section on Quneiṭra.

[34] See Dalman, "Inschriften," pp. 253-254, Inscriptions #9-12.

[35] Dalman, "Inschriften," p. 251, Inscriptions #2-4.

[36] Dalman, "Inschriften," pp. 251-252, Inscription #5.

[37] Dalman, "Inschriften," pp. 249-251, Inscription #1.

[38] See previous note.

In 1967, Quneiṭra was briefly surveyed by a survey team headed by S. Gutman, who reported that "the center of the town, near the old mosque, is built atop an ancient ruin and in the town's homes in this area there are many fine-hewn ancient stones, columns and capitals in secondary use."[39] Near the *khân* the team found a number of stones with Greek inscriptions in secondary use as paving blocks, but the team did not copy or photograph the inscriptions.[40]

Between April 1968 and April 1972, the author resided in Quneiṭra when he served as the Staff Officer in Charge of Archaeological Affairs in the Golan. During that time, he and his team surveyed the town's homes a number of times.[41] Because of the extent of the modern construction there, it was difficult to assess the extent of the ancient ruin in the old center of the town. Still the pottery collected there reveal that the settlement had already begun in the latter days of the Hellenistic period. Many shards of the different stages of the Roman, Byzantine, Arab, and Ottoman periods were also gathered by the author's team. In the course of our surveys, about sixty decorated architectural fragments were recorded that had not been reported by the previous surveyors. Twenty-four items were found with Greek inscriptions, twelve came from architectural items—mainly fragments of lintels—and twelve from tombstones. The inscriptions, some of which were published by Schumacher and Dalman, are discussed at length in the Quneiṭra section of our joint book with R. C. Gregg.[42]

Let us note, however, that some lintels and gravestones stem undoubtedly from pagans who lived there at the end of the Hellenistic period or during the Roman period, others derive from Christians from the Byzantine period, leaving only a few inscriptions that refer to Jews. From the Jewish inscriptions, we shall detail three here.

Inscription #1[43]

This inscription was first mentioned by Dalman and we relocated it in secondary use as a building stone in one of the Circassian houses near the city's old mosque.[44] The inscription was carved into the finely worked basalt slab whose original use is unknown. The height of the stone is 43

---

[39] Epstein & Gutman, p. 262, Site #45.

[40] Epstein & Gutman, p. 262, Site #45.

[41] See D. Urman, "Quneiṭra," *Reports of the Staff Officer in Charge of Archaeological Affairs in the Golan* (from 1968-1972), Archive of the Israel Antiquities Authority, Jerusalem (in Hebrew); Urman, "Golan—1," p. 2; Urman, "Golan—2," p. 11; Urman, *List*, p. 6; Urman, *Golan*, p. 191, Site #47.

[42] See Gregg and Urman.

[43] See Gregg and Urman, Inscription #208.

[44] See Dalman, "Inschriften," p. 251.

cm., its width is 91 cm., and its thickness is 24 cm. The inscription contains two lines and its letters are 6-7 cm. high. Its transcription:

ΑΡΧΕΛΑΟΣ
ΑΝΝΙΑΝΟΥ

We read it: "'Αρχέλαος 'Αννιανοῦ" and translate it: "Archelaos, (son of) Annianos."

The name Archelaos appears again, as we shall see, on a gravestone of a Jew which we discovered at Ṣûrmân, southeast of Quneiṭra.[45] This name was, of course, the name of Herod's son. The name Annianos ('Αννιανὸς) is definitely a Jewish name and appears in its various forms in many inscriptions of the second-temple and rabbinic periods.[46] It appears in identical spelling above arcosolium 1 in room III of Catacomb 13 at Beth She'arim,[47] and in a similar form, Ανιανοῦ, is found in a Greek-Hebrew bilingual inscription discovered at Hall A in Catacomb 14 there.[48]

Inscription #2[49]

This inscription appears on a gravestone fragment made of basalt; it is 54 cm. in height, 38 cm. wide, and 12 cm. thick. The fragment comes from the upper part of the stone and four lines of a Greek inscription were preserved, the letters varying in height between 5 to 7 cm. Its transcription follows:

ΘΑΡΣΙ
ΑΝΙΝΑ
ΣΕΤΩΝ
ΟΕ

It reads: "Θάρσι 'Ανινᾶς ἐτῶν οε" and translates: "Be of good courage, Aninas, Sixty-five years old."

The name 'Ανινᾶς is the Greek transliteration of the name חנינא (Ḥanina). This name was widespread beginning in the second-temple period, especially among the rabbinic sages.[50] It appears on inscriptions at Beth She'arim,[51]

---

[45] See below, inscription #2 in the section on Ṣûrmân.

[46] For examples, see Frey, vol. 1, pp. 88, 310 and *passim*. Frey also wrote: "Le noms juifs Αννιανος, Αννις, Αννία, etc., sont la forme hellénisée de noms hebreux tous dérivés de la racine *hanan*" (p. 62).

[47] Schwabe and Lifshitz, p. 142, Inscription #166.

[48] Schwabe and Lifshitz, pp. 147-148, Inscription #175, and see there more references.

[49] Gregg and Urman, Inscription #212.

[50] See, for example, רבי חנינא בן דוסא in Mishnah Berakot 5:5; Sotah 9:15; Abot 3:9. And for others with this name see in Margalioth, vol. 1, pp. 326-351.

[51] See Schwabe and Lifshitz, p. 33, Inscription #55.

and as one of two artisans who did the mosaic floors uncovered in the Jewish public buildings at Beth Alpha and at Beth-Shean.[52]

Inscription #3[53]

This fragment of a basalt gravestone is 66 cm. in height, 31 cm. wide, and 8 cm. thick. It forms the upper part of the stone and 5 lines of a Greek inscription were preserved on it with letters 6 cm. high. This is the inscription's transcription:

M N H Σ
Θ H A Λ
A Φ Ω Z
H E T Ω
N o I H

Its reading: "μνησθῆ Αλαφω ζή(σας) ἐτῶν ιη" and its translation: "May Alapho be remembered, who lived eighteen years."

The name Alapho (Αλαφω) is found in its Aramaic form חלפו in dedicatory inscriptions of the Jewish public buildings uncovered at Capernaum and Mazra'at Kanaf,[54] and perhaps also in Inscription #3 from Ghâdriyye.[55] A name close in form is Alapheos (Αλαφεος). This name also appears in a Jewish burial stone that we found at nearby Ṣûrmân.[56]

It should be pointed out that the combination of the letters ζη that in the inscription is an abbreviation for a participial form.[57] And it seems that since the small circle in line 5 does not compute as an age, it must represent a 'dot' marking, in this case division of the word from the numerals.[58]

Inscription #4

Another inscription found in our surveys at Quneiṭra is, to be sure, non-Jewish but from it we learn that the name of the ancient settlement there, at least in the late third century and the early fourth century, was Sarisai (Σαρισῶν).[59] This appears on a basalt fragment of a boundary marker. The

---

[52] Concerning the question of whether Marianos (Μαριανος) and his son 'Aninas ('Ανίνας), the artisans of the mosaic floors uncovered at Beth Alpha and Beth-Shean were Jews or not, Lea Roth-Gerson devoted a lengthy discussion claiming they were. See Roth-Gerson, *Greek Inscriptions*, pp. 29-33. And see her complete bibliography concerning these inscriptions there.

[53] Gregg and Urman, Inscription #213.

[54] See Naveh, *Mosaic*, pp. 38-40, Inscriptions #18-19.

[55] See the section on Ghâdriyye.

[56] See below, inscription #2 in the section on Ṣûrmân.

[57] Avi-Yonah, "Abbreviations," p. 67.

[58] Avi-Yonah, "Abbreviations," p. 33.

[59] For other evidence concerning the name of the village, see the boundary marker published by Dalman in Dalman, "Inschriften," pp. 249-251, Inscription #1.

height of the fragment is 49 cm., its width 30 cm., and its thickness 8 cm. Seven lines of the inscription were preserved; the average height of its letters is 4 cm. Below is the inscription's transliteration:[60]

```
Λ Ι . . Ν Δ
Ι Ο Ρ Ι Ζ Ο Ν Τ
Α Α Γ Ρ Ο Υ
Κ Ω Μ Σ Α Ρ
Σ Ω Ν Κ Α Ι
Α Χ Χ Α Ν
Ω Ν
```

It reads: "…λί[θο]ν διορίζοντα ἀγροῦ[ς] κωμ(ῶν) Σαρ[ι]σῶν καὶ Αχχανῶν…" and its translation: "…stone marking the borders of the fields of the villages of Sarisai and Achanai.…" Akin to the other boundary stone discovered in Quneiṭra (published by Dalman), this inscription may be assumed originally to have contained the names of Diocletian and his colleagues, and to be datable to the period 285-305 C.E. Interestingly, this notice of the line separating two villages' fields repeats the reference to Sarisai, found in Dalman's boundary marker and thought by him a candidate for Quneiṭra's "antiken Namen."[61] We may safely conclude that the place was called Sarisai (Σαρισῶν).

The question of the date of the Jewish finds at Quneiṭra is difficult. These were all found when they were in secondary use as building stones in modern buildings. Furthermore, at the ancient site in the city, no systematic archaeological excavations have yet been conducted. Yet, it is logical to suggest that a Jewish community existed at Quneiṭra/Sarisai, like that at nearby Ṣûrmân, in the days of the rule of the Herodians in the region. The abundance of Christian finds of the Byzantine period found at Quneiṭra also hints at the antiquity of the Jewish finds, perhaps from the early Roman period.

ṢÛRMÂN
(SURRAMÂN, EL-'ADNÂNIYYE, EL-QAKHTANIYYE, EL-MÛDARIYYE)

This site appears at an abandoned Circassian village about 2 kilometers southeast of Quneiṭra at coordinates 2286-2784. The village stands on the slopes and at the base of a volcanic mound rising about 40 meters above the surrounding terrain to an elevation of 1016 m. above sea level. A system of roads and paths connects the village to nearby settlements: Quneiṭra, el-Qakhtaniyye, er-Ruhîneh, Mûmsiyye, and 'Ein Ziwân.

---

[60] Gregg and Urman, Inscription #209.
[61] See Dalman, "Inschriften," pp. 249-251, Inscription #1.

Schumacher, who surveyed the region in 1884, included in his survey the village's two areas of monumental buildings (one on the mound's slopes and the other on the western plateau) as well as the area of construction at the village of el-Mûdariyye, which is about one km. north of Sûrmân and appears on modern maps as el-Qakhtaniyye. With regard to the antiquities at the site, Schumacher's description is superficial. This is how he describes the village and its antiquities:

> Surramân—Three large Circassian villages, containing together about 200 buildings, and 900 inhabitants. Near the two south ones there is a large tank and old masonry. The antiquities have almost entirely disappeared, that is to say, they have been used in the walls of the buildings, and white-washed. According to the positive statements of the natives, who were acquainted with the ground before the existence of the villages, this was covered with the remains of a very ancient extended site. The Bedawîn called it Surr el-Mâl (Secret of the Treasure). It was this name, so the officials of el-Kuneitrah (Quneitrah—D.U.) assert, that drew the Circassians hither, who, indeed, have actually discovered several valuable finds, which partly explains the large colony and swift rise of the villages. However, to divert attention from their property, the Circassians have turned the name into Surramân.[62]

The village was surveyed by a team headed by S. Gutman in 1967. This team was the first to report on the existence of complete ancient structures at the site, as well as decorated architectural items and Greek inscriptions, incorporated into the Circassian construction.[63] In addition, Gutman published ground-plans and cross-section drawings of one of the village's ancient structures and a catacomb.[64]

On several occasions during the years 1968-1970, the author and his team explored the village and nearby settlements,[65] and conducted salvage excavations of several tombs discovered on the northern slope of the mound.[66] The author concluded that Sûrmân sits on remains of an ancient town which, according to ceramic and numismatic evidence, was in exis-

---

[62] Schumacher, "Dscholan," p. 349; Schumacher, *Jaulân*, pp. 243-244.

[63] Epstein & Gutman, p. 262, Site #47.

[64] Urman, *Golan*, pp. 262-263.

[65] D. Urman, "Sûrmân," "el-Qakhtaniyye," and "'Ein Ziwân," *Special Survey Reports*, Archive of the Association for the Archaeological Survey of Israel, Israel Antiquities Authority, Jerusalem (in Hebrew); D. Urman, "Sûrmân," "el-Qakhtaniyye," and "'Ein Ziwân," *Reports of the Staff Officer in Charge of Archaeological Affairs in the Golan* (from 1968-1972), Archive of the Israel Antiquities Authority, Jerusalem (in Hebrew); Urman, "Golan—1," p. 3; Urman, "Golan—3," p. 5; Urman, *List*, pp. 8-9; Urman, "Golan—6," p. 2; Urman, *Golan*, p. 191, Sites #48 and #51; and see also our notes for these sites in Urman, *Golan*, p. 211.

[66] Urman, "Golan—1," p. 3; Urman, "Hellenistic," pp. 462-464.

tence in the second century B.C.E.[67] The settlement evidently attained its greatest size (an area of approximately 80 dunams) in the period between the third to seventh centuries. An interruption of the occupation of the village may have occurred around the time of the Arab conquest; later resettlements are associated with the Mamelukes and the Circassians.

Of the 156 houses in the village, the Circassians built 56 on foundations of structures from the late Roman and early Byzantine periods. Some fifteen of the houses, with their original Haurân-style roofing intact, are thought to date to these centuries. On several of the well-preserved buildings upper stories have been added, with lower rooms used for storage and animal shelter.

Space here is too short to detail the abundance of the decorated architectural items that we found in the village, some *in situ* and some in secondary use as building stones in Circassian houses. Let us only point out that some items are decorated with reliefs of rosettes and geometric patterns, motifs common in Jewish public buildings of second-temple and rabbinic periods. Other items are decorated with reliefs of crosses and no doubt belong to the stage of Christian habitation, apparently in the fifth, sixth, and seventh centuries. In addition to the architectural pieces, we recorded 29 items with Greek inscriptions—25 in Ṣûrmân, three in 'Ein Ziwân, and one at el-Qakhtaniyye. Eighteen of the items are gravestones and the rest are lintel fragments, all made of basalt. The inscriptions have been studied by my colleague R. C. Gregg and their full publication appears in our joint work.[68] Here we shall mention only the four tombstones which bear a date—one of which is beyond doubt that of a deceased Jew.

Inscription #1[69]

A complete tombstone, measuring 115 cm. high, 31 cm. wide, and 15 cm. thick. The stone has an eleven line Greek inscription with 4-6 cm. high letters. It reads:

Θ Α Ρ Σ Ι
Μ Ο Ν Ι
Μ Ω Σ Α
Φ Ι Λ Ι Π Π
Ο Υ Ο Υ Δ Ι
Σ Γ Α Ρ Α
Θ Α Ν Α Τ Ο Σ
Ε Τ Ω Ν
Ξ

---

[67] In our surveys, at the location there were also found a few shards of the Early Bronze II period, the Middle Bronze II and the Late Bronze periods, and a larger quantity of shards from Iron Age I—but these are all irrelevant for our discussion here.

[68] Gregg and Urman, Inscriptions #175-203.

[69] Gregg and Urman, Inscription #175.

ΕΤΟΥΣΤΞ
Z

That is: "θάρσι Μονιμωσα Φιλίππου, οὐδὶς γὰρ ἀθάνατος ἐτῶν ξ ἔτους τξζ." Its translation: "Be of good courage, Monimosa, (daughter of) Philippos, for no one is immortal! Sixty years old in the year 367."

Monimosa is apparently a feminine form of the name Μονιμος that was also used by Jews.[70] The name Philippos is, of course, in wide use.

What calendar was used in Ṣûrmân? In Avi-Yonah's opinion, the Seleucid calendar was in effect in the territory of the Golan (Gaulaitis).[71] By this reckoning, then, Monimosa died in the year 55 C.E. In his discussion of the inscription, Gregg raises two further possibilities.[72] First, to the extent that Ṣûrmân belonged to the territory of Caesarea Philippi, Monimosa died in 361 C.E. Second, that according to the Pompeian calendar, the year is 303 C.E. Avi-Yonah's opinion is more acceptable because it is based upon the body of inscriptions of all of South Syria and because Ṣûrmân did not belong to the area of the city of Caesarea Philippi. That region, in our opinion, extended mainly through the Ḥuleh Valley and along the slopes facing this valley, whereas Ṣûrmân lies in the heart of the Upper Golan.

Inscription #2[73]

This tombstone fragment is 69 cm. high, 34 cm. wide, and 12 cm. thick. On the upper part of the fragment there is a lovely engraving of either a 'tree of life' with seven branches or a menorah with seven branches. The latter identification is more likely, given the symbols associated with it. Next to the menorah appear two round engravings symbolizing either (1) a stylized *lulab*, shofar, or *ethrog* or (2) 'rolled Torah scrolls,' like the menorah relief from Priene in Asia Minor.[74] The Greek inscription is intact, consisting of four lines, with letters 4-5 cm. high:

ΘΑΡΣΙΑΛΑ
ΦΕΟΣΑΡΧΕ
ΛΑΟΥΕΤΟΥΣ
ΟΤΕΤΩΝΟ

That is: "θάρσι Αλαφεος Ἀρχελάου ἔτους οτ ἐτῶν ο" and its translation: "Be of good courage, Alapheos, (son of) Archelaos! (Died) in the year 370, at seventy years of age."

---

[70] Orfali, "Capharnaum," pp. 159-163; Wuthnow, p. 78; Frey, vol. 1, p. 379.

[71] Avi-Yonah, *Holy Land*, pp. 167-170.

[72] Gregg and Urman, Inscription #175.

[73] Gregg and Urman, Inscription #176.

[74] For a photograph of the tombstone fragment from Ṣûrmân, see previous note. For a photograph of the item from Priene, see Foerster, "Diaspora Synagogues," p. 165.

Alapheos is a variant of the name Αλαφος which in its Aramaic form
חלפו is also found in the dedication inscriptions of public Jewish buildings
uncovered at Capernaum and Mazra'at Kanaf,[75] and perhaps also in the inscription from Ghâdriyye.[76] The name Archelaos ('Αρχελαος) also appears
in a Jewish inscription found at nearby Quneiṭra.[77] It seems that the combination of the names Alapheos and Archelaos together with the engraved
menorah clearly indicate that this is the tombstone of a deceased Jew. The
question remaining is the date of his death. According to Seleucid count
Alapheos' death occurred in 58 C.E. According to the Pompeian era—
305/306 C.E.—and by the count of Caesarea Philippi—367 C.E. As we
indicated in our treatment of Inscription #1, we hold that the Seleucid
reckoning was in use in the Golan, and therefore the date of the death of
Alapheos son of Archelaos should be fixed at 58 C.E.

Inscription #3[78]

This inscription appears on a complete tombstone, measuring 125 cm.
high, 33 cm. wide, and 12 cm. thick. The stone has an eight-line Greek inscription with 6 cm. high letters.

It reads:

```
Θ Α Σ Ι Ζ
Η Ν Ο Δ
Ω Ρ Ο Σ
Ο Υ Δ Ι Σ
Α Θ Α Ν
Α Τ Ο Σ
. Τ Ω Ν Κ Θ
. Τ Ο Υ Σ Ι Υ
```

That is: "θά[ρ]σι Ζηνόδωρος, οὐδῖς ἀθάνατος [ἐ]τῶν κθ [ἔ]τους ιυ" and
its translation: "Be of good courage, Zenodoros! No one is immortal.
Twenty-nine years old, in the year 410."

In this epigraph, the *alpha* and *rho* in θάρσι seem to have been com-
pressed; otherwise the *rho* has been omitted. Zenodoros is widespread in
Syrian inscriptions, and also appears on a gravestone which we found at
Quneiṭra.[79] According to the Seleucid reckoning, Zenodoros died in 98 C.E.

---

[75] See Naveh, *Mosaic*, pp. 38-40, Inscriptions #18-19.

[76] See the section on Ghâdriyye.

[77] See Inscription #1 in the section on Quneiṭra.

[78] Gregg and Urman, Inscription #177.

[79] See Gregg and Urman, Inscription #211.

Inscription #4[80]

This inscription appears on an intact gravestone, the left side of which has been systematically chipped away—apparently when it was used as a building stone in a Circassian house. It is 100 cm. high, 29 cm. wide now, and 12 cm. thick. It bears a nine-line Greek inscription whose letters are 5 cm. high which reads:

Θ Α Ρ Σ Ι Κ
Α Λ Ε Μ Ο Σ
Φ Ρ Ο Ν Τ Ι
Ν Ο Υ Ο Υ Δ Ι
Σ Α Θ Α Ν Α
Τ Ο Σ Ε Τ
Ω Ν Ι Ε
Ε Τ Ο Υ Σ Ι Ε
Υ

That is: "θάρσι Κάλεμος φροντίνου, οὐδὶς ἀθάνατος. ἐτῶν ιε ἔτους ιευ" and its translation: "Be of good courage, Kalemos, (son of) Phrontinos! No one is immortal. Fifteen years old, in the year 415."

Both names in this inscription are known.[81] The final date poses some difficulty, though the reading given here is not in serious doubt. It is worth commenting, nevertheless, that although an *upsilon* appears in line 9, it is not as clearly legible as other letters, and there is no line incised between line 8 and what stands below. Also, the order of the letter numerals may be a bit unusual, since one would expect consistent sequence from smaller to larger (ε ι υ), but in the preceding line the pattern (ι ε) also occurs. According to the Seleucid calendar, Kalemos died in 103 C.E.

These four inscribed tombstones were all found in Ṣûrmân. The stones, as stated, differ from the other gravestones that we found in the village and those near it in that they have the year of the death of the interred. An examination of the dates indicates that these four gravestones belong to one span of time—the second half of the first century C.E. and the beginning of the second century. This period of time more or less overlaps the years of the reign of Agrippa II. Since the gravestone with Inscription #2 is for a Jew, along with the great likelihood that the Monimosa mentioned in Inscription #1 was also Jewish, one may conclude that Ṣûrmân had a Jewish community in the days of the reign of Agrippa II, and perhaps even earlier than that. It is to this period of time that one may perhaps also attribute the architectural artifacts decorated with the reliefs of rosettes and geometric patterns that we found in the village. It seems that after the death of Agrippa the Jewish community there began to dwindle, and beginning with the fifth

---

[80] Gregg and Urman, Inscription #178.

[81] See previous note.

century, Ṣûrmân became a large Christian village—as a number of the other inscriptions attest.[82]

KAFR NAFÂKH

This abandoned Syrian-Turkoman village was built on the ruins of an ancient settlement at coordinates 2194-2742. Schumacher visited the place in 1884 and described the antiquities that he saw there as follows:

> Kefr Naphâkh—An old Bedawîn village, which has been recently rebuilt by the Turkomans, containing a large well-built corn magazine; old building stones, mostly unhewn and long, appear in large numbers, and, as in the neighbouring Bêdarûs, are heaped up in regular hills, so that one is only able to discover old square foundations with labour. They are all, however, greatly weather-worn; the decoration of a large capital can scarcely be any longer perceived, whilst some shafts of columns are also very much injured. In the south of the ruins the Turkomen have hollowed out a well-shaped cavity some yards square, which is bricked in, and about 25 feet deep. Very interesting are the sliding tombs lying close to the margin of the wâdî (Figs. 122-123 in the German edition, Figs. 70-71 in the English one).[83]

It is interesting to note that even though Schumacher did not mention Jewish finds in the village, the writer of the famous guide to Palestine and Syria, K. Baedeker, theorized at the start of the twentieth century that Kafr Nafâkh was the place from which Rabbi Yohanan Bar Nafkha' had come.[84]

In the 1950's, the Syrian Army set up a number of military camps around the village and the families of the men settled in the village. The construction work done in the village damaged a number of ancient buildings and many architectural items—some decorated—were taken for secondary use as building blocks in the new homes. In 1967, the village was surveyed by a team headed by S. Gutman. In the published report of this survey, Gutman described many houses in the village which had ancient bottom-floors and stone ceilings. He also mentioned arches, capitals, ancient stone doors (in secondary use as troughs), columns, reliefs, decorated finely-hewn stones, as well as a statue of a man whose head was broken, holding a shield decorated with a Medusa head.[85]

In the years between 1968 and 1972, and again in August 1975, the author surveyed the village and the nearby Syrian army camps a number of

---

[82] See Gregg and Urman, Inscriptions #185, 186, 193, 194, 195, 196, 198.
[83] Schumacher, "Dscholan," pp. 339-340; Schumacher, *Jaulân*, pp. 177-178. Parentheses mine.
[84] See Baedeker, *Palestine*.
[85] Epstein & Gutman, p. 264, Site #53.

times.[86] During these surveys, the area of the site was estimated at over 40 dunams. The teams collected a few pottery pieces from the end of the Hellenistic period, and great quantities of shards from stages of the Roman, Byzantine, Arab, and Ottoman periods. At the site area one can clearly see a number of stages of construction, starting with the tops of ancient walls, as far as one can tell, from the late Hellenistic and early Roman periods, through six complete structures of the late Roman and Byzantine periods that were preserved with their original first floor stone ceilings (the roofs are made of long basalt slabs in the Haurân style). Two structures—in which the stone ceiling also survived—were probably reconstructed at a somewhat later period, perhaps in the early Arab or later. The architectural items reported by Gutman were located and some of them were transferred to the Golan Antiquities Collection now in Qaṣrîn. It should be noted that on the headless statue found by Gutman's team, we found a Greek inscription around the outer rim of the shield. This statue, which is treated more extensively in the author's joint volume with R. C. Gregg, provides evidence that during the settlement's Roman period, a pagan population also resided there.[87]

Among the items we found in the village not reported by Gutman, noteworthy is a fragment of an eagle's wing and a number of Ionic capitals of the type common in the Jewish public buildings of the Galilee and the Golan during the second-temple and rabbinic periods. We also found in the village a number of olive-oil presses. On the eastern edge of the site, where today stands a Syrian military camp, what seems to be a Jewish cemetery from the rabbinic period was found. We found fragments of four tombstones bearing Greek inscriptions there.

Inscription #1[88]

This inscription appears on a fragment of a basalt gravestone. The fragment is 105 cm. high, 40 cm. wide, and 26 cm. thick. Three lines of a Greek inscription were preserved, their letters 5-6 cm. in height:

ΓΑΙΣΚΥ
ΡΙΛΛΟΥ
ΕΤ᾽ΛΕ

---

[86] D. Urman, "Kafr Nafâkh," *Special Surveys Reports*, Archive of the Association for the Archaeological Survey of Israel, Israel Antiquities Authority, Jerusalem (in Hebrew); D. Urman, "Kafr Nafâkh," *Reports of the Staff Officer in Charge of Archaeological Affairs in the Golan* (from 1968-1972), Archive of the Israel Antiquities Authority, Jerusalem (in Hebrew); Urman, "Golan—2," p. 11; Urman, *List*, p. 7; Urman, "Hellenistic," p. 467; Urman, "Kafr Nafâkh," pp. 3-4; Urman, *Golan*, p. 192, Site #58.

[87] See the section on Kafr Nafâkh in Gregg and Urman and Inscription #105.

[88] Gregg and Urman, Inscription #106.

The inscription reads: "Γάις Κυριλλου ἐτ(ῶν) λε." Its translation: "Gais, (son of) Kyrillos. Thirty-five years old."

θάρσει (= "Be of good courage") may have stood in the line above the first that is legible here. The name Γάις is a well-known variant of Γάιος, but it is possible that a dim line cut beneath a raised sigma in line 1 is intended to note an abbreviation (i.e., Γάιος). The name Gaios, in spite of its being a typically Roman one, was widespread among the Jews of the Diaspora as well as among those in Palestine.[89] As for the name of the father, Κύριλλος, it is of interest to quote here Lifshitz's remarks about this name in the Beth She'arim inscriptions:

> This name is common in the inscriptions from Beth She'arim (the name Κυρίλλα is also found at Beth She'arim, see #146). A Jew of this name is mentioned in an inscription from Rome. In the (Jewish) inscriptions from Jaffa the name Κύριλλος appears twice. It was a common name among Palestinian Jews. This was also the name of the 7th century Palestinian poet called, in Hebrew, Ha-Kalir. In Hebrew, the lamed and resh were reversed and the Greek ending was omitted.[90]

Inscription #2[91]

This inscription comes from a basalt gravestone fragment. The height of the fragment is 94 cm., its width is 40 cm., its thickness is 15 cm. The inscription is worn but seems to be complete (the average height of its letters is 6 cm.):

ΘΑΡΣΙ
ΑΛΟΥ
ΟΣΑΝΙΝ
.ΥΕΤΟ

The inscription reads: "θάρσι Ἀλου[δ]ος(?) Ανιν[ο]υ(?) ἔτ(ους) ο" and translates as: "Be of good courage, Aloudos(?), (son of) Aninos or Aninas(?). Seventy years old."

Erosion of the stone's surface, especially in line 2, leaves this reading in doubt. The names, if accurately reconstructed, are Semitic, and probably Jewish.[92]

---

[89] See Schwabe and Lifshitz, pp. 193-194, Inscription #207; Roth-Gerson, *Greek Inscriptions*, p. 142, and the references in both to further bibliography.

[90] Schwabe and Lifshitz, p. 5, Inscription #10. Apart from Inscription #10, the name Kyrillos appears at Beth She'arim also in Inscriptions #9 and #107. For the inscriptions cited, see Frey, vol. 1, #133, and vol. 2, #922 and #934.

[91] Gregg and Urman, Inscription #107.

[92] For Ἀλουδος, see Wuthnow, p. 18; for Ἀνιν and Ἀνινας, see Wuthnow, p. 22.

Inscription #3[93]

This inscription appears on a basalt gravestone fragment. Its height is 70 cm.; its width, 35 cm.; and its thickness 19 cm. On the fragment four lines have been preserved from an eroded inscription whose letters are 4-5 cm. tall:

ΣΟΥΛΓΑ
Α.ΟΥΔΟ
ΜΝΟΥ
ΕΤΙΕ

The inscription reads: "Σοῦλ Γα[ι]α[ν]ου Δόμνοῦ ἔτ(ους) ιε" and translates as: "Soul, (son of) Gaianos Domnos. Fifteen years old."

A line at the top of the inscription appears to be a border, so there is no reason to suppose that a Θάρσει (= "Be of good courage") preceded. As in the case of inscription No. 2, the worn condition of the stone makes the names probable, at best, while the name Σοῦλ is a clearly Semitic name.[94] The name Γαιανος, which is similar to the Roman name Γάιος, also appears in Semitic inscriptions[95] whereas the name Δόμνος is found in Jewish inscriptions from Rome.[96] One may, then, suppose that the gravestone before us is of a Jewish young man.

Inscription #4

This basalt fragment seems to be from a gravestone. It measures 50 cm. high, 30 cm. wide, and 17 cm. thick. It preserves only the first letters of four lines of an inscription the height of whose letters was about 8 cm.:

ΘΑ - - -
ΑΓ - - -
ΕΔ - - -
Υ - - -

The inscription reads: "Θά[ρσει] Αγ--- εδ--- υ" and means: "Be of good courage, Ag...."

On the assumption that this stone was a funeral marker with at least the word Θάρσει on the first line (a border runs along the left side of the stone), the preserved piece is the upper left portion. The names are too fragmentary to recover. Yet, since the marker fragment was found with the three gravestones described above it is plausible to assume that this also carried names that were prevalent among Jews in the Roman and early Byzantine periods.

---

[93] Gregg and Urman, Inscription #108.

[94] Wuthnow, p. 112.

[95] Wuthnow, p. 39.

[96] Frey, vol. 1, Inscriptions #20 and #494.

In the latter part of the Byzantine period, Christianity penetrated Kafr Nafâkh and to that several architectural items can attest, primarily lintels decorated with crosses.

It should be noted that in the time that elapsed between our surveys of this site in 1968-1972 and the survey we conducted there in August 1975, the Yom Kippur War had taken place in 1973 in the Golan heights, among other places.[97] In this war, Kafr Nafâkh served as the focal point of blood-drenched armored battles that, among other things, caused severe damage to the site and disruption of the entire agricultural periphery in the region. We mention this here so that the reader will be aware of the limitations that exist in later surveyors' reports of Kafr Nafâkh and its surroundings.

In October and November 1979, the remains of Kafr Nafâkh were surveyed by a team headed by C. Dauphin.[98] This team repeated the survey in October and November 1988 and also surveyed the remains of the site's agricultural periphery.[99] In the reports of these surveys that were conducted, as was said, after the 1973 war, we have found nothing new. Still, it is interesting to quote a section here from C. Dauphin's reports on the Jewishness of the ancient site at Kafr Nafâkh:

> Kafr Nafâkh appears to conform to the definition of the Jewish 'ayara (unfortified small town) as described in rabbinic sources. It lies close to a main road, without either directly abutting on it or straddling it, which would have rendered its defence more difficult. Rectangular in shape, but not strictly planned internally, it conforms to one of the six urban layouts listed in the Tosefta. It thus appears to have developed according to local needs, while following the requirements of rabbinic law. The streets, defined by buildings that were not constructed on carefully gridded plots, were far from straight. The outer defence system, formed by continuous house walls, was reinforced by the internal subdivision of the settlement into independent quarters. Three main north-south streets and east-west offshoots divide Kafr Nafâkh into six smaller, defensible neighbourhoods, each of which offered a continuous outer wall. Each large building unit consisted of a central courtyard around which numerous outbuildings clustered. The way that housing units ('private property') opened onto each other— or onto streets, piazzas, gardens and empty lots ('public property')—is frequently mentioned in the texts.
> The focal point of the Jewish 'ayara was the synagogue, usually situated at the geographical centre of town. Although a synagogue has not yet been identified at Kafr Nafâkh, the alignment in R. 9 and R. 11 of Quarter II of

---

[97] See above, note 86.

[98] See Dauphin, "1979," pp. 223-225; Dauphin, "Golan Heights—1," p. 68; Dauphin, "Settlement Patterns—1," p. 38; Dauphin, "Gaulanitis," *passim*; Dauphin and Schonfield, *passim*.

[99] See Dauphin, "1988a," p. 6; Dauphin, "1988b," pp. 176-177; Dauphin and Gibson, pp. 12-14; Dauphin and Gibson, "Ancient Settlements," pp. 7-9.

fallen pillars drums—the only ones so far found at Kafr Nafâkh—suggests the presence of a monumental building in that area of town.[100]

We can only hope that in the future Dauphin, or another investigator, will excavate and uncover the remains of the monumental building mentioned in the last part of this quotation, and that there will indeed be found clear and well-dated Jewish remains in it.

EL-BREIKAH

This large Circassian village lies at the foot of Tell 'Akâsha at coordinates 2315-2718. Since the village lies outside Israeli-controlled territory in the Golan, we have no details about the ancient remains there except for the brief report of G. Schumacher after his visit to the village in 1884.[101] According to Schumacher:

> In the village itself one finds crosses and lintel ornamentations from ancient times. One of these ornamentations (Fig. 47 in his German text and Fig. 23 in the English text) is worthy of notice, because on it is represented the cross and the Jewish candlestick; it seems, indeed, as if the latter were added as a supplement to the cross.[102]

E. R. Goodenough drew upon the Schumacher's illustration in his analysis of Jewish art. He wrote:[103]

> Another stone, fig. 587, was taken with reason to be a Christian adaptation of the same design, in which the menorah is being equated with or transformed into a cross. If that is true, the Christians were adapting a design whose original value was still so felt that its Christianization was demanded—like the Christianization of many pagan festivals. I am, however, not fully convinced that such crosses are Christian at all, for the round ends of the central cross look very much like what we have been calling the solar, magical cross.[104]

Ma'oz, in his article criticizing C. Dauphin's discussion of her finds at Farj,[105] comments on the el-Breikah lintel: "All these lintels are expressions of one and the same artistic and symbolic approach and they may well

---

[100] Dauphin, "1979," p. 224.

[101] Schumacher, "Dscholan," pp. 289-290; Schumacher, *Jaulân*, pp. 113-114 and Fig. 23 on p. 115.

[102] See previous note. Parentheses mine.

[103] Goodenough, vol. 3, Fig. 587.

[104] Goodenough, vol 1, pp. 222-223.

[105] See Dauphin, "Gaulanitis" and Ma'oz, "Communities." For a discussion of the details of these finds, see below, in the section on Farj.

have been used by a Christian sect, possibly newly converted Jews, which integrated the menorah into its iconographic repertoire."[106]

We shall not get involved in the debate about whether the lintel illustrated by Schumacher at el-Breikah belonged to a Christian, Judeo-Christian, or Jewish building. In our opinion, we should wait until it is possible for investigators to survey the site anew and provide further information on its antiquities.

SOLYMA

The village of Solyma (κώμης Σολύμης) is mentioned only once in the writings of Flavius Josephus, in *Vita* § 187: "The region of Gaulanitis, as far as the village of Solyma, likewise revolted from the king (Agrippa II)" (parentheses mine).

From the context, it seems that Solyma is a Jewish village, yet on the basis of the solitary reference it is impossible to determine anything about its location. B. Bar-Kochva suggested that this village be identified with the site which is known today as the site of Gamala.[107] However, since Bar-Kochva's identification rests upon his mistaken identification of Gamala, it is highly unlikely. We can only say, then, that in the late second-temple period, a Jewish village named Solyma existed on the borders of the Golan but its location remains unknown.

KHUSHNIYYE

This abandoned Syrian town lies at coordinates 2261-2669. Before the Six Day War, Khushniyye was the second largest town on the Golan after Quneiṭra. The town grew during the 1950's and 1960's when a number of Syrian Army camps were erected nearby and it became an important crossroads in the region.

G. Schumacher, who visited the place in 1884, found neither the ancient site nor any archaeological finds at Khushniyye. His brief remark revealed his lack of interest in the town: "A large winter village on the Roman street west of er-Rafîd, with scattered building stones. Most of the huts have fallen to pieces."[108] In 1967, the town was surveyed by teams headed by C. Epstein and S. Gutman, who discerned that the southern part of the town lay on a tell. On the western slopes of the tell, the surveyors made out the remains of ancient walls. These include a restricting wall, part of which served

---

[106] Ma'oz, "Communities," p. 63.

[107] Bar-Kochva, "Gamala," pp. 70-71.

[108] Schumacher, "Dscholan," p. 291; Schumacher, *Jaulân*, p. 194.

as the wall of a *khân*. In one of the yards of a Syrian house, they found the lower part of a basalt statue portraying a man wearing a toga. Epstein and Gutman date the shards found at the site to the Roman, Byzantine and Ottoman periods. They also reported finding a coin from the time of Emperor Diocletian.[109]

From 1968 to 1972, the tell, the town, and the nearby Syrian Army camps were surveyed a number of times by the author and his staff.[110] In these surveys, it became clear that the area of the ancient site there had covered about 30 dunams, its main part resting on the tell, which present-day maps label Tell Khushniyye. But even on the level ground surrounding the tell, it is possible to discern the tops of ancient walls. In addition to the shards reported by Epstein and Gutman, we also found a small amount of pottery from the Hellenistic period and the different Arab periods.

Among the remains of buildings we surveyed, one near the summit of the mound stands in a good state of preservation—a large dwelling with an interior courtyard which, after the Arab conquest, was converted into a *khân*. The antiquity of the structure is indicated by the existence in one room of its original Haurân-style roof.

Within the modern Syrian houses, we discovered architectural fragments such as pedestals, bases, column capitals, and other items. These are typical of types common in the Jewish public buildings in the Galilee and the Golan in the second-temple and rabbinic periods. This find led us to suggest at the time that we search for remains of a Jewish public building, perhaps a synagogue.[111]

Other evidence supports our supposition that Khushniyye had been a Jewish community during the second-temple and rabbinic periods. It comes from the Greek inscriptions found in our surveys.[112]

Inscription #1[113]

This burial inscription has its upper portion broken off. The gravestone is made of basalt and its preserved dimensions are 44 cm. high, 25 cm. wide, and 12 cm. thick. Its upper section contains a number of incisions, but it is difficult to know if they are the remains of letters, such as "EMM." More

---

[109] Epstein & Gutman, p. 270, Site #81.

[110] D. Urman, "Khushniyye," *Special Surveys Reports*, Archive of the Association for the Archaeological Survey of Israel, Israel Antiquities Authority, Jerusalem (in Hebrew); D. Urman, "Khushniyye," *Reports of the Staff Officer in Charge of Archaeological Affairs in the Golan* (from 1968-1972), Archive of the Israel Antiquities Authority, Jerusalem (in Hebrew); Urman, *List*, p. 12; Urman, *Golan*, p. 195, Site #84.

[111] See Urman, "Synagogue Sites," p. 23; Urman, "Hellenistic," p. 467.

[112] The inscriptions were studied at the time by my colleague R. C. Gregg; see Gregg and Urman, Inscriptions #151-153.

[113] Gregg and Urman, Inscription #151.

probably, the curved lines form part of a decorative motif. Beneath these incisions there are five clear lines of a Greek inscription, the height of whose
letters range between 2-5 cm.:

A B O Υ Σ
Z E H P A
Σ E Z H
E T Ω N
O

The inscription reads: "'Αβοῦς Ζεηρας ἔζη ἐτῶν ο." Its translation:
"Abous Zeeras. He lived seventy years."

From the name of the deceased it is clear that he was a Jew. The source
of the name 'Αβοῦς is the name אב or אבא,[114] and is close to the name אבון
which we found in the Jewish inscriptions at 'Ein Nashôt and at Qîsrîn. The
name or the cognomen Ζεηρας derives from זעירא[115] and is common in the
rabbinic literature both as a name and as a cognomen of a number of the
sages.[116]

Inscription #2[117]

This fragment comes from a basalt gravestone. The fragment's dimensions
are 50 cm. high, 32 cm. wide, and 17 cm. thick. Four lines of the Greek inscription were preserved, with letters varying between 5-8 cm. in height:

X A I P E
I O Υ Λ I
A N E
Z H Σ A

The inscription reads: "Χαῖρε 'Ιουλιανὲ ζήσα[ς]..." and its translation:
"Farewell, Julianus, who lived...."

The Roman name Julianus was used among the Jews.[118] It is therefore
possible to argue that this gravestone, too, was of a deceased Jew.

The third inscription which we found in the village was also carved in
Greek on a gravestone made of basalt. However, since of its five lines only
the first two letters of each line was preserved, it is difficult to reconstruct
the inscription's text.[119]

In 1981 or 1982, the site was surveyed again by C. Dauphin and her
team.[120] From this survey's published reports, two new aspects emerge.

---

[114] Wuthnow, p. 10.

[115] Wuthnow, p. 49.

[116] For examples, see Albeck, *Introduction*, pp. 233-236, 323, 388-391.

[117] Gregg and Urman, Inscription #152.

[118] Schwabe and Lifshitz, p. 100; Tcherikover et al., vol. 3, #1439.

[119] See Gregg and Urman, Inscription #153.

[120] See Dauphin, "1981-1982," p. 112; Dauphin, "1981/1982," p. 37.

First, on the western slope of the tell are shards of the Chalcolithic period. Second, Dauphin and her staff found at the site "a rough basalt block (0.39 x 0.24 m.) possibly bearing an incised menorah...reused in a retaining wall."[121]

In sum, the site's archaeological remains indicate that Khushniyye was a large village in the Roman and Byzantine periods. Its nucleus was established during the late Hellenistic period, and the settlement declined after the Arab conquest (until its resurgence around 1950). When the ancient community flourished, its population included both pagans (as the fragment of the statue indicates) and Jews (to judge from the names in the Greek inscriptions). Because it is impossible to date these artifacts precisely, we do not know whether the two groups lived here concurrently. It is possible that the population was initially pagan and subsequently Jewish. Hopefully, in the future there will be systematic archaeological digs at Khushniyye to help identify the periods of the existence of the Jewish community there. Perhaps one or more monumental structures will also be revealed, since we found a number of their artifacts in our surveys.

FARJ (EL-FERJ)

This abandoned Syrian village was built upon the ruins of an early settlement. It stands on a small volcanic hill and at its foot, at coordinates 2284-2627.

G. Schumacher, who visited the place in 1884, wrote: "A small Bedawîn winter village with decaying huts and old building stones. The Tell el-Ferj, against which the village rests, is supposed to contain a large cavern, but it was not possible for me to investigate this statement."[122]

In 1967, the site was surveyed by a team headed by S. Gutman, who reported the existence of ancient houses in the village with stone roofs. The houses were built according to standard plan—a front section serving as an entrance hall and the rear area consisting of a ground floor and an attic. The team also reported on the existence of stones decorated with crosses and various decorations in the village, as well as steps hewn out of a block of basalt, a hewn-out grave, and pits.[123]

In 1968-1972, the author and his staff surveyed the village a number of times.[124] These surveys revealed that the area of the early site was about 40

[121] Dauphin, "1981-1982," p. 112.

[122] Schumacher, "Dscholan," p. 293; Schumacher, *Jaulân*, p. 136.

[123] Epstein & Gutman, p. 273, Site #96.

[124] D. Urman, "Farj," *Special Surveys Reports*, Archive of the Association for the Archaeological Survey of Israel, Israel Antiquities Authority, Jerusalem (in Hebrew); D. Urman, "Farj," *Reports of the Staff Officer in Charge of Archaeological Affairs in the Golan*

dunams. The site produced shards primarily from the different stages of the
Roman and Byzantine periods. About twenty houses of the Syrian village
were built on top of structures of the Roman and Byzantine periods, sometimes using entire rooms from these periods that were preserved up to their
original stone roofs (built in the Haurân style). In a number of the houses,
second-floor rooms of the earlier structures were also preserved.

In several of the early houses, we found decorated architectural items in
secondary use as regular building stones. Indeed, the houses reveal a number
of building stages—as early as the Byzantine period, secondary use was
made of items taken from ruined houses of the Roman period. Of the tens of
architectural items we recorded in the village, most outstanding are the lintels decorated with crosses, a number of segments of a basalt column decorated with engravings of vine branches and crosses, and six gravestones with
Greek inscriptions.

The inscriptions, which were studied by R. C. Gregg,[125] include clearly
Roman names such as Julia, Domittias, Kyrilla, Sabina, and Klaudios, and
also Semitic names such as Barnebos, Alapha, Echoma, and Otaras.[126]

In 1979-1988, the site and its agricultural periphery were surveyed by a
team headed by C. Dauphin.[127] In the village's agricultural periphery—
which they investigated up to a radius of 1.5 kilometers from the site—
Dauphin's team discerned four stages. Stage I revealed a large number of
dolmens scattered over the entire area with Middle Bronze Age shards. Stage
II had rectangular fields with boundary walls, associated with the Late
Hellenistic and Early Roman quarters north-east and south-east of the settlement. Stage III was characterized by a planned complex of field systems
divided into strips with straight enclosure walls. This stage is probably associated with the Late Roman to Byzantine occupation at Farj. Stage IV
consisted of the modern Arab restoration of field systems close to the settlement or beside roads leading out of it.[128]

(from 1968-1972), Archive of the Israel Antiquities Authority, Jerusalem (in Hebrew);
Urman, *List*, p. 13; Urman, *Golan*, p. 197, Site #96.

[125] See Gregg and Urman, Inscriptions #132-137.

[126] Gregg and Urman, Inscriptions #135-137.

[127] Dauphin, "1979," p. 223; Dauphin, "Golan Heights—1," p. 68; Dauphin, "Settlement
Patterns—1," p. 38; Dauphin, "1980-1981," p. 240; Dauphin, "Settlement Patterns—2," p. 40;
Dauphin, "Gaulanitis," pp. 129-142; Dauphin, "Golan Heights—2," p. 75; Dauphin, "1981-
1982," p. 112; Dauphin, "1981/1982," p. 37; Dauphin, "Settlement Patterns—3," p. 1;
Dauphin, "Farj," pp. 233-245; Dauphin, "Settlement Patterns—4," p. 1; Dauphin, "1985a," p.
44; Dauphin, "1985b," pp. 273-274; Dauphin, "1988a," p. 7; Dauphin, "1988b," pp. 178-179;
Dauphin and Schonfield, pp. 189-206; Dauphin and Gibson, "Ancient Settlements," pp. 12-
19.

[128] See Dauphin, "1988a," p. 7; Dauphin, "1988b," pp. 178-179.

Some 200 m. west of the settlement a two-room ancient structure with an eastern-oriented apse was discovered. The building (whose surviving dimensions are 2.85 x 2.85 m.) is built of well-dressed square stones. It was identified by Dauphin as a chapel on the basis of the cross carved into its lintel. A large rounded reservoir (7.60 x 5.95 m.; 2.08 m. deep) was located north-east of the chapel; it is also built of well-dressed square stones.[129]

In the village itself, Dauphin discerns two early stages: "In the first stage, two elaborately laid out buildings were erected on the site, later developing into at least twelve housing units, some of two stories, built of well dressed stones."[130]

Here we must note that between the surveys of Gutman and ourselves on the one hand and that of Dauphin and her team on the other, many of the village's buildings were damaged by developmental activities, so that one must use the figures of the last survey cautiously. According to one report, Dauphin and her team registered in the village 50 "pieces of architectural sculpture,"[131] and according to a second report, 70 such items.[132] It is logical to assume that many of these items had already been reported upon previously, but there is no doubt that the development work on the one hand, and the intensity of Dauphin's survey on the other, uncovered many items heretofore unknown. Up to now, a full report of Dauphin's survey has yet to be published and we therefore do not have a full picture of all these artifacts. Yet, the preliminary publications indicate that Dauphin and her team also found clearly Jewish remains at the site. And Dauphin reports as follows: "The most remarkable finds, however, were the lintel of a monumental Jewish building (perhaps of a synagogue or an academy) bearing two seven-branched candlesticks (*menorot*) and a Greek inscription."[133] "There are also fifteen lintels,[134] at least one of them *in situ* carved in low relief with *menorot* or Trees of Life, palm branches (*lulavim*), rams' horns (*shofarot*) citrons (*ethrogim*), and an Aramaic inscription."[135]

In summing up her report on the Jewish finds at Farj, Dauphin writes: "These discoveries situated outside the area believed to have been occupied by Jews, challenge the hypothesis of a Jewish habitat limited to the western

---

[129] See previous note, and Dauphin and Gibson, "Ancient Settlements," p. 19.

[130] Dauphin, "1981/1982," p. 37.

[131] Dauphin, "Golan Heights—2," p. 74.

[132] Dauphin, "1981-1982," p. 112.

[133] Dauphin, "1980-1981," p. 240. See also Dauphin, "Gaulanitis," pp. 136-137; Dauphin, "Golan Heights—2," p. 75; Dauphin and Schonfield, p. 205; Dauphin and Gibson, "Ancient Settlements," p. 17.

[134] In Dauphin, "Golan Heights—2," p. 75, she wrote 19 instead of 15.

[135] Thus in Dauphin and Schonfield, p. 205. And also see Dauphin, "1980-1981," p. 240. In Dauphin, "Gaulanitis," p. 137 and Dauphin, "Golan Heights—2," p. 75, she reports on "at least two Aramaic inscriptions" but without presenting photographs, copies, or readings of these inscriptions.

edge of the central Golan (Ma'oz, "Synagogues": 100-101) and isolated from the other components of the population of the region."[136] This last remark, together with Dauphin's conclusion which rests upon her Farj finds, that there was "peaceful co-existence" between the Jews in the Golan and their neighbors, the Christian Ghassanid communities,[137] distressed Ma'oz and brought him to write an article disagreeing.[138] We shall not here enter into the controversy between Ma'oz and Dauphin. Instead, let me indicate here that, on the one hand, one should wait until Dauphin has published all her finds from Farj, including the Aramaic inscriptions. On the other hand, in her article which provoked Ma'oz, she presented two illustrations of two window lintels that she found at Farj with seven-branched *menorot* incised upon them.[139] Thus there is no doubt that Dauphin and her team indeed un-covered evidence of the existence of a Jewish community at Farj dating to the second-temple or rabbinic periods.

RAFÎD (ER-RAFÎD)

Rafîd is an abandoned Syrian village, built within and atop of the ruins of an early settlement, at coordinates 234-262. The site is located on the plain east of Tell el-Faras, near the intersection of the principal roads between Ḥammat Gader-Rafîd and Quneiṭra-Sheikh Maskin.

Rafîd was first surveyed by G. Schumacher,[140] who observed two build-ing phases in the site: "Two periods of architecture are distinguishable in the ruins: the old Haurân style below, and the Arabian one above ground."[141] On the basis of the many cross decorations he noted in the village remnants, as well as a structure with apses which he presumed to be a church, Schumacher related the early building phase in Rafîd to Christian village population.[142]

S. Gutman, surveying Rafîd after the 1967 war, found in the eastern part of the village a church structure.[143] It was rectangular in shape, its inner length 14 m. and its width between 7.50-8.50 m. A single apse was built in

---

[136] Dauphin, "Gaulanitis," p. 137. See also Dauphin, "1980-1981," p. 240; Dauphin, "Golan Heights—2," p. 75; Dauphin and Schonfield, p. 205.

[137] See Dauphin, "Gaulanitis," p. 140.

[138] See Ma'oz, "Communities," pp. 59-68.

[139] Dauphin, "Gaulanitis," p. 135, Fig. 6; Dauphin, "Gaulanitis," p. 138, Fig. 10. At the center of the second lintel, the one in Fig. 10, there appears a nine-branched candelabrum and, on either side of it, two smaller *menorot* of seven branches and a *shofar*.

[140] Schumacher, "Dscholan," pp. 312-314; Schumacher, *Jaulân*, pp. 226-229.

[141] Schumacher, "Dscholan," p. 312; Schumacher, *Jaulân*, p. 226.

[142] Schumacher, "Dscholan," pp. 313-314 and Fig. 73; Schumacher, *Jaulân*, pp. 227-228 and Fig. 115.

[143] Epstein & Gutman, pp. 273-274, Site # 97.

its eastern wall, measuring 4.80 m. wide and 4.50 m. long or deep.[144] Gutman claims that this church was constructed above the remains of an earlier one. In the western part of the village he observed a group of ancient, completely preserved buildings, in which were found, in secondary use, hewn stones bearing Greek inscriptions and rosette decorations, as well as column-capitals. In his report, Gutman provided no copies or photographs of these inscriptions.

A short while after Gutman's survey, the author and his team began a prolonged and systematic survey of the site and its agricultural periphery that concluded in 1970.[145] Since the full report of this survey is presently in the last stages of preparation for publication as an independent volume, we will give only a general and brief description of the survey's finds here, with special emphasis on the finds that attest to the existence of a Jewish chapter in the village's history.

The survey revealed that the built up area of the ancient settlement there is about 100 dunams (25 acres) and contains shards of the different stages of the Roman, Byzantine, Arab, and Ottoman periods. The survey identified and measured 140 complete and ruined structures. These range in date from the Roman period to 1967. Our study of the site indicates that the nucleus of the ancient village consisted of two or three wealthy farmers' houses in the Roman era.

It seems that during the later Roman period (third-fourth centuries), additional structures were built in the settlement. Yet without systematic archaeological excavations at the site, it is difficult to know either when the wealthy farmers' houses—the more ancient structures (first and second centuries C.E.?)—were in use, or what the relationship was between those structures and the buildings later added to them. It should be pointed out that it seems the finds which may bear witness to Jewish habitation should be attributed to one of the two stages of the Roman period.

Among the probable Jewish finds are the fragments of a lintel with the compass-produced bas relief rosettes. The fragments were found in secondary use as arch stones in a building of the Byzantine period (Building 15). Other lintel fragments with relief decorations of circles that were set into later buildings in secondary use as construction stones (Building 22 and Building 40). Similarly, a lintel fragment with a bas relief of a shrine (*aedicula*) was found in secondary use as a doorpost-stone in the entrance of a stable of the Byzantine period (Structure 45). Among the fifteen Greek inscriptions we

---

[144] See plan in Epstein & Gutman, p. 274.

[145] See D. Urman, "Rafîd," *Reports of the Staff Officer in Charge of Archaeological Affairs in the Golan* (from 1968-1972), Archive of the Israel Antiquities Authority, Jerusalem (in Hebrew); Urman, *List*, p. 13; Urman, "Golan—6," pp. 1-2; Urman, *Golan*, p. 197, Site #97.

found during the survey, at least two may be attributable to the Jews (see below).

In the Byzantine period, the village numbered sixty buildings, some of which had stables attached. Some of these buildings were found intact—that is, including their original roofs made of stone slabs in the style which Schumacher named the 'Haurân style.' In these buildings, several stages are also discernible but we shall not treat them here, for it seems that in the Byzantine period Jews no longer lived there. Indeed, in the later Byzantine period, Rafîd was without a doubt a large Christian village. During the Arab and Ottoman periods, construction activity was limited, and it seems that the site functioned as a seasonal village for Bedouin tribes. Only in the early 1950's was the village resettled, when some eighty new buildings were added, with secondary use of many ancient building stones and architectural elements.

In these houses, as in a number of the Byzantine buildings, we found fifteen Greek inscriptions, a number of which perhaps are Jewish. Thirteen of the inscriptions are being published in the joint volume of the author and R. C. Gregg,[146] and all are dealt with anew in the final publication of the survey report which should see the light of day shortly. Here we shall present only two of the inscriptions.

Inscription #1[147]

A gravestone made of basalt stone, 96 cm. high. 29 cm. wide, and 14 cm. thick. The inscription is intact, consisting of five lines, with letters 8 cm. high. It reads:

Θ Α Ρ Σ
Ι Α Λ Α
Φ Θ Α
Ε Τ Ε
Ξ

That is to say: "Θάρσι Αλαφθα ἐτ(ῶν) εξ" and translates: "Be of good courage, Alaphtha! Sixty-five years old."

The name Alaphtha = חלפא or חלפתה in its Galilean form, is known from the rabbinic period as the name of several of the Palestinian *tannaim* and *amoraim*.[148] This name is found in precisely the same spelling on a Greek burial inscription discovered in the Jewish cemetery of Jaffa,[149] and in its Aramaic-Galilean form in Inscription #2 at Qîsrîn.

---

[146] See Gregg and Urman, Inscriptions #119-131.

[147] Gregg and Urman, Inscription #129.

[148] See A. Hyman, *Toldoth Tannaim ve-Amoraim* (London, 1910), 2:452-454 (in Hebrew).

[149] See Klein, *ha-Yishuv*, p. 81, Inscription #13.

Inscription #2[150]

This short inscription appears on a basalt fragment whose original use is unclear. The stone was found in secondary use as a doorpost in the entrance of Building 17, which is a modern Syrian building, and it was apparently taken from one of the ancient nearby buildings. The stone fragment is 26 cm. high, 36 cm. wide, and about 20 cm. thick. Two lines of the inscription were preserved on it (the letter heights vary between 6 and 8 cm.)
    It reads:

    Θ Ε Ο Δ
    Ω Ρ Ο Σ

That is to say: "Θεόδωρος," namely, "Theodoros."
    The name Theodoros was widespread in Syria and Palestine in the periods under discussion here, but we also find it in use among the Jews.[151]
    To conclude our discussion of the finds at Rafîd we must note that to our regret the homes of the village were hard hit in the battles of the 1973 war. And after this war, we were no longer able to visit the site because it now lies beyond the Israel Defence Forces' cease-fire lines. In the future, if further archaeological work at the site should become possible, it would be worthwhile to look for the remains of the village's ancient cemeteries which may be east of it in the areas which we could not visit before 1973, because of their proximity to the cease-fire line of those days. In our estimation these cemeteries were not seriously damaged over the course of the various periods in the village's history, for in our survey we found, all told, only two gravestones—a very small number compared to other villages in the Golan. It may be that if the site's cemeteries of the Roman period would be uncovered, our knowledge of the Jews that resided there would be enriched.

BUṬMIYYE

This small abandoned Syrian village near the Rafîd-Ḥammat Gader (el-Ḥammah) road lies about 1.5 km. southwest of Rafîd, at coordinates 2328-2615.
    The village was first surveyed by G. Schumacher, who was impressed primarily by the remains of a Byzantine building which he mistakenly dated to the Arab period and whose use he took to have been a *khân*.[152] In the *khân*-structure Schumacher saw, drew, and published, three broken lintels

---

[150] Gregg and Urman, Inscription #128.

[151] See, for example, the writings of Josephus, *Ant.* XIV §§ 222, 226, & 307; and similarly in the gravestone found at the Jewish cemetery at Jaffa, see Klein, *ha-Yishuv*, p. 82, Inscription #16.

[152] Schumacher, "Dscholan," pp. 292-293; Schumacher, *Jaulân*, pp. 115-117.

that, in his opinion, were ornamented with "Christian symbols—namely, rectilinear crosses, vine-leaf ornamentation, and weather-worn inscriptions— that recall an earlier Christian period."[153] Concerning the third lintel Schumacher adds: "Very peculiar are the greatly weather-worn decorations of a door lintel, on which may still be distinguished some Greek signs, besides a ten-branched figure recalling the Jewish candlestick."[154]

In 1968, the village was surveyed by the survey teams headed by C. Epstein and S. Gutman, who reported briefly that the village was built upon a tell and that there were found in it ancient buildings with stone ceilings that served as cellars for the Syrian village buildings.[155] Epstein and Gutman also reported upon the existence of "decorated hewn stones (in the village), among them an inscription with a cross: 'IOCH,' as well as shards from the Roman-Byzantine period."[156]

In 1969-1970, the author and his team surveyed the village a number of times.[157] In this survey, we discovered that the Syrian village rests upon a small tell, the area of which is estimated at 20 dunams. The tell itself consists of Roman and Byzantine structures once standing on this small hill. Of the forty dwellings in the modern village, four survive, either completely or partially, from the early Byzantine era.

One structure contains a rectangular room built in the Haurân style, having become partly subterranean with the passage of time. In its western wall can be seen nine 'Chorazin windows,' indicating that this room represents only a small portion of a larger building. An edifice which stands atop the tell seems to be Schumacher's *khân*. This building represents, in fact, the joining of two L-shaped halves. The north-eastern wing, which dates from the early Byzantine age, includes seven rooms, with five preserving Haurân-style (corbelled) roofs. The south-western half of the structure is later. In it we found, in secondary use, a fragmentary lintel made of basalt bearing a portion of a Greek inscription. This lintel fragment—128 cm. long, 33 cm. high, and 13-15 cm. thick—is the one that Schumacher copied and published in his time.[158] It was also seen by the Epstein and Gutman survey teams.[159] An close examination of this lintel fragment indicated that it is

[153] Schumacher, "Dscholan," pp. 292-293, Figs. 49-50; Schumacher, *Jaulân*, p. 116, Figs. 25-26.
[154] Schumacher, "Dscholan," pp. 292-293, Fig. 51; Schumacher, *Jaulân*, p. 116, Fig. 27.
[155] Epstein & Gutman, p. 274, Site #99.
[156] Epstein & Gutman, p. 274, Site #99.
[157] See D. Urman, "Buṭmiyye," *Special Surveys Reports*, Archive of the Association for the Archaeological Survey of Israel, Israel Antiquities Authority, Jerusalem (in Hebrew); D. Urman, "Buṭmiyye," *Reports of the Staff Officer in Charge of Archaeological Affairs in the Golan* (from 1968-1972), Archive of the Israel Antiquities Authority, Jerusalem (in Hebrew). See also Urman, "Lintel," pp. 2-3; Urman, *List*, p. 13; Urman, *Golan*, p. 197, Site #101.
[158] Schumacher, "Dscholan," p. 293, Fig. 50: Schumacher, *Jaulân*, p. 116, Fig. 25.
[159] Epstein & Gutman, p. 274, Site #99.

about three quarters of the lintel's original length. In the center of the lintel there is a prominent relief of a stylized flower which erroneously looked to Schumacher and the staffs of Epstein and Gutman like a cross. At both ends of the lintel there were found two additional reliefs of a stylized flower (rosette?) of which only the right one is preserved. The inscription is in-scribed between the three floral reliefs:

...OYC   IΩCH
        A

This reads: "...ουσα (?) 'Ιωση" and means: "...ουσα (?) Yose."

The placement of the letters in relation to the prominent relief of the flowers suggests that the alpha represents the ending of (what remains of) the first word. We have no suggestion for the completion of the inscrip-tion's first word and it seems we shall have to wait patiently until the miss-ing left quarter of the lintel is found. In any case, the second word is undoubtedly the name 'Ιωση (and not 'Ιοση as erroneously published in the Epstein-Gutman report), a widespread Jewish name in the rabbinic period, and also found in the Jewish inscriptions uncovered at 'Ein Nashôt.[160]

In the later section of the complex, we found two additional decorated ar-chitectural pieces made of basalt stone that may also have belonged to the public building or to private homes of Jews. One item is a right fragment of a lintel—75 cm. long, 38 cm. high, and about 17 cm. thick—with a lovely relief of a vine branch. A poor drawing of this lintel fragment was published by Schumacher.[161] The second item is a stone slab (perhaps a doorpost?)— 78 cm. high, 35 cm. wide, and 17 cm thick—on which there was engraved, in sketchy form, a nine-branched candelabrum with a tripod base with circles engraved on its sides (see PL. 26a).

In the early Byzantine section of the complex, we found the broken lintel about which Schumacher reported finding the engraving of "a ten-branched figure recalling the Jewish candlestick."[162] Since lower part of the lintel was broken, Schumacher may have been correct, and indeed, the engraving at the center of the lintel was intended to represent a nine-branched candelabrum (and not ten as Schumacher wrote) set in a circle. Goodenough, who related to the lintel on the basis of the figure published by Schumacher, writes that the illustration "shows the conventionalization of a nine-branched menorah with an arch, and may be a late concession to rabbinic prejudice against the menorah with seven branches."[163] And he adds: "In itself we should presume

---

[160] For a detailed treatment of this name and additional comparisons, see below in our treatment of inscriptions #1 and #3 from 'Ein Nashôt.

[161] See Schumacher, "Dscholan," p. 293, Fig. 49; Schumacher, *Jaulân*, p. 116, Fig. 26.

[162] See Schumacher, "Dscholan," pp. 292-293, Fig. 51; Schumacher, *Jaulân*, p. 116, Fig. 27.

[163] Goodenough, vol. 1, p. 222.

that the stone was a lintel on a synagogue."[164] On both sides of the circle (and not "arch" as Goodenough wrote) that encloses the menorah, there are two complete circles, and on the left edge of the lintel there survived a two-line Greek inscription of which only a few letters are legible. Unfortunately, the Greek letters suggest neither a recognized name nor a familiar abbreviation.[165]

These finds, along with the abundance of hewn basalt stones (ashlar) and a number of Doric and Ionic capitals that were found scattered at the site, led us to speculate at the time that at some time during the rabbinic period there had been a Jewish public building in the village, perhaps a synagogue.[166] In our surveys we did not succeed in locating the site of the building, but it may yet be uncovered if systematic archaeological excavations are conducted there.

The pottery visible at Buṭmiyye is from the various stages of the Roman and Byzantine periods (with some later Arab pieces). Without further archaeological investigation the identity of the village's inhabitants must remain unknown to us; but on the basis of the name Ἰωση in the first inscription treated above and the two schematic nine-branched *menorot*, we are justified in thinking that at least some portion of the population during the late Roman and Byzantine periods was Jewish.

---

[164] See previous note.

[165] See Gregg and Urman, inscription #118.

[166] See Urman, "Synagogue Sites," p. 22. And this is perhaps the place to point out that F. Hüttenmeister and G. Reeg, who visited the site in the summer of 1974, suggested dating this building to the third or fourth centuries C.E. See Hüttenmeister and Reeg, pp. 77-78.

THE LOWER GOLAN

GOLAN (GAULANA, GAULANE, GAULON)

At various times in the history of the Golan region, it contained a settlement called by different names derived from the biblical name גּוֹלָן, (Gôlan). Different literary sources sometime refer to this settlement as a city, other times as a village. It is difficult to know whether the different references to the size of the settlement and different names reflect the existence of different settlements in different locations in different periods of time or whether they reveal a single settlement whose size and name vary over time. The few sources we have indicate that this settlement sometimes had a Jewish population.

Prior the Roman period, a settlement with the name 'Golan' appears only in the Bible.[1] In two of the biblical references, Deuteronomy 4:43 and 1 Chronicles 6:56, the name 'Golan' appears in the form used today, namely, in the 'Plene' Hebrew spelling גּוֹלָן (Gôlan). In two further references, Joshua 20:8 and Joshua 21:27, the name appears in the corrupted form גָּלְלָן.[2] In all four references, the Bible refers explicitly to a city named Gôlan which was designated a city of refuge (Deuteronomy 4:43; Joshua 20:8) and which was given to the Gershonites, one of the Levite families (Joshua 21:27; 1 Chronicles 6:56). In all four passages, the Bible mentions that the city was in the Bashan, in the territory of Manasseh.

The exact boundaries of the Bashan as presented in the Bible are the subject of much scholarly debate.[3] But from an examination of the various references to the Bashan in the Bible, especially from the verse in Deuteronomy 33:22 ("Dan is a lion's whelp, that leaps forth from Bashan"), it is clear that the region known today as the Golan Heights was also a part of the biblical Bashan.

---

[1] In the Tell el-Amarna tablets, a city by the name of *Gi-lu-ni* is mentioned; see S. A. B. Mercer, *The Tell el-Amarna Tablets*, vol. 2 (Toronto, 1939), Site #185 (22, 25). Some scholars believe that this was a city located in the southern Lebanon Valley, while others believe that it is the name of the biblical city of Gôlan. Since the name *Giluni* differs in form from the name "Golan" and since the source of this reference has no connection with sources from the Roman or Byzantine periods, I will not discuss the matter further.

[2] But the *qer'e* reads here גולן.

[3] A good summary of these debates and bibliography can be found in Loewenstamm, "Bashan."

As for the identification of the city of Golan mentioned in the Bible, modern scholarship has offered several suggestions. Most scholars follow Schumacher and have identified the location of the biblical city with the village Saḥem ej-Jaulân (coordinates 2380-2433) because of its name.[4] W. F. Albright, on the other hand, argues that this city must be within the region of the present-day Golan.[5]

The debate over the location of the Levite refuge city of "Golan in Bashan" has not been limited to modern scholarship. Echoes of this debate can be found in late antiquity in the targumic and midrashic literature, as will be seen below. Since our discussion here is devoted primarily to a city or village called "Golan" in the second-temple and rabbinic periods, we will not enter into the debate over biblical Golan's location. We will point out, however, that as long as remains from the Late Bronze Age and/or Iron Age are not found in Saḥem ej-Jaulân, it is difficult to identify this village with the biblical city solely on the basis of the name; the same logic would enable us to identify the city with the village of Jillîn or Jallîn (coordinates 2432-2400), with Kh. el-Jelabinâ (coordinates 2110-2719), or with the Roman-period settlement called Galania, whose existence we know only from inscriptions.[6]

The name "Golan" does not again appear in Jewish literature until the writings of Josephus. In fact, Josephus is the first to use "Golan" not only as the name of a city or a settlement but also as the name of a region. Seventeen instances of his use of the name refer to the region of Golan. In only four references, Josephus applies the name "Golan" to a settlement.[7] The first of these references appears in *Antiquities* IV § 173, Josephus presents the list of the three refuge cities of the Transjordan which includes Γαυλανὰν δ'ἐν τῇ Βατανίδι, that is, "Gaulana in Batanaea." Note that Josephus uses the form Γαυλανά rather than one of the transliterations found in the Septuagint or Γωλάν—forms used by Eusebius in the fourth century (see below).

In *Antiquities* XIII § 393, Josephus again uses the form Γαυλανά. The context makes clear that the name designates a city. The city appears in a description of Alexander Jannaeus' military campaign against the cities of Gaulana and Seleucia. The sentence immediately following confirms the identification of Golan as a city here—"After taking these cities as well...."

---

[4] On Schumacher's identification, see Schumacher, *Jordan*, pp. 91 ff. Of the numerous scholars agreeing with this suggested identification, we only mention here B. Mazar, who maintains this identification in the latest version of his article "Gshur ou M'achah," in Mazar, *Cities*, p. 199.

[5] See Albright, "Cities," p. 57.

[6] See Aharoni, "Golan," pp. 94 ff.; Aharoni, "Huleh," p. 136.

[7] For a comprehensive discussion of the rest of the references of the name "Golan" in the writings of Josephus, see Urman, "Toponym Golan."

In the parallel version which appears in *War* I § 105, Josephus calls the city Γαυλάνην—Gaulane. The same form of the name, Gaulane, identifies the city in *War* I § 90 as a place near which the army of Jannaeus was defeated by that of Obedas, the king of Arabia.

It is hard to know if the location of Gaulana, the city of refuge, is the same as that of Gaulana or Gaulane from the days of Alexander Jannaeus. It is even more difficult, as already indicated above, to identify their location in the area. If we accept Josephus' version that Alexander Jannaeus had to conquer Gaulana (or Gaulane), then it is clear that at that time the city had no Jewish inhabitants. What happened to the city after its capture, Josephus never reveals. In fact, he never mentions the city again. This silence suggests two possibilities for the town's fate—either Alexander Jannaeus destroyed the city at the time of its conquest and it was never again settled, or the town was repopulated by Jews and continued to exist without the status of a city.

A settlement named Golan, Gaulana, or Gaulane goes unmentioned by any literary source discussing the Roman period. Only in the early fourth century, at the beginning of the Byzantine period, does the name "Golan" as a name of a settlement appear, and then in only one paragraph of Eusebius' *Onomasticon*. The entire paragraph as it appears in Klosterman's edition, together with the Latin translation of Jerome appearing in the same edition, are presented below:[8]

Γαυλὼν ἢ Γωλάν, Φυλῆς	Gaulon sive Golan in tribu
Μανασσῆ, Πόλις ἱερατικὴ	Manasse, civitas sacerdotalis
τῶν φυγαδευτηρίων ἐν τῇ	et fugitivorum in regione
Βασανίτδι. καὶ νῦν Γαυλὼν	Basanitide. sed et nunc
καλεῖται κώμη μεγίστη ἐν	Gaulon vocatur villa
τῇ Βαταναίᾳ, ὁμωνυμεῖ δὲ	pergrandis in Batanaea, ex
τῇ κώμῃ καὶ ἡ περίχωρος.	cuius nomine et regio sortita
	vocabulum est.

Gaulon or Golan in the tribe of Manasseh, a priestly city among the cities of refuge in the Bashan. And today Gaulon is called a very large village in the Bashan; and also the district is called by the same name as the village.

The forms Γωλάν and Γαυλὼν in Eusebius are identical to those appearing in the Greek translation of the Bible. Indeed it is clear that Eusebius has quoted the Greek translations in his work.[9] Most important for our purposes is that Eusebius—whether he had firsthand experience with the Golan region

---

[8] Eusebius, *Onomasticon*, E. Klosterman, ed. (Leipzig, 1904), 64 (6-8) and 65 (6-8).

[9] On the use of the Greek translations of the Bible in the *Onomasticon*, see the introduction of Klosterman's edition, *passim*.

or only derived his information from hearsay or other contemporary sources—emphasizes that, in his time, Γαυλών signified both a very large village and the surrounding district.

But where was this "very large village" located? Scholars have proposed three candidates. The two modern villages of Sahem ej-Jaulân and Kh. el-Jelabinâ both contain remains from the early fourth century—the time of the *Onomasticon*'s composition.[10] The third possibility is settlement of Galania (Γαλανία). Archaeologists have discovered boundary stones which indicate that a village called Galania existed in the late third or early fourth centuries on the northwestern Golan slopes descending to the Huleh Valley.[11] Several different ruins near the markers have been suggested as the actual site of Galania.

If we accept Eusebius' statement that "Gaulon" was a very large village, the possibility of identifying it with Kh. el-Jelabinâ is remote, since the size of this site—approximately 12 dunams—is too small for a "very large village" during this period. The same can be said about the sites for which an identification with Galania is possible.[12] This leaves only Sahem ej-Jaulân, for both Eusebius and Jerome write that the "very large village" was in the Batanaea, where this village is situated.

The close link between Eusebius and the Septuagint, however, reveals that Eusebius wrote under the inspiration of the biblical passages. We therefore need not necessarily restrict our search for the site of Eusebius' "very large village" to the Batanaea. This being the case, I suggest the identification of Eusebius' "very large village" with Tell el-Jûkhadâr (coordinates 2302-2594). The latter has revealed decisive archaeological evidence indicating that it flourished during the time of both Eusebius and Jerome.[13] Furthermore, it is one of the largest sites in the Golan region (ca. 200 dunams). Of course, this identification depends on the reliability of the *Onomasticon* with regard to contemporary conditions. But, except for the fact that the *Onomasticon* identifies the village of its time known as Gaulon

---

[10] For the remains at Sahem ej-Jaulân, see Schumacher, *Jordan*, pp. 91-99. On the remains in Kh. el-Jelabinâ, see Schumacher, *Jaulân*, pp. 162-163; C. Epstein, "Kh. el-Jelabinâ," *Golan Survey—Phase B*, Reports in the Archive of the Association for the Archaeological Survey of Israel, Israel Antiquities Authority, Jerusalem (in Hebrew); D. Urman, "Kh. el-Jelabinâ," *Reports of the Staff Officer in Charge of Archaeological Affairs in the Golan* (1968-1972), Archive of the Israel Antiquities Authority, Jerusalem (in Hebrew); Urman, *Golan*, p. 193, Site #64.

[11] See Aharoni, "Golan," pp. 94 ff.; Aharoni, "Huleh," p. 136.

[12] On the possible identifications of the site of Galania, see Aharoni, "Golan," p. 95. An examination of additional possibilities in the region, such as Kh. el-Beida' (coordinates 2144-2857) and Kh. el-Fureyish (coordinates 2132-2851), also reveals sites of small area (15-18 dunams).

[13] On the results of the archaeological excavations at Tell el-Jûkhadâr see Urman, "Golan—1," p. 3; Urman, "Golan—2," pp. 11-12; Urman, "Hellenistic," pp. 457-458.

(Γαυλῶν) with the biblical city, there is no plausible reason for doubting its veracity.[14]

To our regret, neither Eusebius nor Jerome's translation provide any details concerning the ethnic or religious character of the population of the "very large village" of Gaulon. However, if there is an identity between the Gaulon of Eusebius and Gaulana (or Galvanic [גוולנה], or Govlana [גובלנה]) mentioned in the Palestinian Talmud, as S. Klein claimed,[15] then Jews lived in this village and probably had a synagogue.[16] The Palestinian Talmud twice refers to Rabbi Jeremiah, an *amora* of the third and fourth generations (late third and early fourth centuries—a contemporary of Eusebius), who lived in Tiberias and traveled to Gaulana. The first passage appears in Y. Megillah 3:1, 73d, where it says: "Rabbi Jeremiah went to Gaulana (Galvanic—גוולנה) saw them putting a bell in the Ark." The second passage appears in Y. Abodah Zarah 2:5, 41c: "R. Jeremiah went to Gaulana (Govlana—גובלנה) and taught there about big barrels...."

In an earlier article, I showed that there is no certainty that R. Jeremiah went to a settlement named "Gaulana," "Galvanic," or "Govlana," but rather the Palestinian Talmud possibly refers to the Golan region in general and not to a specific settlement.[17] Still, whether the settlement or the region is meant here, none of the sites so far suggested for identification as the Gaulon of Eusebius or the "Gaulana" of the Palestinian Talmud (including Tell el-Jûkhadâr) have revealed any remains of Jewish public buildings. So again we must wait patiently for further archaeological research in the region in general, and in the sites mentioned in particular.

DABÛRA

This abandoned Syrian village was built upon the ruins of an ancient Jewish settlement on the northern bank of Naḥal Gilbon (Wâdî Dabûra), approximately 5 km. northeast of the Benot Ya'aqov Bridge, at coordinates 2125-2724.

---

[14] Thus far remains from the Late Bronze or Iron Age have not been uncovered at Tell el-Jûkhadâr. However, considering the fact that the excavations at this site were conducted along its edges and not on its acropolis, we are unable, at this stage of research, to determine —either positively or negatively—the identification of Tell el-Jûkhadâr with the biblical site of Golan.

[15] See Klein, "Estates," pp. 549-550; Klein, *Transjordan*, p. 51; Klein, *ha-Yishuv*, pp. 26-27.

[16] See Hüttenmeister and Reeg, pp. 139-140. Note that Hüttenmeister and Reeg follow Schumacher and Klein and identify the place of Gaulana, Gavlana, or Govlana, with Saḥem ej-Jaulân.

[17] Urman, *Golan*, pp. 20-21.

G. Schumacher was the first to report, albeit briefly, the existence of antiquities at this site, which he visited in 1885. And this is what he wrote:

> A winter village of tolerable size, close to the Wâdî Dabûra, above the Lake
> of Huleh. Near the wretched Bedawîn huts a large modern corn magazine
> stands. The old site is north of the village, where a number of very large
> unhewn building stones and foundation walls, like in Bêdarûs, are to be met
> with. Here also they lie in confused heaps upon one another. Fine oaks and
> terebinths grow out of the once inhabited places. The remains, even at the
> present day, proclaim a large, firm, and carefully built settlement. The po-
> sition is certainly a peculiarly fine one, inasmuch as it commands the Lake
> of Huleh and its lowlands. On some art-worked fragments I observed a
> small basaltic column, which is inserted in the wall of one of the huts de-
> serted in summer...in the village itself as well as in the neighbourhood
> there are a great number of liquorice trees (Umm es-Sûs). This ruin, so I
> have lately heard, is to be again colonized, by the Jews who have settled
> on the slopes of the Jaulân near Dabûra.[18]

In 1967 the site was surveyed by a team headed by S. Gutman and A.
Druks. They reported that the western part of the Syrian village was built
upon the remains of an early settlement, and that the cemetery west of the
village also stood on top of the ancient site.[19] Gutman and Druks also reported the presence of a large dolmen and the remains of ancient buildings
near the cemetery of the Syrian village; that in the village itself there was
much construction with ashlars in secondary use; and that there were
"structures with arches and large halls that survived from the ancient settlement, a gabled sarcophagus, pillars, as well as hewn stones decorated with
eagles, fish, a child with a basket, a vase, birds and geometric forms."[20] The
surveyors also identified four inscriptions with "Hebrew letters," but did not
provide their texts.

In the years of 1968-1970, the site was surveyed several times by the author and his staff.[21] These surveys discovered that the area of the ancient settlement was about 100 dunams. They found a few shards from the
Hellenistic period, an abundance of pottery from the different stages of the
Roman period, as well as smaller quantities of shards from the Byzantine
and Arab periods. The homes of the Syrian village were built of stones
taken from the remains of the ancient houses; as a result their walls con-

---

[18] Schumacher, "Dscholan," p. 266; Schumacher, *Jaulân*, pp. 117-118.

[19] Epstein & Gutman, p. 265, Site #62.

[20] Epstein & Gutman, p. 266.

[21] D. Urman, "Dabûra," *Special Surveys Reports*, Archive of the Association for the
Archaeological Survey of Israel, Israel Antiquities Authority, Jerusalem (in Hebrew); D.
Urman, "Dabûra," *Reports of the Staff Officer in Charge of Archaeological Affairs in the
Golan* (1968-1972), Archive of the Israel Antiquities Authority, Jerusalem (in Hebrew). See
also, Urman, "Lintel," pp. 1-2; Urman, "Golan—1," p. 3; Urman, "Golan—2," p. 11; Urman,
List, p. 7; Urman, "Hellenistic," p. 464; Urman, *Golan*, p. 192, Site # 61 and *passim*.

tained scores of architectural items, decorated and undecorated, some of which had been already reported by Gutman and Druks. In addition to the architectural items, we located in the village houses eight items (seven broken and one intact) with inscriptions. When assembled, these fragments produced one Hebrew and five Aramaic inscriptions—all Jewish dedicatory inscriptions (see below).

Throughout the area of the Syrian village and the open areas north, west, and south of the village, one can see the tops of walls of early buildings. In four different places in the ruin, we found the tops of walls from monumental structures built of basalt ashlars. In our opinion, if systematic archaeological excavations were conducted at these four places, the remains of a *bet midrash* and other Jewish public buildings from the rabbinic period would be found. Indeed, the inscriptions discussed below clearly point to the existence of such buildings at Dabûra.

The largest concentration of monumental construction stands at the southwest edge of the Syrian village where the slope begins to descend southward to Naḥal Gilbon. There one can discern the remains of two monumental buildings between which a street apparently passed.[22] A second concentration of monumental construction exists north of the Syrian houses, at the highest point of the ruins. Here one can also identify, in addition to the tops of the walls, two Attic column bases and a number of column sections, all of well-hewn basalt.[23] A third concentration exists west of the Syrian village, more or less at the center of the ruins; like the previous area, this site also contains several column sections of well-hewn basalt.[24] The fourth concentration lies at the western edge of the ruin, near the grove of the large eucalyptus trees. Here too one can make out parts of basalt columns, an Attic base, and a number of Doric capitals.[25]

In the houses of the Syrian village, we found weights from ancient olive-oil presses incorporated in secondary use as building stones. On the periphery of the ruin—in the east, north, and west—we found preserved *in situ* four nearly intact olive-oil presses as well as parts of two others.[26] The large number of olive-oil presses that operated here in antiquity undoubtedly points to the growth of olive trees and the production of olive oil as a central staple of Dabûra's economy during the second-temple and/or rabbinic periods.[27]

---

[22] D. Urman, "Dabûra," *Special Surveys Reports*, Archive of the Association for the Archaeological Survey of Israel, Israel Antiquities Authority, Jerusalem, p. 13 (in Hebrew).

[23] *Ibid.*, p. 15.

[24] *Ibid.*, p. 16.

[25] *Ibid.*, pp. 17-18.

[26] *Ibid.*, pp. 20-22. And also see Urman, *Golan*, p. 159, Figs. 68-69.

[27] See Urman, "Economy."

We turn now to a brief discussion of the Jewish inscriptions that were discovered at the site. Since we have already devoted a number of detailed articles, in both Hebrew and English, to the reading of the inscriptions and their significance, I shall only set out their text and translation here.[28]

Inscription #1

On three fragments of a basalt architrave, traces of an Aramaic inscription carved in two lines, and part of a one-line Greek inscription are visible (see PL. 26b). The overall length of the fragments is 110 cm.; the height of the letters is about 6 cm. The inscription reads:

אלעזר בר[ן... ר]בה עבד עמודיה דעל מן

כפתה ופצ̇נ̇ימיה... EKT[ICEN]YCTIKOC[PO]

Its translation:

> El'azar the son of...made the columns above
> the arches and beams...Rusticus built (it).

The juxtaposition of a Greek inscription mentioning the craftsmen with one in Aramaic referring to the donors also occurs on the mosaic floor of the Beth Alpha synagogue. As in this inscription, the Beth Alpha mosaic mentions in Greek the craftsmen who made the mosaic, Marianos and his son Hanina, while the Aramaic inscription commemorates the benefactors.[29]

Inscription #2

This fragment of an Aramaic inscription was engraved on a basalt lintel (see PL. 27a). The fragment measures 36 cm. in length, 28 cm. in height; the letters are 8 cm. high. The inscription reads:

...בר̇ יודה

Its translation:

> ...son of Yudah

---

[28] See Urman, "Dabûra Inscriptions—1," pp. 399-408; Urman, "Dabûra Inscriptions—2," pp. 131-133; Urman, "Dabûra Inscriptions—3," pp. 16-23; Urman, "Dabûra Inscriptions—4," pp. 72-81 (see also pp. 82-83 and 318); Urman, "Dabûra Inscriptions—5," pp. 154-156.

[29] See Sukenik, *Beth Alpha*, p. 47. A few years ago Lea Roth-Gerson suggested "that it is more plausible to see Rusticus of Dabûra as a contributor to the synagogue or its founder, and the inscription as an inscription of dedication for the synagogue and not as an inscription of the artisan who executed the work." (Roth-Gerson, *Greek Inscriptions*, p. 52). We find no basis for her suggestion.

Inscription #3

This fragment of a two-line Aramaic inscription was engraved on a basalt lintel. The fragment measures 30 cm. in length, 34 cm. in height; the letters are about 8 cm. high. The inscription reads:

...חן]ינה
...ב]רכתן]ה[

Its translation:

Ḥ]inenna   [May he (or they)] be blessed.

Inscription #4

This basalt-lintel fragment contains three lines of an Aramaic inscription (see PL. 27b). The fragment measures 26 cm. in length and 28 cm. in height; the letters are 3 cm. high. The inscription reads:

עבדו בית
תהי לה
ברכהת

Its translation:

They made the house of...
May he
be blessed.

To the right of lines 2 and 3 are traces of a wreath of leaves in relief. From the dressing of the stone, the decorative form of the wreath, and the text of the inscription, the lintel seems to have belonged to a synagogue or school from around the third century.

Inscription #5

This fragment of an Aramaic inscription was engraved on a narrow strip of relief work, at the top portion of a basalt lintel. The stone measures 108 cm. in length, 60 cm. in height. The letters of the inscription are 1.5 to 2 cm. high. The inscription reads:

עבד תרעה

Its translation:

Made the gate.

It is reasonable to assume that on the missing piece of the lintel was written the name of "X son of Y" who made the gate. The lintel probably belonged to one of the Jewish public structures in Dabûra. This assumption is further strengthened by the ornament on the fragment. In the center appears a

spread-winged eagle, head facing left, with a small wreath in its beak. The
head, throat, breast, feet, and remaining wing are carefully executed.[30] A
similar decoration has been found on a lintel in Safed, and was identified by
N. Avigad as part of an ancient synagogue.[31] On our lintel, a fish in relief
appears next to the wing of the eagle; a second fish is shown below, suggesting that this may have been a representation of the zodiac constellation
Pisces. The inscription is engraved above the outstretched wing between the
wreath and the fish next to it.

Inscription #6

This Hebrew inscription was engraved on a basalt lintel (see PL. 28a). The
lintel measures 170 cm. in length, 42 cm. in height. The letters are 5-10
cm. high. The inscription reads:

זה בית
מדרשו
שהלרבי
אליעזר הקפר

This is the *bet midrash* of Rabbi Eliezer ha-Qappar.

This formula, its meter, and the spelling of the word שהלרבי, resembles a
contemporary inscription found at Beth She'arim.[32] The spelling שהלרבי as
one word is unusual and deserves a separate study. The writer may either
have intended to write שה/לרבי as two words or indeed as one word; in the
light of the parallel quoted above and of similar biblical usage, the second
possibility seems preferable.[33]

Rabbi Eliezer ha-Qappar was a famous tannaitic sage active in the late
second to early third centuries. Only one saying of his appears in the
Mishnah: "Jealousy, lust, and ambition put a man out of the world" (M.
Avot 4:21). However, in the Tosefta, the two talmuds, and the midrashic
literature, he is mentioned frequently, both by his Hebrew name—Eliezer
ha-Qappar—and by his Aramaic nickname—Bar-Qappara.[34]

---

[30] An eagle grasping a wreath in its beak is a recurring motif in ancient Jewish public
structures. This image was found, among others, on the lintel of the synagogue at Japhia. See
Goodenough, vol. 3, Fig. 569.

[31] Avigad, "Jewish Art," pp. 18-19.

[32] See Mazar, *Beth She'arim*, pp. 39, 199-200, Inscription #23: הקבר הזה שלרבי יצחק בר
מקים—This grave belongs to Rabbi Isaac bar Maqim.

[33] Eccl. 6:10: ולא יוכל לדין עם שהתקיף ממנו—And he is not able to dispute with one
stronger than him.

[34] For a discussion demonstrating that the sage mentioned in the sources by the nickname
of Bar-Qappara is Rabbi Eliezer ha-Qappar, see my article Urman, "Eliezer ha-Qappar,"
pp. 7-25. It seems that this article was not known to Dr. Lea Roth-Gerson when she wrote a
discussion on "Jews in Dabûra" in her book. Roth-Gerson, *Greek Inscriptions*, pp. 52-53.

By any reckoning, Rabbi Eliezer ha-Qappar, seems to have been recognized in his era as an important teacher and sage. The sources reveal he was Rabbi Judah ha-Nasi's opponent in daily life as well as in the halakah.[35] It is known that Rabbi Eliezer ha-Qappar collected many *halakot*, or laws, which he arranged in a treatise called "The Mishnah of Bar-Qappara," or "The Great *Mishnayot* of Bar-Qappara."[36] J. N. Epstein and S. Lieberman concluded that Bar-Qappara was the final editor of Sifre Zuta.[37] Particularly eminent among his students were Rabbi Hoshaya the Great and Rabbi Joshua b. Levi, among the most celebrated sages of the first amoraic generation. It has been established that Rabbi Eliezer's first student, Rabbi Hoshaya the Great, lived also in the Golan, at Qîsrîn.[38]

The lintel bearing the inscription is decorated in relief. On both sides are carved two harrier-eagles with outspread wings, each of which grasps a snake in its beak. The two snakes, whose heads are carefully represented, intertwine and form a plaited wreath. It should be noted that another lintel was found in Dabûra with a relief of two harrier-eagles, each grasping a snake in its beak. But on this lintel a wreath was carved between the birds, and in the center of the wreath a stylized rosette appears.

The six inscriptions discovered at Dabûra, along with the decorated architectural elements, point to the existence of a large Jewish community during the late Roman period with comparatively rich resources, both material and religious/educational. We must imagine several imposing Jewish public buildings in ancient Dabûra, among which there could be counted one or two synagogues as well as the *bet midrash* of Rabbi Eliezer ha-Qappar in the late second or early third century.[39]

---

[35] For example, see Y. MQ 3:1, 81c; B. MQ 16a; B. Ned. 50b-51a; B. Nazir 52b; B. BB 16b.

[36] See Y. Horayot 3, 48c; Lamentations Rabbah 23; Pesikta de R. Kahana 15:7 (ed. Mandelbaum, p. 257); Song of Songs Rabbah 8:2; Ecclesiastes Rabbah 6:2; Midrash Tehillim 104:22 (ed. Buber, p. 446).

[37] See Epstein, *Introduction*, pp. 741-746; Lieberman, *Siphre Zutta*, pp. 92-124.

[38] See Urman, "Bar Qappara—2," pp. 163-172. And see further on this, below, in the chapter devoted to Qîsrîn.

[39] Z. Ma'oz claims "in 1982 Ma'oz discovered the location of the synagogue or school" at Dabûra (Ma'oz, "Golan—1," p. 297). In Ma'oz, "Golan—2," p. 544, he states: "In 1982, Z. Ma'oz identified the location of the synagogue or school *(bet midrash)*." It only remains for us to congratulate Christopher Columbus and hope that he will in the future publish further details of his discovery. Although Ma'oz gives credit to the discoverers of the inscriptions and the architectural artifacts that come from the Jewish public buildings at Dabûra, he unfortunately omitted Muhammad 'Ali 'Amashah and Hsein Shams, who along with S. Bar-Lev and M. Hartel, helped transfer the inscriptions to the Golan Antiquities collection which was at that time housed in Quneitra.

ḤORVAH EAST OF THE BENOT YA'AQOV BRIDGE

The ruins of an ancient settlement built upon a low hill sloping from east to west toward the Benot Ya'aqov Bridge lie at coordinates 2106-2687. The ruin, nameless and unmentioned on the maps, was designated by the late Zvi Ilan as "the Benot Ya'aqov Bridge site."[40]

The author first learned about the existence of antiquities at this site in 1970 from members of Kibbutz Gadot. In a survey conducted by the author and his staff that same year,[41] it turned out that the ruin occupied an area of about 10 dunams and that the shards found there were from the Roman, Byzantine, early Arab, and medieval periods.[42] An agricultural village occupied the site as early as the early Roman period. Its water supply was provided by a group of flowing springs on the site's western edge. The remains of an olive-oil press indicates that local residents earned their livelihoods in part from growing olives and producing olive-oil.

On the northern slope of the ruin we found the remains of a monumental rectangular structure built of ashlars. The building's lengthwise axis is east-west, and its estimated external dimensions are about 14 x 6.5 m. We could see on the surface two to three courses of sections of the structure's north, east, and south walls. Nothing of its west wall was preserved on the surface, but its outline could be made out. Inside and around the building, we registered two Attic column bases, eight column sections, and three Doric capitals—all made of basalt and of excellent quality. At some stage of the structure's use, its walls and a number of its architectural items were covered with a thick layer of plaster.

In our survey of this site, we found neither remains of Jewish inscriptions nor any architectural items ornamented with Jewish decorations. Therefore, despite the presence of remains of the monumental structure at the site and even though the ruin lies at the edge of the area of Jewish settlement in the Golan during the rabbinic period, our survey report neither declared that the remains are those of an ancient Jewish settlement nor did it define the structure as a synagogue. Zvi Ilan and Zvi Ma'oz, who visited the ruin a few years after our survey, suggested that the settlement there had been Jewish and that the remains of the monumental building we had found were those of a synagogue.[43] Still, until the site in general and the remains

---

[40] See Ilan, *Israel*, p. 70.

[41] See D. Urman, "A Ḥorvah East of the Benot Ya'aqov Bridge," *Reports of the Staff Officer in Charge of Archaeological Affairs in the Golan* (1968-1972), Archive of the Israel Antiquities Authority, Jerusalem (in Hebrew).

[42] See previous note, and also Urman, *Golan*, p. 194, Site #73.

[43] See Ilan, *Israel*, p. 70; Ma'oz, *Golan* (rev. ed.), pp. 40-41. It should be pointed out that we found in their reports no new data about the site or its finds.

of the monumental structure in particular become the objects of systematic archaeological excavation, their suggestion remains a hypothesis.

GHÂDRIYYE
(EL-GHADÎRÎYEH, KHÂN BÂNDAK, DANNIKLEH, EL-DÂNQALLE)[44]

The southern part of this small abandoned Turkoman village was built upon the ruins from a Jewish settlement of the rabbinic period. The village lies at coordinates 2154-2694, about 800 m. north of the site called 'Ein Nashôt. On the western edge of the village there is a flowing spring.

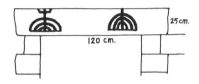

FIG. 1 Lintel with two seven-branched *menorot*. (After Schumacher.)

G. Schumacher was the first to publish a Jewish item from this site—a lintel decorated with engravings of two seven-branched candelabra (Fig. 1).[45] Alongside this find, Schumacher published a lintel fragment with reliefs of a wreath and a rosette (Fig. 2)—motifs that are common in the Jewish public structures in the Golan—as well as an item decorated with a cross in relief (Fig. 3) that was discovered in the village.[46] As for the item with the cross, Schumacher did not indicate whether it was on a lintel, a column, or the like. This item was not found at the site by later surveys. However, this fact in no way impugns the reliability of Schumacher's reports. Indeed, Schumacher himself had already written in his book, *The Jaulân*, that in the Golan region it is difficult to date of cross reliefs found in secondary use or

---

[44] In G. Schumacher's writings, two different Turkoman villages are mentioned; one he calls el-Ghadîrîyeh (Schumacher, "Dscholan," p. 293; Schumacher, *Jaulân*, p. 147) and the other Khân Bândak and Dannikleh (Schumacher, "Dscholan," pp. 257-258; Schumacher, *Jaulân*, p. 183). The descriptions of the two villages are very similar except for the fact that in his description of Khân Bândak and Dannikleh, Schumacher mentions finds with Jewish and Christian decorations. In surveys conducted in the Golan after 1967, the Jewish artifacts mentioned by Schumacher were found in a village the maps labeled as both Ghâdriyye and ed-Dânqalle (see Epstein & Gutman, p. 267, Site #70). On the maps of recent years, it is only called Ghâdriyye.

[45] Schumacher, "Dscholan," pp. 257-258, Figs. 9-11; Schumacher, *Jaulân*, p. 183, Figs. 74-76. Also see Goodenough, vol. 3, Fig. 581.

[46] See previous note.

not lying *in situ*, they could be from either the Byzantine period or the Crusader period.[47]

In 1968, the site was surveyed by a team headed by S. Gutman.[48] This team found in the walls of the abandoned Turkoman structures many ancient hewn stones in secondary use: a basalt stone with an engraved candelabrum, (Fig. 5), bases of columns and additional architectural artifacts decorated with reliefs of rosettes and geometric designs. The team also reported finding a stone fragment with remains of an Aramaic inscription (see Fig. 4 and our discussion below).[49]

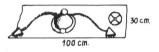

FIG. 2 Lintel with wreath and rosette.
(After Schumacher.)

FIG. 3 Cross in relief.
(After Schumacher.)

During 1970-1972, the author examined the ancient remains in the village and its vicinity a number of times.[50] These investigations uncovered an abundance of decorated architectural items there—gables, cornices, architraves and the like. These are all characteristic of Jewish public buildings in the Golan and the Galilee in the second-temple and rabbinic periods. Among these items we should here point out a cornice fragment with a relief of a trailing branch, a gable fragment of the Syrian type decorated with the egg-and-dart motif and a rosette (Fig. 6), a lintel fragment with a rosette relief at its end and at its center a relief of an *aedicula* within a relief of a geometric motif (Fig. 7). In addition to these artifacts, we found in the houses a lintel fragment with an engraving of a seven-branched candelabrum and a tripod base (see PL. 28b)—which may be a fragment of the lintel with the engraved candelabra first published by Schumacher (see above, Fig. 1)—as well as the stone fragment with the remains of the Aramaic inscription about which the S. Gutman survey team reported.

These finds, along with those of the earlier surveyors, led us to search for remains of the public structure itself. And indeed, at the beginning of 1972, we succeeded in locating in the village remains of walls of a monumental

---

[47] See Schumacher, *Jaulân*, pp. 3-4.

[48] Epstein & Gutman, p. 267, Site #70.

[49] See previous note.

[50] D. Urman, "Ghâdriyye," *Reports of the Staff Officer in Charge of Archaeological Affairs in the Golan* (1968-1972), Archive of the Israel Antiquities Authority, Jerusalem (in Hebrew); Urman, *List*, p. 9; Urman, "Golan—6," pp. 2-3; Urman, "Synagogue Sites," pp. 23-24; Urman, "Golan—7," p. 1; Urman, "Hellenistic," p. 466; Urman, *Golan*, p. 193, Site #69, and see also the note for Site #69, p. 211.

structure oriented north-south, like the orientation of the public Jewish
structure we uncovered at Qîsrîn.[51] In the brief exploratory excavations of
the structure's remains (partially buried under a Turkoman house), we suc-
cessfully uncovered 14 m. of the southern wall and 19 m. of the western
one.[52] The structure's walls were built of basalt ashlars like those of the
structure at Qîsrîn and at other Jewish public structure sites in the Golan.
Our surveys at the village also revealed that the area of the ancient site was
about 10 dunams, and that the site, according to the shards found there, had
been settled intermittently from the Roman period up to our day.[53]

The Inscription

The stone fragment with the engraved inscription was discovered by the
Gutman survey team incorporated in secondary use as a building stone in a
Turkoman house (see PL. 29a). After the stone was removed from the wall
of the house, it turned out to be a basalt door-lintel fragment (to be more
precise, the left end of the lintel). The fragment is 23 cm. long, 33 cm.
high, and 46 cm. thick. Only two lines of the inscription have been preserved, and the height of the letters ranges from 4 to 7 cm. A copy of the
inscription is to be found in Fig. 4:

FIG. 4 Aramaic Inscription.

The possibility that the inscription is Aramaic becomes clear with the
finding of the word "בר" at the end of the first line. Therefore we suggested
in an earlier publication that the inscription be completed as follows:[54]

...חל[פ]ּו בר

...בר[כ]תֿה

---

[51] See below, in the section on Qîsrîn.

[52] See Urman, "Synagogue Sites," pp. 23-24; Urman, "Golan—7," p. 1; Urman,
"Hellenistic," p. 466.

[53] See above, note 50.

[54] See Urman, "Synagogue Sites," pp. 23-24; Urman, "Golan—7," p. 1; Urman,
"Hellenistic," p. 466; Urman, "Kazrin Inscriptions," pp. 523-524.

This dedicatory inscription names a donor called Ḥalfo or Ḥalfu son of X who contributed to some part of the public structure to which the lintel belongs. The name Ḥalfo (Ḥalfu) is also found in dedicatory inscriptions of public Jewish structures uncovered at Capernaum and at Mazra'at Kanaf.[55] It seems that the inscription ends on the second line, with the blessing formula common in the dedication inscriptions of Jewish public structures from the rabbinic period: "תהי לה ברכתה," that is, "תהא לו הברכה" ("may he be blessed.")[56]

FIG. 5 Lintel fragment with menorah.   FIG. 6 Gable fragment.

J. Naveh, who included the inscription in his book, reads the first letter that is preserved in the upper line as a shin (שׁ)—שׁו בר[....[57] In light of this reading, we examined the stone again and were convinced that it is indeed difficult to determine whether it is a shin (שׁ) or a peh (פ), for the stone is broken at the letter. If the letter is a shin, then it is possible to complete the name of the donor and read ישׁו instead of חלפוּ. The name ישׁו was common among the Jews of Palestine in the second-temple and rabbinic periods.

FIG. 7 Lintel fragment with reliefs of an *aedicula* and a rosette.

To conclude our treatment of the finds at the village of Ghâdriyye, we need to point out that Z. Ma'oz recently published a basalt lintel (?) fragment with a five-branched candelabrum with a tripod base engraved upon it

---

[55] See Naveh, *Mosaic*, pp. 38-40, Inscriptions #18-19.

[56] See Naveh, *Mosaic*, pp. 27-28 (Inscriptions #9-10); pp. 30-31 (#12); pp. 38-39 (#18); p. 48 (#26); pp. 52-53 (#30-31); p. 62 (#35); pp. 66-68 (#39); pp. 77-78 (#46).

[57] Naveh, *Mosaic*, p. 146, Inscription #108.

(see PL. 41b) and attributed it to Ghâdriyye.[58] But in fact, the fragment was discovered at Qîsrîn and is now preserved in the collection of the Golan Antiquities Museum at Qaṣrin.[59]

Ma'oz has also claimed that the Jewish architectural artifacts found in Ghâdriyye belong to the public structure uncovered at 'Ein Nashôt.[60] This is simply wrong. Indeed, many of the items we found at Ghâdriyye were uncovered in or near the monumental building which we had begun to excavate. These artifacts surely belong to the building just a few meters away, rather than to a structure eight hundred meters distant. Ma'oz also attributes to the 'Ein Nashôt structure items found at 'Ein Semsem and at Fâkhûra![61] Could it really be that the public structure uncovered at 'Ein Nashôt, whose external measurements are only 12.65 x 11.40 m., could have contained all the architectural items uncovered there (see our discussion of 'Ein Nashôt) plus all the items found at Ghâdriyye, 'Ein Semsem, and Fâkhûra? Certainly not.

'EIN NASHÔT ('EN NASHUṬ)

There is a ruin located at coordinates 2151-2687, about 2.5 kilometers northwest of Qaṣrin, known today as 'Ein Nashôt, after the spring which flows at its foot. The ruin, with an area of about 20 dunams (5 acres), was first surveyed by the author as part of the investigations carried out at the nearby village of Ghâdriyye.[62] On our first visit at the site, we could immediately see that the ruin was the remains of an impressive Jewish agricultural village from the rabbinic period. The settlement's houses had been built on a high hill, well-protected by the wadis surrounding it on three sides. Remnants of the ancient village's cultivated areas were still visible on the slopes of the hill and in areas across the wadis: to the west, north, and east. Among the ruins of the village's homes were two well-preserved olive-oil presses (see PL. 29b). These attest to the villagers' occupation with, among other things, the production of olive oil—a central part of the economy of the Jewish Golan in the rabbinic period.[63] However, the prize result of the survey was the discovery of a public building's remains in the

---

[58] Ma'oz, "Golan—1," p. 293; Ma'oz, "Golan—2," p. 540.

[59] Item no. 816 in the museum collection.

[60] See Ma'oz, *Golan*, p. 36; Ma'oz, "Golan Synagogues," p. 145; Ma'oz, "'En Nashuṭ—1," p. 1203; Ma'oz, "'En Nashuṭ—2," p. 414.

[61] See previous note.

[62] Urman, "Synagogue Sites," p. 24; Urman, "Golan—7," p. 1; Urman, "Hellenistic," p. 466 (In this article there is a corruption in the name of the site, instead of "Ein Nashôt," it was erroneously printed as "En Natosh."); Urman, "Kazrin Inscriptions," pp. 524-528.

[63] Urman, *Golan*, pp. 257, 272-277; Urman, "Economy," pp. 35-66.

site's western part. Among the building's rubble were many decorated architectural items, two of which are particularly worth mentioning because they reveal the building's Jewish character. One item is decorated with a relief of a lioness (see PL. 30a), while the other is decorated with a relief of a seven-branched menorah (see PL. 30b). These two items, plus others, led us to conclude that the remains of the public structure were Jewish and from the rabbinic period.[64] This conclusion was confirmed in 1987, when Z. Ma'oz began to excavate the site.[65]

In the excavations conducted thus far, a room has been completely excavated which Ma'oz designated as "the prayer hall."[66] This room is nearly square in shape and its external dimensions, in the excavator's first publications, were given as 12.50 x 11.30 m.[67]—but, in his later publications, as 12.65 x 11.40 m.[68] According to Ma'oz's subsequent publications, the room's internal dimensions are 10.45 x 9.35 m.[69] The plan he published indicates that the roof of the room rested on two rows of columns, three to a row.[70] Of these columns, only five square stylobates were preserved *in situ.* On one of them, a pedestal was also preserved with a basalt column base, decorated with a rosette in relief.[71] On the floor of the room, a variety of architectural items were found including fragments of the architrave's beams,

---

[64] In November 1972, S. Bar-Lev carried out an additional survey of the site and discovered among the building's ruins another relief of a seven-branched menorah. See Ben-Ari and Bar-Lev, "Golan—1," p. 1.

[65] Ma'oz, "'Ein Nashôt" pp. 27-29; Ma'oz, *Golan* (rev. ed.), pp. 22-25; Ma'oz, "'En Nashuṭ—2," pp. 412-414, and see the additional bibliography there.

[66] Ma'oz, "'En Nashuṭ—2," p. 413.

[67] Ma'oz, *Golan* (rev. ed.), p. 23; Ma'oz, "Synagogues," p. 108; Ma'oz, "Ancient Synagogues," p. 122.

[68] Ma'oz, "'En Nashuṭ—1," p. 1201; Ma'oz, "'En Nashuṭ—2," p. 413.

[69] See previous note.

[70] The plan appears in Ma'oz, "Ancient Synagogues," p. 121. It was reproduced by Rachel Hachlili and Zvi Ilan in their books (Hachlili, *Art*, p. 145; Ilan, *Israel,* p. 109). Unfortunately, the plan fails accurately to represent the site. A comparison of the plan with photographs of the room made at the time of the excavations (and before the reconstruction work), Ma'oz's own writings concerning the site, and studies I conducted at the room during the excavations, place great doubt on many of the plan's details. In particular, the location of the room's entrances are misplaced. Furthermore, Ma'oz inserts a podium for a Torah Ark (a *bemah*), even though none was uncovered at the site during the excavation. The excavator himself does not reproduce the plan in his later publications, for example, in *The New Encyclopedia of Archaeological Excavations in the Holy Land* in its Hebrew and English editions (Ma'oz, "'En Nashuṭ—1," p. 1201; Ma'oz, "'En Nashuṭ—2," p. 413).

[71] A photograph of the pedestal was published by Ma'oz in the site's earlier publications (see, for example, Ma'oz, *Golan* (rev. ed.), p. 23; Ma'oz, "Synagogues," p. 108). In later publications (Ma'oz, "'En Nashuṭ—1," p. 1202; Ma'oz, "'En Nashuṭ—2," p. 413), however, he presents a photograph of another pedestal decorated by a relief of a menorah, which he calls "the northeastern pedestal." But this second pedestal was not discovered in the 'Ein Nashôt excavations; it was found ten years earlier north of the village of Fâkhûra by the survey team headed by S. Gutman (see Epstein & Gutman, p. 268, Site #72). Concerning the further adventures of this pedestal, see the section on Fâkhûra.

sections and fragments of column shafts, bases, and Ionic and Corinthian
capitals. Two of these items require further discussion: an Ionic capital, and
the architrave beam fragments.

The Ionic capital is made of basalt, chiseled in the diagonal Ionic style
with different motifs appearing on each of its four faces. On one face appears
a relief of a large, ten-branched (!) menorah with a two-legged base (see PL.
31a). On the sides of the menorah's base are reliefs of two items, apparently
unsuccessful attempts by the artisan to depict a shofar and a fire-pan. These
objects often appear alongside representations of *menorot* from the rabbinic-
period Palestine in general and from rabbinic-period Golan in particular. On
another face of the capital appears a relief of a large egg next to a baseless
seven-branched candelabrum (see PL. 31b). On the capital's two remaining
faces, the motif of the large egg again appears, along with reliefs of birds,
an amphora, an altar, and a rosette (see PL. 32a).

The architrave beam fragments reveal that the beam's edges were decorated with reliefs of rosettes and that its center portrayed the motif of
Hercules' knot of snakes (see PL. 32b). On the sides of the knot are two
points, one designed as a flower. Under the relief of the snake knot, engraved
on the beam, is the inscription "Abun bar Yose," which will be treated below.

Inside the room, three steps, or rows, of benches built of finely hewn
basalt stones have been preserved along the full length of the northern and
eastern walls. These rows of benches perhaps continued along the room's
southern and western walls, but only a few remains of the bottom bench
have been preserved, mainly in the northwest corner of the room.

The walls of the room and its floor were covered with white plaster, parts
of which have been preserved, but most of it was found in the collapsed
rubble on the floor. From the excavator's reports we learn that on a few
plaster fragments "red lines were found and among them remains of inscriptions. On one of the large pieces an engraved inscription colored with a red
line was found which read: 'Amen Amen Selah Shalom.'"[72] To our regret,
the excavator has not yet published any reproductions or photographs of
these inscriptions and we therefore cannot discuss them here.

In his later publications, Ma'oz presents the stratigraphy uncovered in
the excavation.[73] He distinguishes four layers or stages. The top stratum
(Stratum I) he attributes to the modern period. In this stratum, he says,
"stones were robbed, many engraved architectural elements were smashed,
and the synagogue remains were destroyed."[74]

---

[72] Ma'oz, "'Ein Nashôt" pp. 28-29; Ma'oz, *Golan* (rev. ed.), p. 24. And lastly, see also, Ma'oz, "'En Nashut—2," p. 414.

[73] See Ma'oz, "'En Nashut—1," p. 1201; Ma'oz, "'En Nashut—2," p. 412.

[74] See previous note.

Beneath this stratum, Ma'oz identifies Stratum IIA which he attributes to
the sixth century. This is the stratum, he claims, in which the synagogue
underwent repairs and in which the structure (which he says was erected during Stratum IIB) was last used. Among the repairs which the excavator discerns in Stratum IIA, he lists the broadening of the base of the Torah Ark,[75]
the addition of a column to the western row of columns, the building of a
wall for the narthex, which Ma'oz makes out in the building's forecourt to
the south, and also the laying of a new floor in this narthex. According to
Ma'oz, "these repairs may have been carried out in the wake of an earthquake
in the sixth century C.E. (551 C.E.?)."[76] The excavator adds:

> This stage continued until the synagogue fell into disuse and the village
> was abandoned. On the basis of a few coins and an intact lamp found on a
> bench in the synagogue, this abandonment occurred at the end of the sixth
> or the beginning of the seventh century C.E.[77]

According to Ma'oz, the synagogue was erected in the period of Stratum IIB.
The excavator dates this stratum to the fifth century. Indeed, based upon
"eight coins from the fourth century C.E., mainly from the end of the century (383-395 C.E.)" which were found in "probes dug in the earth-fill of the
Synagogue's foundations," with groups of coins uncovered outside the structure, he postulates that the synagogue was erected in the middle of the fifth
century C.E.[78]

A careful study of Donald T. Ariel's report on the coins from the Ma'oz
excavations at 'Ein Nashôt reveals several contradictions between the information Ma'oz gave Ariel about the site and that which Ma'oz has published
himself.[79] According to Ariel, in the probes conducted in the foundations,
four coins were found and not *eight,* as Ma'oz reports in his publications in
the *New Encyclopedia*.[80] Ariel dates one coin to the days of Valerian (253-
259 C.E.), one coin to the years 330-335, and the remaining two coins to
383-395 C.E. It is clear that from the view of stratigraphic analysis, it
makes no difference whether four or eight coins were found in the probes.

On the basis of the two coins from the late fourth century, Ariel also differs with Ma'oz concerning the date of the synagogue's erection. He states:

> Dates for the construction and occupation of the synagogue may be conjec-
> tured from the finds of four coins from undisturbed deposits below the floor
> level...the latest coin of those from below floor level is one of the com-
> mon SALUS REIPUBLICAE victory-dragging-captive type. While an iden-

---

[75] See my comment on this Torah Ark above in note 70.

[76] See Ma'oz, "'En Nashuṭ—1," p. 1201; Ma'oz, "'En Nashuṭ—2," p. 412.

[77] Ma'oz, "'En Nashuṭ—1," p. 1201; Ma'oz, "'En Nashuṭ—2," p. 412.

[78] Ma'oz, "'En Nashuṭ—1," p. 1201; Ma'oz, "'En Nashuṭ—2," p. 412.

[79] Ariel, "'En Nashuṭ," pp. 147-157.

[80] Ariel, "'En Nashuṭ," Table 1, pp. 150-151.

tification neither of emperor nor of mint is possible, a cross in the left field of the reverse restricts the type's chronological range to 383-395 C.E. This yields a *terminus post quem* date for the construction of the synagogue building at the end of the fourth century C.E.[81]

The problem facing us is that of the reliability of the different reports—contradictions appear not only between Ma'oz and Ariel but also among Ma'oz's different publications. Should we rely upon the first reports of the excavator,[82] his later ones,[83] or upon the reports Ma'oz gave the investigator of the coins? To our regret, this problem continually appears in Ma'oz's publications on his finds in the Golan. This problem makes it difficult to evaluate his conclusions about the earliest stratigraphic layer, Stratum III, which he dates to the third and fourth centuries C.E. According to Ma'oz,[84] "Stratum III lies beneath the remains of the synagogue, in the western part of the building and outside it to the southwest."[85] Ma'oz continues, "The stratum consists of the remains of walls leveled before the construction of the building in Stratum II.... However, the true nature of this stratum, which has been *tentatively* dated to the fourth century C.E. is not sufficiently clear. Shards and coins dating from the first century C.E.,[86] as well as some shards from the Chalcolithic period, were found in various earth fills" (emphasis mine). Two questions must be asked of Ma'oz's excavations for a clear understanding of this statement: First, did Ma'oz reach bedrock in his excavations? If he did, we hope he left behind enough unexcavated area in the room for the benefit of the future generations of archaeologists. Second, in precisely what context were the four coins found that provide the excavator and the numismatist as a basis for dating the structure to the fifth century? Perhaps, as Y. Tsafrir has already noted concerning the excavations of Ma'oz at Ḥorvat Kanaf, the structure at 'Ein Nashôt was built at an early period—second, third, or fourth century C.E.—and in the fifth century was restored or had its floor replaced.[87]

---

[81] Ariel, "'En Nashut," p. 149.

[82] Ma'oz, *Golan* (rev. ed.), Ma'oz, "Synagogues," Ma'oz, "Ancient Synagogues."

[83] Ma'oz, "'En Nashut—1," Ma'oz, "'En Nashut—2."

[84] See previous note.

[85] The photographs of the excavation published by Ma'oz clearly reveal that the southwest area of the room was not well preserved (see, for example, the photograph in Ma'oz, "Synagogues," p. 107). Ariel likewise reports that "the synagogue building was badly damaged by robbing for building materials, and the south-western corner was completely missing as a result of the robbers' pits." Ariel, "'En Nashut," p. 147.

[86] Ma'oz writes "coins" in the plural, whereas in Ariel's Table 1 no "coins" of the first century appear except one. It appears in the column devoted to the 132 non-stratified coins! See Ariel, "'En Nashut," p. 150.

[87] See Tsafrir's article in this book, note 20 on page 76. Here, too, the coin report was written by D. T. Ariel. See Ariel, "Ḥorvat Kanef."

The small dimensions of the room's interior, a considerable portion of which was occupied by the three rows of stone benches, casts doubt upon Ma'oz's conclusion that the room is "the synagogue prayer hall."[88] The room's architecture suggests rather that it perhaps served as a study room or a *bet midrash*. But before we make any definitive statements about its original use, we should wait until all the rooms of the complex have been systematically excavated and we receive complete and precise reports on those excavations.

Further evidence of a Jewish community on this site during the rabbinic period was discovered about 500 m. west of the ruin. A tractor digging a sewage ditch dug up the lids of two sarcophagi upon which were engraved the names of two Jewish departed (below, Inscriptions #2 and #3). It seems that the tractor came across the village cemetery. This fact, however, has not yet been finally clarified, for shortly after the two lids were discovered, the work at the site halted.[89]

Inscription #1

This inscription was found engraved, as mentioned above, under the snake-bow relief that was found in the center of the architrave beam whose pieces were uncovered on the floor of that room defined by Ma'oz as "the prayer hall of the synagogue." The dimensions of the architrave beam piece: length—268 cm., height—25 cm., thickness—24 cm. (see Pl. 30b). The height of the inscription's letters is 4-5 cm. (see Fig. 1). The inscription clearly reads: אבון בר יוסה. Its translation is: Abun bar Yose.

FIG. 1 Inscription #1.

Until the discovery of the "Rabbi Abun" inscription at Qîsrîn (see the section on Qîsrîn), which preceded that of Inscription #1, the name Abun was unknown in Hebrew or Aramaic inscriptions of the Land of Israel and its environs.[90] Yet rabbinic literature makes it quite clear that this name was

---

[88] See, for example, Ma'oz, "'Ein Nashôt" pp. 27-29; Ma'oz, *Golan* (rev. ed.), pp. 22-25; and his other publications on the site detailed above.

[89] It is my pleasant duty at this point to thank Mr. S. Bar-Lev, who served at that time as the Deputy Staff Officer in charge of Archaeological Affairs in the Golan, for providing me with this information and graciously permitting me to publish the lids and their inscriptions.

[90] Among the Greek inscriptions from the Land of Israel, a burial inscription from the Jewish cemetery of Jaffa presents the name Abun once as Ἀββωνες. See Klein, *ha-Yishuv*, p. 84, Inscription #30.

widespread among the Jews living in the Land of Israel and in Babylonia.[91] As we shall see below, the name Abun also appears in Inscription #2.

The name Yose, which is short for Yosef (Joseph, with the final "ph"—peh—dropped), is common in dedicatory inscriptions of public Jewish buildings in the Land of Israel,[92] and is even mentioned in the Palestinian Talmud.[93] This name also appears in Inscription #3 of 'Ein Nashôt.

Since the content of the inscription is the name of a person only, it is difficult to know if he was a donor, a builder, or a *parnas* (leader) of the community. If it should become clear that the room to which the architrave beam bearing the engraved inscription belongs served as a house of study, it could also be possible that this is the name of a sage.[94]

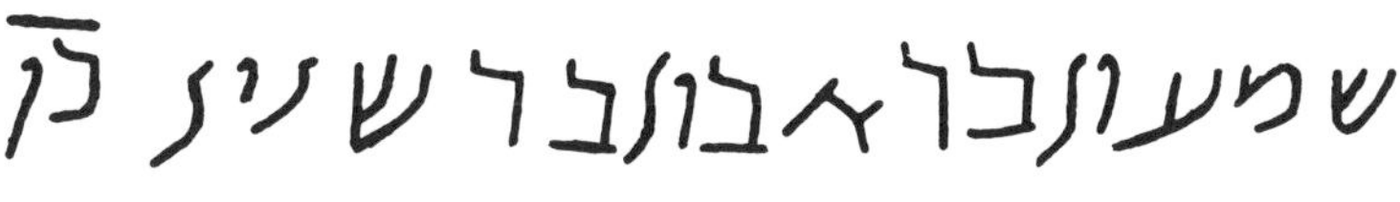

שמעונ/בר/אבונ/בר/שינ/ כו

FIG. 2 Inscription #2.

The inscription is engraved on the long side of a lid of a gabled sarcophagus, made of basalt (see Fig. 2 and PLs. 33a and 33b). The length of the lid is 139 cm., the width at its base is 55 cm., and its height is 35 cm. Each of its broad sides has a carved relief of a rose and in the foreground between them a relief of a stylized tree was engraved. The inscription, whose letters are 5-8 cm. in height, is in Aramaic. It reads:

שמעון בר אבון בר שנין כו

---

[91] See "Index of the *amoraim*" in Albeck, *Introduction*, pp. 669-681; as well as the discussion below on the "Rabbi Abun" inscription from Qîsrîn.

[92] See Naveh, *Mosaic*, pp. 19-20 (Inscription #1); 22-23 (Inscription #3); 30 (Inscription #12); 39-40 (Inscription #19); 52-53 (Inscription #30); 57 (Inscription #33); 62 (Inscription #35); 86 (Inscription #50); 97 (Inscription #63); 105-109 (Inscription #70).

[93] For examples, see the tens of citations of Rabbi Yose in the Jerusalem Talmud collected by J. Omansky in his *Hakhmei ha-Talmud* (Jerusalem, 1952), pp. 88-90 (in Hebrew).

[94] The joining of the name Abun with the name Yose is very reminiscent of the name of two of the Palestinian *amoraim* of the third, fourth, and fifth generations who were both called Rabbi Yose bar Abun. (Concerning these *amoraim* see Ch. Albeck remarks in Albeck, *Introduction*, pp. 336-337 & 395-396). Was there a family relationship between either or both of the two and the person mentioned in this inscription? It is difficult to answer this question either way, but it should be noted that in Genesis Rabbah 46:9 (p. 466 in the Theodor-Albeck edition) an *amora* by the name of R. Abun (as it appears in the texts that follow the Venice 1545 edition and the Yemenite manuscript of R. Elhanan Adler) son of R. Yose, in whose name R. Berekiah and R. Helbo, the *amoraim* of the third and fourth generations, delivered homilies.

And its translation: Shim'on son of Abun [died at] the age of 26.

It is difficult to know if there is any family connection (and hence also a chronological connection) between Shim'on bar Abun and Abun bar Yose, mentioned in Inscription #1. The latter might have been the father of the former, but we cannot demonstrate it.

Inscription #3

This inscription was also engraved on the long side of another gabled basalt sarcophagus lid. The lid's length is 140 cm.; its width at the base, 54 cm.; and its height, 35 cm. On the broad front side, there is a geometrical rose in the center of a circle made with a compass. The rose has six petals. Above the circle, a small stylized tree was engraved.

IO CHC ZANNEOYETIO

FIG. 3 Inscription #3.

The inscription was written in Greek. The average height of its letters is 5 cm. Its transcription reads:

Ἰοσῆς Ζαννεου ἔτ(ῶν) ο

It translates: Yose son of Zanno(?) [died at the age of] 70.

As we indicated above, the name Yose was common in the Land of Israel during the rabbinic period. The Greek form Ἰοσῆς is exceptional and the form that generally appears in the inscriptions is Ἰωσῆς,[95] but changes of "ω" to "o" were common in that period.[96]

The form of the name Ζαννεος is to this point unknown in Jewish inscriptions. It has not been found in other epigraphic sources either.[97]

In concluding our treatment of the 'Ein Nashôt findings, let us point out that the similarity between the two sarcophagus lids—upon which inscriptions #2 and #3 were engraved—in form, dimensions, and decoration, leads us to conclude that these coffins are from Jewish graves of the same genera-

---

[95] For examples, see Frey, vol. 1, pp. 88-89 (Inscription #126); 271-272 (Inscription #347); 398-399 (Inscription #538); 428 (Inscription #585); 518-519 (Inscription #719).

[96] See Schwabe and Lifshitz, p. 9 (in the discussion of Inscription #23).

[97] The form of a somewhat similar name—Ζαννάις—appears twice on an ostracon from Edfu, the estimated date of which is 49 B.C.E., and see *CPJ*, vol. 1, p. 255 (#140). Another close form—Ζαννος—appears in a list of payers of head tax from Nessana the estimated date of which is 689 C.E. It should be pointed out, however, that from the name of the father of that self-name Zannos—Αβδαλλος—his Arabic extraction becomes clear. See Kraemer, *Nessana*, pp. 215-221 (#76.41).

tion. It turns out, then, that 'Ein Nashôt was a Jewish agricultural village in the Golan whose residents, whether or not any of its residents were scholars, used both the languages then current among the Jews of the Land of Israel— Aramaic and Greek.

DÂBIYYE

This abandoned Syrian village was built in part over the remains of a Jewish, rabbinic-period settlement that lies at coordinates 2184-2684. The Syrian village was apparently erected only at the beginning of the twentieth century, for it is not mentioned in G. Schumacher's first reports. He visited the location but was not impressed by the remains—describing them as "insignificant building remains of different ages, and some sheep folds."[98] After his visit to the region in June 1913, Schumacher reported that Turkomans had built nine huts there.[99]

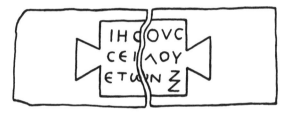

FIG. 1 A Jewish burial inscription.

S. Gutman surveyed the site in 1967 and made out the ruin, reporting that "in the village there are scattered bases, capitals, columns, and lintels."[100] About a year later, the author and his team conducted another survey of the village, in the course of which it became clear that the ancient settlement covered about 20 dunams. It was settled from the late Roman period through the various stages of the Byzantine period.[101] In this survey and in subsequent visits, it was discovered that one of the Syrian village houses was built on the remains of a Jewish public building whose walls and entrances were preserved on the surface to a height of 2-3 courses. In the walls of this Syrian house, as well as in nearby houses, we found various

---

[98] Schumacher, "Dscholan," p. 267; Schumacher, *Jaulân*, p. 120.

[99] Schumacher, "Ostjordanlande," p. 148.

[100] Epstein & Gutman, p. 269, Site #73.

[101] D. Urman, "Dâbiyye," *Special Surveys Reports*, Archive of the Association for the Archaeological Survey of Israel, Israel Antiquities Authority, Jerusalem (in Hebrew); Urman, *List*, p. 9.

architectural items taken from the Jewish public structure incorporated in secondary use as building stones.[102]

In the roof of the Syrian house built atop the remains of the Jewish public structure, we found incorporated in secondary use two basalt fragments on which a Greek inscription was engraved. The inscription was engraved within a *tabula ansata* relief that was broken in the middle into two parts. Because the two parts of the stone were incorporated in the ceiling of the modern house, we were unable to take the stone's measurements and ascertain its precise original use. It is possible that the two fragments once comprised the side of a sarcophagus or a lintel of a mausoleum. A combination of the drawings of both parts of the stone (see Fig. 1) allows for the reading of the three line inscription:[103]

I H Σ O Y Σ
Σ E I Λ O Y
E T Ω N Ξ

It should be transcribed as: Ἰησοῦς Σειλου ἐτῶν ξ. It translates as: "Jesus (son of) Seilos. Sixty years old."

The content of the inscription clearly shows that it is a Jewish burial inscription. The name ישי or ישוע, is the shortened form of the Hebrew name יהושע[104] and similarly written, it is mentioned in Jewish inscriptions and papyri from Hellenistic and Roman Egypt.[105] It is common in the writings of Josephus,[106] in the papyri discovered at Naḥal Ze'elim,[107] and also appears in inscriptions from Jerusalem[108] and from Beth She'arim.[109] This name in its Hebrew and Aramaic forms is used as a Jewish name in the Bar Kokhba letters,[110] in the talmudic literature,[111] in dedication inscriptions

---

[102] See previous note. And also see D. Urman, "Dâbiyye," *Reports of the Staff Officer in Charge of Archaeological Affairs in the Golan* (1968-1972), Archive of the Israel Antiquities Authority, Jerusalem (in Hebrew); Urman, "Synagogue Sites," p. 23; Urman, "Golan—7," p. 2; Urman, *Golan*, p. 194, Site #75.

[103] See Urman, "Kazrin Inscriptions," pp. 520-522; Gregg and Urman, Inscription #94.

[104] See M. D. Herr, "Continuum in the Chain of Torah Transmission," *Zion* 44 (1979): 51, note 52 (in Hebrew), and compare Tcherikover, *Jews*, p. 184.

[105] For specifics see the previous note and *CPJ*, vol. 3, p. 180.

[106] See Schalit, *Josephus*, pp. 60-61.

[107] B. Lifshitz, "The Greek Documents from Naḥal Ze'elim and Naḥal Mishmar," *Yedi'ot* 25 (1961): 66-69 (in Hebrew).

[108] Frey, vol. 2, p. 253, Inscription #1231.

[109] Schwabe and Lifshitz, pp. 31-32, Inscription #51.

[110] See Y. Yadin, "Maḥaneh Dalet," *Yedi'ot* 25 (1961): 53 ff. (in Hebrew); Y. Yadin, *Bar Kokhba, The Discoveries in the Judaean Wilderness and the Letters of the Leader of the Revolt against Rome* (Jerusalem, 1971), pp. 124-139 (in Hebrew).

[111] Generally, it appears as יושע. For examples, see the references of the fourth generation Palestinian amora, R. Joshua (יושע) of the South, in Y. Shabbat 10:5, 12c; Y. Erubin 1:7, 19b; Y. Erubin 4:4, 21d; Sukkah 4:9, 54d. It should be noted that in the section of the Y. Erubin 1:7, 19b that has been preserved in the Geniza, the name of this *amora* appears

from the ruins of Susiya,[112] and even in an inscription discovered at Pompeii.[113] On the other hand, the name Σειλου, which we transliterate as שׂילא, has not yet been found in ancient Jewish inscriptions.[114] This name is common, however, in talmudic literature as the name of some *tannaim* and *amoraim* of Palestine and Babylonia.[115]

In 1975, the site was examined once more by S. Bar-Lev and M. Hartal. In this examination, in one of the modern buildings near the ancient public structure, a lintel fragment was discovered with two seven-branched candelabra engraved upon it. (see PL. 35a).[116] This find provides further evidence of a Jewish community at Dâbiyye in the rabbinic period.

In August 1982, Z. Ma'oz conducted a week-long salvage excavation in the southern part of the Jewish public structure at Dâbiyye.[117] Following this limited excavation—which neither uncovered the whole structure nor examined adjacent ancient structures—the excavator issued an announcement that the structure had served as a synagogue, published its reconstructed plan, and dated it to the late fifth or early sixth century.

In his excavation report, Ma'oz points out specifically that "the designation of the building as a synagogue was established on the basis of its ground plan—a colonnaded hall with its main entrance facing south toward Jerusalem—and on the stone with the incised *menorot*."[118] This conclusion is premature, for the entire building has yet to be excavated and the lintel

---

as "ר׳ יֵשׁוּ דרומייה" and see L. Ginzberg, *Yerushalmi Fragments from the Genizah* (New York, 1909), p. 93, line 22.

[112] Naveh, *Mosaic*, pp. 118-120, Inscriptions #77-78.

[113] Frey, vol. 1, pp. 414-415, Inscription #562.

[114] It is interesting to note that a similar form of the name appears in the bi-lingual dedication inscription at Palmyra (Tadmor) whose date is 254 C.E. In the Aramaic version, the name is שׁאילא, whereas the Greek version has Σεειλᾶ. See Cooke, *Inscriptions*, pp. 282-283, Inscription #123.

[115] See the "Index of the *amoraim*" in Albeck, *Introduction*, pp. 669-681. It should be noted that an examination of the manuscripts and printed editions of the talmuds indicates that the name שׁילא was also often written as שׁילה. See, for example, the different spellings of the name of the Palestinian *amora* of the second generation, R. שׁילא of K'far T'marta in the Palestinian Talmud (ed. Venice): Rosh Hashanah 2:9, 58b (רבי שׁילה דכפר תמרתה); Hagigah 3:8, 79d (רבי שׁילה דכפר תמרתה); Gittin 9:11, 50d (רבי שׁילא דכפר תמרתא). And see also the variants of his name in the Mandelbaum edition of Pesikta de-Rab Kahana 5:1 (p. 78) and 5:10 (p. 99). Sometimes, instead of שׁילא or שׁילה, the name forms שׁאול, שׁאולה, or שׁאילה also appear; see the variants of the name of the first-generation Palestinian *amora*, R. Johanan (or Jonathan) בר שׁילא (or בר שׁאול), in the Theodor-Albeck edition of Genesis Rabbah 91:8 (p. 1130); 94:3 (p. 1173). The last form—שׁאילה—is very reminiscent of the form of the name שׁאילא which appears in the Palmyra bi-lingual inscription mentioned in the previous note.

[116] See Ben-Ari & Bar-Lev, "Survey," p. 2.

[117] See Ma'oz, "Dâbiyye—1," p. 2; Ma'oz, "Dâbiyye—2," p. 21; Ma'oz, "Golan Synagogues," p. 150; Ma'oz, "Excavations," pp. 49-65; Ma'oz, "Dâbiyye—3," pp. 383-384; Ma'oz, "Dâbiyye—4," p. 318.

[118] Ma'oz, "Excavations," p. 49.

fragment with the *menorot* (whose photograph is presented at PL. 35a was not found in the structure itself nor even *in situ*.[119]

In Ma'oz's reconstructed plan, he suggests the existence of two continuous, complete rows of benches built, in his opinion, inside of the hall and attached to the western, northern, and eastern walls.[120] He writes in the text of his report:

> As noted above, a gap of 0.80-1.00 m. was found between the edges of the pavers and the interior of the western wall. *Although no remains were found*, two rows of benches may be restored here, the depth of each about 0.45 m. It is thus likely that a pair of stepped benches ran along two or three walls of the hall, with the probable exception of the southern wall, where the pavement reached all the way up to the wall.[121]

Anyone who scrutinizes the plan of the excavation and the cross-sections that accompany it,[122] will indeed see the existence of "a gap...between the edges of the pavers and the interior of the western wall" above wall W16. Yet Ma'oz presents no clear details about this wall and does not discuss the relationship between the top of this wall and the remains of the paving which he attributes to the "synagogue phase." Before sketching the "reconstructed plan," it would have been better carefully to examine the relationship between W16 and the remains of the paving, and to conduct examinations next to the northern and eastern walls of the hall to search for the remains of the two hypothesized rows of benches.

Another point worth noting in Ma'oz's "reconstructed plan" are the imaginary lines he draws west of the hall's main entrance, inside the hall, adjacent to the southern wall. This is the supposed location of Ma'oz's hypothesized "Torah-shrine" or "ark-of-law."[123] He writes, "The presumed ark-of-law at Dâbiyye seems not to have had a stone base, for the pavement here extended to the wall.[124] The ark was probably constructed entirely of wood and was laid directly upon the stone pavement."[125] This imaginary "ark-of-law" Ma'oz suggests here is like the imaginary "ark-of-law" which he added to the Jewish public structure at 'Ein Nashôt.[126] For Dâbiyye, however, Ma'oz forgot the end of his own report, where he suggests that the construction of the "synagogue" at Dâbiyye was never completed, since he found no clear remains of the existence of a roof.[127] If so, why, in the rainy Golan,

---

[119] See Ben-Ari & Bar-Lev, "Survey," p. 2.

[120] See Ma'oz, "Excavations," p. 57, Plan 3.

[121] Ma'oz, "Excavations," pp. 57-58. Emphasis mine.

[122] Ma'oz, "Excavations," pp. 52-53, Plan 1 and Plan 2.

[123] Ma'oz, "Excavations," p. 57.

[124] If this is so, then why does he sketch such a base in his reconstructed plan?

[125] Ma'oz, "Excavations," p. 57.

[126] And see our comment in the section on 'Ein Nashôt.

[127] Ma'oz, "Excavations," pp. 60, 62.

would the residents have built wooden ark and left it exposed to the forces of nature?

We turn now to a brief examination of the excavator's dating of the structure—the end of the fifth or beginning of the sixth century C.E. In the report of the excavation and the publications that appeared thereafter,[128] Ma'oz divides the strata that he found during his brief excavation of the structure thus:[129]

Stratum I: Modern Period. The ruined synagogue was inhabited in the modern period. To this end, the walls were rebuilt and other walls, arches, and rooms were added. The ancient pavement and column footings were partially destroyed.

Stratum II: Byzantine Period. The synagogue was erected in the Byzantine period and was paved with dressed basalt slabs. When some of them were removed, a hoard of coins (more than five hundred) mostly from the fourth to fifth centuries C.E. was discovered, including a gold coin of Gratianus, from about 400 C.E. The coins and pottery date the construction of the synagogue to the late fifth or early sixth century.

Stratum III: Late Roman Period. A series of small rectangular rooms separated by a paved alley were uncovered from the Late Roman period. The walls of the rooms are carefully built of roughly cut stones. Many of the walls served as the synagogue's foundations. There were traces of ash on the floor in one of the rooms. Potsherds and coins from the Late Roman period (third to fourth centuries) were found on the floors.

Still, any archaeologist who carefully reads the reports on the coins and pottery found at the excavation[130] in comparison with Ma'oz's excavation report,[131] cannot help but notice that despite the attempts of the scholars who published the pottery and the coins to examine the finds according to the stratigraphic schema provided by the excavator, there is no coordination between their conclusions and those of Ma'oz.[132] Especially evident is the contradiction between the date Ma'oz sets for Stratum II and that which D. T. Ariel provides after an analysis of the coins. Ariel writes *inter alia*: "No occupation phase of the Synagogue was found. Five of the seventeen loci

---

[128] Ma'oz, "Excavations"; Ma'oz, "Dâbiyye—3," p. 384; Ma'oz, "Dâbiyye—4," p. 318.

[129] Ma'oz, "Dâbiyye—4," p. 318.

[130] Killebrew, "Dâbiyye," pp. 66-73; Ariel, "Dâbiyye," pp. 74-80.

[131] Ma'oz, "Excavations," pp. 49-65.

[132] Ann Killebrew, instead of examining the pottery and dating it independently, relied upon the coins that were found in each individual stratum for the pottery dating—see the end of each discussion where she deals with each of the three groupings in Killebrew, "Dâbiyye," pp. 66-73. With regard to the date of the founding of the "synagogue," one should pay attention to Killebrew's statement (p. 67), "The second assemblage of ceramics was recovered from fills associated with the construction of the synagogue. Due to the fragmentary nature of the original synagogue floor, none of these loci was sealed and the possibility of later contamination cannot be completely ruled out."

containing coins were wholly or partly sealed. L120 was the only sealed locus which could date the pre-synagogue phase. However, the only coin
found in it was unfortunately unidentifiable...."[133] And after many twists
and turns—given that the latest Byzantine coins that were identifiable from
the hundreds of coins found at the excavation were from the years 395-408
C.E.—he summarizes as follows: "In spite of the paucity of coins of the
fifth century C.E. observed in excavations in Syria-Palestine, the weight of
the numismatic evidence suggests that the synagogue at Dâbiyye was constructed in the early fifth century C.E., shortly after the date of the site's latest coins."[134] This final conclusion of Ariel's is odd, given his earlier
statement (quoted above), "No occupation phase of the synagogue was
found."[135] But despite this oddity, a gap of about 100 years (!) remains between the date suggested by Ariel and that suggested by Ma'oz.

We will not tire the reader further with comparisons between Ma'oz and
Ariel. Let us only hope that one day, when the structural complex in its entirety has been excavated, we will receive more reliable reports and analyses.
From our familiarity with the structure, let us only point out that the floor
which Ma'oz attributes to "a synagogue," is a pavement that laid by those
who used the structure in the later periods. Thus, the date of the building is
probably the third or fourth century C.E. But for firm conclusions, we must
wait for the excavation of the entire structure and, preferably, of the nearby
buildings as well.

SANÂBER (ES-SANÂBIR)

This abandoned Syrian village lies at coordinates 2129-2675. G.
Schumacher visited there in 1884 and was not impressed by its ancient remains. He wrote, "es-Sanâbir—a ruin with 15 winter huts, between the similarly named wâdî and the Wâdî el-Fakhûreh. The remains of antiquity are
unimportant."[136]

In 1967, the village was surveyed by S. Gutman and his team, who reported that the southern part of the Syrian village is earlier than its northern
part, and that the early part rests upon a ruin.[137] Gutman also reported that
"in the village there are hewn stones, fragments of columns, and a capital
with four spirals with reliefs of pomegranates between them."[138]

---

[133] Ariel, "Dâbiyye," p. 74.
[134] Ariel, "Dâbiyye," p. 78.
[135] Ariel, "Dâbiyye," p. 74.
[136] Schumacher, "Dscholan," p. 318; Schumacher, *Jaulân*, p. 236.
[137] Epstein & Gutman, p. 269, Site #76.
[138] See previous note.

A short time after Gutman's survey, the site was surveyed again by the author and his team.[139] This survey established that the area of the ancient ruin is about 20 dunams and has shards mainly from the Roman and Byzantine periods. We found an abundance of basalt ashlars incorporated in secondary use in the houses of the Syrian village; these apparently came from one or more public buildings of the second-temple and/or rabbinic periods. During the survey, the shafts of columns and the capital which Gutman had reported were rediscovered. In addition, the survey also found two Attic column bases and three Ionic capitals. In the southeast area of the ruin, it was possible to make out the tops of the walls of a monumental building, but without systematic excavation it was difficult to estimate its precise dimensions.[140]

In 1976, Z. Ilan published a photograph of a basalt lintel fragment, on which a seven-branched candelabrum was incised. A square had been incised beside it, which perhaps represented a fire-pan.[141] According to Ilan, the stone was found by S. Ben-Ami of Kibbutz Merom Golan and its source was the village of Sanâber. In light of the discovery of the lintel fragment, Ilan came to the conclusion "that Jews also lived in this village in antiquity."[142] In his last book, Ilan included the village of Sanâber in the list of sites in which there may have been synagogues.[143]

Ilan's conclusions are acceptable to us primarily because of the site's location in the heart of the Jewish settlements in the Golan in the second-temple and rabbinic periods. A comparison of the Attic bases and the Ionic capitals found at the site with those from Jewish public buildings in the Galilee and the Golan of the same era strengthens the possibility that Sanâber had at least one Jewish public building.

FÂKHÛRA

This abandoned Syrian village can be found at coordinates 2148-2674. The village was first surveyed in 1967 by S. Gutman and his team, who reported that "the village is new and has no antiquities."[144]

North of the village, near a volley ball court beside a new, isolated Syrian house, Gutman's team found a concentration of four basalt column

---

[139] D. Urman, "Sanâber," *Special Surveys Reports*, Archive of the Association for the Archaeological Survey of Israel, Israel Antiquities Authority, Jerusalem (in Hebrew); Urman, *List*, p. 10; Urman, *Golan*, p. 194; Site #78 and see the note for this site on p. 212.

[140] D. Urman, "Sanâber," *Special Surveys Reports*, p. 4 (in Hebrew).

[141] Ilan, *Golan*, p. 167.

[142] Ilan, *Golan*, p. 168.

[143] Ilan, *Israel*, p. 323.

[144] Epstein & Gutman, p. 269, Site #77.

shafts, and near them, a basalt pedestal, on which there are lovely reliefs of meander, flowers, and an eight-branched candelabrum (see PLs. 35b and 36a). The stones were not found *in situ*.[145]

In 1968, the author surveyed the village and found ancient building stones in secondary use in some of the Syrian houses and a few shards of the Roman and Byzantine periods.[146] On this occasion, the area of the volley ball court was also investigated, but while the column shafts reported upon by Gutman and his team were rediscovered, the pedestal decorated with the candelabrum had disappeared. Later, the pedestal was discovered in the late Moshe Dayan's collection and was transferred to the Golan Antiquities Museum in Qaṣrin when it was erected.[147]

In his publications on 'Ein Nashôt, Z. Ma'oz determined that the pedestal mentioned above had been taken from the Jewish public building at 'Ein Nashôt.[148] He even published its photograph as if it had been uncovered at that site.[149] He provides no sound basis for this link, however. Indeed, the facts of the pedestal's travels just related makes clear that Ma'oz's identification is incorrect. As we mentioned in our discussion of the 'Ein Nashôt site (see above), Ma'oz's attempt to 'adopt' architectural items from various sites for the rather small structure at 'Ein Nashôt suggest that it was as tall as the famed Tower of Babel. Furthermore, if the pedestal with the candelabrum had been plundered from 'Ein Nashôt, then the four column shafts found beside it also originated there (increasing the building's height even more!). These observations all suggest that the remains of a Jewish public building should be sought at Fâkhûra itself.

Support for this possibility appeared in 1972 when a new bed was cut south of Fakhûra for a paved road to the new Israeli urban settlement of Qaṣrin. During the initial cutting of the roadbed, a large site was discovered at coordinates 2144-2676 "with the remains of many buildings and much pottery from the Roman period."[150] A Roman coin found at the site was identified as a coin of the city of Tyre from 182/183 C.E. Also found at the site were the remains of an olive-oil press and an ornamented architectural artifact.[151]

Shortly after the road was cut, S. Bar-Lev conducted salvage excavations at this site in which he excavated a few rooms in two private structures. A

---

[145] Epstein & Gutman, p. 268, Site #72.

[146] See D. Urman, "Fâkhûra," *Special Surveys Reports*, Archive of the Association for the Archaeological Survey of Israel, Israel Antiquities Authority, Jerusalem (in Hebrew); Urman, *Golan*, p. 195, Site #79.

[147] Ilan, "Menorot," p. 118.

[148] See above, note 65 in the section on 'Ein Nashôt.

[149] See, for example, Ma'oz, "Golan—1," p. 1202; Ma'oz, "Golan—2," p. 413.

[150] Ben-Ari and Bar-Lev, "Golan—1," p. 1.

[151] Ben-Ari and Bar-Lev, "Golan—1," p. 1.

full report on these excavations have not yet been published, but according to Bar-Lev's preliminary report, he uncovered "fragments of Herodian lamps and many bowls and cooking pots of the second and third centuries C.E."[152]

During a visit the author made to Bar-Lev's dig, it became clear that the site extends over 5 dunams and it is possible also to make out ancient ashlar building stones.

The dates of the pottery uncovered by Bar-Lev and the remains of an olive-oil press characteristic of the Jewish settlements in the Golan, combined with the fact that this settlement lies in the heart of the Jewish region in the Golan in the second-temple and rabbinic periods, permit us to hypothesize that the remains are of a Jewish settlement. It is possible that the source of the pedestal with the candelabrum relief is a public building once located at this site, but its precise location has yet to be identified.

<h2 style="text-align:center">AHMADIYYE</h2>
(EL-AHMEDÎYEH, 'ÂMÛDIYYE, EL-ḤAMEDÎYEH, SHUWEIKEH)

Ahmadiyye is an abandoned Turkoman village which lies on two low hills near a group of springs about two kilometers northeast of Qaṣrin at coordinates 2160-2679.

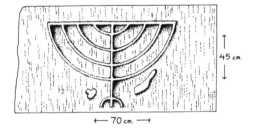

FIG. 1 Relief of menorah, shofar, and incense shovel. (After Schumacher.)

The village was first surveyed by G. Schumacher in 1884,[153] and was visited by him once again in June 1913.[154] Schumacher discovered a number of decorated architectural items that we now know belonged to a Jewish public structure of the rabbinic period. One item is decorated with a relief of a nine-branched menorah, a shofar, and a fire-pan (Fig. 1).[155]

---

[152] Ben-Ari and Bar-Lev, "Golan—2," p. 1.

[153] Schumacher, "Dscholan," pp. 281-282; Schumacher, *Jaulân*, pp. 70-72.

[154] Schumacher, "Ostjordanlande," pp. 149-150.

[155] See Schumacher, "Correspondenzen," p. 333; Schumacher, "Dscholan," p. 282, Fig. 34; Schumacher, *Jaulân*, p. 71, Fig. 7.

A similarly decorated item was discovered in the late 1960's in the village of Yahûdiyye and published by Z. Ilan.[156] At first, Ilan thought the decorated stone from Yahûdiyye was the same item seen by Schumacher here at Aḥmadiyye. In his last book, however, he added the possibility that they were two similar items produced by the same artisan.[157]

Schumacher also published a sketch of a window lintel with two *menorot* incised in its ends (Fig. 2).[158] The candelabra are seven-branched and the one to the left lacks a base. Schumacher registered a similar lintel at Khân Bândak (Ghâdriyye)—a site found about two kilometers northwest of Aḥmadiyye (see the discussion of Ghâdriyye). Schumacher's report includes a sketched copy of the Jewish inscription in Greek, which the surveyor neither read in its entirety nor explained.[159] (See Fig. 3 and the discussion of Inscription #1.)

FIG. 2 Lintel with two *menorot*. (After Schumacher.)

In 1968, the village was surveyed by a team lead by S. Gutman.[160] In this survey, a section of a Hebrew inscription was found, hitherto unknown (see PL. 36b and Inscription #2). Two years later, a survey was conducted there by the author.[161] Its purpose was to measure the area of the site and determine the periods of settlement from pottery remains—the details of which had not been reported by the earlier surveyors. Our examination produced few shards of the Hellenistic period but an abundance of shards from the various stages of the Roman and Byzantine periods. Tops of ancient walls led us to conclude that, at its greatest extent, the ancient settlement covered approximately 35 dunams.[162] Around and within the abandoned Turkoman houses, we found several architectural artifacts whose source was one or more Jewish public buildings which had been dismantled by the

---

[156] Ilan, "Menorot," pp. 117-118.

[157] Ilan, *Israel,* p. 65.

[158] See Schumacher, "Correspondenzen," p. 333.

[159] Schumacher, "Dscholan," p. 282, Fig. 33; Schumacher, *Jaulân,* p. 70, Fig. 6.

[160] Epstein & Gutman, p. 269, Site #78.

[161] D. Urman, "'Aḥmadiyye," *Reports of the Staff Officer in Charge of Archaeological Affairs in the Golan* (1968-1972), Archive of the Israel Antiquities Authority, Jerusalem (in Hebrew); Urman, *List,* p. 10; Urman, *Golan,* p. 195, Site #80.

[162] See previous note.

Turkoman settlers (as Schumacher testified).[163] Among the items found in the survey were a lintel with a relief of a garland with a 'knot of Hercules,' pedestals with pillar bases, and sections of columns and Doric capitals—all made of basalt. These are all items typical of Jewish public buildings in the Galilee and the Golan.[164] In the village, we also found a boundary-stone fragment with part of a Greek inscription (see Inscription #3 below).

In 1978, the site was surveyed yet again by Z. Ma'oz, but this effort produced no new finds.[165]

Inscription #1

On a (basalt?) stone tablet, whose nature and dimensions were not given by Schumacher, an incised two-line Greek inscription was found, which he copied and published.

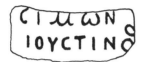

FIG. 3 Inscription #1.

Its transcription is Σίμων 'Ιουστινο[υ], which translates as "Simon, son of Justinu[s]."

Since the stone has not been found by later surveyors, it is difficult to determine if this was a section of a dedicatory or burial inscription. The latter possibility seems to us more plausible, but only the stone's rediscovery can provide a certain answer. It is well-known that Schumacher often made imprecise copies.[166] It is therefore doubtful if we can attribute any significance to the sign which appears in the sketch above the "o" (omicron) at the end of the second line of the inscription.[167]

The name "Simon" (Σίμων), which is the Greek pronunciation of the Hebrew name "Shim'on,"[168] is known as a Jewish name both from the lit-

---

[163] Schumacher, "Dscholan," pp. 281-282; Schumacher, *Jaulân*, pp. 70-72.

[164] See above, note 161, and also Urman, "Synagogue Sites," p. 25; Urman, "Hellenistic," p. 467.

[165] Ma'oz, "Golan—1," p. 293; Ma'oz, "Golan—2," p. 541.

[166] See, for example, the sketch of the incised menorah and the inscription, "I Yehudah the Hazzan," that appears in Schumacher's book (*The Jaulân*, p. 141, Fig. 45). Its source is the column from Fîq that stands today in the Golan Antiquities Museum at Qasrin.

[167] The possibility that this sign is the letter 'C' does not seem likely to us. See Gregg and Urman, Inscription #91.

[168] See Cassuto-Salzmann, pp. 188-189; Schwabe and Lifshitz 1967, p. 208.

erary sources of the second-temple and rabbinic periods,[169] and also from the burial inscriptions uncovered at Beth She'arim,[170] and other places.[171] The form of the name Ἰοῦστινος, however, is so far unknown as a Jewish name in the inscriptions of this period.[172] Yet a check of the talmudic literature reveals that this name—like similar names such as Ἰοῦστας or Ἰοῦστος, which stem from Latin renderings of the Hebrew name 'Zadok'—was common among the Jews of Palestine in this period.[173] We find evidence of this primarily in the Palestinian Talmud where the Palestinian *amora*, Rabbi Justini, is mentioned.[174] It should be noted that in talmudic literature, the forms of the names Simon, Justa, and Justini are attached only to Palestinian *amoraim* of the third, fourth, and fifth generations,[175] that is, those living in the late third and the fourth centuries. Two inscriptions in which the name Simon appears at Beth She'arim were discovered in a burial hall dated to the fourth century C.E.[176] These facts suggest that the inscription under consideration likewise derives from the fourth century—a period when the names Simon, Justa, Justini, or Justinos were common among the Jews of Palestine.[177]

---

[169] Examples of the appearance of the name "Simon" as a Jewish name in the second-temple period abound in the writings of Josephus, see Schalit, *Josephus*, p. 113. For examples from talmudic literature, see the many passages concerning Rabbi Simon in the Jerusalem Talmud, collected by Omansky in Omansky, *Sages*, p. 121.

[170] Schwabe and Lifshitz, pp. 35-36, Inscriptions #59-60.

[171] See, for example, Frey, vol. 2, Nos. 880, 920, 1173, 1184; as well as Ovadiah, "Sarcophagus," pp. 225-230.

[172] This name appears once in a Jewish inscription from Palestine—in a dedication inscription written in Aramaic in a mosaic floor of a public structure that Sukenik uncovered at Beth Alpha; see Sukenik, *Beth Alpha*, pp. 43-47. However, in this instance it is clear beyond any doubt that the person by this name mentioned in the inscription is one of the emperors known as Justinos; and See Naveh, *Mosaic*, pp. 72-73.

[173] See Tcherikover, *Jews*, p. 192; Schwabe and Lifshitz, p. 98.

[174] See, for example, Y. BB 8:6, 16b. And for details, see Urman, "Kazrin Inscriptions," p. 517, note 20.

[175] See Albeck, *Introduction*, pp. 669-681.

[176] Schwabe and Lifshitz, p. 35; Mazar, *Beth She'arim*, p. 97.

[177] It should be pointed out that the combination of the forms of the name *Simon* with *Justi*(!) appears in the talmuds in the name of the fourth-century Palestinian *amora*—(third generation—Albeck, *Introduction*, p. 246), Rabbi Justi ben Rabbi Simon (Y. Erubin 6:5, 23c; Y. Sheqalim 2:1, 46c; and perhaps also in Y. MS 4:3, 54d). Without detailing the variant readings regarding the name of this sage, let us point out that the form of the name as it appears above derives from the main readings as well as variants with which we have dealt elsewhere (see Urman, "Kazrin Inscriptions," p. 517, note 20). Was there a family relationship of any sort between the *amora* R. Justi ben Rabbi Simon and Simon ben Justinos (or Justini) mentioned in this inscription? To this question, we have no answer. But it should be clear from my comments that it is a question worth pursuing.

Inscription #2

The stone upon which this inscription was engraved was not found in its original site.[178] It is 56 cm. long, 35 cm. high, and 23 cm. thick. It is a fragment of an architrave decorated on its upper portion with a relief of a vase from which there is an emerging leafy vine branch with a cluster of grapes (see PL. 36b). On the fragment's bottom portion appears the following inscription, engraved in Hebrew letters (7-9 cm. high):

תכן שלשמר

FIG. 4 Inscription #2.

This should be transcribed as: ...תמוש משמר....

J. Naveh speculates that this is a segment of a text in Biblical style: [לא]—תמוש משמר]וחקותיו ומעשות מצוותין "[You shall not] stray from observing [his laws and doing his commandments]."[179]

It is difficult to reconstruct its content, as Naveh has indicated, in spite of the relatively large number of letters that have been preserved. Nevertheless, until an additional fragment of the architrave is discovered, we suggest also weighing the possibility that this inscription comes from the list of the 24 Levitical courses that served in the Temple along with the 24 Priestly watches during the second-temple period.[180] I suggest the following reconstruction, ...[ומשמר]ת מוש משמרות.... It would be translated as "...the course] (of) Mush, (the) course [(of)...." Mush was the second son of Merar, son of Levi,[181] and the father of the Mushi family mentioned in most of the genealogical lists of the families of Levi preserved in the Bible.[182]

---

[178] See Epstein & Gutman, p. 269, Site #78.

[179] Naveh, *Mosaic*, p. 147, Inscription #109.

[180] There is clear evidence of the existence of Levitical courses during the second-temple period. The most outstanding of these is Tos. Taa. 3:2-3 (pp. 336-337 in the Lieberman edition), "Moses ordained eight courses for the Priests and eight for the Levites. After David and Samuel the seer arose, they made them into twenty-four priestly courses *and twenty-four Levitical courses,* as is written, 'David and Samuel the seer established them in their office of trust.' (1 Chron. 9:22); these are the Priestly and Levitical courses. Came the Prophets that were in Jerusalem and set twenty-four stands there parallel to the *twenty-four Priestly and Levitical courses* as is written, 'Command the Israelite people and say to them, "My food which is presented unto Me"' (Num. 28:2). This cannot mean all the Israelites, but it teaches us that one's delegate is as himself. When it is time for the course, its Priests and Levites go up to Jerusalem, and the Israelites of that course, who cannot go to Jerusalem, gather in their cities and read the section of the Creation and are excused from work that entire week." (Italics mine.) See also *Antiquities* VII §§ 366- 367; M. Taa. 4:2; Y. Taa. 4:2, 67d; Y. Pesahim 4:1, 30c; B. Taa. 27a; Numbers Rabbah 3:10.

[181] It seems that the form of the name *mush* appearing in the inscription (assuming my proposal is correct) is the correct form of the name, rather than the form *mushi*, which is preserved in the genealogical lists of the Levites in the Bible (see following note). The *mushi*

The inscriptions (all fragmentary) of the list of the 24 Priestly courses so far discovered can be reconstructed on the basis of the list of courses in 1 Chronicles 24:7-18.[183] By contrast, completing the above inscription is difficult because no complete formulation of the 24 Levitical courses has been preserved in the Hebrew Bible,[184] certainly none similar to the courses of priests and musicians.[185] That a complete text of the Levites' 24 courses was not preserved in the Bible may be explained by the fact that during the second-temple period, the Levites were forced out of their positions in the Temple courtyard by the priests.[186] It is also reasonable to assume that after the destruction of the Second Temple, some people (perhaps of the Levitical families?) wished to preserve the memory of the Levitical courses,[187] just as others preserved the memory of the 24 Priestly courses.[188]

Inscription #3[189]

This basalt fragment is 26 cm. high, 28 cm. wide, and 28 cm. thick. Four lines of a Greek inscription have been preserved (the average letter height: 3 cm.). It reads:

Λ Ι Θ Ο Ν Δ Ι Ο
Ρ Ι Ζ Ο Ν Τ Α Ο Ρ
Α Ω Σ Α Ρ Ν . Μ
. Ε Υ Η . Ω Ν

---

form is a possessive indicating "belonging to," and meaning "of *mushi*." Compare, for example, 1 Chron. 6:3 ("And the sons of Kohath: Amram, Izhar, Hebron, and Uzziel...") with Numbers 3:27 ("To Kohath belonged the clan of the Amramites [*ha-amrami*], the clan of the Izharites [*ha-izhari*], the clan of the Hebronites [*ha-hebroni*], and the clan of the Uzzielites [*ha-uzzieli*]; these were the clans of the Kohathites [*ha-kohathi*].". The phenomenon of the presevation (or, more precisely, the "absorption") of name forms that in their origin were possessives in biblical genealogical lists is quite common. See, for example, "...the sons of Merari: Ethan son of *kishi* son of Abdi..." (1 Chron. 6:29) in contrast to "...and of the sons of Merari, *kish* son of Abdi..." (2 Chron. 29:12).

[182] See Exod. 6:19; Num. 3:20, 3:33, 26:58; 1 Chron. 6:4, 6:32, 23:21, 23:23, 24:26, 24:30.

[183] See Naveh, *Mosaic*, pp. 87-89, 91, 142-143, Inscriptions #51, 52, 56, and 106.

[184] And see on this, J. Liver under the rubric "Course, Priestly and Levitical Courses" in the *Encyclopedia Biblica*, vol. 5, pp. 569-580; Liver, *Priests and Levites*, pp. 11-32.

[185] 1 Chron. 24:7-18, 25:9-31.

[186] See Safrai, "Ritual," pp. 370-371.

[187] Some support for this premise we find in the fact that even though the early *paytanim* (Jewish liturgical poets) devoted many of their *piyyutim* (liturgical poems) and lamentations to the memory of the 24 Priestly courses, lamentation-*piyyutim* devoted to the memory of the courses of the Levites-musicians have also been preserved till our day. See *Siddur R. Saadja Gaon*, pp. 414-416 (in Hebrew) as well as the *kerovot* of Ha-Kalir published by E. Fleisher in "On the Courses in the Piyyutim," *Sinai* 62 (1968): 19 ff. (in Hebrew).

[188] On this see Urbach, "Mishmarot," pp. 304-327.

[189] The inscription was read and translated by R. C. Gregg, see Gregg and Urman, Inscription #92.

The inscription should be transcribed as: …λίθον διορίζοντα ὄρ(ου?)ς Αρν.μ . ευη[ν]ων…. Its translation: "…a stone demarking (the) boundaries (?) of…."

The first two lines, no doubt originally preceded by several others, fit the form familiar from a number of Diocletian boundary stones discovered in the Golan.[190] It is difficult to know how ΟΡΑΩΣ is to be interpreted; it would be an unusual spelling of ὄρους, the word tentatively proposed here. In the third and fourth lines, we would expect the name of a landowner, a village, or a people, but the letters' illegibility makes reconstruction futile.

To sum up our discussion of the Jewish finds from the village of Aḥmadiyye, we must note that despite the damage to the ancient site done by the nineteenth-century Turkoman settlers, we have no doubt that systematic archaeological excavations at the site will reveal remains of one or more Jewish public buildings from the fourth century C.E., and perhaps earlier.[191]

ED-DÛRA (KH. ED-DÛRA)

This abandoned Syrian army post was built upon the ruins of an ancient settlement and stands on a lofty spur at coordinates 2124-2664.

Ed-Dûra was first surveyed by G. Schumacher in 1884, who wrote: "A ruin with eight winter huts of the 'Arab el-Wesîyeh, between the Wâdî el-Fâkhûra and the Wâdî es-Sanâber. In the west and south, where the city was not so well protected by nature as in the east, there are basalt terraces of steep incline, and a triply thick wall of great unhewn blocks of basalt. It leads south to a pile of ruins, out of which stems of pillars and Doric capitals, and also a corner pillar, rises. This, I presume, was the old city gate. From here the old city walls run in a sharp angle for a little distance further towards the southeast. On the city gate carefully hewn stones, 6 feet long, are to be found; there are also capitals lying about in other places. In the village itself, which lies inside the city wall, I noticed nothing of interest."[192]

After the Six Day War, the site was surveyed by teams led by C. Epstein and S. Gutman, who reported that at the summit of the spur there are remains of buildings built of hewn stones in secondary use, and that a carved-

---

[190] See, e.g., Gregg and Urman, Inscriptions #10, 11, 42, 43, 209, 240.

[191] Here we must note that Hüttenmeister and Reeg expressed their opinion that the segment of the architrave upon which Inscription #2 was found is characteristic of the architraves that were found in synagogues of the third century (See Hüttenmeister and Reeg, pp. 4-5). Still, in their opinion, on the basis of this find alone it is difficult to be definite about the fact that there was a synagogue in Aḥmadiyye. If these investigators had seen the abundance of architectural items that we found in the village during our survey, their opinion would certainly have been different.

[192] Schumacher, "Dscholan," pp. 279-280; Schumacher, *Jaulân*, pp. 130-131.

out ditch separates the settlement from the spur's south part.[193] Epstein and
Gutman also reported that among the buildings on the spur there are shards
from the Hellenistic, Roman, Byzantine, and Ottoman periods, whereas at
the foot of the spur, in the trenches of the Syrian Army post, they found a
great quantity of shards from the early Canaanite period (Early Bronze
Age).[194]

In 1968 and again in 1972, the author surveyed the site and found pottery
from the Middle and Late Bronze Ages, and from the Middle Ages (the
Middle Arab period)—in addition to the periods noted by Epstein and
Gutman.[195] In the survey it was possible to make out both the remains of
the walls described by Schumacher and the ditch which Epstein and Gutman
reported. I discussed these fortifications in a previous publication and
pointed out that "without an archaeological excavation it is impossible to
determine to which period these fortifications belong."[196]

At the location Schumacher identified as the city gate, we found many
well-hewn, basalt stones (ashlars) as well as several column shafts. There is
little to indicate that this structure was a gate rather than a building. If systematic archaeological excavations are conducted there, perhaps remains will
be found there of a monumental building from the second-temple and/or rabbinic periods.

Near the ruins of the houses of the Arab village that preceded the Syrian
Army outpost, we also found an abundance of ancient finely-hewn stones
and several pillar shafts, as well as Doric and Ionic capitals of the types
common in Jewish public buildings of the Galilee and the Golan during the
second-temple and rabbinic periods. The quantity of remains suggests that
more than one public structure existed at the site.

At the southern and western edges of the ruin, we found parts from a
number of olive-oil presses, and on the spur's southern slope a complete
olive-oil press was located *in situ*. The presence of several olive-oil presses
at the site reveals that during the second-temple and/or rabbinic periods olive
oil was one of the staples, perhaps the only one, of the local economy.

In October-November 1988, the site was surveyed yet once more by A.
Golani, who reported finding Chalcolithic shards at the site, in addition to
those found in earlier surveys.[197] The surveyor estimated the area of the ruin

---

[193] Epstein & Gutman, p. 270, Site #83.

[194] See previous note.

[195] D. Urman, "ed-Dûra," *Special Surveys Reports*, Archive of the Association for the
Archaeological Survey of Israel, Israel Antiquities Authority, Jerusalem (in Hebrew); D.
Urman, "ed-Dûra," *Reports of the Staff Officer in Charge of Archaeological Affairs in the
Golan* (1968-1972), Archive of the Israel Antiquities Authority, Jerusalem (in Hebrew);
Urman, *List*, p. 10.

[196] See Urman, *Golan*, p. 195, Site #82 and the note for this site on p. 212.

[197] Golani, "Golan," p. 8.

as 75 dunams and reported uncovering the remains of a bath-house of the Byzantine period at the site. Nevertheless, his most important find, for our focus was a fragment of a basalt stone slab measuring about 30 cm. high and about 48 cm. wide. On it was incised an Aramaic inscription with letters some 4 to 8 cm. high. The inscription reads:

אמֹה ברת
שמעון

It translates: "Amah (or Umath) daughter of Shim'on."

This is a fragment of a Jewish female's gravestone whose father's name was Shim'on, one of the most common Jewish names in the second-temple and rabbinic periods. The name Shim'on also appears in other Golan inscriptions.[198] It seems that the man who incised the inscription first left out the third letter in the maiden's or girl's name and added it sometime after completing the next word. As a result, it is unclear whether the letter is a ה or a ת. If her name was Umath, this may be the Aramaic form of the name Εὐμάθη, which also appears on a burial stone we unearthed at el-'Âl.[199]

The find of the tombstone fragment of a Jewish female enables us to postulate that a Jewish settlement existed at ed-Dûra during the second-temple and/or rabbinic periods. This settlement, like most of the Jewish settlements of the time in the Golan, supported itself at least partially by growing olives and producing olive oil, as the remains of the olive-oil presses attest. From the size of the site, the abundance of the ancient building stones (ashlar), and the quantity of architectural items identified by the various surveys, it is possible to suggest that this settlement contained a number of Jewish public buildings.

QÎSRÎN (QAṢRÎN)

This abandoned Syrian village was built at coordinates 2161-2660, upon and within the ruins of a Jewish settlement from the rabbinic period. Today the area serves as a tourist park for the display of antiquities, near the new Israeli urban settlement of Qaṣrin which was erected in the mid-1970's.

G. Schumacher, who visited the place in 1884, did not discern the Jewish remains and described the site in a few words: "A small Bedawîn winter village, with a group of beautiful oak trees and old ruins, south of el-Aḥmadiyye."[200] In 1967, the site was surveyed by a survey team led by S.

---

[198] See Inscription #2 in the section on 'Ein Nashôt, as well as Inscription #1 in the section on Aḥmadiyye.

[199] See the section on el-'Âl, as well as Gregg and Urman, Inscription #61.

[200] Schumacher, "Dscholan," p. 340; Schumacher, *Jaulân*, p. 194.

Gutman. They were the first to report the remains of a Jewish public building.[201]

In 1970, the author and his team surveyed the abandoned village again,
and determined that the area of the ancient site had once spread out over 50
dunams across a low hill with moderate slopes. This hill may actually be a
tell containing construction remains to a depth of at least three meters. The
survey gathered small amounts of pottery from Middle Bronze Age IIb, from
the Late Bronze Age, the Iron Age, (especially Iron Age II), and the
Hellenistic period. A larger quantity of shards was collected from the different stages of Roman, Byzantine, early Arab, middle Arab (Mameluke) and
later Arab (Ottoman) periods.[202] In the Syrian houses, the survey found a
number of decorated architectural items in secondary use as building material
that had gone unreported by Gutman's team. The origin of these items was
apparently the Jewish public building complex. Of these architectural items,
two basalt doorposts require further mention. On one of them, an eleven-
branched menorah with a tripod base was incised (see PL. 37a).[203] On the
second doorpost were found stone reliefs of a five-branched menorah and, beside it, a peacock pecking at a cluster of grapes or a pomegranate (see PL.
37b).[204]

In April 1971, the author began to excavate the Jewish public building's
remains at Qîsrîn. In two seasons of excavation, the boundaries of a large
rectangular hall were uncovered (18 x 15.40 m.), which our first reports designated as "the synagogue hall" (see PL. 38b).[205] Leading into the hall is a
central doorway located in the center of its northern wall (see PL. 38a). This
doorway, whose width on the inner side of the wall is 1.90 m. and on the
outer side is 1.45 m., has been preserved to its full 2.45 m. height. The
doorway frame is composed of sculpted bands with a flat architrave, a
convex frieze, and a cornice with an egg-and-dart design. On the lintel of the
doorway, in addition to these sculpted bands are also reliefs of a wreath tied
in a 'Hercules knot' flanked by two pomegranates and two vases (amphorae).
At the foot of the doorposts, two Attic pilaster bases project from the wall.
In the southeast corner of the hall, in the eastern wall, there is a small

---

[201] Epstein & Gutman, p. 270, Site #84.

[202] D. Urman, "Qîsrîn," *Reports of the Staff Officer in Charge of Archaeological Affairs in
the Golan* (1968-1972), Archives of the Israel Antiquities Authority, Jerusalem (in Hebrew);
Urman, *List*, p. 10.

[203] This engraving could be interpreted as a 'tree of life,' although the presence of the
tripod base makes this interpretation less likely.

[204] See note 202, and also Urman, "Golan—3," p. 4.

[205] See Urman, "Qaṣrin Synagogue," p. 8; Urman, "Synagogue Sites," pp. 25-27; Urman,
"Golan—7," p. 2; Urman, "Hellenistic," pp. 460-462. As for the definition of the use of the
hall as a *bet knesset*, see my comments in Urman, "Kazrin Inscriptions," p. 513, note 2, as
well as in my article "The House of Assembly and the House of Study: Are They One and
the Same?" appearing in volume 1 of this collection, pp. 232-255.

doorway whose width on the inner side of the wall is 0.85 m. and, on the outer side, 1.05 m. This doorway, which narrows toward the inside of the hall, leads to an adjacent room and provides evidence that the hall we excavated is only part of a large complex of a Jewish public building. Further evidence that the hall comprises part of a larger complex is the fact that the hall's western wall continues southward across the corner formed where the hall's southern wall converges upon it.[206]

Within the hall, along all four walls, we found the remains of two rows of benches constructed of well-hewn basalt stones (ashlar). Parts of column shafts, as well as the bases and capitals of the hall's columns, were found scattered in the rubble or in secondary use in the later construction within the hall, adjoining rooms, or nearby structures. It seems that the roof of the hall originally rested upon two rows of columns—four in each row—and upon a pair of pilasters found incorporated in the construction of the southern wall (see PLs. 39a-40a). It should be noted that the capitals we found in the Qîsrîn excavation are identical with those Schumacher found at Yahûdiyye.[207] These capitals, which are a variation of the Ionic capitals widespread in sites of southern Syria, are characteristic of the Golan's Jewish public buildings from the second-temple and rabbinic periods.

---

[206] In Z. Ma'oz's writings, he has published a plan of the hall in which he places an entranceway in the western wall, larger in width (according to the plan) than the one in the northern wall. (See Ma'oz, "Qasrin," p. 4; Ma'oz & Killebrew, "1982/1984," p. 92; Ma'oz & Killebrew, "1983/1984," p. 290, Fig. 1; Ma'oz & Killebrew, "Ancient Qasrin," p. 8; Ma'oz & Killebrew, "Qasrin—1," p. 1423; Ma'oz & Killebrew, "Qasrin—2," p. 1219). Recently he wrote, "Traces of another entrance were found in the western wall. Its lintel bears a double meander relief (swastika). A geometric relief of rhomboids and triangles, with a rosette in the center probably belonged to a window above this entrance." (Ma'oz & Killebrew, "Qasrin—2," p. 1220). In Ma'oz & Killebrew, "Qasrin—1," p. 1423 he points out that the width of the entranceway in the hall's western wall is only 1.20 m., and in Ma'oz & Killebrew, "Ancient Qasrin," pp. 18-19, note 7 he states, "Because this door was eliminated in a later remodeling, its presence was indicated only by an inner threshold-stone and a gap in the benches along the west wall of the prayer hall. Fragments of it, however, were found in secondary use incorporated into a recent lean-to structure adjacent to the synagogue in the west. These included the threshold stone and the doorjamb stones, one of which was incised with a tree of life." Ma'oz's identification of a door in the western wall is unfortunately mistaken. In the two seasons of excavations we conducted at Qîsrîn—prior to Ma'oz's excavations—we uncovered the entire layout of the hall's outer walls and some tops of the hall's walls and the rooms near it on the west, south, and east. We also excavated the external surface of the hall's northern wall to the foundations and most of the length of the external surface of its western wall. Therefore, as the one who was the first to excavate in the structure, and who, among other things, excavated the west wall of the hall designated by Ma'oz as a "prayer hall," and as the one who, in the course of excavation, disassembled the later structure adjacent to the western wall of that hall, I must note the hall's western wall contained no traces of an entranceway. Today's visitor to the site, unfortunately, will find an entranceway in the western wall because of Ma'oz' involvement in the site's preservation and reconstruction. I regret to say, however, the door has no true scientific basis.

[207] See Schumacher, "Dscholan," p. 303, Figs. 60-61; Schumacher, *Jaulân*, p. 271, Figs. 142-143; and see more about this farther on in the chapter on Yahûdiyye.

From the stratigraphy, the shards, the coins that were uncovered in the hall's excavation and other areas of excavation around it, it became clear that this hall was built in the first half of the third century C.E. From then on, it went through several stages until the end of the thirteenth century. In its first stage, which lasted until the mid-fourth century, along its four walls there were two rows of well-hewn basalt stone benches. The hall floor, at this stage, was made of a layer of thick plaster grooved to imitate stone slabs. During the second stage of the hall's use a mosaic floor was laid on top of the plaster floor (greatly damaged in later stages of occupation). At this time, a low platform near the center of hall's southern wall was also built. The date at which the second stage began is not clear, but it appears that it occurred sometime in the second half of the fourth century. The third stage opened at the start of the seventh century with the laying of a plaster floor atop the mosaic one. From this period, a cache of 82 coins dating from 598-603 C.E. was discovered, near the northeast corner of the platform.[208] A date for the destruction of the hall after the third stage is not known, but it is clear that it was destroyed by an earthquake. Sometime after its destruction, the northern part of the hall was rebuilt and it appears that this rehabilitated section served as a prayer hall at least until the thirteenth century. When the northern part was restored, a wall containing a small niche was built facing south. The stones for this wall were taken from the ruins of the southern part of the hall (which was restored only after our excavations). One of these stones contained part of an Aramaic inscription (see Inscription #1). A second, rectangular niche was opened in the inner side of the western wall, in the center of the northern part of the hall. Incised on a stone at the bottom of the niche was a five-branched menorah.

It is difficult to ascertain the identity of the people who repaired the northern part of the hall and used it until the thirteenth century. Were they Jews or Muslims? Ma'oz, in his various publications, ignores the incised candelabrum and the niche above it, and argues emphatically that the place served as a mosque.[209] During our excavations of this part of the hall—which examined the hall entirely—we found no artifacts or other evidence to support this conclusion (excluding the niche facing southward). It is possible, additionally, that some time after the third stage of the hall's history, it was also used by Christians (perhaps only in the twelfth century). The first indication of this is that on the upper plaster floor we uncovered in the northern part of the hall, ceramics were found typical of the Crusader sites in twelfth-century western Palestine. The second indication is that a careful pe-

---

[208] The cache of coins was discovered during the preservation and reconstruction work at the site under the supervision of M. Ben-Ari and S. Bar-Lev. My thanks go to Mr. Bar-Lev who placed this information at my disposal.

[209] See note 206.

rusal of the lintel over the central doorway of the hall's northern wall reveals that the center of the wreath contains a carved cross.

In the decades immediately preceding our excavations at the site, the area of the building complex was the cemetery of the Syrian village, and just outside the doorway in the hall's northern wall, a large structure of a sheik's tomb had been built, which we dismantled at the start of the excavations there. A platform built in recent decades served as a base for the sheik's tomb using building stones and decorated architectural items taken from the complex surrounding the Jewish public building. When we dismantled parts of this platform, we found an Ionic capital upon which a three-branched menorah was incised, as well as a fragment of a window lintel containing a bas relief of a five-branched menorah (see PL. 41b).[210]

Upon the conclusion of our excavations at the site and after a new road was paved nearby in preparation for the new urban center of Qaṣrîn, many interested parties began to visit the site. At the beginning of 1974, near the ruins of a Syrian house east of the Jewish public building complex, one visitor accidentally discovered a basalt stone on which was carved a complete Hebrew inscription (below, Inscription #5). In September 1975, the author together with D. Groh, conducted another survey of the ruins of the Syrian village houses and the site's agricultural periphery.[211] In the course of the survey, a number of architectural items hitherto unknown to us were discovered, including two lintel (?) fragments with segments of inscriptions (below, Inscriptions #2 and #3). In 1975-1976, M. Ben-Ari and S. Bar-Lev completed the excavation and restoration of the hall and supervised the clearing of part of the ruins of the Syrian village, when the place was turned into a tourist site, as mentioned above. In the process of this work, two Aramaic inscription segments were discovered.[212] One of these belongs to Inscription #1, and we shall therefore designate it as Inscription #1a. The second inscription will be identified as #4.

This history of archaeological investigation at Qîsrîn has unfortunately been abbreviated in the entry on "Qasrin" in the *New Encyclopedia*. In the article's opening remarks, Z. Maʿoz writes:

> In 1978, a stratigraphic probe was conducted under the synagogue floor by Bar-Lev and Z. Maʿoz. A new series of excavations was carried out in the synagogue from 1982 to 1984, on behalf of the Israel Department of

---

[210] In continuation of the mosque theory which Maʿoz especially developed in his 1988 article with Ann Killebrew, he insists that the platform upon which we found the sheikh's tomb is "a 13th century platform outside of the mosque; this was used for prayer in the summer." (Maʿoz & Killebrew, "Ancient Qasrin," p. 5). We can only note that this determination has no basis.

[211] See Urman, "Qasrin," pp. 2-3.

[212] My thanks to S. Bar-Lev here also, who generously allowed me to publish these inscription segments.

Antiquities and Museums (today the Israel Antiquities Authority), under the
direction of Ma'oz, R. Hachlili, and A. Killebrew. Excavations in the village were begun in 1983, directed by Killebrew. An area of about 1,250 sq.
m. was cleared in the northern part of the village, including the synagogue
and domestic buildings.[213]

This paragraph leads the reader to several inaccurate conclusions. First,
Ma'oz and Bar-Lev were not the first to carry out exploratory stratigraphic
excavations beneath the so-called "synagogue floor." The excavations I carried out in the northern part of the hall over two seasons conducted such
probes. M. Ben-Ari and S. Bar-Lev carried out similar excavations in 1975-
1976, in both the southern and northern parts of the hall.[214] Second, the excavations conducted by Ma'oz, Hachlili, and Killebrew in the years of 1982-
1984 were primarily in the rooms east of the synagogue and not within
it.[215] Third, in the final sentence of the quote, Ma'oz attributes to himself
and Killebrew the excavation of "An area of about 1,250 sq. m....in the
northern part of the village, *including the synagogue* and domestic buildings."[216] But in 1988 he wrote: "During the 1983-1986 seasons, we opened
a 1200 square-meter segment (40 meters north-south and 30 meters east-

[213] Thus in Ma'oz & Killebrew, "Qaṣrin—1," p. 1423 and Ma'oz & Killebrew,
"Qaṣrin—2," p. 1219. Parentheses mine.

[214] To our regret, from the mid-1970's until the writing of these lines, M. Ben-Ari and S.
Bar-Lev have not published the results of their seasons of excavation there, for the two
ceased their archaeological work and turned to other things. Perhaps their new work is
important, for Bar-Lev became a leader of the Israeli settlements in the Golan and has
served as head of the Qaṣrin City Council since this new city was established. Still, it is to be
hoped that when they free themselves of these occupations, they will publish the results of
their excavations at the site.

[215] See note 1 on page 18 of Ma'oz & Killebrew, "Ancient Qaṣrin," "Rachel Hachlili
was also one of those asked by the council (the local council of Qaṣrin—D.U.) to begin a
new excavation (at Qîsrîn—D.U.). *The spring 1982 season concentrated on the cleaning and
recording of the architectural fragments.*" (emphasis mine—D.U.) This last sentence
indicates that, in the first season, the excavators did not concern themselves with excavation
at the area but only with cleaning and recording the archaeological items. Unfortunately,
Ma'oz fails to give proper credit to the archaeologists who studied the site prior to him. His
implication that the author, as well as M. Ben-Ari and S. Bar-Lev in their turn, did not clean
and register all the archaeological artifacts that were discovered in the excavations and
various surveys conducted at the site is preposterous. Indeed, a filing cabinet full of
material—reports concerning these sites and others, including photographs—was transferred
by M. Ben-Ari and S. Bar-Lev to Z. Ma'oz when he became the archaeologist for the Golan
District in the Israel Antiquities Authority. He continues his lack of courtesy to previous
excavators when he says, "The later, medieval additions to the synagogue were recorded,
examined, and partially dismantled;" Who did the work he fails to give credit for? Primarily
the expeditions led by the author, Ben-Ari, and Bar-Lev—not by the team led by Ma'oz,
Hachlili, and Killebrew. He goes on to say, "In 1983, investigations of the village
commenced. From 1983 through 1987, excavations of the village and synagogue have been
under the directorship of the authors." Again, he fails to acknowledge the site's previous
excavators.

[216] See note 213. Emphasis mine.

west) *east of the synagogue*."[217] Thus, although Ma'oz and his colleagues excavated the ancient village of Qîsrîn, the synagogue was largely excavated by others well before their arrival on the scene.

Finally, it should be noted that a final report detailing the shard finds and the plans of the stratigraphic cross-sections has not yet been published from the "stratigraphic probe" conducted in 1978 by Bar-Lev and Ma'oz.[218]

To summarize our criticism of the publications on the excavations at Qîsrîn by Ma'oz, and Ma'oz and Killebrew, we emphasize that the problem is not one of giving credit to previous excavators but rather one of the reliability of their writings. One hopes that Ma'oz and Killebrew, instead of overlooking archaeological excavations prior to their work in the Golan area, will dedicate their efforts to full and reliable publication of the excavations they conducted around the complex of the Jewish public structure at Qîsrîn. Until such a publication appears, it is better that the readers and publishers of encyclopedias be aware of the incomplete and misleading character of the Ma'oz-Killebrew reports on the excavations at Qîsrîn.

We shall now turn to the various inscriptions discovered at the site, from which we can learn more about the Jewish community that lived there during the rabbinic period.[219]

Inscription #1

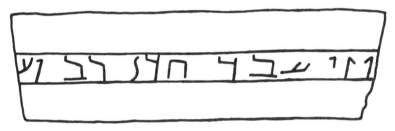

FIG. 1 Inscription #1.

---

[217] Ma'oz & Killebrew, "Ancient Qasrin," p. 11. Emphasis mine.

[218] Instead of such a report, we find in Ma'oz & Killebrew, "Ancient Qasrin," p. 7, the following statement by Ma'oz, "In the summer of 1978, Bar-Lev and I excavated *a small probe* in the south-western corner of the synagogue. Three main floors and one working surface that was related to the use and construction of the synagogue were recovered. Based on the ceramic evidence from this probe *and on my survey and excavations at the synagogues of Horvat Kanaf and 'Ein Nashôt,* I have concluded that the synagogue (at Qîsrîn—D.U.) was first erected in the Byzantine period (approximately the 4th-6th centuries C.E.)." (Emphasis mine—D.U.) It seems that there is nothing better than this statement to attest to the scientific standards of its author and his ability, as an archaeologist, to provide research with firmly based dates.

[219] I discussed these inscriptions at length about ten years ago, but in Hebrew. See Urman, "Kazrin Inscriptions," pp. 531-544. There the reader will be able to find copies and photographs which, for technical reasons, we are prevented from presenting here.

This portion of an Aramaic inscription was engraved between two parallel straight lines on a well-hewn basalt stone. The stone's exact place in the public structure is unclear; it may have served as an architrave in the hall's first stage. The stone fragment is 1 m. long and 32 cm. high. The height of the inscription's letters is 5-7 cm. The reading of the inscription is clear: "[...]וזי עבד הדן רבוע[...]"

At the first reports of this find, we suggested completing the reading thus:[220] "....ע]וזי עבד הדן רבוע[ה." That is: "...X son of U]zzi made (in the sense of "donated to make") this accommodation[...."[221] J. Naveh, who included the inscription in his book, accepted our reading and added: "There is no way of knowing the nature of this accommodation mentioned here; it may be that it was some architectural part of the synagogue structure."[222]

After a prolonged study of this inscription, we suggest interpreting this רבוע ("square") as a room or hall in which it was customary to have 'רבעות' that is, 'סעודות,' group meals or ritual repasts. These meals often followed the fulfillment of an obligatory religious ceremonial.[223] J. N. Epstein and S. Lieberman have already shown that the 'רבעה' (feast) is mentioned in Y. Shabbat 4:2, 7a: "R. Yonah and R. Yose visited the house of study of Bar Ulla where there was a 'feast.'" And in Y. Shabbat 20:1, 17c, they found, "In the days of R. Judah b. Pazi there was a 'feast' in the house of study...." In his book Ha-Yerushalmi ki-Peshuto, S. Lieberman further explained the second passage: "It seems that the regular 'reclining' (at a meal) in the talmud and the special place where one reclined during the meal was called רבעה.'"[224] The revuah should therefore be explained as "a known term for some sort of gathering with food and drink at which people were reclined."[225]

Y. Megillah 3:4, 74a, suggests that some sages held that synagogues and houses of study should not be a place for eating:[226] "Houses of assembly [that is, synagogues] and houses of study, one does not behave in them

---

[220] Urman, "Golan—7," p. 2; Urman, "Hellenistic," p. 462.

[221] See Naveh, Mosaic, pp. 9-10.

[222] Naveh, Mosaic, p. 147, Inscription #110.

[223] Concerning group meals and meals associated with religious occasions in the traditions and customs of the Jews of the Land of Israel in the rabbinic period, see A. Oppenheimer, "Groups that were in Jerusalem," in A. Oppenheimer, U. Rappaport and M. Stern, eds., Chapters in the History of Jerusalem during the Second Temple—In Memory of Abraham Schalit (Jerusalem, 1981), pp. 178-190 (in Hebrew). See, especially, pp. 185-189, and the references there to earlier research. On the רבועה, see also Meitlis, "Revua," pp. 465-466.

[224] S. Lieberman, The Literal Jerusalem Talmud (Jerusalem, 1935), p. 213 (in Hebrew).

[225] J. N. Epstein, "On the Remains of the Jerusalem Talmud," Tarbiz 3 (1932): 243 (in Hebrew); S. Lieberman, "Jerusalem Talmud Fragments," Tarbiz 6 (1935): 234 (in Hebrew); J. N. Epstein, "On the Jerusalem Talmud Fragments," Tarbiz 6 (1935): 236-237 (in Hebrew).

[226] See J. N. Epstein, "On the Jerusalem Talmud Fragments," Tarbiz 6 (1935): 236 (in Hebrew).

frivolously, one does not eat or drink in them...."[227] There seems to be significant disagreement on this matter, however, for Y. Pesahim 1:1, 27b, relates the following story. "R. Jeremiah inquired: 'What of houses of assembly and houses of study regarding checking for leaven?' It is required because (leaven) is brought in on Sabbath and New Moons." Y. Moed Qatan 2:3, 81b (=Y. Sanh. 15:2, 26a-b) relates: "R. Yohanan said: 'One may borrow money even at interest for a society [whose purpose is fulfilling a specific] religious commandment and for sanctifying the New Month....' R. Yohanan would go to the synagogue in the morning and collect crumbs, eat them, and say: 'May my lot be among those who ate here last night.'" These passages reveal that on Sabbaths, New Moons, and gatherings of the "religious commandment societies," it was customary to feast in the synagogues and the houses of study. These meals linked to religious ceremonies, as well as other meals,[228] were probably held in special rooms or halls set aside for this purpose in the synagogues and houses of study of the rabbinic period.[229]

Until the inscription's continuation is found, we will not know how to complete the word רבוע— [ה]רבוע or רבוע[תה]—for this is the first time that this word occurs in Jewish dedicatory inscriptions. Support for the completion [רבוע[תה comes from the appearance of the word רבעתא in Nabatean dedication inscriptions. In a bilingual inscription—Nabatean Aramaic and Greek—that was discovered in 1866 in Sidon, the editor of the *CIS* reads:[230]

דא רבעתא די...
אסרתגא בר זנ]אל...
לדושרא אלה[נ]א בירח...שנת]
5 לחרתת]מלך נבטו...

and completes the Greek formula: [Ξεῶ Δουσαρῆ ὁ δεῖνα Ζ]ωίλου σδρατη-γός [ἀνέσδη]σεν.

Similar formulas have also been found in an inscription at Ḥaraba, near Boṣrâ:[231]

---

[227] And also see Tos. Meg. 3(2):7 (pp. 224-225 in the Zuckermandel edition; p. 353 in the Lieberman edition); as well as B. Meg. 28a.

[228] See above, note 223.

[229] Following a conversation on this matter with my teacher Professor S. Lieberman, he wrote me the following, "...From the sources (Jerusalem Talmud Shabbat 4, 7a; 20, 17c) it is clear that in the houses of study there were 'רבעתה' places where they ate."—from his letter to me of Wednesday, Rosh Ḥodesh Elul [Elul 1], 5733 [1973].

[230] See *Corpus Inscriptionum Semiticarum,* vol. 2 (Paris, 1893), pp. 188-189, Inscription #160.

[231] R. Dussaud and F. Macler, *Voyage archéologique au Safâ et dans le Djebel ed-Druse* (Paris, 1901), p. 195, Inscription #77; *idem, Mission dans les régions désertiques de la Syrie moyenne* (Paris, 1903), p. 313, Inscription #19.

דא רבעתא די עבדו ענמו
ומענאלהי בני יענמרו...

and in Boṣrâ itself:[232]

[דא ר]בעתא די ע]נבד]
...[בר (ב)דרו לאלה

These three inscriptions are undoubtedly dedicatory inscriptions. In all three, the names of the donors who contributed for the erection of the רבעתא are mentioned. From the Sidon inscription, we also learn that the רבעתא was dedicated to the god Dushara, the head god of the Nabatean pantheon.

The scholars who dealt with these three Nabatean inscriptions had difficulty translating the word ר,רבעתא,[233] and have in fact provided no satisfactory explanation. But this has no impact on our study, for I brought these inscriptions to point out the ending 'תא—' at the end of the word רבעתא. This suggests that Inscription #1 should be completed רבוע[תה]. And furthermore, our analysis which links Qîsrîn's רבוע[ה] or רבוע[תה] with the Nabatean רבעתא sheds light on the latter's meaning—it signifies a hall for ritual meals.[234]

Inscription Segment #1a

This second inscription fragment forms part of Inscription #1. Its letters were carved between two straight parallel lines, with a space of about 10 cm. between them—just like the letters of Inscription #1. The manner of formation and the style of the two fragments' letters is quite similar, and their heights are identical, about 5-7 cm. The length of the second stone fragment is 38 cm., its height is 33 cm., and its thickness is 22 cm.

FIG. 2 Inscription #1a.

[232] E. Littmann, *Publications of the Princeton University Archaeological Expedition to Syria in 1904-1905 and 1909, Division IV, Semitic Inscriptions, Section A, Nabatean Inscriptions from the Southern Hauran* (Leyden, 1914), pp. 58-59, Inscription #71.

[233] See the publications mentioned in notes 230-232 and especially that of E. Littmann (note 232), pp. 4-5.

[234] On the halls for feasts and ritual feasts among the Nabateans see, for example, Nelson Glueck's comments in his book *Deities and Dolphins* (New York, 1965), pp. 163-191.

Its reading is clear: "...[ר]ין מנין[...." We suggest completing it as either
"...[ת[רין מנין]..." or "...עש[רין מנין]...." That is to say, "...two minahs..." or
"...twenty minahs...."

Of course, two or twenty may not be the entire number. It may be that
before the number "two" or "twenty" there was another number indicating
"tens" (before the two) or "hundreds," similar to that written in Daniel 6:2,
"It pleased Darius to set over the kingdom *one hundred and twenty* satraps,
who should be throughout the whole kingdom...." Still, this possibility depends upon the value of the *minah* coin at the time of the inscription. The
minah, or *maneh* in Hebrew, as we know, is mentioned many times in the
talmudic literature, but its exact value in Palestine at different times during
the rabbinic period has yet to be ascertained.[235] This makes it difficult to estimate the position of this inscription fragment relative to Inscription #1. It
may be that Ben Uzzi was the donor of a number of *minah*s, but this remains speculation at the present. For answers to these and other questions,
we must wait until other parts of the inscription are uncovered.

Let us further point out that this is the first time that the *minah* appears
in a dedication inscription of a public Jewish building of the rabbinic period.
In the rabbinic-era Jewish dedication inscriptions found thus far in Palestine,
the only contributions mentioned are of "one *tremis*,"[236] "three grams,"[237]
"a half *dinar*,"[238] "one *dinar*,"[239] "three *dinars*,"[240] and "five gold *dinars*."[241]

Inscription #2

FIG. 3 Inscription #2.

---

[235] See D. Sperber, "On the Value of the Maneh," *Talpioth* 9 (1970): 591-611 (in
Hebrew), especially p. 611, note 74.

[236] See Naveh, *Mosaic*, p. 57, Inscription #33; p. 60, Inscription #34; p. 62, Inscription
#35; p. 114, Inscription #74.

[237] Naveh, *Mosaic*, p. 57, Inscription #33.

[238] Naveh, *Mosaic*, pp. 62-64, Inscription #35.

[239] Naveh, *Mosaic*, p. 60, Inscription #34.

[240] Naveh, *Mosaic*, pp. 92-93, Inscription #57.

[241] Naveh, *Mosaic*, p. 54, Inscription #32.

The original use of this basalt fragment is unclear. The stone was found with its upper part and sides broken; only on the bottom can the remains of the original edges be seen. The length of the stone fragment is 42 cm. and its height is 30 cm. Its thickness is unclear because it was examined while part of the wall of an abandoned Syrian building. Of the inscription, the remains of two lines were preserved (letter height, 4-6 cm.):

The reading of the upper line is difficult since its letters were severely damaged when the stone fragment was set into the wall of the Syrian building. In the bottom line we read: "...]זֹקחלפתהֹהוֹעֵ[...." I suggest completing it as, "...אתח]זֹק חלפתה וע]בד...," that is, "...Halafta contributed and made...."[242]

The formula אתחזק ועבד ("contributed and made") has been known for some time from the Jewish dedication inscriptions in Palestine. For example, the Aramaic dedication inscription discovered by J. Braslavi (Braslawski) at 'Ibillîn[243] has been deciphered by Naveh as follows:[244]

דכיר לנֹטב] ברוֹך
כֹסֹדֹריי דהכה
[א]תֹחזק וע]בד]
הֹ]ד]ין תרעה
[אמ]ן] שלום

Naveh translates it as, "May he be remembered for [good] Baruk/the Alexandrian (?) who (?) here/contributed and ma[de] /th[is] gate/[Ame]n Peace."

Another Aramaic dedication inscription contains this formula. It was uncovered in the mosaic floor of a Jewish public structure at Jericho. Naveh renders it as follows:[245]

דכירן לטב יהוי דכרנהון לטב כל
קהלה קדי]שה רביה ווערירה דסיע
יתהון מלכיה דעלמה ואתחזקון ועבדון
פסיפסה דידע שמהתון ודבניהון ודאנשי
בתיהון יכתוב יתהון בספר חייה]עם כל]
צדיקיה חברין לכל ישראל שלֹ]ום אמ]ן]

---

[242] In translating the word 'אתחזק' as 'תרם' ('contributed') we have followed Naveh (Naveh, *Mosaic*, p. 10).

[243] See J. Braslawski, "The New Inscription of 'Abellîn," *Yedi'ot* 2, no. 1 (1934): 31 (in Hebrew); "A Synagogue Inscription at 'Abellîn," *Yedi'ot* 2, nos. 3-4 (1935): 10-13 (in Hebrew).

[244] See Naveh, *Mosaic*, pp. 43-44, Inscription #21. And also see what H. L. Ginsberg and S. Klein noted about this inscription, *Yedi'ot* 2, nos. 3-4 (1935): 47-48 (in Hebrew).

[245] Naveh, *Mosaic*, pp. 103-105, Inscription #69. For a recent discussion of this inscription, see N. Wieder, "The Jericho Inscription and Jewish Liturgy," *Tarbiz*, 52, no. 4 (1983): 557-579 (in Hebrew) (and especially see there pp. 563-565); and similarly in the comment of M. A. Friedman, "The Verb 'אתחזק' in Palestinian Synagogue Inscriptions," *Tarbiz* 53, no. 4 (1984): 605-606 (in Hebrew).

Naveh translates it as:

> Remembered for good. May their memory be for good. All
> the h[ol]y congregation, adults and children, who
> with the King of the Universe's help contributed and built
> the mosaic. He Who knows their names, and their children's, and of the
>   members
> of their households, may He inscribe them in the Book of Life [with all]
> the righteous friends of all Israel. Pea[ce. Amen]."

Similar formulations have been found in other Aramaic dedication inscriptions uncovered at Beth-Shean,[246] at Na'aran,[247] and at Khirbet Susiya.[248]

The name חלפתה appears here in its Galilean form.[249] This name is
known from rabbinic literature as the name of a number of palestinian *tannaim* and *amoraim*.[250] It is also found in Greek in a burial inscription from
the Jewish cemetery of Jaffa.[251]

If the suggested completion of the bottom line of Inscription #2 is correct, then the inscription was written in Aramaic. It was a dedicatory inscription which identified a donor named חלפתה who contributed to building
some part—or perhaps all—of a Jewish public structure at Qîsrîn.

Inscription #3

The inscription was discovered incorporated in secondary use in the same
abandoned Syrian building in which Inscription #2 was found. It may be a
continuation of the other, but this is uncertain. The inscription was carved
on a basalt stone whose location and function in the ancient building remains unclear. The stone's dimensions: length—36.5 cm., height—29 cm.,
thickness unknown (the stone is embedded in the wall of a Syrian building).

FIG. 4 Inscription #3.

---

[246] Naveh, *Mosaic*, pp. 77-78, Inscription #46.

[247] Naveh, *Mosaic*, pp. 93-101, Inscriptions #58, 60, 64, 65.

[248] Naveh, *Mosaic*, p.117, Inscription #76; pp. 122-123, Inscriptions #83-84.

[249] See E. Y. Kutscher, *Hebrew and Aramaic Studies* (Jerusalem, 1977), pp. 178 ff. (in
Hebrew).

[250] See Hyman, *Toldoth,* vol. 2, pp. 452-454.

[251] See Klein, *ha-Yishuv*, p. 81, Inscription #13.

The inscription contains two lines, the height of its letters: 4-8 cm. The transcription is:

‫...הבל...‬

‫...זר שובי...‬

From the transcription, it is clear that we have here only a segment of an inscription. To our regret, most of the letters in the top line were damaged when the stone was set into the wall of the Syrian building, and we therefore cannot complete anything there. I suggest this completion of the lower line, "....‫אליע]זר שובי...‬."

The name ‫אליעזר‬ or ‫אלעזר‬ was widespread among palestinian Jews during the rabbinic period and need not be discussed here.[252] The name ‫שובי‬, by contrast, has so far not been found among the inscriptions of the period. It may be that it comprises a nickname based on a place-name, like the fourth generation *tanna*, R. Simeon Shezori, who is named after the Galilean village Shezor.[253] Another possibility is that it constitutes a form stemming from the biblical name "Shobi" or "Shobai." Shobi is mentioned in 2 Samuel 17:27 as one of the men who supported David when he fled from Absalom—Shobi son of Nahash from Rabbath-Ammon. The second form, Shobai, appears in Ezra 2:42 and in Nehemiah 7:45 as the name of a family of Levite gatekeepers. It is possible, therefore, that the Eliezer or Elazar mentioned in the inscription was called ‫[ה]שובי‬, "(the) Shobi," because of his relationship to this family. If this explanation is correct, we might expect to find the definite article, 'ha,' with this name-form, but it is often missing, as in the case of R. Simeon Shezori.

The name "Shobi" or "Shobai" appears in a number of archaeological finds. In 1914, P. Schroeder published a Hebrew seal that seems to have been found at Usha. Upon it appears the inscription ‫לשבי ב/ן אלוכר‬.[254] The name "Shobi" also appears in a Hebrew letter from the seventh century B.C.E. uncovered at Meẓad Ḥashavyahu. In lines 7-8 of the letter, the name ‫חשביהו בן שבי‬ is written.[255] J. Naveh, who deciphered the letter, theorizes that the Hasbayyahu who is mentioned was a Levite.[256] Finally, the name

---

[252] We shall only point out that these name forms have already been found in the Jewish dedication inscriptions from the Golan, and see the section on Dabûra, Inscriptions #1 and #6.

[253] Maimonides, in his introduction to the Order of "Seeds," explained that he was called "Shezori" because of his craft; but recent generations have explained it as did the author of *Kaftor va-Ferah*, i.e. "he was called Shezori after the name of his city...." And see *Kaftor va-Ferah* (Lunz edition), p. 614. See Margalioth, pp. 871-872, and also Klein, *ha-Yishuv*, p. 154.

[254] P. Schroeder, "Vier Siegelsteine mit semitischen Legenden," *ZDPV* 37 (1914): 174-176.

[255] J. Naveh, "A Hebrew Letter from Meẓad Ḥashavyahu," *Yediot* 25 (1961): 120 (in Hebrew).

[256] *Ibid.*, pp. 123, 126.

"Shobi" or "Shobai" is also found incised on two ossuaries from the second-temple period, published by E. L. Sukenik in 1932. On one ossuary Sukenik read, "שבי בן...‏" and on the second, "שבי בן יהוסף‏."[257]

Inscription #4

This basalt architrave fragment is decorated with a relief band in the egg-and-dart style. The fragment's dimensions are: length at the top—27 cm., length at the bottom 23 cm., height—25 cm., and thickness at the bottom—20 cm. Of the Aramaic inscription, only one word survived, "דמבר....‏"[258] It can be translated as, "...that is from the outside." From the fact that after the word, for a length of about 10 cm. until the break in the stone, there is no indication of anything written, we deduce that the inscription originally had a second line under the word that now remains; indeed, the bottom part of the stone is missing.

דמבר

FIG. 5 Inscription #4.

It seems that this fragment derives from a dedication inscription concerning an unknown donor who contributed to building something *outside* the walls of a public Jewish building in Qîsrîn. A description of a place, a part, or an item contributed in a public Jewish building during the rabbinic period is not new among Jewish dedication inscriptions discovered in Palestine.[259]

In an attempt to assess what might be set *outside* a public Jewish structure in Palestine in the period under discussion, we turn to the Y. Erubin 1:1, 18c:

> Rabbi permits an *exedra* in Beth-She'arim. How many columns did it have? R. Jacob bar Aḥa said, "(This is a dispute between) R. Hiyya (and) R. Yose —one says 'six' and one says 'eight.'" Said R. Jacob bar Aḥa, "They do not differ: he who says 'six' is not counting the two *outside;* he who says 'eight' is counting the two *outside*." (Emphasis mine.)

In line with this passage, perhaps the anonymous donor of Qîsrîn contributed to the building of 'outside columns'?[260] We must wait until the

---

[257] E. L. Sukenik, "Two Jewish Hypogea," *JPOS* 12 (1932): 26-27.

[258] The height of its letters is 2.5 cm.

[259] See, for example, the section on Dabûra, Inscription #1.

[260] Remains of *exedrae* with 'exterior columns' were uncovered near a number of public Jewish buildings of the rabbinic period in Palestine. Typical are those discovered at Nabratein, Eshtemoa, Bar'am and also at Umm el-Qanâtir in the Golan. And see Avigad,

bottom part of the inscription is found to determine whether our suggestion is correct.

Inscription #5

On a basalt stone slab discovered lying between the houses of the Syrian village and out of its original location, the Hebrew inscription copied below was found:

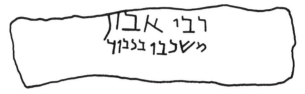

FIG. 6 Inscription #5.

The slab is 108 cm. long; 28 cm. high, and 22 cm. thick (see PL. 40b). The height of its letters ranges between 3 and 9 cm. The inscription is whole and its transcription is clear:

רבי אבון
משכבו בכבוד

The translation is: "Rabbi Abun, may his resting place be in honor."

The formulation "may he rest in honor" makes it clear that this is a burial inscription. The form of the stone slab, crafted with great simplicity, indicates that the slab was set in a memorial structure erected over the grave. The location of the grave has not yet been discovered because, as stated, the slab was not lying in its original site.

Among the Jewish burial inscriptions discovered previously in Palestine, only one bears an inscription with a similar formulation. This inscription was discovered in Catacomb 20 at Beth She'arim and is dated between the late second century and the mid-fourth century C.E.[261] It reads:[262]

רבי יהושע בירבי הלל
בן אטיון משׁ[כ]בׁן
בשלום

Nabratein, Eshtemoa, Bar'am and also at Umm el-Qanâṭir in the Golan. And see Avigad, "Bar'am," p. 148; Yeivin, "Eshtemoa," p. 423; Meyers, "Nabratein," pp. 1077-1079. And for Umm el-Qanâṭir see our discussion of the site below.

[261] Avigad, *Beth She'arim*, p. 115.

[262] *Ibid.*, p. 243, Inscription #16.

Avigad translates it:[263] "Rabbi Joshua, son of Rabbi Hillel, son of Ation (may his) res[ting place] be in peace."

The dates of the corpus of the Hebrew burial inscriptions at Beth She'arim in general, and the date of the "Rabbi Joshua" inscription in particular, suggest that the date of the "Rabbi Abun" inscription belong to the same time frame, namely, between the second and the fourth centuries. We could propose a more precise date for the inscription only if we could identify more precisely the "Rabbi Abun" mentioned.

The rabbinic literature, especially the Palestinian Talmud, and the palestinian *midrashim*, reveal how common the name Abun was among the palestinian and babylonian *amoraim*.[264] Yet only two *amoraim*, whom scholarship identifies as father and son,[265] are cited as "Rabbi Abun" without further specification.[266] Rabbi Abun, the father, lived from the late third century into the early fourth century,[267] and Rabbi Abun the son who was apparently born close to the time of his father's death[268] and lived, then, in the second half of the fourth century.[269]

It is possible that this inscription belongs to the grave of Rabbi Abun the father. Two points suggest that it is the father rather than the son. First, it is logical to assume that on the tombstone of Rabbi Abun the son there would have been some a word or symbol to differentiate him from his father. Second, Bacher and others have shown that Rabbi Abun the son is the Rabbi Abun whose relationships with Rabbi Mana were strained.[270] One of the passages which alludes to the controversies between them indicates that Rabbi Abun the son resided in Tiberias, not in the Golan.[271] Qohelet

---

[263] *Idem, ibid.*

[264] See Albeck, *Introduction*, pp. 669-681.

[265] See Albeck, *Introduction*, p. 385; W. Bacher, *Die Agada der Palästinischen Amoräer*, (3 vols. 1892-1899), vol. 3, Part 3, p. 1; Margalioth, pp. 782-786; and also Y. D. Gilat, "Avin," *EJ*, vol. 3, p. 971.

[266] When we write "without further specification" we mean there is designation neither of the father's name, as, for example, in the case of R. Abun bar Bisna (Y. Yeb. 1:1, 2d), nor of his ancestry, such as R. Abun the Levite (B. Ber. 64a).

[267] An *amora* of the third and fourth generation. See Albeck, *Introduction*, p. 352; Bacher (above note 265), pp. 1-8; Margalioth, p. 782.

[268] See "Said R. Abun, I am free of the obligation to Honor Thy father and mother." They said that when his mother conceived him, his father died. When she gave birth to him, she died." (Y. Peah 1:1, 15c; Y. Qiddushin 1:8, 61b); "The day Rav Abin died (alternate reading: Abun) R. Abin (alternate reading: Abun,) his son was born...." (Genesis Rabbah 58:2, p. 620 in the Theodor-Albeck edition).

[269] A fifth-generation Palestinian *amora*; see Albeck, *Introduction*, p. 385; Bacher (above, note 265), p.1; Margalioth, p. 784.

[270] Albeck, *Introduction*, pp. 385-386; Bacher (see above, note 265), p. 7; Margalioth, pp. 784-785.

[271] "Rabbi Abun made these gates of the Great House of Study. Came to him Rabbi Mana and asked, 'Father-in-law, what have you done?' Answered he, 'Israel has ignored his Maker and built temples—Are there no people who will tire themselves in the study of

Rabbah to Qohelet 11:3 even hints that he died in Tiberias and was buried there:[272]

> R. Isaac said: "If you see troubles approaching, [know that] they come upon the earth, meaning, on account of Israel who are called earth, as it is said, 'For ye shall be a delightsome land.' (Malachi 3:12). If the time has come for a rabbinical scholar to depart from the world—as, e.g., R. Mona (Mana) in Sepphoris and *R. Bun (Abun) in Tiberias*—in the south, or in the north, in the place where the tree falleth, there shall it be. There will all Israel [gather] and bestow loving kindness upon him...." (Emphasis mine.)

By contrast, later sources suggest that Rabbi Abun the father lived not only in the Golan, but specifically in Qîsrîn. The *Midrash ha-Ne'lam* to the Book of Ruth (29a), states, "Rabbi (A)bun spent his whole life in Qîsrîn." Without becoming entangled in the problems of the accuracy of the information about Palestine in the Zohar literature,[273] let us only say that in this citation, it is possible that the author of *Midrash ha-Ne'lam* to the Book of Ruth had an authentic tradition—for it is written in Palestinian Aramaic and with the palestinian custom of dropping the initial 'aleph' of a name. If Rabbi Abun had not "been in Qîsrîn all of his life," he certainly would not have been buried there, for—in the words of Qohelet—"in the place where the tree falleth, there shall it be" (Qoh. 11:3).

If our argument that Inscription #5 belongs to the tombstone of Rabbi Abun the father, then this inscription dates to the middle of the fourth century C.E.

Finally, let me point out that the Qîsrîn in the Golan is the same Qîsrîn mentioned in our sources as the residence of a number of the most important palestinian sages in the third and fourth centuries. Following the discovery of the inscription of Rabbi Eliezer ha-Qappar's academy at Dabûra, I suggested that Qîsrîn in the Golan was the Qîsrîn where the Academy of Rabbi Hoshaya the Great was located.[274] The late Prof. Lieberman, in his work, *The Talmud of Caesarea*, concluded at that time "that the Qîsrîn Academy

---

Torah?'" (Y. Shekalim 5:7, 49b). From a baraita at Y. Sanhedrin 17:1, 28a (or its parallel at Y. Shabbath 6:2, 8a)—"a person should not wear new shoes or sandals unless he has walked in them during the [previous] day. How far should he walk in them?...The Tiberians say, 'The distance from the Great House of Study until Rabbi Hoshaiyah's shop.'" And likewise, from additional places in our sources, it is clear that "the Great House of Study" was in Tiberias. Also see S Klein, "When was Mosaic Pictorial Art Introduced into Palestine?" *Yedi'ot* 1, no. 2 (1933): 15-17 (in Hebrew).

[272] Bacher also held the same opinion (see above, note 265), p. 7, note 3.

[273] G. Scholem, "Questions in the Critique of the Zohar from His Knowledge of Palestine," *Zion* 1 (1926): 40-55 (in Hebrew).

[274] See Urman, "Bar Qappara—2," pp. 163-172; Urman, "Eliezer ha-Qappar," pp. 7-25. I recommend that the interested reader first read the 1985 article and only then that of 1983.

did not cease (to function) from the time of Rabbi Hoshaya Rabbah (and perhaps even Bar Qappara) until the days of R. Yose bar Bun...."[275] He also suggested that "perhaps R. Yose b. Bun also resided in Qîsrîn," and brought support for his theory.[276] Now that the inscription of the tombstone of Rabbi Abun has been discovered at Qîsrîn in the Golan, it is time to re-examine the tangle of the references to Rabbi Yose bar Abun in our sources[277] and to determine if there is any ground for the conclusion of the researchers who postulated that Rabbi Yose bar Abun was the son of Rabbi Abun, the father.[278] In any case, it seems to me that the proof which is the most supportive of the identity suggestion, is the picture of the density of Jewish settlement around Qîsrîn of the Golan during the rabbinic period.[279]

SELEUCIA (Σελεύκεια)

This Golan city, founded in the second century B.C.E., was apparently named after a Seleucid king who ruled the region during that time.[280] The city was captured in 83-80 B.C.E. by Alexander Jannaeus,[281] and after the conquest Jews apparently began to settle there.[282] Its status as a city disappeared over time,[283] and by the Great Rebellion against the Romans in 66-74 C.E. it is mentioned as one of the two Golan villages (in addition to Gamala) that Josephus fortified when he commanded the rebellion in Galilee.[284] From Josephus' description it appears that Seleucia was well-defended by nature, but despite it natural defenses—improved upon by Josephus—he relates that the villagers decided not to fight.[285] As a result, it played an unimportant role in the rebellion and earns only a brief description—not enough to learn anything significant about this Jewish Golan set-

---

[275] Lieberman, *Caesarea*, p. 10.

[276] Lieberman, *Caesarea*, p. 10.

[277] Albeck, for example, theorized that there were two *amoraim* by this name, and see in his book Albeck, *Introduction*, pp. 336-337. And also see Z. W. Rabinowitz, *Sha'are Torath Babel: Notes and Comments on The Babylonian Talmud*, E. Z. Melamed, ed. (Jerusalem: Jewish Theological Seminary of America, 1961), p. 446 (in Hebrew).

[278] See, for example, Hyman, *Toldoth,* vol. 2, p. 717.

[279] Study the map of the Jewish sites in the Golan accompanying this article and see that around the new city of Qasrîn—within a radius not exceeding three miles, there have been discovered to date ten sites containing the remains of Jewish public buildings. Until now, scholars remained unaware of this great density of Jewish settlements in Palestine in the rabbinic period; it was known neither from archaeological finds nor from literary sources.

[280] See Avi-Yonah, *Palestine,* p. 35; Ilan, *Golan*, p. 191.

[281] See *Ant.* XIII §§ 393-394; *War* I §§ 104-105; *Syncellus* I §§ 558-559.

[282] See Stern, "Judea," p. 31.

[283] See Avi-Yonah, *Palestine,* p. 49.

[284] *War* II § 574; *Vita* § 187.

[285] *War* IV § 4.

tlement. He reveals only, in *War* IV § 2, that "Seleucia was near Lake Semechonitis (=Lake Ḥuleh)" and this remark makes clear that the site of Seleucia should be sought on the slopes of the Golan facing Lake Ḥuleh.

Despite Josephus' comment in *War*, Schumacher in the 1880's suggested identifying Seleucia with a ruined called Selûkîyeh, near which the Syrians later established a village called Quṣbiyye el-Jdeideh (sometimes designated as Selûkîyeh or Selûkiyye). In this identification, he followed an earlier suggestion by W. M. Thomson. Schumacher describes it as follows:

> Selûkîyeh—A ruin on the same named wâdî, not far from a spring also sim-
> ilarly named, situated on a small hill with a number of large unhewn build-
> ing stones. The ancient remains, spreading over a large area, appear liter-
> ally to have been made level with the ground, for it is only at the highest
> point that one can perhaps distinguish the foundations of a large square
> building and some smaller ones. On the southern bank of the wâdî extended
> remains are also to be found. At the present day only cattle folds rise out of
> the ruins. Although without any further evidence than that presented by the
> affinity of names, I nevertheless believe to have found again the old
> Seleucia, built during the dominion of the Selenkiden, according to
> Josephus...a fortified city on the border of Agrippa's kingdom. It is true
> that the place of modern Selûkîyeh does not exactly correspond with the
> statement of Josephus, that Seleucia lay on the Lake Semechonitis,
> whereas in fact by its position the place is naturally protected....[286]

The identification suggested by Schumacher and Thomson was accepted until the Six Day War (1967).[287] After the war, the site was surveyed by a
team headed by S. Gutman; they named the site, at coordinates 2190-2653,
"Tell Seleucia."[288] Gutman reported a tell with a ruin on it, and to the west,
at its foot, he described springs, some of them hot. At the northern and
western part of the tell, Gutman and his team made out the remains of a city
wall with a number of entrances in it. At the tell's southern end, the team
found foundations of buildings, and at its northern end, the remains of a
large building of hewn stones. Most shards at the site, according to
Gutman's publication, were found in the tell's southern area, and derive
from the Early Bronze Age. They also found flint items from the Early and
Middle Paleolithic periods.[289]

In 1968, the author surveyed the site and found that the area of the ancient site was about 35 dunams, yielding shards from the Hellenistic,

---

[286] Schumacher, "Dscholan," p. 347; Schumacher, *Jaulân*, p. 237. At the end of the section, Schumacher points out that the present Selûkîyeh had been already mentioned by W. M. Thomson in his book, *The Land and the Book* (New York, 1883), p. 440.

[287] See Avi-Yonah, *Palestine*, p. 152.

[288] Epstein & Gutman, p. 271, Site #87.

[289] See previous note.

Roman, and Byzantine periods as well as the Bronze Age.[290] An examination of Gutman's unpublished original report shows that he too found shards from the Roman and early Byzantine periods near the remains of the monumental structure in the site's northern section,[291] but for some reason this was omitted from the survey's final publication.[292] Within the Syrian village of Quṣbiyye el-Jdeideh we found no antiquities, but occasionally we could see ancient building stones in the houses of residents that had been taken for secondary use as building stones.

The conclusion of our survey's report stated that without systematic archaeological excavation at the site, it would be difficult to date either the remains of the wall at the site or the monumental building whose remains appear at the site's northern end.[293]

Three years after our survey of Seleucia, and following our survey at nearby Kh. Quṣbiyye (see this ruin's discussion below), we suggested that the location of Seleucia should be identified with Kh. Quṣbiyye.[294] Today, I am no longer sure of this suggestion. Z. Ilan's suggestion that Seleucia should be identified with Dabûra is appealing, for Dabûra is naturally well fortified and is near Lake Ḥuleh.[295]

Today, then, three sites are candidates for identification as the ancient Seleucia. First, "Tell Seleucia," was proposed by Schumacher and Thomson primarily because the name of Selûkîyeh was preserved there. Second, Kh. Quṣbiyye was suggested by the author because of the survey's finds and because the name Selûkîyeh was preserved nearby. Third, Z. Ilan suggested Dabûra primarily because of its proximity to Lake Ḥuleh and its natural fortifications. To decide among these candidates is difficult. Systematic archaeological excavations at the sites may not solve the puzzle, but it would certainly increase our knowledge of Jewish communities on the Golan in general, and at these sites in particular, in the second-temple and/or rabbinic periods.

---

[290] D. Urman, "Selûkiyye," *Special Surveys Reports*, Archive of the Association for the Archaeological Survey of Israel, Israel Antiquities Authority, Jerusalem (in Hebrew); Urman, *List*, p. 11; Urman, *Golan*, p. 195, Site #85 and see the note for this site on pp. 212-213.

[291] The original report is in the site file in the Archive of the Association for the Archaeological Survey of Israel, Israel Antiquities Authority, Jerusalem.

[292] Epstein & Gutman, p. 271, Site #87.

[293] See D. Urman, "Selûkiyye," *Special Surveys Reports*, p. 11 (see note 290).

[294] See Urman, "Synagogue Sites," p. 28; Urman, "Golan—7," p. 2.

[295] Ilan, *Golan*, pp. 150-151.

KH. QUṢBIYYE (EL-KUSBÎYEH, EL-KUSEBÎYEH)

This ruin stands on a high hill west of the Yahûdiyye—Khushniyye road, at coordinates 2173-2645.

The ruin was first surveyed in 1884 by G. Schumacher. He described it in these words:

> El-Kusbîyeh—also called el-Kusebîyeh, is a heap of ruins south-west of Selûkîyeh. The highest point is occupied by a totally destroyed square building, on the slopes of which several foundations are to be seen, built of unhewn stones and fitted without mortar. A quantity of building rubbish and stones cover the immediate surroundings. At the western base of the hill a spring set in careful old masonry rises, which is overshadowed by a wild fig tree, and in the abundance, clearness, and purity of its water leaves nothing to be desired.[296]

In December 1971, the site was surveyed twice by the author and his team.[297] These surveys revealed that the ruin's area covered about 35 dunams, and that it primarily contained shards of the Roman and Byzantine periods. Throughout the ruin, the tops of ancient walls could be made out; on its western edge remains of an olive-oil press were found, apparently *in situ*. In the center of the ruin, we discovered a fragment of a basalt lintel which had a relief of an eagle, wings deployed, with the tail of a snake or the end of a wreath clutched in its beak. Its appearance recalled the snake-eagles reliefs found on the lintels of Dabûra.[298] On the lintel's edge, there is a relief band with the egg-and-dart motif. A bit south of this find, another eagle relief in stone was found; which may have stood at the head of the facade wall's gable. In addition to the two items with the eagles, in the area of the center of the ruin yielded sections of columns, an Ionic column base, an Ionic capital, cornice fragments, and an abundance of ashlar building stones. These finds led us to suggest at the time that a search for remains of a Jewish public building from the rabbinic period be mounted.[299] The validity of this suggestion received further support when additional items were discovered at the site, among them a lintel on which an eleven-branched menorah was incised.[300]

---

[296] Schumacher, "Dscholan," p. 308; Schumacher, *Jaulân*, p. 215.

[297] See D. Urman, "Kh. Quṣbiyye," *Reports of the Staff Officer in Charge of Archaeological Affairs in the Golan* (1968-1972), Archive of the Israel Antiquities Authority, Jerusalem (in Hebrew); Urman, "Golan—7," p. 2; Urman, *Golan*, p. 195, Site #87 and the note for this site on page 213.

[298] See the section on Dabûra.

[299] See above, note 297, as well as Urman, "Synagogue Sites," p. 28; Urman, "Hellenistic," p. 467.

[300] Ben-Ari and Bar-Lev, "Golan—1," p. 1.

Z. Ilan surveyed the ruin twice more, in 1974 with D. Ben-Ami, and in 1986 with H. Ben-David and Y. Kentman. In these surveys, the artifacts which we had left in the area were registered, along with a number of new items. Outstanding among these was a basalt column fragment with a relief of an eagle standing upon a pedestal.[301] Concerning the location of the public building at the site, Ilan initially wrote, "Approximately in the center of the ruin we made out a building with broad foundations, apparently a synagogue, the dimensions of whose interior hall is about 10 x 7.5 m. Near the place where the reliefs of the eagles were discovered the heads of 2-3 hewn stones are visible, perhaps a wall of the local public building."[302] But in his last book, Ilan only made brief reference to the wall section built of hewn stones, and indicated that its orientation was east-west.[303]

Ilan's suggestion brings us back, in fact, to the "totally destroyed square building" mentioned by Schumacher. Hopefully, the remains of this structure will soon be excavated and its use clarified. But already it is clear that the remains at Kh. Quṣbiyye are those of a Jewish settlement from the second-temple and/or rabbinic periods. The inhabitants of this settlement, like those of most of the Jewish settlements in the region, earned their livelihood in part from growing olives and producing olive oil—as the remains of the ancient olive-oil press can attest.

'ASÂLIYYE (EL 'ASELÎYEH)

This abandoned Syrian village was built over part of a Jewish settlement from the rabbinic period. The village is about three kilometers southwest of the modern town of Qaṣrin, at coordinates 2134-2636. Northwest of the village, at its foot, a spring spills its waters into an ancient pool known in Schumacher's time as 'Ain esh-Sheikh Mûsa.[304] A second, nameless, spring flows south of the village.

G. Schumacher was the first to survey the village and the ruin, but his reports mention no Jewish remains.[305] In 1968, the place was surveyed by a team headed by C. Epstein.[306] This survey likewise revealed no Jewish remains; but the team did report "architectural items in secondary use (in the

---

[301] See Ilan, *Galilee and Golan*, pp. 106-108; Ilan, "Quṣbiyye," pp. 20-21.

[302] Ilan, *Galilee and Golan*, pp. 107-108.

[303] Ilan, *Israel,* p. 108.

[304] Schumacher, "Dscholan," p. 288; Schumacher, *Jaulân,* p. 96.

[305] Schumacher, "Dscholan," pp. 287-288; Schumacher, *Jaulân,* pp. 96-97.

[306] This survey was done within the framework of Phase B of the Golan Survey under the auspices of the Association for the Archaeological Survey of Israel (See Kochavi, *Survey,* p. 12). The results of the Phase B Surveys have not yet received proper scientific publication, but the surveyors' reports are preserved in the Association's Archive—now in the care of the Israel Antiquities Authority, Jerusalem.

Syrian village houses), including bases of columns and a segment of a stone
decorated with a likeness of a branch."[307] Some time after the survey, Y.
Gal reported on the finding of an engraved five-branched candelabrum at one
of the village houses.[308]

In July 1976, T. Eshel, an instructor at the Golan Field School, reported
the "discovery of the remains of a large public building, apparently a synagogue, at 'Asâliyye."[309] In the wake of this announcement, M. Ben-Ari, S.
Bar-Lev, and H. Ben-David conducted another survey at the site, where they
examined the ruins of the public structure and discovered the remains of
many ancient buildings and an olive-oil press.[310] In and near the ruins of the
public building, they found an abundance of decorated architectural items
typical of Jewish public buildings from the Galilee and the Golan in the
rabbinic period. In the houses of the Syrian village, the surveyors found
more ornamented items in secondary use. Especially noteworthy among
these was a basalt door lintel with an *aedicula* relief at its center and two
seven-branched candelabra engraved on its two sides. Another architectural
item was discovered in the Syrian village with an engraved seven-branched
candelabrum, as was a basalt fragment with a partial Aramaic (?) inscription
(see below).

A short time after the 1976 survey, the author visited the site to examine
the remains of the public structure and the inscription.[311] I discovered that
only a section of a wall (the northern wall?) of the structure remained standing—to a height of 7 courses. This section, about 6 m. long, was built of
basalt ashlars and incorporated into a later Syrian house. Barring a systematic archaeological excavation (including the house's destruction), archaeologists cannot determine the plan of the structure's walls, its entrances, its
orientation, or its dimensions. In the area of the ruin not covered by the
Syrian village, I made out Ionic and Doric capitals—a type prevalent in
Jewish public structures in the Golan. One may then hypothesize that the
abundance of architectural items scattered at the ruin and among the Syrian
village houses, as well as those incorporated into village houses indicates
the presence of several Jewish public buildings at the site.[312] The area of the
early site extends over 25 dunams, and according to the shards found there it

---

[307] C. Epstein, "'Asâliyye," *Golan Survey—Phase B*, Reports in the Archive of the
Association for the Archaeological Survey of Israel, Israel Antiquities Authority, Jerusalem
(in Hebrew).

[308] Ilan, *Golan*, p. 163.

[309] Ben-Ari & Bar-Lev, "'Asâliyye," p. 7.

[310] Ben-Ari & Bar-Lev, "'Asâliyye," p. 7.

[311] The author's thanks go to S. Bar-Lev, who in those days served as the Deputy Staff
Officer in Charge of Archaeological Affairs in the Golan. He showed me the findings of the
survey in which he participated.

[312] See Z. Ilan, *Israel,* p. 105.

seems that the settlement was occupied throughout the Roman and Byzantine periods.[313]

FIG. 1 Sketch of the lintel.

In 1978, Z. Ma'oz also investigated the public structure and afterwards published a suggested reconstruction of the building's plan and its entrance. His suggestions, unfortunately, are based more on imagination than on evidence found at the site.[314] The height of his speculation appears when he adds egg-and-dart reliefs (for which there is no evidence) to the lintel (see FIG. 1). On the basis of the similarity between the style of this imagined lintel from 'Asâliyye and that from the public structure at Qîsrîn—as well as between the imagined dimensions he attributes to the 'Asâliyye structure in comparison to those of the Qîsrîn structure—he also suggests that the structure at 'Asâliyye "was built at around the same time (as the one of Qîsrîn), probably at the beginning of the sixth century C.E."[315] The date proposed for the Qîsrîn structure, however, finds no basis in the stratigraphy revealed by its excavations. It is regrettable that serious investigators have in good faith used Ma'oz's baseless reconstructions and suggestions.[316]

The Inscription

The precise use of the stone tablet on which the inscription was engraved remains unclear. Based upon the relief of a narrow, vertical band on the right edge of the stone fragment, we could hypothesize that this is a segment of a memorial tablet that had been set in a structure's wall (see PL. 42a). Yet it could alternatively be a lintel fragment which had a setting for the inscription carved out.[317] The stone fragment is 29 cm. high, 38 cm. wide, and 20 cm. thick.

---

[313] See Urman, *Golan*, p. 196, Site #90.

[314] See Ma'oz, *Golan*, pp. 17-18; Ma'oz, "'Asâliyye," pp. 185-188; Ma'oz, "Synagogues," p. 105; Ma'oz, "Golan Synagogues," pp. 159-161.

[315] Ma'oz, "Golan—1," p. 296; Ma'oz, "Golan—2," p. 544. Parentheses mine.

[316] See, for example, Hachlili, *Art*, pp. 200 ff. and *passim*; Ilan, *Israel,* pp. 103-105.

[317] Compare it to the fragments from the lintel of the Jewish public building discovered at Kokhav-Hayarden. See Ben-Dov, "Kokhav-Hayarden," p. 96.

FIG. 2 A section of the Aramaic (?) inscription.

The stone tablet was carved in very porous basalt. This fact certainly
made the task of incising the inscription difficult and can explain the differences that exist in the shape of the same letters. The fragment was exposed
to the forces of nature for many generations and therefore is difficult to read
without a hands-on examination. The letters of the inscription are not carved
in deeply, and their average height is 4.5 cm. Of the inscription, the remains
of six lines have been preserved, the left part of which is broken; the top and
bottom lines are broken along their entire length. Of the six lines, only the
fifth is legible with any degree of certainty:

...ושכלל מן קניינו/ה.

Without the ending of the word "קנין," it is difficult to determine whether the
inscription is Aramaic or Hebrew.[318] However, from a reading of the line it
is possible to conclude that it is a dedication inscription from a public building; it mentions the donor who contributed part of his wealth toward the
building's completion,[319] or toward its decoration.[320] The line before us has

---

[318] J. Naveh a few years ago suggested a reading for this inscription which he called
"conjectural and temporary" (see Naveh, "Aramaic and Hebrew," pp. 305-306). His
suggestion shows that he sees this inscription as Aramaic. Regrettably, his reading is based
upon a photograph and not on a hands-on "reading" and so remains "conjectural and
temporary."

[319] The verb שכלל (in the שפעל mode), which is of Akkadian origin, appears in Biblical
Aramaic in the sense of "to complete"; see Rosenthal, *Aramaic,* p. 52 #157. Thus we also
find in Hebrew, for example, in Pesikta Rabbati 2 (6b in the Ish-Shalom edition), "Shall you
(build the Temple), that you are laying the foundation for it? You shall not build it, for you
shall not finish it (משכללו)." (Also compare Yalkut Shimoni on the book of Samuel, #144).

[320] The verb שכלל in the sense of "to decorate" is found many times in rabbinic
literature. For examples, "R. Joshua ben Levi said, 'The heaven was adorned [ונשתכלל] with
the sun, moon, and planets; the earth was adorned [ונשתכללה] with trees, herbs, and the garden
of Eden...'" (Genesis Rabbah 10:5, Venice edition); "...speaks of Solomon. When he had
built the Temple and decorated it [ושכללן], he arranged a seven-days' dedication and then
brought in his guests..." (Numbers Rabbah 17:2); "...like a king of flesh and blood who built
palaces and decorated them [ושיכללן] and prepared a banquet and then brought in his
guests...." (B. San. 38a).

no identical parallel in the Hebrew or Aramaic dedicatory inscriptions published thus far. Its formulation, however, is reminiscent of the formulation found in the (Aramaic) dedication inscription of Chorazin: "...who made this colonnade and the staircase from his possessions," that is to say, "...who contributed of his wealth to the construction of the colonnade and its staircase."[321] It also recalls the formulation of the (Aramaic) dedicatory inscription at Eshtemoa: "...who gave one *Tr[em]is* (a Roman coin) of his wealth."[322]

KH. ER-RAFÎD

Now lying in ruins, this abandoned Arab village was built atop ancient remains above the east bank of the Jordan River at coordinates 2092-2624. The ruin was first surveyed by G. Schumacher in 1889. He reported the existence of twenty-five Bedouin winter houses at the site, as well as ancient remains.[323] Schumacher published drawings of several decorated architectural items he found at the site; they include a fragment of a cornice, a fragment of a frieze with a relief of a vine branch and clusters of grapes, another frieze fragment with reliefs of two fishes and a flower, and an Ionic capital.[324]

C. Watzinger, in his preface to the account of the German excavations of synagogues in Galilee, suggested that the remains at Kh. er-Rafîd, like those excavated at Kh. ed-Dîkkeh further to the south, were synagogue ruins.[325]

On September 28, 1933, E. L. Sukenik visited the ruin. He describes what he and his staff found there as follows:

> We found only one Bedouin family living there in a hut. Unfortunately we were only able to stay there a little over two hours as we had to return early on account of the bad weather. We were not able in this short space of time to locate the synagogue among the many other ruins, but we managed to examine a number of architectural fragments belonging to it. Some of these have already been described by Schumacher, but others were not found by him. The stone with the fishes (Fig. 32) we found built into a straw bin, together with other ancient remains: viz. the base and pedestal of a column in one piece (Fig. 33), a portion of an Ionic capital (Fig. 34), part of a lintel (Fig. 35a), a fluted frieze-stone (Fig. 35b), a fragment of a frieze ornamented with a vine (Fig. 35c), and two small bases (Fig. 35d and e). More important than all these were three carved stones which were found lying on the ground in about the centre of the ruins (Pl. XXIII): a) The greater part of a stone decorated in its lower middle with a shell surrounded by guilloche, astragal and egg-and-dart, and crowned by a gable.

---

[321] Naveh, *Mosaic*, pp. 36-37, Inscription #17.

[322] Naveh, *Mosaic*, p. 114, Inscription #74.

[323] Schumacher, "Tiberias," p. 71.

[324] See Schumacher, "Tiberias," pp. 71-73, Figs. 4-10.

[325] See Kohl and Watzinger, p. 2.

The blank spaces were originally occupied by carvings of living creatures, which at one time were deliberately defaced. Within the gable there are traces of a frontal view of a standing bird. To the right of the bird, part of an animal, apparently a lion, is visible and, to the left, the outline of some unidentifiable beast. b) A smaller stone, almost completely preserved, ornamented with the same elements as (b) but now entirely lacking the animal figures which probably also decorated its upper part. c) A still smaller stone ornamented with a shell enclosed in a guilloche.[326]

Sukenik concluded the description of his findings on the spot by saying, "A thorough exploration, even without excavation, will surely reveal many other parts remaining of the synagogue of er-Rafîd."[327] Regretfully, Sukenik's vision has not been realized. Thirty years after his visit to the site, it was surveyed twice: once by a team led by C. Epstein,[328] and the second time by the author.[329] In neither instance, however, were "many other parts" found, nor even the location of the building itself. It seems that the rubble of the Syrian houses (abandoned at the end of the 1940's, when the area became the front-line between Syria and Israel) covers the remains of the building; without systematic archaeological excavations it will never be found.

Our survey estimated that the area of the ancient ruin occupies about 15 dunams and we identified shards from the different stages of the Roman, Byzantine, and Arab periods. At the eastern part of the site remains of an olive-oil press were identified. Northwest of the olive-oil press two items were recorded that may have originally belonged to the structure defined as a synagogue: one, a large basalt doorpost, with lovely profiles, that originally stood at the building's main entrance, and second, a fragment of a pedestal like the illustration published by Sukenik (Fig. 33 in his report). In various places at the center of the ruin several items were found that had been published by Schumacher and Sukenik, as well as fragments of Ionic and Doric columns and capitals, all of basalt. In the ruin's western part, another concentration of column and capital fragments was found.[330] (See PLs. 42b-43b.)

---

[326] Sukenik, "el-Ḥammeh," pp. 179-180. For further discussion of these finds see Goodenough, vol. 1, p. 211. Some of the items mentioned by Sukenik can be seen in PLs. 42b and 43a.

[327] Sukenik, "el-Ḥammeh," p. 180.

[328] C. Epstein, "Kh. er-Rafîd," *Golan Survey Phase B*, Reports in the Archive of the Association for the Archaeological Survey of Israel, Israel Antiquities Authority, Jerusalem (in Hebrew).

[329] D. Urman, "Kh. er-Rafîd," *Special Surveys Reports*, Archive of the Association for the Archaeological Survey of Israel, Israel Antiquities Authority, Jerusalem (in Hebrew); D. Urman, *Reports of the Staff Officer in Charge of Archaeological Affairs in the Golan* (1968-1972), Archive of the Israel Antiquities Authority, Jerusalem (in Hebrew). See also Urman, *Golan*, p. 196, Site #93.

[330] See previous note.

In two further surveys conducted at the site later on—one in 1979 by Z. Ma'oz, and the other in 1987 by Z. Ilan—the location of the structure was still not found. Ma'oz writes: "The synagogue was probably located in the eastern sector of the site, but its walls were completely robbed and its architectural elements scattered."[331] Ilan suggests that if it becomes clear that the place of the doorpost that we registered in our survey is not the place of the structure, then "the synagogue should be sought on the western side of the ruin, opposite the Jordan gorge."[332]

JARABÂ

This abandoned Syrian village was built in part on the remains of an ancient settlement upon a hill located west of Naḥal Meshushim, at coordinates 2112-2617.

G. Schumacher, who visited the village twice (in 1884 and 1913), saw that it contained ancient remains, but did not report upon them in detail.[333] After the Six Day War, the village was surveyed by a team, headed by S. Gutman, which reported that the ancient ruin extended southwest from the cemetery at the center of the village. The village itself revealed many hewn stones, remains of columns, bases, capitals, and other architectural pieces.[334]

In 1968, the author and his team conducted a systematic survey of the abandoned village and the ruin.[335] In the course of the survey it became clear that the area of the ancient ruin extended over about 25 dunams and that there were a few shards from the late Hellenistic period, a large number from the different stages of the Roman and Byzantine periods, as well as a few from the early Arab up to the modern periods.[336] In the area of the ruin and in the houses of the village, we registered the remains of many ancient walls, several of them had been built with carefully hewn basalt blocks. Two walls deserve further comment: one was found in the northwest part of the cemetery of the abandoned village, of which two courses, 8.5 m. long, were preserved; and the second on top of the cemetery hill, was about 11 m. long, and had only one course preserved on the surface. In both walls, which

---

[331] Ma'oz, "Golan—2," p. 541. See also, Ma'oz, "Golan Synagogues," p. 155; Ma'oz, "Golan—1," p. 292.

[332] Ilan, *Israel,* p. 112.

[333] Schumacher, "Dscholan," p. 273; Schumacher, *Jaulân,* p. 163; Schumacher, "Ostjordanlande," pp. 157-158.

[334] Epstein & Gutman, p. 274, Site #98.

[335] See D. Urman, "Jarabâ," *Special Surveys Reports,* Archive of the Association for the Archaeological Survey of Israel, Israel Antiquities Authority, Jerusalem (in Hebrew).

[336] See previous note and also Urman, *List,* p. 11; Urman, *Golan,* p. 197, Site #98.

belonged to two different buildings, we found *in situ* doorpost-stones of the type common in Jewish public buildings of the Golan. On the basis of these walls, the existence of fragments of basalt benches, and the abundance of decorated architectural items in the village, we predicted in our report that any future excavations near the aforementioned walls would uncover Jewish public buildings of the rabbinic period.[337]

FIG. 1 Fragment of an eagle.

Among the architectural items that we registered in the survey, three are especially noteworthy: a basalt capital with its upper part carved in Ionic style and its lower in Corinthian style; a basalt fragment with a relief of an eagle (see Fig. 1 and PL. 44a), which from all appearances, was part of the gable decoration on the facade of one of the village's magnificent structures (the quality of the eagle relief is reminiscent of a relief from Chorazin); and a lintel fragment, also made of basalt, on which a seven-branched menorah is engraved.

In 1979, the site was examined by Z. Ma'oz, but his publications reveal no new information.[338] In the years of 1987-1989, Z. Ilan surveyed the site and registered an item not previously observed: this was a fragment of a convex frieze made of basalt with "a continuous design of winding foliate branches forming medallions." The image or images that had been on the medallions of that section had been destroyed.[339] On the basis of this find, Ilan hypothesized "that perhaps the synagogue at Jarabâ belonged to the group of synagogues of Chorazin, Capernaum, Kh. Khawkha, and Kh. ed-Dîkkeh that had been decorated by a single group of craftsmen, or that these were buildings whose decoration had been influenced by one another."[340] It

---

[337] See note 335, as well as Urman, "Synagogue Sites," p. 18.

[338] Ma'oz, *Golan* (rev. ed.), p. 33; Ma'oz, "Golan Synagogues," p. 157; Ma'oz, "Golan—1," p. 294; Ma'oz, "Golan—2," p. 542.

[339] See Ilan, *Israel*, p. 75, Fig. 1.

[340] See previous note.

is difficult to decide between Ilan's two hypotheses. In any case, his last find undoubtedly is one more in the series of archaeological finds from Jarabâ that attest to the existence of Jewish public buildings on this site in the rabbinic period.

KH. ZUMÂIMÎRA'

This small abandoned Syrian village was built upon an ancient ruin lying at coordinates 2139-2613. The site was first surveyed in 1968 by a survey team headed by C. Epstein, which discovered the remains of a Jewish public building.[341]

Between 1968 and 1972, the village and the ruins were surveyed a number of times by the author and his staff.[342] These surveys revealed that the area of the ancient site was about 20 dunams. Its pottery remains were primarily from the Roman and Byzantine periods. At the edges of the ruin a number of olive-oil presses were preserved, sufficient to attest that one of the sources of livelihood for the ancient village was growing olives and producing olive oil. This may have even been their main source of income.

In the western part of the site, remains of a Jewish public building were found, which Epstein's team identified as a synagogue. Of the structure, two to three courses of its western external wall were well preserved above ground level, while one or two courses remained of its other walls. The building's dimensions were 19.00 x 15.50 m. and it was oriented east-west. The building stones are of well-hewn basalt (ashlar). The west wall revealed remains of an entranceway about 1.65 m. wide. The lower stones of the doorpost were preserved *in situ* with well-crafted profiles. Near the entrance were stones, also with lovely profiles, preserved from an arch that had apparently been set over the entrance's lintel. In the rubble filling the building, one can discern an Attic base, sections of columns and Doric capitals— all carefully crafted from basalt. The rubble also contains a stone slab with a fine relief of a lion resting upon a pillar with a base and a capital. This item may have been part of the structure's facade or its Torah Ark—if excavations ever indicate that the building once contained an ark.

In the walls of the Syrian houses, we found many building stones and architectural items taken from the ancient ruin. Some of them perhaps came

---

[341] C. Epstein, "Kh. Zumâimîra'," *Golan Survey—Phase B,* Reports in the Archive of the Association for the Archaeological Survey of Israel, Israel Antiquities Authority, Jerusalem (in Hebrew).

[342] D. Urman, "Kh. Zumâimîra'," *Reports of the Staff Officer in Charge of Archaeological Affairs in the Golan* (1968-1972), Archive of the Israel Antiquities Authority, Jerusalem (in Hebrew). See also Urman, *List,* p. 11; Urman, "Synagogue Sites," p. 21; Urman, "Golan—7," p. 2; Urman, "Hellenistic," p. 467; Urman, *Golan,* p. 197, Site #99.

from the so-called synagogue. These include a basalt slab with a seven-branched menorah on a tripod base incised upon its face and a stylized *lulav* and *ethrog* on its sides. Another basalt slab depicts a similar seven-branched, tripod-based menorah, but with two circles incised on its sides.[343]

In 1978, Z. Ma'oz surveyed the site again, but we found nothing new in his reports.[344]

Finally, let us point out that Hüttenmeister and Reeg suggested dating the structure identified as a synagogue to the third and fourth centuries C.E., although with a question mark.[345] Without systematic archaeological excavation, however, it is difficult to determine its date. Perhaps it was erected before the third century.

ET-TAIYIBA (ET-TAIYBEH)

The ruins of an ancient settlement on a low hill above Wâdî Yahûdiyye, at coordinates 2178-2614, provided the site for this small, now-abandoned, Syrian village.

G. Schumacher, who visited the village in June 1913, was enthused by the view of the landscape it provided, and related the presence of 14 Bedouin houses but did not mention any ancient remain.[346]

The village was first surveyed in 1968 by a survey team headed by C. Epstein, who briefly reported that the Syrian village was built on an ancient ruin and that there were a number of ancient architectural items in secondary use as building blocks in the modern houses.[347] A short time after Epstein's survey, this author surveyed the site. He found the area of the ancient ruin to be about 20 dunams and that the shards there were primarily from the various stages of the Roman and Byzantine periods.[348] Most of the houses of the Syrian village were built of stones taken from the remains of the ancient structures. Among them we could identity many dressed basalt ashlars, whose source was one or more public buildings. In the southeast part of the ruin, an area not covered by modern construction, we registered a number of sections of basalt columns and Ionic capitals similar to those usually in the

---

[343] See previous note.

[344] Ma'oz, *Golan*, p. 15; Ma'oz, "Synagogues," p. 103; Ma'oz, "Golan Synagogues," p. 156; Ma'oz, "Golan—1," p. 292; Ma'oz, "Golan—2," p. 541.

[345] Hüttenmeister and Reeg, p. 518.

[346] Schumacher, "Ostjordanlande," p. 158.

[347] C. Epstein, "et-Taiyiba," *Golan Survey—Phase B*, Reports in the Archive of the Association for the Archaeological Survey of Israel, Israel Antiquities Authority, Jerusalem (in Hebrew).

[348] D. Urman, "et-Taiyiba," *Reports of the Staff Officer in Charge of Archaeological Affairs in the Golan* (1968-1972), Archive of the Israel Antiquities Authority, Jerusalem (in Hebrew). See also Urman, *Golan*, p. 197, Site #100.

Golan's Jewish public buildings. This last find caused the author to conclude his report by suggesting that these remains were from a Jewish settlement of the rabbinic period that had at least one public building, perhaps
a synagogue.[349]

In 1977, H. Ben-David and G. Peli found a lintel ornamented with reliefs, incorporated as construction material in secondary use in one of the
Syrian houses in the middle of the village (see PL. 44b). In the center of the
lintel appears a relief of a wreath with a 'Hercules knot' accompanied by a
relief of a rosette at its center. On both sides of the wreath there are reliefs of
round medallions with geometric rosettes within them. Alongside the medallions with the rosettes are two reliefs of stripes between which are engraved
two trees of life (or palm branches). The entire complex of reliefs and engravings are enclosed in a relief framework of with the egg-and-dart motif,
itself enclosed in a relief framework of a stripe on both sides of which, at
the edges of the lintel, there are two additional reliefs of rosettes.

Z. Ma'oz, who surveyed the site in 1979, found near the above-men-
tioned lintel two consoles decorated on the front with reliefs of acanthus
leaves and on their sides with S-like spirals (see PL. 45a). This find, along
with that of the lintel, led him to theorize that the later Syrian structure in
which the lintel had been found was built on the foundations of a synagogue; and since this structure is oriented north-south and the lintel was
found in the base of its southern wall, it seemed to him that the synagogue
had also been built north-south and that its facade wall had been the south
wall.[350] It is clear, however, that without systematic archaeological excavation, Ma'oz's suggestion remains mere speculation.

In the 1980's, Z. Ilan visited the site and apparently in the southeast of
the site made out some of the sections of the columns and the Ionic capitals
that this author had registered in the report of the 1968 survey. In his last
work, the late Ilan wrote as follows:

> In the southeast of the site there stand two columns 60 cm. in diameter, and
> the distance between them on a east-west axis is 2.60 m., which is the reg-
> ular distance between columns in the synagogues. Near them lies a large
> Ionic capital, mostly buried. Near it lies a carved cornice stone. It may be
> that these two columns are standing *in situ* and that it was the site of a syn-
> agogue. In this instance it is possible to posit that the structure's facade
> was in the west. It is clear that this was an extremely fine structure, most of
> whose stones are still buried in the ground.[351]

---

[349] See previous note.

[350] Ma'oz, *Golan*, p. 33; Ma'oz, "Golan Synagogues," p. 158; Ma'oz, "Golan—1," p.
294; Ma'oz, "Golan—2," p. 542.

[351] Ilan, *Israel*, p. 94.

To sum up our discussion of this site let us point out that even though no Jewish inscriptions and/or stones decorated with *menorot* have yet been found in the village or the ruin, no one doubts that this site is a Jewish settlement of the rabbinic period. This settlement had at least one public building whose architectural items have been registered by surveyors and visitors to the village in 1968 and later. Still, until systematic archaeological excavations are conducted, we will not know whether the public building was at the center of the Syrian village or in the southeast section of the ruin; it is even possible that remains of Jewish public buildings may be uncovered in both places.

YAHÛDIYYE
(EL-YAHÛDIYYE, EL-YÊHUDÎYEH, YA'RÂBIYYE)

This abandoned Syrian village was built upon an ancient ruin at the end of a spur below the Naḥal Yahûdiyye (Wâdî el-Yahûdiyye) cliff at coordinates 2162-2605. Apparently, when Schumacher visited the place in 1885, the site showed no signs of modern habitation. But in the 1950's, the Syrians established a village, using the walls and building stones of the ancient structures in the new houses. During the first decade of the village's existence, the Syrians preserved the ancient name of the site, Yahûdiyye, but in 1961 they decided to change it on their maps to Ya'rabiyye.

Schumacher reported, *inter alia*, a 6-foot thick wall surrounding the ruin,[352] and this fact led to suggestions identifying this place as Sogane (Σωγανη), mentioned by Josephus as one of the villages he fortified in the Golan (*Vita* 187).[353] It is still possible to make out sections of this fortification wall, but without systematic excavation it is difficult to date it.

In his description of the ruin, Schumacher writes:

> In the north the mountain ridge widens to a plateau, upon which there are indistinct traces of the kind described, whereas remains of former buildings on a square plan are still to be found. The chamber enclosed by the wall is covered with ruins of all kinds; most of all one sees large hewn basalt building stones, lying in heaps near greatly weather-worn shafts of columns. Besides these, most peculiar capitals (Figs. 60-61 in the German text; Figs. 142-143 in the English text) are to be found, which exhibit a very primitive application of the combined Ionic and Corinthian styles. These are already very weather-worn, and like the other ruins point to a great age. Near the column remains two well preserved top stones lie; they are of the same shape and still in their original position, opposite one another (Fig. 62 in the German text; Fig. 144 in the English text). If the ruins on the surface are not important, they at any rate exhibit characteristic

---

[352] Schumacher, "Dscholan," p. 302; Schumacher, *Jaulân*, p. 270.

[353] See the section on Sogane.

construction and peculiar forms found nowhere else in the Jaulân. Excavations will certainly bring to light more important discoveries, and by this means yield information as to whether el-Yehudîyeh, its name and tradition, are of Jewish origin or not.[354]

It should be pointed out that the figures of the capital published by Schumacher (Figs. 60-61 in the German text and Figs. 142-143 in the English text) clearly show an Ionic capital identical in decoration and dimensions to capitals uncovered by the author in his excavations of the Jewish public building at Qîsrîn. Perhaps the capitals at Yahûdiyye and those at Qîsrîn were made by the same craftsman. Another architectural item published by Schumacher (Fig. 62 in the German text and Fig. 144 in the English text) is hard to identify. This stone may have been incorporated above the lintel of a window in a monumental building. Its relief of concentric geometric forms is common among remains of Jewish public buildings uncovered in the Galilee and the Golan. It may be possible, then, to conclude that Schumacher apparently found the remains of a public Jewish building—the shafts of the columns, the capitals, and the gabled stones—but lacked the knowledge to define it as such.

In 1967, the village and the ruin were surveyed by a team headed by S. Gutman. They reported that "in the center of the village there is a concentration of capitals, columns, and architraves, and that scattered throughout the village there are hewn stones with five-branched menorah decorations, rosettes, and other decorations."[355] Gutman also saw the remains of the wall Schumacher had reported, as well as flint utensils of the Early Neolithic period and shards from "the Roman-Byzantine period."[356]

In 1968, the author and his team surveyed the site.[357] The survey determined that the area of the ruin is about 40 dunams. It found shards from the different stages of the Roman and Byzantine periods as well as a few from the Hellenistic period and the various Arab periods. At the southwest edge of the site there were well-preserved remains of an olive-oil press *in situ*.

At the time of the survey it was possible to make out the tops of walls of ancient structures throughout the Syrian village and the ruin. These had occasionally been integrated into later construction. This phenomenon is especially common near the cliff. There, we could tell that a number of ancient walls were built of well-hewn basalt ashlars. In addition to the items

---

[354] Schumacher, "Dscholan," pp. 302-303; Schumacher, *Jaulân*, pp. 271-272. Parentheses mine.

[355] Epstein & Gutman, p. 275, Site #102. The five-branched menorah appears in PL. 46a.

[356] See previous note.

[357] D. Urman, "Yahûdiyye," *Special Surveys Reports*, Archive of the Association for the Archaeological Survey of Israel, Israel Antiquities Authority, Jerusalem (in Hebrew); Urman, *List*, p. 11; Urman, *Golan*, p. 198, Site #102.

Gutman registered and published,[358] this survey located and recorded about twenty decorated architectural items that had originally belonged to public buildings from the second-temple and/or rabbinic periods; most of these lay in the ruin or were placed in secondary use in the modern structures. Of these items, four Ionic capitals deserve mention (one identical to that published by Schumacher), as well as two pedestals with Attic column bases, an Ionic column base, and fragments of a cornice with a meander relief.

I should also note a decorated lintel with high reliefs, found with its upper section partially broken, which we transferred to the museum in Quneiṭra (see PL. 45b).[359] At the center of this lintel appears a relief of a wreath with a rosette of six leaves within it. On both sides of the wreath are reliefs of pomegranates and branches. The lintel's right end reveals a relief of a square frame with a four-leaf rosette within it, all surrounded by a vine branch. The lintel's left section has a relief of a vase with vine branches emerging from its two sides.

The stone with the five-branched menorah (reported by Gutman and transferred by us to the Quneiṭra Museum, see PL. 46a), and the great similarity existing between the architectural items we found in Yahûdiyye and those of other Jewish public buildings from the rabbinic period in the Galilee and the Golan, led us at the time to conclude that there had been a Jewish community in the village with at least one public structure, perhaps a synagogue.[360]

From the mid-1970's, the site has been surveyed by a number of investigators who reported the same finds registered by Gutman and myself.[361] In 1979, D. Ben-Ami noticed one of the ashlar walls near the cliff and suggested that this was a wall of the synagogue.[362] Z. Ilan suggested that the remains of a different building near the cliff were the synagogue's remains.[363] Without archaeological excavation of these buildings and others nearby, however, it is difficult to decide between the two suggestions; it is even possible that several Jewish communal buildings existed at the site.

In 1980, Z. Ilan published an item taken from the site before the surveys of Gutman and the author.[364] The item, which served originally as a *voussoir*, bears a relief of nine-branched menorah and a tripod base, with a relief of a shofar on one side and a shovel on the other (see PL. 46b). Given the similarity between the decorations of this stone and the illustration of an ar-

---

[358] Epstein & Gutman, p. 275, Site #102.

[359] Today it is in the collection of Golan antiquities at the Qaṣrin Museum.

[360] See note 357, and also Urman, "Synagogue Sites," p. 22; Urman, "Hellenistic," p. 467.

[361] For examples, see Ilan, *Israel,* pp. 95-96; Maʿoz, "Golan—2," p. 544.

[362] See previous note.

[363] Ilan, *Israel,* p. 96.

[364] Ilan, "Menorot," pp. 117-118.

chitectural item found at Aḥmadiyye published by Schumacher (see Fig. 1 in the section on Aḥmadiyye), Ilan suggested at first that they were the same item, "that was perhaps shifted to Yahûdiyye since Schumacher's survey."[365] In his last book, however, he added the possibility that these are two similar items made by the same artisan.[366] I find this possibility more probable.

Undoubtedly, the item published by Ilan dovetails with the architectural items attesting to the early Jewish settlement at Yahûdiyye, at least in the rabbinic period. If systematic excavations were carried out at the site and at the remains of the wall that surrounds it, it might become evident that the Jewish settlement was built in the second-temple period.

"ḤORVAT ZAWITAN"

This nameless ruin was discovered in 1968 by M. Inbar and Y. Gal. After the remains of a public building were identified there, it was given the name of "Ḥorvat Zawitan." The ruin, about eight dunams (2 acres) in area, lies on the bank of Naḥal Zawitan near its confluence with Naḥal Meshushim, at coordinates 2131-2595.

A short time after the ruin was discovered, the author visited the site and dated the shards found there to various stages of the Roman and Byzantine periods.[367] During that visit, which took place during stormy winter weather, the ruins of the public building built of ashlars were also discovered but it was impossible to examine them thoroughly or to measure them. At some distance from the building's remains, I also made out remains of a moat.[368]

In 1979, Z. Ma'oz surveyed the site and he was the first to identify the remains of the public structure as those of a synagogue. According to his reports, the orientation of the public building was east-west, and its length about 13.10 m.[369] In the south wall of the structure, Ma'oz made out the remains of an entranceway whose doorposts had Attic bases. He also reported finding several Doric capitals in the river bed at the foot of the ruins.[370]

Zvi Ilan, who visited the site during the 1980's, claims that the orientation of the building is northeast-southwest and that its dimensions are about

---

[365] Ilan, "Menorot," pp. 117-118.

[366] Ilan, *Israel,* p. 65.

[367] See Urman, *Golan,* p. 198, site #104.

[368] See previous note.

[369] Ma'oz, *Golan,* p. 33; Ma'oz, "Golan Synagogues," p. 158; Ma'oz, "Golan—1," p. 294; Ma'oz, "Golan—2," p. 542.

[370] See previous note.

13 x 8 m.[371] Since the entranceway which Ma'oz reported as being in the south wall is found on the lengthwise wall of the structure, Ilan assumes that the main entrance to the building was in the west wall.[372]

It is quite possible that these remains are of a Jewish public building—the location of the ruin is at the heart of an area of Jewish settlement in the Golan of the second-temple and rabbinic periods, and it has yielded architectural items that are characteristic of Jewish public buildings uncovered in the region. Nevertheless, until systematic excavations are conducted at the site in general and on the public structure in particular, the identification of the building as a synagogue remains hypothetical.

EṢ-ṢALABE

This abandoned Syrian village was built near an ancient ruin, re-using the stones of the ruin's buildings. The village and the ruin are located on top of a lofty spur at coordinates 2170-2596. The spur is surrounded on three sides by wadis: on the north by Wâdî el-Khârîq, on the west by Wâdî el-Batrâ, and on the south by Wâdî Nûkheile (also known as Wâdî eṣ-Ṣalabe).

The village and the ruin were first surveyed in 1968 by a team led by the author, and again by Y. Gal in 1969.[373] These first surveys showed that the houses of the Syrian village were built from ancient stones and architectural items taken from the ancient ruin. Among these were found several column sections and Doric capitals. The ruin's area was about 10 dunams. The shards found were mainly from the Roman and Byzantine periods.[374] Several buildings were identified that had walls of well-hewn ashlars; among their debris sections of columns, a few Ionic and Doric capitals, and parts of olive-oil presses could be seen.[375]

About ten years after the first surveys, Z. Ma'oz visited the site. From that time, he has identified one of the structures on the site's northwest slope as a synagogue.[376] In his words:

> It is a small building (8.50 by 11 m.) built on a terrace formed by large boulders and incorporating parts of olive presses. Only the facade of the building, in the southwest, was built of ashlars; it has survived to a height of five courses. In the center was a single entrance (1.70 m. wide) with

[371] Ilan, *Israel,* p. 86.
[372] See previous note.
[373] See D. Urman, "eṣ-Ṣalabe," *Special Surveys Reports*, Archive of the Association for the Archaeological Survey of Israel, Israel Antiquities Authority, Jerusalem (in Hebrew).
[374] See previous note and also Urman, *Golan*, p. 198, Site #105.
[375] See previous note.
[376] See Ma'oz, *Golan*, p. 34; Ma'oz, "Golan Synagogues," p. 159; Ma'oz, "Golan—1," p. 296; Ma'oz, "Golan—2," p. 543.

plain doorposts and a lintel. The prayer hall was divided by two rows of three columns each into a nave and two aisles. An unfinished Ionic capital and a Doric capital are visible in the building's debris. In the northwestern wall were traces of a doorway leading into a narrow space running along the entire length of the hall.[377]

Elsewhere he adds:

> The synagogue at eṣ-Ṣalabe is a small unadorned building; such simple synagogues, which are difficult to identify in ruins, were probably more common than once believed.[378]

In March of 1989, Z. Ilan visited the site. In the building identified by Ma'oz as a synagogue, he found another Ionic capital.[379] On the slope north-west of the structure, Ilan made out a basalt crosspiece 120 cm. long, 29 cm. high and 20 cm. thick. with various engravings on it, one of which is, in his opinion, a three-branched menorah with a shofar to its left.[380] The bottom part of the stone is fractured along its entire length, but this fact did not prevent Ilan from suggesting "that it served as a lintel which perhaps belonged to a private home or to the nearby synagogue."[381] At the center of the ruin, a short distance from Ma'oz's so-called synagogue, Ilan noticed a high knoll with the remains of a large building built of ashlars. In his opinion, this building also served as a public building "not only because of the large size of its stones but because among its debris and near it are buried about ten column sections of which one was apparently carved with the base."[382] The architectural items that Ilan found in this building (the sections of the columns and the large doorposts) are, in his words, different from the synagogue items identified by Ma'oz, and from this he concludes that they were not transferred from the synagogue to be reused in this building, but that they were originally part of the building. Ilan concludes his description of the building at the center of the ruin thus: "The lengthwise axis of the building, as far as it can be ascertained without excavation, is north-west to southeast. The location of the building is excellent—it is built at the center of the settlement, whereas the earlier building (Ma'oz's so-called synagogue) is at its edge."[383] In his opinion, "The possibility that we have here a public building, another synagogue or house of study should not be ruled out."[384]

---

[377] Ma'oz, "Golan—2," p. 543.

[378] See previous note.

[379] Ilan, *Israel*, p. 107.

[380] See Ilan, *Israel*, p. 107, Fig. 2.

[381] Ilan, *Israel*, p. 107.

[382] Ilan, *Israel*, p. 107.

[383] Ilan, *Israel*, p. 107. Brackets mine.

[384] Ilan, *Israel*, p. 107.

No new information concerning this site has appeared since the visits of
Ma'oz and Ilan. Our 1968 survey report had registered the structures described by Ma'oz and Ilan—as well as another building on the ruin's northwest slope built of well-hewn, ashlar, basalt stones.[385] We hesitated to identify them as Jewish public buildings, however, since no decorated architectural items and/or dedicatory inscriptions had yet been found supporting such
an identification. The possibility that the ruin at eṣ-Ṣalabe is the remains of
a Jewish village of the rabbinic period is quite plausible. After all, the site
lies at the heart of the area of Jewish settlement in the Golan during that period. It is also possible that Ma'oz and Ilan may be correct in their theories
concerning everything related to the buildings they described. But it is clear
that without systematic excavation of the site and the buildings discussed
here, we cannot determine with any certainty either the village's identification as Jewish or the function of the buildings.

WÂKSHARÂ (ḤORVAT BET LAVI)

An ancient ruin about 2.5 kilometers northwest of Gamala (coordinates
2189-2588) provided the location for a small, now-abandoned, Syrian village. G. Schumacher, who visited the site in the 1880's, described the village as a Bedouin winter village. He briefly mentioned the presence of a few
antiquities, but failed to describe them.[386]

All the survey teams of the Association for the Archaeological Survey of
Israel—those led by C. Epstein, S. Gutman, and the author—skipped the
site in their surveys of the region. It remained unstudied until 1979, when
Z. Ma'oz surveyed it.[387] From the surveyor's report, it appears that there are
remains of an ancient building built of hewn ashlars near the southwestern
edge of the Syrian village. Its facade wall, which has been preserved only to
a height of two courses, faces south. Even though the other walls of the
building, in the words of Ma'oz, "had mostly been robbed,"[388] he claims
that the dimensions of the building are 13.10 x 10.80 m. In his reports,
Ma'oz observed that the building's central entrance (1.60 m. wide) was not
in the middle of the south wall. He explained this unusual placement by
saying that the entrance "was moved from the central axis in order to allow
for building the Torah Ark in this wall from the inside."[389] Without a sys-

---

[385] See above, note 373.

[386] Schumacher, "Dscholan," p. 362; Schumacher, *Jaulân*, p. 268.

[387] Ma'oz, *Golan* (rev. ed.), p. 34; Ma'oz, "Golan Synagogues," p. 156; Ma'oz,
"Golan—1," p. 292; Ma'oz, "Golan—2," p. 541.

[388] See the previous note.

[389] Thus, for example, in Ma'oz, "Golan Synagogues," p. 156 and also, in Ma'oz,
"Golan—1," p. 292.

tematic excavation of the building, however, we do not and cannot know whether the building contained a Torah Ark, let alone whether its location explains that of the door.[390]

North of the hewn ashlar building that Ma'oz calls a synagogue, he found a basalt lintel broken at both ends. It depicts a lion in relief, its body viewed from the side and its face from the front. Only the outline of the body and the mane have been preserved; the head has been mutilated. To the right of the lion's head was a *tabula ansata* containing a badly worn Aramaic inscription that has not been deciphered.[391]

Around this building and in the houses of the Syrian village, Ma'oz found additional architectural items which he believes were originally in the synagogue. Among them he lists a pedestal, parts of Ionic and Corinthian capitals, part of a conch, parts of a convex frieze with floral scrolls and rosettes, a cornice decorated with floral motifs, and a relief of a wreath around a rosette.[392]

Zvi Ilan, who visited the site after Ma'oz's survey, pointed out that the designation 'Horvat Bet Lavi' was given the ruin in light of the find of the lintel with the image of the lion.[393] Ilan also reported finding other items at the site whose origin would seem to be from the so-called synagogue. These include a small Doric capital, (that he suggests may have belonged to the second story or to the Torah Ark), and a doorpost (?) fragment with parts of a relief of vine branches and an egg-and-dart decoration.[394]

Whether or not the structure served as a synagogue, it is plausible that these are remains of a Jewish settlement which includes at least one public building. It is to be hoped that in the future Ma'oz will publish a full report of his finds at the site, including details about the area of the ruin and the dates of the shards found in it. This will enable other scholars to know whether it is from the second-temple and/or rabbinic period. The proximity of this ruin to Gamala makes imperative a clear answer to this question.

KH. ED-DÎKKEH

During the rabbinic period, a Jewish settlement was built on a low hill near the east bank of the Jordan River. Its ruins now lie at coordinates 2087-2588.

---

[390] See Ma'oz, "Golan—2," p. 541.

[391] Ma'oz, "Golan—2," p. 541. Here we must note that it is not clear upon what Ma'oz bases his decision that the inscription is in Aramaic. One hopes that in the future he will publish at least a photograph of the inscription, if not its full reading.

[392] See above, note 387.

[393] Ilan, *Israel,* p. 71.

[394] See previous note.

L. Oliphant visited Kh. ed-Dîkkeh in December 1884 and was the first to report its archaeological remains. He identified a particular area of the rubble as the remains of a Jewish public building. In his description, Oliphant describes his difficulty determining that the remains of the public structure should be identified as a synagogue. For this reason, I will cite his description in full:

> After following the course of the Jordan, on its east bank, for another mile, we reached a spot on the barren slope of a hill a few hundred yards from the river, where some native huts had been recently built, and where large cut stones, carved cornices, capitals, and fragments of columns were strewn in profusion, while from the midst of them rose the walls of what appears to have been a synagogue; owing, however, to a later superstructure having evidently been reared upon the original foundation, I feel somewhat diffident in pronouncing upon this point decidedly. I will, however, state my reasons for coming to this conclusion, while the accompanying sketches of the ornamentation I found here may enable others more competent to form an opinion than myself to judge of their origin. The dimensions and ground plan of the building with the columns still *in situ* closely resembled those of the small synagogue at Kefr Birim. The length was 45 feet, the breadth 33 feet. The building had an east and west orientation, and the door was in the centre of the wall on the western side. This does not, so far as I know, occur in the case of any synagogue hitherto found, but it was doubtless due to the necessities of the case, as the site for the building was excavated from the hill-side, the floor at the east end being about 9 feet below the surface of the earth at the back of the wall, while the slope of the hill would have made it inconvenient to place the door, as usual, on the south side. A more serious objection to this being a synagogue lies in the fact that the stones were set in mortar, which does not occur in the case of other synagogues; but there were indications to show that these walls had been erected upon older foundations. They were now standing to a height of 8 feet. There were no door-posts or lintel to the entrance. The floor, which was thickly strewn with building stones, fragments of columns, and of carved cornices and capitals, was below the level of the ground, and was reached by a descent of two steps, while opposite, running along the whole length of the eastern side, were two benches or steps, the face of the upper one decorated with a thin scroll of ornamental tracery; these may have served for seats. The depressed floor and stone benches are both features which occur in the synagogue at Irbid [=Arbel]. Upon the upper bench stood the fragments of two columns about 4 feet in height, and 1 foot 2 inches in diameter. They were evidently not *in situ*, being without pedestals, and I can only account for their being in their present position by the supposition that they had been placed there recently. The other two appeared to be *in situ*, but their bases were much hidden by the blocks of stone heaped on the floor. These blocks averaged 2 feet 6 inches by 18 inches. The capitals of the columns were in Corinthian style, 2 feet 3 inches in height, and consisted of a double row of leaves, which differed somewhat from the usual acanthus, apparently of a later or more composite order. The ornamentation and character of the niches (see figs. 4 and 5) so closely resembled those found at the synagogue at Kerazeh [=Chorazin] and

elsewhere, being of the same florid and somewhat debased type, that they seemed to me to set at rest the question of the original character of this building, though it may subsequently have been diverted to other uses. Time did not allow me to do more than make rough drawings of the architecture, but I trust they are sufficient to enable a comparison to be made between them and the engravings in the "Memoirs."[395] If I am right in my conjecture, this synagogue would probably date from about the second century of the Christian era. I also found a stone which consisted of the upper portion of two small semi-attached fluted columns with Doric capitals, almost exactly similar to the one found at Irbid. Also one cut into a round arch, which may have been placed over the lintel on the plan of the arch on the lintel over the entrance to the great synagogue at Kefr Birim. It measured 39 inches across the base of the arch (fig. 1). A most interesting object was a winged female figure, holding what was apparently a sheaf (fig. 2). The ornamentation of the cornice does not resemble any which I have observed either in the "Memoirs" or elsewhere, and is not unlike the so-called egg and dart pattern (fig. 3). Other specimens of the ornamentation are seen in fig. 7. I have not been able to form any conjecture which should identify this most interesting spot with any Biblical or historical locality. Its modern name is ed-Dikkih, meaning platform, a name not inappropriate to its position. It is possible that during the next dry season the natives may continue their excavations, as stones are needed. I have urgently impressed upon them not to deface or destroy any remains that may be unearthed; but they unfortunately watched my proceedings with an uneasiness and suspicion which I am afraid a gratuity failed altogether to dispel.[396]

Schumacher claims he visited ed-Dîkkeh twice, in 1883 and in 1884—that is, before Oliphant.[397] But since Oliphant's 1885 report was reprinted as an addendum to Schumacher's *Across the Jordan*, which appeared in 1886, and Schumacher's 1886 report on the remains at ed-Dîkkeh refers to Oliphant's report, scholars credit Oliphant as the discoverer of the ed-Dîkkeh site.[398] Since Schumacher describes different aspects of the site from Oliphant, we will also cite his report in its entirety.

This ruin, which is not extensive, but rich in ornamentation, lies close to the Jordan, and immediately north of the Batîhah. Close by the stream one sees a decayed mill with an aqueduct, whose construction is far better than that of the mills of modern Jaulân. The old place stood close by on a small elevation. One's eye is first struck by a rectilinear building, 55 feet in length and 33 feet in breadth, whose surrounding walls project over the ruins for several feet (Fig. 27 in the German edition, Fig. 28 in the English

[395] When Oliphant wrote "Memoirs," he meant the publication by C. R. Conder and H. H. Kitchener, *The Survey of Western Palestine, Memoirs of the Topography, Orography, Hydrography and Archaeology* (London, 1881-1883).
[396] Oliphant, "Lake Tiberias," pp. 83-85 (=Oliphant, "Jaulan," pp. 245-251). Brackets mine. References to figures are Oliphant's. The "winged female figure" appears in PL. 47b, other architectural fragment can be seen in PL. 47a.
[397] Schumacher, "Tiberias," p. 70.
[398] Ilan, "Horvat Dîkkeh," p. 65.

one). On the north-west corner an entrance leads into the interior, which has two flights of steps 18 inches in height, running all round it. There are traces of good ornamentation on the walls and also on the columns. Between the outer wall and the steps on the east side are two basalt columns standing; they are only 5 feet high. Whilst in the inner room four more of these at irregular intervals tower forth out of the ruin. Thus the inner was supported by columns. The surrounding walls were 3 feet thick; the building stones throughout have been carefully hewn. Near the two upper column shafts a winged basaltic figure (Fig. 28 in the German edition, Fig. 29 in the English one=Oliphant's Fig. 2), cut in bas relief, lies, which, in opposition to the other ornamentation, lies upon a low artificial step. The stone is 19 inches long and 17 inches broad. Outside the buildings are to be found gable-like decorations adorned with grapes (Fig. 29 in the German edition, Fig. 30 in the English one=Oliphant's Fig. 7), or with the Haurân moulding (Fig. 30 in the German edition, Fig. 31 in the English one =Oliphant's Fig. 5), beautiful "egg and pearl" moulding with the native tooth ornamentation, especially found in ed-Dera'ah (Haurân), (Fig. 31 in the German edition, Fig. 32 in the English one=Oliphant's Fig. 3), and several twisted double columns (Fig. 32 in the German edition, Fig. 33 in the English one; Oliphant did   not publish this detail), also some with smooth shafts. The ruins present a Byzantine character. Nevertheless, if one compares the discoveries in Western Palestine, in the districts of Safed and Meiron, with those in ed-Dîkkeh, a most striking resemblance between the two appears. After a searching examination they there appear evidently as the remains of Jewish synagogues, and, therefore, perhaps it would not be too audacious to include ed-Dîkkeh among the number of Jewish buildings (see *Across the Jordan*, p. 243). Four winter huts of the 'Arab et-Tellawiyeh have been erected on the ruined places; their inhabitants, however, did not present a very friendly face to archaeological research.[399]

Oliphant and Schumacher both published a conjectural plan of the building. The plans differ on the location of the structure's entrance. Whereas Oliphant sketches a wide entrance in the center of the building's west wall,[400] Schumacher indicated only a small entrance in the northern part of the west wall, near the northwest corner of the building.[401] It is also important to note that Schumacher did not mention that the remains of the early building were covered by the remains of a later structure—which included architectural items from the early building in secondary use.[402]

The later building's remains did not make the task of Kohl and Watzinger easy when they decided a brief exploratory excavation of the building. This was done as part of the project investigating the ancient synagogues in Galilee conducted by the Deutsche Orient-Gesellschaft in the years 1905 and

---

[399] Schumacher, "Dscholan," pp. 278-279; Schumacher, *Jaulân*, pp. 120-123. Parentheses mine.

[400] See Oliphant, "Lake Tiberias," p. 83

[401] Schumacher, "Dscholan," p. 278, Fig. 27; Schumacher, *Jaulân*, p. 120, Fig. 28.

[402] See, for example, Fig. 242 in Kohl and Watzinger, p. 122.

1907. Kohl and Watzinger's team spent three days (April 29, 1905—May 1, 1905) at Kh. ed-Dîkkeh and managed to clean out the northern part of the early building down to its stone-slab floor.[403] In general, Kohl and Watzinger's research concentrated on the architecture of the buildings which, following their predecessors, they called synagogues (=houses of prayer) without any reservations. They used this procedure at sites in the Galilee (Arbel, Chorazin, Capernaum, Ḥorvat ha-'Ammudim, Meron, Bar'am, Nabratein, and Gush Ḥalav), other sites in the Golan (Umm el-Qanâṭir), and in the Carmel (Ḥorvat Sumaqa). At Kh. ed-Dîkkeh, their work followed this same pattern. Their goal was to obtain as many details as possible of each building's plan and its architectural elements. They did not occupy themselves with systematic excavation, which is primarily concerned with determining a structure's stratigraphy and its dating. The latter interest of course requires the study of pottery remains and other small finds such as glass, and coins. Therefore the Kohl-Watzinger report was devoted primarily to the description and analysis of architectural items found in and near the structure.[404] As the final result of their work, they present a conjectural plan of the early building[405] and a suggested reconstruction of the wall of the structure's western facade.[406]

Since the remains of the early building are no longer visible on the surface, it is difficult to verify the accuracy of the ground plan suggested by Kohl and Watzinger. According to this plan, the external dimensions of the building are 15.30 x 11.92 m. Comparing the drawing of the building's unearthed ruins with Kohl and Watzinger's hypothetical plan raises several questions difficult to answer without systematic excavation. The first question focuses on the presence of "the portico," or paved expanse, that Kohl and Watzinger's plan places west of the building's western facade. In the drawing of the remains, there appears a small paved segment at a distance of about a meter west of the facade wall, but there are no traces of the stairs apparently leading to the "portico," or to the paved expanse that Kohl and Watzinger drew on the hypothetical plan. Indeed, Kohl and Watzinger themselves put a question mark on the stairs drawn leading to the "portico" from the south. I think their reconstruction was influenced by the Jewish public structure at Capernaum which has a "portico" with stairs leading to it from both sides. There is no clear evidence, however, that the facade of the ed-Dîkkeh structure was built in the same way. In addition, the complex at Capernaum influenced Kohl and Watzinger to add to their hypothetical reconstruction of the ed-Dîkkeh structure continuations towards the south of

---

[403] See Kohl and Watzinger, p. 120, Fig. 237.

[404] Kohl and Watzinger, pp. 112-124.

[405] See Kohl and Watzinger, Tafel XVI and also see PL. 47a

[406] Kohl and Watzinger, p. 124, Fig. 251. And also see PL. 47b.

both the east and west walls. These suggested extensions likewise have no basis in the drawing of the remains. It is not surprising, then, that Kohl and Watzinger themselves either ignored or forgot the continuations of these supposed walls in their suggested reconstruction of the west wall of the structure's facade.[407]

Another question concerns the presence of a second bench within the hall along its north and south walls. In the drawing of the remains, it is possible to make out the existence of only one bench. The east wall has a second bench, but this is insufficient to attest to the existence of a second bench along the north and south walls.

As for Kohl and Watzinger's suggested reconstruction of the structure's western facade wall, with its decorated architectural items, there is no doubt that their contribution is important to future discussion. We shall not enter upon such a discussion here,[408] but shall only point out that prior to such a discussion, it is necessary to determine whether the west wall actually has three entrances. Oliphant and Schumacher reported the existence of only one entrance in the structure's west wall (although they placed it in different locations), and in Kohl and Watzinger's drawing of remains it is hard to discern more than two entrances. Furthermore, whether another entrance to the hall existed in the building's south wall should also be investigated—a question which Kohl and Watzinger did not solve, for they had insufficient time to uncover the southern part of the building.

Thanks to the Kohl and Watzinger team, which in three days managed to do what in our day sometimes takes a team of archaeologists a week or more, we have important documentation about the remains of the public structure at ed-Dîkkeh. Since 1905, most of these items have disappeared from their positions. Even though the German team uncovered no items with Jewish symbols (such as a menorah) nor any Jewish inscriptions, there is no doubt in the research that the structure was a public Jewish building, and that nearly all the investigators call it "a synagogue."

Immediately following the Six Day War in 1967, C. Epstein surveyed the site and identified a number of architectural items that had been reported by the earlier surveyors.[409] A short time later, in 1968, the site was surveyed by the author and his team.[410] This survey, conducted when the site had been heavily overgrown, did not succeed in estimating the site's area,

---

[407] See previous note.

[408] Cf. Goodenough, vol. 1, pp. 205-206.

[409] C. Epstein, "Kh. ed-Dîkkeh," *Golan Survey—Phase B*, Reports in the Archive of the Association for the Archaeological Survey of Israel, Israel Antiquities Authority, Jerusalem (in Hebrew).

[410] See D. Urman, "Kh. ed-Dîkkeh," *Reports of the Staff Officer in Charge of Archaeological Affairs in the Golan* (1968-1972), Archive of the Israel Antiquities Authority, Jerusalem (in Hebrew); Urman, *List*, p. 13; Urman, *Golan*, p. 198, Site #109.

but we did find an abundance of shards from the different stages of the Roman, Byzantine, Arab and Ottoman periods. On the area's surface almost nothing has remained of the public building, except for architectural items such as sections of columns, capitals, and fragments of cornices that had already been reported by Kohl and Watzinger. These items were found both at the site of the building and among the ruins of the later Arab houses north and east of the structure. It seems that the inhabitants of the Arab houses—which were erected after Oliphant's and Schumacher's visits and Kohl and Watzinger's excavation—used building stones and architectural items from the public structure. After the war in 1948-1949, the place was abandoned because of its proximity to the Israeli-Syrian cease-fire line.

Hüttenmeister and Reeg visited the site in 1974 and dated the public structure to the third century C.E.[411] In 1979, Z. Ma'oz surveyed the site and claimed that he documented "some additional architectural remains," but did not detail them.[412] In his publications, he fails to mention that the building no longer appears on the site's surface, but instead debates with Kohl and Watzinger (and with G. Foerster who discussed the building in his doctoral thesis [Foerster, "Galilean Synagogues," pp. 53-54]) about the building's date. Ma'oz has suggested several different dates: "the fifth century,"[413] "the fourth or the beginning of the fifth century C.E.,"[414] "the first half of the fifth century C.E.,"[415] and "the mid-fifth century C.E.[416]

Z. Ilan, who surveyed the site in November 1988 and February 1989, found no new items. He suggested "that this synagogue was built in the fourth or fifth century C.E."[417]

It is clear that until a systematic excavation of the public building at Kh. ed-Dîkkeh is conducted, we shall know neither the date of the building in general nor those of its different phases in particular. Furthermore, a basic examination of the extent of the site's area is needed, for the impression exists that the site is small even though the wealth of ornamentation found in its public building suggests an economic wealth usually associated in a larger settlement. A large-scale excavation might also reveal the sources of the residents' livelihoods. In our survey, we found no remains of olive-oil presses that generally are found in Jewish sites in the Golan. These may perhaps yet be found at the site.

[411] Hüttenmeister and Reeg, p. 105.
[412] Ma'oz, "Golan—1," p. 292; Ma'oz, "Golan—2," p. 540.
[413] Ma'oz, *Golan* (rev. ed.), p. 12.
[414] Ma'oz, "Golan Synagogues," p. 155.
[415] Ma'oz, "Ancient Synagogues," p. 121.
[416] Ma'oz, "Golan—1," p. 292; Ma'oz, "Golan—2," p. 541.
[417] See Ilan, *Israel,* pp. 84-85.

DARDÂRA (KH. ED-DURDÂRA, EL-KHASHSHE)

This small abandoned Syrian village was built on an ancient ruin on the bank of Naḥal Meshushim—also known by its Arabic name, Wâdî eṣ-Ṣâffah—at coordinates 2114-2575. It seems that the Syrian village was only built in the twentieth century, for in the 1880's it did not exist. Schumacher, who visited Dardâra in 1884, devotes only a sentence to it in his reports: "A ruin with scattered building stones on the Wâdî eṣ-Ṣâffah of the Batîḥah...."[418] Oliphant, who visited the site in December 1885, likewise found no special finds there and wrote:

> From El Hasanîyeh I proceeded for a mile and a half up the Wâdî eṣ-Ṣâffah to a ruin called Dardâra, but found nothing beyond rough basalt blocks, and traces of foundations.[419]

With the building of the small Syrian village (apparently in the late 1940's or the early 1950's), decorated architectural items and other antiquities began to appear. When a team headed by C. Epstein first surveyed the site in 1968, they reported parts of an olive-oil press in a courtyard of a village house and several decorated hewn stones.[420] Epstein dated the shards gathered there to the Roman, Byzantine, and Ottoman periods.[421]

Shortly after Epstein's survey, the site was surveyed once again by the author and his team.[422] This survey determined that the ruins covered about 20 dunams. In addition to the pottery fragments collected by Epstein's team, the site yielded a few shards from the late Hellenistic period and the Middle Ages. The Syrian houses and their courtyards revealed more parts from ancient olive-oil presses as well as bases of two Attic columns, six column sections, three Doric capitals, and a fragment of a carved cornice. All the items were made of finely crafted basalt.[423]

In the southeast part of the village, I discovered that one of the Syrian buildings was erected upon the remains of an early monumental structure while making secondary use of its walls. Four to six courses of the early building's northern and southern walls survived in good condition, as well as a section of the eastern wall (including its corner with the southern wall). The stones in the early walls were of basalt ashlar, and were laid using the

---

[418] Schumacher, "Dscholan," p. 261; Schumacher, *Jaulân*, p. 188.

[419] Oliphant, "New Discoveries," p. 74.

[420] Epstein & Gutman, p. 277, Site #122.

[421] See previous note.

[422] D. Urman, "Dardâra," *Special Surveys Reports*, Archive of the Association for the Archaeological Survey of Israel, Israel Antiquities Authority, Jerusalem (in Hebrew); Urman, *List*, p. 14.

[423] See previous note, and Urman, *Golan*, p. 199, Site #113.

'head-beam-head-beam' system.[424] The building's long axis was apparently east-west, but its exact dimensions were difficult to determine without removing the walls of the later Syrian house and the systematic excavation of the site.

The remains of the monumental building and the well-crafted architectural items preserved in and around it, led us to suggest at the time that these remains were from a Jewish settlement of the rabbinic period, and that the structure may have served as a synagogue.[425] Until further supporting evidence is found, such as Jewish inscriptions or architectural items decorated with *menorot*, this conjecture will remain only that. Hopefully, the remains of the monumental structure will be excavated in the future, so that we will be able to determine a more precise date for it.

BATRÂ ("BATHYRA," "KH. BÂṬRAH," ḤORVAT BATRÂ)

This ruin, whose area covers about 15 dunams, lies at the end of a spur north of the junction of Naḥal Daliyyot (Wâdî ed-Dâliyye) and Naḥal Batrâ, at coordinates 2138-2568. The ruin was first discovered in 1968 by survey teams led by C. Epstein and S. Gutman.[426] The surveyors found the ruin unnamed, but over the years, in light of the remains of a public structure identified by investigators as a synagogue, the names "Kh. Bâṭrah," "Ḥorvat Batrâ," "Bathyra," or just "Batrâ," stuck to the site—names borrowed from that of the nearby wâdî. Since the first survey by the Epstein and Gutman teams, the site has been surveyed a number of times by the author (from 1968 to 1972),[427] by Z. Ma'oz (1978),[428] and by Z. Ilan (September 1984, April 1985).[429]

Z. Ilan theorized that the Aramaic name "Batrâ" which survived as the name of the nearby wâdî, was perhaps the early name of the site,[430] and even proposed the theory that the site was one of the villages of the Bnei

---

[424] See Urman, *Golan*, p. 213, Site #113.

[425] See above, note 422. Also see Urman, "Synagogue Sites," p. 19, Urman, "Hellenistic," p. 466.

[426] Epstein & Gutman, p. 278, Site #117.

[427] D. Urman, "Batrâ," *Special Surveys Reports*, Archive of the Association for the Archaeological Survey of Israel, Israel Antiquities Authority, Jerusalem (in Hebrew); D. Urman, "Batrâ," *Reports of the Staff Officer in Charge of Archaeological Affairs in the Golan* (1968-1972), Archive of the Israel Antiquities Authority, Jerusalem (in Hebrew); Urman, *List*, p. 14; Urman, "Synagogue Sites," p. 19; Urman, "Hellenistic," p. 464; Urman, *Golan*, p. 199, Site #114.

[428] Ma'oz, *Golan* (rev. ed.), p. 33; Ma'oz, "Golan Synagogues," p. 157; Ma'oz, "Golan—1," p. 293; Ma'oz, "Golan—2," pp. 541-542.

[429] Ilan, *Ancient Synagogues*, pp. 137-144; Ilan, *Galilee and Golan*, pp. 95-98; Ilan, *Israel*, p. 72.

[430] See Ilan, *Ancient Synagogues*, pp. 138-139.

Bathyra who he thought settled around Gamala in the time of Herod.[431] It is difficult to confirm or disprove Ilan's theories without a systematic excavation of the site, and such has yet to be conducted. Still, to the credit of Ilan's theories, it should be noted that the site has yielded a few shards from the early Roman period, in addition to those of the later Roman and Byzantine periods.[432]

The public structure identified as a synagogue (not yet excavated), is located at the top of the hill on which the settlement was built. The remains of the settlement's houses appear mainly on the hill's southern slope, but here and there one can make out the remains of ancient buildings on its western and northern slopes. At the end of the latter slope, at the foot of the settlement, the remains of an olive-oil press have been well preserved. North of the community structure—indeed, upon it—and on the slopes of the hill it is possible to discern that the site was built in a number of stages. But without archaeological excavation, the dates of the stages of occupation and construction cannot be determined.[433]

Of the public building, a section of the western wall about 8 m. long has been preserved to a height of one course, as well as the remains of a wall, visible on the surface for about 1.50 m., extending eastward from the northern end of the western wall. The stones of these walls are well-hewn ashlars. Continuing northward in line with the building's western wall is an additional wall segment about 7.50 m. long. This wall segment, compared to the section of the western wall described above, is of inferior construction. At the northern end of the wall segment doorpost stones of an entrance about 1.35 m. wide were preserved *in situ*. Lying near the entrance, a basalt lintel about 1.90 m. long was found. Without excavation it is difficult to know whether the segment of wall continuing northward in line with the western wall segment indicates another room of the structure or that it belongs to the remains of a wall of the public building's courtyard—as does the entrance found at its northern end. The latter possibility seems more likely from the quality of construction. In the southern part of the structure, several areas hewn out of the rock were found. Without systematic excavation it is difficult to know whether they preceded the structure, belong to the leveling process of the area before construction, or were hewn out as channels for the foundations of the building's walls.[434]

It is possible to estimate that the overall measurements of the public structure complex were about 17 m. x 10 m., and that it was oriented east to west. It is difficult to determine with any certainty which of the structure's

---

[431] See Ilan, *Ancient Synagogues*, p. 139; also Ilan, "Bathyra."

[432] See above, note 427.

[433] See above, note 427.

[434] See above, note 427.

walls was the facade. Ma'oz suggests that it was the wall which he defines as southwestern, but later construction on this wall's line makes it difficult to accept his idea without excavation.[435]

In and around the structure, many architectural items were found, all of basalt and some decorated with reliefs. These include fragments of a lintel with a relief of a wreath tied with a 'knot of Hercules' whose ends become leafy vine branches with grape clusters, as well as Doric capitals, half an Ionic capital, a capital with a relief of a vine branch emerging from a vase with a partridge-like bird standing between its leaves and the grape clusters. Many parallels can be found to these artifacts and their decorations among the Jewish public buildings identified as synagogues in the Galilee and the Golan. Indeed, this fact caused the various surveyors of the site to suggest that the public structure there served as a synagogue.

It is clear, however, that until systematic excavation of the structure and its immediate area is conducted, we cannot know its date. Hüttenmeister suggested attributing the building to the third century C.E.,[436] but the structure may predate this century. By contrast, the building may have undergone several stages of construction and/or periods of use.

GAMALA (ES-SÂLAM)

The remains of this Jewish city from the second-temple period can be found on the southern slope of a high spur above deep, dry wadis. The ruin, called es-Sâlam on Syrian maps, lies at coordinates 219-256. The top of the spur is shaped like a camel's hump and, this seems to be the instigation for the city's name in the second-temple period.[437]

After the city's destruction during the Great Rebellion of 67 C.E., Gamala remained unpopulated. At first, apparently, Roman regimes forbade its reinhabitation, but later its topographical situation mitigated against resettlement. During the Byzantine period, however, a Christian village—known in the twentieth century as Deir Qrûkh—was founded on the height overlooking the city from the east.[438]

During the Arab periods, the Jewish ruins of the city sank into oblivion. As a result, the investigators of Palestine from the nineteenth and early twentieth centuries struggled to identify the site of Josephus' fortified city. In addition to the writings of Josephus, the searchers also had a small

---

[435] See Ma'oz, "Golan Synagogues," p. 157; Ma'oz, "Golan—1," p. 293; Ma'oz, "Golan—2," p. 542.

[436] Hüttenmeister and Reeg, pp. 38-39.

[437] See *War* IV § 5.

[438] It is still not clear if the site at Deir Qrûkh served in the days of the Second Temple as a suburb of Gamala or not. And see our comments on that in Urman, *Golan*, p. 137, note 98.

amount of information from rabbinic literature. Now that its ruins have been discovered and the uncovering of its secrets has been begun, there is no reason to discuss the previous suggestions concerning the location of Gamala. They are simply no longer germane. This site was correctly identified as Gamala in 1968 by Y. Gal, who published his identification suggestion in 1971.[439]

After Y. Gal's discovery, S. Gutman surveyed the site, concluding that Gal's suggestion that this was Gamala was correct.[440] In 1971-72, the author and Z. Ilan conducted further surveys at this site and at nearby sites where remains of the Roman siege camps may lie.[441] Our survey revealed that the site's area was about 180 dunams. The site yielded large quantities of shards from the first century B.C.E. and first century C.E. as well as a few shards from the Early Bronze I and II periods.[442] We also recorded the remains of settlement's wall and a number of basalt architectural artifacts—mainly column sections. We also found catapult stones made of local basalt. Two things in our survey convinced us that Gal and Gutman were correct in identifying the remains as the site of Gamala: the site's topographical situation fits Josephus' description of Gamala, and the discovery of the wall's remains with catapult stones near it.[443] In his surveys, Z. Ilan also focused on the remains that, if excavated in the future, might contain traces of the Roman army camps that besieged the city; he even published a plan indicating the place of these presumed camps.[444]

Josephus first mentions Gamala as a Hellenistic-Seleucid fortress captured by Alexander Jannaeus on his expedition to conquer Gilead and the Golan in 83-80 B.C.E. (*War* I § 105; *Antiquities* XIII §§ 394-397). It seems that after this conquest, Gamala was inhabited by Jews, for after the Roman conquest in 63 B.C.E., Gabinius attempted to settle a non-Jewish population there (*War* I § 166), an unnecessary action if the town already had non-Jewish inhabitants. This attempt was unsuccessful and during the reign of Herod and his heirs, it was again primarily inhabited by Jews. Furthermore, the Zealot movement develops out of Gamala. The leading figure in this movement—Judas of Galilee or Judas the Galilean (as he is called occasion-

---

[439] See Gal, "Gamala," pp. 156-158.

[440] Gutman, "Gamala."

[441] See *War* IV § 13. On these separate surveys, see D. Urman, "es-Sâlam and Deir Qrûkh," *Reports of the Staff Officer in Charge of Archaeological Affairs in the Golan* (1968-1972), Archive of the Israel Antiquities Authority, Jerusalem (in Hebrew); Urman, *List*, pp. 14, 18; Urman, *Golan*, p. 199, Sites #115 and 116, and also see the notes on these sites on p. 213; Ilan, "Gamala"; Ilan, *Golan*, pp. 296-308; Ilan, *Israel*, pp. 73-74.

[442] See D. Urman, "es-Sâlam and Deir Qrûkh," *Reports of the Staff Officer in Charge of Archaeological Affairs in the Golan*, p. 8 (in Hebrew).

[443] *Ibid.*, p. 11.

[444] See Ilan, *Golan*, p. 299.

ally in Josephus and Acts 5:37)—is in fact from Gamala in the Golan. He founded this movement which Josephus labels "the Fourth Philosophy" along with Zadok the Pharisee. In 6 C.E., he led the civil insurrection against the Roman regime during the census of Quirinius (*War* VII § 253; *Antiquities* XVIII §§ 4-10). Judah's son Menahem continued his father's activities in the Zealot movement and, from 66 C.E., led it until his death (*War* II §§ 433-449). Josephus relates that Eleazar, son of Jairus—who was the last leader of the Zealots including their final stand on Masada—was related to Menahem and was a descendant of Judah of Gamala, but he provides no details of that relationship or of his town of origin; he, too, may have been from Gamala (*War* II § 447; VII § 253).

Despite Josephus' references to Gamala's professed loyalty to the Romans at the start of the rebellion (*Vita* §§ 46-47), it seems that the city's Zealot elements continued to be strong. King Agrippa tried to block the connections between Gamala and the Galilean rebels (*Vita* § 398) and even attempted to destroy the city's fortifications (*War* IV § 10; *Life* § 114). In the battle to break Agrippa's siege, Josephus led the Galilean rebels (*War* II § 568) and claims to have fortified the city (*War* II § 574; IV § 9). It should be pointed out that Josephus knew the city well, for in his writings we find detailed descriptions of it and its fortifications (*War* IV §§ 4-8). But he draws on both Jewish and Roman sources (*War* IV §§ 4-53, 62-83) for his description of the Roman siege of the city, the heroic actions of the Zealots against it, and its capture and destruction by the Romans.

Turning from ancient to recent history, from June 1976 to the end of the 1980's, S. Gutman conducted about fourteen seasons of excavations at the site.[445] In the first season, Gutman excavated two of the site's most important finds—the city wall and the public structure today called the "synagogue."[446] The city wall, which was apparently built at the start of the rebellion, is not uniform and was built section by section. It extends about 350 meters, surrounding the city's eastern end. The builders used the outer walls of earlier buildings and occasionally erected it over existing structures. The wall's thickness was achieved by making the rooms fully or partially impenetrable. Discovered along the length of the wall were hundreds of catapult stones of different sizes, and large quantities of iron arrow-heads, and in some spots signs of forced entry—mute witness to the hard battle which

---

[445] For the excavator's preliminary reports, see Gutman, *Gamala—2*; Gutman, *Gamala—3*; Gutman, *Gamala*; Gutman, *Rebellion*. For further bibliography see Gutman, "Gamla—2," p. 348 (there is a full list there also including most of his publications on the excavation in Hebrew), as well as Gutman, "Gamla—3," p. 463 (a list restricted to his publications in English).

[446] See Gutman, *Gamala—2* and recently, in an abbreviated and updated form, Gutman, "Gamla—3," p. 460.

had taken place in 67 C.E. between the Roman forces and the defenders of Gamala.[447]

The public structure identified as a synagogue lies at the eastern entrance to the settlement, and the city wall was erected adjacent to it at the start of the rebellion. It is a rectangular building whose exterior dimensions are 25.50 x 17 m., while the hall inside is 13.40 m. long and 9.30 m. wide. The center of the inside hall is unpaved, but it is surrounded by paved surfaces as well as three or four rows of benches built from finely-hewn, basalt ashlars. (See PL. 48a.) We shall not describe all aspects of the building, for it has already been detailed in the excavator's reports.[448] But we shall mention several issues and problems concerning this important edifice.

With regard to dating, there is no doubt that these remains represent the earliest Jewish assembly hall yet uncovered by archaeologists in Palestine and Syria. According to Gutman, the structure's date ranges between the time of Alexander Jannaeus—after the capture of Gamala by his forces[449]—and that of John Hyrcanus II (63-40 B.C.E.).[450] Z. Ma'oz, by contrast, delays structure's date to "sometime between 23 B.C.E. and 41 C.E."[451] Unfortunately, we can only wait until the full report of the building's excavation is published and hope that it will provide sufficient stratigraphic, ceramic and numismatic information to help decide the question. If archaeological tools and methods do not provide a precise date, we will be forced to limit our conclusions to saying only that the structure was erected for certain sometime in the decades prior to the rebellion and was undeniably destroyed in 67 C.E.

There is an interesting link among Gamala, Masada, and the Zealot movement that deserves further exploration. First, Gamala was the home of the family that led Jewish opposition to the Roman government for three generations. Second, Gamala contains the earliest assembly hall so far discovered. Third, the next earliest assembly hall was found at Masada, which Menahem, the son of Judah of Gamala and the founder of the "Fourth Philosophy" used as a base in the early stages of the Great Rebellion. Furthermore, his relative Eleazar ben Yair, as I mentioned, commanded Masada during the last stages of the Rebellion. These facts suggest an avenue of investigation to which until now has received little attention. Is there perhaps a link between early assembly halls and the Zealot movement? Although the answer to this question lies beyond the scope of this article, I

---

[447]See Gutman, *Gamala—2*; Gutman, *Rebellion*, pp. 83-98; and Gutman, "Gamla—3," p. 460.

[448] See note 445, and especially Gutman, "Gamla," pp. 30-34.

[449] See Gutman, "Gamla—3," p. 460; Gutman, *Rebellion*, p. 109.

[450] See Gutman, "Gamla," p. 34.

[451] See Ma'oz, "Gamla," p. 35.

will point out that a movement with an ideological-religious program—
such as the Zealots—is precisely the kind of group that needs a large building in which to meet.

At the present stage of research, we lack the data conclusively to demonstrate architectural continuity between this Gamala structure and later
Galilean and Golan buildings. However, several items suggest such a continuity. First, the assembly hall at Gamala has benches built along the inside
of its four walls, as do the Jewish public buildings at 'Ein Nashôt and at
Qîsrîn, and perhaps also at Kh. ed-Dîkkeh, Umm el-Qanâṭir and other sites.
Second, at the Gamala structure, an Ionic capital was uncovered of a type
common to later Jewish public buildings in the Golan and the Galilee from
the rabbinic period (see PL. 48b). Third, a fragment of a lintel with a rosette
decoration made with a compass—a widespread motif in the Jewish archaeological finds of the second-temple and rabbinic periods—was also found
there.[452] This suggests that archaeologists should be careful about dating all
Jewish remains of this type in the Golan to the later Byzantine period; the
Gamala finds suggest they could be as early as the first century.

Adjacent to the assembly hall, Gutman uncovered two additional structures important for the investigation of Jewish public construction in
Palestine during the second-temple and rabbinic periods in general, and of
the Golan region in particular. The excavator defines one structure as a ritual
bath, a *miqweh*. Its exterior dimensions are 4.50 x 4.00 m. and it was uncovered west of the assembly hall. The second structure is a small room east
of the assembly hall. Benches were also built along its four walls. Gutman
calls this room "the Study Room." He concludes, "The synagogue, adjoined
by a study room, a ritual bath, and a courtyard, thereby constituted a community center of sorts for study and prayer, while the Temple in Jerusalem
was still in existence."[453] It seems that if we understand this complex as a
center specifically for the men of the "Fourth Philosophy" (and compare it
to the finds at Qumran), we should refrain from expecting to find all these
components around all public Jewish buildings that date from after the destruction of the Temple.[454]

During later seasons, Gutman excavated private structures as well as craft
and production installations, including presses for olive-oil production.[455] In
some of these buildings, evidence was discovered revealing they had been
covered with stone roofs. A comparison of the presses of Gamala with the

---

[452] For a photograph of the lintel fragment with the rosette decoration, see Gutman,
"Gamla," p. 34.

[453] Gutman, "Gamla—3," pp. 461-462.

[454] See, for example, Z. Safrai's article in volume 1 of this collection. The whole subject
requires more study.

[455] See above note 445.

remains of presses found at other Jewish sites in the Golan shows clear continuity of Jewish settlement in the Golan despite the events of the Great Rebellion.[456]

I conclude this discussion of the Jewish finds at Gamala by mentioning the coins first uncovered at this instructive site. These are bronze coins on one side of which is minted the Hebrew word "לגאלת" ("For the redemption of") and on the other side "...הק. ירשלם" that is, "h[oly] Jerusalem."[457]

"KH. DÂLIYYE"

This nameless ruin lies on a slope of the southern bank of Wâdî ed-Dâliyye at coordinates 2201-2560. The ruin was first discovered by Y. Gal and D. Peri. They reported its location to the author and he led a team to survey it.

During the survey, it became clear that these remains were from a small village with an area of about 15 dunams. According to the shards found there, the village had been inhabited from the early Roman to the late Byzantine period. Apparently, after the Byzantine period the site remained uninhabited.[458]

In the site's southeast section, there were well-preserved remnants of a monumental structure whose walls were built of hewn basalt ashlars. Since the building was full of debris and vegetation, we were unable to measure it during the survey. Nevertheless, it was possible to determine that its lengthwise axis ran east-west and that sections of its walls were sometimes preserved to a height of three courses. Lying on the eastern wall of the building was a basalt lintel, 170 x 50 centimeters, with a slightly blurred relief of three rosettes. Another lintel of the same size was found west of the building. This lintel was carved with reliefs of vine branches issuing from two vases and forming in the center a plaited wreath with a 'Hercules knot.' At each of the lintel ends were a relief of a stylized rosette.[459]

Since the monumental structure was built of well-hewn ashlars and the decorations are similar to those found in public Jewish buildings of the Galilee and the Golan, I suggested at the time that this ruin was the remains of a Jewish village from the second-temple and rabbinic periods, and that the ruin of the monumental building was originally a synagogue.[460] Without a

---

[456] And see my comments in the section on historical background.

[457] See the photographs in Gutman, "Gamla—3," p. 461.

[458] D. Urman, "Kh. Dâliyye," *Reports of the Staff Officer in Charge of Archaeological Affairs in the Golan* (1968-1972), Archive of the Israel Antiquities Authority, Jerusalem (in Hebrew); Urman, *Golan*, p. 200, Site #117.

[459] I published the photograph of the latter lintel, which was found broken in two, in Urman, *Golan*, p. 101, Fig. 42.

[460] See Urman, "Synagogue Sites," p. 19; Urman, "Hellenistic," p. 464.

systematic archaeological excavation in the village and at the building, however, these suggestions will remain no more than that. Finally, it should be
pointed out that near the monumental building our survey also found fragments of a sarcophagus, but to our disappointment these pieces contain no
inscription or decoration which could reveal the ethnic identity of the deceased.

BETHSAIDA

This Jewish settlement of the second-temple and rabbinic periods is well
known from written sources. It was situated somewhere in the Bateiḥah
Valley (designated on today's Israeli maps as the Bethsaida Valley), east of
the spot where the Jordan River enters the Sea of Galilee. The exact location
of this settlement, as we shall yet see below, has not been identified with
certainty.[461]

To begin our discussion, let us examine the literary information concerning Bethsaida. Josephus states that at its beginning, Bethsaida was a Lower
Gaulanitis village on the Sea of Galilee (*War* II § 168; *Antiquities* XVIII §
28). A few years before the start of the Common Era, Philip, Herod's son,
raised the village to the status of city by adding residents and strengthening
its fortifications. He named it Julias—after the emperor's daughter (*War* II §
168; *Antiquities* XVIII § 28).

The New Testament gospels describe the activities of Jesus in and near
the city. They also state that it was the home for the disciples Philip, Peter,
and Andrew. See Matthew 11:20-24; Luke 9:10-17; 10:13-15; Mark 6:45;
8:22-26; John 1:44; 6:5-9; 12:20-22.[462]

In 34 C.E., Philip, Herod's son, died in Bethsaida-Julias, and apparently
was buried there. Emperor Tiberius annexed his territory to Syria
(*Antiquities* XVIII § 108). But later we find that Bethsaida-Julias is included
in the kingdom of Agrippa II (*War* III § 57). Under the rule of Agrippa II, it
seems that the Jewish community at Bethsaida continued to exist unharmed.
After his death, 400 years of rabbinic literature provides evidence that
Bethsaida's Jewish community existed.

The lack of space in this essay prevents us from discussing all the many
references to the Jews of Bethsaida in the rabbinic material.[463] But before we

---

[461] And this the reason why on the map accompanying this article three different sites
are marked around #40 (=Bethsaida).

[462] In sixth-century Christian tradition, Bethsaida was also considered as the home of the
fisherman Zebedee and his sons James and John. See Theodosius, *De Situ Terrae Sanctae*, in
P. Geyer, ed., *Itinera Hierosolymitana* (Vienna, 1898) § 2.

[463] And here we must comment that S. Klein erroneously attributed appearance of this
place name to the Jewish community of Sidon (Saida), on the coast of Lebanon. See Klein,

mention a few of them, we must indicate that the name Julias is nowhere included in them.[464] From the time that Bethsaida began to play an important role in Christian traditions and writings, apparently, the Jewish sources refrained from even using its name. They instead called it Saidan (צײדן) or Saidin (צײדין).

In the second generation of Yavneh (early second century C.E.), Hananiah ben Hakinai probably lived in Bethsaida, for Tosefta Niddah 6:6 says: "Said R. Simeon: I found Hananiah ben Hakinai in Saidan and he told me that when he went to R. Aqiba...."[465] As is known, Hananiah ben Hakinai is considered one of the Ten Martyrs, and in the Babylonian Talmud, at Ketubot 62b, we find that his home was in a Jewish city on the bank of a river. This fits with Bethsaida, which lay on the bank of the Jordan River.

During the persecutory decrees promulgated both during and after the Bar Kokhba Rebellion (135-138), Rabban Simeon b. Gamaliel hid in Bethsaida, and only after the decrees were rescinded did he move to Usha. During his stay in Bethsaida, Rabban Simeon b. Gamaliel found there an active group of sages. This experience explains his many comments about Bethsaida in his halakic discussions. For example, Y. Sheqalim 6, 50a reads: "Said Rabban Simeon b. Gamaliel, It happened that I went to Saidan and they brought me more than 300 kinds of fish...." Mishnah Gittin 7:5 states, "Rabban Simeon b. Gamaliel said, 'It once happened in Saidan that a man said to his wife, "Lo, this is your bill of divorce on condition that you give me my cloak," and the cloak was lost. But the sages said, "Let her give him its value."'" And Tosefta Gittin 1:4 reads: "Rabban Gamaliel said to the Sages at Saidan...." These passages make it clear that a group of sages lived at Bethsaida and made halakic decisions. This group may have included the local sages such as Abba Gurion of Saidan who cited in the name of Rabban Gamaliel, the father of Rabban Simeon b. Gamaliel, as we find in the Midrash Abba Gurion on Esther (Buber edition 1):

> Abba Gurion of Saidan said five things in the name of Rabban Gamaliel: When false judges increased, false witnesses also increased; when the brazen increased, people lost their glory; since the lesser say to the greater

---

ha-Yishuv, pp. 129-130. Z. Safrai, who realized this, collected many, but not all, of the references (see Safrai, *Settlement*, pp. 37-39).

[464] Nor is this anything to be surprised at, as Z. Safrai correctly noted (Safrai, *Settlement*, p. 35), for the rabbinic sources generally refrain from calling settlements in the Land of Israel by the Greek or Roman names given them. For example, Acre (Akko) remains Akko in rabbinic literature and not Ptolemais; Emmaus remains Emmaus and not Nicopolis.

[465] In the Tosefta versions of this story (צײדי) appears, but the *Hasdei David* spells it (צײדן). The story also occurs in B. Niddah 52b.

'I am greater than you,' men's years were shortened; since beloved children angered their Father in heaven, He set over them a wicked king.[466]

Another sage of this group may have been Abba Yudan of Saidan who is mentioned in Tosefta Yebamot 14:7 and Oholot 18:7.

In the amoraic period, Rabbi Yose Saidania is mentioned (Y. Ketubot 11:7, 34c; Y. Berakot 4:4, 8a). We also find that Resh Laqish taught the Law at Saidan "on a menorah that is removed by hand" (B. Shabbat 45b). Even this limited selection of passages clearly reveals that a Jewish community existed in Bethsaida and at one point during the rabbinic period it had a rabbinic academy.

In the modern period, the ruin was visited by Sir Laurence Oliphant, the pioneer investigator of the Jewish settlements in the Golan. After his stop there in 1884, he wrote the following:

> I commenced my investigations immediately on crossing the Jordan, at the point of its debouchure into the lake. Here, at a distance of half a mile east from its mouth, are situated the ruins of el-'Araj, which consists of foundations of old walls, and blocks of basaltic stone, cut and uncut, which have been used for building purposes. The ruins cover a limited area. A little over a mile north of el-'Araj there rises from the fertile plain of el-Bateihah a mound strewn with blocks of stone, and remains which cover a considerable area. This is et-Tell, a spot which it has been sought by more than one traveler to identify with Bethsaida Julias. I will not here enter into the much vexed question of whether there were two Bethsaidas, as insisted upon by Reland and many others, or only one; or whether "the desert place apart," upon which was performed the miracle of the five loaves and the two fishes, was on a desolate spur of the range immediately to the north of this Tell, which would necessitate two Bethsaidas, or whether it was not, as Dr. Thomson supposes, at the northeast corner of the Lake on the shoulder overhanging Mes'adiyeh, upon which assumption he constructs a theory which would involve only one; or whether, as suggested by Captain Conder, the Sinaitic Manuscript is right in omitting the definition (Luke 9:10) of the desert where the 5,000 were fed, as "belonging to the city called Bethsaida," in which case the necessity for a second city of that name ceases to exist, and the miracle may have been performed in the plain at the south-east of the Lake. It is possible that excavations at et-Tell might enable us to decide positively whether it is the site of Bethsaida Julias, which we know was in this vicinity.[467]

But 110 years after Oliphant wrote these remarks—and despite the systematic archaeological investigations have been conducted in recent years at et-Tell—many of the questions this pioneer investigator articulated remain.

---

[466] Other information concerning this sage has been preserved. See B. Qiddushin 82a; Tos. Yeb. 4:7; Tos. Oh. 18:7, and B. Yeb. 122a, etc.

[467] Oliphant, "Lake Tiberias," p. 82.

Most early investigators of Palestine in recent centuries were interested in the question of the location of Bethsaida and Julias mainly because of its appearance in the New Testament. But we wish to know the location of the *Saidan* or *Saidin* of Hananiah ben Hakinai, Abba Gurion, Abba Yudan, and R. Yosi. So we shall not survey here the extensive writings of Christian clerics and researchers who concerned themselves with the location of Bethsaida over the last 1400 years (!).[468]

We shall only examine, following Oliphant's remarks, what we know from the archaeological point of view about each of the three sites Oliphant mentioned.

el-'Araj

The remains of this ruin lie on the shore of the Sea of Galilee between the Jordan River (to the west) and Wâdî ez-Zâkiyye (to the east), at coordinates 2082-2554. Oliphant saw there foundations of old walls, and basalt blocks but he described it as a small area.[469] Schumacher, who also surveyed the site in the 1880's, was more impressed by the ruin's size and described it as follows: "A large, completely destroyed site close to the lake in the Batîhah. The building stones of basalt are unusually large; also the foundations, which are still visible, and are built in part with white mortar."[470]

At the start of the twentieth century, G. Dalman visited the place and found shards which he attributed to the Roman period and remains of a monumental structure which he identified as a synagogue.[471] In the 1930's, R. de Haas reported on the existence of remains of a mosaic floor near "Beth ha-Beq" mentioned by Schumacher in his description as the "Hâsil of the famous leader of the Mecca pilgrims, Muhammed Sa'îd Pasha."[472]

Between the years 1950-1967, the place served as a position of the Syrian Army and was designated on maps as el-Hâsel and "Beth ha-Beq." After the Six Day War in 1967, the site was surveyed by the author and his team.[473] In these surveys, it was difficult to estimate the full area of the site since some of it was covered by lagoons and swamps, while other areas were

---

[468] For some of this literature, the reader should consult the article by Bargil Pixner, "Searching for the New Testament Site of Bethsaida," *Biblical Archaeologist* (December 1985): 207-216, and this article's accompanying bibliography. It is not clear why Pixner did not mention the works of Oliphant and Schumacher.

[469] Oliphant, "Lake Tiberias," p. 82.

[470] Schumacher, "Dscholan," pp. 286-287; Schumacher, *Jaulân*, p. 93.

[471] Dalman, "Bethsaida," pp. 45-48; Dalman, *Jesu*, p. 173

[472] See R. de Haas, *Galilee, the Sacred Sea: A Historical and Geographical Description* (Jerusalem, 1933), p. 114. See also Schumacher, "Dscholan," p. 287; Schumacher, *Jaulân*, p. 94

[473] See D. Urman, "el-'Araj, el-Hâsel, and Beth ha-Beq," *Reports of the Staff Officer in Charge of Archaeological Affairs in the Golan* (1968-1972), Archive of the Israel Antiquities Authority, Jerusalem (in Hebrew); Urman, *List*, p. 14; Urman, *Golan*, p. 200, Site #118.

covered by the Sea of Galilee; yet other areas of the ruin were covered by tangled vegetation.

In any case, it seems that Schumacher was correct in judging that this is a large ruin. In the areas of the site we could examine, we found the tops of walls of a number of buildings, although we did not locate the remains of the monumental building Dalman reported. In addition to a few shards from the end of the Hellenistic period, we identified many shards from different stages of the Roman and Byzantine periods as well as the Ottoman period. We found two coins at the site; one was identified as a coin of Philip from 29 or 33 C.E. and the other as a coin of Agrippa II. (The latter has a secondary minting.) Near the 'Beth ha-Beq' structure, we found a concentration of architectural items. These included the remains of a limestone Corinthian column, a limestone Attic pedestal, and a drum of a heart-shaped corner column as well as fragments of column drums made of limestone and basalt. Since we found no items with obviously Jewish decoration (such as a menorah), we concluded our report by pointing out the possibility that two monumental buildings once existed at the site, one built of basalt and the other of limestone (although it could have been a single building in which two types of stone were incorporated). Without archaeological excavation at the site, however, it is difficult to know whether the remains stem from a Jewish public building or a Christian church.[474]

In 1974, M. Nun surveyed the site and wrote:

> In 1974 the author found near Beth ha-Beq architectural items—a capital, a base, and a cornice stone that belonged to a public building of the Roman period whose exact location is not yet known. There is reason to theorize that these are the remains of the Bethsaida synagogue, that was built as were all the other synagogues on the shores of the Kinneret, in the second and third centuries C.E. The building was outstanding with its white stones against the black basalt setting, like the synagogue at Capernaum.[475]

In 1983, the site was examined once again by Mendel Nun and Bargil Pixner, and in this visit they found the drum of the heart-shaped corner-column that had already been reported in the author's survey.[476]

In the course of March and April 1987, R. Arav conducted a limited exploratory dig in the site area. Unfortunately, he has yet to publish a full report on the excavation; he has written only the following

> El-'Araj is a low mound extending over 10 dunams near the mouth of the Jordan River, Remains of a monumental building are visible. The excavation of el-'Arajrevealed a single level, dating from the fourth to the sixth centuries C.E. A few Hellenistic and mediaeval shards testified to some sort

---

[474] See previous note.
[475] Nun, *Kinneret*, p. 20.
[476] See Pixner, "Bethsaida," pp. 213-214.

of activity during these periods. It is noteworthy that we did not find a Hellenistic or Roman city level at el-'Araj. In the light of the finds from the probe excavations, it seems more reasonable to identify ancient Bethsaida with et-Tell than with el-'Araj.[477]

el-Meṣ'adiyye

This Syrian Army position (now in ruins) was built upon the remains of an ancient site on the shore of the Sea of Galilee south-east of el-'Araj, at coordinates 2088-2548. The similarity of the Arabic name of the site to the names Saidan and Bethsaida drew the attention of many Christian researchers, but none of them reported the existence of antiquities prior to Schumacher. Schumacher, who surveyed the site in the 1880's, described it as:

> A ruin and winter village of the 'Arab et-Tellawîyeh, on an artificial elevation of the Bateîḥah on the Lake of Tiberias. The ruins with a few palms and fruit trees, the last remains of a once large vegetation, are unimportant, although extensive; the building stones are mostly unhewn. The place is surrounded by marshes, and consequently unhealthy. The Wâdî el-Meṣ'adiyye or Wâdî es-Saffah, bouches west of the Wâdî ed-Dâliyye, and east of the ruins, into the Lake. To me it appears that the old site corresponds to the Biblical Bethsaida Julias, because, at the present time, it lies quite close to the Lake, and in earlier times must have lain immediately on the Lake (see, however, under et-Tell).[478]

After the Six Day War, the Syrian outpost and the site were surveyed by the author and his team.[479] Despite the thick vegetation that covered the site at the time of the survey, it was possible to determine that the houses of the Syrian position were built in part on the tops of the walls of ancient structures, with many ancient building stones in secondary use. We did not find any architectural items worth mentioning here. But it was possible to make out on the shoreline the remains of an ancient fishing anchorage. Among the shards that were collected at the site, there were few from the late Hellenistic period and an abundance of shards from the different stages of the Roman, Byzantine, Arab, and Ottoman periods. In the survey's report, we raised the possibility that this ancient site is a direct continuation of the site at el-'Araj.[480] The fact that at the time of the survey the outflow of Wâdî ez-

---

[477] Arav, "el-'Araj," pp. 187-188. See also Kuhn and Arav, pp. 93-94.

[478] Schumacher, "Dscholan," pp. 310-311; Schumacher, *Jaulân*, p. 221.

[479] See D. Urman, "el-Meṣ'adiyye," *Special Surveys Reports,* Archive of the Association for the Archaeological Survey of Israel, Israel Antiquities Authority, Jerusalem (in Hebrew); D. Urman, "el-Meṣ'adiyye," *Reports of the Staff Officer in Charge of Archaeological Affairs in the Golan* (1968-1972), Archive of the Israel Antiquities Authority, Jerusalem (in Hebrew); Urman, *Golan*, p. 201, Site #128.

[480] See previous note and especially the note on Site #128 in Urman, *Golan*, p. 214.

Zâkiyye separated the two sites does not affect this suggestion, for
Schumacher states that the Wâdî's outflow (which he calls Wâdî el-
Meṣ'adiyye or Wâdî es-Saffah) was east (!) of el-Meṣ'adiyye.[481]

et-Tell

These ruins of a Syrian military position were built on the remains of an
ancient site at coordinates 2093-2574. In the past, an Arab village located
here was designated on the maps by various names: el-'Amîriyye, et-
Tellâwiyye, and Mashfa'. Oliphant, who visited the place in 1884, noticed
that the Arab village was built among ancient ruins but he did not tarry to
examine them. He wrote: "A small native village has been built among the
ruins, which do not at present afford to the passing traveler any indications
of former magnificence; but I was unable at the time to examine
them...."[482]

Schumacher, who surveyed the site thoroughly, was well aware that
many investigators were trying to identify this as Bethsaida-Julias, wrote:

> A large winter village of 'Arab-et-Tellâwiyye, who take their name from
> this ruin. It contains 60 carelessly built huts on the north-west margin of
> the Bateîhah. These huts, *with extremely few antique remnants*, cover the
> south-west slope of a small hill, past the foot of which the spring, 'Ain
> Mûsmâr flows, turning a mill at the Jordan. From ten to fifteen persons
> from et-Tell have built huts round this latter, which they inhabit perma-
> nently; they have also laid out some gardens. At the foot of et-Tell, on the
> spring 'Ain-Mûsmâr, stands the tomb of the Sheikh 'Abdallah; it is sur-
> rounded by a great stone circle and overshadowed by bramble bushes. East
> of et-Tell rises a volcanic hill, between which a small wâdî stretches. Et-
> Tell has been frequently connected with Bethsaida-Julias by Seetzen,
> Smith, and others. But this place appears to me to be too far inland for a
> fishing village, being one and a quarter miles distant from the Lake. From
> this point of view el-Meṣ'adiyye has manifestly more recommendations.
> Besides which, *up to the present, there have not by any means been more
> ornaments or inscriptions discovered in et-Tell which would lead to con-
> clusions as to the past of this place than in el-Meṣ'adiyye*. In one respect
> only, et-Tell favours the widely spread assumption, viz., in its elevated
> position commanding the plain. Is it not possible that el-'Araj marks the
> fishing village; et-Tell, on the other hand, the princely residence, and that
> both places were closely united by the beautiful roads still visible? In this
> case, if the industry of earlier days had disappeared in the former, the glory
> and the splendour of the seat of the Tetrarchs would have given way to a
> heap of wretched huts.[483]

[481] Schumacher, "Dscholan," pp. 310-311; Schumacher, *Jaulân*, p. 221.

[482] Oliphant, "Lake Tiberias," p. 82.

[483] Schumacher, "Dscholan," pp. 318-319; Schumacher, *Jaulân*, pp. 245-246. Emphasis
mine.

The survey teams led by C. Epstein and S. Gutman surveyed the site in 1967 and reported that it is possible to make out within the defense trenches of the Syrian Army position the remains of ancient walls. The shards that were collected in this survey were dated to the following periods: Early Bronze Age II, Middle Bronze Age I and II, Iron Age I, Iron Age II, Roman, Byzantine, and Ottoman.[484]

In 1968, the Syrian position and the ruins of the Arab village were surveyed by the author and his staff.[485] This survey estimated the area of the ancient site at about 45 dunams.[486] In addition to shards from periods identified by the previous teams, we also found a few shards from the Hellenistic period and a large number from the various stages of the Arab period. In concluding our report, we commented that "we share Schumacher's disappointment over the finds at the site, for at a place identified by many researchers as Bethsaida, we expected to find many decorated architectural artifacts and inscriptions—as are found at almost every one of the Jewish sites in the Golan that are not mentioned in the sources."[487]

In 1970, M. Nun reported to us that he found a broken lintel among the ruins of the Arab village. The lintel had reliefs of a meander motif and rosettes.[488] This single find, which may have originally belonged to a Jewish public building, has been attributed by R. Arav to a structure he dates to the Late Hellenistic-Early Roman period and whose remains were unearthed in Area A of his excavations.[489] Arav claims that in this structure he found additional decorated stones.[490] Arav has yet to publish any details or photographs of these stones, however, so it is difficult to assess whether he is correct in 'adopting' the lintel fragment for the building excavated in Area A.

---

[484] Epstein & Gutman, pp. 276-277, Site #111.

[485] See D. Urman, "et-Tell, el-'Amîriyye," *Special Surveys Reports*, Archive of the Association for the Archaeological Survey of Israel, Israel Antiquities Authority, Jerusalem (in Hebrew); D. Urman, "et-Tell, el-'Amîriyye, et-Tellâwiyye and Mashfa'," *Reports of the Staff Officer in Charge of Archaeological Affairs in the Golan* (1968-1972), Archive of the Israel Antiquities Authority, Jerusalem (in Hebrew); Urman, *List:*, p. 14; Urman, *Golan*, p. 199, Site #112.

[486] Here we must indicate that R. Arav, the excavator at the site in recent years, claims that its area is about 80 dunams (see, for example, Arav, "el-'Araj," p. 187). Practically speaking, he includes the hill called et-Tell, which is basically a volcanic mound. Since at this stage his excavation is focused only on the center of the site, we are not yet sure that he is correct in his assessment.

[487] See D. Urman, "et-Tell, el-'Amîriyye," *Special Surveys Reports*, p. 3. See also note 485.

[488] For a photograph of the lintel, see Nun, *Kinneret*, p. 21 as well as Pixner, "Bethsaida," p. 207.

[489] See Arav, "Bethsaida-1," p. 185.

[490] Arav, "Bethsaida-1," p. 185. See also Kuhn and Arav, pp. 95-97.

Since March 1987, R. Arav has been excavating this site. With regard to the location of Bethsaida-Julias, Arav is convinced that at et-Tell he is excavating its remains.[491] His first reports reveal that he has found strata from the Early Bronze Age, Iron Age I and II, and from a period he calls Late Hellenistic-Early Roman.[492] Most impressive are his finds from Iron Age I and II which he relates to the Geshurites mentioned in the Bible as a kingdom that had special relationships with King David.[493] By contrast, his finds from the Hellenistic and Roman periods are spotty. I should note that Arav has found several coins of Alexander Jannaeus and Philip, son of Herod,[494] but he has not yet raised the possibility that one of the late Hellenistic strata at the site was from the time Bethsaida was either destroyed or resettled by Alexander Jannaeus (as Z. Ma'oz found in his excavations at Mazra'at Kanaf).[495]

To conclude our discussion of the archaeological finds uncovered at el-'Araj, el-Meṣ'adiyye, and et-Tell, let us again point out here that we wish to find at one of these three sites either the remains of Bethsaida-Julias from the time of Philip son of Herod and of Jesus, or the Saidan or Saidin of H,)ananiah ben Ḥakinai, Abba Gurion, Abba Yudan, and R. Yosi Saidania. To our regret, the excavation of R. Arav at el-'Araj was brief and limited, his excavations at et-Tell have thus far not yielded the finds we hoped for, and at el-Meṣ'adiyye he has not excavated at all. In the light of our knowledge of these sites and of our experience with the el-Kûrsî excavations—where we found the impressive remains of a monastery and a church completely buried under the silt of Wâdî es-Samekh—we suggested to R. Arav and the members of his expedition[496] that they return and renew the excavations at el-'Araj, inaugurate excavations on a broad scope at el-Meṣ'adiyye, and in the area between this ruin and el-'Araj. This could become a continuation of their fruitful work at et-Tell. For it is possible that the silt of the streams of the Bateiḥah Valley still hides the missing remains of Jewish Bethsaida at el-Meṣ'adiyye and el-'Araj. Whether or not they follow our advice, we hope that the Bethsaida Expedition uncover clear Jewish finds at et-Tell.

---

[491] And so it is that in all of his recent articles the name et-Tell has disappeared from the title and in its place only Bethsaida appears. See below, note 492.

[492] See Arav, "el-'Araj"; Arav, "Et-Tell—1"; Arav, "Et-Tell—2"; Arav, "Et-Tell—3"; Arav, "Bethsaida—1"; Arav, "Bethsaida—2"; Arav, "Bethsaida—3"; Arav, "Bethsaida—4"; Arav, "Bethsaida—5"; Arav, "Bethsaida—6"; Kuhn and Arav, pp. 94-106.

[493] See Arav, "Bethsaida—3," p. 173.

[494] See Arav, "Et-Tell—1," p. 178; Arav, "Et-Tell—2," p. 100; Arav, "Bethsaida—3," p. 174; Arav, "Bethsaida-4," p. 9; Arav, "Bethsaida-5," p. 9; Kuhn and Arav, p. 97.

[495] See the section on Mazra'at Kanaf.

[496] The suggestion was made during my lecture in a special session entitled "New Testament Archaeology and Bethsaida" at the 1993 *Society of Biblical Literature* International Meeting held July 25-28, 1993 in Münster, Germany.

EL-ḤÛSEINIYYE (EL-AḤSENIYEH, ḤÛSNIYÂT ESH-SHEIKH 'ALI)

These ruins of a now-abandoned Syrian village lie on the north bank of
Naḥal Yahûdiyye at coordinates 2114-2559. The ancient site was first reported by Sir Laurence Oliphant who visited the village in December, 1884
and saw how its Bedouin residents were digging among the remains of the
ancient structures for any dressed stones that seemed worth taking for their
buildings.[497] Oliphant estimated the area of the ancient site as larger than
that at Kh. ed-Dîkkeh (which he had visited prior to his visit to El-
Ḥûseiniyye), "and that it was in ancient times probably the centre of a larger
population."[498]

In describing the remains of a monumental structure uncovered by the
Bedouins, he writes:

> The character of the remains now exposed to view is very difficult to deter-
> mine, owing to the confusion which has been created by their representing
> two periods, the building of the later having apparently been placed diago-
> nally on the one that preceded it. They were situated upon a terrace of solid
> masonry about 5 feet high, now strewn with building stones. The upper or
> more recent chamber measured 20 feet across one way, but there was noth-
> ing to determine its length, no walls having been left standing; the dimen-
> sion in one direction, however, could be gathered from the cement floor
> which still remained, a considerable portion of which was visible at a
> depth of 18 inches below the surface of the earth. There appeared, 18
> inches below it, a floor of solid stone, and this was evidently a portion of a
> building of some size, to judge from the blocks of stone which apparently
> were the foundations for the pedestals of columns. These consisted of five
> cubes of stone, each 2 feet every way, and 6 feet apart. As the stone floor
> on which they stood was 3 feet below the surface of the ground, the upper
> surface was 1 foot below it, and there may therefore have been more in con-
> tinuation of the line in which they were, which the excavations of the vil-
> lagers had not revealed. They ran north and south, and diagonally to the
> upper flooring of cement. There were some fragments of columns,
> pedestals, and carved cornices and capitals lying among the ruins of the
> vicinity, but they were much broken, and not sufficiently noteworthy to
> stop to sketch.[499]

Oliphant's description is important, for today's visitor to the site can no
longer see what this pioneering investigator described. From what he wrote
it is clear that the site contains the remains of a monumental structure
which, at its bottom stage, has a north-south lengthwise axis, and its floor
was built of stone slabs. From the description of the stones of the stylobate
of the row of the five columns which Oliphant saw and from the compari-

---

[497] Oliphant, "Lake Tiberias," pp. 85-86.
[498] Oliphant, "Lake Tiberias," p. 85.
[499] Oliphant, "Lake Tiberias," pp. 85-86.

son he made between the remains of this structure and those at Kh. ed-Dîkkeh, there is a reasonable possibility that the structure, at least in its bottom stage, served as a Jewish public building.[500]

G. Schumacher, who visited the village some time after Oliphant, apparently did not see the remains of the monumental building. He reported, by contrast, finding remains of a bath-house on the site, as well as walls with cell-work and, near them, decorated items that seemed to him to be of the Roman period.[501] It may be that some of the items that Schumacher saw originally belonged to the Jewish public building; one of the items was decorated with a relief of a wreath with a 'Hercules' knot' that had grape clusters at its edges. At the center of the wreath there is an additional relief of a rosette.[502]

In December of 1885, Oliphant learned that the villagers had uncovered more decorated stones on two of which there were lions carved.[503] In light of this information, Oliphant visited the village again and found that the villagers had incorporated a relief with a lion's head into the wall of a granary which had been built since his previous visit, whereas the second relief had not yet been taken for use in building again and showed the body of a lion but its head was missing.[504] The two architectural items with lions strengthen the probability that the public building which Oliphant reported was Jewish, for on many of the Jewish public buildings in the Golan and the Galilee of the rabbinic period reliefs of lions were found.

Since the 1880's, the village has apparently undergone many changes—especially since 1950, when it began to be used as a military outpost on the front line against Israel. In 1968, the author and his staff surveyed the village and found that the area of the ancient site was about 15 dunams.[505] The shards scattered there attest to the settlement's occupation off and on from the ancient Roman period and up until the time of the survey.[506] It seems that the location of the public building described by Oliphant became the later village's cemetery; today it lies north of the ruins of the mid-twentieth

[500] Oliphant, "Lake Tiberias," p. 85.

[501] Schumacher, "Dscholan," pp. 283-284; Schumacher, *Jaulân*, pp. 73-74.

[502] Schumacher, "Dscholan," p. 284, Fig. 39; Schumacher, *Jaulân*, p. 74, Fig. 12.

[503] Oliphant, "New Discoveries," p. 73.

[504] Oliphant, "New Discoveries," pp. 73-74, Figs. 1-2.

[505] The staff that assisted me in the survey of the abandoned villages in the Golan in 1967-1968 included many good people, most of them from the founding nucleus of Kibbutz Merom Golan—which in those days resided in Quneitra—as well as volunteers from Israel and abroad who came to this kibbutz. Actually the survey of the abandoned villages in those days served as a source of livelihood for the founders of Merom Golan. Four of the staff in one way or another remained involved with the investigation of the Golan antiquities and were my partners in many discoveries in the region: S. Bar-Lev, D. Ben-Ami, Y. Gal, and M. Hartal. My thanks go to them and all the staff not mentioned by name.

[506] See Urman, *List*, p. 15; Urman, *Golan*, p. 200, Site #120.

century Syrian village. The area of the cemetery at the time of the survey looked like a low tell and it was possible to make out upon it a great number of tops of ancient walls. The thickness of a number of these wall tops indicate monumental construction there. On top of one wall we found a basalt doorpost stone standing *in situ*, decorated with profiles of the kind found in a number of the Jewish public buildings in the Golan and in the Galilee. Near the doorpost, we found part of an architectural item made of basalt which was decorated with a relief of an eagle with outspread wings (of which only the left wing survived). This item was taken from the area and transferred at the time to the Golan antiquities collection housed in Quneiṭra; at time of this writing, it is in the Golan Antiquities Museum in Qaṣrîn. Among the other architectural items registered by us in the survey, all made of basalt, were two Attic column bases, an Ionic column base, six column shafts, three Doric capitals, and two fragments of a richly ornamented cornice.[507]

In 1985, the site was surveyed once again by Z. Maʿoz but his reports reveal no new information.[508] In Z. Ilan's last book, he reveals that he visited the site during the 1980's. The book includes a photograph of an item decorated with vine branches which we had not seen in our survey.[509]

KH. KHAWKHA (EL-KHÔKA, EL-KOKA)

This abandoned Syrian village was built on an ancient ruin above the south bank of Naḥal Daliyyot (Wâdî ed-Dâliyye), at coordinates 2153-2556. G. Schumacher, who visited the region in 1884, does not mention any antiquities there and writes only: "El-Khôka—A little winter village with a few huts, containing about twenty inhabitants. Its position on the rising high plateau above the Batîhah is a peculiarly beautiful one."[510] It is clear, by contrast, that L. Oliphant actually visited the site. He published an illustration of the remains of the early spring house near the ruin, and noted that he found at the site: "numerous fragments of columns and a block which was built into the wall of a granary...upon which there was carved a very beautiful scroll of flowers and foliage."[511] In summing up the description of

---

[507] See D. Urman, "El Ḥuseiniyye," *Special Surveys Reports*, Archive of the Association for the Archaeological Survey of Israel, Israel Antiquities Authority, Jerusalem (in Hebrew).

[508] See See Maʿoz, "Golan—1," p. 293; Maʿoz, "Golan—2," p. 542.

[509] Ilan, *Israel*, p. 66. Fig. 2. The late Z. Ilan suggested that the item "may perhaps be part of the lintel that Oliphant had described." But it seems that he was referring to the item ornamented with the grape clusters published by Schumacher (see above), because Oliphant5 never described a lintel from this site. According to Ilan, the item was transferred from the area to the Golan Antiquities Museum in Qaṣrîn.

[510] Schumacher, "Dscholan," pp. 290-291; Schumacher, *Jaulân*, p. 186.

[511] Oliphant, "New Discoveries," pp. 74-75.

his findings there, Oliphant writes: "el-Koka was evidently a place of some importance."[512]

In 1967, the site was surveyed by C. Epstein who reported that the Syrian houses and courtyards contained many ancient building stones, including columns, capitals, and parts of an olive-oil press.[513] North of the village, on a small hill, the surveyor and her team made out ruins of early houses, whose walls and yards were well preserved. Epstein reported that her team found shards from the Roman, Byzantine, and Ottoman periods.[514]

In 1968, the abandoned Syrian village and the ancient ruin were surveyed by the author and his team.[515] In this survey it became clear that the area of the ancient ruin was about 20 dunams. The modern Syrian houses had been built on nearly the entire ruin, with secondary use of wall sections and building stones from the ancient structures. Among the architectural items recorded in our survey, especially noteworthy are an Attic pedestal, a number of column fragments, Doric and Ionic capitals, cornice and architrave fragments—all well crafted out of local basalt. Our survey also registered the remains of the spring house depicted by L. Oliphant and the sections of olive-oil presses reported by Epstein. The pottery remains we gathered in the village included, in addition to those reported by Epstein, shards from different Arab periods. In our survey's conclusion, we wrote that "the architectural items that had been incorporated in secondary use in the houses of the abandoned Syrian village were perhaps taken from a monumental Jewish structure that had been there from the periods of the Mishnah and the Talmud, but we were unable in our survey to locate its site and its remains."[516]

In January 1976, the site was again surveyed by Z. Ilan and S. Bar-Lev.[517] In this survey, the location of the monumental building in the southern part of the village was found. Z. Ma'oz claims that he too surveyed the site in 1979, but in his publications thereafter—in which he ignores the reports of all previous investigators, including that of Ilan and Bar-Lev—we found no new information not already in the reports of Ilan and Bar-Lev.[518]

In 1985, Ilan continued his survey of the site and, in his last book, he described the remains of the monumental building thus:

---

[512] See previous note.

[513] Epstein & Gutman, p. 279, Site #119.

[514] See previous note.

[515] D. Urman, "Kh. Khawkha," *Special Surveys Reports*, Archive of the Association for the Archaeological Survey of Israel, Israel Antiquities Authority, Jerusalem (in Hebrew); Urman, *List*, p. 15; Urman, *Golan*, p. 200, Site #121.

[516] See previous note as well as Urman, *Golan*, p. 214, note for Site #121.

[517] Ben-Ari and Bar-Lev, "Survey," p. 2.

[518] See Ma'oz, *Golan*, p. 33; Ma'oz, "Golan Synagogues," p. 156; Ma'oz, "Golan—1," p. 292; Ma'oz, "Golan—2," p. 541.

The synagogue was built in the southern part of the village, at its highest point. Later buildings were built within its compound, but it is still possible to make out the east and the south walls that remained to a height of 4-5 courses of ashlar. From the west wall, one or two courses were preserved and upon them some later construction. The northern wall was not found. From the southern wall westward, a wall built of hewn stone extends with an original complete entranceway in it. (Perhaps another entranceway survived.) It forms a corner with a north-south wall, and if it is ancient, it is the western end of the complex. If these are really parts of the building, then the building's lengthwise axis is east-west and its length is 40.65 m.—longer than usual. The hall length is 17 m. and the section west of it apparently served as a courtyard. The construction system characteristic of the building, and especially obvious in the south wall, is the existence of a course of large stones atop a number of courses medium-sized stones. It could be that this layer indicates the transition from the first floor to the second floor. In the east side of the south wall there apparently was an entranceway. The facade of the building was apparently in the west, like the buildings at Mazra'at Kanaf and Deir 'Azîz, located 3-4 kilometers south of Kh. Khawkha. This hypothesis rests on the assumption that the courtyard was on the west, and the fact that near the west wall a large supporting stone lug (console) was found. Carved into its facade was the head of an animal with its head smashed, apparently a lion's head (we at first thought it to be an eagle's head). There are tens of architectural items that belonged to the building scattered at the site, including a stone fragment with deep grooves, apparently the left branches of an ordinary menorah. Also found were an Attic pedestal of the sort characteristic of synagogues, and columns. Round one of the columns there are triangular hollows (for candles?). A few Ionic and Doric capitals were found as well as small bases. In the building's inner wall and beside it there are two frieze sections on which there are scrolls of leaves of the sort known at Kh. ed-Dîkkeh, Jarâba, Capernaum, and Chorazin. Especially noteworthy is the Corinthian capital found at the site, and one or two parts of similar capitals.[519]

Ilan concludes his description with the following remark: "According to the remains of the building and its stones, it was a complex and magnificent building. Would that we shall have the funding to uncover and preserve it."[520] Of this it has been said, "Whoever adds, detracts!"

ZEIṬA

This small abandoned Syrian village was built upon an ancient ruin on top of a low hill situated above the south bank of Naḥal Daliyyot (Wâdî ed-Dâliyye), at coordinates 2168-2554. Schumacher, who visited it in 1884,

---

[519] Ilan, *Israel,* p. 88.
[520] See previous note.

described it as "A small Bedawîn village with some ruins, in the neighbourhood of the Wâdî Joramâyeh."[521]

L. Oliphant, who toured the region in December 1885, likewise devoted
only one sentence to this site: "I passed one small unimportant ruin called
Zeiṭa, with blocks of basalt and foundations; near a spring were two or three
date palms, but no traces of ruins near them."[522]

In 1968, the site was surveyed briefly by C. Epstein's team. They reported the existence of a ruin among the olive groves near two springs, and
the lower part of an olive-oil press hewn into the rock on the hill near the
eastern spring. Epstein dated pottery found at the site to the Roman III,
Byzantine, and Ottoman periods.[523]

A short time after Epstein's survey, the author and his team surveyed the
Syrian village and the ruins. They estimated the ancient ruin's area at about
15 dunams. It also became clear that ancient architectural items and a large
quantity of ancient well-hewn ashlars were incorporated in secondary use in
some modern buildings. The architectural items included a number of column bases and shafts as well as Doric capitals apparently taken from the
remains of a monumental building. The survey team did not succeed in locating this building.[524]

In 1985, Z. Ilan and S. Adam surveyed the site and recorded several architectural items mentioned in our report but left at the site, as well as several
items that had been transferred to the yard of a house in the nearby moshav,
Ma'ale Gamala.[525] In summarizing the discussion of his survey at Zeiṭa,
Ilan wrote, "It seems that this was one of the Jewish settlements in the region of Naḥal Daliyyot—Bâṭrah, Kh. Khawkha, and Mazra'at Kanaf, part of
the continuous Jewish region of the Golan in the days of the talmud."[526]
Since Ilan and his colleague were unable to locate the site of the monumental building in their survey, Zeiṭa was only included in Ilan's last book in
the list of "additional possible synagogues" that appears at the end of his
book.[527]

In October-November 1988, a team led by A. Golani surveyed the site
once again. In this survey's brief published report, Golani thinks he identified the monumental public structure. He states, "The foundations of a large
ashlar structure were examined. Scattered ashlar blocks and architectural ele-

[521] Schumacher, "Dscholan," p. 363; Schumacher, *Jaulân*, p. 273.
[522] Oliphant, "New Discoveries," p. 74.
[523] Epstein & Gutman, p. 279, Site #120.
[524] D. Urman, "Zeiṭa," *Special Surveys Reports*, Archive of the Association for the
Archaeological Survey of Israel, Israel Antiquities Authority, Jerusalem (in Hebrew);
Urman, *List*, p. 15; Urman, *Golan*, p. 200, Site #122.
[525] See Ilan, *Ancient Synagogues*, pp. 153-154; Ilan, *Galilee and Golan*, pp. 98-99.
[526] Ilan, *Ancient Synagogues*, p. 154.
[527] Ilan, *Israel*, p. 323.

ments were recorded, which may be remains of a synagogue, like the structures in the nearby sites of Khawkha, Bâṭrah and Kanaf."[528] We must await the building's excavation to determine the date of its construction and use.

MAZRA'AT KANAF (KANEF, KH. KÂNEF, Ḥ. KANAF)

This now-abandoned Syrian village was built among the ruins of an ancient Jewish settlement at coordinates 2145-2531. The ancient settlement was built on the top of a lofty spur surrounded on three sides by steep slopes, with a spectacular view of the Sea of Galilee. Today it is about two kilometers north of the Israeli moshav Ma'ale Gamala.

The site's Jewish remains were discovered by L. Oliphant, who visited it in December 1885. He described his finds thus:

> On the high bluff which separates the Wâdî Shebib from the Wâdî Shukeiyif, and two miles and a half east of el-Akib, are situated the ruins of Kanef. Hearing from the Vakeel that I should find important remains there, I rode up to examine them, under the guidance of a Bedouin sheikh. Kanef is situated about 1,300 feet above the level of the lake, and the latter part of the ascent is somewhat steep. The whole of this region belongs to Mohammed Said Pasha, who has a hasil, or granary here; but the only inhabitants are some Diab Arabs, who are his tenants, and whose tents were pitched not far from the Khurbet. This consisted of a considerable area of ruin, and numerous fragments of columns were scattered about; a row of five, some standing to a height of seven feet, supported the roof of a cowshed, but of these only one was a monolith, the others consisted of fragments which had been placed one upon another, and I could not trace on the spot the foundation of the building of which they may have formed part. They probably belonged to the ruin which I immediately afterwards discovered on the other side of the hasil, about 50 yards distant, and which unquestionably was that of a synagogue, as will appear from a fragment of a cornice which I have found here, measuring 7 feet by 2 feet 8 inches, on which was à Hebrew [should be Aramaic] inscription (Fig. 4). Close by were other carved fragments, pedestals, etc., and two square stones, on which were carved circular devices, both of them 18 inches in diameter (Figs. 5 and 6). The ground was so thickly strewn with huge basalt building stones that I could only discover here and there traces of the foundations, and was unable to measure the dimensions of the building, About two hundred yards from the ruin was a spring, which had also been masoned like the one at el-Koka [=Kh. Khawkha], but which was not in such a good state of preservation.[529]

It is not clear whether G. Schumacher visited the site or only described it from hearsay, for he mentions no Jewish finds at the site. "Kanef—A Bedawîn winter village east of Batîhah and a magazine of Muhammed Sa'îd

[528] Golani, "Golan," p. 8.
[529] Oliphant, "New Discoveries," pp. 75-76. Brackets mine.

Pasha of Damascus, occupied by ten to fifteen inhabitants, and is conspicuous from its high position. There are some old building stones."[530]

Oliphant, as we noted, erred in identifying the language of the inscription he had found. He published a drawing of it without any transcription or explanation. We shall discuss the inscription below, but at this stage we shall note that in 1914 G. Dalman republished Oliphant's copy with a transcript and short commentary.[531] His reading was adopted by S. Klein several years later.[532] Klein subsequently published it again, with a slight change.[533]

In November 1932, after completing his excavations of the synagogue at Ḥammat Gader, Prof. E. L. Sukenik took his team to examine the Jewish remains at Mazra'at Kanaf. After this visit, he published short articles in English and Hebrew on the remains of the Jewish public building at the site.[534] The articles included drawings and photographs of artifacts that have since been broken and used as building stones in the Syrian village built in the 1950's. Sukenik measured the remains of the public structure and describes it thus:

> On the site of the ancient structure a stone building has been erected, in which is stored the grain reaped by the Bedouin tenants of the local landowner, a wealthy Damascene. Of the synagogue there remains *in situ* the north-east corner, which has been included in the modern building (Pl. XXb). This corner comprises the foundation and five additional courses of the wall. They are of basalt blocks of unequal size, but well cut, and hold together without cement. At the north side (16.30 m. long) a stone floor appears, which seems to be the only surviving part of the synagogue's paved court. It is possible that the entrance to the modern building near the east corner of this wall is simply being re-used, and that it once led from the court into the synagogue. Many well-hewn and well-dressed basalt stones lie about this side, and undoubtedly belong to the ancient structure.
>
> Of the west wall there remains *in situ* only the foundation course to the extent of 11 m. No part of the upper courses has survived in place. In front of the wall there are still a few steps, and in one corner the remains of a pavement, 1.35 m. lower than that of the north side of the court. Among the numerous stones strewn about there are some drums of columns, a lintel. door-posts, jambs, and various decorated stones (Fig. 29). One may consequently conclude that the facade of the synagogue was here on the west side, as was customary in Transjordanian Synagogues. It seems to me that a kind of a small porch was built in front of this facade, and that some steps led up from it to the synagogue.[535]

---

[530] Schumacher, "Dscholan," p. 334; Schumacher, *Jaulân*, p. 169

[531] Dalman, "Palästina," p. 138.

[532] Klein, *Inscriptionum*, p. 82.

[533] S. Klein, "Inscriptions from Ancient Synagogues in the Land of Israel," *Yedi'ot ha-Makhon le-Mada'ei ha-Yahadut*, (Hebrew University in Jerusalem, 1925), vol. 2, p. 33 (in Hebrew).

[534] Sukenik, "Khirbet Kànef," pp. 74-80; Sukenik, "el-Ḥammeh," pp. 174-178.

[535] Sukenik, "el-Ḥammeh," pp. 175-176.

In his articles, Sukenik also published a more exact copy of the inscription Oliphant discovered, and identified the stone upon which it was carved as a lintel fragment, 2.40 m. long and 0.82 high. Sukenik found that the right end of the upper part of the lintel had been broken and pointed out that the lintel's left end was also missing. According to Sukenik, the length of the remaining portion of the inscription is 1.58 m., the letters are 4.5-6.5 cm. high. It reads:[536]

...[ברכ]תה דכיר לטב יוסה בר חלפו בר חנ...

The translation is:

...the blessing. Remembered for good Yose bar Ḥalfo bar Ḥan...

Sukenik also published, as we mentioned, drawings and photographs of decorated architectural items which he also attributed to the site's Jewish public structure.[537]

In 1967, the site was surveyed by C. Epstein and S. Gutman, who reported that the Syrian village contained many ancient building stones in secondary use, and that the synagogue's location is now the site of a cross-vault building using the ancient building's foundations and the corners of its ashlar walls. Near the building, the surveyors found part of the decorated lintel, but the remains of the inscription were found set as building stones in the Syrian houses. At the foot of the Syrian village the surveyors gathered shards from periods they identified as "Roman-Byzantine, and Ottoman."[538]

In 1968, the author and his team also surveyed the site.[539] In the survey it became clear that whereas the area of the Syrian village is about 15 dunams and is built mainly on top of the spur, the ancient settlement also spread over the slopes of the spur and covered about 25 dunams. In many instances, the Syrian houses had been built using walls of the ancient Jewish buildings. The survey counted sixteen such Syrian structures, and about another twenty built over ancient buildings without using the ancient walls. All the Syrian structures were built of ancient building blocks, some of which were re-dressed by the Syrians. Thus, many architectural items were found incorporated in Syrian houses in secondary use, some decorated with the reliefs described by Oliphant and Sukenik. A small amount of the shards collected during the survey derived from the Hellenistic period, but most

[536] Sukenik, "el-Ḥammeh," pp. 176-177.

[537] Sukenik, "el-Ḥammeh," pp. 177-178 and Sukenik, "Khirbet Kànef," pp. 77-80.

[538] Epstein & Gutman, pp. 279-280, Site #129.

[539] See D. Urman, "Mazra'at Kanaf," *Special Surveys Reports,* Archive of the Association for the Archaeological Survey of Israel, Israel Antiquities Authority, Jerusalem (in Hebrew); D. Urman, "Mazra'at Kanaf," *Reports of the Staff Officer in Charge of Archaeological Affairs in the Golan* (1968-1972), Archive of the Israel Antiquities Authority, Jerusalem (in Hebrew); Urman, *List,* p. 15; Urman, *Golan,* p. 201, Site #132.

stemmed from the different stages of the Roman, Byzantine, and Arab periods.

During 1978-1980 and in 1985, Z. Ma'oz conducted four short seasons of excavation at the site. As I write these lines, the excavator has yet to publish a full, detailed report of his excavations.[540] We must therefore make do here with his remarks in the English edition of the *New Encyclopedia of Archaeological Excavations in the Holy Land*.[541] Ma'oz dug in two areas of the site: Area A—the public building and its surroundings; Area B—a residential structure on the southern slope of the site.

Under the heading of *Stratigraphy and Chronology* he writes:

> A stratigraphic sequence (with extended gaps) from the Middle Bronze Age to the 1950's was found only in Area A, north of the synagogue. It has been identified as follows:
> Stratum VIII: Middle Bronze Age II (17th century B.C.E.). A tomb on the north slope of the site.
> Stratum VII: Late Bronze Age to Iron Age (13th-10th centuries B.C.E.). Parts of walls, foundations, and floors.
> Stratum VI: Middle Hellenistic period (150-81 B.C.E.). Foundations of a watchtower and a chamber roofed with stone slabs.
> Stratum VA: Late Hellenistic to Early Roman periods (first century B.C.E.). Orderly construction of a set of rooms (barrack?)
> Stratum VB: Early Roman period (first century C.E.). Changes in the rooms of the barrack, floor raising, and abandonment during the First Jewish Revolt against Rome in 67 C.E.
> Stratum IV: Late Roman to Early Byzantine periods (fourth-fifth centuries C.E.). Pottery and numismatic finds in the foundations of the synagogue.
> Stratum IIIA: Middle Byzantine period (beginning of the sixth century C.E.). Construction of a synagogue and a pavement on the north side of a street.
> Stratum IIIB: Late Byzantine period (second half of the sixth century C.E.). Reconstruction of the synagogue following an earthquake (?); construction of a platform in front of the synagogue on the west; and changes in the paved street.
> Stratum II: Mameluke to Ottoman periods (13th-16th centuries). Dwellings next to the synagogue; (undefined) use of the synagogue and its front platform.
> Stratum IA: modern period (late 19th-early 20th centuries). Seasonal Bedouin occupation around a vaulted storehouse.
> Stratum IB: modern period (1950's-1967). Repavement of a granary that served as a pen for animals, and dwellings around the synagogue.[542]

---

[540] For the full list of the publications in which the excavator has so far reported his finds, see Ma'oz, "Horvat Kanaf—1," p. 810.

[541] Ma'oz, "Ḥorvat Kanaf—2," pp. 847-850.

[542] Ma'oz, "Ḥorvat Kanaf—2," pp. 847-848. Once again, without a full report of the excavations, including plans, photographs, and drawings of the crosscuts of the excavations, it is difficult to study and evaluate—positively or negatively—the stratigraphy and the chronology that Ma'oz lays out. From our acquaintance with the pottery found at the site—

A number of the finds from the Maʻoz excavations undoubtedly make an important contribution to our knowledge of the Jewish settlement that existed here during the second-temple and rabbinic periods. Maʻoz attributes the destruction of the Hellenistic-Seleucid tower (and the end of Stratum VI) to the conquest of the Golan by Alexander Jannaeus in 81 B.C.E.[543] In previous publications, he wrote that during the next stratum in the history of the settlement (that is, Stratum V according to his division) the site was settled by Jews. "This stratum, which was settled by Jews, existed with variations until the Great Revolt in 67 C.E. Then the site was abandoned and its inhabitants found refuge apparently in nearby Gamala."[544] As we commented in note 542, it is unclear to us why Maʻoz ignores the existence of ceramic and numismatic finds at the site from the second and third centuries C.E. In any case, both in his earlier publications about the site and in his most recent publication (in the *New Encyclopedia*), Maʻoz writes:

> Jewish settlement on the site was renewed only in the second half of the fourth century C.E. A spacious village was built, whose economy was based on field irrigation and the cultivation of crops in the fertile surroundings, as well as on olive-oil production. The village reached its zenith at the end of the fifth and the beginning of the sixth centuries C.E., when a large synagogue was built on the crest of the ridge...During the course of the sixth century there was already a visible decline in the economic strength of the village. At least one earthquake (551 C.E.) shook the structure of the synagogue, requiring its rebuilding, which was limited to the lower story.[545]

It is unclear upon what data Maʻoz determines the economic decline in the village in the course of the sixth century. What evidence has he of the occurrence of an earthquake in the village specifically in 551 C.E.? And upon what does he base his conclusion that when the public building was rebuilt, it had only one floor?

The date that Maʻoz assigns to the public structure—the sixth century C.E.—seems to us to lack any foundation. The excavator himself writes: "Of its inner part, only the foundations of the columns remain. The original stone pavement, benches, and Torah Ark, which undoubtedly existed in the structure, were completely destroyed."[546] And he goes on to write under the

---

both during the survey which we conducted in 1968, and from the visits to the site during the Maʻoz excavations—it is unclear to us why pottery found at the site from the second, third, eighth, and twelveth centuries do not appear in Maʻoz's chronology.

[543] Maʻoz, "Ḥorvat Kanaf—2," p. 848.

[544] The quotation is from Maʻoz, "Golan Synagogues," p. 149.

[545] Maʻoz, "Ḥorvat Kanaf—2," p. 850.

[546] Maʻoz, "Ḥorvat Kanaf—2," p. 848. This quote reveals the excavator's power of imagination. After he decided that the Jewish public building served as a synagogue, he assigned to it benches and a Torah Ark—even though there is no evidence for them. In his

heading *The Finds and Date of the Synagogue*, "No contemporary finds for the synagogue exist, as a result of the secondary use of construction material and its destruction in strata I and II."[547] In other words, the excavator has no sealed stratum from the synagogue because of secondary usage of the building's materials and the disturbances in strata I and II—that is, from the Middle Ages until now. The date he sets is based upon coins and shards which he believes belong to the fill layers of the structure. I suspect that Ma'oz failed to read the stratigraphy correctly. However, until he publishes the full report of his excavations, the dating of this structure will remain questionable.[548]

According to Ma'oz,

> The synagogue was built as a trapezoid, oriented east-west. Its western side is 12.5 m. long; its eastern side, 13.25 m.; its southern side, 15.85 m.; and its northern side, 16.4 m. One course of stone at the northwest corner of the structure and three to five courses at the south wall (all below floor level) have been preserved. The northeast corner is preserved to height of seven courses, adjacent to which are the doorjambs of the side entrance, which were found *in situ*. The walls are 1 m. thick; their external side is constructed of well-dressed and precisely fitting, unmortared ashlars.... The lower part of the side entrance, which is 1.25 m. wide, has been preserved *in situ*.[549]

In the continuation of this passage, Ma'oz exaggerates his descriptions and conclusions so that they support his imaginary reconstruction of the building, including a single central entrance in the western wall which, he claims, was 1.65 m. wide, 2.30 m. high.[550] This detail is quite incredible, since Ma'oz found preserved *in situ* not even a single doorpost stone of this imaginary entrance.

Based upon five "ashlar stylobates" which were found under the paving of layer IB (the layer from 1950 to 1967), Ma'oz concludes "that there were two rows of eight columns, dividing the hall into a nave (about 4.5 m. wide) and two aisles (each about 2.75 m. wide). The column drums and capi-

---

opinion, they "undoubtedly existed." Before concluding that the building had benches, we need to find such evidence—even a crumpled piece of bench *in situ* would do.

[547] Ma'oz, "Horvat Kanaf—2," p. 849.

[548] The date that Ma'oz fixed for the community structure at Mazra'at Kanaf, by depending on the Preliminary Report of the finds of coins (Ariel, "Horvat Kanef"), also draws criticism from Y. Tsafrir in his article in this collection [vol. 1, pp. 70-86—eds.]. Tsafrir concludes his critique with the sentence, "In our opinion it would be better to weigh the possibility that the building was built at an early period and that it was restored or had its floor replaced in the sixth century." (p. 76, note 20).

[549] Ma'oz, "Horvat Kanaf—2," p. 848.

[550] He has even published a drawing of this reconstruction. See, for example, Ma'oz, "Ancient Synagogues," p. 127.

tals were found in secondary use in strata IIIB and IB, inside and near the synagogue."[551] In his more recent publications, Ma'oz presents no plan of the public building.[552] However, in his article, "Ancient Synagogues of the Golan" (Ma'oz, "Ancient Synagogues"), he published a sketch with a layout of complete walls, eight columns *in situ* as well as the single (imaginary) entrance in the western wall.[553] In the building's northwest corner, he draws the northern wall of the hall as having an extension westward (as he found it during his excavations), but nowhere in his many publications on the site has he even suggested that the hall was part of a larger complex or that it had a westward extension.

We conclude our discussion of the Ma'oz excavations by examining three epigraphic finds. The first is a basalt fragment, of which Ma'oz has published neither its measurements nor a good photograph. An examination of the photograph which Prof. J. Naveh received from Ma'oz and published in the *Yigael Yadin Memorial Volume*, suggests, on the basis of the forms of the letters, that the fragment is a segment of the inscription discovered by Oliphant.[554] Its transcription was published by Sukenik (see above). The poor quality of the photograph Naveh published, however, makes this uncertain. For the photograph cuts off the fragment at the last letter and is blurry on the right side.

Naveh reads the first letter in the segment as a ' י,' or a 'ו,' and the rest of the letters as דעבדה.[555] We are not confident that the last letter is indeed a 'ה.' In our opinion the actual stone must be examined (which we have till now been unable to do), for the final letter may be a 'ח.' Ma'oz sees the segment as a direct continuation of the inscription Sukenik read and suggests completing it as follows:

[הדה איסכופ]תה דכיר לטב יוסה בר חלפו בר חניו דעבדה

He translates it:

[This is the lintel] remembered for good (be) Yose ben Halfo ben Honyo that I made.[556]

Naveh—who provides an earlier version of Ma'oz's translation of the word דעבדה, "who made it" and not "that I made"—writes that the Ma'oz reading

---

[551] Ma'oz, "Horvat Kanaf—2," p. 848.

[552] Ma'oz, "Horvat Kanaf—1"; Ma'oz, "Horvat Kanaf—2."

[553] Ma'oz, "Ancient Synagogues," p. 126.

[554] See Naveh, "Aramaic and Hebrew," p. 306, Fig. 5.

[555] See previous note.

[556] Thus the translation in Ma'oz, "Horvat Kanaf—1," p. 808; in Ma'oz, "Horvat Kanaf—2," p. 848, there again appears for some unknown reason, a translation close to that of Sukenik, without the section that Ma'oz found, "...in blessed memory of Yose son of Halfu son of Han..."— the solutions are with Ma'oz.

"is difficult, but I have no better suggestion,"[557] and adds, "perhaps it is possible to read the name of the donor's grandfather 'חַנָנָי'"?[558] The reading is indeed difficult, but that makes it even more important to know whether this section is actually the end of the inscription. If it is not, it may be that the 'ה' (if indeed it is a 'ה' and not a 'ח') is the first letter in the word הדן, that is, 'this' or 'this one,' and therefore a noun follows it. This would suggest that Yose ben Ḥalfo donated part of the building or perhaps even the entire building.

The two additional epigraphic finds Ma'oz uncovered were discovered in Area B—a residential building the excavator designated "Building 300." These finds are copper amulets upon which there are adjurations in Aramaic that include blessings in Hebrew. One amulet (measuring about 6 x 6 cm), whose inscription testifies that it was written for יאיתה ברתה דמרין ("Ya'itha the daughter of Marian"), was found in a depression in the floor of the corner of a room (Locus 301) in the southern apartment of the building.[559] The second amulet (measuring about 7.5 x 5 cm.), inscribed לרבי אלעזר ברה דאסתיר ("to Rabbi Eleazar the son of Esther"), was found in another room of the building (Locus 308), in the stone debris on the floor.[560] Naveh and Shaked, who published these amulets,[561] depend upon Ma'oz and date them to the later part of the occupation of Building 300, that is, the late sixth or early seventh century C.E.[562]

To conclude our discussion of this interesting site, we can only once again express our hope that a complete, scientific publication of the Ma'oz excavations will be published soon. Perhaps further excavations at the site will yield additional finds from the Jewish communities that lived there for hundreds of years.

DEIR 'AZÎZ

Using the ruins of an ancient settlement, this now-abandoned Syrian village was built on a hill above Wâdî Deir 'Azîz, at coordinates 2170-2523. G. Schumacher described the site as "a small winter village, consisting of ten huts on the Wâdî Deir 'Azîz (Wâdî esh-Shuqayyif). It belongs to the 'Arab ed-Diâb, but is not inhabited in summer."[563] Since he mentions no antiqui-

---

[557] Naveh, "Aramaic and Hebrew," p. 306.

[558] See previous note.

[559] See Ma'oz, "Ḥorvat Kanaf—2," p. 849; Naveh and Shaked, pp. 44-49, Amulet #2.

[560] Ma'oz, "Ḥorvat Kanaf—2," p. 849; Naveh and Shaked, pp. 50-55, Amulet #3.

[561] The bibliography in the publications mentioned in the previous two notes will direct the reader to complete transcriptions of the amulets along with English translations.

[562] Naveh and Shaked, p. 46.

[563] Schumacher, "Dscholan," p. 267; Schumacher, *Jaulân*, pp. 118-119.

ties, it is possible to conclude that he did not visit the village but wrote on the basis of information received from residents of the area.

In December 1885, Sir Laurence Oliphant visited the site, led by a Bedouin guide, and was the first to report the presence of antiquities— Jewish remains in particular. He writes,

> My guide now offered to conduct me to another Khurbet..., the Khurbet of Deir 'Azîz. Here I found a large encampment of Arabs, their tents huddled amid the flat-roofed granaries in which they store their crops, and which were constructed as usual from the stones of the Khurbet. These ruins were enclosed on two sides by a massive ancient wall, measuring 140 feet one way by 90 feet the other, and with an average height of 6 feet. Many of the beautifully squared blocks of which it was constructed measured 6 feet by 18 inches, and were laid on each other without cement. Within this enclosure were many fragments of columns and traces of foundations, besides two small arches, 10 feet high with a 13-feet span; but these, I think, were of a later date than the wall: one of them supported the roof of a granary; the other connected with it, though enclosed by walls, supported nothing. I also found a piece of a cornice with moulding of the unornamented Jewish type. But the most interesting discovery was that of the synagogue. This stood a little way down the slope of the hill, on the northern flank of the Wâdî esh-Shuqayyif, near the head of which this Khurbet is situated. The walls were still standing in places to a height of 9 feet, and the whole character was clearly defined (Fig. 7 in Oliphant's article). The dimensions were 60 feet by 37 feet; the diameter of the columns, of which none were standing *in situ*, 2 feet. The lintel over the door, 6 feet by 18 inches; width of door, 4 feet 6 inches. It was oriented, and the entrance was in the eastern wall. I searched in vain for cornices or carving of any sort. The whole architecture was of the plainest and simplest description, but the interior was so thickly strewn with masses of building stone that some of the more ornamental features may have been concealed.[564]

Oliphant also describes remains of an olive-oil press which he saw, as well as remains of the ancient settlement's spring house.[565]

After the Six Day War, the site was surveyed by teams led by C. Epstein and S. Gutman. In their survey report,[566] Epstein and Gutman described ancient buildings with stone roofs in the village. In its southwest corner, they found the remains of a large building built of finely-hewn stones with a subterranean structure beside it, both of which they measured and published their plans. On the wâdî's slope, the surveyors located the remains of the spring house which Oliphant had reported. They also pointed out that between the village and the fountain were remains of ancient buildings. Among these they found large columns, capitals, frieze fragments, and so

---

[564] Oliphant, "New Discoveries," pp. 76-77. Parenthesis mine.

[565] Oliphant, "New Discoveries," pp. 77-78.

[566] Epstein & Gutman, pp. 280-281, Site #132.

on. The pottery remains found at the site were dated by the surveyors to the period they call "Roman-Byzantine."[567]

A short time after the Epstein-Gutman survey, the author and his staff surveyed the village and the ruin.[568] This survey indicated that the ancient ruin's area occupied about 50 dunams. In addition to pottery remains reported by Epstein and Gutman, we found shards from the late Hellenistic and the early Roman periods (the second and first centuries B.C.E. and the first century C.E.). Examination of the remains of the ancient buildings in the village and the ruin revealed at least two, if not three, phases of ancient construction. These phases can easily be recognized, especially in the buildings with Haurân-style roofs. But without systematic archaeological excavation, it is difficult to fix the phases' dates.

In our survey, we registered and photographed the remains of the two monumental structures which Oliphant had reported. The one structure, on top of the hill on which the ruin lies, is built of large, finely-hewn basalt ashlars. The building is oriented north-south; its plan was published by Epstein and Gutman.[569] Of the original structure, three courses of its western and southern walls are well-preserved on the surface, while only one or two courses are sometimes visible of its eastern and northern walls. Within the structure, in the southeast corner, a long, narrow room (about 10 x 2.5 m.) has been preserved with its roof built of long basalt slabs. An entrance in the northern wall (near the main entrance to the building which is in the center of its eastern wall) leads into the room. In its western wall there are thirteen 'Chorazin windows.' Without archaeological excavation, it is difficult to determine whether this room belonged to the original phases of the building or was built into it in a later period. The structure's original dimensions—about 25 x 15 m.—do not fit the measurements reported by Oliphant—140 x 90 feet. Still, it is possible to resolve this contradiction if we add to the structure's original dimensions those of the later construction that was attached to it on the south, north, and east. Previously, we suggested that the original stage of this building, was a synagogue[570] or a house of study.[571] Today, however, without a systematic excavation of the structure, we can only conjecture that these are the remains of a Jewish public building of the second-temple and/or rabbinic periods.

On the slope between the aforementioned structure and the remains of the early spring house, we found the ruins of the building that Oliphant defined

---

[567] Epstein & Gutman, p. 281.

[568] D. Urman, "Deir 'Azîz," *Special Surveys Reports*, Archive of the Association for the Archaeological Survey of Israel, Israel Antiquities Authority, Jerusalem (in Hebrew); Urman, *List*, p. 16; Urman, *Golan*, p. 202, Site #136 and the note for this site on page 214.

[569] Epstein & Gutman, pp. 280-281, Site #132.

[570] See Urman, "Synagogue Sites," p. 17.

[571] Urman, "Hellenistic," p. 466.

as a synagogue. It seems that since Oliphant's visit, more stones were taken from the structure to serve as building material for the Arab-Syrian village. This building itself was built of basalt ashlar and measures, as Oliphant wrote, about 18.30 x 11.30 m. The axis of the building is east-west and appears to have had two entrances, one in the east wall and another in the west wall. Inside the structure it was possible to make out that most of its height was buried by debris. Within it, column shafts can be seen, two of which may be standing *in situ*. Outside the building, we found more sections of column shafts as well as three Doric capitals. West of the building, a lintel fragment was preserved, measuring 104 cm. long, 52 cm. high, and an average of about 42 cm. thick. Preserved on the lintel fragment was a relief of a wreath with a 'Hercules' knot.' About 8 meters southwest of the lintel fragment, we registered a frieze fragment about 94 cm. long with smooth profiles. On the slope leading down to the spring house, more architectural items were seen (including cornice fragments) which originated either in the structure identified by Oliphant as a synagogue or in some other monumental building that may be in that part of the ruin.

The great similarity between the architectural items which we recorded at Deir 'Azîz and others that were found at Jewish sites of second-temple and rabbinic periods in the Galilee and the Golan, as well as the fact that no pagan or Christian remains were found in the village, lead us to conclude that these remains are those of a Jewish settlement. Without systematic archaeological excavation, however, it is difficult to determine with any certainty the functions of the two or three public structures.

In 1978, Z. Ma'oz surveyed the site once more.[572] For some reason, Ma'oz decided that the teams of the Epstein, Gutman and the author "mistakenly identified [Oliphant's synagogue] with an ashlar building at the summit of the hill."[573] Instead, according to Ma'oz, "In 1978, Z. Ma'oz rediscovered Oliphant's synagogue on the southern slope, a short distance below the summit."[574] The preceding discussion reveals two problems with Ma'oz's claim. First, anyone who checks Epstein and Gutman's publication will find that these careful, pioneering investigators never refer to the question of "Oliphant's synagogue."[575] Second, the public structure found by the author and his team fits Oliphant's description of the synagogue precisely. Ma'oz seems to have confused Epstein's and Gutman's report with that of the author, thus resulting his claim that he found Oliphant's synagogue. The discovery was actually made by the author.

---

[572] See Ma'oz, *Golan*, p. 14; Ma'oz, "Golan Synagogues," pp. 157-158; Ma'oz, "Golan—1," p. 294; Ma'oz, "Golan—2," p. 542.

[573] See, for example, Ma'oz, "Golan—2," p. 542. Brackets mine.

[574] See, for example, Ma'oz, "Golan—2," p. 542.

[575] Epstein & Gutman, pp. 280-281, Site #132.

Apart from the matter of the synagogue, there is nothing new in Ma'oz's report and, at its end, he concludes, "The remains indicate that the synagogue was very similar to that excavated at Ḥorvat Kanaf, and the probable date of construction was therefore the beginning of the sixth century C.E."[576] Since the structure at Deir 'Azîz remains unexcavated, however, we cannot fix its date with any certainty. It is regrettable that Zvi Ilan took Ma'oz's comments seriously and accepted them in his last book.[577]

LÂWIYYE (EL-LAWIYEH)

This small abandoned Syrian village was built upon a hill on the western slope of a spur descending from the Golan toward the Sea of Galilee at coordinates 2140-2503.

G. Schumacher who visited the region in 1884 described it as "a miserable Bedouin winter village and some ruins, surrounded by beautiful oak trees, on the northern margin of the Wâdî es-Samekh."[578]

L. Oliphant, who surveyed the site in December 1885, led by a Bedouin guide, found at the ruin "three columns *in situ*, a piece of cornice with the egg-and-dart pattern, and a block on which was carved a small oblong panel, which seems a characteristic of Jewish ornamentation."[579] In his report he added, "I could also trace the foundations of the building in which the columns were placed, and although it was impossible to determine its dimensions, enough was visible to convince me that the few remains existing were those of a synagogue...."[580]

In 1967, the site was surveyed by C. Epstein's team. In the houses and courtyards of the Syrian village, this team found decorated hewn stones. They gathered shards from the Early Bronze Age II, the late Roman, Byzantine, and Ottoman periods.[581]

At the beginning of 1968, the site was surveyed yet again by a team led by the author. While the houses of the Syrian village were built for the most part of ancient building stones—some of which were ashlar—it was difficult to make out the remains of the ancient site and to estimate its area. At one of the Syrian houses, we found a basalt capital worked in the Ionic style prevalent in the Jewish public buildings in the Golan of the rabbinic period. We did not succeed in locating, however, the remains of the structure

---

[576] See previous note.
[577] See Ilan, *Israel,* pp. 81-82.
[578] Schumacher, "Dscholan," p. 309; Schumacher, *Jaulân,* p. 217.
[579] Oliphant, "New Discoveries," p. 78.
[580] See previous note.
[581] Epstein & Gutman, p. 282, Site #141.

described by Oliphant.[582] It should be noted that at the time of our survey
the village was covered with tall vegetation, which made conducting the
survey quite difficult. Since the 1968 survey, we have had no opportunity to
return to the village. However, since Oliphant's reports on the archaeological finds in the Golan have generally been found reliable, we hope that the
structure which he saw will yet be found and uncovered in the future.[583]

UMM EL-QANÂṬIR (UMM EL-KANÂṬIR, UMM EL-KANATAR, EL-MANSHIYYE, 'EIN EṢ-ṢUFEIRA)

This abandoned Syrian village was built in the first half of the twentieth
century on two levels of a cliff overlooking the Sea of Galilee at coordinates
2194-2505.

The ruins of the ancient settlement were first surveyed by L. Oliphant in
1884.[584] Oliphant first examined the remains of the ancient spring house at
the site, whose arches provide, as far as one can tell, the source for the
Arabic name of the ruin: Umm el-Qanâṭir—that is, "the Mother of the
Arches." Near the spring house, Oliphant found a basalt slab with a relief of
a lion on it (see PL. 49b).[585] About 50 meters north of the spring, he
discovered the remains of a Jewish public structure known today as "the
synagogue of Umm el-Qanâṭir." Oliphant describes the structure's remains
in this way:

> They are situated about fifty yards from the spring to the north, and consist
> of ruined walls enclosing an area apparently as nearly as possible of the
> same dimensions as the synagogue at ed-Dîkkeh, but the traces of the west-
> ern wall were concealed by such piles of large blocks of building stones
> that it was impossible to determine them. The southern wall was standing
> to a height of about 7 feet, and consisted of three courses of stone averag-
> ing a little over 2 feet each in height by about 2 feet 6 inches in breadth.
> The door was situated 15 feet from south-east angle of the wall, and was 4
> feet 9 inches in width; the stones forming the door-post were slightly
> carved into a plain moulding. On entering, the area presented a mass of
> stone debris, and columns, and pieces of carving, tossed about in the
> wildest confusion; six columns from 10 to 12 feet in height rose above the
> piles of stone at every angle, as though they had been partially overturned
> by an earthquake; the shaken condition of one of the stones which formed
> the door-post, and which projected from the others, as well as the general
> aspect of such of the ruin as was still standing, confirmed my impression

[582] D. Urman, "Lâwiyye," *Special Surveys Reports*, Archive of the Association for the
Archaeological Survey of Israel, Israel Antiquities Authority, Jerusalem (in Hebrew). See
also Urman, *List*, p. 16; Urman, *Golan*, p. 202, Site #142 and the note for this site on page 214.

[583] Urman, "Synagogue Sites," p. 18; Urman, "Hellenistic," p. 467.

[584] Oliphant, "Lake Tiberias," pp. 89-91; Oliphant, *Haifa*, pp. 262-265.

[585] Oliphant, "Lake Tiberias," p. 90, Fig. 1.

that the building had been destroyed by a convulsion of nature. It was difficult under the circumstances to determine the true position of the columns,
or the exact plan of the building; but the character of the fragments of ornamentation which still remained, the fact that the columns were all within
the enclosure of the building, that the walls were without cement, the position of the door, and the moulding of the door-posts, all rather lead me to
the same conclusion with respect to this building which I have arrived at in
the case of ed-Dîkkeh, and to regard it as having been formerly a synagogue. There was one stone on which was carved the representation of an
eagle (Fig. 3), a fragment of egg-and-dart cornice, closely resembling the
one at ed-Dîkkeh, a large triangular slab cut in the shape of an arch and
highly ornamented, measuring 3 feet 6 inches along the base line, and 5
feet 8 inches between the two extremities, and which I assume to have been
placed on the lintel of the main entrance (Fig. 4); and there were fragments
of Corinthian capitals.[586]

G. Schumacher surveyed the site together with Oliphant,[587] but added nothing new in his report except drawings and dimensions of five architectural
items, four of which were not described in Oliphant's report.[588]

In May 1905, the expedition headed by H. Kohl and C. Watzinger conducted four days of intensive excavation in the remains of the public building. In the course of this excavation, they uncovered sections of the north,
west, and south walls of the building, remains of the stylobate and the bases
of the five columns of the hall's western row of columns *in situ*, and the
western end of the stylobate of the northern row of columns. They also unearthed the remains of the porch built outside the structure's southern facade.
It was reached by ascending a staircase to the main entrance (width—about
1.63 m.) at the center of the southern facade wall. An entrance 1.55 m. wide
was also uncovered in the structure's west wall.[589]

As a result of their excavation, it became clear that the outer length of
the building's hall was 18.80 m. and its estimated width was 16.80 m
(according to the conjectural plan published by Watzinger in Tafel XVII). It
should be pointed out that the excavators did not uncover the hall's east
wall, nor even the parallel row of columns inside the hall. Yet these facts

---

[586] Oliphant, "Lake Tiberias," pp. 90-91.

[587] See Oliphant's note in Oliphant, *Haifa*, p. 267 and see also Schumacher, "Dscholan,"
pp. 358-360; Schumacher, *Jaulân*, pp. 260-265.

[588] See Schumacher, "Dscholan," p. 360, Figs. 140-144; Schumacher, *Jaulân*, pp. 264-
265, Figs. 137-141.

[589] Kohl and Watzinger, pp. 125-134. Here we must note that in the plan of the remains
of the structure and the suggestion for its restoration which Watzinger published (Tafel
XVII), there is an error of about 60 degrees in marking the north. As a result, Watzinger and
those who based themselves upon his publication erred in everything related to the orientation
of the building. The length-wise axis of the building is more south-north than east-west.

and the measurement of its estimated width escaped the eyes of the good
people who have made use of Watzinger's conjectural plan.[590]

Watzinger also drew a reconstruction of the building's southern facade
wall—including the remains of the porch in front of it.[591] According to his
proposal, the structure had two stories. He placed architectural items found
in the excavation into the drawing as parts of assumed windows in the two
stories of the facade wall. On the basis of the capitals of the porch columns,
which are of the so-called 'basket' capital type, Watzinger dated the structure
to the fifth century.[592] This suggested date was accepted by E. L. Sukenik
who visited the site in the autumn of 1928.[593] According to him,
"Watzinger's conclusion regarding the date is further confirmed by the fact
that the facade and main entrances are on the east side, that is, on that *opposite* the wall of orientation; as contrasted with the synagogues of the older
type, where the facade is on the side of the orientation."[594] It is interesting
to note that Sukenik, too, who visited the site, did not pay attention to the
exact orientation of the structure, instead depending on Watzinger's ground
plans.

During his visit, Sukenik found a stone near the spring with an inscription enclosed in a *tabula ansata*. Sukenik did not succeed in reading it because its letters were blurred, but he made it out to be Greek.[595]

In the region of the public structure, Sukenik saw the porch's 'basket'
capital as well as the stones with the reliefs of the eagle and the lion—drawings of which were published by Oliphant, Schumacher, and Watzinger.
Sukenik expressed his opinion that these reliefs originally belonged to the
structure's facade wall.[596]

A few years before Sukenik's visit to the site, S. Klein had suggested—
in light of the archaeological finds then known—identifying Umm el-
Qanâṭir as קמטרא (Qamtra), the abode of the *amora* Simeon Qamtria, who is
mentioned in the Jerusalem Talmud at Berakoth 9:2, 13d.[597] Sukenik rejected this suggestion, writing:

---

[590] See, for example, Avi-Yonah, "Synagogues—2," pp. 104; Avi-Yonah,
"Synagogues—3," pp. 1137.

[591] Kohl and Watzinger, pp. 134.

[592] See previous note.

[593] Sukenik, "el-Ḥammeh," pp. 172-174.

[594] Sukenik, "el-Ḥammeh," pp. 172-173. Emphasis original.

[595] Sukenik, "el-Ḥammeh," p. 172. It seems that Sukenik found the same blurred
inscription Oliphant and Schumacher had reported. See Oliphant, "Lake Tiberias," p. 90;
Oliphant, *Haifa*, pp. 263-264; Schumacher, "Dscholan," p. 359; Schumacher, *Jaulân*, p. 261.
To our regret, the inscription was not found by the surveys conducted at the site after 1967.

[596] See Sukenik, "el-Ḥammeh," p. 172.

[597] Klein, *Transjordan*, pp. 49-50.

What the ancient name of this site was we do not know. The Arabic Umm el
Qanâṭir, "mother of arches," is derived from the arches over the spring.
Klein's suggestion that Simeon Qamtria, Y. Ber. 12d [i.e., 13d] top, derived his surname from this locality is therefore highly improbable. קמטרא
is a fairly frequent loanword from the Greek κάμτρα or κάμπτρα, "chest,"
in Mishnah, Talmud, and Targum, and קמטריא (Qamtria) as a family name
may mean "cabinet maker"; cf. the proper name קבוטר (other reading קבוטל)
M. Yoma 1: 6 etc. = κιβωτάριος "joiner" (also in Aramaic as a common
name קבוטריא, "joiners," Y. Abodah Zarah, 40c)[598]

At the same time Sukenik also rejected Gildemeister's suggestion identifying Umm el-Qanâṭir with the site of Gamala, and added, "It is an interesting
fact that for קולפא דקנסיר, Zohar, Gen. 57b., which is named as a bay
(קולפא=κολφυς, κόλπος) the happening at which the miracle-worker R.
Simeon b. Yoḥai was able to see from the gate of Tiberias, the Ma'arikh
(16th century) has קנטיר which he glosses as follows: 'קנטיר a locality on the
other side of the Sea of Tiberias, still known by that name.'"[599]

In spite of Sukenik's criticism, Klein continues to hold to his opinion
that Umm el-Qanâṭir may be identified with the place of the third-century
amora Simeon Qamtria, that is, Simeon of Qamtra,[600] and perhaps he is
right.[601]

After the Six Day War, the site was surveyed by teams led by C. Epstein
and S. Gutman, who first reported houses of a new Syrian village on the
cliff's upper ledge which incorporated a number of architectural items, originally from the ancient Jewish public structure.[602]

In 1968, the site was surveyed by the author and his team.[603] In this
survey it became clear that most of the remains of the ancient settlement lie
on the lower ledge of the cliff (about 20 dwellings), but that the upper ledge
has remains of several ancient buildings (8-10 structures). Remains were
found of olive-oil presses on both the upper and lower ledges, but it seems
that the ancient settlement's main working areas were on the upper ledge.
The overall area of the ancient settlement is estimated at about 35 dunams,
but it may have been larger. The houses of the Syrian village were generally

---

[598] Sukenik, "el-Ḥammeh," p. 173. Brackets mine.

[599] Sukenik, "el-Ḥammeh," p. 174.

[600] See Klein, *ha-Yishuv*, p. 143.

[601] See Ilan, *Golan*, p. 291 and Ilan, *Israel*, p. 64.

[602] Epstein & Gutman, p. 283, Site #148.

[603] See D. Urman, "Umm el-Qanâṭir, el-Manshiyye, and 'Ein eṣ-Ṣufeira," *Special
Surveys Reports*, Archive of the Association for the Archaeological Survey of Israel, Israel
Antiquities Authority, Jerusalem (in Hebrew); D. Urman, "Umm el-Qanâṭir, el-Manshiyye,
and 'Ein eṣ-Ṣufeira," *Reports of the Staff Officer in Charge of Archaeological Affairs in the
Golan* (1968-1972), Archive of the Israel Antiquities Authority, Jerusalem (in Hebrew);
Urman, *List*, p. 17; Urman, "Synagogue Sites," p. 16; Urman, *Golan*, p. 203, Site #146.

built between 1950-1967, primarily on the upper ledge, but several were
constructed between the spring and the ruins of the Jewish public building.
A number of architectural items were found—apparently from the public
building—incorporated into the Syrian houses as building stones. These
include the stone with an eagle with outstretched wings whose drawing was
published by both Oliphant and Schumacher. Another decorated architectural
item, which was not seen by the surveyors and excavators prior to 1967, is
the corner-capital on which lovely reliefs of an eagle with outstretched
wings appears (alongside its wings is an egg-and-dart pattern) as well as a
pattern of arches with rosettes above and under it (see PL. 50a). It should be
noted that the two items just described were found in a single Syrian house
(whose owner seems to have been an antique fancier). We also found reliefs
of grape vines and birds pecking at the grape clusters in that building. In the
courtyard of a Syrian house southwest of the public structure, we found the
archstone decorated with different relief bands reported by previous surveyors
and excavators. Among the structure's ruins, we saw several Ionic capitals
unreported by our predecessors; on one was a relief of a three-branched
menorah. Also found west of the structure were fragments of the lion relief
reported by Watzinger.

In 1970, M. Avi-Yonah, in the article "Synagogues" which he wrote for
the Hebrew edition of the *Encyclopaedia of Archaeological Excavations in
the Holy Land*, published a short segment on the Jewish public building at
Umm el-Qanâṭir. In it he expressed his opinion that the lack of an apse in
the structure, the existence of a third row of columns (transverse), and a
stone floor are evidence that the structure should be attributed to an period
earlier than that set forward by Kohl, Watzinger, and Sukenik.[604]
Hüttenmeister and Reeg followed Avi-Yonah and ascribed the building to the
third century C.E.[605] In support of the earlier date, our survey of the ancient
settlement found shards from the various stages of the Roman period, as
well as from the Byzantine and Arab periods.[606] Still, without systematic
archaeological excavation, it is doubtful whether we can determine a sure
date.

In the 1980's, the site was surveyed by Z. Ilan[607] and Z. Ma'oz.[608] Their
publications reveal no new information. Ma'oz, however, seems to have
forgotten those who studied the site prior to him. He also published a hypothetical plan of the structure in which the third row of columns consists of

---

[604] See M. Avi-Yonah, "Synagogues—2," pp. 103-104; and also M. Avi-Yonah,
"Synagogues—3," pp. 1137-1138.

[605] Hüttenmeister and Reeg, p. 468.

[606] See above, note 603.

[607] Ilan, *Israel,* pp. 63-64.

[608] Ma'oz, "Golan Synagogues," pp. 158-159; Ma'oz, "Ancient Synagogues," p. 125;
Ma'oz, "Golan—1," pp. 294-296; Ma'oz, "Golan—2," pp. 542-543.

only one column and not two as Watzinger had suggested.[609] Likewise, Ma'oz decided that the entrance in the building's south wall was not built in the center of the wall but a bit to the east "probably in order to leave room for the Ark of the Law inside."[610] On this, it has been said that "whoever adds, detracts." It is to be hoped that in the future, systematic excavations will be conducted from which we will be able to answer the many questions concerning this site.

KFAR 'AQABYAH (KAFR 'AQÂB, KAFR 'AQIB, ED-DUGÂ, ED-DUKÂ, DUKÂTH KAFR 'AQÂB)

In one of the inscriptions uncovered in the mosaic floor of the synagogue at Ḥammat Gader (el-Ḥammeh),[611] a contributor by the name of "Patric of Kfar 'Aqabyah" was mentioned. Sukenik, who had excavated the synagogue and first published the inscription, transcribed it:

וקנ]ירוס פ]טריק ד(כ)פר עקביה

He translated it:

and K[yros Pa]tric of (K)far 'Aqabyah

He claimed that the כ was omitted through inadvertence.[612] Naveh, who examined the inscription in the 1970's, claims that the remains of the 'כ' are clear in the mosaic but the 'ד' cannot be made out.[613] Naveh suggests, therefore, correcting Sukenik's reading to either "כפר עקביה<ד>" or "<דמ> כפר עקביה."[614] Neither suggestion changes the meaning.

In dealing with the question of the location of Kfar 'Aqabyah, Sukenik writes that Kfar 'Aqabyah "is mentioned in Y. Nazir 57d, in connection with R. Abba bar Cohen, a scholar of the late third century, but there is no indication of its location. Nevertheless it can hardly be anything other than the modern Kafr (or Khirbet) 'Aqib, near the northern end of the eastern shore of the Sea of Galilee."[615] Naveh, who also dealt with the question of the site's location, writes: "Kfar 'Aqabyah, mentioned in Y. Nazir, ch. 9, 57d, is identified by Klein with Khirbet 'Uqbah which is south of Safed (S. Klein, *Sefer*

---

[609] See Ma'oz, "Ancient Synagogues," p. 125. And this is an unfortunate occurance because the plan was copied in Z. Ilan's publication (see above, note 607). Many good people will continue to err and rely on this erroneous plan.

[610] Thus in Ma'oz, "Golan—1," p. 294 and in Ma'oz, "Golan—2," p. 543.

[611] On the synagogue at Ḥammat-Gader (el-Ḥamma) and its inscriptions, see the section on Hammat-Gader.

[612] Sukenik, "el-Ḥammeh," pp. 138-141.

[613] Naveh, *Mosaic*, p. 58.

[614] Naveh, *Mosaic*, pp. 58-59.

[615] Sukenik, "el-Ḥammeh," p. 141.

ha-Yishuv, vol. 1, [Jerusalem, 1939], p. 96). However, more plausible is its identification with Kfar 'Aqâb which is on the eastern shore of the Sea of Galilee."[616]

The archeological surveys of this site identified as Kfar 'Aqabyah have had varying success. Schumacher, who visited the region in 1884, describes the site as "Ruins on the coast of the Sea of Galilee, with scattered building stones, but few foundations."[617]

Oliphant, who traveled the region a short time after Schumacher, found no antiquities whatsoever, and discussed only the different names of the place. He wrote:

> Following the Lake shore, we passed at the mouth of the Wâdî Ejgayif the ruins of 'Akib; these consist of nothing but heaps of basaltic stones. There is near here a spot marked "ruins" in some maps, and called Dukah; they are also mentioned by more than one traveler. I found on inquiry, however, that a projecting cliff near 'Akib was called the Dukah Kefr 'Akib, or the precipice of 'Akib, and this has doubtless given rise to the confusion. A mile and a half beyond 'Akib we turned up the great Wâdî of es-Samekh.[618]

In 1967, C. Epstein surveyed the ruins of the Syrian military settlement, Kafr 'Aqâb, that was set up in 1950 about a kilometer east of the Sea of Galilee shore, at coordinates 2117-2521. She reported:

> A village sitting upon a ruin, at the center of a protruding hill with a concentration of natural rocks around it. In the Syrian Army's defensive trenches one can discern the accumulation of waste materials from the ruin to a depth of 1.5 meters. The shards find: from the MB II Age (a few fragments), the Byzantine, and the Ottoman periods.[619]

In 1968 the author surveyed the Syrian Army settlement ruins once again and found that on this site there are also shards from Iron Age I and a few from the Roman period. As a result of the modern Syrian construction it was difficult to estimate the area of the early site there.[620]

As a continuation of the survey at Kafr 'Aqâb, the author also surveyed a nearby site on the shore of the Sea of Galilee at coordinates 2106-2521, then designated on the maps as ed-Dugâ; ed-Dukâ; and Dukâth Kafr 'Aqâb. At this site, visited by Schumacher but not surveyed by Epstein, there is actually a tell created by ruins of ancient houses with an area of about 40 dunams. At the site area we found large quantities of shards from the

---

[616] Naveh, *Mosaic*, p. 59.

[617] Schumacher, "Dscholan," p. 277; Schumacher, *Jaulân*, p. 133.

[618] Oliphant, "Lake Tiberias," p. 86.

[619] Epstein & Gutman, p. 280, Site #131.

[620] D. Urman, "Kafr 'Aqâb," *Special Surveys Reports*, Archive of the Association for the Archaeological Survey of Israel, Israel Antiquities Authority, Jerusalem (in Hebrew); Urman, *List*, p. 16; Urman, *Golan*, p. 201, Site #135 and also see the note for this site on p. 214.

Roman, Byzantine, early Arab, medieval, and late Arab periods. The tops of early walls could be seen throughout the tell area, yet we found no architectural items that could attest to the existence of monumental buildings at the site. In the site's southwest section, we made out the remains of a bathhouse and near it, on the shoreline, we discerned the remains of an ancient artificial anchorage.[621] We examined the anchorage again in 1970 with M. Nun, who published its data at length.[622]

In light of the ceramic findings at both sites—Kafr 'Aqâb and ed-Dugâ—it seems that it may be possible to identify this area as the location of the ancient Jewish settlement of Kfar 'Aqabyah mentioned in the Palestinian Talmud and in the inscription uncovered at the Ḥammat Gader synagogue. Hopefully, future archaeological excavations will be conducted at the two related sites that will clarify the relationship between them and will fix their identification.

---

[621] See D. Urman, "Dukâth Kafr 'Aqâb," *Reports of the Staff Officer in Charge of Archaeological Affairs in the Golan* (1968-1972), Archive of the Israel Antiquities Authority, Jerusalem (in Hebrew); Urman, *List*, p. 15; Urman, *Golan*, p. 201, Site #134.

[622] See Nun, "Kinneret" and Nun, *Kinneret*, pp. 81-82.

DISTRICT OF SÛSÎTA

EṢ-ṢUFEIRA (EṢ-ṢÂGHÎRA, SAFFÛREH)

This small abandoned Syrian village was built on the ruins of an ancient settlement at coordinates 2242-2503. G. Schumacher, who visited the site in 1884, found no ancient remains, reporting only, "A crumbled winter village, the better huts of which are inhabited by from two to six persons. There is some woody and arable land in the surrounding country, but few old remains."[1]

After the Six Day War in 1967, the village was surveyed by teams led by C. Epstein and S. Gutman. The joint report published by these surveyors reported for the first time that the village was built upon a ruin making secondary use of the ancient building stones. The surveyors also reported a number of decorated architectural items in the village, including a column base and a section of a cornice decorated with a rosette. The shards they found were dated to the Byzantine period.[2]

After the surveys of Epstein and Gutman, the site was surveyed in 1968 by the author. In this survey, it became clear that the area of the ancient site was about 40 dunams. In addition to the Byzantine pottery remains, the site also yielded shards from various stages of the Roman period.[3]

The center of the site lies on a low hill which is actually a tell. On top of this hill we made out the tops of the walls of a monumental structure, oriented north-south. Unfortunately, its dimensions are difficult to ascertain without archaeological excavation. In and around the structure, we found a number of architectural items, including two column bases and three Ionic capitals of the type prevalent in Jewish public buildings of the Galilee and the Golan from the second-temple and rabbinic periods. This find led us to

---

[1] Schumacher, "Dscholan," p. 345; Schumacher, *Jaulân* p. 236.

[2] Epstein & Gutman, p. 283, Site #149.

[3] See D. Urman, "eṣ-Ṣufeira," *Special Surveys Reports*, Archive of the Association for the Archaeological Survey of Israel, Israel Antiquities Authority, Jerusalem (in Hebrew); *Idem,* "eṣ-Ṣufeira," *Reports of the Staff Officer in Charge of Archaeological Affairs in the Golan* (from 1968-1972), Archive of the Israel Antiquities Authority, Jerusalem (in Hebrew); Urman, *List*, p. 19; Urman, *Golan*, p. 203, Site #147.

conjecture that if the structure was excavated, it might be identified as a Jewish public building—perhaps a synagogue—of the rabbinic period.[4]

Since 1968, however, the site has not been investigated (to the best of our knowledge); certainly no new finds have been reported. Today the regional center of Ḥisphît is near the site.

KHISFÎN (CASPEIN, HASFIYA, KHISFIYYA, ḤASPIN)

This large, now-abandoned, Syrian village on the el-Ḥammeh—Rafîd road can be found at coordinates 2266-2506. It was built upon the ruins of a large ancient town, making use of the ancient building stones. Many scholars have identified this ruin as the location of Χασφών or Κασπείν mentioned in 1 Maccabees 5:26 and in 2 Maccabees 12:13.[5] It is generally identified with חספייה, one of the 'forbidden towns' in the territory of Sûsîta,[6] mentioned in Tos. Sheb. 4:10 (66, 4-6), Y. Demai 2:1, 22d, and the halakic inscription discovered in the mosaic floor of the Jewish public structure at Rehob.[7]

The mention of חספייה as one of the forbidden towns in the territory of Sûsîta indicates that the place had a large Jewish population during the third and fourth centuries C.E. This population may have continued even after Christianity began to penetrate the region. A hint about this possibility may be found in the Syriac manuscript describing the life of Maximus the Confessor. It appears that the Christians still hesitated being baptized at Khisfîn in the late sixth century C.E.[8]

---

[4] See Urman, "Synagogue Sites," p. 16; Urman, "Hellenistic," p. 467; Urman, *Golan*, p. 214, Site #147.

[5] See, for example, Klein, *Transjordan*, p. 5 and Avi-Yonah, *Palestine*, p. 158 and the additional bibliography there. It should be pointed out that recently Z. Ma'oz stated, "The absence at the site of ceramic finds from the Hellenistic period raises the possibility that hellenistic Haspin was not here, but at Tell edh-Dhahab, about 1.5 km. (1 mile) to the southeast." (Ma'oz, "Haspin—1," p. 523; Ma'oz, "Haspin—2," p. 586). There is no basis for this suggestion because in the surveys and excavations conducted at Khisfîn, hellenistic ceramics *were* found, although not in great quantity because the excavations did not proceed below the strata of the Byzantine period.

[6] For further discussion of the 'forbidden towns,' see pp. 384-385.

[7] See Klein, *Transjordan*, p. 38; Avi-Yonah, *Palestine*, p. 158; Ilan, *Golan*, p. 288; Safrai, *Settlement*, p. 17.

[8] See Brock, "Maximus." Information about the life and career of Maximus (d. 662) is preserved in a work composed by one of his Monothelite adversaries. The manuscript is no later than the eighth, and perhaps as early as the seventh, century. According to the treatise, Maximus was the son of a Persian maidservant and a Samaritan textile producer of the village Sekar, close to Shechem. Relatives of Maximus' father, Avna, were hostile to the couple's marriage, and the pair fled to Khisfîn, where they took refuge in the house of the local priest named Martyrius. Baptizing Avna, his wife Shanda, and their son secretly, Martyrius gave them the names Theonus, Miriam, and Muskhaion. Upon the death of his parents, Muskhaion was admitted to a monastery where he acquired the name Maximus. The secrecy of the baptisms and the suggestion in the text that Martyrius gained protection from

After the Arab conquest, no mention of any Jewish inhabitants appears again. In the ninth century, the Arab historian and geographer al-Ya'qûbi described Khisfîn as a prominent town in "the Damascus province."[9] Yâqût, writing in the thirteenth century, mentioned it as "a village of the Hauran, on the road down to Egypt, lying between Nawâ and the Jordan."[10]

In the 1880's, both L. Oliphant and G. Schumacher visited this site. Oliphant was excited by the remains of a massive building which he identified as a Crusader fortress. This identification came largely from the influence of architectural items decorated with crosses that he found in the village—many of which we now know belong to the Byzantine period.[11] He describes the structure and the village as follows:

> The walls of the principal fort now standing measure 68 yards one way, by 54 the other. They are 9 feet in thickness, and are eight courses of stone in height, the stones from 1 foot to 1 foot 6 inches square, but some are much larger. Within the fort are the traces of a second or inner wall forming a sort of keep in the centre, but the whole area is so encumbered with ruin that it would require more time than I was able to give to it to make accurate measurements, or a plan of the building. The village had almost the appearance of a quarry, so thickly piled were the blocks of hewn stone which enclosed the courtyards and formed the walls of the houses, while they were strewn thickly or stacked in heaps over all the neighbouring fields. The lintels of the doors consisted frequently of large stones, some of which possibly had served the same purpose in old times, on which were tablets, rosettes, crosses, bosses, and other crusading devices.[12]

It should be noted that Oliphant added drawings of three architectural items to his description. He thought these were Christian, apparently from the Crusader period.[13] A survey team led by the author found these items many decades later. Two of them may not be Christian at all and are surely not Crusader. One item is a lintel with a relief of a *tabula ansata* with rosettes on both sides of it, and the other (see PL. 50b) is an arch stone with a relief of a garland with a clear rosette at its center; it does not combine a cross and rosette, as Oliphant drew it. A few years after he visited Khisfîn, Oliphant wrote about the site as follows:

Samaritans in his community, from his cousin, the governor of Tiberias, may hint at the status of Christians in Khisfîn. Were they a relatively weak group in the latter half of the sixth century, perhaps contending with a considerable number of non-Christians (Jews and/or Samaritans) in the area? For this argument, see Kedar, "Khisfîn," pp. 238-241.

[9] See Ibn-Wâdih al-Ya'qûbi, *Kitab al-Buldân,* ed. M. J. De Geoje (Leiden, 1892), p. 115 (in Arabic).

[10] Yâqût ibn 'Abdullâh al-Hamawi, *Mu'jam al-Buldân,* ed. F. Wüstenfeld (Leipzig, 1867), vol. 2, p. 443 (in Arabic).

[11] See Oliphant, *Haifa,* pp. 250-255, and especially p. 252.

[12] Oliphant, "Lake Tiberias," pp. 88-89.

[13] Oliphant, "Lake Tiberias," p. 88

The important question which I could not determine was whether, in the old
Roman times, it had been a place of note. There can be little doubt that a future examination, of a more minute character than I was able to give, would
determine this point, and it is not at all impossible that upon the old
stones might be found seven-branched candlesticks, pots of manna, or em-
blems of a still older date, which would carry it back to Jewish times.[14]

Schumacher was aware of the possibility of identifying Κασπείν or Χασφών
mentioned in the Books of the Maccabees with Khisfîn, but he did not report any Jewish finds at the site.[15] Oliphant's Crusader fort Schumacher understood as a fortified *khân*, and even published a sketch of its ground
plan.[16] This is how Schumacher describes Khisfîn:

> Today Khisfîn, although extensive, is a miserable village, consisting of
> scarcely 60 inhabited huts with a census of about 270 souls, But three
> times as many huts are destroyed and deserted, and good hewn and unhewn
> basalt stones lie in confusion across one another. Here and there Roman
> ornamentation appear (Figs. 16 and 17 in his German edition; Figs. 77 and
> 78 in the English one),[17] and the sign of the cross in a variety of forms on
> the same stone as shown on Fig. 119 (in the English edition; Fig. 78 in
> the German edition). Most of these, however, are buried beneath the ruins.
> The ruined huts are roofed with basalt slabs in the style of the Haurân; sev-
> eral are to be found beneath the ground. In the western end of the city the
> ruin of a large building is to be found, measuring 133 feet from east to west
> and 160 feet from south to north (Fig. 18 in the German edition; Fig. 79 in
> the English edition). There is a gate entrance 11 1/2 feet wide in the south.
> In the west, outer walls, 6 1/2 to 9 feet thick (?), enclose a passage 19 1/2
> feet in width; then comes an inner wall only 3 feet in thickness, which sur-
> rounds a rectangular court-yard. The outer wall makes a kind of oblique
> slope and in the east has a buttress; it is very solidly built; the whole gives
> the impression of a fort or fortified Khân, the architecture of which would
> probably be about the time of Yâqût, and which, like Khisfîn, served a mil-
> itary purpose.[18]

At the beginning of the 1950's, Syrian military camps were erected in and
around Khisfîn, doing considerable damage to its antiquities. Immediately after the Six Day War, the teams led by C. Epstein and S. Gutman surveyed
the village. They reported remains of ancient buildings with arches and stone
slab roofing, a mosaic floor in a courtyard of a Syrian building, as well as
architectural artifacts attesting to remains of a church. The shards collected

---

[14] Oliphant, *Haifa*, p. 254.

[15] Schumacher, "Dscholan," pp. 264-265; Schumacher, *Jaulân*, p. 184.

[16] Fig. 18, p. 265 in the German edition; Fig. 79, p. 186 in the English edition.

[17] Fig. 16 in the German edition and Fig. 77 in the English edition is a drawing of the arch
stone with the relief of a garland with a rosette at its center that was also published by
Oliphant. Our photograph of this item appears as PL. 50b.

[18] Schumacher, "Dscholan," pp. 265-266; Schumacher, *Jaulân*, pp. 184-186. Parentheses
mine.

by the survey teams were identified as belonging to the Byzantine period.[19] Epstein and Gutman attached to their report two photographs and a drawing of an ancient lintel decorated with lovely reliefs, which had been found in secondary use as a lintel of a door in a Syrian military medical clinic (see PL. 51a, and the discussion below).

Between the years of 1968 and 1972, the village was surveyed a number of times by the author and his team.[20] These surveys determined that the area of the ancient site was about 100 dunams. In addition to a large quantity of shards from the Byzantine period (as reported by Epstein and Gutman), we found a few shards from the Hellenistic period and large quantities of shards from various stages of the Roman and Arab periods, as well as a few shards from the Ottoman period.

As earlier surveyors indicated, a number of structures of the Byzantine period were preserved with their original ceilings. Nevertheless, it seems that as a result of the intensive Syrian construction in the 1950's, many of the ancient buildings seen by Oliphant and Schumacher had been dismantled, including the fort, or fortified *Khân*, they mentioned. In the Syrian houses, we found incorporated as building stones dozens of decorated architectural items. Some of these undoubtedly belonged to Christian church buildings (see below), and some may have also served in the buildings of the Jews who lived here during the Roman and early Byzantine periods. Two items deserve further discussion: a doorpost stone—78 cm. high and 54 cm. wide—upon which was engraved a three-branched menorah with a tripod base, and the lintel found in the Syrian army medical clinic (PL. 51a). The lintel is 41 cm. high, 155 cm. long, and 24 cm. thick. An interesting arrangement of reliefs appears on the lintel, mostly paralleling items found in Jewish public buildings from the second-temple and rabbinic periods in the Galilee and the Golan. On the left of the lintel appears a relief of a palm-tree on which a serpent crawls and on whose branches a bird perches. To the right of the tree are triglyphs and, between them, rosettes in circles made by compass. Further to the right appears a vine branch with clusters of grapes, and to the right of that is a garland with a 'Hercules' knot.' In the garland appears a three-line inscription engraved in Greek. Its letters average 3 cm. in height. Its transcription is:[21]

[19] Epstein & Gutman, pp. 283-284, Site #150.

[20] See D. Urman, "Khisfîn," *Special Surveys Reports*, Archive of the Association for the Archaeological Survey of Israel, Israel Antiquities Authority, Jerusalem (in Hebrew); D. Urman, "Khisfîn," *Reports of the Staff Officer in Charge of Archaeological Affairs in the Golan* (from 1968-1972), Archive of the Israel Antiquities Authority, Jerusalem (in Hebrew); Urman, "Golan—3," p. 5; Urman, *List*, p. 19; Urman, "Hellenistic," pp. 458-459; Urman, *Golan*, p. 203, Site #148.

[21] See Gregg and Urman, Inscription #74.

    Σ Η Φ
    Ο Σ Α Ι Ο
    Υ

It reads: Σηφος Αιου. Its translation is: "Sephos, (son of) Aios."

The name Σηφος is similar to Σηφις mentioned in Wuthnow.[22] Αιος is also listed in Wuthnow's collection of Semitic personal names in Greek inscriptions and papyri.[23] There may be a connection between the name Σηφος and the name Σαφω or Σαφου, the name of a woman found twice in the Beth She'arim inscriptions.[24] This inscription probably is the Greek form of the name of a Jewish male.[25]

Our surveys located seventeen more items with Greek inscriptions. Five were found on gravestones in secondary use in the Syrian houses. All the inscriptions are published in the chapter on Khisfîn in Urman and Gregg.[26] Some of the inscriptions are doubtless Christian[27] and others pagan.[28] But it is also possible that some are Jewish. Here let us mention only one basalt gravestone whose height is 100 cm, its width 30 cm., and its thickness 16 cm. Preserved on the gravestone were three lines of an inscription, the height of its letters varying between 5-7 cm. Its transcription:[29]

    Θ Α Ρ Σ Ι
    Ζ Η Ν Ω Ν
    ΕΤ Ϙ

It reads: Θάρσι Ζήνων ἐτ(ῶν) Ϙ. The translation is: "Be of good courage, Zenon! Ninety years old."

Also engraved on the stone is a 'tree of life' decoration. This decoration appears primarily on Jewish architectural items, but occasionally on Christian items found in the Golan region.[30] The name Zenon (Ζηνών) also appears on a gravestone we found at Kafr Hârib and which may also be that of a Jew.[31]

In February 1972, the author, with the assistance of S. Bar-Lev, excavated the remains of a church with three external apses in the western part of

---

[22] Wuthnow, p. 108.

[23] Wuthnow, p. 15.

[24] Schwabe and Lifshitz, p. 19, Inscription #27 and pp. 97-99, Inscription #127, and also see the additional bibliography there.

[25] These forms of the name merit further study and investigation.

[26] Gregg and Urman, Inscriptions #71-73, 75-82, 84, 86-90.

[27] Gregg and Urman, Inscriptions #79-82, 84, 86.

[28] See for example Inscription #71 which is of a veteran of the Legion III Cyrenaica.

[29] Gregg and Urman, Inscription #78.

[30] See Ma'oz, "Communities," p. 62, Fig. 1.

[31] See Gregg and Urman, Inscription #5.

the village.[32] At the end of that year, M. Ben-Ari conducted a salvage excavation of the remains of another church from the Byzantine period uncovered by workers digging a trench for a water line in the eastern part of the site.[33] In June 1975, S. Bar-Lev uncovered sections of two mosaic floors one placed atop the other, about 130 meters north of M. Ben-Ari's excavation and about 200 meters east of the other church.[34] Preserved in a section of the upper mosaic was a Greek inscription from which reveals that the floor was part of a church building, perhaps a monastery.[35]

To conclude our discussion of Khisfîn, we should point out that despite the construction in the village during the later Byzantine and later periods, the site is worthy of archaeological excavation on a greater scope. Such excavations, we believe, will realize Oliphant's vision presented above.

EL-KÛRSÎ (TELL EL-KÜRSÎ, TELL KH. EL-KÛRSÎ, KÛRSÎ, QÛRSÎ)

These remains of an ancient settlement can be found on the eastern shore of the Sea of Galilee at coordinates 2106-2481.

Since the collection of names Kûrsî—Korsia (χορσία), Gergesa (Γέργεσα), Gerasa and Keráze (=כורזין)—are connected in different traditions to the place mentioned in the New Testament where Jesus' miracle of the swine took place (Mark 5:1-25; Matthew 8:23-34; Luke 8:22-37), the site's name became the subject of frequent scholarly discussion during the nineteenth and early twentieth centuries. These scholars, on the one hand, tried to clarify the different versions appearing in the Christian pilgrimage literature and, on the other hand, attempted to identify the place where the miracle occurred.[36] Our interest here is not in the site at which the miracle oc-

---

[32] See Urman, "Hellenistic," pp. 458-459; Gregg and Urman, Inscription #85. It should be pointed out that a complete report of the excavation has not yet been published. But this did not prevent Z. Ma'oz from extracting information from the excavation's file—protected in the Archive of the Israel Antiquities Authority and restricted for the excavator's use only—a photograph of the mosaic floor with the inscription uncovered in the excavation and a copy of the church's ground plan. These he published without the excavator's permission. Let it also be noted that Ma'oz's descriptions of the excavation and its finds are deficient and erroneous in many details. It is only to be regretted that the editors of the *New Encyclopdia* did not pay attention to this. See Ma'oz, "Haspin—1," pp. 523-525; Ma'oz, "Haspin—2," pp. 586-588.

[33] See Ben-Ari & Bar-Lev, "Golan—1," p. 2. To our reget, here too, we must note that in the publications mentioned in the previous note, Ma'oz presents incorrect details about this excavation, and determines—on what basis is unclear—that the remains uncovered by Ben-Ari are of dwelling and not of a church.

[34] Bar-Lev, "Khisfîn," p. 3.

[35] See Tzaferis and Bar-Lev, pp. 114-115; as well as Gregg and Urman, Inscription #83.

[36] For example, see the articles of Abel, "Koursi" and Kopp, "Sea of Galilee" and the references there to an extensive earlier literature.

curred,[37] but rather with the location of the Jewish settlement of Qûrsî which Prof. S. Klein suggested was the origin of the sage, R. Ya'aqov ben Ḥanilai, also identified in our sources as R. Ya'akov ben Qûrsî. Klein wrote:

> At home in the household of Rabban Simeon ben Gamaliel the Prince and teacher of R. Judah the Prince in his youth was R. Ya'akov ben Ḥanilai (Sifre Deuteronomy 322=Midrash Tannaim, p. 184, line 24 in the D. Z. Hoffman edition; see the editor's note), who is also mentioned as R. Ya'akov ben Qûrsî or R. Ya'akov Qûrsî (Y. Shabbat 10:5; Y. Pesahim 10:1; Leviticus Rabbah 3:1; Ecclesiastes Rabbah 4:6). It seems that he was from a place named Qûrsî (and Qûrsî is not his father's name, because that was Ḥanilai), and that is Kûrsî near the Sea of Galilee where Wâdî es-Samekh empties into the sea. The place is further mentioned in the fourth century as Qorsin in the Y. (Y. Ketubot 6:5; "R. Jose's students went up to Qorsin." The term "went up" is used here because from Tiberias one "goes up" to there)....[38]

We accept the late Prof. Klein's argument, based on Y. Ketubot 6:5, that Qorsin or Qûrsî was a name of a settlement. R. Ya'aqov ben Qûrsî was a household intimate of Rabban Simeon ben Gamaliel II when he served as Patriarch and also served as the teacher of Rabbi Judah the Patriarch. This information fits with the long list of evidence we have concerning the special ties that these two patriarchs had with the Jews in the Golan and the Bethsaida Valley north of Kûrsî in general, and the town of Bethsaida in particular.

When we turn to this site's archaeological finds and to the question of whether any Jewish remains were found before 1970, we find a more meager harvest. This is because the investigators of the nineteenth century and early twentieth century focused primarily on identifying the site as the location of the miracle of the swine. Thus, for example, it is unclear whether Schumacher, who surveyed the region in the 1880's, visited the site being discussed here, or whether he saw the remains of the other site where we in 1970 excavated a monastery and a church. This is what Schumacher writes in the English edition of his book about Kûrsî, which he calls Kersa:

> A ruin on the shore of the Sea of Tiberias, lying close to the discharge of the Wâdî es-Samekh. The remains date from two periods: a more ancient one, from which only scattered building stones and foundations are still extant, and a more recent one, probably Roman, whose long walls, 3 feet

---

[37] It seems that the place of this site was finally clarified when, in 1970, the author for the first time uncovered the remains of the impressive monastery and church found at coordinates 2103-2480, and known today also by the name of el-Kûrsî or, for short, Kûrsî. For the first reports of this discovery, see Urman, "Golan—3," p. 5; Urman, "Golan—4," pp. 1-3; Urman, List, p. 20; Urman, "Unclean Spirit," pp. 72-76; Urman, "Kursi," pp. 1-12; Urman, "Hellenistic," pp. 459-460.

[38] Klein, Transjordan, p. 38.

thick, are built of small stones joined with white mortar similar to those found in Tiberias. They enclose square rooms. A round tower, built above the ruin on the lower ledges of the slopes, dates from the same period. According to the statements of the Bedawîn, it bears the name Kersa, or Kursu, because it is not unlike a stool, whilst the already-mentioned walls on the lake are called es-Sûr. Nevertheless, what is usually understood by Kersa is the ruin generally, which is distinguished by a splendid Butmeh. The ruins are extended, and it is thought that traces of aqueducts can be distinguished....Up to now the site has been identified with the Gergesa (Matthew 8:28)....It would be well to strike it out. Mark 5:1, Luke 8:26 etc., refer to Gadara.[39]

In the surveys conducted in the region immediately after the Six Day War, the site was not surveyed. So only in 1970, when the author began his excavations at the nearby monastery and church, was the site surveyed and a few brief exploratory digs were carried out.[40] It became clear in the survey that the site contained a tell whose area was about 10 dunams, and which stood about 5 m. above its surroundings. East and north of the tell, on an area of about 30 additional dunams, it is possible to make out the tops of the walls of ancient buildings that seem to have been covered by alluvial layers from the nearby Wâdî es-Samekh. It seems, then, that the entire area of the ancient settlement spread over approximately 40 dunams.[41] Of the pottery remains gathered at the site, a few shards stem from the Hellenistic period, a large quantity from the Roman period, and an even larger quantity from the end of the Roman period and the stages of the Byzantine and Arab periods.[42] In a short exploratory dig we conducted by means of 5-meter long trench in the southern slope of the tell, we found remains of thick walls— apparently a *khân* of the Arab period. In the main, ceramics collected in this dig were dated to the Byzantine period, the early Arab period, the middle Arab (Crusader) period, and the later Arab periods.

About 100 meters north of the tell, we found the remnants of a structure with thick walls. Within these walls, several basalt architectural items were found. These included two column-shaft fragments and an Ionic capital of the type prevalent in Jewish public buildings of the second-temple and rabbinic periods in the Golan and the Galilee. (The capital is now on display in the Kibbutz 'Ein Gev collection.) In the short exploratory dig we conducted of the structure (a grid of 3 x 3 meters), an additional column shaft and Ionic capital were uncovered, as well as pottery remains. The shards included ones

---

[39] Schumacher, "Dscholan," pp. 340-341; Schumacher, *Jaulân*, pp. 179-180.

[40] See D. Urman, "el-Kûrsî," *Reports of the Staff Officer in Charge of Archaeological Affairs in the Golan* (from 1968-1972), Archive of the Israel Antiquities Authority, Jerusalem (in Hebrew).

[41] See the previous note. And also see Urman, *Golan*, p. 204, Site #154, and also the note for this site on p. 215.

[42] See above, note 40.

which could be dated to the second and third centuries C.E. These shards led us to speculate, at the time, that if the excavation there would be completed,[43] the remains might be shown to be those of a Jewish synagogue.[44] North of this structure, we located remains of another building that may have had a mosaic floor, for within its confines were many mosaic stones of different colors.

North of the buildings mentioned, remnants were also found of an artificial anchorage and various fishing installations. These were examined by a team from the Undersea Exploration Society of Israel headed by A. Raban and S. Shapira.[45]

To conclude our discussion of this site, we again point out that Prof. Klein's proposed identification seems the most probable to us. We hope that the archaeological exploration of this interesting but neglected site will continue.

NÂB

This small, now-abandoned, Syrian village is located on an ancient ruin near the Rafîd-Ḥammat Gader (el-Ḥammeh) road at coordinates 2241-2483. The village was apparently not established before the twentieth century, for Oliphant and Schumacher, who surveyed the site in the 1880's, did not report its existence. Oliphant visited Nâb on his way to Khisfîn in December 1884 and wrote:

> After riding for an hour we came to the ruins of Nâb, situated on a small mound. They consist of blocks of basalt building stone, some traces of foundations, some fragments of columns and capitals, and a tank, dry at the time of my visit, but which evidently holds water for some portion of the year; it had apparently been much deeper at a former period, only the two upper courses of masonary being now visible. It was oval in shape, and measured about 60 yards by 30. This place does not appear to have been previously visited or described.[46]

Schumacher visited Nâb shortly after Oliphant and described the site as follows:

> Ruins on a hill in the ez-Zawîyeh el-Ghurbîyeh district, with the spring 'Ain Nâb in the north-east, and an old stone enclosed pool in the southwest, which is partly fed by the spring. Beneath the debris lie large unhewn

---

[43] And here we must note that our main activity in the region in those days was focused on uncovering the adjacent monastery and church.

[44] See Urman, "Synagogue Sites," p. 18.

[45] For the first reports on these remains, see Urman, "Golan—4," p. 2; Urman, "Unclean Spirit," pp. 75-76; Urman, "Kursi," p. 6; Nun, "Kinneret," pp. 212-218.

[46] Oliphant, "Lake Tiberias," p. 87; Oliphant, *Haifa*, p. 252.

and hewn stones, basalt columns, and the usual Haurân ornaments, very much defaced. The walls of the fallen-in old buildings are 29 1/2 inches in thickness, and arranged in courses as shown by Fig. 107.[47]

Epstein and Gutman surveyed the site in 1968 and reported that the Syrian village is situated atop a ruin and that ancient building stones—fragments of columns and capitals—and shards from the Roman and Byzantine periods can be seen there.[48]

The author and his team surveyed the site shortly after Epstein and Gutman and collected a few shards from the Hellenistic period and the different Arab periods, in addition to those identified by Epstein and Gutman.[49] The capitals reported by Epstein and Gutman were also found. These were made of basalt and hewn like the Ionic capitals common in the Jewish public buildings in the Galilee and the Golan during the second-temple and rabbinic periods. If we combine these capitals with the column shafts and the large number of finely hewn ancient building stones found in secondary use in the houses of the Syrian village, we may conclude that there had been a public building there during the second-temple and rabbinic periods. The site appears on a low hill, but it is difficult to determine whether the hill was natural or a result of generations of ruins without archaeological excavations. The area of the ancient site including the tell is about 20 dunams, and at the time of the survey, it was possible to make out traces of the ancient settlement's fields.[50]

Many investigators identify Nâb as the site of Nob, one of the 'forbidden towns' in the territory of Sûsîta, mentioned in Tos. Sheb. 4:10 (66, 4-6), Y. Demai 2:1, 22d, and the halakic inscription in the mosaic floor of the Jewish public building at Rehob.[51] Our finds at the site support this identification.

---

[47] Schumacher, "Dscholan," p. 342; Schumacher, *Jaulân*, p. 223. In Fig. 107 of the English edition and Fig. 124 of the German edition, Schumacher shows that the walls were built of one or two stones that were placed as 'heads' and two as 'beams', one stone placed as a 'head' and two as 'beams', and so forth, over and over. This form of building is very reminiscent of the remains of the walls of the public building that we found at Dardâra (see above), but it is not clear from Schumacher's figures if the stones of the walls that he saw at Nâb were ashlar.

[48] Epstein & Gutman, p. 285, Site #162.

[49] D. Urman, "Nâb," *Special Surveys Reports*, Archive of the Association for the Archaeological Survey of Israel, Israel Antiquities Authority, Jerusalem (in Hebrew); Urman, *List*, p. 23; Urman, *Golan*, p. 204, Site #161.

[50] See previous note.

[51] For examples, see Klein, *Transjordan*, p. 37; Avi-Yonah, *Palestine*, p. 158. For further discussion of these towns, see above, pp. 384-385.

'AWANÎSH (EL-'AWANÎSH)

The ruins of this ancient village lie at coordinates 2125-2471. The village
was built on a slope facing Wâdî es-Samekh near a flowing spring called by
the name of the village, 'Ein 'Awanîsh. Schumacher, who surveyed the
place in the 1880's, saw ancient remains at the site, but did not specify
them. He pointed out, "According to the statement of the natives, the place
was once important, and this is confirmed by the fact that the same name is
attached to several places in the neighborhood; but all the same, the place
cannot have been of great extent."[52]

In 1968, the site was surveyed by a team led by C. Epstein. They reported the existence of a ruin, the remains of early buildings and walls, and
ancient graves on both sides of the spring. The pottery remains Epstein's
team found were dated to the Roman and Byzantine periods.[53]

At the end of 1968, the author investigated the site and, in addition to the
pottery of the Roman and Byzantine periods, also saw a few shards from various stages of the Arab periods. The author's survey indicated that the ruin's
area was about 13 dunams. Among the remains of the houses, one can discern walls that were built of well-hewn basalt ashlars.[54]

The name "'Awanîsh' that was preserved for the place is very close to
the pronunciation and sound of the name 'Ayyanosh—one of the 'forbidden
towns' in the territory of Sûsîta, mentioned in Tos. Sheb. 4:10 (66, 4-6),
Y. Demai 2:1, 22d, and the halakic inscription in the mosaic floor of the
Jewish public building at Rehob. Therefore, many scholars have already
suggested identifying this place as the town mentioned in the written
sources.[55] If this identification is correct, we hope that systematic archaeological excavations—to the extent that such will be held at the site—will
reveal the existence of a Jewish community there during the second-temple
and rabbinic periods.

SQÛFIYYE (SQÛPIYYE, SKÛFIYEH, SKÛFIYYÂ, SEKÛFIYE)

This abandoned Syrian village was built on an ancient ruin at coordinates
2147-2452. The ancient settlement, whose area was about 30 dunams, was
built on a hill with a spectacular view of the Sea of Galilee. In 1970, the
Benei Yehudah Regional Center was erected beside the site.

---

[52] Schumacher, "Dscholan," p. 288; Schumacher, *Jaulân*, p. 97.

[53] Epstein & Gutman, p. 285, Site #164.

[54] D. Urman, "'Awanîsh," *Reports of the Staff Officer in Charge of Archaeological Affairs
in the Golan* (from 1968-1972), Archive of the Israel Antiquities Authority, Jerusalem (in
Hebrew); Urman, *List*, p. 21; Urman, *Golan*, p. 205, Site #163.

[55] For further discussion of these towns, see the section on Sûsîta.

The village was first surveyed in the 1880's by G. Schumacher, who reported 70 houses and 350 residents in the village.[56] In the eastern part of the village, Schumacher made out several artificial caves. In its southern part, he found remains of an ancient rectangular structure called by the residents *el-kal'a*[57] or *el-Kûl'ah*, that is, 'the fortress.' Near the fortress, Schumacher saw a number of choked up cisterns[58] and, without clearly indicating where in the village, he reports finding a number of stones with reliefs of "rectilinear crosses."[59]

In the 1950's, the village enjoyed accelerated construction following the erection of Syrian Army camps nearby. In 1968, the village was surveyed by the staffs of Epstein and Gutman, who reported finding shards of the Roman, Byzantine, and Ottoman periods, as well as looted burial caves and a number of columns and capitals in secondary use near the village's new mosque.[60]

A short time after the Epstein and Gutman survey, this author conducted an extensive survey at the site which uncovered a number of finds not seen in the earlier surveys.[61] These include shards of the early Arabic and medieval periods—in addition to the Roman, Byzantine, and Ottoman ceramics reported by Epstein and Gutman—parts of olive-oil presses, and three basalt items that bear segments of Greek inscriptions.[62]

Two of the items with Greek inscriptions are tombstone fragments. One of them is part of the lower section of a gravestone. It preserves only the letter N and an incised 'tree of life.'[63] On the second tombstone, which may be complete, an inscription was preserved that reads: θάρσ(ει) ΣωΦόνι ἐτ(ῶν) μ. Its translation: "Be of good courage, Sophonios! Forty years old."[64] The third item is a fragment of a lintel which preserved a section of the dedication inscription. It reads:

[ἐ]πὶ τοῦ θεοσ[εβ] (εστά του)
'Ιλία ἀρχ[ι]μα[νδρ](ίτου) 'Ιάνης μαθ[ητὴς] ἔκτισεν τον ο...

---

[56] Schumacher, "Dscholan," p. 348; Schumacher, *Jaulân*, p. 242.

[57] Schumacher, "Dscholan," p. 348.

[58] Schumacher, *Jaulân*, p. 242.

[59] Schumacher, *Jaulân*, p. 242.

[60] Epstein & Gutman, p. 287, Site #180.

[61] See D. Urman, "Sqûfiyye," *Special Surveys Reports*, Archive of the Association for the Archaeological Survey of Israel, Israel Antiquities Authority, Jerusalem (in Hebrew). Also see Urman, *List*, p. 22; Urman, *Golan*, p. 206, Site #177.

[62] For complete details, dimensions, and photographs of these inscriptions, see Gregg and Urman, Inscriptions #45-47.

[63] Gregg and Urman, Inscription #45.

[64] Gregg and Urman, Inscription #46.

Its translation is: "Under the most pious archimandrite, Ilias, Ianes (the) disciple, built the...."[65] According to the reading suggested by our colleague R. C. Gregg, the last inscription—along with several architectural items decorated with crosses also found in our survey—clearly indicates that sometime during the Byzantine period (its last phases perhaps) some of the settlement's inhabitants were Christian.[66]

Nevertheless, despite the existence of Christian remains at the site, we suggested in the early 1970's that the site be searched for remains of a Jewish public structure.[67] Our suggestion flowed from the similarity between the Ionic columns and capitals that Epstein and Gutman saw near the village's new mosque (as well as additional items such as pedestals, Corinthian capitals, other Ionic capitals, and fragments of a decorated cornice registered by our survey) and similar items uncovered in the Jewish public buildings elsewhere in the Golan. We further suggested that the location of the Jewish structure or structures be sought at or near the site of the mosque.[68]

In the 1980's, a fragment from the center of a basalt lintel, about 50 cm. long and about 45 cm. high, was discovered at the site. It depicts a well-preserved relief of an *amphora* (a two-handled vase) with reliefs of lions on both sides.[69] The two-lion motif in general, and of a pair of lions on each sides of a vase in particular, is common in the Jewish art of the rabbinic period.[70] It is likely, then, that this find supports our conjecture that a Jewish settlement of some sort existed in Sqûfiyye during the Roman period and at least part of the Byzantine period; this settlement had at least one public building of which further remains are likely to be uncovered in the future.

---

[65] Gregg and Urman, Inscription #47.

[66] On the basis of Inscription #47 it may be possible to conjecture that "Ianes the disciple" erected a monastery, the remains of which should perhaps be sought in those of the "fortress" which Schumacher reported.

[67] See Urman, "Synagogue Sites," p. 18; Urman, "Hellenistic," p. 467.

[68] See D. Urman, "Sqûfiyye," *Special Surveys Reports*, Archive of the Association for the Archaeological Survey of Israel, Israel Antiquities Authority, Jerusalem, p. 23 (in Hebrew).

[69] The lintel fragment, its details and photographs were first published by the late Z. Ilan. See Ilan, *Ancient Synagogues*, pp. 154-155; Ilan, *Galilee and Golan*, p. 99; Ilan, *Israel*, p. 100, Fig. 1.

[70] See Hachlili, *Art*, pp. 321-328.

EL-ʿÂL

This large, now-abandoned, Syrian village was built on the ruins of an ancient settlement on the southern tributary of Wâdî es-Samekh (Naḥal or Wâdî El-ʿÂl), at coordinates 2200-2457.

The Syrian village was probably built in the second half of the nineteenth century, for in April-May of 1812, when J. L. Burckhardt passed through, he described the site as a "ruined village."[71] G. Schumacher, who surveyed the site in 1884, found 65 dwellings there and 320 adult inhabitants; he described the settlement as "a large well-built village on the point of reviving."[72] In his words, "The whole neighbourhood of the village contains several antiquities of strikingly Roman characters."[73] In the courtyard of the sheik's home, he saw and described a basalt statue of a woman[74] as well as fragments of a tombstone with a Greek inscription. He sketched a drawing of the tombstone and copied its inscription, but provided no transcription or translation in his publications.[75] The inscription reads: Δημητρία ...χαῖρε which means "Demetria...farewell."[76] In the stable of the sheik who hosted Schumacher, he saw a number of column shafts and, here and there, fragments of what he described as a "Roman cornice."[77] According to Schumacher, the residents discovered a large number of basalt sarcophagi east of the village, and in his reports he presents a drawing of the side of one depicting a relief of the head of the deceased in a medallion or wreath held by two winged Nikes.[78] Schumacher concluded the description of the village and its finds with the sentence, "Avarice and curiosity will prompt the inhabitants of El-ʿÂl to further investigations, which will result in bringing more discoveries to light."[79]

In December 188, Sir Laurence Oliphant visited the village and it appears his host was the same sheik who had hosted Schumacher.[80] According to Oliphant, the village is one of the largest in the Golan region and was built "on the site of an ancient ruin, but the place has been so much built over that little can be seen, though in the walls and yards of the houses are many vestiges of antiquity."[81] In the sheik's stable, Oliphant made out a column

---

[71] Burckhardt, *Travels*, p. 281.

[72] Schumacher, "Dscholan," p. 284; Schumacher, *Jaulân*, p. 81.

[73] Schumacher, "Dscholan," p. 285; Schumacher, *Jaulân*, p. 83.

[74] Schumacher, "Dscholan," p. 285, Fig. 42; Schumacher, *Jaulân*, pp. 83-84, Fig. 15.

[75] Schumacher, "Dscholan," p. 285, Fig. 43; Schumacher, *Jaulân*, p. 84, Fig. 16.

[76] Gregg and Urman, Inscription #62.

[77] Schumacher, "Dscholan," pp. 285-286, Fig. 44; Schumacher, *Jaulân*, p. 84, Fig. 17.

[78] Schumacher, "Dscholan," p. 286, Fig. 45; Schumacher, *Jaulân*, pp. 84-85, Fig. 18.

[79] See previous note.

[80] Oliphant, "Lake Tiberias," p. 87; Oliphant, *Haifa*, pp. 250-251.

[81] Oliphant, "Lake Tiberias," p. 87.

in situ standing to a height of six feet. In the yard of the house he apparently saw the statue Schumacher had drawn and he identified it as a statue of Diana.[82] On that same visit, Oliphant found in the village three coins of Alexander Jannaeus, which he later placed in the collection of the Palestine Exploration Fund in London.[83]

In the 1950's and 1960's, the village enjoyed a surge of renewed building when a number of army camps were built in and near it as part of the Syrian Army's deployment along the front line with the State of Israel. After the end of the battles in 1967, the village was surveyed by teams led by C. Epstein and S. Gutman who reported briefly:

> A large village. Its western side, which is on the bank of the Wadi El-'Âl, is built on a ruin. Many decorated building stones and a number of inscriptions. Ceramic survey: Hellenistic (?), Roman, Byzantine, and Ottoman periods.[84]

In 1969, a two-week systematic survey of the site was carried out by the author and his team.[85] The survey determined that the ancient ruins in the center of the village extended over an area of about 100 dunams (approximately 25 acres). In addition to the pottery types noted by Epstein and Gutman, the author's team recorded pottery from the Early Arab and medieval periods, including wares exclusive to the Crusader period. Traces of walls built of large ashlars with chiseled margins were visible beneath the densely-built modern village. These remains suggested the presence of a large medieval building which would have protected the spring in the wâdî below. Perhaps this building is to be associated with the fortress of Qaṣr Bardawil built in the early twelfth century?

We discovered that several Syrian houses in the village center had been built over Haurân-style houses of Late Roman and Early Byzantine periods. The ancient rooms were used as cellars in the modern houses. Some of the internal walls were pierced with 'Chorazin windows,' and a few had troughs which were used as mangers. Nearly all the Syrian houses in the village center had been built out of ancient stones. Among the various finds uncovered in this part of the village were sections of olive-oil presses, a fragmentary basalt statue depicting the lower portion of a draped figure, a fragmentary basalt statue of a female figure dressed in a belted chiton, and a cube-shaped basalt fragment which is probably the lower portion of an altar. This last item has reliefs on four sides depicting an eagle, a bust of a human

---

[82] Oliphant, "Lake Tiberias," p. 87; Oliphant, *Haifa*, p. 251.

[83] Gibson and Urman, pp. 67-72.

[84] Epstein & Gutman, pp. 287-288, Site #181.

[85] See D. Urman, "El-'Âl," *Reports of the Staff Officer in Charge of Archaeological Affairs in the Golan* (from 1968-1972), Archive of the Israel Antiquities Authority, Jerusalem (in Hebrew). See also Urman, *List*, p. 22; Urman, *Golan*, p. 206, Site #178.

figure in a toga, a rosette, and a garland. This area also yielded a number of architectural items and tombstones with Greek inscriptions (see below).

In the eastern part of the village, south of the Syrian mosque, the author and his team found an abundance of large hewn basalt stones and ashlars. This area also yielded several Ionic and Attic bases, shafts, and sections of columns, as well as many decorated Ionic and Corinthian capitals—all made of finely hewn basalt. Fragments of carved cornices and architraves were found here—some of them with reliefs of vine branches and the egg-and-dart motif—and several gravestones with Greek inscriptions (see below). Other finds in this area of the village include a fragmentary basalt stone from a doorpost (?) depicting a relief of a winged figure in what appears to be a chiton (the head is missing). The figure is modeled after a winged Nike/Victory, and may originally have been one of two such figures guarding an entranceway (the arm of the figure hangs in such a way as to suggest vertical rather than lateral position). A similar depiction of a Nike was found on a lintel fragment in Kh. ed-Dîkkeh (see the section on this ruin). Another item found is the dome of a basalt niche, some 60 cm. high and 90. cm. wide.

The finds south of the mosque—especially the abundance of Ionic capitals of the type prevalent in Jewish public buildings in the Golan—led the author to suggest that the ancient settlement of El-ʿÂl had contained at least one Jewish public building.[86] This conclusion was not accepted at that time by my colleague Prof. R. C. Gregg who joined me in publishing the collection of Greek inscriptions found in the Golan, including the eighteen found at El-ʿÂl as well as the one from the village published by G. Schumacher in his time.[87] Gregg, who edited the summary of the book's section concerning El-ʿÂl, writes:

Archaeological and epigraphical data from El-ʿÂl are, in comparison with evidence from most of our other sites, uniform and definite. The town seems to have flourished in the late Hellenistic and Roman periods, its prosperity indicated by two statues (in addition to that drawn by Schumacher *Jaulân*, p. 84, Fig.15), by traces of one or more large buildings, the dome of a stone niche, a well-cut, three-sided capital, and several decorated architectural elements (including the doorpost with the Victory in relief). Not discovered in recent surveys of El-ʿÂl was the sarcophagus seen by Schumacher (*Jaulân*, p. 85, Fig. 18), adorned with a medallion-framed head of a man, flanked by two Victories; this piece adds to the impression of the town's Roman ethos.
Particularly striking is the absence of inscriptions with typical early Byzantine traits, and neither epigraphs nor architectural remnants provide a trace of Christian inhabitants of El-ʿÂl. We might speculate that the

---

[86] See Urman, "Synagogue Sites," p. 15; Urman, "Hellenistic," p. 466.

[87] See Gregg and Urman, the section on el-ʿÂl.

town diminished in importance and population at the time when nearby Fiq came to prominence.

A question remains whether there was a Jewish population in El-'Âl. Onomastic evidence does not suggest this, but the three-sided Ionic capital with egg-and-dart decoration is very similar to capitals discovered in the region and having close connection with Jewish religion—e.g., at Jibîn, Yahûdiyye (Epstein and Gutman, *Survey*, pp. 275, 289, resp.), Qîsrîn, and 'Ein Nashot (Levine, *ASR*, pp. 104, 111, resp.). However, because Aramaic and Hebrew inscriptions failed to turn up in the town, as did menorah symbols, the presence of Jews cannot be positively confirmed. And yet the three coins of Alexander Jannaeus at least raise the possibility of the early 'Jewishness' of the site.

El-'Âl gives no evidence of any other than pagan inhabitants. Beyond that, there is the evidence, in inscription 64, of a Roman military encampment in the town probably in the time of Julia Domna.[88]

In writing this article, I have once again reviewed the architectural items and inscriptions found at El-'Âl, and my conclusions differ from those of Prof. Gregg. It is correct that the pagan element is prominent in these finds (especially the statues), but some of the items which Prof. Gregg sees as pagan, or as attesting to the "Roman ethos," can also be construed as Jewish or in Jewish use. These include the doorpost with the winged figure and the dome of a basalt niche, to which parallels can be found in Jewish public buildings in the Galilee and the Golan.

A similar picture emerges from the Greek inscriptions found in the village, most of which (15 of 19) were preserved on tombstones.[89] Names such as Antonia ('Αντωνία—inscr. #48), Gaia (Γαîα—inscr. #49), Agathe ('Αγάθη—inscr. #51), Diodoros (Διόδωρε—inscr. #53), Demetria (Δημητρία—inscr. #62), Gaianos (Γαιανός—inscr. #63) and Augusta (Αὐγοῦστα—inscr. #64), are undoubtedly Greek names and/or also Roman, but it may be that some of these inscriptions bearing these Greek or Roman names were Jews. The phenomenon of the use of Greek and Roman names among the Jews of Palestine and the Diaspora during the time of the second-temple and rabbinic periods is well known.[90] Furthermore, on another gravestone appears a clearly Jewish name from the rabbinic period—Hona or Huna (Hωνα—inscr. #50). This gravestone (80 cm. high, 25 cm. wide, and 14 cm. thick) was found in secondary use as a building stone in a Syrian house. The four-line inscription on the tombstone is clear, with an average height of the letters of 4 cm. It reads:

---

[88] See Gregg and Urman, the section on el-'Âl.

[89] For a comprehensive treatment of these inscriptions see Gregg and Urman, in the section on el-'Âl.

[90] For a definitive treatment of this phenomenon, see Roth-Gerson, *Greek Inscriptions*, pp. 147 ff. and the additional bibliography there.

Θάρσι
Ηωνα
ετ(ῶν)
οε

Its translation is: "Be of good courage, Huna! Seventy-five years old." Prof.
Gregg attempted to read, in the second line, the name Ηωρια but immediately realized that this name is problematic and wrote "Ηωρια is unfamil-
iar.... Possibly the reading could be Ηωμα or Ηωνα. The latter is at least
conceivable."[91] Recently I reexamined the tombstone and there is no doubt
that the correct reading is Ηωνα. This name is known from rabbinic literature as the name of several *amoraim*.[92]

Another gravestone which may designate a Jewish woman was found in
secondary use as a building stone in a Syrian house in the eastern part of the
site. Although its upper part has been broken off, it has been preserved to a
height of about 45 cm., a width of 33 cm., and a thickness of 14 cm. The
fragment preserves four lines of a Greek inscription (the height of the preserved letters averaged about 6 cm.). It reads: ...νι Εὐμάθη ἐτ(ῶν) ξε. The
translation is: "Eumathe, sixty-five years old."

Prof. Gregg, who studied the inscription,[93] was aware that forms of the
name Eumathe are attested in burial inscriptions from Beth She'arim—
Εὐμαθία and Εὐμαθεία μήτηρ Ἰακώβου καὶ Ἰούστου—but he did not con-
sider the possibility that our deceased woman was also a Jewess.[94]

To summarize, it seems that the Jewish settlement at El-'Âl began as
early as the days of Alexander Jannaeus. This settlement, which appears to
have been part of the territory of Sûsîta (Hippos), was for extended periods a
mixed community of pagans and Jews. Since Christianity did not succeed in
penetrating the village in the fourth, fifth, and sixth centuries, we conclude
that the village had a strong Jewish community. This community had at
least one public building whose architectural artifacts we found south of the
modern mosque. Indeed, it is in this area that the foundations of the building
itself should be sought in future archaeological excavations. The pagan population most likely had its public buildings as well, but alternatively the
statues found in the village may originally have stood in private homes.

Finally, let us point out that El-'Âl should perhaps be identified as one
of the two 'forbidden towns' in the territory of Sûsîta—'Ein Harrah and
Ya'arot—whose names have not been preserved in the region even though
they appear in the lists preserved in Tos. Sheb. 4:10, in Y. Demai 2:1, 22d,

---

[91] See Gregg and Urman in the section on el-'Al.

[92] See Albeck, *Introduction*; Omansky, *Sages*.

[93] See Gregg and Urman, Inscription #61.

[94] Schwabe and Lifshitz, Inscriptions #113 & 125.

and in the halakic inscription in the mosaic floor of the Jewish public building at Rehob.[95]

"TELL HA-YE'UR"

The remains of this ancient village lie on a hill northeast of Kibbutz 'Ein
Gev, at coordinates 2106-2435. The site is not indicated on the maps and its
designations are local, given by the people of 'Ein Gev who, led by M.
Nun, discovered it many years ago.[96] Over the years, they found many antiquities there, some of which they moved to their kibbutz.

In 1985, Z. Ilan, M. Nun, and P. Porat—along with members of
Kibbutz 'Ein Gev and Kibbutz HaOn—surveyed the site and measured the
remains of a building, which Z. Ilan identified as a synagogue.[97] The building stands on top of the hill on which the site lies; its longitudinal axis
runs north-south and its exterior measurements are 10.10 x 7.10 m. The
building is built of large basalt stones, some of which have chiseled margins. The structure has two entrances in its eastern wall. In the south entrance, which is about 1.60 m. wide, the doorpost stones, crafted with
lovely profiles, were preserved *in situ*.[98] The building's northern wall,
which was repaired during its use, still stands about 3 meters high. Under
the northwest part of the building there is a hewn-out cistern, which was
completed with excellent construction. In Ilan's opinion, this may have
served as a *miqweh*.[99] North of the structure, the survey team found two
column sections and, west of it, a fragment of a heart-shaped corner-column.
In Kibbutz 'Ein Gev are two Ionic capitals from the building; they are of the
type common in Jewish public buildings of the Galilee and the Golan during the second-temple and rabbinic periods. A basalt lintel was also brought
to Kibbutz 'Ein Gev from the site; it is decorated with roses and various geometric figures set in four square frames. The lintel decorations recall the
decorations found on coffins of Jews from the second-temple period.[100]

In the site's eastern section, the survey found remains of olive-oil presses
and at the foot of the hill they identified several burial caves. Unfortunately,
the surveyors did not report on the ceramic finds at the site. But without a
systematic archaeological excavation of the structure, however, we cannot
determine its date.

Ilan concludes his report with the following:

---

[95] On these lists, see pp. 384-385.

[96] Nun, *Kinneret*, p. 34.

[97] Ilan, *Ancient Synagogues*, pp. 155-157; Ilan, *Israel*, p. 113.

[98] See photograph No. 2 in Ilan, *Israel*, p. 113.

[99] Ilan, *Israel*, p. 113.

[100] See photograph No. 3 in Ilan, *Israel*, p. 113.

The building is small, among the smallest known synagogues (whose size varies from place to place) and was suited to the needs of the village in which it was erected. This was apparently a Jewish daughter-village of Sûsîta, whose ancient name is unknown.[101]

If indeed Ilan is right in his last sentence—and this we can know only after archaeological excavation of the building—then we can identify this as one of the 'forbidden towns' in the territory of Sûsîta—mentioned in Tos. Sheb 4:10, Y. Demai 2:1, 22d, and the halakic inscription at Rehob—whose location has not yet been identified.[102]

SÛSÎTA (HIPPOS, HIPPUS, QAL'AT EL-ḤÛṢN)

These remains of an ancient city are located about 2 kilometers east of the Sea of Galilee at coordinates 212-242. The city was built in the Hellenistic period on a lofty spur rising about 300 m. above its surroundings. It functioned as a major city and district center until the Arab conquest. It is reasonable to assume that during Sûsîta's existence Jews lived there. Yet, as we shall see, our knowledge of the existence of a Jewish community in Sûsîta remains uncertain.

Josephus reveals that the city was captured (and perhaps even destroyed) by Alexander Jannaeus. Later, in 63 B.C.E., after the conquest of Palestine by the Romans, Pompey returned the inhabitants to their city and, along with other Greek cities, annexed it to Syria (*War* I § 156; *Antiquities* XIV § 75). In the year 30 B.C.E., the city was given to Herod by Caesar Augustus (*War* I § 396; *Antiquities* XV § 217), but after Herod's death the city was re-annexed to the province of Syria (*War* II § 97; *Antiquities* XVII § 320). When the Great Rebellion erupted, Zealots attacked the villages in the territory of Sûsîta and set them afire (*War* II § 459; *Vita* § 42), but no evidence suggests that the Zealots attacked Sûsîta itself.[103] Josephus recounts that in response to this attack the people of Sûsîta-Hippos killed the "boldest" among the Jews and imprisoned the "timid" (*War* II §§ 477-478). Indeed it is not clear whether Josephus speaks of killing the Jews of the city or of the district, but it is probably the first possibility.[104] C. Epstein writes that "Jews from the city were among the defenders of Taricheae (Magdala)."[105] However, if one reads closely the Josephus passage upon which she relies—*War* III § 542, which deals with the battles of Vespasian around the Sea of

---

[101] Ilan, *Israel*, p. 113.

[102] For further discussion of these towns, see pp. 384-385.

[103] In contrast to what C. Epstein has recently written, see Epstein, "Sûsîta," p. 1102; Epstein, "Hippos," p. 634.

[104] See Safrai, *Settlement*, p. 28.

[105] Epstein, "Sûsîta," p. 1102; Epstein, "Hippos," p. 634.

Galilee in 67 C.E.—it appears that Hippos (Sûsîta) is mentioned with Gadara, Gaulanitis, and Trachonitis. These are names of districts, not cities, so it remains uncertain whether Josephus speaks of Jews from the city itself.

It is interesting to note that after the rebellion and the destruction of the Second Temple a small amount of evidence about Jews in Sûsîta continues to appear. Y. Ketubot 2, 26c, for example, cites Sûsîta as an example of "a city most of whose population is Gentile [non-Jewish]" and whose Jews are not known. But the passage goes on to discuss two Jews who came from Sûsîta, one of whom "everybody knows to be an Israelite and the other no one knows, (but) his friend knows (that he is an Israelite)...."

During the Byzantine period, Sûsîta continued to fulfill its central role in the district, but most of its inhabitants were Christians. The city served as the seat of the episcopate and we know of episcopal representation from Hippos at the councils of Seleucia and Antioch in the fourth century, and at two sixth-century synods in Jerusalem.[106] Just before the Arab conquest, the city was abandoned and destroyed, and it was not populated again until 1937, when Kibbutz 'Ein Gev was established at the foot of the hill.

As for archaeological investigation, Sûsîta has not yet received the attention it deserves. To be sure, Schumacher investigated it. He presented a long account in his books describing the site and its remains,[107] but he identified it as Gamala, not Sûsîta-Hippos. Among the antique traces he observed were an impressive fortification, a "principal street" 600 yards in length, burial chambers with several sarcophagi (none bearing inscriptions), and a substantial structure he took to be either "a synagogue or a Place of Justice."[108]

With the establishment of Kibbutz 'Ein Gev, a number of its members—including C. Epstein, M. Neishtat and his brother, M. Nun—began to explore the site and its remains. Nothing about these investigations and surveys was published except for a forgotten article in a Hebrew periodical called 'Atidot written by Neishtat in 1946.[109] With the establishment of the State of Israel and the outbreak of the 1947-1949 war, the site became a battleground and, at the war's end, remained as a forward outpost of the Israel Defense Forces that defended Kibbutz 'Ein Gev till the conquest of the Golan in 1967.

Despite the site's sensitive location on the Israeli-Syrian cease-fire line, a number of salvage excavations were conducted in the years 1950-1955.

---

[106] See Epiphanius, *Panarion* LXXIII, 26; Socrates, *Historia Ecclesiastica* III, 25; Hierocles, *Synecdemus*, DCCXX, 6 (Buckhardt edition, 1893); Stephanus Byzantinus, *Ethnika*, CCXXII, 4 (Dindorf edition, 1825); also see B. Bagatti, *The Church from the Gentiles in Palestine*, (Jerusalem, 1971), pp. 56, 94.

[107] See Schumacher, "Dscholan," pp. 327-334; Schumacher, *Jaulân*, pp. 194-206.

[108] Schumacher, "Dscholan," p. 332; Schumacher, *Jaulân*, p. 204.

[109] M. Neishtat, "Sûsîta: the City and its Area," *'Atidot* 19-20 (1946): 218-222.

These focused mainly on uncovering parts of Byzantine-period dwellings and the remains of one of the city's four churches, apparently a cathedral. Since no Jewish remains were found in these excavations, we shall not describe the finds here; the reader can find these items in the excavators' reports and the articles published by C. Epstein on Sûsîta.[110]

Since these excavations, no further excavations have been conducted at the site. In the 1980's, P. Porat found a fragment of a marble tablet which preserved a segment of a Hebrew inscription whose origin, according to Z. Ilan, seemed to be a synagogue that had been there.[111] In September 1988, after a great fire cleared the site of brush, Z. Ilan, P. Porat, and Y. Gal toured the site. During this tour, they investigated the remains of a structure in the western part of the site which, according to Ilan, apparently served as the synagogue of the Jewish community in Sûsîta.[112] Since we have not had the opportunity of examining the building's remains up close, we will cite Ilan's description:

> The building is entirely built of basalt with two-three columns *in situ*. It seems that the columns belong to different rows. The distance between them, in a north-south direction, is 4.80 m. This was also the width of the nave. It therefore seems that the lengthwise axis of the building was east-west, like the synagogues in the western Golan, such as at Kanaf. Near the columns were found a cornice stone (part of a raking cornice?) carved with decorative bands, a base, and an Ionic capital of the type common in the synagogues. All told, there are in the building and beside it more than ten columns whose diameter is 46 cm. It seems that a fragment of a lintel with a *tabula ansata* (a tablet with handles) upon it belongs to the building in whose vicinity it was found. Near its right edge, which is all that survived, is an eagle at rest, contracted, in the style of a number of descriptions of beasts and birds found in various places in the Golan, and which were carved in such a contracted fashion, perhaps because of a poor division of the stone's area. There is an example of this in the carving of the eagle at Kh. ed-Dîkkeh which is north of the Sea of Galilee. Apparently there also was an eagle on the second side of the lintel, with a wreath or inscription in the center, and perhaps these parts will be found sometime. The stone is preserved at the Gordon House in Deganya "A." North of the building there is a capital in the upper part of which was hewn out a round basin in secondary use. South of the building lie two Ionic capitals, a Doric capital and

---

[110] See A. Schulman, "Sûsîta," *'Alon* 5-6 (1957), pp. 30-31 (in Hebrew) ; E. Anati, "Sûsîta," *'Alon* 5-6 (1957), pp. 31-33 (in Hebrew); M. Avi-Yonah, "An Inscription in the Oratorio of Sûsîta," *'Alon* 5-6 (1957), p. 33 (in Hebrew); C. Epstein and V. Tzaferis, "The Baptistry at Sûsîta-Hippos," *'Atiqot* 20 (1991): 89-94; Epstein, "Sûsîta," pp. 1102-1104; Epstein, "Hippos," pp. 634-636.

[111] We learn of this discovery from Ilan's book—Ilan, *Israel*, p. 99. The tablet and the section of the inscription on it have yet to be published and we have no further details about them.

[112] See Ilan, *Israel*, p. 99. Ilan does not specify the period to which he attributes the structure—Second-Temple, Mishnaic, or Talmudic period? Without a systematic excavation of the building we cannot determine its date.

additional sections of a column. A pretty Ionic capital of basalt, found near
the way down to 'Ein Gev, apparently slid down from the building.[113]

FÎQ (FÎK, APHIK, APHEK, APHEKA, AFECA, AFÎQ)

This large, now-abandoned, Syrian village was built on a tell and an ancient
ruin. It stands above the gorge of a deep wâdî bearing the same name, at coordinates 216-242. Today Kibbutz Afiq is nearby.

The Fîq site has attracted the attention of many investigators in the past
one hundred and ten years for two reasons. First, in the fourth century,
Eusebius identified this place as the biblical Aphek, and in recent generations many scholars have followed his lead. Second, in the 1880's,
Schumacher reported the existence of Jewish remains in the village.

When Eusebius, in his *Onomasticon*, describes the town of Aphek that
appears in Joshua 13:4, he writes: "Ἀφεκά ὅριον τῶν' Ἀμορραίων ὑπὲρ
τὸν 'Ιορδάνην, ὁ γέγονε φυλῆς 'Ρουβίν καὶ νῦν ἐστι κώμη 'Ἀφεκὰ
λεγομένη μεγάλη περὶ τὴν ῞Ιππην πόλιν τῆς Παλαιστίνης." In English,
"Apheka: [the] territory of the 'Amorites' above the Jordan, which fell to the
tribe of Reuben. And presently [the] village Apheka is called great,
[standing] near the city of Hippos in Palestine."[114] Jerome's translation into
Latin reads: "Afeca terminus Amorraeorum super Iordanem in sorte tribus
Ruben, sed et usque hodie est castellum grande Afeca nomine iuxta Hippum
urbem Palestinae."[115]

After the Arab conquest, the place was mentioned by al-Balâdhuri (d.
892) in his *Conquests of the Lands*; he lists Aphek among the villages and
fortresses vanquished by the Arabs in 638.[116] And in the thirteenth century,
Yâqât (d. 1229) mentioned Aphek in his *Dictionary of the Lands*, recording a
complaint that the people call the place Fîq.[117]

On May 6, 1812, J. L. Burckhardt visited Fîq and reported it as a large
village, inhabited by more than 200 families, and containing "a few remains
of ancient buildings...amongst others, two small towers on the two extrem-

---

[113] Ilan, *Israel*, p. 99.

[114] Eusebius, *Onomasticon*, 22 (20-21) (Klosterman ed.).

[115] *Ibid.* The fact that Jerome defined Afeca as a *Castellum* (fort) and not as a village
(χώμη) as did Eusebius, greatly occupied the scholars of the nineteenth century (see for
example Schumacher, *Jaulân*, pp. 144-145). However, in spite of the prolonged survey we
carried out in Fîq, no remains were found which could confirm Jerome's version—such as
evidence for the existence of a fort at Fîq during the fourth and fifth centuries. It would be
worthwhile, in the future, to search for remains of this fort either at Rujm Fîq (see Urman,
Golan, p. 206, Site #181), or in the mound located in the southern section of Fîq (see Urman,
"Golan—5," p. 1).

[116] Al-Balâdhuri, *Futuh al-Buldân*, ed. M. J. de Goeje (Leiden, 1866), p. 112 (in Arabic).

[117] Yâqût ibn 'Abdullâh al-Hamawi, *Mu'jam al-Buldân*, ed. F. Wüstenfeld (Leipzig,
1866-73), vol. 1, p. 332 and vol. 3, p. 932 (in Arabic).

ities of the cliff."[118] Seventy-two years later, Schumacher found the village dying out, the cause of which he describes thus:

> Fîk—a large village of southern Jaulân, which till recently belonged to the Kada Tubariya (Tiberias), but as the natives felt themselves thereby injured and in great part deserted it and settled in the environs, it was added to El-Kuneiṭrah (Quneiṭra), for which it is adapted by its situation. Fîk, however, is scarcely more flourishing since that time. Of the 160 existing tolerably well-build stone houses, only about 90 are inhabited, containing scarcely 400 persons, the others are quickly going to ruin.[119]

It appears that Schumacher surveyed Fîq quite thoroughly and he describes the archaeological finds he made there as follows:

> About 220 yards from the most southern house one comes upon a hill covered with ruins and olive trees, which is marked as a former site by its remains of old columns and building stones. At the present day the inhabitants of Fîk bury their dead there, and with the object of honoring a Moslem tomb, called the place Jâmat el-'Umeri; perhaps a mosque stood there at one time. In the neighbourhood there is a second tomb, that of the Sheikh Faiyâd Abd el-Ghani: to each of these saints is entrusted a heap of firewood. An old graveyard, with a longish hill called El-Mujjenneh, borders these places eastward. The Kusr el-'Ulliyeh lies in the south of the village, on the rising ground commanding the whole neighbourhood (see Fig. 84 in the German edition or Fig. 39 in the English one). It is a Moslem building, formerly destined for the reception of strangers, and, judging from the *enceinte* walls, was also fortified. At the time that Fîk, according to the testimony of the natives, formed the central point of the land, Kusr el-'Ulliyeh was the seat of Government, the Serai. Several Ionic basalt and granite capitals of pillars and a quantity of basalt shafts of columns lie round about; old door lintels, with totally defaced Cufic inscriptions, are situated on the entrances.
> The village possesses an extraordinary number of oil mills, for large olive trees are to be found round this village, as well as on the slopes and in the wâdî. Besides old cisterns, there is a circular well, 25 feet deep, with an edge of hewn stones. In the courtyard of the summer Menzûl of Sheikh Diâb, besides remains of columns, the ornaments of Figs. 85 and 86 (in the German edition, Figs. 40 and 41 in the English one)[120] are found, and in the wall there is a fragment of a defaced Arabic inscription from the year 741 of the Hegira....
> In the neighbourhood of the Menzûl the more ancient inscription of Fig. 87 (in the German edition, Fig. 42 in the English one)[121] may be observed. Further distant, the Greek inscription of Fig. 88 (in the German edi-

---

[118] Burckhardt, *Travels*, pp. 279-280.

[119] Schumacher, "Dscholan," pp. 319-320; Schumacher, *Jaulân*, p. 136. Parentheses mine.

[120] The decorated items that Schumacher published in these illustrations seem to be segments of cornices decorated with reliefs of grapevines and grape clusters, that may have belonged to a Jewish public building of the rabbinic period.

[121] The item that appears in this illustration is a burial monument with a Cufic inscription.

tion, Fig. 43 in the English one)[122] lies on the street. I found the inscription of Fig. 89 (in the German edition, Fig. 44 in the English one)[123] over the door of a dwelling-house. Mention must be made of the defaced Hebrew signs (Fig. 90 in the German edition, Fig. 45 in the English one), with the seven-branched candlestick, found on a small basalt column.[124] Another form of this latter is presented on a doorpost, which has already been given in the *ZDPV* VIII, p. 333 (=Schumacher, "Correspondenzen").[125]

Further on, Schumacher presents illustrations of additional finds, especially lintels decorated with reliefs of altars, rosettes, garlands, and incised crosses (Figs. 91-96 in the German edition, Figs. 46-51 in the English one), and he concludes: "Although the figures rendered only represent a small part of the things still extant, they are quite enough to prove that Fîk was once an important as well as an ancient place."[126]

After the Six Day War in 1967, the village was surveyed by the teams of C. Epstein and S. Gutman. They reported:

> A large village with a tell beside it on which a (Syrian) army camp was built. In the village there are a large number of hewn stones in secondary use: capitals, bases, decorations carved in the stone. A synagogue column (know from literature),[127] that was at Fîq, was found in Quneiṭra in the Syrian Army cemetery. In the defensive trenches dug in the tell: remains of buildings, graves, and shards. The debris reaching a depth of about 3 meters contains shards from the Middle Bronze Age II (a few lone shards); the Roman-Byzantine, Arab, and Ottoman periods.[128]

In 1968-1970 the author and his team conducted a systematic survey of the site. They surveyed the town, the large Syrian village, and the army camps that had been erected nearby. They discovered over 200 architectural items—most of which were decorated—that had not been reported by Schumacher, Epstein, or Gutman.[129] Some of these items have been published in Gregg

---

[122] The inscription is of a gravestone. For its suggested reading, see Gregg and Urman, Inscription #37.

[123] This Greek inscription is also on a burial stone, see Gregg and Urman, Inscription #36.

[124] And here we must note that Schumacher erred in identifying the written language as Hebrew, since the inscription is written in Aramaic, and also in defining the column on which the inscription was engraved as "kleinen Basaltsaüle," for its height is 180 cm. See PL. 51b. See Inscription #1 below.

[125] Schumacher, "Dscholan," pp. 320-322; Schumacher, *Jaulân*, pp. 138-141. Parentheses mine.

[126] Schumacher, "Dscholan," p. 323; Schumacher, *Jaulân*, p. 143.

[127] The reference is to the column with the incised menorah and the inscription about which Schumacher reported—see below, Inscription #1.

[128] Epstein & Gutman, pp. 288-289, Site #187. Parentheses mine.

[129] D. Urman, "Fîq," *Special Surveys Reports*, Archive of the Association for the Archaeological Survey of Israel, Israel Antiquities Authority, Jerusalem (in Hebrew); D. Urman, "Fîq," *Reports of the Staff Officer in Charge of Archaeological Affairs in the Golan* (from 1968-1972), Archive of the Israel Antiquities Authority, Jerusalem (in Hebrew);

and Urman,[130] and, in the future, I hope to publish a complete report of all the finds of our survey at Fîq in an separate volume. For the moment, we shall mention only the outstanding Jewish finds. First, we turn to a shaft of a complete, basalt column (180 cm. in height; 41 cm. diameter at its base; and 37 cm. in its upper portion) upon which is engraved Inscription #1 (see below) with a seven-branched menorah with a three-legged base. (Even though Schumacher drew the base with two legs, which sometimes even appear as two in photographs, a close examination of the column reveals three legs.) The column was discovered after the Six Day War as Epstein and Gutman had already reported, when it was standing in one of the two rows of ancient columns that the Syrians had set up along the path leading to the grave of the Unknown Soldier in the military cemetery at Quneiṭra. The column is now in the Golan Antiquities Museum at Qaṣrîn (see PL. 51b).

Inscription #1

Because Schumacher's copy of this inscription was unclear and erroneous, it has been scrutinized by some of the best scholars of ancient Palestine during the late nineteenth century and the early twentieth century (PL. 51b).[131] The inscription is in Aramaic and reads: אנה יהודה חזאנה. It translates as "I (am) Yehudah the Cantor."

J. Naveh discussed this inscription[132] and noted that the source of the title חזן (=Cantor) is in the Akkadian *hazannu*.[133] In Assyrian literature appears the title *hazannu ha ali*, which was borrowed by an Aramaic text of the beginning of the sixth century B.C.E.: חזן קריתא that is, a sort of 'city head' or 'mayor.'[134] According to rabbinic literature, the *hazzan* generally fulfilled the functions of *shammash* (sexton) but from a Greek inscription that was discovered in the synagogue of Apamea in Syria we learn that the function of the *hazzan* was quite important, since the period that he held office served to mark the date. The inscription reads, Ἐπὶ Νεμία ἀζζανα, that is, "under (=in the time of) Nehemiah the Ḥazzan."[135] In the course of time, the im-

---

Urman, "Golan—1," p. 2; Urman, "Golan—3," p. 6; Urman, *List*, p. 22; Urman, "Golan—5," p. 1; Urman, "Synagogue Sites," p. 14; Urman, "Hellenistic," pp. 466-467; Urman, *Golan*, p. 207, Site #187.

[130] See in the section on Fîq in Gregg and Urman. The section also presents a number of Greek inscriptions and one in Latin.

[131] For the extensive bibliography dealing with this inscription, see Hüttenmeister and Reeg, p. 2, especially items 5-13.

[132] Naveh, *Mosaic*, pp. 50-51, Inscription #28.

[133] Naveh, *Mosaic*, pp. 41-42.

[134] See Caquot, *Dupont—Sommer*, p. 14.

[135] See Lifshitz, Inscription #40.

portance of the Ḥazzan diminished, and his functions were restricted to those of *shammash* of the synagogue, the rabbinic court, and the school.[136]

It is interesting to note that in addition to the Greek inscription uncovered in the Apamea synagogue, we find the title "the *ḥazzan*" in an Aramaic dedication inscription in the remains of a public Jewish structure at Ḥorvat ha-'Ammudim.[137] While the mosaic floor at Apamea is dated to the late fourth century C.E.,[138] the public structure at Ḥorvat ha-'Ammudim is dated to the late third century and was in use for only about a hundred years, mainly during the fourth century.[139] It is possible, then, that at Fîq the public structure was also in use during the fourth century C.E. and perhaps even earlier.[140]

Inscription #2

To our regret, of this inscription only the letter ו (waw) survived, so that it is difficult to know if the inscription was in Hebrew or Aramaic. It was engraved like the inscription at the academy of Rabbi Eliezer ha-Qappar at Dabûra in a relief of a lovely garland at the center of a well-made basalt lintel (see PL. 52a). The preserved length of the lintel fragment is 78 cm. (and it is possible that its full length was about 170 cm. like the length of the lintel mentioned above at Dabûra); its height, 40 cm.; and its thickness, 14 cm. The height of the preserved letter is 6 cm. Left of the garland relief appears a whole relief of a rosette. One can conjecture that a similar relief appeared on the lintel's right end as well. It is plausible to assume that this lintel originally stood in a central entranceway in a Jewish public building. Whether it stood in the building to which the column with Inscription #1 belonged or in another building is difficult to know. In any case, we hope that in the future its right half—with the continuation of the inscription—will be found.

Another lintel which may also have belonged to a Jewish public building was seen and reported by Schumacher[141] and was found anew by us set in secondary use in one of the Syrian homes at the western edge of the village, near the cliff overlooking Wâdî Fîq (see PL. 52b). This basalt lintel's length is 137 cm.; it is 37 cm. high, and 16 cm. thick. The lintel's length indi-

---

[136] See Lieberman, "Hazzanut," pp. 222-224; Kutsher, *Words*, p. 47.

[137] See Avigad, "Umm el-'Amed."

[138] See Foester, "Diaspora Synagogues," p. 165.

[139] See Levine, "Ḥorvat ha-'Ammudim," p. 80.

[140] In the opinion of M. Sokoloff, the plene spelling "חזאנה" is indicative of the antiquity of the inscription. Except for foreign words this is unusual in later Galilean Aramaic, whereas in the tannaitic period it was common. See Naveh, *Mosaic*, p. 51.

[141] See Schumacher, "Correspondenzen," p. 333; Schumacher, "Dscholan," p. 322; Schumacher, *Jaulân*, p. 141.

cates that it served in a relatively small entranceway (a side entrance?) in a public building, or perhaps in a private building (?). At the lintel's center appears a lovely relief of a circle and within it, a relief of a seven-branched menorah and, on both sides, reliefs of a shofar and an ethrog (?).[142]

Another basalt lintel, unmentioned by the early surveyors, was found in secondary use in a later house in the western part of the village. It is 183 cm. long, 29 cm. high, and 25 cm. thick. At the lintel's center appears a circular relief and, within it, a relief of a five-branched menorah or 'tree of life' (see PL. 53a). It is difficult to know whether this lintel belonged to a Jewish or Christian building. In any case, the first possibility is plausible, and it seems that whoever designed this lintel may have been influenced by the previously discussed lintel, which also has a relief of a menorah within a circle.

Other finds that might be Jewish include about a dozen Ionic capitals of the type prevalent in the Jewish public buildings during the second-temple and rabbinic periods in the Galilee and the Golan, as well as column bases and shafts to which these capitals belonged, and fragments of cornices ornamented with grapevines and grape clusters (some of which was reported by earlier surveyors). It is also possible that some of the Greek inscriptions we found in the village were also Jewish. For example, the name Gaios (Γαίου), that appears in a segment of an inscription preserved on a lintel fragment,[143] despite its being a typical Roman name, was widespread both among the Jews of the Diaspora and those in Palestine.[144] Similarly the name Magnos (Μάγνος), which appears on a tombstone without a cross,[145] was used by Jews who were buried in Beth She'arim.[146] As we have already noted above, we hope in the future to publish all the finds of our survey at Fîq. We will add here only that the area of the ancient site there is about 100 dunams, and that, in addition to the shards reported by Epstein and Gutman, we found a few pottery remains from the late Hellenistic period.

In 1973, during the excavation of a ditch for laying a telephone line across the site, M. Ben-Ari and S. Bar-Lev uncovered remains of private dwellings. In one of the rooms of these houses, six cooking pots were found

---

[142] Or perhaps an incense shovel? As these lines are being written the possibility occurs to us that maybe the object defined as an ethrog or incense shovel is in fact a bell or knocker, of the kind Rabbi Jeremiah saw when he visited Gaulana or Govlana. See Y. Megillah 3:1, 73d. The matter still needs investigation.

[143] See Gregg and Urman, Inscription #23.

[144] See Schwabe and Lifshitz, pp. 193-194, Inscription #207; Roth-Gerson, *Greek Inscriptions*, p. 142, and in both, the references to other bibliography.

[145] See Gregg and Urman, Inscription #29. The Christian gravestones that we found at Fîq are easily identifiable because of the carved cross, generally at the head.

[146] See Schwabe and Lifshitz, p. 130, Inscription #145.

(three of them whole) dating from the fourth century.[147] According to the excavators, "in the excavated area no material was found antedating the Roman-Byzantine period."[148] Nevertheless, in a conversation I had with the excavators, it became clear that their excavation had been limited to the depth of the telephone line ditch and that they did not excavate below this depth to earlier strata.[149]

In 1975, Z. Ilan surveyed the site and, according to his report, found "a small column of finely carved basalt that was perhaps attached to the synagogue's *bemah*."[150] Since the late Ilan did not publish a photograph or further data about this "small column," it is difficult to know on what basis he connected it with a synagogue *bemah*. Commenting on the remarks by Ma'oz concerning this site,[151] Ilan writes:

> In the village there were found remains from the second century C.E. to the Mamelukes period. There is no reason to place the founding of the synagogue later than the late sixth or the early seventh century C.E. It existed, apparently, in the latter part of the Byzantine period and also continued to exist for sometime in the early Arab period.[152]

Although Ma'oz tries to mislead, Ilan is also incorrect. Indeed, until archaeologists find the location of the Jewish public structure(s) at Fîq and conduct excavations, it is difficult to determine its date. The date suggested by Hüttenmeister and Reeg—the second or third centuries C.E.—seems more reasonable to me.[153]

---

[147] See Ben-Ari & Bar-Lev, "Golan—2," p. 1.

[148] See previous note.

[149] Conversation with Ben-Ari and Bar-Lev in August 1973.

[150] Ilan, *Israel*, p. 68.

[151] See Ma'oz, *Golan* (rev. ed.), pp. 36-37, where he writes of the lintel with the relief of the seven-branched menorah (which Schumacher first reported and which was found again in our survey), "After the Six Day War there was found in the village a lintel with a relief of a seven-branched menorah, a shofar, and an incense-shovel within a round medallion. The style of the menorah within the medallion points to a synagogue date in the seventh or eighth century." It should be pointed out that Ma'oz continues to claim (without any basis) that, "Judging from some synagogue fragments found in Fîq—including a lintel with a medallion containing a menorah, a shofar, and an incense shovel, as well as a column with an incised menorah and the inscription, 'I, Judah the Ḥazan'—there must have been a Jewish community in Fîq in the eighth century C.E." (Ma'oz, "Golan—1," p. 545.)

[152] Ilan, *Israel*, p. 69.

[153] See Hüttenmeister and Reeg, p. 4. And see also Sokoloff's suggestion about the plene spelling "חזאנה" in note 140.

KAFR HÂRIB (KEFAR YAHRIB, KEFAR IAHRIV, KAFAR HARUV)

This large, now-abandoned, Syrian village was built atop an ancient ruin on the western edge of the southern plateau of the lower Golan. The site lies above the cliffs overlooking the Sea of Galilee, at coordinates 2121-2405.

The site was first surveyed in 1884 by G. Schumacher, who described its antiquities as follows:

> In the village itself there are few antiquities, although the old building stones point to large buildings.... The old site south of the present village is marked out by a number of scattered stones, mostly unhewn, with foundations of the Arabic age. Here and again one discovers quadrangular subterranean rooms, very carefully built of hewn stones without mortar; they have a base area of 6.5 by 5 feet, and a depth of 5 feet, and were probably formerly sepulchres; they are now turned into grain chambers. One of the basalt coverings of these appears to me to have been adopted later than the remains lying around. After the old site is passed, we reach broad traces of a wall which can be followed along the western margin of the plateau as far as the Sultaneh, stretching down to Khân el-'Akabeh. Probably they are the remains of a Roman road, which was bounded by a wall.[154]

To his description, Schumacher appended sketches of two items which he found in the village. In one appears a lintel, two meters long, decorated with the reliefs of a garland and two encircled rosettes.[155] In the other appears a damaged stone—about 25 cm. high and 35 cm. wide. Engraved upon this artifact is a four-line Greek inscription. Schumacher presents this without interpretation.[156] R. C. Gregg recently studied the inscription, and he identifies it as a fragment of a gravestone of a Roman soldier of the Tenth Legion (Legio X Fretensis).[157]

In 1967, the village was surveyed by a team headed by S. Gutman, who reported the existence of columns, capitals, and remains of an olive-oil press with weights at the site, along with shards of the Roman, Byzantine, and Ottoman periods.[158]

In 1968, the village and the ruins upon which it is built were surveyed by the author and his team.[159] In this survey, it became clear that the area of the Syrian village is about 300 dunams (as a result of increased building

---

[154] Schumacher, "Dscholan," pp. 337-339; Schumacher, *Jaulân*, pp. 170-172.

[155] Schumacher, "Dscholan," p. 338, Fig. 120; Schumacher, *Jaulân*, p. 171, Fig. 64.

[156] Schumacher, "Dscholan," p. 338, Fig. 121; Schumacher, *Jaulân*, p. 171, Fig. 65.

[157] Gregg and Urman, Inscription #1.

[158] Epstein and Gutman, p. 289, Site #190.

[159] D. Urman, "Kafr Hârib," *Special Surveys Reports*, Archive of the Association for the Archaeological Survey of Israel, Israel Antiquities Authority, Jerusalem (in Hebrew); D. Urman, "Kafr Hârib," *Reports of the Staff Officer in Charge of Archaeological Affairs in the Golan* (from 1968-1972), Archive of the Israel Antiquities Authority, Jerusalem (in Hebrew); Urman, *List*, p. 23; Urman, *Golan*, p. 207, Site #191.

there after 1950), and the area of the ancient ruin is about 100 dunams.[160] In
addition to the ceramics Gutman reported, we also found a few shards from
the late Hellenistic period and the different Arab ones.

In the houses, courtyards, and alleys of the Syrian village, we recorded
dozens of ancient architectural artifacts—both decorated and undecorated.
Some of these had been incorporated in secondary use as building material in
the modern houses and some were just lying in courtyards and alleys. We
shall not detail the scores of items, but will just point out that among them
are a large number of column bases, shafts, and capitals—whole and damaged—of the Doric and Ionic styles common in Jewish public buildings in
the Galilee and the Golan dating to the second-temple and rabbinic periods.
These findings led us, at the time, to suggest searching this site for the remains of a Jewish public building (a synagogue?),[161] even though we also
found a number of pagan artifacts and a fragment of a lintel decorated with a
simply carved cross and a *chi-rho* symbol.

It seems that the inhabitants of the Syrian village damaged the ancient
settlement's cemeteries, for we found four sarcophagi (one of basalt and
three of limestone) serving as water-troughs in courtyards. A fragment of
another sarcophagus was found in secondary use as a building stone; this
was decorated with a rosette(?) between two bands. In addition to the sarcophagi, we also found in secondary use in village houses as building
stones, eight basalt gravestones with Greek inscriptions upon them. A full
treatment of these inscriptions appears in Gregg and Urman.[162]

The names of the deceased on these gravestones do not reveal any clearly
Jewish names. Still, unlike my colleague Gregg, who sees all of these
gravestones as monuments of deceased pagans, in my opinion it is possible
that some are of Jews. Thus, for example, the name Dionysia (Διονυσια)
that appears on monument #2 at Kafr Ḥârib also appears as the name of a
deceased Jewish woman buried in Catacomb No. 1 in Beth She'arim.[163]

In the center of the modern village we found a subterranean chamber
(2.76 m. long; 1.20 m. wide; 1.50 m. high) built in five tiers of smoothly
hewn stones resting on bedrock. Originally, the vault was covered by basalt
slabs, several of which were removed in modern times to enable construction of descending steps. It is unclear if modern inhabitants used this chamber for storage of grain, as Schumacher reported about similar structures

---

[160] See Urman, *Golan*, the note for Site #191 on p. 215.

[161] See Urman, "Synagogue Sites," p. 13; Urman, "Hellenistic," p. 467.

[162] See Gregg and Urman, Inscriptions #2-9.

[163] Schwabe and Lifshitz, Inscription #52. And see Lifshitz's comments on the
phenomenon of theophoric names among Jews, and the parallels that he brings there that also
includes a Jew from Tiberias who bore the name of Dionysius (Διονύσιους).

observed during his visit to Kafr Ḥârib, but we share his suspicion that this room (and others like it) "were probably formerly sepulchres."[164]

In the area of the village and the ruin, we found many parts of olive-oil presses, some *in situ*. This evidence reveals that the village inhabitants in the second-temple and rabbinic periods gained their livelihoods in part by growing olives and producing olive oil.[165]

Following our survey, two additional Greek inscriptions were found near the village, both of them boundary stones dating to an imperial survey and registration of lands for taxation which took place between 293-305 C.E. The two inscriptions were published and it shall suffice us here only to note the publishers and the translation of the inscriptions. The first inscription was published by S. Applebaum, B. Isaac, and Y. Landau, and its translation is: "[Diocletian] and Maximian, Augusti, and Constantius...illustrious Caesars (have erected this) stone demarking (the) fields [or boundaries] (of)...."[166] The second inscription, more complete, was published by P. Porat. Its translation is: "The Augusti Diocletian and Maximian, and the most illustrious Caesars Constantius and Maximian, have ordered the erection of a boundary stone on the borders of the village Kapar Haribo in the place (called) REO [...] GA, by the tax assessors AM [..] D [.]OLYOY and Agelippos."[167]

The latter inscription, which was found near lands cultivated today by the kibbutzim Kafar Ḥaruv and 'Afiq at coordinates 2154-2420,[168] confirms the accepted identity of this site as Kafr Ḥârib (=Kefar Yaḥrib or Kefar Iaḥriv) as one of the 'forbidden towns' in the territory of Sûsîta, as set out in Tos. Sheb. 4:10, Y. Demai 2:1, 22d, and in the halakic inscription from the Jewish public building at Rehob.[169] This find also strengthens our opinion that one should continue to search at Kafr Ḥârib for the remains of the Jewish public building or buildings, for in our survey we registered a great quantity of its (their) architectural items.

It seems that Kafr Ḥârib has had a fascinating ethnic history. The settlement began in the latter part of the Hellenistic period (and perhaps by Jews in the days of Alexander Jannaeus, like El-'Âl). It continued as a mixed Jewish and pagan settlement during the Early and Late Roman periods. At the start of the Byzantine period, a large Jewish population apparently continued to live in the village, but it gradually became smaller in the later stages of this period, when Christianity began to penetrate. It is hard to

---

[164] Schumacher, "Dscholan," p. 338; Schumacher, *Jaulân*, p. 171.

[165] See Urman, *Golan*, pp. 145-148; Urman, "Economy," pp. 35-66.

[166] Applebaum, Isaac & Landau, p. 134.

[167] Porat, "Golan," pp. 130-133.

[168] Porat, "Golan," pp. 130.

[169] For further discussion of these towns, see pp. 384-385.

know whether the local pagan population adopted Christianity or whether Christian families were added to the village population. Mention of Kefar Yaḥrib in the list of the forbidden towns in the territory of Sûsîta appearing in rabbinic sources also constitutes evidence of the ethnic changes that overtook this important village in the course of the fourth century.

KFAR ṢEMAḤ

One of the 'forbidden towns' in the territory of Sûsîta, mentioned in Tos. Sheb. 4:10, Y. Demai 2:1, 22d, and in the halakic inscription at Rehob.[170] In all versions of the forbidden-towns list, including the Rehob Inscription, the following sentence is added, "and Rabbi (that is Rabbi Judah the Prince) released Kfar Ṣemaḥ." We shall not address the differing conclusions drawn by scholars about this sentence, but shall only discuss suggestions for the identification of this town's location.

S. Klein identified Kfar Ṣemaḥ with the Arab village of Semakh located, until the end of the 1940's, south of the Sea of Galilee.[171] Avi-Yonah was apparently also impressed by the preservation of the name there, but put a question mark with this identification.[172]

Our knowledge of the archaeological finds at Arabic Semakh is limited because no systematic archaeological excavations have been conducted there. The site is presently covered with piles of ruins of the Arab village, which was built mostly out of clay bricks. Schumacher, who visited the site in the 1880's, indicates that "In the Menzûl of the Sheikh there are several basalt columns, about 36 inches in length and 12 inches in diameter, which have been used as props for the rooms. Otherwise the village, which is lacking in building stone, has few antiquities."[173]

In the opinion of M. Nun, there are no remains of an ancient settlement in Arab Semakh, and he therefore suggests identifying Kfar Ṣemaḥ with Samra which is south of Kibbutz HaOn. Nun calls the site Tell Samra.[174] He claims that

> the remains of the large construction on the surface of the tell attest to the importance and wealth of the settlement. In its cemetery, found on the Tell Katzir hill opposite, from time to time coffins made of limestone and basalt are found that testify to the well-to-do status of the inhabitants....At the time of the [British] Mandate, a Byzantine church mosaic was found at Samra, and, indeed, in the 1960s, during excavation work at the north end

---

[170] For further discussion of these 'forbidden towns,' see pp. 384-385.

[171] Klein, *Transjordan*, p. 38.

[172] Avi-Yonah, *Palestine*, p. 158.

[173] Schumacher, "Dscholan," p. 345; Schumacher, *Jaulân*, p. 238.

[174] Nun, *Kinneret*, pp. 34-35.

of the tell, a complex of buildings with mosaic floors was uncovered and destroyed. It seems to have been a Byzantine monastery.[175]

It should also be noted that during Nun's investigations on the Kinneret and its region he discovered, foundations of an ancient anchorage—about 70 meters long—on the shore of Samra.[176]

In 1970, the author surveyed the site at Samra. This survey showed that the area of the ancient tell there was about 40 dunams. It yielded many shards from the various stages of the Roman, Byzantine, and Arab periods.[177] During the survey it was possible to see the remains of the tops of walls of various structures over the entire area of the site, but without archaeological excavation it was difficult to determine which of them were ancient and which belong to buildings of the more recent Arab village.

Nun's suggested identification is attractive, to be sure, but we must wait for further archaeological study of the ruins at both Semakh and Samra.

EL-'UYÛN (KH. 'AYÛN, 'IYYON)

This small, now-abandoned, Syrian village was built upon an ancient tell in the southern extremity of the lower Golan plateau above the cliffs of Wâdî Masaûd (which descends into the Yarmuk gorge), at coordinates 2129-2360.

The village was first surveyed by G. Schumacher in the 1880's. He realized the importance of its topographic location and wrote:

> The old settlement covered a space of several hektars, and presents traces of different masonry of modern, mediaeval, and ancient times. A number of large, mostly unhewn, basalt stones lie heaped up between the falling huts of a Bedawîn winter village; the foundation walls of buildings in Moslem times, and Roman remains in the form of basaltic shafts of columns, still exist; these last measure 5 feet in length, and 12 inches across. There, are also some old subterranean corn magazines with traces of basalt roofing.[178]

Schumacher published a drawing of a gravestone with a Greek inscription which, at the time, served as a doorpost in one of the Arab buildings.[179] The inscription reads: θάρσι Αντίοχ[ε] αἰτῷ[ν]. It translates: "Be of good courage, Antiochus. ? years old."[180]

---

[175] Nun, *Kinneret*, pp. 34-35. Brackets mine.

[176] Nun, *Kinneret*, p. 84.

[177] D. Urman, "Samra," *Special Surveys Reports*, Archive of the Association for the Archaeological Survey of Israel, Israel Antiquities Authority, Jerusalem (in Hebrew); Urman, *Golan*, p. 209, Site #203.

[178] Schumacher, "Dscholan," pp. 244-245; Schumacher, *Jaulân*, pp. 97-98.

[179] See Schumacher, "Dscholan," p. 244, Fig. 6; Schumacher, *Jaulân*, p. 98, Fig. 19.

[180] See Gregg and Urman, Inscription #12.

In 1924, J. Barslavi visited the site and found another gravestone with a Greek inscription set in secondary use in one of the buildings in the Bedouin village. Barslavi, who copied the inscription, gave the author the copy which reads: εὐμοίρι [Κ]λεοπάτρα. It translates as: "May your lot be good, Cleopatra!"

We should point out that Braslavi reported the first letter of the name Cleopatra as a *sigma*. Perhaps the error was on the tombstone he inspected, though the error points to possible provision by the copyist of a Greek C=sigma, rather than the K which we expect on the stone.[181]

In 1968, the village was surveyed by C. Epstein who found ceramic remains from the Middle Bronze Age I, Middle Bronze Age II, Iron Age I, Iron Age II, Byzantine, and Ottoman periods.[182]

In 1969, the site was surveyed again by the author and his staff. This survey determined that the area of the ancient site was about 15 dunams. It found shards from the different stages of the Roman and Arab periods as well those reported by Epstein.[183] We were unsuccessful in locating the inscriptions copied by Schumacher and Barslavi, but we did identify in the abandoned Syrian houses a large number of ancient building stones in secondary use, some of which were ashlars. We also found fragments of columns as well as Doric and Ionic capitals. As a result of these finds, we suggested searching for remains of a Jewish public building from the rabbinic period which might turn out to be a synagogue.[184] Since this survey, however, we have not had the opportunity to visit the village again.

In 1978, S. Applebaum, B. Isaac, and Y. Landau published a Greek inscription that was found in el-'Uyûn a few years earlier.[185]

The inscription reads:

Αγαθῆ τύχῃ
Ἰσίδωρος καὶ
Δομιττιανός οὐεττ(ερανοὶ)
ἐξ ἱεροῦ πρετωρίου
τῆ κυρίᾳ πατρῖδι

Its translation is: "Good fortune! Isidoros and Domittianos, veterans from (the) praetorian guard in (the) sovereign land."[186] Applebaum et al., associate ἱεροὺ πραιτώριον with the Praefectus Praetorio Orientis at Con-

[181] See Gregg and Urman, Inscription #13.

[182] Epstein & Gutman, p. 291, Site #203.

[183] D. Urman, "el-'Uyûn," *Special Surveys Reports*, Archive of the Association for the Archaeological Survey of Israel, Israel Antiquities Authority, Jerusalem (in Hebrew); Urman, *List*, p. 26; Urman, *Golan*, p. 209, Site #204.

[184] Urman, "Synagogue Sites," p. 13; Urman, "Hellenistic," p. 467.

[185] See Applebaum, Isaac & Landau, pp. 134-135.

[186] See previous note. See also Gregg and Urman, Inscription #14.

stantinople, and suggest a fourth-century dating, perhaps "subsequent to Constantius II's reunification of the empire in 350."[187]

El-'Uyûn remains today a puzzling site. On the one hand, there are no significant remains to be seen above ground level; on the other hand, a place bearing the name el-'Uyûn or 'Ayûn, thought to be in this area, is well-attested in the primary literature (in contrast to the majority of sites in the Golan, which go unmentioned in literary sources). In the description of the territory of Canaan in Numbers 34:10-11, we read, "To the east you shall draw a line from Hazar-enen to Shepham; it shall run down from Shepham to Riblah east of *Ain*, continuing until it strikes the ridge east of the Sea of Kinnereth" (New English Bible). The passage seems to point to the area of el-'Uyûn, and its phrase about the "ridge" could refer to the cliff that runs south to north, from Kh. et-Tawâfîq to Kafr Hârib.[188]

In the rabbinic period, a settlement named 'Iyyon is mentioned in the list of 'forbidden towns' in the territory of Sûsîta (see Tos. Sheb. 4:10, Y. Demai 2:1, 22d and the halakic inscription from Rehob).[189] The existence of shards from the Roman and Byzantine periods at el-'Uyûn, on the one hand, and the existence of archaeological items that might have belonged to a Jewish public building, alongside the inscriptions mentioning pagan residents in the village in these periods, on the other, strengthen the conclusion that the 'Iyyon mentioned in the halakic list should be identified with the remains found in the village of el-'Uyûn. On the basis of this identity and the architectural items found in our survey, the investigation of the site should be continued. Hopefully, discoveries will be made that will attest to a Jewish community of the rabbinic period.

DEMBAR (OR DEMBAR 'IYYON)

One of the 'forbidden towns' in the territory of Sûsîta[190] mentioned in the Tos. Sheb. 4:10,[191] Y. Demai 2:1, 22d,[192] and in the halakic inscription in the mosaic floor of the Jewish public structure at Rehob.[193]

S. Klein, who wrote before the discovery of the Rehob inscription, preferred the version of the name that appeared in the Yerushalmi manuscripts,

---

[187] Applebaum, Isaac & Landau, p. 135.

[188] The existence of shards from the Bronze and Iron Ages at the tell upon which the village is built supports the identification.

[189] For further discussion of this list, see pp. 384-385.

[190] See previous note.

[191] In the manuscripts of the Tosefta, the name of the town appears in different forms, see the editions of Zuckermandel and Lieberman.

[192] In the manuscripts of the Yerushalmi, the name רם ברין appears.

[193] In the Rehob Inscription, the version is דמבר or דמבר עיין.

רם ברין, but he emended it to רום ברך,[194] and suggested identifying the place
with the Breik'ah mentioned by Schumacher.[195]

Avi-Yonah followed Klein and emended the name to רָם בְּרָק ("Ram
Baraq") and followed the identification of the site with Schumacher's
Breik'ah.[196]

What is interesting in Schumacher's report on Breik'ah is that there is no
description of any particularly impressive antiquities at that site. So it
appears that Klein and Avi-Yonah based their conclusions on the similarity
between the Arabic name Breik'ah and רום ברך or רם ברק. Schumacher describes the site thus: "Breik'ah—A small crumbled ruin on the western de-
clivity of the Wâdî Masaûd. A few splendid old trees spring out of the ruins,
under which are some winter huts fallen into decay."[197]

In 1967, C. Epstein surveyed the region of the site and reported finding a
ruin lying on a spur overlooking Wâdî Masaûd (at coordinates 2147-
2374).[198] At the top of the spur, Epstein and her team made out the remains
of buildings and a wall section. Southeast of the ruin, the surveyors found
the remains of an ancient cemetery with caves and pits carved into the rock.
The shards found at the site, according to Epstein's report were "from Middle
Bronze Age II, the Late Bronze Age, the Iron period (the Israelite), the
Roman period, the Middle Ages, and the Ottoman period. In the pit
graves—from the Middle Bronze Age II."[199]

In 1968, the author surveyed the site.[200] This survey determined that the
ancient ruin's area was about 15 dunams and that the cemetery covered at
least 7 dunams. Remains of the ancient buildings are most impressive but
without systematic archaeological excavation it is difficult to date the various buildings and the fortification enclosing the site. It should be pointed
out that in addition to the shards C. Epstein reported, we also found shards
from the various phases of the Byzantine period.[201] As for the possibility of
identifying the place as Dembar or Dembar 'Iyyon, we must indicate that we
found no archaeological remains there that reveal either the origin or the re-

---

[194] See Klein, *Transjordan*, p. 37.

[195] Klein, *Transjordan*, p. 37.

[196] See Avi-Yonah, *Palestine*, p. 158.

[197] Schumacher, "Dscholan," p. 257; Schumacher, *Jaulân*, p. 115.

[198] Epstein & Gutman, p. 291, Site #202.

[199] Epstein & Gutman, p. 291, Site #202.

[200] D. Urman, "Breik'ah," *Special Surveys Reports*, Archive of the Association for the
Archaeological Survey of Israel, Israel Antiquities Authority, Jerusalem (in Hebrew); D.
Urman, "Breik'ah," *Reports of the Staff Officer in Charge of Archaeological Affairs in the
Golan* (from 1968-1972), Archive of the Israel Antiquities Authority, Jerusalem (in Hebrew);
Urman, *List*, p. 25; Urman, *Golan*, p. 208, Site #202.

[201] See previous note.

ligion of the site's inhabitants. Yet, it is possible that if systematic archaeological excavations were conducted at the site, such remains might be found.

As was indicated above (note 193), the version of the name appearing in the Rehob inscription discovered in 1974 is דמבר (Dembar). Nevertheless, Sussmann, who published the inscription, noted that it is possible that the reading should be דמבר עיון (Dembar 'Iyyon), because between the names דמבר and עיון there is no conjunctive 'ו' (waw) as there is before the other place names in the inscription.[202] If Sussmann is correct, then the list of 'forbidden towns' in the Sûsîta territory contains only eight, not nine, towns as has been accepted by all the scholars who dealt with this list previously. And if this is so, we should stop searching for דמבר (Dembar) separately and עיון ('Iyyon) separately.

Sussmann's comment was published in 1974, but that did not prevent Z. Safrai four years later from renewing the suggestion of identifying Dembar and 'Iyyon separately.[203] In referring to Dembar, Safrai writes: "דמבר—in the literature: רום ברך, and on the basis of this erroneous version it was suggested to identify it with Breik'ah, northeast of Khushniyye.[204] According to the version of the inscription one should suggest el-Môbarah, about a kilometer north of Wâdî es-Samekh and about 3 kilometers east of el-Hârrath."[205]

At the place suggested by Safrai, we found no antiquities whatsoever. In Schumacher's writings, however, we found reference to another site in the Golan bearing the name of Môbarah, which he describes as follows: "Môbarah—Extremely rocky and wild slopes on the northern bank of the Rukkâd, near Kafr el-Mâ. Some remains of ruins and caves are to be found in the basalt rocks bounding the plateau; they are called Tâket el-Harîreh."[206] Regrettably, the site Schumacher describes is on the Syrian-Israeli cease-fire line and we were unable to visit it. Nevertheless, if one studies Schumacher, one will find that immediately after his description of Môbarah which is near Kafr el-Mâ, he mentions an area then called Môbarat 'Ayûn.[207] And he writes, "Môbarat 'Ayûn—A district close to the precipice

---

[202] See Sussmann, "Beth-Shean," p. 122.

[203] See Safrai, Settlement, p. 17.

[204] Here we should note that to the best of our knowledge, no one has suggested identifying Breik'ah which is northeast of Khushniyye with רום ברך. Had Safrai carefully read what Klein and Avi-Yonah had written (see Klein, Transjordan, p. 37 and Avi-Yonah, Palestine, p. 158), he would have seen that both, in their footnotes, were referring to the other Breik'ah that appears in Schumacher, which was discussed above in this chapter, and not to the one northeast of Khushniyye.

[205] See Safrai, Settlement, p. 17.

[206] Schumacher, "Dscholan," p. 342; Schumacher, Jaulân, pp. 221-222.

[207] See Schumacher, "Dscholan," p. 342; Schumacher, Jaulân, p. 222.

of the Wâdî 'Ayûn, north of the same-named ruin."[208] It seems that Schumacher's mention of Môbarat 'Ayûn and Sussmann's version of the name found in the Rehob Inscription, together lead to the conclusion that we alluded to above, that one should cease seeking דמבר (Dembar) apart from עיון ('Iyyon).[209] It may also be that the location of דמבר עיון, (Dembar 'Iyyon) was el-'Uyûn (see the section on el-'Uyûn).

'EIN ḤARRAH (OR 'EIN ḤADDAH)

This name designates one of the 'forbidden towns' in the territory of Sûsîta,[210] mentioned in Tos. Sheb. 4:10,[211] Y. Demai 2:1, 22d,[212] and the halakic inscription from Rehob.[213]

Nowhere near the ruins of Sûsîta nor in its district has the name 'Ein Ḥarrah been preserved. In the attempts by different researchers over the last hundred years to identify the site of 'Ein Ḥarrah or 'Ein Ḥaddah, we have found no proposal with enough factual evidence to be worthy of discussion.[214] We can only conjecture that this site should be identified with one of those in which Jewish finds of the rabbinic period have been, or will be, uncovered in the Sûsîta territory. At this stage, we are unable to point to any specific site.

YA'AROT (YA'ARUT)

Ya'arot was one of the 'forbidden towns' in the territory of Sûsîta.[215] Its name has not been preserved in the area and therefore there is no certainty about its location. S. Klein suggested identifying it with Kh. el-'Arâis, ap-

---

[208] See previous note. And we are unable to understand how this fact escaped Z. Safrai and even Y. Sussmann, who also 'sinned' in his attempts to locate the towns mentioned in the Tosefta, the Yerushalmi, and the Rehob Inscription. See, for example, his suggestion for 'Ein Ḥarrah or 'Ein Ḥaddah—Sussmann, "Beth-Shean," p. 122, note 204.

[209] See Sussmann, "Beth-Shean," p. 122.

[210] For further discussion of these 'forbidden towns,' see pp. 384-385.

[211] In all manuscripts of the Tosefta, the name appears as עין תרעא.

[212] In the manuscripts of the Yerushalmi, the name appears as עין תרע and עין חדע.

[213] In the Rehob Inscription, the form appears as עין תרע or עין חדע. See Sussmann, "Beth-Shean," p. 122, note 204.

[214] See Klein, *Transjordan*, p. 37; Sussmann, "Beth-Shean," p. 122, note 204; Ilan, *Golan*, p. 291; Safrai, *Settlement*, p. 16.

[215] See Tos. Sheb. 4:10 (66, 4-6), Y. Demai 2:1, 22d, and the halakic inscription uncovered in the mosaic floor of the Jewish public building at Rehob. For further discussion of these 'forbidden towns,' see pp. 384-385.

parently as a result of Schumacher's finds at this ruin.[216] Avi-Yonah followed the lead of both Klein and Schumacher.[217]

Unfortunately, because the location of Kh. el-'Arâis is near the cease-fire line between Israel and Syria, we have been prevented from surveying the site and so we must make do with Schumacher's description of the site, which offers no a hint about the origin or religion of the site's inhabitants in antiquity. He writes:

> Khurbet el-'Arâis—'The ruins of the bride,' lies a little way from the discharge of the Rukkâd into the Yarmûk, on the steep margin of the high plateau of southern Jaulân. Today it is only a heap of ruins with a strong wall against the incline, which is a few layers in height and 3 feet thick. Foundation walls 30 feet broad by a length of 13, 22, 25, and even 65 feet, are found ranged one upon another on the highest places of the ruins, whilst other traces of the same extend as far as the plain and down the slope. This was once a settled and important place, as is shown by its solid construction of large unhewn basalt blocks set together without mortar. There are also several bent angled embossments to be found here. On the slope, about 131 feet below the ruins, an excellent spring, the 'Ain el-'Arâis, flows down into the ravine and joins the 'Ain el-Fejjeh below, which is overgrown with splendid fig trees, and which trickles down into the Rukkâd.[218]

ḤAMMAT GADER (EL-ḤAMMA, EL-ḤAMMEH)

Ḥammat Gader lies in a valley north of the present bed of the Yarmuk River at coordinates 212-232. The valley is about 1500 m. long, about 500 m. wide, and its over-all area is about 750 dunams. The valley has a number of hot springs known by their Arabic names. Two of them, 'Ein ej-Jarab and 'Ein Bûlus flow alongside the hill of Tell el-Bâni (or Tell el-Ḥammeh, that is, "the mound of the bath") upon which the remains of a synagogue were uncovered (see below). Two additional springs, 'Ein er-Rîḥ and 'Ein el-Mâqlle or Ḥammet Selîm flow in the southern part of the valley. Near the latter spring, remnants of magnificent ancient baths have been uncovered. A fifth spring, the water of which Schumacher attests is good for drinking,[219] flows in the north-east corner of the valley and is called by the Arabs 'Ein es-Sakhneh or 'Ein Sa'âd el-Fâr.

Space does not allow me to detail the list of travelers and investigators who have visited the site from the days of Estori ha-Parḥi until the first excavations in 1932. The essence of their remarks is devoted, of course, to the

[216] Klein, *Transjordan*, p. 37.
[217] Avi-Yonah, *Palestine*, p. 158.
[218] Schumacher, "Dscholan," p. 261; Schumacher, *Jaulân*, p. 187.
[219] See Schumacher, "Dscholan," p. 295; Schumacher, *Jaulân*, p. 151.

description of the valley, the hot springs, and the baths. In the spring of 1932, officials of the Department of Antiquities of the British Palestine Government became aware of the discovery of the remains of a mosaic at Tell el-Bâni, and after a short check by these officials, an expedition under the auspices of the Hebrew University of Jerusalem, led by E. L. Sukenik, went out to excavate the site. The excavations concentrated on uncovering the structure in which the mosaic had been discovered, that is, the synagogue and its annexes, which covered an area of about 700 square meters. The expedition also cleaned the central part of the ancient theater that was found about 300 m. east of Tell el-Bâni, and dug a number of exploratory trenches near the remains of the ancient bath at Hammet Selîm.[220] A short time after the work of the Sukenik expedition, C. S. Fisher and N. Glueck conducted excavations at Tell el-Bâni intended to examine the ancient strata in this tell. Their excavations showed strata of settlement there from Early Bronze Age I-III, but the site was uninhabited from this period until the late Roman or Byzantine period.[221]

Because of the political and military events that took place in the region from the mid-1930's up to the Six Day War in 1967, there was a 36-year hiatus in the investigation of the site. In 1968, S. Tammari investigated the ancient baths and cleared the ruins of the rubble of the various Arab structures that filled them.[222] During the years 1979-1982, Y. Hirschfeld and G. Solar excavated large parts of the baths complex.[223] In March 1982, G. Foerster and P. Porat conducted further excavations in the area of the synagogue that Sukenik had uncovered.[224]

In our discussion here we shall describe neither the theater—whose date of erection and patrons have yet to be clarified—nor the baths, for no Jewish finds whatever have as yet been discovered in them (according to the preliminary publications of Hirschfeld and Solar).[225] We shall only point out that since neither the theater nor the baths are mentioned by Josephus, they were probably not built prior to the beginning of the second century.

With the construction of the baths in the course of the second century C.E.,[226] a small settlement began to flourish alongside them and remained

---

[220] See Sukenik, "Hammath-by-Gadara"; Sukenik, "el-Hammeh"; Sukenik, *el-Hammeh*.

[221] Glueck, "Yarmûk," pp. 22-23; Glueck, "el-Hammeh," pp. 321-330; Glueck, "Palestine," pp. 137-140.

[222] To the best of our knowledge Tammari has not yet published the results of his investigations.

[223] For a list of the many early publications that appeared following these excavations, see Hirschfeld, "Hammat Gader-1," p. 514; Hirschfeld, "Hammat Gader-2," p. 573. A full report has yet to be published.

[224] Foerster, "Hammat Gader-1," pp. 11-12; Foerster, "Hammat Gader-2," p. 41.

[225] See above, note 223.

[226] See Hirschfeld, "Hammat Gader-1," p. 505; Hirschfeld, "Hammat Gader-2," p. 565.

there for several centuries. The residents certainly provided services to the
baths' many visitors. The remains of the town itself have not yet been excavated systematically and, to our regret, in the twentieth century, buildings
for various services to the bathers have arisen on much of it. However, the
rabbinic sources, on the one hand, and the remains of the synagogue at Tell
el-Bâni, on the other, make it clear that Jews were among the town's residents and the visitors that frequented the baths.

Clear testimony to the existence of a Jewish community at Hammat
Gader at the end of the second and the beginning of the third centuries appears in B. Erubin 61a (parentheses mine):

> It has been taught: Rabbi (Rabbi Judah the Prince) permitted the inhabi-
> tants of Gader (=Gadara) to go down to Hamethan (=Hammat Gader) but did
> not allow the inhabitants of Hamethan to go up to Gader. Now what could
> have been the reason? Obviously, that the former did put up a partition;
> while the latter did not put up a barrier.
> When R. Dimi came, he explained: The people of Gader used to molest the
> people of Hamethan....Then why should Sabbath be different?—Because
> intoxication is not uncommon on such a day....Rav Safra explained: Gader
> was a town that was built in the shape of a bow. Rav Dimi bar Hinena ex-
> plained: The former were the inhabitants of a large town (=Gadara) while
> the latter were inhabitants of a small town (=Hammat Gader).

It seems that the existence of the baths, and, concomitantly, the hospitality
of the local Jews, drew many sages to Hammat Gader who, despite the presence of Gentiles, came for relaxation or to seek relief for their illnesses.
Apparently, they conducted Torah discussions and, among other things, determined the halakah for the local Jews. Thus, for example, in Y. Erubin 6,
23c, we read:

> R. Hanina and R. Jonathan went to Hammat Gader. They said: Let us wait
> until the Elders of the South come here.

And in Y. Qid. 3, 64d we find:

> Rabbi Jonathan accompanied Rabbi Judah the Prince to Hammat Gader.
> There, there were (a Gentile and a slave who had intercourse with a Jewish
> girl), the offspring is legitimate....R. Hama bar Hanina, on his way up to
> Hammat Gader, came to his father. Said he to him: "Express your opinion,
> since there are disqualified (people or things) there that one should not
> have contact with."

And indeed, Hirschfeld and Solar, in their excavations in the baths, found
much instructive evidence of the many "disqualified" there. Nevertheless, it
seems that the Jews of Hammat Gader and the Jews who came as guests
generally got along well with the non-Jews there. One can see instructive
evidence of the relationships that were formed there between Jews and
Gentiles in Y. Abodah Zarah 45b:

> If a person bought utensils from a Gentile...as in this instance: Rav Ami
> went up to Ḥammat Gader with Rabbi Judah the Patriarch and they borrowed
> silver from the house of Ossinus.

From the sections quoted above and from other places in rabbinic literature,[227] it is clear that Jews lived at Ḥammat Gader and that sages visited the
place from at least the mid-second century and throughout the third and
fourth centuries C.E. When Sukenik excavated the remains of the synagogue
at the site, he dated its erection between the fourth century and the first half
of the fifth century C.E.[228] M. Avi-Yonah, who at the time wrote the
"Ḥammat Gader" entry in the *Encyclopedia of Archaeological Excavations in
the Holy Land*,[229] suggested on the basis of a comparison between the mosaic of the Ḥammat Gader synagogue and that of the Hammath-Tiberias
synagogue, to move the dating of the former to the middle of the sixth
century C.E. at the earliest.[230] Yet in the brief excavations carried out in the
building in March 1982 by G. Foerster and P. Porat, it became clear that
beneath the level of the synagogue uncovered by Sukenik there are two
earlier stages in the history of the synagogue that Foerster attributes to the
third and fourth centuries C.E.[231] It turns out, then, that we have
archaeological evidence of a Jewish public complex from the third century
up to the end of the Byzantine period.

Since the synagogue complex, at least in its last stage, has already been
discussed at length by its excavator and others, there is no reason to repeat
its description here.[232] But we shall present the inscriptions uncovered in
the building, for Sukenik's readings and interpretations have been emended
by J. Naveh[233] and they contain material that illuminates the strong ties
that remained between this site and Jewish communities in the Galilee and
the Golan.

---

[227] See Y. Shabbat 3, 5d; 4, 7a; 18, 16c; Y. Abodah Zarah 2, 40a; 2, 40d; Y. Terumot 2,
41b & 41c; Ecclesiastes Rabbah 5:10, 11 etc.

[228] See Sukenik, "Hammath-by-Gadara," p. 59; Sukenik, "el-Ḥammeh," p. 170.

[229] Avi-Yonah, "Ḥammat Gader," pp. 469-473.

[230] Avi-Yonah, "Ḥammat Gader," p. 473.

[231] See Foerster, "Ḥammat Gader—1," pp. 11-12; Foerster, "Ḥammat Gader—2," p. 41.
And also see his article in this collection, vol. 1, pp. 87-94.

[232] See Sukenik, "Hammath-by-Gadara"; Sukenik, "el-Ḥammeh"; Sukenik, *el-Ḥammeh*;
Avi-Yonah, "Ḥammat Gader," pp. 469-473.

[233] Naveh, *Mosaic*, pp. 54-64, Inscriptions #32-35.

Inscription #1[234]

This dedication inscription of ten lines in Aramaic was found in the mosaic floor of the nave (the middle hall) of the synagogue, within a wreath between two lions.

According to Sukenik the inscription reads as follows:·

1 ודכיר לטב

2 קירס הופליס וקירה

3 פרוטון וקירס סלוסטיס

4 חתנה וקומס פרורוס ברה

5 וקיריס פוטיס חתנה וקירס

6 חנינה ברה הננון ובניהון

7 דמיצוותון תדירן בכל אתר

8 דהבון הכה חמישה דינרין

9 דהב מלר עלמה יתן ברכתה

10 בעמלהון אמן אמן סלה

which he translates:

1. And remembered be for good
2. Kyris Hoples, and Kyra
3. Protone, and Kyris Sallustius
4. his son-in-law, and Comes Phroros his son
5. and Kyris Photios his son-in-law, and Kyris
6. Haninah his son—they and their children—
7. whose acts of charity are constant everywhere
8. (and) who have given here five denarii
9. (of) gold. May the King of the Universe bestow the blessing
10. upon their work, Amen. Amen. Selah.

Naveh accepts Sukenik's reading literally as written and only adds a few comparisons that were unknown in Sukenik's day.[235]

Inscription #2[236]

This dedication inscription in Aramaic of four lines was found in the mosaic floor of the nave, within the right part of a *tabula ansata* under the pair of lions and the wreath in which Inscription #1 was set. The inscription is 2.58 m. in length, is read by Sukenik thus:

1 ודנכיר לטןב רב תנחום הלוי בנר חלןיפה דהב
חד טרימיסין ודכיר לטב מוניקה דסוסי(ת)ה צפוריה

2 וקנירוס פןטריק ד(כ)פר עקביה ויוסה בר דוסתי
דמן כפר נחום דיהבון תלתיהון תלת גרמין מלך

[234] See Sukenik, "el-Hammeh," pp. 129-137, Inscription #I; Naveh, *Mosaic*, pp. 54-57, Inscription #32.

[235] See previous note.

[236] See Sukenik, "el-Hammeh," pp. 137-143, Inscription #II; Naveh, *Mosaic*, pp. 57-60, Inscription #33.

עולמה יתן ברכתה בעמלנ[הון] אמן אמן סלה שלום   3
ודכיר לטב יודן ארדה מן חימאים (?) דיהב תלת

תדכירין לט[ו]ב ארביליי דיהבון מחי(ת)הון מלך   4
עלמ(ה) יתן ברכתה בעמלהון אמן אמן סלה

and he translates it as follows:

> 1. And r[emembered be for] good Rab (*sic!*) Tanhûm the Levite, the s[on of Hal]îpha, who has donated one *tremissis*; and remembered be for good Monikos of Sûsîtha (?), the Sepphorite
> 2. and [Kyros Pa]tricius, of (Ke)far 'Aqabyah, and Yôse, the son of Dositheus, of Capernaum, who have, all three, donated three scruples. May the King
> 3. of the Un[iverse best]ow the blessing upon their work, Amen! Amen! Selah! Peace! And remembered be for good Yûdân…of…who has donated three (that is, 3 scruples?);
> 4. and remembered be for good the people of Arbela who have donated of their cloths. May the King of the Universe bestow blessing upon their work. Amen! Amen! Selah!

In the first sentence Naveh emended Sukenik's reading of "חל[י]פה"· to "ח[ל]פה" (=Halafa or Halfa). This name in its Greek form Αλαφα is found in the Golan on a burial stone discovered in the village of Farj.[237] It should be pointed out that forms of the name that originate in "h-l-f" root are common enough in the Jewish inscriptions on the Golan; in the Aramaic inscriptions the name חלפו is found at Mazra'at Kanaf and perhaps also in the inscription from Ghâdriyye. In its Greek form, Αλαφω it appears in Inscription #3 from Quneiṭra. The Greek form Αλαφθα appears in Inscription #1 from Rafîd, while the form Αλαφεος is found in Inscription #2 at Sûrmân. The name form חלפתה appears in Aramaic in Inscription #2 from Qîsrîn.

In the continuation of the first line, Naveh suggests emending Sukenik's reading of "מוניקה דסוסי(ת)ה צפוריה" to "מינוקה דסיסיפה וצ[נ]פוריה," that is, instead of "Monikos of Sûsîta (?) the Sepphorite," Naveh suggests reading it "the child of Sisifos the Sepphorite." It is interesting to mention here that Sukenik indeed translated the name "צפוריה" as "the Sepphorite" but nevertheless also raised the second possibility that the man was "a native of Saffûreh in Jaulân."[238] Ṣaffûreh is eṣ-Ṣufeira (see Site #49 on the map on pp. 386-387 and the above discussion). Since the continuation of the inscription mentions donors from settlements near Hammat Gader such as Kfar 'Aqabyah and Capernaum, I prefer Sukenik's second suggestion.

As already mentioned in our treatment of Kfar 'Aqabyah (see above), Naveh suggests reading the second line of the inscription "עקביה <כפ>ר" or

---

[237] See our discussion of Farj, and for the full details on this gravestone, see Gregg and Urman, Inscription #136.

[238] Sukenik, "el-Ḥammeh," p. 140.

"דמן> כפר עקביה>," instead of "ד(כ)פר עקביה" as Sukenik read it. There is nothing in this emendation that changes the translation or meaning of the inscription which, according to both Sukenik and Naveh, commemorates a donor from Kfar 'Aqabyah.

In the third line Sukenik struggled with the reading of the line's last words, "יודן ארדה מן חימאים (?) דיהב תלת," therefore he left spaces in the inscription's English translation. In his discussion of this section he wrote:

> This phrase bristles with difficulties. The rare biblical name ארד, and ארך— "tall," are equally unsatisfactory; the latter would have to be either Hebrew—הארוך—or Aramaic—אריכא (the real name of the great second century scholar was, of course, אבא אריכא). המן is also meaningless, and it is no help to correct it to דמן as no place by the name of חימאים or חימאים is known. It is further remarkable that the denomination of the coin should have been left out after תלת, though it might be meant to be understood from the foregoing to be גרמין. It is therefore from sheer perplexity, and with all reserve, that I suggest that the mosaic-maker may have jumbled the letters, and that the first three words should be יודן דמן אריח. A place called אריח in the neighbourhood of the Sea of Galilee is known from several passages. It is supposed to have been identical with בית ירח, the site of which we are enabled by the contexts in which it occurs to locate with certainty at Khirbet Kerak, at the southwestern corner of the Sea of Galilee, just above the issue of the Jordan.[239]

About twenty years after Sukenik wrote these words, P. Bar-Adon uncovered the remains of a Jewish public structure complex at Khirbet Kerak (=Beth Yeraḥ), which he defined as a synagogue dated to the fourth or fifth century C.E.[240]

Naveh suggests here, instead of ארדה, to complete the word as "ארד<כלל>ה," that is, "the architect," and instead of חימאים or חימאים as Sukenik read it, he follows Kutscher who reads "אמאוס" or "עמאוס"[241] Between Sukenik's speculation and that of Naveh the decision is difficult, and the section is still in need of reconsideration. In any case, the settlement חימאים or חימאים (or עמאוס = אמאוס as Kutscher and Naveh suggest), is to be sought in the Lake Kinneret basin near Ḥammat Gader and not in Judaea.

In the fourth line Naveh reads "ארביליי דיהבון מחירהון," that is, "the people of Arbela who have donated the cost of (?)."[242]

---

[239] Sukenik, "el-Ḥammeh," pp. 142-143.

[240] See Bar-Adon, "Beth-Yerah," pp. 53-54; Bar-Adon, "Synagogue," p. 185. See also Applebaum, "Beth-Yeraḥ," pp. 181-184.

[241] Naveh, *Mosaic*, p. 59, and the reference to Kutscher appears there.

[242] Naveh, *Mosaic*, p. 59. Naveh's reading is preferable to Sukenik's but see his hesitations and reservations there.

Inscription #3[243]

This Aramaic dedication inscription had four lines and was also found on the mosaic floor of the nave. It continues Inscription #2, and appears within the left part of the *tabula ansata* formed as a framework for the two inscriptions. The length of the inscription is 2.20 m. and it is read by Sukenik thus:

1   ודכ(י)ר לטב קיריס ליאנטיס וקירה קלניק דהנבון
                                        לי]קרה דכנישתה

2   מלך עלמה יתן ברכתה בעמלה אמן אמן סלה
                            שלום ודכירה לטב חדה אתה

3   אנטוליה דניהב]ה חד דינר ליקרה דכנישתה מלך
                               עלמה יהן ברכתה בעמלה

4   אמן אמן [סלה] שלום ודכירין לטב עיריא דהבון
                                       חד טר(ימ)יסין

And he translates it:

1. And remembered be for good Kyris Leontios and Kyra Kalonike, [who have donated...denarii in ho]nour of the synagogue.
2. May the King of the Universe bestow blessing upon his work. Amen. Amen. Selah. Peace. And remembered be for good one woman
3. Anatolia, [who has donate]d one denarius in honour of the synagogue. May the King of the Universe bestow blessing upon her work.
4. Amen. Amen. [Selah]. Peace. And remembered be for good the wakeful who have donated one *tr(em)issis*.

This inscription is important because it is the only published inscription found *in situ* in an ancient Jewish public structure in Palestine that specifically states that the structure served as a synagogue! Another inscription with expression "ליקרה דכנישתה," that is to say, "in honour of the synagogue," was found on a fragment of a stone column which is reported to have been found at Beth Govrin,[244] but even if the origin of the column fragment is Beth Govrin, it was not found *in situ*. My teacher and friend J. Naveh taught me years ago that it is possible that the term 'synagogue' also appeared in an inscription uncovered at the public Jewish structure at 'Ein Gedi, but to this day the inscription remains unpublished and we know nothing of its details.[245]

Naveh argues that the name *Anatolia*, which appears at the beginning of the third line, is to be explained as an adjective and not as a private name, and that the words "חדה אתה אנטוליה" he suggests, then, be translated "a righteous woman."[246]

---

[243] See Sukenik, "el-Ḥammeh," pp. 143-145, Inscription #III; Naveh, *Mosaic*, pp. 60-62, Inscription #34.

[244] See Urman, "Beth Guvrin," pp. 151-162 and the additional bibliography there.

[245] See Naveh, "Aramaic and Hebrew," p. 308.

[246] See Naveh, *Mosaic*, p. 61.

Inscription #4[247]

This inscription was found in the northern panel of the mosaic floor of the nave surrounded by a frame of a *tabula ansata*, its length 1.25 m, and its height 0.35 m. The inscription was written in Aramaic and in Sukenik's opinion its letters were set in the mosaic by a different craftsman than the one who worked on the letters of the three previous inscriptions.[248] The inscription contains five lines which Sukenik reads:

1]ודכיר ל[ט]ב אדה בר תנחום
2]בר מוני[ן]קה דיהב חד טרימיסין ויוסה
3]בר[קרוצה ומוניקה דיהב(ו) חד פלגות
4]די[ן]ר לגו הדן]פסיפ[ס]ה תהוי להון
5 ברכרה אמ[ן] סל[ה] שלום

and translates it:

1. [And remembered for] good be Ada, the son of Tanḥûm
2. [the son of Moni]kos, who has contributed one *tremissis*, and Yôse,
3. the son of Qaroṣah(?) and Monikos, who have contributed [one]-   half
4. denarius towards th[is mosai]c. May theirs be
5. the blessing. Am[en Sel]ah. Peace.

Naveh's reading of the first three lines of the inscription presents a slightly different version from that of Sukenik:

1]דכירין ל[ט]ב אדה בר תנחום
2]ומ[נ]ֹקה דיהב חד טרימיסין ויוסה
3]בר[קרועה ומינוקה דיהב חד פלגות

and translates it:

1. [And remembered be for] good Ada, the son of Tanḥûm
2. [and his] child, who has contributed one *tremissis*, and Yôse,
3. [the son of] Qrw'h and his child, who has contributed one-half denarius...

Fragments of Inscription #5

Fragments of a dedication inscription in Greek were found engraved on a marble panel within a chancel screen of the synagogue. The fragments were found during the excavation scattered in the region of the apse, and the inscription is difficult to complete. Sukenik describes the fragments and the remains of the inscription that is on them:

---

[247] See Sukenik, "el-Ḥammeh," pp. 145-147, Inscription #IV; Naveh, *Mosaic*, pp. 62-64, Inscription #35.

[248] See Sukenik, "el-Ḥammeh," p. 145.

Three consecutive fragments (Pl. XIIb), from a slab which was ornamented with a wreath enclosing a shell (or rosette) and inscribed with Greek writing, were found. Their preserved length is 46 cm., height 25 cm., and thickness 5.5 cm. They preserved the following letters: ΟΣΠΑΡΗΓΟΡΙΟΥ; which is perhaps to be restored e.g. as υἱòς Παρηγορίου, that is, X, the son of Paregorios. The name Παρηγόριος (cf. פריגרי, name of an Amora, *Yer. Ter.* 47d), which is equivalent to the Hebrew, מנחם, נחמן, נחום, תנחום, etc., occurs a number of times elsewhere in Jewish epigraphy. Apparently another son of Paregorios is referred to in a further fragment of a slab, (30 cm. by 14 cm. by 3.5 cm.), the legend of which may perhaps be restored as: Υ υἱòς Παρη]γορίου καὶ τόν (?)[. A smaller fragment (16 cm. by 19 cm. by 4,5 cm.) whose left edge is thinned so as to fit into a vertical groove in a pillar, is inscribed καὶ τόν[. Still another (11 cm. by 16 cm. 4.5 cm.) bears the letters ου κ(αι). Other fragments preserved only a few letters, from which it is impossible to extract any meaning.[249]

It should be pointed out that in the area between the theater and 'Ein er-Rîh a fragment of another chancel tablet was discovered made of marble which may also have belonged originally to the chancel of the synagogue. This tablet fragment, published by M. Avi-Yonah, is the upper part of the tablet whose original measurements seem to have been: length—1.00 m., height—0.84 m., and thickness—4 cm.[250] The tablet was decorated with a lovely relief of a wreath with a seven-branched menorah within it.

Finally, let us mention a small find made by Sukenik in his excavation of the synagogue. This find is a signet ring with an engraved bezel, a drawing of which the excavator published.[251] About it he wrote only, "...(it) evidently served as a signet, on whose bezel are deeply incised one above the other an eagle, a lion, and a serpent."[252] It is hard to know if the ring belonged to a Jew, even though Sukenik found another ring in the synagogue which undoubtedly was a Christian's—for upon it appears the Christian legend: Χε (that is, Χριστὲ) Βοήθ(ε)ι 'Ανδρέᾳ, that is, "O Christ, help Andrea."[253] Even so, we can suggest that the ring belonged to a Jew, because we found on it an interesting combination of three living things most widespread in the decorations of the Jewish public buildings in the Golan of the rabbinic period. Can it be that this triple combination on one ring and the order in which they appear from top to bottom may hold an artistic idea which reflects the world of living things? Each domain is represented by a ruling animal: the eagle—king of the birds; the lion—king of the beasts on

[249] Sukenik, "el-Hammeh," pp. 148-149. See also Roth-Gerson, *Greek Inscriptions*, pp. 132-133.

[250] Avi-Yonah, "Remains," pp. 17-19, and see especially p. 17, Fig. A.

[251] See Sukenik, "el-Hammeh," p. 160, Fig. 24.

[252] Sukenik, "el-Hammeh," p. 161.

[253] Sukenik, "el-Hammeh," pp. 160-161, Fig. 23.

earth; the serpent—here representing the subterranean living creatures or those that live in the oceans.

To conclude our discussion of Ḥammat Gader, we shall only note that the archaeological investigation of this important and interesting site is not complete. In the future, it behooves us to continue to clarify fully the plans of the stages that Foerster and Porat uncovered beneath the synagogue which Sukenik had revealed. It is also fitting to excavate in the areas between Tell el-Bâni and the Roman theater, and between Tell el-Bâni and the baths complex, with the purpose of uncovering the remains of houses of the town's residents—where we look forward to further Jewish finds.

THE GOLAN JEWISH PUBLIC STRUCTURES:
TYPOLOGY AND CHRONOLOGY

In my preface to this article, I observed that the archaeology of the Jewish communities in the Golan Heights region is still in its infancy. The remains have just begun to undergo study and so it would be an error to attempt to summarize their implications. Nevertheless, Z. Ma'oz has rushed to do so in his recently written essay, "Golan," in both editions of *The New Encyclopedia of Archaeological Excavations in the Holy Land*.[1] The English-language essay provides a good example of the problems caused by our current lack of knowledge about the Golan, for he has presented an incomplete, erroneous, and distorted picture of the Jewish settlement in the Golan during the second-temple and rabbinic periods. In addition, he has proposed a typological and chronological scheme for the Jewish public structures uncovered in the region. His scheme, like his picture of Jewish settlement, presents an inaccurate portrait. But before we discuss the shortcomings of Ma'oz's scheme, we must first analyze his presentation of Jewish settlement in the Golan, for this distorted picture serves as the basis for his proposed typological scheme.

In his survey of Golan history from the Hellenistic period till the time of the Great Rebellion against the Romans (which Ma'oz labels 'Early Roman') in light of the archaeological findings, Ma'oz mentions the name of Judah the Maccabee only once; there is no hint of a single Jewish settlement or community in the Golan during the entire period from the time of Judah Maccabee until the Great Rebellion in 66/67.[2] By contrast, Ma'oz writes extensively about the Itureans who dwelt in the northern Golan, in his opinion, from the early second century B.C.E. up to *the last days of the Byzantine period*! This picture is based upon excavations that "have been conducted on a limited scale at only three Iturean sites in the Golan— Horvat Zemel, Horvat Namra, and Bâb el-Hawâ."[3] In comparison, Ma'oz treats the Jewish archaeological finds that were found at sites in the northern Golan—for example, at the same Bâb el-Hawâ, as well as other sites from the second-temple and rabbinic periods, such as Ṣûrmân and Quneiṭra—as if they had never existed. He deals neither with the Jewish communities on the

---

[1] See Ma'oz, "Golan—1" and Ma'oz, "Golan—2."

[2] See Ma'oz, "Golan—1," pp. 286-288; Ma'oz, "Golan—2," pp. 534-536.

[3] See Ma'oz, "Golan—1," pp. 287-288; Ma'oz, "Golan—2," pp. 535-536. The quotation is from Ma'oz, "Golan—2," p. 535.

Golan from the days of the conquests of Alexander Jannaeus, through the days of his heirs, nor even in the days of Herod's heirs such as Philip and Agrippa II.

In his treatment of the period he designates the 'Early Roman' (66 B.C.E. to 67 C.E.), Ma'oz writes: "Sherds from 143 sites throughout the Golan indicate the magnitude of the settlement in the Early Roman period; many additional sites from the Byzantine period were probably settled in the Early Roman period as well, but their remains have disappeared beneath the massive construction of later periods."[4] But despite the "143 sites," he bases his description of this period primarily upon the excavations at Gamala and Mazra'at Kanaf. Even then, he fails to mention that they are Jewish communities, except for a brief mention of the existence of a synagogue at Gamala. In continuing his discussion of the Early Roman Period, under the heading of "The Aftermath of the First Revolt Against Rome in the Jewish Settlements in the Golan," Ma'oz first reveals that there were Jewish settlements in the Golan before the Great Rebellion, but then —immediately after the heading—he manages to massacre nearly all of them, with the help of the Romans. He writes:

> The excavations at Gamala confirmed that the site was abandoned after its conquest by the Romans and the massacre of all its inhabitants, never to be resettled. A similar picture emerges from the excavations at Horvat Kanaf—the occupation level from the first century CE precedes a hiatus of two or three centuries in the site's occupation. The Kanaf villagers probably sought refuge at nearby Gamala and met their fate there. Excavations of the synagogues at "En Nashut', Qaṣrin, and Dâbiyye also testify to an archaeological gap, lasting from the late first to the early fourth centuries CE. Moreover, there is almost no mention of places in the Golan in the Mishnah or the Talmud. It would seem, therefore, that its Jewish population was almost completely obliterated in the First Revolt, following which there was a drastic decline—if not a complete halt—of Jewish settlement in the region. An echo of this catastrophe can be discerned in a redemption homily dating to the time of the sages of Yavneh: "And the Galilee shall be destroyed and the Gaulan desolate and the people of the border [of the Galilee] shall wander from city to city and none shall pity them..." (Mishnah *Sot.* 9:16). Moreover, the Roman authorities may have forbidden the renewal of Jewish settlement in the rebellious Golan, as they did in the area of Jerusalem, with the prohibition remaining in effect until the beginning of the Byzantine period. A similar pattern of destruction, followed by a palpable gap in Jewish presence, has been detected in other districts that took part in the revolt, such as Peraea and Narbata. The disappearance of the Jewish population of the villages in the territory of Sussita (Hippos), mentioned in the *Baraita di-teḥumin*, may also be linked to the aftermath of the First Revolt. The remains identified by the archaeological survey at the locations figuring on that list, such as Khisfîn, Nov, and

---

[4] Ma'oz, "Golan—1," p. 288; the quotation is from Ma'oz, "Golan—2," p. 536.

Kefar Ḥaruv, among others, did not include synagogues—only evidence of Christian occupation in the Byzantine period.[5]

It is difficult to imagine a more mistaken picture of the Jewish settlement in the Golan following the Great Revolt than the one Ma'oz sketches above. I will not take the time to correct all his errors, but shall only indicate some of them in brief.

(A) It is not true that Jewish settlements in the Golan are not mentioned in the Mishnah and in the Talmud. Many of them are explicitly mentioned by name, while other appears as part of the names of sages who were identified with specific Golan villages or towns.

(B) Ma'oz completely misunderstands the aggadah preserved in Mishnah Sotah 9:15 (mistakenly cited as 16). In fact, the homily speaks of the future which will come "with the footprints of the Messiah"—a time which is also referred to as "in the generation when the son of David comes."[6] This homily does not reflect a historic situation from the past or present, but rather *what will be* when the Messiah comes. And even if we for a moment set aside the Messiah and the problems of the use of the term *Gavlan* (נבלן) in this homily, the implications of Ma'oz's statement are that in the Galilee as well as in the Golan no Jewish settlements remained after the Great Revolt!

(C) Josephus makes it clear that only one of the three Golan settlements he claims to have fortified participated in the Revolt—Gamala. The other two, Sogane and Seleucia, finally decided not to fight and so were spared Gamala's fate (*War* IV § 4). Gamala, indeed, was laid waste and not resettled, but the great majority of the Jewish settlements in the Golan were not harmed; they remained under the protection and rule of Agrippa II. Could it be true that the Romans decreed "no Jewish resettlement in the Golan...and the prohibition did not lose effect until the start of the Byzantine period"? If so, we would expect to find some recollection of so harsh a decree in the writings of Josephus and/or the Church Fathers.

(D) No Christian finds have as yet been found in Nov (=Nob or Nâb). Furthermore, with only one exception, none of the sites identified with the list of "the forbidden towns in the territory of Sûsîta" (not in *Baraita di-teḥumin*—a term which Ma'oz borrowed from others and is inapplicable here), have undergone extensive archaeological excavations.[7] So it is pre-

---

[5] The quotation is from Ma'oz, "Golan—2," p. 536.

[6] See Y. Sotah 9, 23b; B. Sotah 49a-b; B. San. 97a; Shir ha-Shirim Rabbah 2, 13; Pesikta de R. Kahana 51, 2; Pesikta Rabbati 15, 75b; Derekh Eretz Zuta 10, 59a; Seder Eliahu Zuta 16. For a more extensive discussion of this homily and the question of its date, see Urman, *Golan*, pp. 14-18.

[7] The exception is Khisfîn, where some small excavations have been conducted.

mature to declare that they contain no remains of structures that Ma'oz calls "synagogues," that is, public Jewish buildings.

Before Ma'oz gets to the Byzantine period, he addresses the situation during the Middle and Late Roman Periods (67-365 C.E.). His discussion of these 300 years opens with this inaccurate statement: "As the surveys have produced almost no pottery from the Middle and Late Roman periods, information about the settlement pattern then is vague."[8] This statement is simply false; shards and coins from this period have been found at over 150 sites in the Golan in surveys and excavations (including those of Ma'oz!). Following the above sentence, Ma'oz writes, "The excavations at Qaṣrin and Dâbiyye exposed occupation levels from the fourth century C.E." He immediately proceeds to deal with Roman Sûsîta and Baniâs. From there, through a lengthy discussion of Roman roads in the Golan, he goes on to deal with the Golan of the "Byzantine period (365-636 C.E.)." Thus 300 years slip by for which he mentions almost no settlements in the Golan in general and no Jewish communities in particular. The sages of the Yavnean period residing in the Golan and those visiting its Jewish communities fail to receive a mention. The events of the Bar Kokhba Revolt and its results, the generation of Usha, the sages of Bethsaida, the generation of Rabbi Judah the Prince and R. Eliezer ha-Qappar, the academy at Dabûra, and the sages of Qîsrîn—none are worthy of attention. Apparently, they potentially disturb and undermine the conclusion towards which he is striving, namely, that synagogues did not appear in the Golan before the fifth and sixth centuries C.E.

When he reaches the Byzantine period, Ma'oz writes:

> The archaeological data from the Byzantine period has made it possible *for the first time* to determine the ethnic and religious identity of the population of the Golan. Public buildings, such as synagogues and churches, inscriptions in Hebrew, Aramaic, and Greek, and artistic and religious symbols, such as seven-branched candelabra and crosses, provide clear guidelines to the ethno-religious map of the Golan in this period.[9]

Ma'oz apparently knows how to identify the continuity of the existence of the Itureans in the northern Golan from the Hellenistic through the last stages of the Byzantine period through the evidence of shards,[10] but do not statues and dozens of Greek pagan inscriptions found at sites throughout the Golan indicate these peoples' existence in the region during these periods? Could none of the dozens of Hebrew, Aramaic, and Greek inscriptions, and dozens of menorah decorations have appeared before the Byzantine period?

---

[8] Ma'oz, "Golan—1," p. 288; The quotation is from Ma'oz, "Golan—2," p. 536.

[9] Ma'oz, "Golan—1," p. 290; The quotation is from Ma'oz, "Golan—2," p. 538 (emphasis mine).

[10] *Idem, ibid.*

According to Ma'oz, "the main impetus for the renewal of Jewish settlement in the Golan—after it was interrupted in the Middle Roman period—was provided by migration from the Galilee during the fourth century
C.E."[11] The problem with this statement is that Ma'oz fails to explain what
happened in Galilee in the fourth century that led to this wave of migration.
Nor does he explain why the destruction of the Jewish settlements in Judea
after the Bar Kokhba Revolt in the second century C.E. produced no
migration into the Golan, but an unknown event in the fourth century did?

After Ma'oz establishes the renewal of Jewish settlement on the Golan,
he turns to explicate his typological and chronological scheme. He bases his
scheme on the synagogues, that is, the Jewish public buildings that have
been discovered there. This is what he writes:[12]

> *Synagogues.* Surveys carried out in the western part of the central Golan
> (the Lower Golan) identified remains of seventeen synagogues; at eight
> other sites, architectural fragments were found from synagogues whose ex-
> act locations are unknown.[13] Four of those synagogues have been exca-
> vated: at Ḥorvat Kanaf, 'En Nashuṭ, Qaṣrin, and Dabiyye.[14] The synagogue
> was generally the only public building in the typical Jewish village in the
> Golan.[15] It was built on the best site available, which, given the topo-

---

[11] *Idem, ibid.*

[12] Ma'oz, "Golan—1," pp. 290-291; The quotation is from Ma'oz, "Golan—2," p. 539.

[13] It is clear that Ma'oz's numbers are erroneous and misleading. Any one who reads the
earlier chapters of this article will find, in the Lower Golan alone, another eight or more
"synagogue" buildings. But Ma'oz's count is ever increasing. He began his count of
synagogue buildings in the Golan with only eight in 1981 (See Ma'oz, "Excavations," p. 101).
Now, in 1993, he counts seventeen, and it appears, then, that he needs only another twelve
years to reach the number known today.

Here we should clarify that our sharp criticism in this essay is intended first and foremost
to warn against the uncritical use that a number of the important figures in ancient synagogue
research have made over the past twelve years of Ma'oz's material to support their
conclusions. See, for example, the articles of E. M. Meyers and G. Foerster in Levine, *SLA*
(Meyers, "Current State"; Foerster, "Art"). Y. Tsafrir, who, in the same collection, writes an
article headed "The Byzantine Setting and its Influence on Ancient Synagogues" (Tsafrir,
"Synagogues," pp. 147-157), is somewhat more careful in depending upon Ma'oz—see p.
154, note 2, as well as his comments in his article in this collection (vol. 1, pp. 70-86).

[14] What happened to the excavations of Sukenik and Foerster at the synagogue in
Hammat Gader? Here Ma'oz can argue that one should not see Hammat Gader as part of
the Lower Golan. But what happened to S. Gutman's excavations of the Jewish public
building at Gamala? This of course does not belong to the homogeneous all-Byzantine picture
which Ma'oz wishes to present to us. But to where have the excavations of Kohl and
Watzinger at Kh. ed-Dîkkeh and Umm el-Qanâṭir disappeared? These apparently are
unworthy of mention as excavations, even though later on he incorporates the finds of these
digs into his treatment of the synagogues when they suit the picture he is creating.

[15] Since the archaeological investigation of the remains of the Jewish communities in the
Golan is still in its infancy, it is still too early to decide with certainty that the synagogue was
the only public building in "the typical Jewish village in the Golan." Ma'oz himself admits to
the possibility, when he writes about the Jewish remains discovered at Yahûdiyye and at
Dabûra, acknowledging that at these sites there were at least two different public Jewish
buildings. See Ma'oz, "Golan—1", pp. 296-298; Ma'oz, "Golan—2," p. 544.

graphical and climatic conditions of the Golan, was not necessarily the highest or most central point in the village. Rather, it was the highest point on a slope or somewhere near a spring. The Golan synagogues constitute a regional architectural group, sharing certain common features: basalt ashlar masonry, thick (0.8-1 m) dry-stone walls, a single entrance in an ornamental facade, columns and stone architraves, an internal division by two rows of columns, and gabled roofs made of tiles laid on wooden trusses. At the same time, different subgroups of buildings, the work of different masons' "schools," can be discerned, each with its distinctive plan, elevation, and carved decorations. The differences between these schools may be attributable in part to the date of construction (fifth as opposed to sixth century CE), but also to the different economic constraints on the builders.

Ma'oz goes on to detail the division of the Golan 'synagogue' into three 'schools.' He describes the first in the following manner:[16]

> The Chorazin-'En Nashut "School" includes the synagogues at Chorazin, Khirbet Shura, and Khirbet Tuba west of the Jordan, and 'En Nashut, Kh. ed-Dikkeh, Rafid, Kh. Khawkha, Horvat Bet Lavi (Wâkhsharâ), and Khirbet Zumeimira in the Golan. These synagogues have richly decorated facades, and the gables are surrounded by convex friezes with floral scrolls in relief and decorated cornices. The facade is pierced by windows whose frames are carved with a gable with colonnettes, and sometimes also with conches and animal reliefs. The outer walls are decorated with pilasters crowned by diagonal Ionic capitals. The columns in the synagogue hall stand on pedestals: the lower order of columns has Doric or Ionic capitals and the upper story has Corinthian capitals (or sometimes Doric columns without bases). The architraves resting on the columns are of the "'En Nashut type":[17] an abundance of sculpture in relief, with subjects taken from the world of flora and fauna. Miniature animals carved in relief on architectural elements, such as capitals and parts of windows, are very common.
> Based on the excavations at 'En Nashut and on some specific architectural details, the date of this group has been assigned to the mid-fifth century CE.

The second 'school' Ma'oz describes as follows:

> The Kanaf "School" includes the synagogues at Horvat Kanaf, Deir 'Aziz, and probably also Taiybeh. This school lacks the ornate decoration of the preceding school. What decoration there is in its generally simple style is concentrated mainly on the outer facade, usually around the portal. The columns in the prayer hall have no pedestals and their capitals are Doric (Deir 'Aziz, Horvat Kanaf) or schematic Ionic (Taiybeh). Based on the

---

[16] Ma'oz, "Golan—1," p. 291; The quotation is from Ma'oz, "Golan—2," p. 539.

[17] Here we must direct the reader's attention once again to Ma'oz's imaginative ability to reconstruct large structures out of a few remains. How many architrave fragments did he find in his 'Ein Nashôt excavations? Can two architrave fragments on which 'Abun bar Yose' is incised indeed be worthy of having a 'type' named after them? And this in comparison with the rich find at Chorazin that he includes in the 'school' under discussion here?

Kanaf excavations, the school has been dated to the beginning of the sixth century CE.[18]

The third 'school' is that of Qîsrîn or Qaṣrîn, and includes the structures at Qîsrîn, 'Asâliyye, Kh. Quṣbiyye, and Yahûdiyye. According to Ma'oz:[19]

> The decoration in these buildings is concentrated on the outer entrance. All of them have the same type of frame around the main entrance: a convex frieze merges at the bottom of the doorposts with a kind of engaged pillar on an Attic base, and the cornice is decorated with an egg-and-dart motif.... Within the hall the plan is uniform—two rows of columns stand on Attic bases.[20] The columns have Ionic capitals whose design is specific to this school. No stone architraves were found in the synagogues in this sub-group.[21]

Based on the Qîsrîn excavations, Ma'oz dates this 'school' to the beginning of the 6th century C.E. In his opinion, "Its architectural style is not a local development but a new fashion that originated in western Palestine," although he brings no evidence for this declaration. Ma'oz concludes his discussion on the typological/chronological scheme by observing, "In addition to reflecting these well-defined architectural 'schools,' synagogues in the Golan exhibit a distinctive architectural design within the general 'Golan' style, such as those at Umm el-Qanâṭir, Ṣalabeh, and Dâbiyye."[22]

The typological scheme that Ma'oz proposes is not as solidly based as he presents it. Many of the structures upon which he builds his typological framework have not yet been excavated; their exact plan remains unknown, and their architectural details have not yet been uncovered. Even in buildings that have been excavated, Ma'oz presents the reader only with the finds that fit his suggested building scheme. As I noted above, Ma'oz ignores the architrave from the Qîsrîn structure (see my discussion of Qîsrîn, including the notes).

In the "Chorazin-'En Nashuṭ School," Ma'oz includes buildings from sites in the Galilee, and when he sums up his discussion of the "Qaṣrin School," he concludes that this type was "a new fashion that originated in western Palestine." The question is, then, whether it is possible to distin-

---

[18] Ma'oz, "Golan—1," p. 291; The quotation is from Ma'oz, "Golan—2," p. 539.

[19] Ma'oz, "Golan—1," p. 291; The quotation is from Ma'oz, "Golan—2," p. 539.

[20] Here we must note that Ma'oz exaggerates. Whence does he know that "the plane is uniform—two rows of columns stand on Attic bases"? After all, except for the structure excavated at Qîsrîn, the other structures at 'Asâliyye, Kh. Qusbiyye, and Yahûdiyye that are seen on the surface of the area have not been excavated yet, and there is no possibility of knowing their plan and the order of their columns.

[21] In three of the four buildings Ma'oz includes in this sub-group excavations have not yet taken place. Once again Ma'oz leads the reader astray since in the excavations of the structure at Qîsrîn parts and fragments of an architrave were discovered and on one of them Inscription #4 was found—see above, in our discussion of the remains uncovered at Qîsrîn.

[22] Ma'oz, "Golan—1," p. 291; The quotation is from Ma'oz, "Golan—2," p. 539.

guish a 'Golan type' among the Jewish public buildings in Palestine and Syria? According to the "common features" Ma'oz attributes to the Golan structures—"basalt ashlar masonry, thick (0.8-1 m) dry-stone wall, a single entrance"—it is possible to include in this group not only buildings from the eastern parts of the Galilee but also structures in the Lower Galilee and the Issachar Heights. Rather than setting forth a distinctive Golan style, Ma'oz has instead delineated characteristics that identify these structures as part of a larger regional pattern.

More than a dozen years ago, A. Kloner set out a regional-typological scheme of the ancient synagogues in Israel and explored the possible linkages between such a scheme and a chronological one.[23] He wisely included the little material known at the time about the structures in the Golan within the 'Galilean Synagogues' complex.[24] In his conclusion concerning all the regions of Palestine, he wrote: "At the present stage of investigation the most fruitful method seems to be an examination of each building individually. Similar characteristics are shared by buildings in the same or neighboring regions, but there is no chronological distinction between the various regional types."[25]

Despite this observation, we can see that Ma'oz's scheme essentially puts the cart before the horse. He defines a 'Golan type' and divides it typologically and chronologically before most of the Golan sites have undergone complete and systematic excavations. And in Ma'oz's scheme, the cart lacks wheels, for as we noted above, the 'wheels' of Ma'oz's assigned dates are often unfounded. This is particularly true for the sites of Dâbiyye, 'Ein Nashôt, Mazra'at Kanaf, and Qîsrîn, as I demonstrated in my discussions of those sites.

Ma'oz is not alone in his misrepresentation of our knowledge of Jewish settlements and public structures in the Golan region.[26] In L. I. Levine's essay on "Synagogues" in the Hebrew edition of *The New Encyclopedia of Archaeological Excavations in the Holy Land*,[27] Levine 'updates' the state of research on the synagogues in the Golan from the 1970's to the beginning of the 1990's. He writes:

---

[23] See Kloner, "Synagogues," pp. 11-18.

[24] Kloner, "Synagogues," pp. 12-15.

[25] Kloner, "Synagogues," p. 18.

[26] Here I should note that in Ma'oz's discussion of the "schools" he sees in the Jewish public buildings in the Golan, he wrote a section titled "Location of the Entrance and the Direction of Prayer"—see Ma'oz, "Golan—1," p. 291; Ma'oz, "Golan—2," p. 539. This section is based upon imaginary data of locations of Torah arks for which no traces have been found. (I commented on this above in the sections on the relevant sites—it is not worth discussing further here.)

[27] See Levine, "Research," pp. 258-261.

The Golan. Since the end of the nineteenth century three synagogues were known in the Golan—at Kh. ed-Dîkkeh, at Ḥorvat Kanaf, and at Umm el-Qanâṭir, whereas since the Six Day War the remains of six additional synagogues have been discovered here—at Qaṣrîn, 'Ein Nashôt, Deir 'Azîz, Kh. Zumâimîra', 'Asâliyye, and Dâbiyye—as well as other evidence (symbols, inscriptions) of the existence of other synagogues. These structures were built of local basalt stone; the exterior face of their walls are made of ashlar stones, and the interior—of planed stones. The thickness of their walls run from 0.80 to 1 meter; they are of dry-wall construction, i.e., without mortar; and are strengthened by a fill of dirt or small stones. All had a magnificent facade with a Syrian gable and a decorated entrance. These structures generally had a single entrance (except the synagogue at ed-Dîkkeh, which had three entrances), and a few had porticos in their facade. The interior of these buildings was uniform, generally: two rows of columns (except for the Umm el-Qanâṭir synagogue which had three rows of columns), the floors were made of slabs of stone or clay, and in a few of them, such as the synagogue at Qaṣrîn, in the second stage of its existence, they were decorated with mosaics. With the exception of the synagogue at 'Ein Nashôt, the columns had no pedestals, and in all of the structures, inside the room along its four sides, there were two rows of benches. A base for the Holy Ark was found in the synagogues at Qaṣrîn and 'Ein Nashôt. The orientation of the entrance in these structures is not uniform: in four of them the entrance faces west, in one-north, and in four, south. Among the most widespread motifs in their ornamentation are the eagle, the lion, the fish, grapevines, and the double meander.[28]

The picture that Levine sketches for the reader is not only wanting, in error, and misleading, but apparently is intended to belittle the significance of the remains of the Jewish settlement in the Golan for the study of the Jewish people during the second-temple and rabbinic period in general, and for the investigation of Jewish public buildings in particular. Is it really true that from the end of the nineteenth century till the Six Day War only three synagogue sites were known in the Golan? Or indeed, that from the Six Day War until the beginning of the 1990's, the remains of only six more synagogues discovered?[29] If it has accomplished nothing else, my preceding discussion of over sixty Golan sites reveals this is simply untrue.

---

[28] Levine, "Research," p. 260.

[29] And here we must note that in the English edition of the *Encyclopedia*, not only was the essay written by M. Avi-Yonah removed from the "Synagogues" entry (even though it appears in the Hebrew edition which came out just a year earlier)—a grave matter and we regret the loss—but also Levine wrote a different article from the one in the Hebrew edition. In it, he corrects the numbers in everything related to the Golan synagogues, but continues to transmit imprecise data: "Surveys and excavations in the Golan before the 1967 war uncovered only a few scattered synagogue remains. However, in the subsequent twenty-five years, remains of at least sixteen buildings, and evidence of eleven others, have been discovered. Almost without exception, these remains date to the Byzantine period." See Levine, "Synagogues," p. 1422. And to continue, in his new article Levine writes: "Synagogues in the Golan, which in some ways resemble the 'early' Galilean type and in others resemble the 'late' type, were constructed from the fifth to the seventh centuries." See

Levine generally follows Ma'oz when he sets out the common features of the Jewish public structures in the Golan. However, he adds a characteristic not found in Ma'oz: "in all of the structures, inside the room along its four sides, there were two rows of benches." Clearly this sentence is imprecise and as yet unproven. Structures which he himself cites, such as those that were discovered at Deir 'Azîz, Kh. Zumâimîra', and 'Asâliyye, have yet to be excavated, while it remains uncertain whether the structure at Dâbiyye had benches along all four walls (see my discussion of Dâbiyye above).

To conclude my discussion, let me reiterate that the archaeological investigation of the remains of the Jewish communities in the Golan Heights region is still "in its infancy." It would be a serious error at this stage of the research to conclude, as do Levine and Ma'oz, that "Synagogues in the Golan...were constructed from the fifth to seventh centuries C.E." The archaeological and epigraphic remains that were discussed above clearly indicate the continuity of the Jewish settlement in the Golan from the time of Alexander Jannaeus to at least the end of the Byzantine period. The Ionic capitals found in the assembly building at Gamala and in the dozens of Jewish sites in the Golan constitute clear archaeological evidence of this continuum. Of course, some researchers will argue that this constitutes merely a 'conservatism' in decorative style and not necessarily evidence of continuity. It seems to me, however, that a comprehensive study is required of the place, the origins, and the evolution of this capital in Jewish architecture and decorative art in the Golan and the Galilee.[30]

The coming generations of researchers who hopefully will investigate the Jewish archaeological remains in the Golan will face many additional challenges. For example, it is very important to complete the excavation of the two early strata of the building found by G. Foerster and P. Porat in the synagogue at Ḥammat Gader, for here with complete confidence we can claim (at least in the third stage of the building) that we have the remains of a synagogue. It is to be hoped that the Jewish public buildings at Dabûra will also be uncovered soon. For among these is the single building that we know served as a house of study (*bet midrash*). The issue of the benches in the Jewish public construction in the Golan, whose chronological beginning appears in the structure at Gamala, is also worthy of basic investigation.

---

p. 1423. A look at the bibliography list that Levine appends to his article, clearly indicates whence he drew this information—the articles of his student, Z. Ma'oz.

[30] Here we shall only note that in the first surveys we conducted in the Golan after 1967, these capitals served as an indicator of the existence of the remains of a Jewish public building at the site. Thus, after we found such capitals at 'Ein Nashôt, we continued to search the site and found the remains of the lintel with the menorah relief and the item with the lioness relief. On the heels of these, the Jewish public building there was also discovered— see above in the chapter dealing with finds from 'Ein Nashôt.

But above all, it is to be hoped that the dozens of unexcavated Jewish public structures in the Golan will indeed be excavated, and that we will receive from them true dates and reliable, proper excavation reports, for without these, there is no typology, no chronology, and no value to archaeology.

ABBREVIATIONS AND BIBLIOGRAPHY

AASOR	*Annual. American School of Oriental Research.*
ABD	*The Anchor Bible Dictionary*, 6 vols. (New York: Doubleday, 1992).
Abel, "Koursi"	F. M. Abel, "Koursi," *JPOS* 7 (1927): 112-121.
AbhMainz	*Abhandlung der Geistes- und Sozialwissenschaftlichen Klasse der Akademie der Wissenschaften und der Literatur, Mainz.*
ADAJ	*Annual of the Department of Antiquities of Jordan.*
Adan-Bayewitz, "Ceramics"	David Adan-Bayewitz, "The Ceramics from the Synagogue of Horvat 'Ammudim and Their Chronological Implications," *IEJ* (1982): 13-31.
Adan-Bayewitz, "Manufacture"	David Adan-Bayewitz, "Manufacture and Local Trade in the Galilee of Roman-Byzantine Palestine" (Ph.D. Dissertation. Hebrew University, 1985).
Adan-Bayewitz and Perlman	David Adan-Bayewitz and Isadore Perlman, "The Local Trade of Sepphoris in the Roman Period," *IEJ* 40 (1990): 153-72.
Aharoni, "Golan"	Y. Aharoni, "Three New Boundary-Stones from the Western Golan," *'Atiqot* 1 (1955): 94-98 (in Hebrew).
Aharoni, "Huleh"	Y. Aharoni, "Two Additional Boundary-Stones from the Huleh Valley," *'Atiqot* 2 (1958): 136-137 (in Hebrew).
AJA	*American Journal of Archaeology.*
Albeck, *Introduction*	Ch. Albeck, *Introduction to the Talmud Babli and Yerushalmi* (Jerusalem and Tel Aviv: Dvir, 1969; repr. 1975) (in Hebrew).
Albright, "Cities"	W. F. Albright, "The List of Levitic Cities," in A. Marx et al., ed., *Louis Ginzberg Jubilee Volume* (New York: AAJR, 1945), pp. 49-73.
Amir, *Banias*	D. Amir, *Banias—From Ancient till Modern Times*, Beth Ussishkin—Institute for Natural History of the Huleh Valley (Kibbutz Dan, 1968) (in Hebrew).
Amit and Ilan	D. Amit and Z. Ilan, "The Ancient Synagogue at Maon in Judah," *Qadmoniot* 23 (1990): 115-125 (in Hebrew).
ANRW	*Aufstieg und Niedergang der römischen Welt.*
ANRW 19.1	*Aufstieg und Niedergang der römischen Welt* II, *Principat* 19.1 (Berlin and New York: Walter de Gruyter, 1979).
Antiq., Ant.	Flavius Josephus, *Jewish Antiquities.*
Antiquities	Flavius Josephus, *Jewish Antiquities.*
Apion	Flavius Josephus, *Against Apion.*
Applebaum, "Beth-Yerah"	S. Applebaum, "The Synagogue at Beth-Yerah—Its Character and Function," in Kasher, *Synagogues*, pp. 181-184 (in Hebrew).

Applebaum, "Legal Status"	S. Applebaum, "The Legal Status of the Jewish Communities in the Diaspora," in Safrai and Stern, *Compendia*, pp. 420-463.
Applebaum, "Organization"	S. Applebaum, "The Organization of the Jewish Communities in the Diaspora," in Safrai and Stern, *Compendia*, pp. 464-503.
Applebaum, Isaac & Landau	S. Applebaum, B. Isaac and Y. Landau, "Varia Epigraphica," *Scripta Classica Israelica* 4 (1978): 134-135.
Arak.	Arakin.
Arav, "Bethsaida—1"	R. Arav, "Bethsaida, 1989," *IEJ* 41 (1991): 184-186.
Arav, "Bethsaida—2"	R. Arav, "Bethsaida, 1992," *IEJ* 42 (1992): 252-254.
Arav, "Bethsaida—3"	R. Arav, "Bethsaida," in M. Gophen and Y. Gal, eds., *Lake Kinneret* (Tel-Aviv, 1992), pp. 172-174 (in Hebrew).
Arav, "Bethsaida—4"	R. Arav, "Bethsaida, 1990-1991," *HA* 99 (1993): 8-9 (in Hebrew).
Arav, "Bethsaida—5"	R. Arav, "Bethsaida—1990/1991," *EASI* 12 (1994): 8-9.
Arav, "Bethsaida—6"	R. Arav, "Bethsaida—1992," *HA* 101-102 (1994): 22-23 (in Hebrew).
Arav, "el-'Araj"	R. Arav, "Et-Tell and el-'Araj," *IEJ* 38 (1988): 187-188.
Arav, "Et-Tell—1"	R. Arav, "Et-Tell (Bethsaida)—1988," *EASI* 7-8 (1988-1989): 177-178.
Arav, "Et-Tell—2"	R. Arav, "Et-Tell, 1988," *IEJ* 39 (1989): 99-100.
Arav, "Et-Tell—3"	R. Arav, "Et-Tell (Bethsaida)—1989," *EASI* 9 (1991): 98-99.
Arch. Anz.	*Archaeologischer Anzeiger.*
Ariel, "Dabiyye"	D. T. Ariel, "Coins from the Synagogue at Dabiyye," *'Atiqot* 20 (1991): 74-80.
Ariel, "'En Nashut"	D. T. Ariel, "Coins from the Synagogue at 'En Nashut," *IEJ* 37 (1987): 147-157.
Ariel, "Horvat Kanef"	D. T. Ariel, "Coins from the Synagogue at Horvat Kanef: Preliminary Report," *Israel Numismatic Journal* 4 (1980): 59-62.
Aristeas	*The Letter of Aristeas.*
ARN	*Abot de-Rabbi Natan.*
Avi-Yonah, "Abbreviations"	M. Avi-Yonah, "Abbreviations in Greek Inscriptions," *QDAP*, Suppl. 9 (1940).
Avi-Yonah, "Archaeological Sources"	
	M. Avi-Yonah, "Archaeological Sources," in Safrai and Stern, *Compendia*, pp. 46-62.
Avi-Yonah, "Architecture"	M. Avi-Yonah, "Ancient Synagogue Architecture in *Eretz Israel* and the Diaspora," in C. Roth, ed., *Jewish Art* (Tel Aviv: Massada, 1959), cols. 135-164 (in Hebrew).
Avi-Yonah, *Art*	M. Avi-Yonah, *Art in Ancient Palestine* (Jerusalem: Magnes, 1981).
Avi-Yonah, "Comments"	M. Avi-Yonah, "Some Comments on the Capernaum Excavations," in Levine, *ASR*, pp. 60-62. Originally published as "Editor's Note," *IEJ* 23, no. 1 (1973): 43-45. See Loffreda, "Capernaum."

Avi-Yonah, "Courses"   M. Avi-Yonah, "A List of Priestly Courses from Caesarea." *IEJ* 12 (1962): 137-139.

Avi-Yonah, *Gazetteer*   M. Avi-Yonah, *Gazetteer of Roman Palestine* (Jerusalem, 1976) (=*Qedem*, vol. 5).

Avi-Yonah, "Goodenough's Evaluation"
          M. Avi-Yonah, "Goodenough's Evaluation of the Dura Paintings: A Critique," in Gutmann, *Dura-Europos*, pp. 117-135.

Avi-Yonah, "Hammat Gader"   M. Avi-Yonah, "Hammat Gader," in *EAEHL*, vol. 2, pp. 469-473.

Avi-Yonah, *Holy Land*   M. Avi-Yonah, *The Holy Land from the Persian to the Arab Conquest (536BC—AD640), A Historical Geography* (Grand Rapids, MI: Baker Book House, 1977).

Avi-Yonah, *Madaba*   M. Avi-Yonah, *The Madaba Mosaic Map* (Jerusalem, 1954).

Avi-Yonah, *Palestine*   M. Avi-Yonah, *Historical Geography of Palestine: From the End of the Babylonian Exile up to the Arab Conquest* (Jerusalem: Bialik Institute, 1962) (in Hebrew).

Avi-Yonah, "Remains"   M. Avi-Yonah, "Two Remains of our Ancient Art," *Yediot* 12 (1945-46): 15-19 (in Hebrew).

Avi-Yonah, "Synagogue: Architecture"
          M. Avi-Yonah, "Synagogue: Architecture," *EJ*, vol. 15, pp. 595-600.

Avi-Yonah, "Synagogues"   M. Avi-Yonah, "Ancient Synagogues," *Ariel* 32 (1973): 29-43. Reprinted in Avi-Yonah, *Art*, pp. 272-273, and in Gutmann, *Synagogue*, pp. 95-109.

Avi-Yonah, "Synagogues-2"   M. Avi-Yonah, "Synagogues," in *EAEHL*, vol. 1, pp. 100-106 (in Hebrew).

Avi-Yonah, "Synagogues-3"   M. Avi-Yonah, "Synagogues," in *EAEIHL*, vol. 4, pp. 1129-1138.

Avigad, "Bar'am"   N. Avigad, "Bar'am," in *NEAEHL*, vol. 1, pp. 147-149.

Avigad, "Beth Alpha"   N. Avigad, "The Mosaic Pavement of the Beth-Alpha Synagogue and its Place in the History of Jewish Art," in J. Aviram, ed., *The Bet-Shean Valley: The 17th Archaeological Convention* (Jerusalem: IES, 1962), pp. 63-70 (in Hebrew).

Avigad, *Beth She'arim*   N. Avigad, *Beth She'arim, vol. III, (Catacombs 12-13)* (New Brunswick, NJ: Rutgers University Press on behalf of the Israel Exploration Society and the Institute of Archaeology, Hebrew University, 1976).

Avigad, *Jerusalem*   N. Avigad, *Discovering Jerusalem* (Nashville, 1983).

Avigad, "Jewish Art"   N. Avigad, "Relics of Ancient Jewish Art in Galilee," *Eretz Israel* 7 (1964): 18-19 (in Hebrew).

Avigad, "Synagogues"   N. Avigad, "On the Form of Ancient Synagogues in the Galilee," in H. Z. Hirschberg and J. Aviram, eds., *All the Land of Naphtali: The 24th Archaeological Convention* (Jerusalem: IES, 1967), pp. 91-100 (in Hebrew).

Avigad, "Umm el-'Amed"   N. Avigad, "An Aramaic Inscription from the Synagogue at Umm el-'Amed in Galilee," *Rabinowitz Bulletin*, vol. 3, pp. 62-64.

AZ   Abodah Zarah.

B   *Bavli,* Babylonian Talmud, Talmud of the Land of
                                      Babylonia.
B. M. Quarterly   *British Museum Quarterly.*
BA   *Biblical Archaeologist.*
BAAS   *Bulletin of the Anglo-Israel Archaeological Society.*
Bacher, *Agadah*   W. Bacher, *Die Agadah der Palaestinensischen
                                      Amoraeer* (Tel-Aviv, 1927; repr. 1930) (in Hebrew).
                                      Translation of German original, *Die Agada der
                                      Palaestinensischen Amoraer,* 3 vols. (Strassburg, 1892;
                                      repr. Hildesheims: G. Olms, 1965).
Baedeker, *Palestine*   K. Baedeker, *Palestine et Syrie, Manuel du Voyageur*
                                      (Leipzig and Paris, 1912).
Bahat, "Beth-Shean"   Bahat, Dan. "A Synagogue at Beth-Shean," in Levine,
                                      ASR, pp. 82-85.
BAR   *Biblical Archaeology Review.*
Bar-Adon, "Beth-Yeraḥ"   P. Bar-Adon, "Ṣinnabra and Beth Yeraḥ in the Light of
                                      the Sources and Archaeological Finds," *EI* 4 (1956): 50-
                                      55 (in Hebrew).
Bar-Adon, "Golan"   P. Bar-Adon, "A Greek Inscription in the Upper Golan,"
                                      Zion 5 (1933): 187-188 (in Hebrew).
Bar-Adon, "Synagogue"   P. Bar-Adon, "A Possible Fortified Synagogue at Beth-
                                      Yeraḥ," in S. Applebaum, ed., *Roman Frontier Studies—
                                      1967* (Tel-Aviv, 1971), p. 185.
Baras, *Eretz Israel*   Z. Baras et al., eds., *Eretz Israel from the Destruction of
                                      the Second Temple to the Muslim Conquest,* 2 vols.
                                      (Jerusalem: Yad Yitzak ben Zvi, 1982-84) (in Hebrew).
Bar-Kochva, "Gamala"   B. Bar-Kochva, "Gamala and Gaulanitis," *ZDPV* 92
                                      (1976): 54-71.
Bar-Lev, "Khisfîn"   S. Bar-Lev, "Khisfîn," *HA* 56 (1976): 3 (in Hebrew).
Baron   S. W. Baron, *A Social and Religious History of the Jews,*
                                      vol. 2 (New York, 1952).
BASOR   *Bulletin of the American School of Oriental Research.*
BB   Baba Batra.
BCH   *Bulletin du correspondance hellénique.*
BDB   Francis Brown, S. R. Driver, and Charles A. Briggs, *A
                                      Hebrew and English Lexicon of the Old Testament*
                                      (Oxford: Clarendon, 1951).
Bean, *Aegean Turkey*   G. Bean, *Aegean Turkey: An Archaeological Guide*
                                      (London, 1966).
Beer   M. Beer, *The Babylonian Exilarchate in the Arsacid and
                                      Sassanian Periods* (Tel-Aviv: Dvir, 1970) (in Hebrew).
Bek.   Bekorot.
Ben-Ari & Bar-Lev, "'Asâliyye"   M. Ben-Ari and S. Bar-Lev, "'Asâliyye—a Synagogue,"
                                      HA 59-60 (1976): 7 (in Hebrew).
Ben-Ari & Bar-Lev, "Golan—1"   M. Ben-Ari and S. Bar-Lev, "The Golan," *HA* 45
                                      (1973): 1-2 (in Hebrew).
Ben-Ari & Bar-Lev, "Golan—2"   M. Ben-Ari and S. Bar-Lev, "The Golan," *HA* 47
                                      (1973): 1-2 (in Hebrew).
Ben-Ari & Bar-Lev, "Survey"   M. Ben-Ari and S. Bar-Lev, "A Survey in the Golan,"
                                      HA 57-58 (1976): 2-3 (in Hebrew).

Ben-Dov | M. Ben-Dov, *The Dig at the Temple Mount* (Jerusalem: Keter, 1982) (in Hebrew).

Ben-Dov, "Kokhav-Hayarden" | M. Ben-Dov, "Synagogue Remains at Kokhav-Hayarden," in Levine, *ASR*, pp. 95-97.

Ben-Horin (Sukenik) | U. Ben-Horin, "Bibliography of the Writings of E. L. Sukenik," *EI* 8 (1967). pp. אם-כד (in Hebrew).

Benjamin of Tudela | *Itinerary of Benjamin of Tudela*, N. Adler, ed. (London, 1907; repr. New York, n.d.).

Ber. | Berakot.

Bevan, *Egypt* | E. Bevan, *The House of Ptolemy: A History of Egypt under the Ptolemaic Dynasty* (London, 1927; repr. Chicago: Argonaut, 1968).

Bickerman, "Symbolism" | E. J. Bickerman, "Symbolism in the Dura Synagogue," *HTR* 58 (1965): 127-151.

Bickerman, "Warning" | E. J. Bickerman, "The Warning Inscription of Herod's Temple," *Studies in Jewish and Christian History*, vol. 2 (Leiden: E. J. Brill, 1980).

Biebel, "Hamman Lif" | F. M. Biebel, "The Mosaics of Hamman Lif," *Art Bulletin* 18, no. 4 (1936): 541-551.

Bik. | Bikkurim.

BJ | Flavius Josephus, *Bellum Judaicum* (*The Jewish War*).

BJPES | *Bulletin of the Jewish Palestine Exploration Society.*

BM | Baba Metzia.

Bokser, "Sacred Space" | Baruch Bokser, "Approaching Sacred Space," *HTR* 78, nos. 3-4 (1985): 279-299.

Bokser, "Wall" | Baruch Bokser, "The Wall Separating God and Israel," *JQR* 73, no. 4 (1983): 349-374.

Boulanger | A. Boulanger, *Orphée: Rapports de L'Orphisme et du Christianisme* (Paris: F. Rieder et Cie, 1925)

BQ | Baba Qamma.

Branham, "Sacred Space" | Joan R. Branham, "Sacred Space Under Erasure in Ancient Synagogues and Early Churches," *Art Bulletin* 74, no. 3 (1992): 375-394.

Bright, *Jeremiah* | John Bright, *Jeremiah* (Garden City, NJ: Doubleday, 1965).

Brock, "Maximus" | S. Brock, "An Early Syriac Life of Maximus the Confessor," *Analecta Bollandiana* 91 (1973): 302-315.

Brooten | B. J. Brooten, *Women Leaders in the Ancient Synagogue* (Chico, CA: Scholars Press, 1982).

Brown, "Templum" | John Pairman Brown, "The *Templum* and the *Saeculum*: Sacred Space and Time in Israel and Etruria," *Zeitschrift für die alttestamentlich Wissenschaft* 98 (1986): 415-433.

Bruneau, *Recherches* | Philippe Bruneau, *Recherches sur les cultes de Delos a l'epoque hellenistique et a l'epoque imperiale*, Bibliotheque des Ecoles françaises d'Athenes et de Rome, (Paris, 1970).

BSOAS | *Bulletin. School of Oriental and African Studies.*

Burckhardt, *Travels* | J. L. Burckhardt, *Travels in Syria and the Holy Land* (London: John Murray, 1822).

Burkert | Walter Burkert, *Greek Religion*, John Raffan, tr. (Cambridge, MA: Harvard University Press, 1985).

Burtchaell

James Tunstead Burtchaell, *From Synagogue to Church* (Cambridge: Cambridge University Press, 1992).

CA

Cahiers archéologiques.

Caquot, *Dupont-Sommer*

A. Caquot, *Hommages à A. Dupont-Sommer* (Paris: Adrien-Maisonneuve, 1971).

Cassuto-Salzmann

M. Cassuto-Salzmann, "Greek Names among the Jews," *Eretz Israel* 3 (1954): 186-190 (in Hebrew).

Cenival, *Associations*

Françoise de Cenival, *Les Associations religieuses en Égypte d'après les documents démotiques*, Bibliothèque d'Étude, vol. 46, IFAO (Cairo, 1972).

Chen, "Design"

D. Chen, "The Design of the Ancient Synagogues in Judea: Masada and Herodium," *BASOR* 239 (1980): 37-40.

Chiat, "First-Century"

Marilyn J. Chiat, "First-Century Synagogue Architecture: Methodological Problems," in Gutmann, *Synagogues*, pp. 49-60.

Chiat, *Handbook*

Marilyn Joyce Segal Chiat, *Handbook of Synagogue Architecture*, Brown Judaic Studies 29 (Chico, CA: Scholars Press, 1982).

CIG

A. Boeck, ed., *Corpus Inscriptionum Graecarum* (Berlin, 1828-1877).

CII

See Frey.

CIJ

See Frey.

cm

centimeter.

Cohen, "Evidence"

Shaye J. D. Cohen, "Pagan and Christian Evidence on the Ancient Synagogue," in Levine, *SLA*, pp. 159-181.

Cohen, "Menstruants"

Shaye J. D. Cohen, "Menstruants and the Sacred in Judaism and Christianity," in Sarah B. Pomeroy, ed., *Women's History and Ancient History* (Chapel Hill: University of North Carolina Press, 1991), pp. 273-299.

Cohen, "Rabbi"

Shaye J. D. Cohen, "The Place of the Rabbi in Jewish Society of the Second Century," in Levine, *GLA*, pp. 157-173.

Cohen, "Temple"

Shaye J. D. Cohen, "The Temple and the Synagogue" in T. Madsen, ed., *The Temple in Antiquity* (Provo, Utah: Brigham Young University Press, 1984), pp. 151-174.

Cohn

Robert Cohn, *The Shape of Sacred Space* (Chico, CA: Scholars Press, 1981).

Coins

Bluma Trell and Martin Price, *Coins and their Cities* (London: Friary Press, Ltd., 1977).

Contemplative Life

Philo, *On the Contemplative Life.*

Cooke, *Inscriptions*

G. A. Cooke, *A Text-Book of North Semitic Inscriptions* (Oxford: Clarendon, 1903).

Corbett

Peter E. Corbett, "Greek Temples and Greek Worshippers: The Literary and Archaeological Evidence," *Bulletin of the Institute of Classical Studies* 27 (1970): 149-158.

Corbo, *Cafarnao*

V. C. Corbo, *Cafarnao 1, Gli Edifici della citta* (Jerusalem: Franciscan Printing Press, 1975).

Corbo, "L'Herodion—prime campagna"

Corbo, V., "L'Herodion de Giabel Fureidis," *LA* 13 (1962-63): 219-277.

Corbo, "L'Herodion—quarta campagna"

    Corbo, V., "L'Herodion de Giabel Fureidis," *LA* 17(1967): 65-121, esp. 72, 101-103.

Corbo, "Magdala"

    Virgilio Corbo, "La Città romana di Magdala," in *Studia Hieroslymitana. In onore di P. Bellarmino Bagatti, I. Studi archaeologici* (Jerusalem: Franciscan Printing Press, 1976).

Corbo, *Herodion*

    V. C. Corbo, *Herodion I: Gli Edifici della Reggia-Fortezza* (Jerusalem: Studium Biblicum Franciscanum, 1989).

Cowley

    A. E. Cowley, *Aramaic Papyri of the Fifth Century B.C.* (Oxford: Clarendon, 1923).

CPJ

    A. Tcherikover with A. Fuks, eds., *Corpus papyrorum Judicarum*, 3 vols. (Cambridge, MA: Harvard University Press for Magness Press, 1957-64).

CRAI

    Comptes Rendus de l'Academie des Inscriptions et Belles Lettres.

Dalman, "Bethsaida"

    G. Dalman, "Bethsaida Julias," *Palästinajahrbuch*, 8 (1912): 45-48.

Dalman, "Inschriften"

    G. Dalman, "Inschriften aus dem Ostjordanland," *ZDPV* 36 (1913): 249-265.

Dalman, *Jesu*

    G. Dalman, *Orte und Wege Jesu* (Gütersloh: Bertelsmann, 1924).

Dalman, "Palästina"

    G. Dalman, "Inschriften aus Palästina," *ZDPV* 37 (1914): 135-150.

Daremberg-Saglio, *Dict.*

    C. Daremberg and E. Saglio, *Dictionaire des antiquities greques et romaines*, 5 vols. (Paris, 1877-1919; repr. Graz, 1962-1969).

Dauphin, "1979"

    C. M. Dauphin, "Golan Survey, 1979," *IEJ* 29 (1979): 223-225.

Dauphin, "1980-1981"

    C. M. Dauphin, "Golan Survey, 1980-1981," *IEJ* 31 (1981): 239-240.

Dauphin, "1981-1982"

    C. M. Dauphin, "Golan Survey, 1981-1982," *IEJ* 33 (1983): 112-113.

Dauphin, "1981/1982"

    C. M. Dauphin, "Golan Survey—1981/1982," *EASI* 2 (1983): 37.

Dauphin, "1983a"

    C. M. Dauphin, "Golan Survey—1983," *EASI* 3 (1984): 35-36.

Dauphin, "1983b"

    C. M. Dauphin, "Golan Survey, 1983," *IEJ* 34 (1984): 268-269.

Dauphin, "1985a"

    C. M. Dauphin, "Golan Survey—1985," *EASI* 5 (1985): 44.

Dauphin, "1985b"

    C. M. Dauphin, "Golan Survey, 1985," *IEJ* 36 (1986): 273-275.

Dauphin, "1988a"

    C. M. Dauphin, "Golan Survey—1988," *EASI* 9 (1989-90): 6-7.

Dauphin, "1988b"

    C. M. Dauphin, "Golan Survey, 1988," *IEJ* 41 (1991): 176-179.

Dauphin, "Farj"

    C. M. Dauphin, "Farj en Gaulanitide: refuge judéo-chrétien?" *Proche-Orient Chrétien* 34 (1984): 233-245.

Dauphin, "Gaulanitis"

    C. M. Dauphin, "Jewish and Christian Communities in the Roman and Byzantine Gaulanitis: A Study of Evidence

	from Archaeological Surveys," *PEQ* 114 (1982): 129-142.
Dauphin, "Golan"	C. M. Dauphin, "Survey in the Golan," *HA* 84 (1984): 5 (in Hebrew).
Dauphin, "Golan Heights—1"	C. M. Dauphin, "Golan Heights," *PEQ* 112 (1980): 68.
Dauphin, "Golan Heights—2"	C. M. Dauphin, "Golan Heights," *PEQ* 114 (1982): 74-75.
Dauphin, "Settlement Patterns—1"	
	C. M. Dauphin, "Golan, settlement patterns," *HA* 73 (1980): 38 (in Hebrew).
Dauphin, "Settlement Patterns—2"	
	C. M. Dauphin, "Golan, settlement patterns," *HA* 76 (1981): 40 (in Hebrew).
Dauphin, "Settlement Patterns—3"	
	C. M. Dauphin, "Golan, settlement patterns," *HA* 83 (1983): 1 (in Hebrew).
Dauphin, "Settlement Patterns—4"	
	C. M. Dauphin, "The Golan—settlement patterns," *HA* 88 (1986): 1 (in Hebrew).
Dauphin and Gibson	C. Dauphin and S. Gibson, "Ancient Settlements in their Landscapes: the Results of Ten Years of Survey on the Golan Heights (1978-1988)," *BAAS* 12 (1992-93): 7-31.
Dauphin and Gibson, "Ancient Settlements"	
	C. Dauphin and S. Gibson, "Exploring Ancient Settlements and Landscapes in the Golan," *Cathedra* 73 (1994): 3-25 (in Hebrew).
Dauphin and Schonfield	C. M. Dauphin and J. J. Schonfield, "Settlements of the Roman and Byzantine Periods on the Golan Heights: Preliminary Report on Three Seasons of Survey (1979-1981)," *IEJ* 33 (1983): 189-206.
Derrida	J. Derrida, "La Différance," in *Marges de la Philosophie* (Paris: Editions de Minuit, 1972).
Diaspora	M. Stern, ed., *The Diaspora in the Hellenistic-Roman World* (Jerusalem: Am Oved, 1983) (in Hebrew).
DJD	Discoveries in the Judean Desert.
DOPapers	*Dumbarton Oaks Papers.*
Dothan, "Hammath-Tiberias"	M. Dothan, "The Synagogues at Hammath-Tiberias," *Qadmoniot* 1, no. 4 (1968): 116-123 (in Hebrew).
Dothan, *Hammath Tiberias*	M. Dothan, *Hammath Tiberias* (Jerusalem: Israel Exploration Society/University of Haifa/Department of Antiquities and Museums, 1983).
Du Mesnil, "Le Deux synagogues"	
	Comte Du Mesnil de Buisson, "Le Deux Synagogues Successives a Doura-Europos," *RB* 45 (1936): 72-90.
Du Mesnil, *Les peintures*	Comte Du Mesnil de Buisson, *Les peintures de la synagogue de Doura-Europos, 245-256 après J.-Chr.* (Paris, 1939).
EAEHL	*Encyclopaedia of Archaeological Excavations in the Holy Land*, B. Mazar, ed., 2 vols. (Jerusalem: IES & Massada Press, 1970) (in Hebrew).

EAEIHL	*Encyclopedia of Archaelogical Excavations in the Holy Land,* M. Avi-Yonah and E. Stern, eds., 4 vols. (London: Oxford University Press & Jerusalem: IES & Massada Press, 1976).
EASI	*Excavations and Surveys in Israel* (English edition of *Hadashot Arkheologiyot*).
Ed.	Eduyyot.
EI	*Eretz Israel.*
Eissfeld, "Dura-Europos"	O. Eissfeld, "Dura-Europos," *Reallexikon für Antike und Christentum,* vol. 4 (Stuttgart, 1959), pp. 350-370.
EJ	*Encyclopedia Judaica,* 16 vols. (New York & Jerusalem: Macmillan & Keter, 1971).
Elbogen, *Jewish Prayer*	I. Elbogen, *Jewish Prayer in its Historical Development* (Tel Aviv: Dvir, 1972) (in Hebrew). Original German edition: *Der jüdische Gottesdienst in seiner geschichtlichen Entwicklung* (Leipzig, 1913). English translation: *Jewish Liturgy: A Comprehensive History,* R. P. Scheindlin, tr., (Philadelphia: Jewish Publication Society, 1993).
Eliade, "Architecture"	M. Eliade, "Sacred Architecture and Symbolism," in Diane Apostolos-Cappadona, ed., *Symbolism, the Sacred, and the Arts: Mircea Eliade* (New York: Crossroads, 1986). Originally published as "Architecture sacrée et symbolisme" in *Mircea Eliade,* Constantin Tacou, ed., Cahiers de l'Herne, no. 33 (Paris: L'Herne, 1978). That French essay was a revision of "Centre du monde, temple, maison," first published in *Le symbolisme cosmique des monuments religieux,* Guiseppi Tucci, ed. (Rome: Istituto Italiano par il Medio ed Estremo Oriente, 1957).
Eliade, *Myth*	M. Eliade, *The Myth of the Eternal Return* (New York: Pantheon Books, 1954).
Eliade, *Sacred*	M. Eliade, *The Sacred and the Profane* (San Diego: Harcourt Brace Jovanovich, 1959).
"En-Nabratein"	E. M. Meyers, J. F. Strange, C. L. Meyers, "Second Preliminary Report on the 1981 Excavations at en-Nabratein, Israel," *BASOR* 246 (1982): 35-54.
Ephal	I. Ephal, "The Babylonian Exile," in *Restoration,* pp. 17-27 (in Hebrew).
Epstein, "Hippos"	C. Epstein, "Hippos (Sussita)," in *NEAEHL,* vol. 2, pp. 634-636.
Epstein, *Introduction*	J. N. Epstein, *Introduction to Tannaitic Literature* (Jerusalem and Tel Aviv: Magnes & Dvir, 1957) (in Hebrew).
Epstein, "Sûsîta"	C. Epstein, "Sûsîta," in *NEAEIHL,* vol. 4, pp. 1102-1104 (in Hebrew).
Epstein & Gutman	C. Epstein and S. Gutman, "The Survey in the Golan Heights," in M. Kochavi, ed., *Judaea, Samaria and the Golan: Archaeological Survey 1967-1968* (Jerusalem: Carta, 1972), pp. 243-298 (in Hebrew).
Erub.	Erubim.
FA	*Fasti Archaeologici.*

Fine, "Holy Place"	S. Fine, "A 'Holy Place': Palestinian Synagogues During the Talmudic Period," *Direction* (Fall, 1992): 10-20.
Finkelstein, "Origin"	L. Finkelstein, "The Origin of the Synagogue," in Gutmann, *Synagogue*, pp. 3-13. Originally published in *PAAJR* 1 (1928-30): 49-59.
Flaccus	Philo Judaeus, *In Flaccum.*
Flesher, *Slaves*	P. V. M. Flesher, *Oxen, Women or Citizens? Slaves in the System of the Mishnah* (Atlanta, GA: Scholars Press, 1988).
Floriani Squarciapino	See Squarciapino
Foerster, "Art"	G. Foerster, "The Art and Architecture of the Synagogue in its Late Roman Setting in Palestine," in Levine, *SLA*, pp. 139-146.
Foerster, "Diaspora Synagogues"	G. Foerster, "A Survey of Ancient Diaspora Synagogues," in Levine, *ASR*, pp. 164-171.
Foerster, "Galilean Synagogues"	G. Foerster, "Galilean Synagogues and Their Relation to Hellenistic and Roman Art and Architecture," (Ph.D dissertation, The Hebrew University of Jerusalem, 1972) (in Hebrew).
Foerster, "Hammat Gader"	See Foerster, "Hammat Gader-1."
Foerster, "Hammat Gader-1"	G. Foerster, "Hammat Gader—Synagogue," *HA* 82 (1983): 11-12 (in Hebrew).
Foerster, "Hammat Gader-2"	G. Foerster, "Hammat Gader, Synagogue," *EASI* 2 (1983): 41.
Foerster, "Masada"	G. Foerster, "The Synagogues at Masada and Herodium," in Levine, *ASR*, pp. 24-9. This is an abbreviated version of Foester, "Masada & Herodion."
Foerster, "Masada & Herodion"	G. Foerster "The Synagogues at Masada and Herodion," *JJA* 3-4 (1977): 6-11. This article is an expanded version of "The Synagogues at Masada and Herodion," *EI* 11 (1973): 224-228 (in Hebrew).
Foerster, "Menorah"	G. Foerster, "Some Menorah Reliefs from Galilee," *IEJ* 24 (1974): 191-196.
Foerster, "Notes"	G. Foerster, "Notes on Recent Excavations at Capernaum," in Levine, *ASR*, pp. 57-59.
Foerster, "Synagogues"	G. Foerster, "Synagogues in the Galilee," A. Shmueli et al., eds., *The Lands of Galilee*, vol. 1 (Haifa, 1983), pp. 231-256 (in Hebrew)
Foss, *Byzantine and Turkish Sardis*	Clive Foss, *Byzantine and Turkish Sardis*, Archaeological Exploration of Sardis, Monograph 4 (Cambridge, 1976).
Fraser, *Alexandria*	P. M. Fraser, *Ptolemaic Alexandria*, 3 vols. (Oxford: Clarendon, 1972).
Frey	Jean-Baptiste Frey, ed., *Corpus Inscriptionum Judaicarum*, 2 vols. (Rome, 1936-1952; repr. New York: Ktav, 1975 in a single volume).
Gafni, "Synagogues"	I. Gafni, "Synagogues in Talmudic Babylonia: Tradition and Reality," in Kasher, *Synagogues*, pp. 155-164 (in Hebrew). [Translated in this collection as I. Gafni, "Synagogues in Babylonia in the Talmudic Period."]
Gaius	Philo, *On the Embassy to Gaius.*

Gal, "Gamala"	Y. Gal, P. Sela, and M. Livneh, "Suggested Identification of the Site of Gamala in the Golan," *Teva va-Aretz* 13 (1971): 156-158 (in Hebrew).
Gammie	John Gammie, *Holiness in Israel* (Minneapolis: Fortress Press, 1989).
Gerkan, *Milet*	A. von Gerkan, *Milet, Ergebnisse der Ausgrabungen und Untersuchungen seit dem Jahr 1899* (Berlin, 1922).
Gerkan, "Synagogue in Milet"	A. von Gerkan, "Eine Synagogue in Milet," *ZNW* 20 (1921): 177-181.
Gibson and Urman	S. Gibson and D. Urman, "Three Coins of Alexander Jannaeus from El-ʿÂl in the Golan Heights," *BAAS* 10 (1990-91): 67-72.
Gil, *Palestine*	M. Gil, *Palestine During the First Moslem Period (634-1099)*, 3 vols. (Tel Aviv: Tel-Aviv University & the Ministry of Defense-Publishing House, 1983) (in Hebrew). English: (Cambridge & New York, 1992).
Ginzberg, *Commentary*	L. Ginzberg, *A Commentary on the Palestinian Talmud*, 4 vols. (New York: The Jewish Theological Seminary of America, 1941-1961; repr. Ktav, 1971) (in Hebrew).
Ginzberg, *Yerushalmi*	L. Ginzberg, *Yerushalmi Fragments from the Genizah* (New York: The Jewish Theological Seminary of America, 1909) (in Hebrew).
Girard, *Violence*	René Girard, *Violence and the Sacred* (Baltimore: Johns Hopkins University Press, 1977).
Git.	Gittin.
Glueck, "el-Ḥammeh"	N. Glueck, "Tell el-Ḥammeh," *AJA* 39 (1935): 321-330.
Glueck, "Palestine"	N. Glueck, "Explorations in Eastern Palestine, IV," *AASOR* 25-28 (1951): 137-140.
Glueck, "Yarmûk"	N. Glueck, "The Archaeological Exploration of el-Ḥammeh on the Yarmûk," *BASOR* 49 (1933): 22-23.
Golani, "Golan"	A. Golani, "Golan, Survey of Central Area," *EASI* 9 (1989-90): 7-8.
Goldman	Bernard Goldman, *The Sacred Portal* (Detroit, MI: Wayne State University Press, 1966; repr. Lanham, MD: University Press of America, 1985).
Goldstein	J. Goldstein, "The Central Composition of the West Wall of the Synagogue of Dura-Europos," *JAOS* 16-17 (1984-85): 99-142.
Goodenough	E. R. Goodenough, *Jewish Symbols in the Graeco-Roman Period*, 13 vols. (New York: Pantheon Books, 1953-68).
Goodenough, *Christianity*	A. T. Kraabel, ed., *Goodenough on the Beginnings of Christianity* (Atlanta, GA: Scholars Press, 1990).
Goodenough, *Faith*	E. R. Goodenough, *Toward a Mature Faith* (New Haven: Yale, 1961; repr. Lanham, MD: University Press of America, 1988).
Goodenough, "Rabbis"	E. R. Goodenough, "The Rabbis and Jewish Art in the Greco-Roman Period," in Goodenough, *Christianity*, pp. 133-142.
Goodenough, Pilgrimage	R. S. Eccles, *Erwin Ramsdell Goodenough: A Personal Pilgrimage* (Atlanta, GA: Scholars Press, 1985).

Goodenough, *Religion*	E. S. Frerichs and J. Neusner, eds., *Goodenough on The History of Religion and on Judaism* (Atlanta, GA: Scholars Press, 1986).
Goodenough and Avi-Yonah	E. R. Goodenough, and M. Avi-Yonah, "Dura-Europos," *EJ*, vol. 6, pp. 275-298.

Grant, *The Jews in the Roman World*

Michael Grant, *The Jews in the Roman World* (New York: Charles Schribner's Sons, 1973).

GRBS	*Greek, Roman and Byzantine Studies.*
Green, "Question"	W. S. Green, "Introduction: Messiah in Judaism: Rethinking the Question," in Neusner, Green, and Frerichs, *Messiahs*, pp. 1-14.
Gregg and Urman	R. C. Gregg and D. Urman, *Jews, Pagans, and Christians in the Golan Heights—Greek and Other Inscriptions of the Roman and Byzantine Eras* (Princeton, NJ: Darwin Press, 1995).
Groh, "Chronology"	Dennis E. Groh, "Jews and Christians in Late Roman Palestine—Towards a New Chronology," *BA* 51 (1988): 80-96.
Gush Halav	*Excavations at the Ancient Synagogue of Gush Halav*, Meiron Excavation Project V, edited by Eric M. Meyers and Carol L. Meyers, with James F. Strange (Winona Lake, IN: Eisenbrauns for the American Schools of Oriental Research, 1990).
"Gush Halav"	E. M. Meyers, J. F. Strange and Carol Meyers, "Preliminary Report on the 1977 and 1978 Seasons at Gush-Halav (el-Jish), Upper Galilee, Israel," *BASOR* 233 (1979): 33-58.
Gutman, "Die Synagoge"	S. Gutman, "Dura-Europos, Die Synagoge," *Reallexikon zur byzantinischen Kunst*, vol. 1, (Stuttgart, 1966), pp. 1230-1240.
Gutman, *Gamala*	S. Gutman, *Gamala: The Excavations in the first eight seasons* (Tel-Aviv, 1985) (in Hebrew).
Gutman, *Gamala—2*	S. Gutman, *Gamala: The Historical Background and the First Season of Excavations* (Tel Aviv: Hakibbutz Hameuchad, 1977) (in Hebrew).
Gutman, *Gamala—3*	S. Gutman, *Gamala: The Excavation in the First Three Seasons*, (Tel Aviv: Hakibbutz Hameuchad, 1981) (in Hebrew).
Gutman, "Gamala"	S. Gutman, "A Reconsideration of the Identification of the Site of Gamala," in *The Roman Period in Palestine* (editors unnamed) (Tel Aviv, 1973), pp. 199-225 (in Hebrew).
Gutman, "Gamala—2"	S. Gutman, "Gamala," in *NEAEIHL*, vol. 1, pp. 343-348 (in Hebrew).
Gutman, "Gamala—3"	S. Gutman, "Gamala," in *NEAEHL*, vol. 2, pp. 459-463.
Gutman, "Gamla"	S. Gutman, "The Synagogue at Gamla," Levine, *ASR*, pp. 30-34.
Gutman, *Rebellion*	S. Gutman, *Gamla—A City in Rebellion* (Tel Aviv: Ministry of Defense, 1994).
Gutman, Yeivin, and Netzer	S. Gutman, Z. Yeivin, and E. Netzer, "The Excavation of the Synagogue at Horvat Susiya," *Qadmoniot* 20

	(1972): 47-52. English translation: "Excavations in the Synagogue at Ḥorvat Susiya," in Levine, *ASR*, pp. 123-128.
Gutmann, *Ancient Synagogues*	Joseph Gutmann, ed., *Ancient Synagogues. The State of Research*, Brown Judaic Studies 22 (Chico, CA: Scholars Press, 1981).
Gutmann, *Dura-Europos*	Joseph Gutmann, ed., *The Dura-Europos Synagogue: A Re-evaluation (1932—1972)* (Missoula, Montana: Scholars Press, 1973). Revised and reissued as *The Dura-Europos Synagogue: A Re-evaluation (1932-1992)* (Atlanta: Scholars Press, 1992).
Gutmann, "Origin"	Joseph Gutmann, "The Origin of the Synagogue: The Current State of Research," in Gutmann, *Synagogue*, pp. 72-76.
Gutmann, "Origins"	Joseph Gutmann, "Synagogue Origins: Theories and Facts," in Gutmann, *Synagogues*, pp. 1-6.
Gutmann, *Sanctuary*	Joseph Gutmann, *The Jewish Sanctuary* (Leiden: E.J. Brill, 1983).
Gutmann, *Synagogue*	Joseph Gutmann, ed., *The Synagogue: Studies in Origins, Archaeology and Architecture* (New York: Ktav, 1975).
HA	*Ḥadashot Arkheologiyot*.
Hachlili, *Ancient Synagogues*	Rachel Hachlili, ed., *Ancient Synagogues in Israel. Third-Seventh Century C.E.*, BAR International Series 499 (Oxford: B.A.R., 1989).
Hachlili, *Art*	Rachel Hachlili, *Ancient Jewish Art and Archaeology in the Land of Israel* (Leiden: E. J. Brill, 1988).
Hachlili, "Composition"	Rachel Hachlili, "Unidentical Symmetrical Composition in Synagogal Art," in Hachlili, *Ancient Synagogues*, pp. 65-68.
Hag.	Hagigah.
Hal.	Hallah.
Hanfmann, *Letters*	G. M. A. Hanfmann, *Letters from Sardis* (Cambridge, MA: Harvard, 1972).
Hanfmann, *Sardis und Lydien*	G. M. A. Hanfmann, *Sardis und Lydien*, AbhMainz 6 (Mainz, 1960) 499-536.
Hanfmann and Waldbaum, "New Excavations"	
	G. M. A. Hanfmann and J. C. Waldbaum, "New Excavations at Sardis and Some Problems of Western Anatolian Archaeology," in J. A. Sanders, ed., *Near Eastern Archaeology in the Twentieth Century: Essays in Honor of Nelson Glueck* (Garden City, NY, 1970), pp. 307-326.
Hanfmann & Waldbaum, *Survey*	G. M. A. Hanfmann and J. C. Waldbaum, *A Survey of Sardis and the Major Monuments outside the City Walls*, Archaeological Exploration of Sardis, Report 1 (Cambridge, 1975).
Haran, *Temples*	Menahem Haran, *Temples and Temple Service in Ancient Israel* (Oxford: Clarendon, 1978).
Haran, "Vestments"	Menahem Haran, "Priestly Vestments," *EJ*, vol. 13, cols. 1063-1069.
Hartal, "Bâb el-Hawâ"	M. Hartal, "Bâb el-Hawâ," *HA* 97 (1991): 6-8 (in Hebrew).

Heiman, *History*	See Hyman, *Toldoth.*
Hengel, *Hellenism*	Martin Hengel, *Judaism and Hellenism: Studies in their Encounter in Palestine during the Early Hellenistic Period*, 2 vols. (London, 1974; repr. Philadelphia: Fortress, 1981 in a single volume).
Hengel, "Proseuche"	Martin Hengel, "Proseuche und Synagoge: Jüdische Gemeinde, Gotteshaus und Gottesdienst in der Diaspora und in Palästina," in G. Jeremias et al., eds., *Tradition und Glaube, Festgabe für K. G. Kuhn* (Göttingen, 1971), pp. 157-184. Reprinted in J. Gutmann, ed., *The Synagogue: Studies in Origins, Archaeology, and Architecture* (New York: Ktav, 1975), pp. 27-54.
Hengel, "Synagogeninschrift"	Martin Hengel, "Die Synagogeninschrift von Stobi," *ZNW* 57 (1966): 145-183, reprinted in Gutmann, *Synagogue*, pp. 110-148.
Herr, "Chain"	M. D. Herr, "Continuum in the Chain of Torah Transmission," *Zion* 44 (1979): 43-56 (in Hebrew).
Hirschberg	H. Z. Hirschberg, ed., *All the Land of Naphtali: The Twenty-Fourth Archaeological Convention, October, 1966* (Jerusalem: IES, 1967) (in Hebrew).
Hirschfeld, "Hammat Gader-1"	Y. Hirschfeld, "Hammat Gader," in *NEAEIHL*, vol. 2, pp. 505, 508-514 (in Hebrew).
Hirschfeld, "Hammat Gader-2"	Y. Hirschfeld, "Hammat Gader," in *NEAEHL*, vol. 2, pp. 565-566, 569-573.
Hoenig, "City-Square"	S. B. Hoenig, "The Ancient City-Square: The Forerunner of the Synagogue," *ANRW* 19.1, pp. 448-76.
Hopkins, *Discovery*	C. Hopkins, *The Discovery of Dura-Europos*, B. Goldman, ed. (New Haven: Yale, 1979).
Hopkins, "Excavations"	C. Hopkins, "The Excavations of the Dura Synagogue Paintings," in Gutmann, *Synagogue*, pp. 11-22.
Hor.	Horayot.
HTR	*Harvard Theological Review.*
HUCA	*Hebrew Union College Annual.*
Hul.	Hullin.
Hüttenmeister and Reeg	Frowald Hüttenmeister and Gottfied Reeg, *Die Antiken Synagogen in Israel*, 2 vols. (Wiesbaden: Dr. Ludwig Reichert, 1977).
Hüttenmeister, "Connection"	F. Hüttenmeister, "The House of Assembly and the House of Study and Their Connection," *Cathedra* 18 (1981): 38-44 (in Hebrew).
Hyman, *Toldoth*	A. Hyman, *Toldoth Tannaim ve-Amoraim*, 3 vols., (Jerusalem: Boys Town Jerusalem Publishers, 1964) (in Hebrew).
IDB	*International Dictionary of the Bible.*
IEJ	*Israel Exploration Journal.*
IES	Israel Exploration Society.
Ilan, *Ancient Synagogues*	Z. Ilan, *Ancient Synagogues in Galilee and Golan* (Tel Aviv, 1986) (in Hebrew).
Ilan, "Bathyra"	Z. Ilan, "Bathyra," *Teva va-Aretz* 13 (1971): 164-167 (in Hebrew).

Ilan, "Fortified Settlement"	Z. Ilan, "Marous—A Fortified Settlement fo the First Revolt on the Northern Border of *Eretz-Israel*," *Eretz Israel* 17 (1984): 141-146 (in Hebrew).
Ilan, *Galilee and Golan*	Z. Ilan, *Synagogues in Galilee and Golan* [=*Ariel*, vol. 52], (Jerusalem: Ariel & Kannah, 1987) (in Hebrew).
Ilan, "Gamala"	Z. Ilan, "Gamala in the Golan," *Nofîm va-Aṭârim* (a series of pamphlets published by the Israel Defense Forces) (Tel Aviv, 1973) (in Hebrew).
Ilan, *Golan*	Z. Ilan, *The Land of the Golan* (Tel Aviv: Am Oved and Tarbut Wechinuch, 1976) (in Hebrew).
Ilan, "Ḥorvat Dîkkeh"	Z. Ilan, "The Synagogue of Ḥorvat Dîkkeh near the Jordan and the Kinneret," *Teva va-Aretz* 31 (1989): 64-67 (in Hebrew).
Ilan, *Israel*	Z. Ilan, *Ancient Synagogues in Israel* (Tel Aviv: Ministry of Defense-Publishing House, 1991) (in Hebrew).
Ilan, "Kh. Sûjen"	Z. Ilan, "Kh. Sûjen," *HA* 84 (1984): 4-5 (in Hebrew).
Ilan, "Menorot"	Z. Ilan, "Jewish Menorot from the Golan," *Qadmoniot* 13, nos. 3-4 (1980): 117-119 (in Hebrew).
Ilan, "Meroth"	Z. Ilan, "The Synagogue and *Beth Midrash* of Meroth," in Hachlili, *Ancient Synagogues*, pp. 21-42.
Ilan, "Quṣbiyye"	Z. Ilan, "Discoveries in Jewish Quṣbiyye," *The Land of the Golan* 120 (1987): 20-21 (in Hebrew).
Iliffe	J. H. Iliffe, "The ΘANATOS Inscription from Herod's Temple," *QDAP* 6, no. 11 (1936): 1-3.
Irwin, "Song"	E. Irwin, "The Songs of Orpheus and the New Song of Christ," pp. 51-62 in Warden, *Orpheus*.
Is., Isa.	Isaiah.
JAR	*Jewish Art Review.*
Jastrow	Marcus Jastrow, *A Dictionary of the Targumim, the Talmud Babli and Yerushalmi, and the Midrashic Literature* (New York: Judaica Press, 1982).
JBL	*Journal of Biblical Literature.*
JEA	*Journal of Egyptian Archaeology.*
Jewish Symbols	See Goodenough.
JFA	*Journal of Field Archaeology.*
JJA	*Journal of Jewish Art.*
JJS	*Journal of Jewish Studies.*
Johnson, "Asia Minor"	S. E. Johnson, "Asia Minor and Early Christianity," in J. Neusner, ed., *Christianity, Judaism and Other Greco-Roman Cults: Studies for Morton Smith at Sixty*, Studies in Judaism in Late Antiquity 12 (Leiden: E. J. Brill, 1975), vol. 2, pp. 77-145.
Johnson, "Unsolved Questions"	S. E. Johnson, "Unsolved Questions about Early Christianity in Anatolia," in D. E. Aune, ed., *Studies in New Testament and Early Christian Literature: Studies in Honor of A. P. Wikgren*, Supplements to Novum Testamentum 33 (Leiden: E. J. Brill, 1972), pp. 181-193.
Josephus, *AA*	Flavius Josephus, *Against Apion.*
Josephus, *JA*	Flavius Josephus, *Jewish Antiquities.*
Josephus, *JW*	Flavius Josephus, *Jewish War.*
JPOS	*Journal of the Palestine Oriental Society.*

JQR   *Jewish Quarterly Review.*

JThS   *Journal of Theological Studies.*

JTSA   Jewish Theological Seminary of America.

Juster   J. Juster, *Les juifs dans l'empire romain* (Paris: Librairie
                                      Paul Geuthner, 1914).

Kasher   A. Kasher, *The Jews in Hellenistic and Roman Egypt.
                                      The Struggle for Equal Rights* (Tübingen: J.C.B. Mohr
                                      [Paul Siebeck], 1985), Revised English Edition. This is a
                                      translation of A. Kasher, *The Jews of Hellenistic and
                                      Roman Egypt in their Struggle for their Rights*,
                                      Publications of the Diaspora Research Institute, Tel-Aviv
                                      University, vol. 23 (Tel Aviv, 1978) (in Hebrew).

Kasher, *Synagogues*   A. Kasher et al., eds., *Synagogues in Antiquity*
                                      (Jerusalem: Yad Izhak Ben Zvi, 1987) (in Hebrew).

Kaufmann   Y. Kaufmann, *History of the Israelite Religion*, vol. 4
                                      (Jerusalem and Tel-Aviv: Bialik Institute and Dvir, 1960)
                                      (in Hebrew).

Kedar, "Khisfîn"   B. Z. Kedar, "A Dangerous Baptism at Khisfîn in the
                                      Late Sixth Century," in D. Jacoby and Y. Tsafrir, eds.,
                                      Jews, Samaritans and Christians in Byzantine Palestine
                                      (Jerusalem: Yad Izhak Ben-Zvi, 1988), pp. 238-241 (in
                                      Hebrew).

Kee, "Transformation"   H. C. Kee, "The Tranformation of the Synagogue after
                                      70 C.E.: Its Import for Early Christianity," *New Testament
                                      Studies* 36 (1990): 1-24.

Kel.   Kelim.

Ker.   Keritot.

Ket.   Ketubot.

Kid.   Kiddushin.

Kil.   Kilayim.

Killebrew, "Dabiyye"   A. Killebrew, "Pottery from Dabiyye," *'Atiqot* 20
                                      (1991): 66-73.

Kitchener   H. H. Kitchener, "Synagogues of Galilee," *PEFQS* 11
                                      (1877): 179-180.

Kittel, "Kleinasiatische Judentum"

                                      G. Kittel, "Das kleinasiatische Judentum in der
                                      hellenistisch-romischen Zeit," *TLZ* 69 (1944): 9-20.

Kitzinger, "A Survey"   E. Kitzinger, "A Survey of the Early Christian Town of
                                      Stobi," *DOPapers* 3 (1946): 81-161.

Klein, "Estates"   S. Klein, "The Estates of R. Judah Ha-Nasi and the
                                      Jewish Communities in the Transjordan Region," *Jewish
                                      Quarterly Review* 2 (1912): 545-556.

Klein, *ha-Yishuv*   S. Klein, ed., *Sefer ha-Yishuv*, vol. 1 (Jerusalem: Bialik
                                      Institute and Dvir, 1939; repr. Jerusalem: Yad Izhak
                                      Ben-Zvi, 1977) (in Hebrew).

Klein, *Inscriptionum*   S. Klein, *Jüdisch-palästinisches Corpus Inscriptionum*
                                      (Vienna-Berlin, 1920).

Klein, *Land*   S. Klein, *The Land of the Galilee* (Jerusalem: Mossad
                                      Harav Kook, 1967) (in Hebrew).

Klein, "Neues zum Fremdenhaus"

S. Klein, "Neues zum Fremdenhaus der Synagoge," *MGWJ* 77 (1933): 81-84.

Klein, *Transjordan*   S. Klein, *The Jewish Transjordan* (Vienna: Menorah, 1925) (in Hebrew).

Kloner, "Synagogues"   A. Kloner, "Ancient Synagogues in Israel: An Archaeological Survey," in Levine, *ASR*, pp. 11-18.

Kochavi, *Survey*   M. Kochavi, ed., *Judaea, Samaria and the Golan: Archaeological Survey 1967-1968* (Jerusalem: Carta, 1972) (in Hebrew).

Kohl and Watzinger   H. Kohl and C. Watzinger, *Antike Synagogen in Galiläa*, Wissenschaftliche Veroffentlichung der Deutschen Orient-Gesellschaft 29 (Leipzig, 1916; repr. Jerusalem, 1973).

Kopp, "Sea of Galilee"   C. Kopp, "Christian Sites around the Sea of Galilee— III," *Dominican Studies* 3 (1950): 275-284.

Kraabel   A. T. Kraabel, "The Diaspora Synagogue: Archaeological and Epigraphic Evidence since Sukenik," *ANRW* 19.1, pp. 477-510. Reprinted in the present collection.

Kraabel, "Bibliographic Notes"   A. T. Kraabel, "Bibliographic Notes," in Goodenough, *Christianity*, pp. xi-xvi.

Kraabel, *Goodenough*   A. T. Kraabel,

Kraabel (Goodenough)   A. T. Kraabel, "A Bibliography of the Writings of Erwin Ramsdell Goodenough," in Neusner, *Religions*, pp. 621-632.

Kraabel, "*Hypsistos*"   A. T. Kraabel, "*Hypsistos* and the Synagogue at Sardis," *GRBS* 10 (1969): 81-93.

Kraabel, *Jews*   J. A. Overman and R. S. MacLennan, eds., *Diasposa Jews and Judaism: Essays in Honor of, and in Dialogue with, A. Thomas Kraabel* (Atlanta, GA: Scholars Press, 1992).

Kraabel, "Melito"   A. T. Kraabel, "Melito the Bishop and the Synagogue at Sardis: Text and Context," in D. G. Mitten et al., eds., *Studies Presented to George M. A. Hanfmann* (Cambridge, 1971), pp. 77-85. Reprinted in Kraabel, *Jews*, pp. 197-208.

Kraabel, "Paganism"   A. T. Kraabel, "Paganism and Judaism: The Sardis Evidence," in A. Benoit, M. Philonenko, C. Vogel, eds., *Paganisme, Judaisme, Christianisme: Melanges offerts a Marcel Simon*, (Paris, 1979), pp. 13-33. Reprinted in Kraabel, *Jews*, pp. 237-256.

Kraabel, "Synagogues, Ancient"   A. T. Kraabel, "Synagogues, Ancient," *New Catholic Encyclopedia: Supplement 1967—1974* (Washington, D.C., 1974), pp. 436-439.

Kraeling, *Synagogue*   C. H. Kraeling, *The Synagogue: The Excavations at Dura-Europos, Final Report VIII, Part I*, with contributions by C. C. Torrey, C. B. Welles, and B. Geiger (New Haven: Yale, 1956; repr. New York: Ktav, 1979).

Kraemer, *Nessana*   C. J. Kraemer, *Excavations at Nessana, vol. III (Non-Literary Papyri)* (Princeton: Princeton University Press, 1958).

Krauss   S. Krauss, *Synagogale Altertümer* (Berlin-Vienna: B. Harz, 1922; repr. Hildesheim, 1966).

Krueger — Paulus Krueger, *Codex Justinianus* (Berlin, 1877).

Kuhn and Arav — H. W. Kuhn and R. Arav, "The Bethsaida Excavations: Historical and Archaeological Approaches," in B. A. Pearson, ed., *The Future of Early Christianity: Essays in Honor of Helmut Koester* (Minneapolis: Fortress, 1991): 77-106.

Kutscher, *Words* — E. Y. Kutscher, *Words and their History* (Jerusalem, 1961) (in Hebrew).

LA — *Liber Annus Studii Biblici Franciscani.*

LÄ — *Lexikon der Ägyptologie*, W. Helck and E. Otto, 7 vols. (Wiesbaden, 1972-1992).

Landsberger — F. Landsberger, "The Sacred Direction in Synagogue and Church," *HUCA* 28 (1957): 181-203.

Leg. ad Gaium — Philo Judaeus, *Legatio ad Gaium.*

Legat. — Philo Judaeus, *Legatio ad Gaium.*

Leon, *The Jews of Ancient Rome* — H. J. Leon, *The Jews of Ancient Rome* (Philadelphia: The Jewish Publication Society of America, 1960).

Levenson — J. Levenson, *Sinai and Zion* (San Francisco: Harper & Row, 1985).

Levine, "Ancient Synagogues" — L. I. Levine, "Ancient Synagogues—A Historical Introduction," in Levine, *ASR*, pp. 1-10.

Levine, *ASR* — L. I. Levine, ed., *Ancient Synagogues Revealed* (Jerusalem: The Israel Exploration Society, 1981).

Levine, *Caesarea* — L. I. Levine, *Roman Caesarea: An Archaeological Topographical Study, Qedem II.*, Monographs of the Institute of Archaeology, (Jerusalem: The Hebrew University, 1975).

Levine, *GLA* — L. I. Levine, ed., *The Galilee in Late Antiquity* (New York: Jewish Theological Seminary of America, 1992).

Levine, "Ḥ. 'Ammudim" — L. I. Levine, "Excavations at the Synagogue of Ḥorvat 'Ammudim," *IEJ* 32 (1982): 1-12.

Levine, "Ḥorvat ha-'Amudim" — L. I. Levine, "Excavations at Ḥorvat ha-'Amudim," in Levine, *ASR*, pp. 78-81.

Levine, "Research" — L. I. Levine, "Research of Synagogues since the 1970's," in *NEAEIHL*, vol. 1, pp. 258-261 (in Hebrew).

Levine, *Sages* — L. I. Levine, *The Rabbinic Class of Roman Palestine in Late Antiquity* (Jerusalem: Yad Izhak Ben-Zvi, 1985) (in Hebrew). English translation: *The Rabbinic Class of Roman Palestine in Late Antiquity* (New York: JTSA, 1989).

Levine, "Sages" — L. I. Levine, "The Sages and the Synagogue in Late Antiquity: The Evidence of the Galilee," in Levine, *GLA*, pp. 201-222.

Levine, "Sanctuary" — L. I. Levine, "From Community Center to Lesser Sanctuary: The Furnishings and Interior of the Ancient Synagogue," *Cathedra* 60 (June 1991): 36-84 (in Hebrew).

Levine, *SLA* — L. I. Levine, ed., *The Synagogue in Late Antiquity* (Philadelphia: American Schools of Oriental Research, 1987).

Levine, "Synagogues" — L. I. Levine, "Synagogues," in *NEAEHL*, vol. 4, pp. 1421-1424.

Liddell & Scott

H. G. Liddell, R.Scott, and Sr. H. Stuart Jones, *A Greek-English Lexicon* (Oxford: Clarendon Press, 1968).

Lieberman, *Caesarea*

S. Lieberman, *The Talmud of Caesarea*, Supplement to *Tarbiz*, vol. 2 (1931) (in Hebrew).

Lieberman, "Hazzanut,"

S. Lieberman, "Hazzanut Yannai," *Sinai* 4 (1939): 221-250 (in Hebrew).

Lieberman, *Siphre Zutta*

S. Lieberman, *Siphre Zutta* (New York: JTSA, 1968) (in Hebrew).

Lieberman, *Tosefta*

S. Lieberman, *The Tosefta* (New York: Jewish Theological Seminary of America, 1962).

Lieberman, *Tosefta ki-fshutah*

S. Lieberman, *Tosefta ki-fshutah*, 10 vols. (New York: Jewish Theological Seminary of America, 1955-1973) (in Hebrew).

Lifshitz

B. Lifshitz, *Donateurs et fondateurs dans les synagogues juives*, Cahiers de la Revue Biblique, vol. 7 (Paris, 1967).

Lifshitz, "Greek"

B. Lifshitz, "The Greek Documents from Nahal Ze'elim and Nahal Mishmar," *Yediot* 25 (1961): 66-69.

Lifshitz, "Prolegomenon"

B. Lifshitz, "Prolegomenon," in the 1975 reprint of Frey, pp. 21-104.

Lightstone

Jack N. Lightstone, *The Commerce of the Sacred: Mediation of the Divine among Jews in the Graeco-Roman Diaspora* (Chico, CA: Scholars Press, 1984).

Linder

A. Linder, *The Jews in Roman Imperial Legislation* (Detroit-Jerusalem, 1987).

Linforth, *Arts*

I. M. Linforth, *The Arts of Orpheus* (New York: Arno Press, 1973).

Liver, "Courses"

J. Liver, "Course, Priestly and Levitical Courses," *Encyclopedia Biblica*, vol. 5, pp. 569-580 (in Hebrew).

Liver, *Priests and Levites*

J. Liver, *Chapters in the History of the Priests and Levites* (Jerusalem: Magnes, 1968) (in Hebrew).

Loewenstamm, "Bashan"

S. E. Loewenstamm, "Bashan," *Encyclopedia Biblica*, vol. 2, pp. 366-370 (in Hebrew).

Loffreda, "Capernaum"

S. Loffreda, "The Late Chronology of the Synagogue of Capernaum," *IEJ* 23 (1973): 37-42. Reprinted in Levine, *ASR*, pp. 52-56.

Lyttelton, *Architecture*

M. Lyttelton, *Baroque Architecture in Classical Antiquity* (London, 1974).

m

meter.

m, M

Mishnah.

Maa.

Maaserot.

Maas.

Maaser.

MacMullen

Ramsay MacMullen, *Paganism in the Roman Empire* (New Haven: Yale University Press, 1981).

Mak.

Makkot.

Maksh.

Makshirin.

Ma'oz, "Ancient Synagogues"

Z. Ma'oz, "Ancient Synagogues of the Golan," *Biblical Archaeologist* 51 (1988): 116-128.

Ma'oz, "'Asâliyye"

Z. Ma'oz, "'Asâliyye—A Jewish Village and Ancient Synagogue in the Golan," *Teva va-Aretz* 21 (1979): 185-188 (in Hebrew).

Ma'oz, "Communities"   Z. Ma'oz, "Comments on Jewish and Christian Communities in Byzantine Palestine," *PEQ* 115 (1983): 59-68.

Ma'oz, "Dâbiyye—1"   Z. Ma'oz, "Dâbiyye," *HA* 83 (1983): 2 (in Hebrew).

Ma'oz, "Dâbiyye—2"   Z. Ma'oz, "Dâbiyye," *EASI* 2 (1983): 21.

Ma'oz, "Dâbiyye—3"   Z. Ma'oz, "Dâbiyye," in *NEAEIHL*, vol. 1, pp. 383-384 (in Hebrew).

Ma'oz, "Dabiyye—4"   Z. Ma'oz, "Dabiyye," in *NEAEHL*, vol. 1, p. 318.

Ma'oz, "'En Nashut—1"   Z. Ma'oz, "'En Nashut," in *NEAEIHL* vol. 3, pp. 1201-1203 (in Hebrew).

Ma'oz, "'En Nashut—2"   Z. Ma'oz, "'En Nashut," in *NEAEHL*, vol. 2, pp. 412-414.

Ma'oz, "'En Nashut—3"   Z. Ma'oz, "A Synagogue in 'En Nashut (Golan)," *HA* 69-71 (1979): 27-29 (in Hebrew).

Ma'oz, "Excavations"   Z. Ma'oz, "Excavations in the Ancient Synagogue at Dâbiyye," *'Atiqot* 20 (1991): 49-65.

Ma'oz, "Gamla"   Z. Ma'oz, "The Synagogue of Gamla and the Typology of Second-Temple Synagogues," Levine, *ASR*, pp. 35-41.

Ma'oz, *Golan*   Z. Ma'oz, *The Jewish Settlement and Synagogues in the Golan*, The Society for the Protection of Nature, Qasrin (Jerusalem, 1979) (in Hebrew).

Ma'oz, *Golan* (rev. ed.)   Z. Ma'oz, *The Jewish Settlement and the Synagogues in the Golan*, rev. edition (Jerusalem, 1980) (in Hebrew).

Ma'oz, "Golan—1"   Z. Ma'oz, "Golan," in *NEAEHL*, vol. 2, pp. 534-546.

Ma'oz, "Golan—2"   Z. Ma'oz, "Golan," in *NEAEIHL*, vol. 1, pp. 275-277, 286-300 (in Hebrew).

Ma'oz, "Golan Synagogues"   Z. Ma'oz, "Synagogues in the Golan," *Ariel* 50-51 (1987): 141-161 (in Hebrew).

Ma'oz, "Haspin—1"   Z. Ma'oz, "Haspin," in *NEAEIHL*, vol. 2, pp. 523-525 (in Hebrew).

Ma'oz, "Haspin—2"   Z. Ma'oz, "Haspin," in *NEAEHL*, vol. 2, pp. 586-588.

Ma'oz, "Horvat Kanaf—1"   Z. Ma'oz, "Horvat Kanaf," in *NEAEIHL*, vol. 2, pp. 807-810 (in Hebrew).

Ma'oz, "Horvat Kanaf—2"   Z. Ma'oz, "Horvat Kanaf," in *NEAEHL*, vol. 3, pp. 847-850.

Ma'oz, "Qasrin"   Z. Ma'oz, "Qasrin," *HA* 86 (1985): 2-5 (in Hebrew).

Ma'oz, "Synagogues"   Z. Ma'oz, "The Art and Architecture of the Synagogues of the Golan," in Levine, *ASR*, pp. 98-115.

Ma'oz & Killebrew, "1982/1984"   Z. Ma'oz and A. Killebrew, "Qasrein—1982/1984," *EASI* 4 (1985): 90-94.

Ma'oz & Killebrew, "1983/1984"   Z. Ma'oz and A. Killebrew, "Qasrin—1983-1984," *IEJ* 35 (1985): 289-293.

Ma'oz & Killebrew, "Ancient Qasrin"
                            Z. Ma'oz and A. Killebrew, "Ancient Qasrin: Synagogue and Village," *Biblical Archaeologist* 51 (1988): 5-19.

Ma'oz & Killebrew, "Qasrin—1"   Z. Ma'oz and A. Killebrew, "Qasrin," in *NEAEIHL*, vol. 4, pp. 1423-1428 (in Hebrew).

Ma'oz & Killebrew, "Qasrin—2"   Z. Ma'oz and A. Killebrew, "Qasrin," in *NEAEHL*, vol. 4, pp. 1219-1224.

Margalioth

Martienssen

Masada III

Mayer

Mayer & Reifenberg

Mazar, *Beth She'arim*

Mazar, *Cities*

Mazur, *Studies*

Meg.

Meiggs, *Roman Ostia*

Meil.

Meiron

"Meiron"

Meitlis, "Revua"

Men.

Meyer & Mommsen

Meyers, "Current State"

Meyers, "Nabratein"

Meyers, *Khirbet Shema'*

Meyers, "Khirbet Shema'"

Meyers, *Menorah*

Meyers, "Synagogue Architecture"

M. Margalioth, *Encyclopedia of Talmudic and Geonic Literature*, 2 vols. (Tel Aviv: Joshua Chachik, 1970) (in Hebrew).

Rex D. Martienssen, *The Idea of Space in Greek Architecture* (Johannesburg: Witwatersrand University Press, 1956).

E. Netzer, *The Buildings. Stratigraphy and Architecture, Masada III, The Yigael Yadin Excavations 1963-1965* (Jerusalem: IES, 1991).

G. Mayer, *Index Philoneus* (Berlin-New York, 1974).

L. A. Mayer and A. Reifenberg, "The Synagogue of Eshtemoa-Preliminary Report," *JPOS* 19 (1939): 314-326.

B. Mazar (Maisler), *Beth She'arim*, vol. 1 (Jerusalem, 1973).

B. Mazar, *Cities and Districts in Eretz-Israel* (Jerusalem: Bialik Institute & IES, 1975) (in Hebrew).

Belle D. Mazur, *Studies on Jewry in Greece* (Athens, 1935).

Megillah.

R. Meiggs, *Roman Ostia*, 2nd ed. (Oxford: Clarendon, 1973).

Meilah.

Eric M. Meyers, James F. Strange, Carol L. Meyers, *Excavations at Ancient Meiron, Upper Galilee, Israel 1971-72, 1974-75, 1977*, Meiron Excavation Project 3 (Cambridge, MA: American Schools of Oriental Research, 1981).

Eric M. Meyers, James F. Strange, and Dennis E. Groh, "The Meiron Excavation Project: Archaeological Survey in Galilee and Golan, 1976," *BASOR* 230 (1978): 1-24.

I. Meitlis, "The Significance of the 'Revua' in Qaṣrin," *Tarbiz* 53 (1984): 465-466 (in Hebrew).

Menahot.

See Mommsen.

E. M. Meyers, "The Current State of Galilean Synagogue Studies," in Levine, *SLA*, pp. 127-137.

E. M. Meyers, "Nabratein," in *NEAEHL*, vol. 3, pp. 1077-1079.

E. M. Meyers, A. T. Kraabel, J. F. Strange, *Ancient Synagogue Excavations at Khirbet Shema', Upper Galilee, Israel 1970—1972*, Annual of the American Schools of Oriental Research, vol. 42 (Durham, NC: Duke University Press for the ASOR, 1976).

E. M. Meyers, "Khirbet Shema'—The Settlement and the Synagogue," *Qadmoniot* 5 (1972): 58-61 (in Hebrew).

C. L. Meyers, *The Tabernacle Menorah: A Synthetic Study of a Symbol from the Biblical Cult* (Missoula, Montana: Scholars Press, 1976).

E. M. Meyers, "Synagogue Architecture," *Interpreter's*

	Dictionary of the Bible: Supplement (New York/Nashville, 1976), pp. 842-844.
MGWJ	*Monatsschrift für Geschichte unnd Wissenschaft des Judentums.*
Mid.	Middot.
Miq.	Miqvaot.
Mitten, "A New Look"	D. G. Mitten, "A New Look at Ancient Sardis," *BA* 29 (1966): 38-68.
Moe, "Cross and Menorah"	D. L. Moe, "The Cross and the Menorah," *Archaeology* 30 (1977): 148-157.
Mommsen	Th. Mommsen & P. M. Meyer, *Codex Theodosianus*, 3rd ed. (Berolini: Wiedmannos, 1962).
Moses	Philo Judaeus, *On the Life of Moses.*
MQ	Moed Qatan.
MS	Maaser Sheni.
Murray, "Christian Orpheus"	Sister Charles Murray, "The Christian Orpheus, " *CA* 26 (1977): 19-27.
Naveh	Joseph Naveh, "Ancient Synagogue Inscriptions," in Levine, *ASR*, pp. 133-139.
Naveh, "Aramaic and Hebrew"	J. Naveh, "The Aramaic and Hebrew Inscriptions from Ancient Synagogues," *Eretz-Israel* 20 (1989): 302-310 (in Hebrew).
Naveh, *Mosaic*	J. Naveh, *On Stone and Mosaic: The Aramaic and Hebrew Inscriptions from Ancient Synagogues* (Jerusalem: IES & Carta, 1978) (in Hebrew).
Naveh and Shaked	J. Naveh and S. Shaked, *Amulets and Magic Bowls: Aramaic Incantations of Late Antiquity* (Jerusalem: Magnes and Leiden: E. J. Brill, 1985).
Naz.	Nazir.
NEAEHL	*The New Encyclopedia of Archaeological Excavations in the Holy Land*, E. Stern, ed., 4 vols. (New York: Simon & Schuster and Jerusalem: IES, 1993).
NEAEIHL	*The New Encyclopedia of Archaeological Excavations in the Holy Land*, E. Stern, ed., 4 vols. (Jerusalem: IES, Ministry of Defense and Carta, 1992) (in Hebrew).
Ned.	Nedarim.
Neg.	Negaim.
Neusner, *Appointed Times*	J. Neusner, *A History of the Mishnaic Law of Appointed Times*, 5 vols., Studies in Judaism in Late Antiquity, vol. 34 (Leiden: Brill, 1973).
Neusner, *Evidence*	J. Neusner, *Judaism: The Evidence of the Mishnah* (Chicago, 1981).
Neusner, "Forward"	J. Neusner, "Editor's Forward," in E. R. Goodenough, *Jewish Symbols in the Greco-Roman Period*, abridged edition by J. Neusner (Princeton: Princeton University Press, 1988)
Neusner, "Goodenough"	J. Neusner, "Goodenough's Contribution to the Study of Judaism," in Neusner, *Symbol*, pp. 210-234.
Neusner, *Messiah*	J. Neusner, *Messiah in Context* (Philadelphia: Fortress, 1984).

Neusner, *Religions*   J. Neusner, ed., *Religions in Antiquity: Essays in Memory of Erwin Ramsdell Goodenough*, Studies in the History of Religions, vol. 14 (Leiden: Brill, 1968).

Neusner, *Symbol*   J. Neusner, *Symbol and Theology in Early Judaism* (Minneapolis: Fortress Press, 1992).

Neusner, Green, and Frerichs, *Messiahs*
                                        J. Neusner, W. S Green and E. Frerichs, eds. *Judaisms and their Messiahs at the Turn of the Christian Era* (Cambridge: Cambridge, 1987).

New Encyclopedia   See *NEAEHL*.

Nid.   Niddah.

Nock, *Essays*   A. D. Nock, *Essays on Religion and the Ancient World* (Oxford: Clarendon, 1972), 2 vols.

Nötscher, *Jeremias*   F. Nötscher, *Das buch Jeremias* (Bonn: Peter Hanstein, 1934).

Nun, *Kinneret*   M. Nun, *Sea of Kinneret: A Monograph* (Tel Aviv: Hakibbutz Hameuchad, 1977) (in Hebrew).

Nun, "Kinneret"   M. Nun, "Ancient Harbors and Jetties in the Lake of Kinneret," *Teva va-Aretz* 16 (1974): 212-218 (in Hebrew).

Oesterley & Robinson   W. O. E. Oesterley and T. H. Robinson, *Hebrew Religion: Its Origin and Development* (London, 1930; repr. London: S.P.C.K., 1951).

OGIS   *Orientis Graeci Inscriptiones Selectae*.

Oh.   Ohalot.

Oliphant, *Haifa*   L. Oliphant, *Haifa or Life in Modern Palestine* (Edinburgh & London: W. Blackwood, 1887).

Oliphant, "Jaulan"   L. Oliphant, "A Trip to the North-East of Lake Tiberias, in Jaulan," in G. Schumacher, *Across the Jordan* (London: Richard Bentley, 1886), pp. 243-267.

Oliphant, "Lake Tiberias"   L. Oliphant, "Explorations North-East of Lake Tiberias and in Jaulan," *PEFQS* (1885): 82-93.

Oliphant, "New Discoveries"   L. Oliphant, "New Discoveries," *PEFQS* (1886): 73-81.

Omansky, *Sages*   J. Omansky, *Sages of the Talmud* (Jerusalem: Mossad Harav Kook, 1952) (in Hebrew).

Onomastikon   Eusebius, *Das Onomastikon der Biblischen Ortsnamen*, trans. E. Klostermann (Leipzig, 1904).

Oppenheimer, *Am Ha-Aretz*   A. Oppenheimer, *The Am Ha-Aretz: A Study in the Social History of the Jewish People in the Hellenistic-Roman Period* (Leiden: E. J. Brill, 1977).

Oppenheimer, "Study"   A. Oppenheimer, "The Uniqueness of the House of Study," *Cathedra* 18 (1981): 45-48.

Oppenheimer, Isaac & Lecker   A. Oppenheimer, in collaboration with B. Isaac and M. Lecker, *Babylonia Judaica in the Talmudic Period* (Wiesbaden: L. Reichert, 1983).

Oppenheimer, Rappaport and Stern
                                        A. Oppenheimer, U. Rappaport and M. Stern, eds., *Jerusalem in the Second Temple Period, A. Schalit Memorial Volume* (Jerusalem: Yad Izhak Ben-Zvi & Ministry of Defense, 1980) (in Hebrew).

Or.   Orlah.

Or. Lov. Per.	*Orientalia Lovaniensa Periodica.*
Orfali, "Capharnaum"	Pere Orfali, "Une nouvelle inscription grecque découverte à Capharnaüm," *JPOS* 6 (1926): 159-163.
OTP	J. H. Charlesworth, *The Old Testament Pseudepigrapha*, 2 vols. (Garden City, NY: Double-day, 1983-1985).
Otto	Rudolf Otto, *Das Heilige* (1919). See also the English translation, *The Idea of the Holy*, translated by J. W. Harvey, 2nd. ed. (London: Oxford, 1923; repr. 1973).
Ovadiah, "Gaza"	A. Ovadiah, "Excavations in the area of the Ancient Synagogue at Gaza," *IEJ* 19 (1969): 193-198.
Ovadiah, *MPI*	Ruth and Asher Ovadiah, *Hellenistic, Roman and Early Byzantine Mosaic Pavements in Israel*, Biblioteca archeologica, vol. 6 (Roma: "L'ERMA" de Bretschneider, 1987).
Ovadiah, "Sarophagus"	A. Ovadiah, "A Jewish Sarcophagus at Tiberias," *Yediot* 31 (1967): 225-230 (in Hebrew).
Ovadiah, "Synagogue"	A. Ovadiah, "The Synagogue at Gaza" in Levine, *ASR*, pp. 129-132.
Ovadiah and Michaeli	A. Ovadiah and T. Michaeli, "Observations on the Origin of the Architectual Plan of Ancient Synagogues," *JJS* 38, no. 2 (1987): 234-241.
PAAJR	*Proceedings of the American Academy for Jewish Research.*
Par.	Parah.
Parker	Robert Parker, *Miasma: Pollution and Purification in Greek Religion* (New York: Oxford University Press, 1983).
Parkes	J. Parkes, *The Conflict of the Church and the Synagogue* (London: Soncino, 1934).
Pauly-Wissowa	Pauly-Wissowa, *Real-Encyclopädie der classischen Altertumswissenschaft*, 33 vols. (Stuttgart, 1903-1978; repr. Munich, 1962-1987, 16 vols.).
Pedley, *Ancient Literary Sources on Sardis*	
	Pedley, J. G., *Ancient Literary Sources on Sardis*, Archaeological Exploration of Sardis, Monograph 2 (Cambridge, 1972).
PEFQS	*Palestine Exploration Fund Quarterly Statement.*
PEQ	*Palestine Exploration Quarterly.*
Pes.	Pesahim.
Philo, *Flaccum*	Philo Judaeus, *In Flaccum.*
Philo, *Gaius*	Philo Judaeus, *The Embassy to Gaius.*
Pixner, "Bethsaida"	B. Pixner, "Searching for the New Testament Site of Bethsaida," *Biblical Archaeologist* 48 (1985): 207-216.
Porat, "Golan"	P. Porat, "A New Boundary-Stone from the Southern Golan," *Scripta Classica Israelica* 10 (1989-90): 130-133.
Porten	B. Porten, *Archives from Elephantine* (Berkeley-Los Angeles: University of California Press, 1968).
Qad	*Qadmoniot.*
QDAP	*Quarterly of the Department of Antiquities in Palestine.*
Qin.	Qinnim.

Rabello, "Ostia"	A. M. Rabello, "Ostia," *EJ*, vol. 12, pp. 1506-1509.
Rabinowitz Bulletin	*Bulletin, Louis M. Rabinowitz Fund for the Exploration of Ancient Synagogues*, 3 vols. (Jerusalem, 1949, 1951, 1960).
Rabinowitz, "Sefarad"	I. Rabinowitz, "Sefarad," *Encyclopaedia Biblica*, vol. 5, pp. 1100-1103 (in Hebrew).
RB	*Revue Biblique.*
REG	*Revue des études grecques.*
Reicke, *New Testament*	Bo Reicke, *The New Testament Era*, D. E. Green, tr. (London, 1969) (German edn., 1964).
REJ	*Revue des études juives.*
Restoration	H. Tadmor, I. Ephal, and J. C. Greenfeld, eds., *The Restoration: The Persian Period* (Jerusalem: Am Oved, 1983) (in Hebrew).
RH	Rosh Hashannah.
Rivkin, "Nonexistence"	E. Rivkin, "Ben Sira and the Nonexistence of the Synagogue: A Study in Historical Method," in D. J. Silver, ed., *In the Time of Harvest: Essays in Honor of Abba Hillel Silver on the Occasion of his 70th Birthday* (New York/London: Macmillan, 1963), pp. 320-54.
Robert, *Bull. epigr.*	*Bulletin Epigraphique.*
Robert, "Inscriptions grecques"	L. Robert, "Inscriptions grecques de Side," *RPh* 32 (1958): 36-47.
Robert, *Nouvelles inscriptions*	L. Robert, *Nouvelles inscriptions de Sardes I* (Paris: Adrien Maisonneuve, 1964).
Robert & Robert	Jeanne and Louis Robert, "Inscriptions et reliefs d'Asie Mineure," *Hellenica* 9 (1950): 47-48.
Roberts, "Hellenism"	Bleddyn J. Roberts, "Hellenism and Judaism," in J. Gwyn Griffiths, ed., *Cefndir y Testament Newydd* (Llandysul, 1966).
Robinson	E. Robinson, *Biblical Researches in Palestine*, 2 vols. (Boston, 1860).
Rosenthal, *Aramaic*	F. Rosenthal, *A Grammar of Biblical Aramaic* (Wiesbaden: Otto Harrassowitz, 1974).
Roth-Gerson, *Greek Inscriptions*	L. Roth-Gerson, *The Greek Inscriptions from the Synagogues in Eretz-Israel* (Jerusalem: Yad Izhak Ben-Zvi, 1987) (in Hebrew).
RPh	*Revue de Philologie.*
Safrai, *Community*	Z. Safrai, *The Jewish Community* (Jerusalem: Zalman Shazar Center, in press).
Safrai, *Compendia*	S. Safrai, "The Synagogue," in *Compendia Rerum Judaicarum*, vol. 2 (Assen: Van Gorcum, 1976), pp. 908-944.
Safrai, "Functions"	Z. Safrai, "Communal Functions of the Synagogue in Eretz Israel in the Period of the Mishnah and Talmud," in Z. Safrai, ed., *The Synagogue in the Period of the Mishnah and Talmud* (Jerusalem: Zalman Shazar Center, 1986), pp. 105-123 (in Hebrew).
Safrai, "Gathering"	S. Safrai, "Gathering in the Synagogues on Festivals, Sabbaths and Weekdays," in Hachlili, *Ancient Synagogues*, pp. 7-15.

Safrai, "Halakah"	S. Safrai, "Halakah and Reality," *Cathedra* 18 (1981): 45-48 (in Hebrew).
Safrai, "Ritual"	S. Safrai, "The Ritual in the Second Temple," in M. Avi-Yonah, ed., *Sepher Yerushalayim*, vol. 1 (Jerusalem and Tel Aviv: Bialik Institute & Dvir, 1956), pp. 370-371 (in Hebrew).
Safrai, *Second Temple*	S. Safrai, *In the Late Second Temple and the Mishnah Periods* (Jerusalem: Zalman Shazar Center, 1983) (in Hebrew).
Safrai, "Security"	Z. Safrai, "The Security System in the Jewish City," *Cathedra* 22 (1982): 43-50 (in Hebrew).
Safrai, *Settlement*	Z. Safrai, *The Jewish Settlement in the Golan After the Destruction of the Second Temple* (Qesheth, Golan Heights, 1978) (in Hebrew).
Safrai, "Synagogue"	S. Safrai, "The Synagogue and the Worship of God Therein," in M. Avi-Yonah and Z. Baras, eds., *Society and Religion in the Days of the Second Temple*, A History of the Jewish People (Jerusalem, 1983) pp. 44-64, 259-259 (in Hebrew). English translation: (Jerusalem, 1977), pp. 65-98, 338-345.
Safrai, "Temple"	S. Safrai, "The Temple and the Synagogue," in A. Kasher, A. Oppenheimer, and U. Rappaport, eds., *Synagogues in Antiquity*, (Jerusalem: Yad Izhak Ben Zvi, 1987), pp. 31-51 (in Hebrew).
Safrai, "Town"	S. Safrai, "The Jewish Town in the Land of Israel in the Period of the Mishnah and the Talmud" in *The Town and the Community*, (Jerusalem: The Historical Society of Israel, 1967), pp. 227-236 (in Hebrew).
Safrai and Stern, *Compendia*	S. Safrai, and M. Stern, eds., *Compendia Rerum Iudaicarum ad Novum Testamentum*, vol. I.1 (Assen, 1974). Published in the United States under the title *The Jewish People in the First Century* (Philadelphia, 1974).
Saller, *Second Revised Calalogue*	S. J. Saller, *Second Revised Catalogue of the Ancient Synagogues of the Holy Land*, Studium Biblicum Franciscanum, Collectio minor 6 (Jerusalem, 1972).
Salzmann (Avi-Yonah)	M. C. Salzmann, "Bibliography of M. Avi-Yonah," *IEJ* 24 (1974): 287-315.
San.	Sanhedrin.
Sanders, *Judaism*	E. P. Sanders, *Judaism: Practice and Belief, 63 BCE-66 CE* (Philadelphia: Trinity Press International, 1992).
Schalit, *Josephus*	A. Schalit, *Namenwörterbuch zu Flavius Josephus* (Leiden: E. J. Brill, 1968).
Schapiro	Meyer Schapiro, "Ancient Mosaics in Israel: Late Antique Art—Pagan, Jewish, and Christian," in *Late Antique, Early Christian and Mediaeval Art* (New York: George Braziller, Inc., 1978), pp. 20-33.
Schede, *Die Ruinen*	Martin Schede, *Die Ruinen von Priene*, 2nd ed. (Berlin: W. DeGruyter, 1964).
Schrage, "Synagoge"	W. Schrage, "Synagoge," *Theological Dictionary of the New Testament*, vol. 7 (Grand Rapids, MI, 1971), pp. 798-852.
Schultze, *Altchristliche Städte*	V. Schultze, *Altchristliche Städte und Landschaften*, II. Kleinasien (Gütersloh, 1922-1926).

Schumacher, "Correspondenzen"	G. Schumacher, "Correspondenzen," *ZDPV* 8 (1885): 333-334.
Schumacher, "Dscholan"	G. Schumacher, "Der Dscholan," *ZDPV* 9 (1886): 165-363.
Schumacher, "Ergänzungen"	G. Schumacher, "Ergänzungen zu meiner Karte des Dschôlân und westlichen Haurân," *ZDPV* 22 (1899): 178-188.
Schumacher, *Jaulân*	G. Schumacher, *The Jaulân* (London: Richard Bentley, 1888).
Schumacher, "Jedûr"	G. Schumacher, "Notes from Jedûr," *PEFQS* (1897): 190-195.
Schumacher, *Jordan*	G. Schumacher, *Across the Jordan: An Exploration and Survey of Part of Hauran and Jaulân* (London: Richard Bentley, 1886).
Schumacher, "Ostjordanlande"	G. Schumacher, "Unsere Arbeiten in Ostjordanlande," *ZDPV* 40 (1917): 143-170.
Schumacher, "Tiberias"	G. Schumacher, "Von Tiberias zum Hûle-See," *ZDPV* 13 (1890): 65-75.
Schürer	E. Schürer, *The History of the Jewish People in the Age of Jesus Christ*, G. Vermes and F. Millar, eds., 3 vols. (Edinburgh: T&T Clark, 1973-1987).
Schwabe	Moshe Schwabe, "Greek Inscriptions from Jerusalem," in M. Avi-Yonah, ed., *Sepher Yerushalayim* (Jerusalem & Tel Aviv: The Bialik Institute and Dvir Publishing House, 1956), vol. 1, pp. 358-368 (in Hebrew).
Schwabe, "Golan"	M. Schwabe, "Commentaries to the Greek Inscriptions in the Golan," *Zion* 5 (1933): 189-190 (in Hebrew).
Schwabe and Lifshitz	M. Schwabe and B. Lifshitz, *Beth She'arim, vol. II (The Greek Inscriptions)* (Jerusalem: IES & Massada Press, 1974).
Scully	Vincent Scully, *The Earth, the Temple, and the Gods: Greek Sacred Architecture* (New Haven: Yale University Press, 1962).
Seager, "The Architecture"	A. R. Seager, "The Architecture of the Dura and Sardis Synagogues," in Gutmann, *Dura-Europos*, pp. 79-116. Reprinted in Gutmann, *Synagogue*, pp. 149-193.
Seager, "The Building History"	A. R. Seager, "The Building History of the Sardis Synagogue," *AJA* 76 (1972): 425-435.
Seager, "Historiography"	A. R. Seager, "The Recent Historiography of Ancient Synagogue Architecture," in Hachlili, *Ancient Synagogues*, pp. 85-92.
Seager, *The Synagogue*	A. R. Seager, et al., *The Synagogue and its Setting*, Archaeological Exploration of Sardis, Report 5 (Cambridge, forthcoming).
SEG	*Supplementum Epigraphicum Graecum.*
Segal, "Warning"	P. Segal, "The Penalty of the Warning Inscription from the Temple of Jerusalem," *IEJ* 39 (1989): 79-84.
Shab.	Shabbat.
Shabu.	Shabuot.
Shanks and Mazar	H. Shanks and B. Mazar, eds., *Recent Archaeology in the Land of Israel* (Washington and Jerusalem: Biblical

	Archaeology Society and Israel Exploration Society, 1981).
Shebi.	Shebiit.
Sheq.	Sheqalim.
Shiloh, "Torah Scrolls"	Y. Shiloh, "Torah Scrolls and the Menorah Plaque from Sardis," *IEJ* 18 (1968): 51-57.
SIG	*Sylloge Inscriptionum Graecarum*, ed. W. Dittenberger, 3rd ed., 4 vols. (Leipzig, 1915-1924).
Simon, "L'angelolatrie"	M. Simon, "Remarques sur l'angelolatrie juive au debut de l'ere chretienne," *CRAI* (1971), pp. 120-132.
Simon, "Synagogues"	M. Simon, "Remarques sur les synagogues a images de Doura et de Palestine," in M. Simon, *Recherches d'Histoire Judeo-Chretienne*, Etudes juives 6 (Paris, 1962), pp. 188-198, 204-208.
Simons, *The Geographical and Topographical Texts*	
	J. Simons, *The Geographical and Topographical Texts of the Old Testament* (Leiden: E. J. Brill, 1959).
Simpson-Housley & Scott	P. Simpson-Housley and J. Scott, *Sacred Places and Profane Spaces: Essays in the Geographics of Judaism, Christianity, and Islam* (New York: Greenwood Press, 1991).
Skinner, *Genesis*	J. Skinner, *A Critcal and Exegetical Commentary on Genesis*, International Critical Commentary (New York: Charles Scribner's Sons, 1910).
Smallwood	E. M. Smallwood, *The Jews under Roman Rule* (Leiden: E. J. Brill, 1976).
Smallwood, *Philo*	E. M. Smallwood, *Philonis Alexandrini Legatio ad Gaium* (Leiden: E. J. Brill, 1961).
Smith, "Jewish Symbols"	Morton Smith, "Goodenough's JEWISH SYMBOLS in Retrospect," *JBL* 86 (1967): 53-68, reprinted in Gutmann, *Synagogue*, pp. 194-209.
Smith, *Map*	Jonathan Z. Smith, *Map is Not Territory* (Leiden: E.J. Brill, 1978).
Smith, *Place*	Jonathan Z. Smith, *To Take Place: Toward Theory in Ritual* (Chicago: The University of Chicago Press, 1987).
Sokoloff, *Dictionary*	M. Sokoloff, *A Dictionary of Jewish Aramaic of the Byzantine Period* (Ramat Gan: Bar-Ilan University Press, 1990).
Sonne, "Synagogue"	I. Sonne, "Synagogue," *Interpreter's Dictionary of the Bible* (1962), vol. 4, pp. 476-491.
Sot.	Sotah.
Special Laws	Philo, *On the Special Laws*.
Spencer, *Temple*	Patricia Spencer, *The Egyptian Temple. A Lexicographical Study* (London, 1984).
Sperber, "Menorah"	Daniel Sperber, "The History of the Menorah," *JJS* 16 (1965): 135-159.
Squarciapino, "*archisynagogus*,"	M. Floriani Squarciapino, "Plotius Fortunatus *archisynagogus*," *Rassegna mensile di Israel* 36 (1970): 183-191.
Squarciapino, *La sinagoga*	M. Floriani Squarciapino, *La Sinagoga di Ostia* (Rome, 1964).

Squarciapino, "La sinagoga"	M. Floriani Squarciapino, "La sinagoga di Ostia: Seconda Campagna di Scavo," in *Atti del VI Congresso intern. di arch. crist. 1962* (Rome, 1965), pp. 299-315.
Squarciapino, "The Synagogue".	M. Floriani Squarciapino, "The Synagogue at Ostia," *Archaeology* 16 (1963): 194-203.
Stein, *Philo*	Edmund Stein, *Die allegorische Exegese des Philo aus Alexandreia* (Giessen, 1929).
Stern, "Judea"	M. Stern, "Judaea and her Neighbors in the Days of Alexander Jannaeus," in L. I. Levine, ed., *The Jerusalem Cathedra*, vol. 1 (Detroit: Wayne State & Jerusalem: Yad Izhak Ben-Zvi, 1981), pp. 22-46.
Stern, "Orphée"	H. Stern, "Orphée in l'Art Paléochrétien," *Cahiers archéologiques* 23 (1974): 1-16.
Stern, "Orpheus"	H. Stern, "The Orpheus in the Synagogue of Dura-Europos," *Journal of the Warburg and Courtauld Institutes*, 21, nos. 1-2 (1958):1-6.
Suk.	Sukkah.
Sukenik, *ASPG*	E. L. Sukenik, *Ancient Synagogues in Palestine and Greece*, The Schweich Lectures on Biblical Archaeology 1930 (London: Oxford University Press, 1934).
Sukenik, *Beth Alpha*	E. L. Sukenik, *The Ancient Synagogue at Beth Alpha* (Jerusalem: University Press, 1932).
Sukenik, *Dura-Europos*	E. L. Sukenik, *The Synagogue of Dura-Europos and its Paintings* (Jerusalem: Bialik Institute, 1947) (in Hebrew).
Sukenik, *el-Ḥammeh*	E. L. Sukenik, *The Ancient Synagogue of el-Ḥammeh* (Jerusalem: R. Mass, 1935).
Sukenik, "el-Ḥammeh"	E. L. Sukenik, "The Ancient Synagogue of el-Ḥammeh," *JPOS* 15 (1935): 101-180 [=Sukenik, *el-Ḥammeh*].
Sukenik, "Hammath-by-Gadara"	E. L. Sukenik, "The Ancient Synagogue of Hammath-by-Gadara," *Journal of the Jewish Palestine Exploration Society* 3 (1934-35): 41-61 (in Hebrew).
Sukenik, "Khirbet Kànef"	E. L. Sukenik, "The Ancient Synagogue at Khirbet Kànef in the Golan," *Journal of the Jewish Palestine Exploration Society* 3 (1934-35): 74-80 (in Hebrew).
Sukenik, "The Present State"	E. L. Sukenik, "The Present State of Ancient Synagogue Studies," in *Rabinowitz Bulletin*, vol. 1, pp. 7-23.
Sussmann, "Beth-Shean"	Y. Sussmann, "A Halakic Inscription from the Beth-Shean Valley," *Tarbiz* 43 (1973-74): 88-158 (in Hebrew).
Sussmann, "Rehob"	Y. Sussmann, "The Inscription in the Synagogue at Rehob," in Levine, *ASR*, pp. 146-153.
SymbOslo	*Symbolae Osloenses.*
Taa.	Taanit.
Tam.	Tamid.
TAPA	*Transactions and Proceedings. American Philological Association.*
Tcherikover, *Jews*	V. Tcherikover, *The Jews in Egypt in the Hellenistic-Roman Age in the Light of the Papyri*, 2nd rev. ed. (Jerusalem: Magness, 1963) (in Hebrew).
Tem.	Temurah.

Ter.	Terumot.
TLZ	*Theologische Literaturzeitung.*
Toh.	Tohorot.
Tos., tos.	Tosefta.
Trendall, *Shellal*	A. D. Trendall, *The Shellal Mosaic* (Canberra: Australian War Memorial, 1957).
Tsafrir	Y. Tsafrir et al., eds., *Eretz-Israel from the Destruction of the Second Temple until the Islamic Conquest: II: Archaeology and Art* (Jerusalem: Yad Izhak Ben-Zvi, 1985) (in Hebrew).
Tsafrir, "Synagogues"	Y. Tsafrir, "The Byzantine Setting and its Influence on Ancient Synagogues," in Levine, *SLA*, pp. 147-157.
TY	Tebul Yom.
Tzaferis, "Ma'oz Hayyim"	V. Tzaferis, "The Ancient Synagogue at Ma'oz Hayyim," *IEJ* 32 (1982): 215-244.
Tzaferis and Bar-Lev	V. Tzaferis and S. Bar-Lev, "A Byzantine Inscription from Khisfin," *'Atiqot* 11 (1976): 114-115.
Tzori	N. Tzori, "The Ancient Synagogue at Bet-Shean," *EI* 8 (1967): 149-167 (in Hebrew).
Uq.	Uqsin.
Urbach, "Idolatry"	E. E. Urbach, "The Rabbinical Laws of Idolatry in the Second and Third Centuries in the Light of Archaeological and Historical Facts," *IEJ* 9, no. 3 (1959): 149-245.
Urbach, "Mishmarot"	E. E. Urbach, "Mishmarot and Ma'amadot," *Tarbiz* 42 (1972-73): 304-327 (in Hebrew).
Urbach, *Sages*	E. E. Urbach, *The Sages: Their Concepts and Beliefs* (Jerusalem: Magnes, 1975).
Urman, "Bar Qappara—1"	D. Urman, "Regarding the Location of the *Batei-Midrash* of Bar Qappara and Rabbi Hoshaya Rabbah," *Proceedings of the Eight World Congress of Jewish Studies: Division B-The History of the Jewish People* (Jerusalem: World Union of Jewish Studies, 1982), pp. 9-15 (in Hebrew).
Urman, "Bar Qappara—2"	D. Urman, "The Location of the *Batei-Midrash* of Bar Qappara and Rabbi Hoshaya Rabbah," in M. Stern, ed., *Nation and History: Studies in the History of the Jewish People*, vol. 1 (Jerusalem: Zalman Shazar Center, 1983), pp. 163-172 (in Hebrew).
Urman, "Beth Guvrin"	D. Urman, "Beth Guvrin: A History of Mixed Population during the Period of the Mishnah and Talmud," in D. Urman and E. Stern, eds., *Man and Environment in the Southern Shefelah: Studies in Regional Geography and History*, (Ramat-Gan: Massada Press, 1988), pp. 151-162 (in Hebrew).
Urman, "Dabûra Inscriptions—1"	D. Urman, "Jewish Inscriptions from Dabûra in the Golan," *Tarbiz* 40 (1971): 399-408 (in Hebrew).
Urman, "Dabûra Inscriptions—2"	D. Urman, "Jewish Inscriptions from Dabûra in the Golan," *Qadmoniot* 4 (1971): 131-133 (in Hebrew).
Urman, "Dabûra Inscriptions—3"	D. Urman, "Jewish Inscriptions from Dabbura in the Golan," *IEJ* 22 (1972): 16-23.

Urman, "Dabûra Inscriptions—4" D. Urman, "Jewish Inscriptions from the Village of Dabûra in the Golan," in J. Naveh, ed., *A Jewish Epigraphy Reader* (Jerusalem: Magnes, 1981), pp. 72-81 (in Hebrew).

Urman, "Dabbura Inscriptions—5"
D. Urman, "Jewish Inscriptions from the Village of Dabbura in the Golan," in Levine, *ASR*, pp. 154-156.

Urman, "Economy" D. Urman, "The Economy of Jewish Communities in the Golan in the Mishnah and Talmud Period," in N. Gross, ed., *Jews in Economic Life-Collected Essays in Memory of Arkadius Kahan* (Jerusalem: Zalman Shazar Center, 1985), pp. 35-66 (in Hebrew).

Urman, "Eliezer ha-Qappar" D. Urman, "Rabbi Eliezer ha-Qappar and Bar Qappara—Father and Son?" *Beer-Sheva* 2 (1985): 7-25 (in Hebrew).

Urman, *Golan* D. Urman, *The Golan: A profile of a region during the Roman and Byzantine periods*, BAR International Series #269 (Oxford: BAR, 1985).

Urman, "Golan—1" D. Urman, "The Golan," *HA* 30 (1969): 2-4 (in Hebrew).

Urman, "Golan—2" D. Urman, "The Golan," *HA* 33 (1970): 10-12 (in Hebrew).

Urman, "Golan—3" D. Urman, "The Golan," *HA* 34-35 (1970): 4-6 (in Hebrew).

Urman, "Golan—4" D. Urman, "The Golan," *HA* 36 (1970): 1-4 (in Hebrew).

Urman, "Golan—5" D. Urman, "The Golan," *HA* 37 (1971): 1 (in Hebrew).
Urman, "Golan—6" D. Urman, "The Golan," *HA* 38 (1971): 1-4 (in Hebrew).

Urman, "Golan—7" D. Urman, "The Golan," *HA* 41-42 (1972): 1-3 (in Hebrew).

Urman, "Hellenistic" D. Urman, "Golan—Hellenistic to Ottoman Periods," in *EAEIHL*, vol. 2, pp. 456-467.

Urman, "Kafr Nafâkh" D. Urman, "Kafr Nafâkh," *HA* 56 (1976): 3-4 (in Hebrew).

Urman, "Kursi" D. Urman, "Kursi—The Site of the Miracle of the Swine," *Dapim* (May 1972): 1-12 (in Hebrew).

Urman, "Lintel" D. Urman, "The Lintel of the School (Beth-Midrash) of Rabbi Eliezer ha-Qappar," *HA* 30 (1969): 1-2 (in Hebrew).

Urman, *List* D. Urman, *List of Historical Sites in the Golan Heights*, The Headquarters of the Military Government in the Golan Heights (Quneitra, 1971) (in Hebrew).

Urman, "Qaṣrin" D. Urman, "Qaṣrin," *HA* 56 (1976): 2-3 (in Hebrew).
Urman, "Qaṣrin Inscriptions" D. Urman, "Jewish Inscriptions of the Mishnah and Talmud Period from Qaṣrin in the Golan," *Tarbiz* 53 (1984): 513-545 (in Hebrew).

Urman, "Qaṣrin Synagogue" D. Urman, "The Synagogue at Qaṣrin," *HA* 39 (1971): 8 (in Hebrew).

Urman, "Synagogue Sites" D. Urman, "Ancient Synagogue Sites in the Southern Golan Heights and the Eastern Shore of the Sea of Galilee," *Dapim* (May 1972): 13-30 (in Hebrew).

Urman, "Toponym Golan"   D. Urman, "The Usage of the Toponym Golan in
                                Josephus' Writings," in U. Rappaport, ed., *Josephus
                                Flavius—Historian of Eretz-Israel in the Hellenistic-
                                Roman Period* (Jerusalem: Yad Izhak Ben-Zvi, 1982),
                                pp. 6-12 (in Hebrew—for an English summary, see pp.
                                I-III).

Urman, "Unclean Spirit"   D. Urman, "The Site of the Miracle of the Man with the
                                Unclean Spirit," *Christian News from Israel* 22 (1971):
                                72-76.

van der Leeuw   Gerardus van der Leeuw, *Phänomenologie der Religion*,
                                2nd ed. (Tübingen, 1955). English translation: *Religion
                                in essence & manifestation: a study in phenomenology*,
                                translated by J. E. Turner (London: G. Allen & Unwin,
                                Ltd., 1938).

Vita   Flavius Josephus, *Life.*

Vita Mos.   Philo Judaeus, *Life of Moses.*

von Rad, *Genesis*   G. von Rad, *Genesis: A Commentary*, Old Testament
                                Library (Philadelphia: Westminster, 1972).

VT   *Vetus Testamentum.*

VTsup   *Vetus Testamentum. Supplement.*

War   Flavius Josephus, *The Jewish War.*

Warden, *Orpheus*   J. Warden, *Orpheus: The Metamorphoses of a Myth*
                                (Toronto: U. Toronto Press, 1982).

Weill, "David"   R. Weill, "La cite de David," *REJ* 70 (1920): 30-34.

White   L. M. White, *Building God's House in the Roman World*
                                (Baltimore: Johns Hopkins University Press: 1990).

Wiegand and Schrader, *Priene* T. Wiegand, and H. Schrader, *Priene: Ergebnisse der
                                Ausgrabungen understand Untersuchungen in den
                                Jahren 1895-1898* (Berlin, 1904).

Wilken, "Melito"   R. L. Wilken, "Melito, the Jewish Community at Sardis,
                                and the Sacrifice of Isaac," *Theological Studies* 37
                                (1976): 53-69.

Will   E. Will, "L'espace sacrificiel dans les provinces ro-
                                maines de syrie et d'arabie," in Roland Étienne et
                                Marie-Thérése Le Dinahet, eds., *L'espace sacrificiel
                                dans les civilizations méditerranéennes de l'antiquité*
                                (Lyon: Bibliothéque Salmon-Reinach, 1991), pp. 259-
                                263.

Wischnitzer, *The Architecture* R. Wischnitzer, *The Architecture of the European
                                Synagogue* (Philadelphia: Jewish Publication Society of
                                America, 1964).

Wischnitzer, *Theme*   R. Wischnitzer, *The Messianic Theme in the Paintings of
                                the Dura Synagogue* (Chicago: University of Chicago,
                                1948).

Wiseman, *Stobi*   J. Wiseman, *Stobi: A Guide to the Excavations* (Beograd,
                                1973).

Wiseman and Mano-Zissi, "Excavations 1970"
                                J. Wiseman and D. Mano-Zissi, "Excavations at Stobi,
                                1970," *AJA* 75 (1971): 395-411.

Wiseman and Mano-Zissi, "Excavations 1971"
                                J. Wiseman and D. Mano-Zissi, "Excavations at Stobi,
                                1971," *AJA* 76 (1972): 407-424.

Wiseman and Mano-Zissi, "Excavations 1972"

J. Wiseman and D. Mano-Zissi, "Excavations at Stobi, 1972," *AJA* 77 (1973): 391-403.

Wiseman and Mano-Zissi, "Excavations 1973-1974"

J. Wiseman and D. Mano-Zissi, "Excavations at Stobi, 1973-1974," *JFA* 1 (1974): 117-148.

Wolfson, *Philo*

H. A. Wolfson, *Philo: Foundations of Religious Philosophy in Judaism, Christianity, and Islam*, 2 vols. (Cambridge, MA: Harvard, 1947).

Wright

G. R. H. Wright, *Ancient Building in South Syria and Palestine* (Leiden: E. J. Brill, 1985).

Wuthnow

H. Wuthnow, *Die semitischen Menschennamen in griechischen Inschriften und Papyri des vorderen Orients* (Leipzig: Dieterichische Verlagsbuchhandlung, 1930).

Y

Yerushalmi, Palestinian Talmud, Talmud of the Land of Israel.

Yad.

Yadayim.

Yadin, *Bar-Kokhba*

Y. Yadin, *Bar-Kokhba: The Rediscovery of the Legendary Hero of the Second Jewish Revolt against Rome* (Jerusalem: Weidenfeld and Nicolson & Ma'ariv Book Guild, 1971) (in Hebrew). English translation (New York: Weidenfeld and Nicolson, 1971).

Yadin, "Maḥaneh Dalet"

Y. Yadin, "Maḥaneh Dalet," *Yediot* 25 (1961): 49-64 (in Hebrew).

Yadin, *Masada*

Y. Yadin, *Masada: Herod's Fortress and the Zealots' Last Stand* (Jerusalem & New York: Steimatzky, 1966).

Yadin, *Preliminary Report*

Y. Yadin, *The Excavation of Masada 1963/64: Preliminary Report* (Jerusalem: IES, 1965).

Yadin, "Synagogue"

Y. Yadin, "The Synagogue at Masada," in Levine, *ASR*, pp. 19-23.

Yeb.

Yebamot.

Yeivin, *Decade*

Sh. Yeivin, *A Decade of Archeology in Israel, 1948-58* (Istanbul: Nederlands Historish-Archaeologish Institut, 1960).

Yeivin, "Eshtemoa"

Z. Yeivin, "Eshtemoa," in *NEAEHL*, vol. 2, pp. 423-426.

Yeivin, "Susiya"

Z. Yeivin, "Khirbet Susiya—The *Bema* and Synagogue Ornamentation," in Hachlili, *Ancient Synagogues*, pp. 93-98.

Yeivin, "Temples"

Sh. Yeivin, "Non-Existent Temples," *Eretz Israel* 11 (1973): 163-175 (in Hebrew).

Zab.

Zabim.

ZDPV

Zeitschrift für des deutschen Palästina-Vereins.

Zeb.

Zebahim.

Zeitlin, "Origin"

S. Zeitlin, "The Origin of the Synagogue," in Gutmann, *Synagogue*, pp. 14-26. Originally published in *PAAJR* 2 (1930-31): 69-81. Reprinted in S. Zeitlin, *Studies in the Early History of Judaism*, vol. 1 (New York: Ktav, 1973), pp. 1-13.

Zevi, "La sinagoga"

F. Zevi, "La sinagoga di Ostia," *Rassegna mensile di Israel* 38 (1972): 131-145.

ZNW

Zeitschrift fur die Neutestamentliche Wissenschaft.

GENERAL INDEX

Abba, 235, 236

Abba bar Cohen, 552

Abba bar Kahana, 190

Abba b. R. Hiyya bar Abba, 244

Abba Gurion of Saidan, 381, 522, 527

Abba Semuqa, R., 159

Abba Yudan of Saidan, 381, 521, 522, 527

Abbahu, 142, 246, 183

Abbaye, 41-44, 230, 231

Abiathar, 362

Abin, 309

Abraham, 341, 362

Absalom, 476

Abtalyon, 243

Abun, 250-251, 309, 310, 315, 383, 444, 478-481

Abun bar Yose, 441

Academy (see also House of Study), 582

Achanai, 398

Acre, 307

Adam, S., 533

Adan-Bayewitz, D. 56

Adda b. Matna, 226

aedicula, 417, 486

Aegean, 6

Aegina, 126

Aequus Modius, 390

Aeschylus, 101

Afeca, 578

Afîq, 578

Agrippa II, 380, 381, 389, 390, 403, 410, 520, 523, 608, 609

Agrippa, King 515

Ahmadiyye, 386, 455, 461, 464, 499

Aha, 241

Aha of Hutsal, Rav, 45

'Ain esh-Sheikh Mûsa, 485

'Ain Mûsmâr, 525

'Akâsha, Tell, 409

Akbarah, 284

al-Balâdhuri, 578

al-Ya'qûbi, 557

Albright, W. F., xxxiv, 424

Alcman, 101

Alexander Jannaeus, 272, 379, 380, 424, 425, 481, 515, 516, 527, 538, 570-575, 587, 608

Alexander the Great, 337

Alexandria, 5-7, 10, 16, 32, 94, 205, 207, 210, 215-217, 227

Alexandria, Great Synagogue of, 105, 212-213, 217

Alexandrou-Nesos, 215

Alma, 256

Altar, 570

Ami, 225

Ami, Rav, 598

Amidah, xxii

Amit, D., xxix, xxxv, 129-156

Ammi, 240, 244

'Ammudim, Horvat, 63, 64, 69, 71, 76, 88, 507, 582

Amoqa, 287

Amphora, 568

'Âmûdiyye, 455

Anaia, 135, 153

Anastasius I, 273

Anastasius, 367

Anchorage, 564

Anderreg, F., 348

Anderson, R. E., 176

Angels, 305

Anim, xxix, 129, 156

Antioch, 6, 28, 32, 314, 576

Antiochus Epiphanes, 20

Antoninus, 383

Antoninus Pius, 259

Apamea, 582

Aphek, 578

Apheka, 578

LIST OF PLATES

7a   Ḥ. Sumaqa: The entrance to one of the burial caves, adorned with two *menorot*. (Author original.)

7b   Ḥ. Sumaqa: The eastern facade and the narthex of the synagogue. (Author original.)

8a   Ḥ. Sumaqa: The complete northern entrance, blocked by the bench (W20). (Author original.)

8b   Ḥ. Sumaqa: (W2 in L291). The wall is composed of a hard mixture of stones and concrete and makes use of many architectural fragments. View is from west to east. (Author original.)

9a   Ḥ. Sumaqa: A collection of kitchenware pottery from the early Middle Ages. It was discovered in L2. (Author original.)

9b   Ḥ. Sumaqa: The eastern building opposite the facade of the synagogue. It was inhabited during the Middle Ages. (Author original.)

10a   Arbel (Arbela): Looking from south to north over the remains of the synagogue that remained *in situ*. (Permission, Palestine Exploration Fund.)

10b   Arbel (Arbela): Looking from north to south at the remains of the entrance and columns that survived *in situ*. (Permission, Palestine Exploration Fund.)

11a   Bar'am: Looking south-west to north-east at the facade and the remains of the porch of the structure designated as 'the Great Synagogue.' (Permission, Palestine Exploration Fund.)

11b   Bar'am: Looking from south-west to north-east at a segment of the facade wall from the porch in front of it to the Great Synagogue. (Permission, Palestine Exploration Fund.)

12a   Bar'am: Looking from south-east to north-west upon the remains of the Great Synagogue and the Arab structure that was built within it during the nineteenth century. (Permission, Palestine Exploration Fund.)

12b   Bar'am: Looking at the central entranceway in the wall of the southern facade of the Great Synagogue structure. (Permission, Palestine Exploration Fund.)

13a   Bar'am: Looking from north to south at the remains of the 'small synagogue.' (Permission, Palestine Exploration Fund.)

13b   Capernaum: A general view of the area of the ruins of the synagogue in the 1860's. (Permission, Palestine Exploration Fund.)

21b   Dura Europos: David figure in synagogue reredos. Technique 2.
(Author original.)

22a   Gaza Maiumas: Upper part of mosaic floor in synagogue.
(Author original.)

22b   Gaza Maiumas: Lower part of mosaic floor in synagogue.
(Author original.)

23a   Hazor (in Judea): Bottom section of mosaic floor in church.
(Author originals.)

23b   Hazor (in Judea): Middle section of mosaic floor in church.
(Leftmost photographs by courtesy of Israel Antiquities Authority;
right photograph author original.)

24a   Ma'on (Nirim): Drawing of mosaic floor in synagogue.

24b   Ma'on (Nirim): Upper portion of mosaic floor in synagogue
showing menorah flanked by lions. (Author original.)

24c   Ma'on (Nirim): Bottom-right corner of mosaic floor in synagogue
showing peacock. (Author original.)

25   Shellal: Drawing of mosaic floor in church. Note peacocks at
bottom.

26a   Buṭmiyye: Door-post (?) with a nine-branched menorah.
(Zev Radovan, used by permission.)

26b   Dabûra: Inscription #1.
(Zev Radovan, used by permission.)

27a   Dabûra: Inscription #2.
(Zev Radovan, used by permission.)

27b   Dabûra: Inscription #4.
(Zev Radovan, used by permission.)

28a   Dabûra: Inscription #6. The lintel of the *bet midrash* of R. Eliezer
ha-Qappar. (Zev Radovan, used by permission.)

28b   Ghâdriyye: A lintel fragment with an engraving of a seven-branched
menorah and a tripod base. (Zev Radovan, used by permission.)

29a   Ghâdriyye: A lintel fragment with the remains of an Aramaic
inscription. (Zev Radovan, used by permission.)

29b   'Ein Nashôt: Remains of an olive-oil press *in situ*.
(Zev Radovan, used by permission.)

30a   'Ein Nashôt: Architectural fragment decorated with the relief of a
lioness. (Zev Radovan, used by permission.)

30b   'Ein Nashôt: Architectural item with the seven-branched menorah.
(Zev Radovan, used by permission.)

39b   Qîsrîn: Smaller column base.
       (Zev Radovan, used by permission.)

40a   Qîsrîn: Ionic capital.
       (Zev Radovan, used by permission.)

40b   Qîsrîn: Inscription #5, R. Abun's grave marker.
       (Zev Radovan, used by permission.)

41a   Qîsrîn: Decorated window lintel.
       (Zev Radovan, used by permission.)

41b   Qîsrîn: Lintel fragment with a five-branched menorah with a tripod
       base. (Zev Radovan, used by permission.)

42a   'Asâliyye: Inscription.
       (Zev Radovan, used by permission.)

42b   Kh. er-Rafîd: Sketches of architectural fragments.
       (After Sukenik, "el-Ḥammeh.")

43a   Kh. er-Rafîd: Sketches of decorated architectural fragments.
       (After Sukenik, "el-Ḥammeh.")

43b   Kh. er-Rafîd: A decorated architectural fragment from the Jewish
       public structure. (Zev Radovan, used by permission.)

44a   Jarabâ: Eagle.
       (Zev Radovan, used by permission.)

44b   et-Taiyiba: Lintel.
       (Zev Radovan, used by permission.)

45a   et-Taiyiba: Two consoles.
       (Zev Radovan, used by permission.)

45b   Yahûdiyye: Large lintel.
       (Zev Radovan, used by permission.)

46a   Yahûdiyye: Doorpost stone with a five-branched menorah.
       (Zev Radovan, used by permission.)

46b   Yahûdiyye: Architectural item with a nine-branched menorah,
       shofar, and shovel. (Zev Radovan, used by permission.)

47a   Kh. ed-Dîkkeh: Decorated architectural items found near the
       remains of the public structure. (Zev Radovan, used by
       permission.)

47b   Kh. ed-Dîkkeh: Lintel fragment with a relief of a winged female
       figure holding garlands. (Zev Radovan, used by permission.)

48a   Gamala: Synagogue structure, looking toward the east.
       (Zev Radovan, used by permission.)

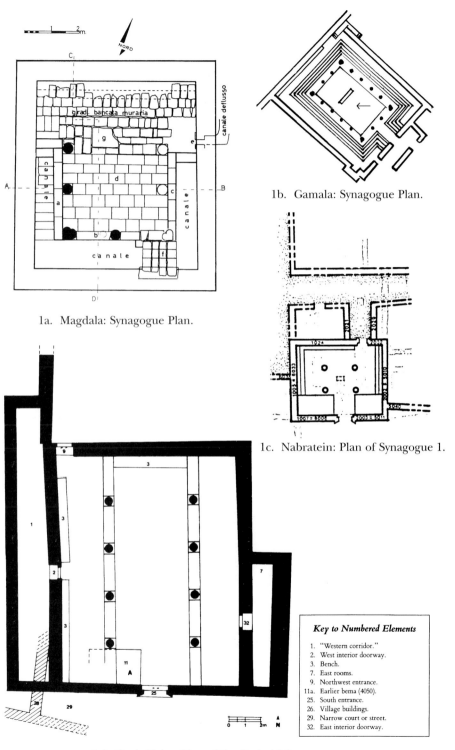

1a. Magdala: Synagogue Plan.

1b. Gamala: Synagogue Plan.

1c. Nabratein: Plan of Synagogue 1.

Key to Numbered Elements

1. "Western corridor."
2. West interior doorway.
3. Bench.
7. East rooms.
9. Northwest entrance.
11a. Earlier bema (4050).
25. South entrance.
26. Village buildings.
29. Narrow court or street.
32. East interior doorway.

1d. Gush Halav: Plan of the Period I Synagogue.

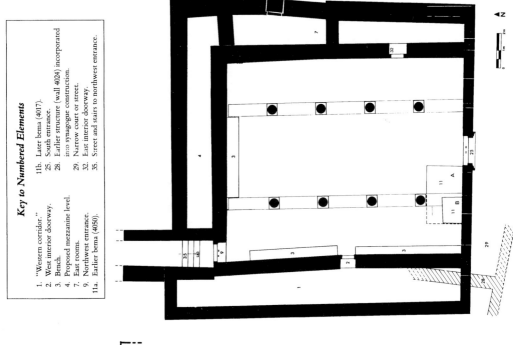

2a. Nabratein: Plan of Synagogues 2a and 2b.

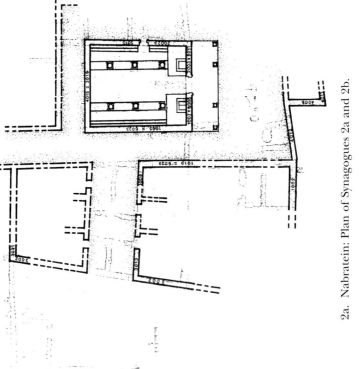

2b. Gush Halav: Plan of Period II-IV Synagogues. →

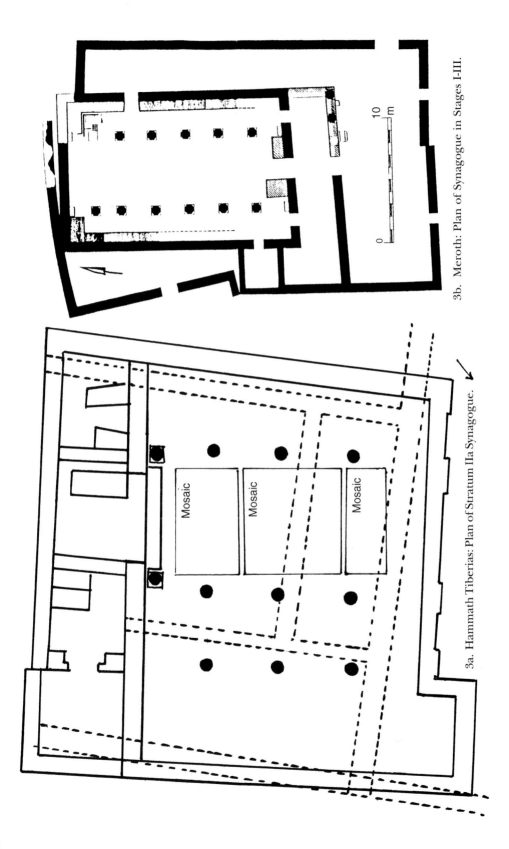

3b. Meroth: Plan of Synagogue in Stages I-III.

3a. Hammath Tiberias: Plan of Stratum IIa Synagogue.

4a. Susiya: General view of synagogue, looking northwest.

4b. Tel Maon: Aerial view towards the southwest. Synagogue is in the middle of the north slope.

5a. Maon: General view of synagogue towards the east.

5b. Anim: General view of synagogue towards the south.

6a. Anim: General view of courtyard, narthex and entrace facade.

6b. Anim: Bemah on north wall of synagogue.

↑

7a. Ḥ. Sumaqa: The entrance to one of the burial caves, adorned with two *menorot*.

→

7b. Ḥ. Sumaqa: The eastern façade and the narthex of the synagogue.

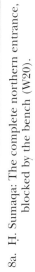

8b. H. Sumaqa: (W2 in L291). The wall is composed of a hard mixture of stones and concrete and makes use of many architectural fragments. View is from west to east.

8a. H. Sumaqa: The complete northern entrance, blocked by the bench (W20).

9a. Ḥ. Sumaqa: A collection of kitchenware pottery from the early Middle Ages. It was discovered in ← L2.

9b. Ḥ. Sumaqa: The eastern building opposite the facade of the synagogue. It was inhabited during the Middle Ages. ↓

10a. Arbel (Arbela): Looking from south to north over the remains of the synagogue that remained *in situ*.

10b. Arbel (Arbela): Looking from north to south at the remains of the entrance and columns that survived *in situ*.

11a. Bar'am: Looking south-west to north-east at the facade and the remains of the porch of the structure designated as 'the Great Synagogue.'

11b. Bar'am: Looking from south-west to north-east at a segment of the facade wall from the porch in front of it to the Great Synagogue.

12a. Bar'am: Looking from south-east to north-west upon the remains of the Great Synagogue and the Arab structure that was built within it during the nineteenth century.

12b. Bar'am: Looking at the central entranceway in the wall of the southern facade of the
Great Synagogue structure.

13a. Bar'am: Looking from north to south at the remains of the 'small synagogue.'

13b. Capernaum: A general view of the area of the ruins of the synagogue in the 1860's.

14a. Capernaum: A view of a number of decorated architectural items found near the ruins of the synagogue by C. W. Wilson and R. E. Anderson, when they conducted a brief exploratory excavation there in 1866.

14b. Capernaum: A view of the various decorated architectural items that were found in the ruins of the synagogue structure in the 1860's.

15a. Chorazin: A view of decorated architectural items in the area of the ruins of the synagogue before its excavation.

15b. Chorazin: Part of a gable on which there is a relief of a lion.

16a. Meiron: Looking from south to north at the remains of the synagogue's facade wall.

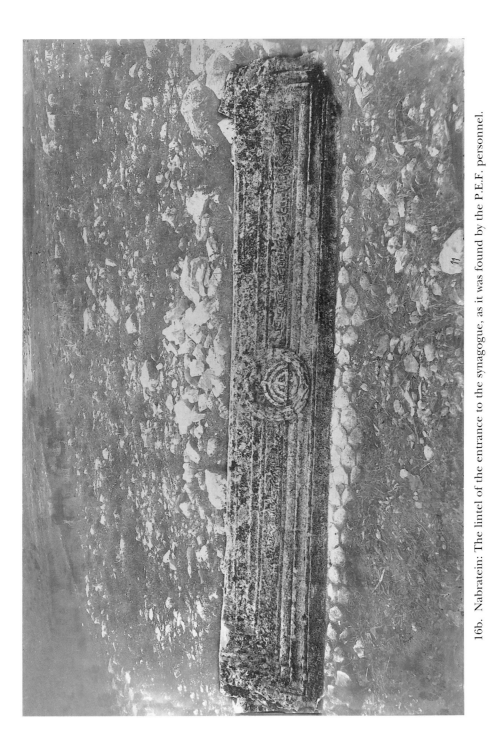

16b. Nabratein: The lintel of the entrance to the synagogue, as it was found by the P.E.F. personnel.

17a. Coin of the Temple of Men at Antioch, 238-244
C.E. A lattice-work screen marks off the *temenos*.

17b. Tiberias: Jewish lattice-work screen.

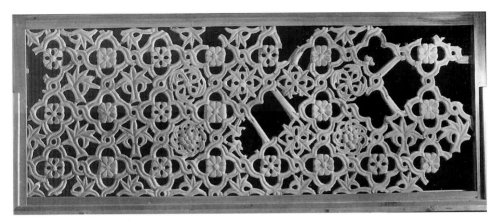

18a. Gaza: Synagogue chancel screen, sixth to seventh century.

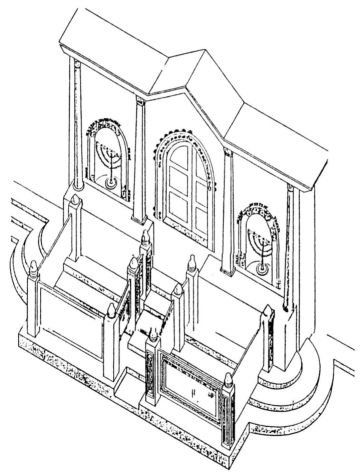

18b. Khirbet Susiya: Reconstuction of chancel arrangement, fourth to
seventh century.

19a. Gaza: Sixth-century inscription to "the most holy place" on the floor mosaic of the synagogue.

19b. 'Ein Nashôt: Nine-branched menorah on capital.

20a. Rome: Seven-branched, solid-based menorah on the Arch of Titus, 81 C.E.

20b. Beth Alpha: Mosaic panels on synagogue floor.

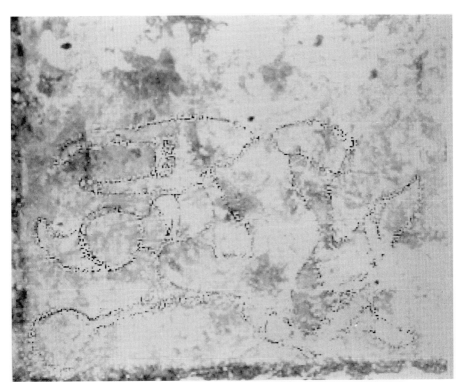

21a. Dura Europos: David figure in synagogue reredos. Technique 1.

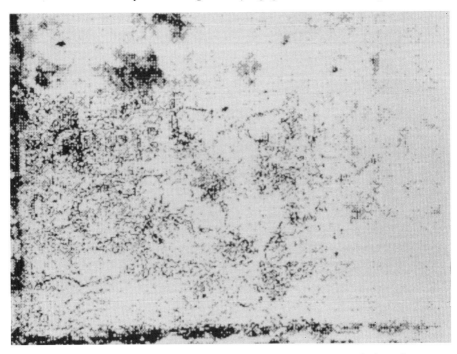

21b. Dura Europos: David figure in synagogue reredos. Technique 2.

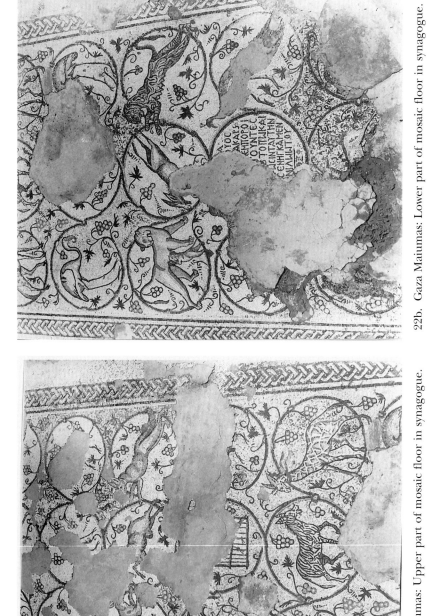

22a. Gaza Maiumas: Upper part of mosaic floor in synagogue.

22b. Gaza Maiumas: Lower part of mosaic floor in synagogue.

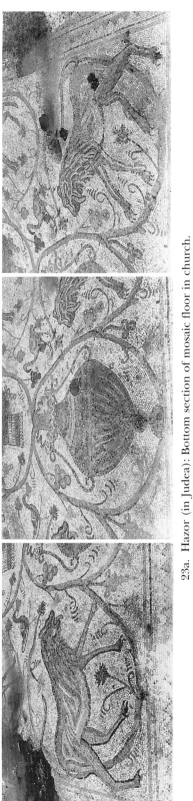

23a. Hazor (in Judea): Bottom section of mosaic floor in church.

23b. Hazor (in Judea): Middle section of mosaic floor in church.

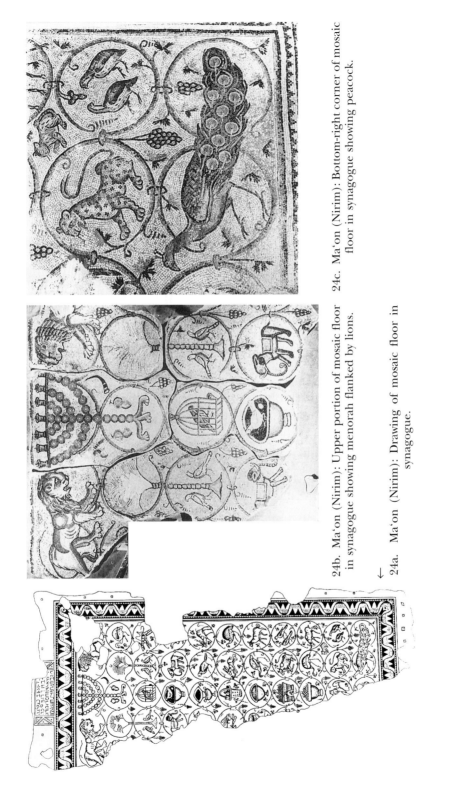

24c. Ma'on (Nirim): Bottom-right corner of mosaic floor in synagogue showing peacock.

24b. Ma'on (Nirim): Upper portion of mosaic floor in synagogue showing menorah flanked by lions.

24a. Ma'on (Nirim): Drawing of mosaic floor in synagogue.

25. Shellal: Drawing of mosaic floor in church. Note peacocks at bottom.

26a. Buṭmiyye: Door-post (?) with a nine-branched menorah.

26b. Dabûra: Inscription #1.

27a. Dabûra: Inscription #2.

27b. Dabûra: Inscription #4.

28a. Dabûra: Inscription #6. The lintel of the *bet midrash* of R. Eliezer ha-Qappar.

28b. Ghâdriyye: A lintel fragment with an engraving of a seven-branched menorah and a tripod base.

29a. Ghâdriyye: A lintel fragment with the remains of an Aramaic inscription.

29b. 'Ein Nashôt: Remains of an olive-oil press *in situ.*

30a. ʿEin Nashôt: Architectural fragment decorated with the relief of a lioness.

30b. ʿEin Nashôt: Architectural item with the seven-branched menorah.

31a. ‘Ein Nashôt: Ionic capital showing the face with a ten-branched menorah.

31b. ‘Ein Nashôt: Same Ionic capital showing the face with a large egg and a baseless, seven branched menorah.

32a. 'Ein Nashôt: Same Ionic capital showing the other faces.

32b. 'Ein Nashôt: Architrave with the inscription of "Abun bar Yose." (Inscription #1.)

33a. 'Ein Nashôt: Inscription #2.

33b. 'Ein Nashôt: End of a sarcophagus lid showing the decorations of a stylized rosette and a 'tree of life.'

34a. 'Ein Nashôt: Lintel fragment with reliefs of a lion and a seven-branched menorah (?).

34b. 'Ein Nashôt: Fragment of a decorated door lintel.

35a. Dâbiyye: Lintel fragment with two seven-branched *menorot*.

35b. Fâkhûra: Pedestal showing the side with the meander.

36a. Fâkhûra: Same pedestal showing the side with the menorah.

36b. Aḥmadiyye: Inscription #2.

37b. Qisrin: Doorpost stone with a five-branched menorah and a peacock with a pomegranate in its beak. Found near the Jewish public structure.

37a. Qisrin: Doorpost with an eleven-branched menorah and a tripod base. Found near the Jewish public structure.

38a. Qîsrîn: Main Entranceway in the northern facade wall of the structure.

38b. Qîsrîn: The Jewish public structure, view from the south-east.

39a. Qîsrîn: Column base.

39b. Qîsrîn: Smaller column base.

40a. Qîsrîn: Ionic capital.

40b. Qîsrîn: Inscription #5, R. Abun's grave marker.

41a. Qîsrîn: Decorated window lintel.

41b. Qîsrîn: Lintel fragment with a five-branched menorah with a tripod base.

42a. 'Asâliyye: Inscription.

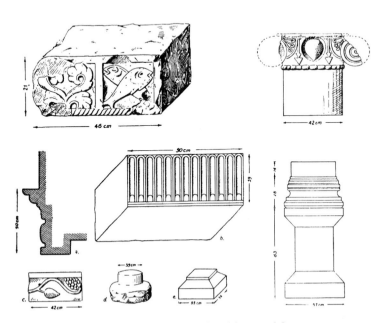

42b. Kh. er-Rafîd: Sketches of architectural fragments.

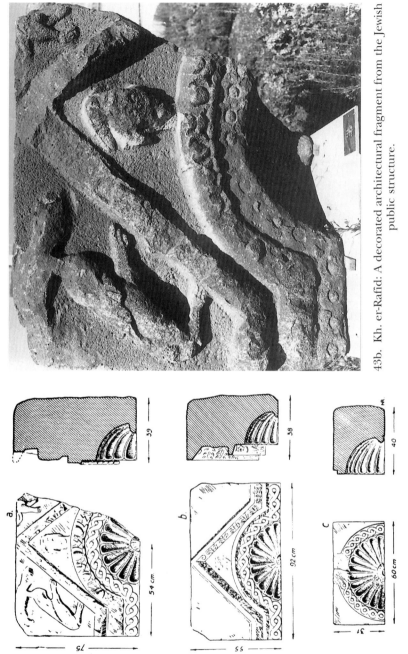

43b. Kh. er-Rafid: A decorated architectural fragment from the Jewish public structure.

43a. Kh. er-Rafid: Sketches of decorated architectural fragments.

44a. Jarabâ: agle.

44b. et-Taiyiba: Lintel.

45a. et-Taiyiba: Two consoles.

45b. Yahûdiyye: Large lintel.

46b. Yahûdiyye: Architectural item with a nine-branched menorah, shofar, and shovel.

← 46a. Yahûdiyye: Doorpost stone with a five-branched menorah.

47a. Kh. ed-Dîkkeh: Decorated architectural items found near the remains of the public structure.

47b. Kh. ed-Dîkkeh: Lintel fragment with a relief of a winged female figure holding garlands.

48a. Gamala: Synagogue structure, looking toward the east.

48b. Gamala: Ionic capital found in the synagogue.

49a. Gamala: Architectural item (a capital?) found in the synagogue structure.

49b. Mazra'at Kanaf: Fragment with lion relief.

50a. Umm el-Qanâ\lo(t,)ir: Decorated capital.

50b. Khisfîn: Voussoir from a Jewish (?) public structure.

51a. Khisfîn: Decorated lintel.

51b. Fîq: Column upon which is engraved Inscription #1 and a seven-branched menorah.

52a. Fîq: Fragment of the door lintel with Inscription #2.

52b. Fîq: Door lintel with a relief of a seven-branched menorah within a circle, with a shofar and ethrog (?).

53. Fîq: Lintel with a relief of a five-branched menorah or 'tree of life.'

STUDIA POST-BIBLICA

1. KOSMALA, H. *Hebräer – Essener – Christen*. Studien zur Vorgeschichte der frühchristlichen Verkündigung. 1959. ISBN 90 04 02135 3
3. WEISE, M. *Kultzeiten und kultischer Bundesschluß in der 'Ordensregel' vom Toten Meer*. 1961. ISBN 90 04 02136 1
4. VERMES, G. *Scripture and Tradition in Judaism*. Haggadic Studies. Reprint. 1983. ISBN 90 04 07096 6
5. CLARKE, E.G. *The Selected Questions of Isho bar Nūn on the Pentateuch*. Edited and Translated from Ms Cambridge Add. 2017. With a Study of the Relationship of Isho'dādh of Merv, Theodore bar Konī and Isho bar Nūn on Genesis. 1962. ISBN 90 04 03141 3
6. NEUSNER, J. *A Life of Johanan ben Zakkai (ca. 1-80 C.E.)*. 2nd rev. ed. 1970. ISBN 90 04 02138 8
7. WEIL, G.E. *Élie Lévita, humaniste et massorète (1469-1549)*. 1963. ISBN 90 04 02139 6
8. BOWMAN, J. *The Gospel of Mark*. The New Christian Jewish Passover Haggadah. 1965. ISBN 90 04 03142 1
11. NEUSNER, J. *A History of the Jews in Babylonia*. Part 2. The Early Sasanian Period. ISBN 90 04 02143 4
12. NEUSNER, J. Part 3. From Shahpur I to Shahpur II. 1968. ISBN 90 04 02144 2
14. NEUSNER, J. Part 4. The Age of Shahpur II. 1969. ISBN 90 04 02146 9
15. NEUSNER, J. Part 5. Later Sasanian Times. 1970. ISBN 90 04 02147 7
16. NEUSNER, J. *Development of a Legend*. Studies on the Traditions Concerning Johanan ben Zakkai. 1970. ISBN 90 04 02148 5
17. NEUSNER, J. (ed.). *The Formation of the Babylonian Talmud*. Studies in the Achievements of the Late Nineteenth and Twentieth Century Historical and Literary-Critical Research. 1970. ISBN 90 04 02149 3
18. CATCHPOLE, D.R. *The Trial of Jesus*. A Study in the Gospels and Jewish Historiography from 1770 to the Present Day. 1971. ISBN 90 04 02599 5
19. NEUSNER, J. *Aphrahat and Judaism*. The Christian-Jewish Argument in Fourth-Century Iran. 1971. ISBN 90 04 02150 7
20. DAVENPORT, G.L. *The Eschatology of the Book of Jubilees*. 1971. ISBN 90 04 02600 2
21. FISCHEL, H.A. *Rabbinic Literature and Greco-Roman Philosophy*. A Study of Epicurea and Rhetorica in Early Midrashic Writings. 1973. ISBN 90 04 03720 9
22. TOWNER, W.S. *The Rabbinic 'Enumeration of Scriptural Examples'*. A Study of a Rabbinic Pattern of Discourse with Special Reference to *Mekhilta d'Rabbi Ishmael*. 1973. ISBN 90 04 03744 6
23. NEUSNER, J. (ed.). *The Modern Study of the Mishna*. 1973. ISBN 90 04 03669 5
24. ASMUSSEN, J.P. *Studies in Judeo-Persian Literature*. [Tr. from the Danish]. (Homages et Opera Minora, 12). 1973. ISBN 90 04 03827 2
25. BARZILAY, I. *Yoseph Shlomo Delmedigo (Yashar of Candia)*. His Life, Works and Times. 1974. ISBN 90 04 03972 4
27. BERGER, K. *Die griechische Daniel-Exegese*. Eine altkirchliche Apokalypse. Text, Übersetzung und Kommentar. 1976. ISBN 90 04 04756 5
28. LOWY, S. *The Principles of Samaritan Bible Exegesis*. 1977. ISBN 90 04 04925 8
29. DEXINGER, F. *Henochs Zehnwochenapokalypse und offene Probleme der Apokalyptikforschung*. 1977. ISBN 90 04 05428 6

30. COHEN, J.M. *A Samaritan Chronicle*. A Source-Critical Analysis of the Life and Times of the Great Samaritan Reformer, Baba Rabbah. 1981. ISBN 90 04 06215 7

31. BROADIE, A. *A Samaritan Philosophy*. A Study of the Hellenistic Cultural Ethos of the Memar Marqah. 1981. ISBN 90 04 06312 9

32. HEIDE, A. VAN DER. *The Yemenite Tradition of the Targum of Lamentations*. Critical Text and Analysis of the Variant Readings. 1981. ISBN 90 04 06560 1

33. ROKEAH, D. *Jews, Pagans and Christians in Conflict*. 1982. ISBN 90 04 07025 7

35. EISENMAN, R.H. *James the Just in the Habakkuk* Pesher. 1986. ISBN 90 04 07587 9

36. HENTEN, J.W. VAN, H.J. DE JONGE, P.T. VAN ROODEN & J.W. WEESELIUS (eds.). *Tradition and Re-Interpretation in Jewish and Early Christian Literature*. Essays in Honour of Jürgen C.H. Lebram. 1986. ISBN 90 04 07752 9

37. PRITZ, R.A. *Nazarene Jewish Christianity*. From the End of the New Testament Period until its Disappearance in the Fourth Century. 1988. ISBN 90 04 08108 9

38. HENTEN, J.W. VAN, B.A.G.M. DEHANDSCHUTTER & H.W. VAN DER KLAAUW. *Die Entstehung der jüdischen Martyrologie*. 1989. ISBN 90 04 08978 0

39. MASON, S. *Flavius Josephus on the Pharisees*. A Composition-Critical Study. 1991. ISBN 90 04 09181 5

40. OHRENSTEIN, R.A. & B. GORDON. *Economic Analysis in Talmudic Literature*. Rabbinic Thought in the Light of Modern Economics. 1992. ISBN 90 04 09540 3

41. GERA, D. *The Role of Judaea in Eastern Mediterranean International Politics*. In Preparation. ISBN 90 04 09441 5

42. ATTRIDGE, H.W. & G. HATA (eds.). *Eusebius, Christianity, and Judaism*. 1992. ISBN 90 04 09688 4

43. TOAFF, A. *The Jews in Umbria*. Vol. I: 1245-1435. 1993. ISBN 90 04 09695 7

44. TOAFF, A. *The Jews in Umbria*. Vol. II: 1435-1484. 1994. ISBN 90 04 09979 4

45. TOAFF, A. *The Jews in Umbria*. Vol. III: 1484-1736. 1994. ISBN 90 04 10165 9

46. PARENTE, F. & J. SIEVERS (eds.). *Josephus and the History of the Greco-Roman Period*. Essays in Memory of Morton Smith. 1994. ISBN 90 04 10114 4

47. URMAN, D. & P.V.M. FLESHER (eds.). *Ancient Synagogues*. Historical Analysis and Archaeological Discovery.
Volume One. 1995. ISBN 90 04 10242 6
Volume Two. 1995. ISBN 90 04 10243 4
ISBN *set* 90 04 09904 2